An Ethnography
of Santa Clara Pueblo
New Mexico

An Ethnography of Santa Clara Pueblo New Mexico

W. W. Hill

Edited and Annotated by
Charles H. Lange

UNIVERSITY OF NEW MEXICO PRESS
Albuquerque

Library of Congress Cataloging in Publication Data

Hill, W.W. (Willard Williams), 1902–1974.
     An Ethnography of Santa Clara Pueblo, New Mexico.

     "Constitution and Bylaws of the Pueblo of Santa Clara"—Appendix B.
     Bibliography: p.
     Includes index.
     1. Tewa Indians—Social life and customs.   2. Indians of North America—New Mexico—Santa
     Clara Pueblo—Social life and customs.   3. Santa Clara Pueblo (N.M.)—Social life and customs.
     I. Lange, Charles H.   II. Title.
     E99.T35H5   1981   970.004'97   80-52277
     ISBN 0-8263-0555-5   AACR2

iv

Contents

v

Illustrations

PLATES

Following page 32

1. Santa Clara Pueblo, vertical air photograph, c. 1950.
2. Santa Clara Pueblo, oblique air photograph looking north.
3. Santa Clara Pueblo, oblique air photograph looking west.
4. View across Santa Clara Pueblo looking toward Black Mesa.
5. View of Santa Clara Pueblo looking south.
6. Santa Clara Pueblo looking northwest.
7. Santa Clara Pueblo looking southwest.
8. Santa Clara Pueblo, two-storied house.
9. Santa Clara Pueblo, architectural detail.
10. Corn, squash, chili and hay drying on *ramadas*.
11. Santa Clara Pueblo's harvested crops drying.
12. Santa Clara Pueblo looking northwest.
13. Threshing floor being used with horses.
14. Three Pueblo cradleboards.
15. Santa Clara men at Omaha Exposition, 1898.
16. Santa Clara men at Omaha Exposition, 1898.

Following page 160

17. Santa Clara men at Omaha Exposition, 1898.
18. The Governor of Santa Clara Pueblo.
19. Painted buffalo robe, Santa Clara Pueblo.
20. Painted buffalo robe, Santa Clara Pueblo.
21. Painted buffalo robe, Santa Clara Pueblo.
22. Painted buffalo robe, Santa Clara Pueblo.
23. Santa Clara Indians.
24. Santa Clara woman's embroidered dress.
25. Beaded moccasins, Santa Clara Pueblo.
26. Beaded moccasins, Santa Clara Pueblo.
27. Pump drill, Santa Clara Pueblo.
28. Elk horn fleshing tool, Santa Clara Pueblo.
29. Elk horn fleshing tool, Santa Clara Pueblo.
30. Quiver of mountain lion skin, Santa Clara Pueblo.
31. José Leandro Tafoya, governor of Santa Clara Pueblo.
32. Powder horn, child's rattle, and arrow wrench.
33. Arrow shart smoother, bone pipe and pottery rest, and clay pipe.
34. Pipe and tobacco bag, gunpowder container.

MAP

Preface

This volume, *An Ethnography of Santa Clara Pueblo, New Mexico*, is, for the most part, the result of data gathered in the course of extended field research by W.W. Hill. In a letter of November 15, 1971 (Hill correspondence), Nibs, as he was most widely known, described his field studies with these words: "Most of the material was obtained during 1940–41. Shorter field excursions were made in 1948, 1952, and 1960–62." Hill further noted that he had used "thirty paid informants." Additional data came from his frequent, unstructured conversations with these and other informants as well as from intermittent, direct observations of varied activities at the pueblo. This field research extended over a period of twenty-five or even thirty years.

In another, subsequent letter of February 8, 1972 (Hill correspondence), the following comments were found:

A little on the background of my involvement at Santa Clara may be useful. In 1940 Dr. Matthew W. Stirling, Chief of the Bureau of American Ethnology [in Washington, D.C.], sent me Jean Allard Jeançon's manuscript on Santa Clara and requested that I edit it and fill in the gaps that I could. It was at his insistence that I began my fieldwork. Currently my manuscript is something over 1200 pages and contains most of the material from Jeançon as well as my own....

Jeançon's manuscript, completed in 1931, represented "some thirty years of observation and study with the Tewa Indians of New Mexico, especially those in Santa Clara," according to Jeançon's Introduction. There was also a considerable number of unpublished field notes made by Jeançon between 1904 and 1930. In addition to those acquired by Hill, a series of notes from 1906 was found at the Denver Art Museum. These were primarily in regard to pottery making.

Early in his field research on Santa Clara, Hill received a letter, dated May 28, 1943, from Barbara Freire-Marreco Aitken, who had done fieldwork at Santa Clara and elsewhere among the Southwestern Indian tribes in the period, 1910–13. Aitken's letter was in response to some inquiries made by Hill, April 10, 1943, concerning certain of his findings at Santa Clara. The following paragraph from Aitken's reply is of interest here:

It is very satisfactory that an anthropologist who has the people's confidence should be working up Santa Clara—not the most romantic of the pueblos by any means, but I do think the "noblest" (in the Spanish sense of the word) ever since Benavides' time! I venture to hope that you speak Spanish and can use it freely with the old people of the place.

While Hill's command of Spanish fell short of Aitken's hope, it is important to point out that in the thirty-year interval between Aitken's fieldwork and Hill's research, the need for facility in Spanish had greatly diminished. This decline has continued to the present time, and today the use of Spanish at Santa Clara is increasingly rare, as is also true of the use of Tewa— particularly among the children, the coming generation. This is a trend that characterizes most of the Rio Grande Pueblo tribes today; members of the older generations deplore this development but have been ineffective in reversing it to any significant degree.

At the time of Hill's correspondence of late 1971 and early 1972, his intention was to publish his Santa Clara material in several smaller volumes: the first were to be two volumes on religion, the largest segment of the work, some 300–350 pages of manuscript; these were to be followed by four additional volumes— the Village, 160 pages, housing and household equipment (including pottery making), food preparation, dress and adornment (including skindressing and weaving); Subsistence, 160 pages, agriculture and agricultural equipment, hunting and hunting equipment, fishing and fishing equipment, gathering, pastoralism, wage work, trade, and warfare; Individual Development, 260 pages, life cycle from birth through death (including socialization and education, marriage, status, men's role, women's role); and Political Organization, 80 pages, law, inheritance, social organization, and kinship. In Hill's own words (correspondence of November 15, 1971), "It is a unique contribution since it is a relatively complete Pueblo ethnology and because most of the informants are now dead and the material is no longer recoverable."

The preparation of the Santa Clara manuscript was at this preliminary stage when Hill unfortunately suffered an incapacitating stroke which ended his anthropological career. Some twenty months later, January 21, 1974, Hill died. Subsequently, Mrs. Hill requested that the editor complete the preparation of the manuscript for publication.

Upon taking over this project, I became aware of several points. There was indeed an impressive accumulation of detailed information regarding Santa Clara Pueblo culture, primarily for the early decades of the present century—a blend of Hill's information with the earlier data from the Jeançon manuscript and field notes, reaching back into the final years of the nineteenth century.

Sections of the material, the data on religion, for example, were more nearly in final manuscript form; other sections, however, were still in rather rough draft. Little, if anything, had been done in integrating the manuscript in terms of introductory material and transitional statements. Cross-references, helping to explain the interrelatedness of various portions of the discussions, were also minimal.

The present volume obviously represents a distinct departure from the original plan of multiple volumes; also, it should be noted that the sequence of topics and subject matter has been revised. Explanatory notes by the editor have been held to the bare minimum; in the editing of the text, the material has been considered as a rough draft rather than a historical document. In other words, editorial changes have been made without resort to brackets, initialing, or similar devices. Rewording has been limited to instances where clarification seemed essential. Such changes would undoubtedly have been made by Hill himself had he been able to complete the manuscript for publication. To use brackets in these instances seemed overly pedantic and really unnecessary.

In addition to noting these revisions and changes in sequence, a somewhat different editorial comment seems appropriate. The long-recognized integrated nature of any culture, dramatically demonstrated in traditional Pueblo Indian cultures, has resulted in a rather unconventional ordering, or clustering, of topics in Hill's ethnography of Santa Clara Pueblo. This is perhaps most evident in Chapter 8. The discussion of "Life Cycle and Social Organization" contains topics such as the extended consideration of "Social Controls," often found elsewhere in an ethnography, usually under the heading of political organization. Frequently there is also a separate chapter on the social organization of the group. Conversely, materials in other chapters of the Santa Clara study are, in most studies, found in the discussion of phases of the life cycle, or individual development.

Such arrangements are clearly not a matter of right or wrong; they reflect the perception of the ethnographer and, ideally, the viewpoint of his informants. They may also reveal the particular emphasis desired by the writer. In this ethnography, the relatively wide compass given by Hill to his discussion of "Individual Development" has been retained. However, elements of this subject still remained in other chapters, where they have been left rather than moving or repeating them. The index will assist the reader in finding such material.

Mention should also be made here of the imbalance to be found among the various chapters insofar as length and the amount of detail are concerned. The very brief Chapter 3, "Property, Ownership, and Inheritance," for example, stands in sharp contrast to Chapter 10, "Ceremonial Organization," the unit most nearly completed by Hill and, as mentioned, planned by him as the first to be published. These units were left essentially intact as there seemed to be no patently logical combination to make, on the one hand, and, on the other, no clear-cut point, or points, at which the discussion might reasonably be broken. Rather than making such a step for the sake of arbitrary "form," it appeared preferable to leave the units as Hill had arranged them. Also, such emphasis on the religious life seemed an accurate reflection of the pervasive importance accorded religion and ceremonialism by traditional Santa Clara culture. Again, it appears reasonable to suggest that the other chapters on aspects of Santa Clara culture would have been appreciably expanded and elaborated upon had Hill been able to engage in further fieldwork. Finally it should be noted that the preferred spelling of *Navajo* has changed since Hill did his work. In this volume, the current preference of the Navajo Tribe has followed—using the *j* rather than *h*—except in direct quotations from published sources.

The Introduction and the initial chapters on geographical and historical context and background have been added by the editor to make the data more meaningful to the reader. In the years to come, these aspects of the study will undoubtedly be more obscure than they are to Southwestern scholars and readers of the present day. Cultural change has been noted among the Southwestern tribes since the sixteenth century advent of the Spaniards—the beginning of the historic period in the area. These changes have accelerated with the passing years—most dramatically in the years of World War II and subsequent decades.

It is precisely this accelerated culture change that makes the ethnographic details compiled by Hill so valuable. As he himself noted, many of his informants had already died as of the time of his letter of November 1971. Others have passed away in the interval since that time.

There can be no doubt that there are individual Santa Clara tribal members who have either retained a sincere interest in their cultural heritage or who have recently come to appreciate their traditional ways and values. For those and others with similar interests and appreciations, it is hoped that a measure of genuine satisfaction will be provided by the contents of this volume.

Judging from the reactions of the Cochiti Pueblo Indians, some thirty miles south of Santa Clara, to a comparable volume authored by the editor in 1959, the present volume most assuredly will, in time, gain acceptance among and provide real satisfaction for many Santa Clara Indians—not all, to be sure, but hopefully the great majority. If so, the fondest aspirations of Professor Hill, Mrs. Hill, and myself will have been realized.

Charles H. Lange
Northern Illinois University
DeKalb, Illinois
February 1980

Acknowledgments

The assistance which W. W. Hill received in the field from numerous Santa Clara Indians, including both those who were compensated for their time and those who volunteered information in the course of more casual conversations, must be gratefully acknowledged first of all. Their cooperation and collaboration, at times at some personal risk to themselves, have been deeply appreciated. The specific contribution of each remains unspecified; the comfort of anonymity is and will be well understood by all who have had any degree of association with Pueblo Indian tribes of the American Southwest. Hopefully, these Santa Clara Indians will deem the final result worthy of their involvement.

In a letter of November 15, 1971, Professor Hill had written:

The manuscript has been read by the late Dr. Edward P. Dozier of the University of Arizona and Dr. Alfonso Ortiz of Princeton University. Dr. Harry W. Basehart has read the section on Political Organization and Dr. J. J. Brody, Dress and Adornment. I wish to acknowledge their help and suggestions.

Elsewhere, Hill expressed his appreciation to Dr. Edward F. Castetter for his identification and analysis of various ethnobotanical specimens, particularly of several varieties of corn.

Additional acknowledgements would undoubtedly have been made by Hill had he been able to complete the manuscript. Those who remain unmentioned here must know that he genuinely appreciated their interest and assistance in his long-term endeavor.

In regard to the subsequent editorial phase of the research, further recognitions are in order. Here, at Northern Illinois University, grateful acknowledgment is made for the support of Jon D. Miller, Associate Dean for Research, and members of the Graduate School Fund Review Committee in providing a "starter grant" for the preliminary stages of the work. Similarly, the interest and assistance of Dr. Ronald Provencher, Anthropology Department Chairman, and Ms. Anita Mozga, Departmental Secretary, are also acknowledged.

Subsequently, the continued interest of Dean Miller and the Research Office, and the effective support of Dr. Provencher and Professors Harry Basehart (University of New Mexico), Fred Eggan (University of Chicago), and Carroll L. Riley (Southern Illinois University at Carbondale) resulted in research grants from the National Endowment for the Humanities (#RO-26221-77-323) and the National Science Foundation (#BNS77-25299). Without such assistance, completion of the project would have been indefinitely delayed, if not impossible.

As a sequel to the support already noted, further acknowledgment must be made of a subvention for publication grant (#BNS79-25691) from the National Science Foundation, received February 28, 1980.

Mr. Lawrence G. Santeford, Curator, NIU Anthropology Museum, kindly assisted with photographic work, and Ms. Maria A. "Toni" Livingston ably and cheerfully typed the final draft of the manuscript.

As typing of the final manuscript progressed, the editing has benefited once again from the critical reading by Basehart. His suggestions have been greatly appreciated.

Finally, the members of Professor Hill's family, especially his widow, Dorothy Hill, should be recognized and thanked for their continued interest, cooperation, and support throughout the research. His daughter, Ms. Martha Hill Nufer, prepared the accompanying map, and a granddaughter, Cynthia Nufer, very effectively transformed the numerous drawings, originally made with black or colored pencils, or water colors, into inked blackline figures.

C.H.L.
February 1980

PHONETIC TABLE AND EXPLANATION
by
WINTER LAITE

[In the preparation of this manuscript for publication, it became readily apparent that the various phonetic transcriptions used by Hill from various sources and writers were in need of some standardization to make them meaningful and useful to the reader. I did not feel comfortable in making these changes and explanations; however, Winter Laite fortunately volunteered for this formidable task. The results of his work follow and constitute a significant contribution to the overall study. CHL]

SANTA CLARA PHONEMES CONSONANTS	bilabial	labiodental	dental	alveolar	retroflex	alveopalatar	velar	glottal
voiceless stops	p	t	t				k	?
voiced stops	b		d				g	
voiceless affricates				c, ts		*ch*		
voiced affricates								
voiceless fricatives		f				*sh*	x	h
voiced fricatives		v	th	s		*zh*		
nasals	m						ŋ	
voiced semivowel	w					y, j*		
flap					r			

*probably a variant of *zh*

xxii

NOTES ON CONSONANTS

Notes: th as in ether (not either)

sh as in she

ch as in children

x as ch in German loch

c as ts as in bits, but occurs initially

ŋ as ng in song

Glottalization: glottalized consonants are followed by an apostrophe ("p'o")

Nasalization: vowels by a raised n are nasalized ("aⁿ")

Labialization: consonants followed by a raised w are pronounced with the lips rounded ("kʷ")

Aspiration: consonants followed by raised "h" (pʰ) are aspirated.

VOWELS

	front	central	back
high	i		u
mid	e		o
low		a	

Note: All vowels except nasalized *o* and *e* have corresponding long vowels, indicated by a raised period following the symbol: (i·).

Symbols appearing in the original manuscript	Equivalents used here
θ	th
ϕ	f
γ	g (Spanish "agua")
č	ch
š	sh
ž	zh
ą, ę, į, ǫ, ų	aⁿ, etc.
ε, æ	e
η	ŋ
p' (consonant & aspiration)	pʰ

The Tewa terms in Hill's manuscript were compiled from various sources; different methods of phonetic transcription were used. For consistency the terms have been transcribed here using (with unavoidable exceptions) equivalents familiar to the English speaker.

Like Chinese, Tewa is a "tone" language, i.e., a change in the tone of a word (high, low, rising, falling) can change its meaning. For example, tsi wi (higher tone) means "animals," and tsi wi (lower tone) means "ceremonial obsidian knife."

Indication of tone was not always available, and therefore does not appear in the Tewa. The terms listed were very likely mnemonic aids to the fieldworkers, rather than attempts to transcribe with phonetic accuracy. For this reason the reader should consider the terms as, at best, approximations.

A native speaker of Tewa should be consulted for truly accurate pronunciation of the terms. Also, some of the terms used are Tewa but not Santa Clara.

In some cases, several transcriptions appear for one specific term. To enable reference to original cited sources, these terms appear as they are in the original manuscript, with the exception of the mnemonic changes listed.

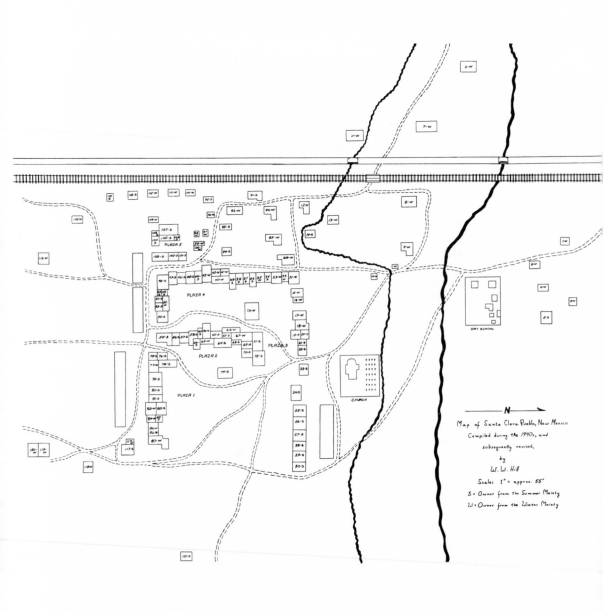

Map of Santa Clara Pueblo, New Mexico. (Compiled during the 1940s and subsequently updated by W.W. Hill.)

Introduction

Over the span of recent decades, ethnographic studies of the Southwestern Pueblo Indian tribes have resulted in an appreciable literature, in terms of both range and depth. Consequently, the ethnological understanding of these tribes, collectively, has attained a relatively favorable position when compared with similar studies of other tribal and regional cultures—both within the Southwest and far beyond. For the Southwestern Pueblo tribes, the greatest depth has occurred in studies of the Hopi of Arizona and the Zuñi of western New Mexico.

Despite this generally acknowledged richness of information, it remains frustratingly true that there is still a great deal more to be learned concerning all of these cultures, particularly at the relatively aboriginal, or unacculturated, time level. For most of these tribal cultures, this relatively unacculturated level may be considered as extending into the present century, perhaps as late as the end of World War I. As the years pass and additional portions of traditional culture disappear from view and even from memory, a considerable share of this cultural heritage is unfortunately being lost forever.

The Pueblo Indians of the upper Rio Grande Valley in New Mexico consist of fifteen distinct tribes, each with a reservation and, for the most part, concentrated in villages, or pueblos. They are the Eastern Pueblo Indians, and presently, they are located in five villages of Eastern Keresan speakers, four villages of Tiwa speakers, one of Towa speakers, and

five villages of Tewa speakers, including those of Santa Clara Pueblo. The amount of information known and recorded varies considerably from one tribe to another and also from one linguistic grouping to another. For example, throughout the historic period there has been at least occasional mention of a sixth Tewa Pueblo and, hence, a sixteenth Eastern Pueblo tribe, Pojoaque. This tribe has numbered far less than a hundred members during the better part of recent decades, has experienced a high proportion of intermarriages with Hispanos, has lost much of its language and culture, and, accordingly, has often been omitted from discussions of Pueblo Indian culture. In recent years, however, something of a revival has occurred at Pojoaque, and limited data concerning the pueblo are appearing from time to time in such discussions.

Limited details concerning the culture of Santa Clara Pueblo have appeared in the form of specific ethnographic studies and also as components of more comprehensive studies of the several Tewa tribes, of the Eastern Puebloans, or even the Southwestern Pueblo Indians. While the following survey, or review, of the pertinent literature is by no means intended to be exhaustive, mentions of the more significant contributions regarding Santa Clara Pueblo have been included for the benefit of the reader or scholar interested in further background or context for the topics discussed in this volume.

While Santa Clara Pueblo and its mission church received some attention in the early Spanish documents, as in those by

Benavides in 1630–34 and Domínguez in 1776, for example, detailed descriptions of the pueblo, the mission, the people, their situation, and their customs did not appear until the latter part of the nineteenth century. Even then, the information was disappointingly incomplete. With few exceptions, Santa Clara was not on the usual route of travelers and expeditions, being on the west bank of the Rio Grande and also rather isolated from the routes leading westward from the Rio Grande Valley through or around the rugged terrain of the Pajarito Plateau and the Jemez Mountains.

Beginning at the end of the 1870s, a slowly expanding body of information on the Santa Clara Indians has grown. Museum collections for the newly formed Bureau of Ethnology, Washington, D.C., were made by Colonel James Stevenson at Santa Clara and also other pueblos, both in 1879 and 1880. Cursory description and observations on Santa Clara are to be found in the 1881 journals of Captain John G. Bourke; the journals and publications of Adolph F. Bandelier provide more extensive details on Santa Clara for the period between 1880 and 1892. Photographers, such as Jack Hillers (1879) and A.C. Vroman (1900), included Santa Clara on their picture-taking itineraries. However, it was not until after the turn of the century that any appreciable amount of information was forthcoming.

At the turn of the century, anthropological activities in the area were steadily increasing, in part a reflection of the growing momentum of the broadly conceived research program of the recently created and newly redesignated Bureau of American Ethnology, Washington, D.C.. Field notes gathered as early as 1895 from various pueblos by Frederick Webb Hodge became integrated in the comprehensive *Handbook of American Indians North of Mexico,* Bulletin 30, that Hodge edited for the BAE. Part 1 was issued in 1907; Part 2, in 1910.

Teams of investigators gathered data on a variety of subjects that led to several other BAE bulletins: from field investigations beginning in 1896 on the Pajarito Plateau came Edgar L. Hewett's *Antiquities of the Jemez Plateau, New Mexico,* in 1906; from

Hewett, Junius Henderson, and Wilfred W. Robbins came *The Physiography of the Rio Grande Valley, New Mexico, in Relation to Pueblo Culture,* in 1913; from Henderson and John P. Harrington came *Ethnozoology of the Tewa Indians,* in 1914; and from Robbins, Harrington, and Barbara Freire-Marreco came *Ethnobotany of the Tewa Indians,* in 1916. A more voluminous report, "The Ethnogeography of the Tewa Indians," by Harrington, based on his fieldwork of 1910–11, was included in the 29th Annual Report of the BAE (for the 1907–8 year), although this did not appear in print until 1916.

While these several reports incorporated certain Santa Clara data, such as designations, names, and usages, the bulk of the material came from other Tewa villages, such as San Juan and San Ildefonso, or was presented in nonspecific "Tewa" discussions.

These activities were paralleled by fieldwork and publication sponsored initially through the Southwest Society of Santa Fe; this was the Santa Fe affiliate of the Archaeological Institute of America and soon changed its name to the School of American Research. Edgar L. Hewett became the first director, beginning his service on January 1, 1907. Under Hewett's leadership, further investigations were carried out; these included archaeological surveys and both test and full excavations. Attention was also given to the Pueblo Indians of that day and to the information from them that could be applied to the interpretation of the remains of the archaeological Puebloan cultures. In present-day terms, these investigations were not very sophisticated, but the value of trying to make associations between prehistoric and historic cultures was clearly recognized, and beginnings were made in this direction.

Over the next few years, archaeological work was carried out on the ruins of the Rito de los Frijoles, especially at Tyuonyi, and on others located on the Pajarito Plateau. Initially, however, excavations were made at ruins still farther north, at Puyé. These remains were generally considered to be the ancestral homes of the Tewa, including the people of Santa Clara Pueblo. In 1908, Hewett, writing in the magazine *Out West,* described the work at Puyé which had begun in the summer of 1907. His remarks are of interest here:

> At first, determined opposition to the excavation of the ruins at Puyé was offered by the Indians from the nearest Tewa village, Santa Clara, ten miles away in the Rio Grande Valley, on whose reservation the site is located. The governor, head men, and representatives of the caciques, or religious rulers, were met in council and the whole matter frankly laid before them. It was explained to them that this was our way of studying the history of the Indian tribes; that we believed that the thoughts and works of their ancestors and of the other peoples with whom they had been in contact constituted a noble record, worthy of being recovered and preserved for all time. Some appeal was made to their sense of gratitude for assistance rendered them in the past in securing from the government a much-needed and justly-deserved extension of their reservation, and a law releasing them from the payment of taxes on their lands, which at one time had threatened the extinction of the titles to their homes. Bare reference was made to the fact that under the permit of the Department of the Interior we were acting entirely within our rights in making excavations on their reservation, for it was desired to rely mostly upon their higher sentiments in the matter. I greatly regret that I am unable to reproduce the speeches of the head men on this subject. They abounded in incisive and cogent argument which demanded unequivocal and logical answer. On the whole, their contention was on a high plane, and their deliberation marked by much lofty sentiment. It ended in all objection being withdrawn and most cordial relations established, which were afterward expressed in a perfectly friendly attitude toward, and interest in, our work.

Another comment on the general situation in which researchers worked early in this century was found in comments by Harrington. In his Introduction to "The Ethnogeography of the Tewa Indians," he noted that the information had been gathered "chiefly in 1910." Harrington continued:

> The difficulties encountered have been many. The Tewa are reticent and secretive with regard to religious matters, and their cosmographical ideas and much of their knowledge about place-names are hard to obtain. Their country is rugged and arid. Most of the places visited were reached on foot in company with one or more Indian informants whose names for obvious reasons are not here given. The region has never been accurately mapped. All of the maps at the writer's disposal are full of errors, many of the features shown being wrongly placed or named, while others are omitted altogether, and still others given where they do not exist. The occurrence of many of the names in a number of dialects or languages has not facilitated the work.

While Harrington's frame of reference was the Tewa, categorically, his characterization may be safely taken as applicable to any Tewa tribe, including Santa Clara. From his discussion, it is clear that his data actually came from informants primarily from the pueblos of Santa Clara, San Juan, and San Ildefonso.

In 1911, Herbert J. Spinden published briefly on pottery making at San Ildefonso, and, in 1915, on Tewa mythology and on home songs of the Tewa. Subsequently, in 1933, Spinden published *Songs of the Tewa* for members of the Explorer's Club of which he was then president. (In 1975, this volume of 144 pages, with newly added supplemental material, was reprinted by the Sunstone Press of Santa Fe.) Between 1913 and 1917, Matilda Coxe Stevenson and W. B. Douglas, separately, published several brief articles on the Tewa, but, all in all, specific information pertaining to Santa Clara was minimal.

Although unfinished and, of course, never published, a manuscript of nearly four hundred pages, "Notes on the Rio Grande

Pueblos," was compiled sometime during this period by Spinden. His fieldwork had been carried out between 1909 and 1913, supported by the Huntington Southwest Fund. As the title suggested, the study was conceived as comprehensive; however, there was enough specific information, identified as such, on Santa Clara Pueblo as of that period of time to attract the interest of Hill who found the data useful as background for his own research beginning with the 1940s.

The 1920s marked the beginning of field-work and publication on the Tewa by Elsie Clews Parsons, a foremost student of the Pueblo Indians and, by that time, a decade into her field studies of Southwestern Indian cultures. In 1924, she published "Tewa Kin, Clan, and Moiety," drawing on the material she had collected in 1923, principally from San Juan, Santa Clara, and San Ildefonso. This paper was followed in 1929 by a considerably larger study, *The Social Organization of the Tewa of New Mexico*. More comprehensive in scope and in depth, the volume included specific data from each of the five Tewa pueblos, including Santa Clara. In her Preface, Parsons remarked on various aspects of her fieldwork, 1923 to 1926; excerpts from her statement warrant inclusion here:

Of all the more visited Pueblo peoples the Tewa have been the least systematically described.... I undertook in November, 1923, the unwelcome task of duplicating research among a people who are past masters of the art of defeating inquiry.

...I settled in Alcalde, the Mexican town two or three miles north of San Juan, and, here,... I secured informants from San Juan, Santa Clara, and San Ildefonso. My informants worked singly or in couples, niece and uncle, sister and brother, mother and daughter, one interpreting for the other....

After three visits at Alcalde, which proved a good base also for work further afield than the Tewa, in 1926 I moved to a ranch between Santa Clara and San Ildefonso, too near either pue-

blo for adventure by the townspeople, always apprehensive of spies....

For the most part I have kept the data from each town particularized. This may seem overmeticulous, and further work among the Tewa will undoubtedly show that in many cases a general statement would have sufficed for what will prove to be a widespread or general practice. But at present, given the incompleteness of our knowledge and the unequal reliability of my informants, I do not mind erring on the side of the meticulous. Moreover, social organization, it is safe to say, will never be found to be quite the same in any two pueblos of any of the Pueblo tribes. The Pueblos offer an unusually interesting field for a study of the distribution of traits within the same general culture area, and this larger study is dependent on intensive studies from town to town, not merely from tribe to tribe. [From the present-day viewpoint, these last two statements need explanation, or clarification. Parsons seems to have been thinking of "tribe" as a linguistic grouping, *i.e.,* Tewa. Today, her "town"—as in the case of each Tewa Pueblo—actually constitutes a tribe; each of these has a recognized political and cultural independence. These tribes, in turn, are affiliated in linguistic groupings, as indicated earlier in this discussion.]

Since I did not reside in any pueblo during my investigation I will not undertake to give an general picture of town life.... With Laguna, the most Americanized of the Keresan towns [*i.e.,* tribes], one might compare Santa Clara. Like Laguna, Santa Clara has experienced a long standing feud between progressive pro-Americans and conservative anti-Americans, in alignment being true to the outstanding pattern of Tewa classification, the moiety pattern, Summer People against Winter People. Recently the Winter people have been electing their own governor; some time they may form one more Pueblo group to found a new town because of religious incompatibilities. Meanwhile, they are not washing their dirty linen in public, a decency I exceedingly regret, since it leaves the history of the quarrel unrecorded. The short-haired English-speaking young man I counted on as historian was one of the most tongue-tied Pueblos it has been my misfortune to meet. There had been recent deaths in the family, I learned later, which were attributed to having told some white person something.

Subsequently, in 1939, Parsons was to publish her prodigious, two-volume, *Pueblo Indian Religion.* Again, she was careful to keep most of the material from each pueblo distinctly identified as such. Some of the Santa Clara information was new—not previously published; a considerable amount, however, had appeared earlier in such works as the 1929 study of social organization already mentioned.

Earlier, in 1931, a manuscript, "Santa Clara: A New Mexico Tewa Pueblo," had been compiled by Jean Allard Jeançon (1931b). Some hundred pages in length, with drawings and photographs in addition, this ethnography and miscellaneous field notes (1904-30) were presented by him to the Bureau of American Ethnology. As Jeançon commented in his brief Introduction, he had spent "some thirty years of observations and study with the Tewa Indians of New Mexico, especially of those living at Santa Clara." Acknowledging the assistance of his Tewa friends, Jeançon also expressed his gratitude to "Mr. M.W. Stirling, Chief of the Bureau of American Ethnology, for making possible the final assembling and publication of these notes." His concluding paragraph is of interest here:

> In a final effort to obtain information in 1930 the writer was amazed to find that fully sixty per-cent of the information contained in this report is unknown to the younger generations, and that the older people are going so rapidly that it will only be a comparatively short period of years until no further information of any value will be obtainable. Many of the men and women of thirty to forty years of age... now know but very little of the material in this report.

As already explained in the Preface to this volume, the Jeançon manuscript was not published. After some years, it was sent by Stirling to W. W. Hill with the request that he check over the material and fill in whatever gaps he could. The present volume is, in large part, the result of that implementation, greatly expanded by the information subsequently gathered by Hill.

In 1930, Hewett, among his remarks in the volume *Ancient Life in the American Southwest,* included this observation:

> It [Santa Clara Pueblo] has the distinction of being the home of Santiago Naranjo (O ye ge pi), four times governor of the pueblo (conservative), best known of all Pueblo Indians, guide, philosopher, and friend of archaeologists, artists and tourists without number, but firm fundamentalist for the old, true, good way.

In more recent years, following World War II, a number of noteworthy publications on the Pueblo Indians and on the Tewa Indians have appeared. Among these was *Bird's Eye View of the Pueblos,* in 1950, by Stanley A. Stubbs. This small volume presented a collection of recent aerial photographs of the pueblos with explanatory diagrams and limited text material for each. While obviously very limited in depth, this volume has been a unique and useful contribution. (Plate 1 is a vertical aerial photograph of Santa Clara taken about the same time, 1950, as the photographs used by Stubbs.)

In 1969, there appeared a volume of even greater interest here. *The Tewa World* was a study by Alfonso Ortiz, a native of San Juan Pueblo with a doctorate from the University of Chicago and teaching experience in California, Princeton University, and currently, at the University of New Mexico. While consistently designated "Tewa," the material was understandably heavily weighted toward San Juan Pueblo. A few specific references were made to Santa Clara, but the greatest portion of the discussion was to Tewa as exemplified by San Juan. Certain basic patterns were deemed common to other Tewa tribes, but allowance must also be made for deviations among the other Tewa pueblos, such as Santa Clara, as Ortiz himself recognized.

The following year, in 1970, *The Pueblo Indians of North America,* by Edward P. Dozier, appeared. Dozier, a native of Santa Clara Pueblo, held a doctoral degree from the University of California at Los Angeles, and was said to be the first Indian to obtain such a degree. He taught at the University of Oregon, Northwestern University, and at the University of Arizona where, at a relatively early age and highly regarded by all who knew him, he died in 1971. Earlier, Dozier had published, in addition to numerous articles, two monographs on the Tewa of First Mesa in Arizona: *The Hopi-Tewa of Arizona,* in 1954, and *Hano: A Tewa Indian Community in Arizona,* in 1966.

Benefiting from his ability to communicate in Tewa with the people of Hano, Dozier was more comfortable working away from his home pueblo. Also, the various New Mexico Tewa villages had attracted earlier and greater attention from researchers, and, of course, Dozier was well aware of Hill's research interests in Santa Clara. As a student at the University of New Mexico before World War II, he had contributed greatly to Hill's acceptance at Santa Clara. Dozier assisted in finding good informants for Hill, and he critically read much of the material as Hill gathered it.

Dozier's general publication (1970a) contained a certain amount of Santa Clara data, but, for the most part, the discussions were balanced, through time and in area, among the various Pueblo Indians.

In 1975, three additional publications deserving of mention here made their appearance. The first, a smaller, more specialized book, *Santa Clara Pottery Today,* was by Betty LeFree. The second, by Vincent Scully, was entitled, *Pueblo: Mountain, Village, Dance.* Almost four hundred pages in length, it was profusely illustrated; the treatment of Santa Clara Pueblo, together with Puyé, covered somewhat over twenty pages, primarily photographs. The third, another general book, *Indians of the American Southwest,* was by Bertha P. Dutton. Again, of necessity in view of the title and purpose

of the volume, only a few paragraphs dealt specifically with Santa Clara.

In 1976, there appeared yet another general book, *The Pueblo Indians,* by Joe S. Sando, a native of Jemez Pueblo. It presented a more general discussion, again with few references to Santa Clara, although one interview with Joseph Filario Tafoya of Santa Clara Pueblo was specifically listed (p. 247) by Sando. There was also a brief biographical sketch of Dozier (pp. 171-76).

In this review of the pertinent literature, one further commentary is appropriate. During his years in the Southwest, from the latter half of 1880 through the early months of 1892, Adolph F. Bandelier visited Santa Clara Pueblo a number of times. Information gained from informants at the pueblo, both Indian and non-Indian, was incorporated to some extent in several of his publications, particularly the *Final Report* of 1890-92. In addition, however, Bandelier maintained a journal almost daily throughout his Southwestern years. Planned on the basis of four volumes, these journals have been edited and annotated by the present editor, together with my colleagues Carroll L. Riley and Elizabeth M. Lange. To date, three volumes have appeared in print: 1880-82, in 1966; 1883-84, in 1970; and 1885-88, in 1975. The manuscript for the final volume, 1889-92, is presently well along toward completion and publication. Considerable previously unpublished material pertaining to Santa Clara Pueblo, the archives once kept there, and the people was recorded by Bandelier in his journals during his numerous visits to the village and several periods of residence there.

From the foregoing overview, it is readily apparent that there has been a rather continuous awareness of Santa Clara Pueblo on the part of numerous researchers for many years. It should be equally apparent that a broad, in-depth treatment of this tribal culture has not yet appeared in print. Hence, Hill's diligence in gathering such materials as the unpublished earlier data of Spinden and, more importantly, the data compiled by Jeançon, and his success in integrating these materials with his own more extensive and intensive field data constitute obviously significant achievements. An additional value of the material stems from the fact that, as of this point in time, much of the information is simply no longer available to anyone, Indian or non-Indian. Comments to this effect were already being made at the turn of the century and also in 1930 by Jeançon, as brought out earlier in this discussion.

A further benefit to Hill's presentation came when, very early, he was able to obtain a critical reading of Jeançon's manuscript by Elsie Clews Parsons, since deceased. In returning the manuscript to Hill, Parsons offered comments in an accompanying letter of September 5, 1940, which has been reproduced here.

Dear Dr. Hill:

Under separate cover I am returning Jeançon's paper. There are several points suggestive for inquiry. But if possible most of the material should be checked or verified. See marginal comments. Jeançon is sometimes a poor observer and recorder. His English is faulty and some of his interpretation questionable.

The clanship situation at Santa Clara is very confused. Unfortunately Jeançon throws no light on it. This will be one of your problems. It can be worked out, if at all, only genealogically, it seems to me. Generalization won't do, merely leaving the situation in a speculative condition, as you may see from the reprint I sent you.

Curiously enough, Jeançon says nothing about the notorious Santa Clara feud (see Parsons, Pueblo Indian Religion, 1137 n.* for a historical note on this). It should be checked up, its history and present day circumstances.

Several ceremonial matters have been noted among the other Pueblos but not recorded before for the Tewa, e.g., second-sight through water gazing; the pregnancy doll (Cochiti); the Earth Mother who sleeps or rests in winter and may not be disturbed (Taos) which accounts for the December period of "staying still." Again the December retreats which are like those of Taos-Isleta—an important parallel. Some of the witchcraft theory of disease is novel.

The pictures are very interesting. We have a few Tewa kachina pictures or altar pictures. My kachina pictures for Santa Clara were drawn, miserably, by a woman. Jeançon pictures should also be compared with mine from San Juan. A great many details differ, as is to be expected, but the general impression is similar.

I have not compared Jeançon *intensively* with "Tewa Social Organization" [Parsons's 1929 publication, CHL] but this should be done. Each study would enrich the other. I hope you will let me see your ms. before you publish it.

Sincerely
Elsie Clews Parsons

Thus, the preparation of this manuscript for publication has been seen as a challenging opportunity, a heavy, but satisfying, responsibility. Every effort has been made to keep the finished form faithful to Hill's rendering of it; at the same time, certain modifications have been made on the premise that much of the manuscript was in no more than preliminary draft and the same or comparable changes would certainly have been made had Hill been able to complete the writing himself.

Throughout the text, the initials of informants as recorded by Hill have been replaced by less revealing numbers enclosed in brackets; in this manner, the sources of specific items of information have been preserved, but the risk of unintentionally revealing the identities of informants has been virtually eliminated. Despite the fact that many of Hill's informants are no longer living, the need still exists to safeguard the others and also the families of all concerned.

Once again, the Preface and this Introduction, as well as the initial chapters on Geographical Setting and Pre-History and History have been written by the editor. Hill's work had not progressed to the point of preparing these units, even in rough draft. Nonetheless, it seems entirely reasonable that he would have done so before considering the work ready for publication. The remainder of the chapters are essentially as prepared by Hill. The number of notations inserted into the discussion of Chapters 3 through 10 have been held to a minimum; they have been enclosed in brackets with an accompanying "WWH" or "CHL" for purposes of identification and clarification.

1

Geographical Setting

Santa Clara Pueblo lies in the "Tewa Basin" of north central New Mexico; it is two miles south of Española, the nearest town (Plate 2), and is almost thirty miles, by highway, northwest of Santa Fe, and fifteen miles north of Los Alamos, on State Highway 30. The pueblo has been in its present location since sometime in the fourteenth century according to Stubbs, who also noted that its present name came from the early Spaniards, in honor of St. Clare of Assisi (1950:43). At the same time, Stubbs, citing Harrington, gave the native name for the pueblo as Kapo'onwi. Hodge (1907–10: II, 456), in an earlier listing of native names for the pueblo, gave preference to K'hapóo, meaning "where the roses (?) grow near the water." Among the variants also given by Hodge were: Ca-po, or Ka-po (perhaps the most commonly used); Capoo, or Kapou; Caypa, or Kai'pa; Kap-ho', and K'ha-po'-o.

For many years, the Indians of Santa Clara have been the second largest Tewa-speaking tribe; as of 1972–73, the tribe had 1,168 members, a total surpassed only by San Juan Pueblo's population of 1,627 (Sando 1976:237). Other Tewa-speaking tribes have been appreciably smaller.

Situated on a low, gravel bench above the Rio Grande Valley where most of the irri-gated fields are, Santa Clara Pueblo is at an elevation of about 5,600 feet (Plate 3). The Tewa Basin is surrounded by mountains and high plateaus; the most abrupt rise, to nearly 12,000 feet, is found in the Jemez Mountains to the west. Farther away and to the east is the Sangre de Cristo Range of the southern Rocky Mountains, with Santa Fe Baldy Peak, 12,622 feet, and North Truchas Peak, 13,102 feet. The Tewa Basin is divided from north to south by the Rio Grande; several permanent tributaries are important in the natural and cultural life of the basin. The Rio Chama, from the northwest, joins the Rio Grande just north of Española, and on the eastern side of the Rio Grande there are the Santa Cruz River and the Pojoaque River, with its tributaries, the Nambé and Tesuque rivers.

Westward from the pueblo, the canyon of the ephemeral Santa Clara Creek leads up into the Jemez Mountains toward Santa Clara, or Tschicoma (Chicomo) Peak, 11,950 feet. Nearer the village, irrigated fields have been made possible by Santa Clara Creek. Higher up, Santa Clara Canyon has been made into a recreation area, administered by the tribe and open to campers, fishermen, and other users on a fee basis. This is part of the Santa Clara Reservation, which extends westward from the original Santa Clara Grant. The grant includes the pueblo, and its rectangular area is more or less divided in half by the Rio Grande flowing through it from north to south.

According to Aberle (1948:80), the original Santa Clara Grant was from the King of Spain, date uncertain, and amounted to 12,244.30 acres; the grant was confirmed by Congress, December 22, 1858. An additional parcel, the "Shoe String Grant," was also given by the King of Spain, July 19, 1763; this grant was confirmed by the Court of Private Land Claims, September 29, 1894, and was subsequently patented, November 15, 1909. By Executive Order, July 29, 1905, the Santa Clara Reservation of 33,044.30 acres was created. These acquisitions came to a total of 45,741.78 acres, most commonly referred to as 45,742 acres.

In an accompanying footnote (p. 80n136), Aberle stated that an official survey of the original grant gave a total of 16,308.01 acres "less 4,079.71 acres non-Indian private claims and 4.00 acres school site (Gov't. land)." She further noted that the resulting total, 12,228.3 acres, included 252.10 acres that had been purchased for the tribe with Compensation Funds during the period from 1937 to 1941.

Elsewhere (p. 84), Aberle gave a figure of 547 acres for agricultural [irrigated] land, with the remainder classified as grazing land. Figures from other sources have varied, perhaps simply a matter of different time references rather than actual errors. Smith (1966: 135), citing the same total of 45,742 acres, indicated 700 irrigated acres and 44,818 acres of rangeland, "including 10,400 acres of forest containing an undetermined amount of commercial timber." Sando (1976: 238) gave a total area, as of 1972–73, of 44,589 acres of which 1,150 acres were irrigated and available for agriculture.

A few observations should be made regarding the nature of soils in the Santa Clara area. Two soils dominate: one is a permeable form, ranging from grayish- or light-brown to reddish-brown and is on the higher slopes where it has been washed down from higher elevations. Alluvial fans of this soil occur along the edges of the valley, or basin.

More important to Santa Clara agriculture is the sedimentary soil carried by the Rio Grande and its tributaries, especially the Rio Chama. This soil is comprised of sands, gravels, and clays ranging from a dark- to a grayish-brown, often with reddish hues.

Before 1880, the flow of the Rio Grande was sufficient to scour the channel of sediment, but since that date the decreased flow and the increasing production of silt on the watershed has brought about results of disastrous importance to the people of the Middle Valley (Harper, Cordova, and Oberg 1943:39).

Earlier in their discussion (p. 37), these authors had noted that the silt received in the Rio Grande as it crossed the Colorado-New Mexico line was negligible; in the next 75 miles to Chamita, or approximately at San Juan Pueblo, 1,000 acre-feet of silt were being carried but only a negligible amount was being deposited. In the 35-mile stretch from Chamita to the White Rock Dam, a few miles north of Cochiti Pueblo, another 4,000 acre-feet of silt had been received from the Chama, Santa Cruz, and Pojoaque rivers. However, of the new total of 5,000 acre-feet, only a negligible amount of silt was being deposited. In other words, silting was not a major problem in the area of the Santa Clara Grant.

Physiographically, Santa Clara Pueblo lies near the southern tip of the Southern Rocky Mountain Province of the Rocky Mountain System, a Major Physical Division of the country (Fenneman n.d.). The province is characterized by complex mountains of various types and intermontane basins, features in which the Santa Clara Grant and Reservation are typical.

Long-term weather records for Santa Clara itself do not exist; however, those for nearby Española extend back more than sixty years and may be taken as essentially valid for Santa Clara (Dorroh 1946). The growing season covers 164 days, from April 29 to October 10. Annual precipitation amounts to only 10.05″ and ranges from a December low of 0.39″ to an August high of 1.71″. Mean temperature averages 51.1°, with a January low of 29.3° and a July high of 72.2° (pp. 37, 42, 45). Typically, the greater incidence of precipitation occurs during the latter portion, mid-July to mid-September, of the agricultural season. These summer storms are often short but violent, and the rain is frequently accompanied by thunder, lightning, and hail. At times, considerable damage to the crops results from the hail, and both crops and the irrigation systems suffer at times from the flash flooding.

The Santa Clara Grant falls entirely within the Upper Sonoran Life Zone, but the Reservation, to the west, is partly within the Transition Life Zone also. The Upper Sonoran zone has sparse vegetation dominated by desert shrubs, cacti, yucca, and short grasses. Where more moisture occurs, there are scattered junipers and piñons, and also the grass is better. Agriculture seldom is possible without irrigation (F. Bailey 1928: Pl. 2; V. Bailey 1913: 19-52). Travel accounts and similar records, however, suggest that a century or more ago, there was limited success with various forms of dry and floodwater farming. Such success has been generally attributed to a better balance among precipitation, water table, and vegetation rather than to any appreciable increase in rainfall (Bryan 1925, 1929, 1941; see also Hack 1942).

Along the Rio Grande and in the mountain canyons, several species of cottonwood are common. West of the Grant, the Santa Clara Reservation extends up into the Transition Zone, as mentioned; higher still is the Canadian Life Zone. These higher elevations, their forests and their game, have been and continue to be important to the Indians of Santa Clara and neighboring tribes. Various species of pine, spruce, and fir are important, with junipers and piñons continuing to appear at the lower levels.

Important animals for the Santa Clara Indians, more particularly in the past than in recent years, include deer, bear, wildcat, badger, coyote, wolf, fox, rabbit, skunk, and squirrel. Mountain sheep and elk have not been seen in the area for decades; mountain lions, or cougars, are more prominent but have not been common in recent years. To hunt bison, the Santa Clara Indians had to go at least to the Pecos Valley, if not farther east.

Principal birds of the area include various eagles, hawks, owls, and ducks as well as turkey, quail, dove, and a variety of songbirds. The bull snake, king snake, and prairie rattlesnake are all native to the area, but, for the most part, they are less numerous than in former times. Numerous small lizards and turtles are also present.

Of these various faunal forms, some were of particular interest to the Indians for food, clothing, implements, and other practical purposes; other forms were useful and even vital as elements in ceremonies; and some were of value in both respects.

Although not specifically concerned with Santa Clara, Ford (1972) has provided a recent, general discussion of ecological phenomena pertaining to Eastern Pueblo culture. His remarks are of value in seeking an understanding of Santa Clara Pueblo culture.

2

Prehistory
and History

PREHISTORY

Precise knowledge of Santa Clara culture history remains tenuous and rather scanty, particularly that of the prehistoric, or pre-Spanish, period. Stubbs (1950:43) was of the opinion that Santa Clara Pueblo had existed in its present location "for some time prior to the coming of the Spanish." More specifically, he stated that the pueblo was "probably founded in the fourteenth century." From these generalities, a few more detailed comments are justified in terms of the limited archaeological evidence.

As a basis for such a discussion, it is helpful to note several admonitions expressed by Dozier (1970b: 203–5) in his perceptive paper, "Making Inferences from the Present to the Past," which appeared in the volume *Reconstructing Prehistoric Pueblo Societies* (Longacre 1970). Dozier warned of the fallacies in assuming too much similarity between the present and the past, including the persistence of such cultural traits and behavioral patterns as language, social and political structures, and ceremonial organization.

Ford, Schroeder, and Peckham (1972: 20-21) have recently summarized the principal hypotheses regarding the reconstruction of

Puebloan prehistory. Taking note of earlier papers by Reed (1949, 1950), Hawley (1950), Wendorf (1954), and Wendorf and Reed (1955), they recognized the alternative suggestions of either a Tewa origin at Mesa Verde prior to the migration to the Tewa Basin of north central New Mexico or a beginning as a Tewa component, in their present location, the northern portion of a long development in the Rio Grande Valley, citing earlier literature for each hypothesis.

In a somewhat detailed discussion of Tewa prehistoric origins, specifically, Ford, Schroeder, and Peckham (1972: 31-32) presented their own preferences in this reconstruction. While some deference to Schroeder's ideas was noted (p. 31), the views of all three were expressed and some divergence of opinion retained in their summary statement.

Tewa-speaking peoples shared a common prehistoric heritage with Towa-speakers in the upper San Juan drainage until about A.D. 700. After that date, the makers of Piedra Black-on-White pottery, "presumably ancestral Tewa living in the Piedra district," could be distinguished from others, such as the Rosa Black-on-white Towa potters. As late as A.D. 900, after the Tewa-Towa split, the Tewa remained in the upper San Juan. "About A.D. 1000 they moved southward down the Chama as well as the Puerco to an area northwest of Albuquerque."

During that period, there were Tewa in the vicinity of Cuba, Española, north of Albuquerque, and in the Galisteo Basin and even in the area east of the Sangre de Cristo Mountains. By A.D. 1250, the Tewa east of the mountains had shifted into the Española region and also on up the Chama Valley to the northwest. Other Tewas were pressured out of the Jemez-Salado area by Towa and Keresan speakers, and they moved into the unoccupied Pajarito Plateau and also into the Chama Valley.

Fords and Peckham's interpretations were in general agreement with Schroeder's reconstruction although they differed somewhat regarding certain details of chronology and of various migrations insofar as places and directions were concerned (pp. 31–32).

Unanimity prevails regarding Tewa prehistory commencing with Wiyo B/W pottery. Following a short period, around A.D. 1300, of small unit villages, good sized villages were built along the Chama and its major tributaries as well as tributaries of the Rio Grande from northern sections of Bandelier [National Monument] north to Velarde... In other words, the Tewa and Chama basins were both occupied by Tewa speakers. However, through the last prehistoric century a gradual concentration into larger communities such as Sapawe occurred. These withdrawals to pueblos on the Rio Grande from the Chama and Pajarito Plateau in the late 1500s are generally attributable to droughts of that period (cf. Schroeder 1968). The two Tewa language groupings continued into historic times. The Tano group in 1680–96 moved into the Santa Cruz valley north of Santa Fe prior to moving to Hopi in 1706. These southern Tewa still speak a dialect quite distinct from that of the northern Tewa. (p. 32)

It is clear from examining the ethnogeographic data collected by Harrington (1916: 147–57, 231–60) that the Santa Clara Indians, along with other Tewa tribes, had names and gave other evidence of associations with innumerable archaeological Pueblo sites in the vicinity of Santa Clara Pueblo, either at Puyé and elsewhere on the Pajarito Plateau to the south or in the Chama Valley to the northwest. Occupation of these sites had virtually ceased in all of these locations, however, by the time the first Spaniards arrived in the mid-sixteenth century.

HISTORY

Sixteenth century contacts between the Spaniards and the Tewa-speaking villages of north central New Mexico were relatively minimal and of little direct consequence in the overall culture history of the area. The early expeditions of Coronado (1540–42), Chamuscado-Rodríguez (1581–82), and Espejo (1582) recorded little, if any, significant data regarding the Tewa tribes beyond their number and location, rather vaguely perceived in most instances, and several Pueblo designations (Hammond and Rey 1940, 1966).

Less than a decade after Espejo's visit, Castaño de Sosa made brief contacts with most of the Tewa villages, very probably being at Santa Clara Pueblo on January 16, 1591. However, this visit was for no more than a part of that one day as Castaño and his companions promptly left for San Ildefonso Pueblo, across the Rio Grande and several miles downstream (Schroeder and Matson 1965:133–34).

Gutiérrez de Humaña's party, according to Schroeder (1972:47), spent "a good part of 1593 among the Tewa of San Ildefonso"; unfortunately, no ethnographic information concerning the neighboring village of Santa Clara has yet come to light. For that matter, Gutiérrez left hardly any information regarding San Ildefonso Pueblo.

Shortly thereafter, the much larger expedition of Don Juan de Oñate left Mexico and proceeded up the Rio Grande Valley. After religious and civil ceremonies along the way, as at Santo Domingo Pueblo, July 7, 1598, Oñate reached San Juan Pueblo

(Ohke) July 11, 1598. His followers established a headquarters among the Tewa—at San Juan de Caballeros, on the east bank of the Rio Grande. After several weeks, the headquarters, or capital, was shifted to Yunque Pueblo, designated San Gabriel, which was located at the junction of the Chama River and the Rio Grande. A church there was dedicated September 8, 1598, and missionaries were assigned to various Indian pueblos. Fray Cristóbal de Salazar and Fray Juan de San Buenaventura, a lay brother, were assigned to the Tewa villages near San Juan, undoubtedly including Santa Clara Pueblo. San Gabriel remained the capital of the province until Governor Don Pedro de Peralta, Oñate's successor, founded Santa Fe in 1610 (Hammond and Rey 1953:I, 10–18).

In summarizing Spanish relations with the Tewa pueblos surrounding them, Schroeder (1972: 50) made a number of observations that merit inclusion here. Although these remarks pertained to the Tewa generally rather than to Santa Clara specifically, they nonetheless provide a context for some understanding of the early seventeenth century situation in the Tewa Basin.

Oñate was well aware of the deep enmity that had resulted from the contacts of the earlier Spanish expeditions with the Pueblo tribes to the south of the Tewa—the Keresans and, perhaps especially, the southern Tiwa. Wishing to avoid the shorter growing season of the northern Tiwa (Taos and Picuris), Oñate decided to settle among the Tewa, aware that they had pledged their obedience to the king during Castaño's visit. The plentiful crops of the Tewa area were undoubtedly a further attraction.

During these initial years, Schroeder suggested that Oñate had introduced several new items, including "fireplaces, sundried adobe bricks, a church, and associated architectural features as well as the tools used for construction" (p. 50). The missionaries seldom remained for extended periods in their parishes during these early years, except perhaps among the neighboring Tewa villages.

Prior to 1610 and the establishment of the new capital of Santa Fe in the relatively unoccupied region between the Tewas and the Keresans, there were no additional Spanish settlements. This failure to expand their holdings may well have resulted from a general concern over hostilities that had reached fresh intensity among Apaches and other traditional enemies against the Tewa tribes and their newly acquired allies. As these attacks increased and continued droughts exerted further pressure upon the Tewas in the Chama Valley, they moved to join their Tewa relatives along the Rio Grande. Partly because of the attacks and partly because of the increased crowding, the Spanish may have hastened the decision to shift their headquarters to the new location at Santa Fe. At any rate, during this first decade of the seventeenth century, it was the Tewa rather than the other Puebloan tribes who seem "to have [been] exposed . . . to things Spanish" (p. 51).

For the remaining decades prior to the Pueblo Indian Revolt of 1680 against the Spaniards, tensions steadily mounted throughout the Puebloan area of New Mexico. Both religious and civil authorities abused the Indians; relations between the two groups of Spanish officials also deteriorated as each group rivaled the other for advantages with the Indians. (See Scholes 1937 and 1942 for details of this often bitter rivalry that was a major factor among the causes of the 1680 Revolt. See also Schroeder 1972: 51–56.)

In summarizing the acculturative impact of the period 1680–96, from the time of the Revolt to the completion of the Reconquest under Governor Don Diego de Vargas, Schroeder (p. 56) offered these comments:

Though little detail concerning cultural change among the Puebloans is known during this period of little recordation, after the Spaniards had been expelled from New Mexico, the avowed intent of the leaders of the rebellion was to do away with all things Spanish. Their success in accomplishing this was minimal, even though force was used in one known case against Isleta. The Pueblo people retained horses, some cattle, metal objects, carts, still spoke Spanish, possibly as a *lingua franca,* and continued to grow Spanish-introduced crops. Churches were used for other purposes, few were destroyed, and in some instances altar pieces and other material were saved.

This was a period of strife among the Pueblo peoples themselves, and some groups fled to the more remote Hopi mesas; these refugees included a number of Tewas, among them Indians from Santa Clara Pueblo (p. 58). It was at this time that the Tewa-speaking village of Hano appeared among the Hopi towns of First Mesa. It is also of interest (and something of a surprise in view of Hill's noting the deep animosity expressed at Santa Clara regarding the Navajo in subsequent chapters of this volume) that Santa Clara Indians similarly found refuge among the Navajo Indians who happened to be on friendly terms with the Tewas at that time.

Further commenting upon the intertribal relations during this period of unusual movements between the eastern and western pueblos, Schroeder (p. 59) expressed his strong belief in the probability that a number of western customs were brought back to the Rio Grande villages when these people returned to their former homes. "As late as the 1880s, aboveground rectangular kivas (perhaps society houses in some cases?) among the Rio Grande pueblos were reported at Tesuque, San Juan, and Santa Clara ..."

Following the Reconquest and continuing on through the 1700s to 1821, when formal rule of the area passed from Spain to Mexico, the earlier animosities between the Spaniards and the Pueblo tribes returned. Missionaries attempted to eradicate native ceremonials and to discredit religious leaders, although their efforts were far from successful. Civil authorities similarly tried to increase their control over the tribes, strictly limiting the ownership of firearms and restricting the free movement of Indians from one pueblo to another. At times, however, raids by the Comanche and other "wild," i.e., non-Puebloan tribes succeeded in making temporary and somewhat uneasy allies of the Spaniards and the Pueblo Indians. In Schroeder's words (p. 61),

... when the Spaniards were not constantly campaigning against the surrounding tribes who were deeply involved in their own hostilities, Pueblo Indians became more involved in Spanish justice, obtaining acquittals or judgments in their favor ... as well as sentences, including banishment to other pueblos with different languages ... Spaniards were fined for employing Indians as shepherds or mistreating them ... Indians purchased land from Spaniards... and had judgments in their favor on land suits ... Santa Clara even filed a complaint in 1788 against its own governor...!

In summarizing his discussion of these and other relations between the Spaniards and the Indians, Schroeder (p. 65) commented as follows:

Adjustments of the Pueblo and Spanish people between 1700 and 1821 to a life without *encomenderos,* to many wild tribes through cooperative campaigns, to integration through mutual enterprises and some intermarriage, to common use of Spanish civil procedures, and so forth, had developed a society with two different cultures that lived fairly amicably side by side.

The relatively brief period under the government of Mexico, 1821–46, brought few actual changes to the Pueblo Indians of New Mexico.

... under the Plan of Iguala, the racial origin of citizens no longer was mentioned. This put the Pueblo Indians and genízaros on an equal footing with the remnant of the Spanish population. All citizens were concerned with the Santa Fe Trail trade, Navajo and Apache raids, American trapping ventures, and trade to the south. Independence had little effect in the way of direct influence from Mexico itself. The Puebloans and their villages coexisted with their neighbors throughout this period. (p. 65)

The processes of adoption, and adaption,

were at times slow and sometimes difficult. A brief quotation from Stephen's Hopi Journal (Parsons 1936:II, 848) provides a valuable perspective on the actual thinking of individuals during the process of acculturation among the Pueblos, applicable to the Rio Grande Valley and to Santa Clara Pueblo as well as to the Hopi towns.

A long while ago our old people got their first metal knives from the Spaniard. These were much better than the stone knives and they used them to fashion the prayer-sticks, but the portions of the prayer-stick touched with the metal knife were always rubbed upon stone to dispel the evil influence of the Spaniards. They denounced our kiva devotions and the making of prayer-sticks and they tried to compel our old people to have their heads washed by their long-robe men, the *tota'ichi*, (i.e. to be baptized by their priests) but our old people would not submit and they never had their heads washed by the Spaniards. But the people of Awa'tobi and Sikya'tki did, but the people of these two villages were bad.

Many traditional religious and political patterns continued with little modification. Religious rites continued to be generally closed to outsiders—the New Mexicans and the genízaros. Intertribal relations, particularly with the non-Puebloans, alternated between times of peace and trading and periods of hostilities marked by raids and countermeasures. Captives were commonly taken and traded as either servants or slaves. Increasingly, the Pueblo Indians participated in various aspects of New Mexican life.

In 1846, the arrival of General Stephen W. Kearny and his troops marked the end of Mexican governing in the area and the beginning of New Mexico as a territory of the United States. Immediate attempts to secure statehood for New Mexico found insufficient support in Congress, and on September 9, 1850, a compromise measure, the Organic Act of the Territory of New Mexico, was passed. This also served to settle a long-standing controversy with Texas concerning lands east of the Rio Grande.

On March 3, 1851, James C. Calhoun (as of March, 1849, the first Indian agent west of the Mississippi) became the first governor under the Organic Act. That summer, John B. Lamy became bishop of the newly created Roman Catholic Vicarate Apostolic of Santa Fe and, upon his arrival in Santa Fe, he began an extensive series of reforms, including an educational program. (See Horgan 1975 for a recent biography of this important figure; while a number of Pueblos appear in the index of this volume, there was no mention of Santa Clara Pueblo. The study nevertheless has value for anyone interested in the general historical background of Santa Clara Pueblo.)

The land laws of the United States were extended to New Mexico by Congress in July, 1854, and the territorial office of United States Surveyor-General was created. In 1856, this official, following an investigation of Pueblo Indian land claims, recommended confirmation of titles to eighteen pueblos, including Santa Clara. As noted in Chapter 1, the Santa Clara Grant was confirmed by Congress, December 22, 1858.

While slavery was not prevalent in New Mexico, sympathies in the Civil War tended to be initially with the South. However, an invasion of the Territory by Texans shifted the support of most New Mexicans to the Union. Several battles occurred in New Mexico, and finally, by 1862, the Territory of New Mexico was secured for the North.

With the depletion of garrisons and a general diversion of the army's attention to the more major actions of the Civil War in the East, the non-Puebloan tribes took advantage of the situation to renew their raids on the pueblos and other settlements of the territory. In the early 1860s, countermeasures resulted in the removal of several thousand Navajo Indians to the Bosque Redondo near Fort Sumner in eastern New Mexico, where they were held along with several hundred Mescalero Apaches. The reeducational program at Bosque Redondo was a failure, and the survivors were allowed to return to their former areas and the newly created reservation in western New Mexico and Arizona in 1868. Subsequently, the attacks on the pueblos and other communities all but ceased.

At about this time, the sale by Governor William A. Pile of the Spanish Santa Fe archives for waste paper in 1869–71 was a severe blow to those interested in learning about and preserving the history of the area. It was estimated that no more than about a quarter of these records were later recovered.

In 1875, on February 12, Bishop Lamy was named Archbishop of Santa Fe when the diocese was elevated to a metropolitan see by papal bull.

The first railroad track was laid in New Mexico on November 30, 1878; on December 7 of that year, the first locomotive crossed Raton Pass. In the 1880s a narrow-gage track reached Española from the north; after a few years, a new line connected this stretch of track to Santa Fe (Gjevre 1969: 1–7).

Other signs of progress and development continued during the last decades of the nineteenth century; to help establish titles to land grants in New Mexico and elsewhere in former Mexican territory, a Court of Private Land Claims was established, March 3, 1891. (By the middle of 1904, some 2,000,000 acres had been confirmed by this court.)

On May 12, 1892, the capitol building in Santa Fe burned, and many public documents and records were destroyed. These losses, in addition to Governor Pile's unfortunate act some twenty years earlier, as well as the destruction by the Indians of innumerable early records in the Pueblo Revolt of 1680, have resulted in making the reconstruction of New Mexican history—Spanish, Mexican, and early American—a very difficult if not impossible task, particularly for certain periods of time.

However, especially in the early American period, there are a number of generalized statements that have come down to us in the form of reports, letters, and diaries; few of these, unfortunately, can be related to specific communities, tribes, or events. Exceptions tend to be concentrated in the final decades of the nineteenth century—as, for example, the diary of Lieutenant John G.

Bourke, U.S. Army, who recorded observations and other information regarding various pueblos, tribes, places, events, and people. Fortunately, Bourke visited Santa Clara Pueblo on July 15, 1881. Because of the relative uniqueness of his notes, and to provide details in terms of time perspective, Bourke's comments are reproduced here with only minor changes in the account as edited by Bloom (1936: 255–58).

[From Santa Cruz] Drove through Española to the Pueblo of Santa Clara, six miles below. This is on the bank of the Rio Grande, on a low promontory of no elevation jutting out into the stream. The population numbers only [Bourke did not fill in the blank he left for the population figure. For the previous year, 1880, Bandelier, noting figures obtained from the office of Dr. B.M. Thomas, the Pueblo Agent, showed a population of 212 for Santa Clara Pueblo in his journal entry of July 16–17, 1882 (Lange and Riley 1966: 341). CHL], and is not deserving of any elaborate description, having in mind that already given of the people of Zuni, whom they resemble closely in everything save language. I saw rafters that had beyond a doubt been cut with stone axes, although such an assumption does not carry with it a belief in the antiquity of the present pueblo. It is a well ascertained fact that in repairing or reconstructing their dwellings and villages the Sedentary Indians have incorporated in new structures all the serviceable material saved from the old. There are a few windows glazed with selenite, feather plumes of sacrifice to be buried in their harvest fields, an abundance of down and plumage of eagle and parrot in all the houses and a gentile organization, as in Zuni, while there is also the sacrifice of bread or meal at the hours of eating. The Pueblo has an untidy, slouchy appearance, the streets being dirty and the houses themselves much worn at the corners.

I succeeded in hiring Francisco Naranjo—Ah-co an-ye, and Pablo Tafoya, or Tso-bocu—Nublina—Foy,

Indians of this Pueblo as interpreters: afterwards, I joined to these Rafael Vigil or Mahuehuevi—the Kicker (i.e., in the Kicking game of the Two Little Gods, played with the sticks). It must be borne in mind that the Pueblos on the Rio Grande have been so long under Spanish domination that each and every one of them has received a Castilian name to which he responds and by which he is known in all the ordinary business of life, but each has jealously guarded the tribal name given by his own people, in his own language.

I questioned these men during the day, on matters concerning their people. Their first reluctance to talk upon these subjects was gradually overcome as we became better acquainted and I began to gain their confidence. They told me that they were the one people and spoke the same language with those of San Ildefonso, Tesuque, Nambi, Pojuaque, Santa Clara, San Juan and Tegua, the last the easternmost pueblo of the Moquis—[All of these pueblos were of the Tewa (Tegua) language. Taos (mentioned below) was of the northern Tiwa (Tigua). LBB]

They call their own pueblo, Ca-po. The C being an "exploded" consonant.

San Juan is Otque
San Ildefonso is Patwo-que
Tesuque is Tesuque
Nambi is Nambi
Po-jua-que is Po-suna-cue

The people of Taos call those of Santa Clara, Tar-weo. The great similarity between the pronunciation of the names given by them to San Ildefonso and Pojuaque led me to believe that there must be a mistake somewhere; repeated questioning, however, failed to shake their statements in the least. To put them in good humor, I not only hired these men as guides, but purchased freely of pottery, baskets and apricots, a fruit that is raised extensively by all the villages south of, and including, San Juan. Santa Clara, as a pueblo, presents little in the way of beauty, to attract the eye; it is in a very tumble-down condition, is not at all clean and the houses are nearly all in one story, none of the exceptions being over two. The main part of the village faces upon a "plaza," in the center of which is an "estufa," in poor condition, but from the fresh ashes on the floor I conjecture that it must have recently been in use for purposes of religion or business.

Two or three other buildings, all small, also infringe upon the plan of the plaza. My guides were anxious to show me the ruined church of "Santa Clara" and under their care, I made a brief examination. It is 41 paces from main entrance to chancel, 5 paces wide, 18 ft. high, and lighted by two square, unglazed windows, 8' by 5'. The ceiling is formed of pine "vigas" with a "flooring" of roughly split pine slabs, upon which is laid the earthen roof. In one arm of the transept, were a collection of sacred statues, dolls, crosses, and other appurtenances of the church. The altar-piece, although much decayed, is greatly above the average of the church paintings to be found in New Mexico. It is a panel picture, with an ordinary daub of Santiago in the top compartment and a very excellent drawing of Santa Clara in the principal place. The drawing, coloring and expression of countenance are [un]usually good and I don't blame the Indians for being so proud of their Patroness. A confessional and pulpit occupy opposite sides of the nave.

The following list of clans or gentes, given me by the interpreters above named, I give just for what it is worth, without believing it to be exact. The Rio Grande Pueblos have become so shy and so timorous that duplicity and dissimulation are integral features of their character and in all conversations with strangers, especially such as bear upon their religion or their prehistoric customs and their gentile divisions, they maintain either an absolute reserve, or, if that be broken down, take a malicious pleasure in imparting information for no other object than to mislead and confuse. I had prepared myself for such an experience and determined that nothing should cause me to lose patience in the performance of my task; feeling that if at one pueblo I might be completely baffled, at another better fortune might await me and feeling also that after making a commencement, progress would each day become more and more easy. Accordingly I wrote down the list which follows, annexing to each name in Spanish, its Indian and English equivalents:

1 Sol	Pau-towa	Sun
2 Luna	Oxtowa	Moon
3 Estrella	Agoya-towa	Star
4 Maiz Azul	Iunt-owa	Blue Corn
5 Calabaza	Poxtowa	Pumpkin
6 Maiz Blanco	Iuntzi-towa	White Corn
7 Tortuga		Tortoise
7 Agua	Box-towa	Water
8 Nube	Ojua-towa	Cloud
9 Pino	Tze-et-towa	Pine
10 Tierra	Non-towa	Earth
11 Aguila	Ize-towa	Eagle
12 Tejon	Qua-a-towa	Badger
13 Oso	Que-towa	Bear
14 Lobo	Iuni-towa	Wolf
15 Venado (Venuda)	Pen-towa	Antelope
16 Palo Amarillo	I-can-towa	Yellow Stick
17 Alamo	Textowa	Cottonwood
18 Bunchi		

Towa is "people," or "clan"

[In the above listing, there were duplicate "7" designations, seemingly an error in the original recording by Bourke. Venado, No. 15, is often given as deer, or elk, by other Pueblos; Bunchi, or Punche, refers to native tobacco—see White 1943. CHL] Concerning No. 16, I was unable to find out what plant was meant. The Indians say that this plant is "un palo duro para teñir," a hard wood to be used in dyeing," a definition corresponding with that given by the Zunis who have the same gens, a fact of which the Santa Clara Indians seemed fully aware. They denied having the Guakamayo [Guacamayo: Macaw CHL], Turtle, Buffalo, or Snake gentes, but admitted after some conversation that there were representatives of the "Bunchi-towa," or Tobacco gens among them. Gentes rise up and disappear with comparative rapidity among the savage tribes; casualties destroy them or over

population induces a segmentation of the parent gens into new gentes bearing names not to be found in other tribes and Pueblos of same language and blood; consequently, I was less anxious to obtain an exact nomenclature than I was to demonstrate, at least to my own satisfaction, that the gentile organization still existed in all its pristine vigor among these Pueblos on the Rio Grande.

My guides next took me to see an old eagle which they have had for 30 yrs. There are others in the Pueblo, just as good to the ordinary eye but not so worthy of attention as this one. These eagles are kept for their feathers which, as elsewhere stated, are made into sacrificial plumes to be buried in the harvest fields. Stone implements can still be found in quantity. The Indians will soon have sold the last of those in their possession, together with all that remains among them of prehistoric lance and arrow heads of obsidian.

I have said that in my opinion, some of the old rafters in this village must have been cut with stone axes. I was strengthened in this conviction by the remark of an old man who seeing me examine one critically said that it had been cut by a "hacha de piedra," in the time of "Cuanto hay." Which in intelligible language means that it was cut with a hatchet of stone in the time of "how long since?"—an expression used by the natives to denote a period anterior to anything of which they have record or tradition.

Following Bourke's visit to Santa Clara in 1881, Indians of that Pueblo were mentioned a number of times in the journals kept by Adolph F. Bandelier. In his entry of July 3, 1882, he noted meeting Santa Clara Indians in Santa Fe Canyon—"They had black shining pottery, platos [plates], which they called *saua-pi-i,* and little pitchers of yellow micacious pottery, called *sam-be*" (Lange and Riley 1966: 331). Several days later, in visiting Cochiti Pueblo on their Feast Day, July 14, Bandelier noted that among the Indians there from various pueblos, there were a number from Santa Clara (p. 340).

In his journal entries for 1883 and 1884, Bandelier made additional notes pertaining to Santa Clara Indians or their village (Lange and Riley 1970). On October 26, 1883, he noted, "The Indians of Santa Clara make today black vessels with indentations of a plastic nature, grooves and channels for decorative purposes" (p. 153). On November 25, 1883, he wrote that he had "Painted all day at the 'Qu'-huanifi,' or macana [war club] from Santa Clara...." (p. 171). A few days later, on November 29, Bandelier made a more extended entry regarding Santa Clara.

... He [Don Juan Garcia of San Juan Pueblo] told me of an occurrence at Santa Clara which clearly shows the power and office of cacique. On a first day of January (he being then County Judge) he was called to Santa Clara by an Indian to settle a dispute between the young and the old men of the Pueblo about the election of a new governor. The young men claimed to elect through a majority of votes; the old people claimed the usual form of nomination by the cacique! He decided in favor of the young men... (p. 172). [This brief account assumes special importance in terms of culture history and as additional background for the long-standing and often bitter factionalism experienced at Santa Clara Pueblo as described by Hill in Chapter 9, Political Organization. It clearly demonstrates that these troubles go back considerably further in time than is often assumed. CHL]

In his entry of December 1, Bandelier recorded the following information:

... Father Francolon told me that the people of Nambé were disappearing fast, and that it was attributed to a custom either of infanticide or of abortion prevailing among them. At all events there were some dark and singular agencies at work there, and he had noticed their introduction also

among the people of Santa Clara. What it is, he is not capable of defining or finding out ... (p. 173).

As the index for the volume of edited journals from Bandelier's subsequent years in the Southwest, 1885–88 (Lange, Riley, and Lange 1975:683), reveals, there were more frequent and longer visits to Santa Clara by Bandelier during that period. Journal entries recorded comments and observations regarding the Indians and their activities, the village, and other data pertaining to Santa Clara. These comments are of sufficient volume to make their inclusion here impractical, but the interested reader will find much of value in the indicated entries. Similar information was included in entries associated with visits to Santa Clara during Bandelier's final Southwestern years, 1889–92, the period covered in the fourth and final volume of his journals, still being prepared for publication (Lange, Riley, and Lange n.d.).

Special attention should be directed to the somewhat lengthy account by Bandelier of his investigation of the church archive at Santa Clara where he found considerable documentation concerning earlier Puebloan and missionary church history. This account appeared in his volume *The Gilded Man* (Bandelier 1893:289–302), and it was also condensed and used anonymously in the American Guide Series volume on New Mexico in the discussion of Santa Clara Pueblo (1940:352). More recently, it again appeared in complete form in the third volume of Bandelier's Southwestern Journals (Lange, Riley, and Lange 1975: 454–56n618).

In his "Documentary History of the Rio Grande Pueblos of New Mexico," Bandelier (1910:23–24) referred to these documents as "formerly at the Pueblo of Santa Clara and now preserved in Santa Fe through the efforts of the late Archbishop J.B. Salpointe." However, Chavez (1957:3–4) did not mention any archival collection from Santa Clara Pueblo, although his index indicated scattered Santa Clara documents in the Archives of the Archdiocese of Santa Fe. In a number of instances, one suspects that a number of documents exist today only in the copied form made by Bandelier, the originals having been destroyed or lost.

As of the end of the nineteenth century, the United States Indian Service was represented in the Territory of New Mexico by four agencies. These included the Mescalero Agency and the Jicarilla Agency in the south and the north, respectively; also, there were two Pueblo jurisdictions, one administered from Albuquerque (the Southern Agency) and one based in Santa Fe (the Northern Agency), the office responsible for Santa Clara Pueblo.

Dale (1949:149) summarized the situation for the early decades of the twentieth century as follows, noting that "... it remained almost the same throughout the period from 1901 to 1933 and was not greatly changed even in 1948." (In 1912, New Mexico was admitted as the forty-seventh state of the Union, but little change, if any, occurred in regard to the Indians and their reservations.)

> Critics of the Indian Service have pointed at instances of shameful neglect, of treaties made and never kept, of agreements ignored, and of corruption and graft and incompetence. But these instances were, on the whole, outweighed by other examples of patient effort on the part of agents of the Service who wrought great changes for bettering the condition of their charges. The mistakes that were made were due mainly to ignorance on the part of officials in Washington, and even of agents in the field, about the nature of the Indian. The allotment of land in severalty, for instance, proved to be a mistake because of the very nature of the region and the Indian's attitude toward ownership. By 1920 more than 96 percent of the Indian land was still held in common ownership....
>
> The outbreak of the first World War greatly affected the Indians and their relations with the federal government. Many of them entered the armed forces, serving ably and well; others, attracted by high wages, left the reservation to work on the railroads or in mines, shops, or factories....
>
> Although this was a period of great

scientific advancement which brought about radical changes in the manner of living of most of the people of the United States, it brought comparatively little change in the life of the Indians of the Southwest, or in the methods pursued by the federal government in administering their affairs. The Indian, always conservative and wedded to his old customs, progressed with what seemed to many persons as astonishing slowness.... (Dale 1949:151–52)

Dale, noting widespread criticism of the Indian Service for not achieving more tangible progress despite great expenditures, explained that Secretary of the Interior Herbert Work was ultimately prompted "to make an honest effort to learn the truth about conditions among the Indians of the United States as a whole." Government responsibility was to be assessed, and corrective measures were to be recommended. In 1926, the Institute for Government Research was requested by Work to make such a survey; with a specialist in each of the fields of education, health, sociology, economics, agriculture, statistics, and law, a group of nine was assembled under the leadership of Lewis Meriam of the Institute for Government Research. It is interesting that the funds for this study were obtained from private sources. According to Dale (p. 153), a member of this study group, a rough draft of the collective findings was prepared after the field investigations and three months of writing. Meriam, as technical director, completed the report, and it was published in 1928 under the title of *The Problem of Indian Administration*. Subsequently, it has come to be known as "the Meriam Report."

In 1929, the Commissioner of Indian Affairs, Charles H. Burke, after eight years in office, was succeeded by Charles J. Rhoads. While considerable improvement occurred in the schools and health services, and better methods were introduced in the administration of the Indian Bureau and various agencies, progress continued to be slow (p. 156).

John Collier, in 1933, became the successor to Rhoads. Collier had served for a number of years as executive secretary of the Indian Defense Association and also for some time as editor of the *American Indian Life Magazine*. As Dale (p. 124) commented,

> He had, therefore, for a long time been deeply interested in the American Indians, especially those of the Southwest. He was an experienced social worker and brought to his task an able and aggressive personality. He had been one of the most outstanding critics of the Indian Bureau, and he now had the opportunity to put into effect the reforms which he had so long advocated. He served as commissioner for more than twelve years, which was a far longer tenure than that of any of his predecessors, and during all of that time had the full confidence and support of both the President and the Secretary of the Interior.

New programs were initiated, and greatly increased appropriations were forthcoming from Congress. The Pueblo Indian Land Board was created by Congress to settle non-Indian claims to land within, or in conflict with, the Pueblo Land Grants. Some of these problems have continued almost to the present day. However, as Dale (p. 217) remarked, the Board acted to award several Pueblo villages of New Mexico monetary compensation for lands wrongfully taken from them, "and by an act of Congress approved May 31, 1933, an appropriation of more than three-quarters of a million dollars was granted to these Indians to be used for the purchase of additional lands and water or other permanent economic aids."

> To carry out Commissioner Collier's program was impossible without additional legislation by Congress. He therefore sponsored and, with the aid of both the President and the Secretary of the Interior, succeeded in securing the passage and approval of the Indian Reorganization Act, commonly called the Wheeler-Howard Act. This is one of the most important pieces of legislation with respect to the Indians ever enacted by Congress. It marks the definite beginning of a new regime, and its effects upon the Indians and the Indian

> Service have been enormous. (p. 217)

This legislation, approved June 18, 1934, was discussed in some detail by Dale for the next several pages (pp. 217–32) with particular attention being given to the impact it had upon the tribes of the Southwest, where, in most instances, the Indian Reorganization Act was the focal point for continued factionalism and debate in individual tribes.

As an instance of such factionalism, an obvious reflection of the persistent attempt by some tribal members to preserve traditional patterns and procedures, some remarks of Dozier are of interest. In his discussion of cases where elected councils had been adopted under the new Indian Service policies (see Appendix B), Dozier noted that there were tribes where "candidates for the various offices are furnished by a nominating committee." He continued, describing a variation of this situation at his home village, Santa Clara Pueblo (1970a:191):

> ... or as at Santa Clara, by permitting each of several sociopolitical factions recognized in the pueblo's constitution to provide a slate of candidates. It is interesting to note the persistence of traditional methods of choosing the secular officers even in those pueblos which have shifted to an elective system. In Santa Clara, for example, in the faction that contains the Summer moiety chief, this revered priest is permitted to "choose" the slate of officers. Thus, this faction is continuing the moiety chief's traditional prerogative of choosing the secular officers; in this case, of course, in only providing one of several rosters of candidates. The other factions decide on their candidates by discussion and voting....

In summarizing the years of Indian Service administration under Collier, Dale (1949:231–32) noted that:

> Even the bitterest opponents of Commissioner Collier's theories must agree that the Indian Service made great strides in the Southwest from 1933 to 1945. The large additions to Indian land

holdings, the checking of erosion, the new roads, trails, bridges, irrigation works, homes, hospitals, and schools built are tangible accomplishments which speak for themselves....

Important as were the accomplishments of the New Regime, there still remained in 1947 many ancient problems whose complete solution lies far in the future. They are human problems to be found to a greater or less degree among the peoples of every race and country in the world. The standard of living for many thousand Indians of the Southwest was still distressingly low....

In March, 1945, Commissioner Collier resigned; his successor was William A. Brophy. "The new commissioner had been closely associated with the Indian Service for ten years and had married Dr. Sophie Aberle, formerly superintendent of the United Pueblos jurisdiction" (p. 233). Through several subsequent reorganizations, the Northern Pueblos, with which Santa Clara Pueblo is affiliated, has shifted between the United Pueblos Agency, in Albuquerque, and Santa Fe, where the Northern Pueblos Agency was located at times when this was separated from the Southern Agency remaining in Albuquerque.

In the years of World War II and subsequently, to the present time, numerous Santa Clara Indians have obtained employment in the neighboring communities of Los Alamos, Española, Santa Fe, and others. With increasing recognition, several of the Santa Clara potters, painters, and other artisans and craftsmen have gained prominence and have enjoyed steadily expanding incomes.

Smith (1966: 5–7) included a "Summarization of Indian Labor Force, Employment and Unemployment within the Gallup Area for 1963." Her data for Santa Clara Pueblo are presented below, along with similar information for the United Pueblos Agency and the total area for comparative purposes.

	Santa Clara	UPA Totals	Totals—Area
Resident Population	535	15,259	112,727

	Santa Clara	UPA Totals	Totals—Area
Labor Force	183 (34.2%)	5,842 (38.3%)	43,772 (38.8%)
Permanent Employment	104 (56.8%)	2,212 (37.9%)	8,440 (19.3%)
Temporary and Seasonal Employment	48 (26.2%)	2,915 (49.9%)	8,795 (20.1%)
Unemployment	31 (16.9%)	715 (12.2%)	26,537 (60.6%)
Recurrent Unemployment	79 (43.2%)	3,630 (62.1%)	35,332 (80.7%)

From the figures presented in the above table, it is clear that Santa Clara Pueblo enjoyed a relatively favorable position in comparison with other Southwestern Puebloan and other tribes. Compared with national averages, however, the situation at Santa Clara was not so favorable. In this latter instance, the long-standing handicaps and limited opportunities for American Indians were clearly evident.

Physical modernization of Santa Clara Pueblo has kept pace with other changes during the period since the end of World War II. A number of new houses have been built along the northern edge of the village; these homes, arranged on a grid pattern of surfaced streets rather than following the scrambled pattern of past years, extend over much of the area between the old town of Santa Clara and Española. These dwellings are modern, with electricity, running water, and sewage lines associated with a sewage disposal facility.

In a volume entitled *The Indian: America's Unfinished Business,* Brophy and Aberle (1966:106) mentioned as one of the three more successful programs from a total of twenty-nine approved under Title II (A) of the programs under the Office of Economic Opportunity, 1965, the following: "...the Santa Clara, New Mexico, Community Action Program, called 'Operation Head Start,' which was cited by the Office of Economic Opportunity as one of the nation's best pre-school programs."

Despite such overt changes, a surprising

amount of traditional culture persists. Ceremonials are held at which visitors are cordially welcomed; photographic permits are ordinarily for sale. However, other ceremonials are also scheduled at which outsiders are not permitted—and one can only assume that many of the old ways continue to be followed, although there is unquestionably an inexorable, steady decline in the degree of meticulous detail involved—and from time to time, outright loss in paraphernalia or procedures occurs.

Hopefully, material gathered and assembled by Hill and presented here will serve as a positive factor in maintaining and even rekindling interest in such traditional matters before they are irretrievably lost from Santa Clara culture.

3

Property, Ownership, and Inheritance

Both real and personal property have long been recognized at Santa Clara Pueblo. However, the concept of incorporeal property was foreign to the culture. One informant, a cacique, thought the whole idea of incorporeal property extremely funny. Possibly, the lack of this concept could be attributed to the existence of an organized priesthood as opposed to individual religious practitioners.

REAL PROPERTY

The principle of individual ownership was well developed and included rights of disposition, both testamentary and otherwise. The bases for the establishment of ownership were creation, utilization, and gift.

Agricultural land was acquired in several ways: assignment, inheritance, loan, exchange, or sale. When a person desired an assignment, he selected the plot and made application to the governor. The governor called a meeting of the council, and this group visited the tract in question to determine whether there were prior claims or request commitments. If the "title" was clear, the plot was given to the person who requested it [14, 44]. While the land was granted to the head of a family, or consump-

tion group, it was understood that he acted merely as trustee for the family unit as a whole. "Land was given to the family or household rather than to the head of the family" [36, 62, 65]. Requests from unmarried persons were denied. "He is alone and has older people above him to which land has already been given. He would help his parents" [27].

An exception to this rule was made, however, in the case of unmarried orphans [27]. Assignments were made in the order in which requests were received. Farms were located without regard to moiety affiliations. Need and the number of persons in the consumption unit were factors in determining the size of the allotment [23, 36, 52, 72].

Confusion existed as to whether continuity of use was necessary for retention of title. According to several [14, 23, 30], if land remained idle for five years, it reverted to the pueblo for reassignment. However, this ruling was easily circumvented by lending the farm to a relative or friend during the five-year interval. According to another [6], once an assignment was made, use or lack of use had no effect on the validity of the claim.

This uncertainty was illustrated by an ownership dispute in 1934. Some years earlier, an assignment had been made by the governor and council. The assignee, because of illness, was unable to utilize or to improve it. In 1934, a request for the same acreage was granted to another man by the then incumbent governor. No settlement was reached on the conflicting claims, possibly because of the chaotic political situation of the moment. "Now they do not know who it belongs to." Perhaps the whole question was academic since a surplus of land has normally existed. However, once land passed into heirship, title was established.

Lending of land to relatives and friends was not uncommon. Occasionally, this was done to obviate the question of the nonuse ruling; at other times the motives were more altruistic. Leasing also occurred. Rental was commonly fifty percent of the crop. Most lease and lend agreements involved owners who were indigent or whose outside occupational interests precluded their engaging in agricultural pursuits.

Land exchange was also practiced between members of the pueblo, often in order to consolidate holdings. The parties first sought approval from the governor, and contractual features were negotiated before witnesses. Land could be sold to villagers, but not to outsiders. However, if the seller wished to acquire land at a later date he was forced to purchase it, since he was considered to have forfeited his right of assignment [30, 62]. There was no separate ownership of the land and of trees planted on it. All land other than farm tracts and house sites was open to communal exploitation. There was no individual ownership of gathering plots, clay deposits, grazing rights, or hunting, fishing, and wood-gathering areas [68].

House sites were acquired in the same manner as agricultural plots. Houses were predominantly owned by males. This was the result of several factors. First, residence was normally patrilocal or separate. A father usually built a house for his son at the time of the son's marriage, or he established the son in a unit of his own home. Finally, the pattern of house inheritance was prevailingly patrilineal. "A woman has more authority in the home than a man has. However, this does not hold for ownership. In house inheritance a man could say who

would get it" [23]. In those rare instances when a man and wife built a home together, title was vested in both spouses. However, dual ownership was unusual and existed only for the lifetime of one or the other principal [23, 36].

PERSONAL PROPERTY

Individual ownership and right of disposal of personal property were both recognized and were extended to include children as well as adults. Rights were established when an item was created or was acquired through gift or inheritance. "If a man gave a woman a gourd ladle it was hers to dispose of" [12]. Ownership of household furniture and equipment was vested in women whether or not they had manufactured it. Men owned the tools and equipment used in agriculture and hunting [18, 52].

A person had absolute right of testamentary disposition of property and could will it to a particular relative or not as he or she saw fit. When an individual reached advanced age or was seriously ill, it was customary to make an oral will. This was witnessed by someone unrelated to the family [68]. In recent years, written wills have become common [18, 61]. Instances were reported of wills being contested; however, in all cases, the wishes of testator or testatrix were honored. "If a person wanted he could contest a will. He presented his case to the governor and the governor took it to the council. The governor would say, 'If you thought injustice was done why did you not speak up at the time the oral will was made?' He would say, 'No change can be made now.' This was to make a person realize that the father's decision was final" [6].

Personal effects were usually bequeathed to children, although occasionally nieces and nephews inherited them [12]. Normally an equal distribution was made. "If a woman had two daughters and two metates, she gave the fine one to one daughter and the coarse one to the other" [36]. When an equal distribution was impossible, the testator or testatrix selected the heir he or she preferred. "If a man had a bow and arrows, or other articles, not enough to go around, he would give them to the son most dear to him. This was not necessarily the eldest" [36].

House inheritance was overwhelmingly patrilineal. The property normally passed from father to married son. In forty-eight cases on which data were available, sons inherited directly from fathers in twenty-five cases. There were six instances in which sons acquired houses from their mothers. These can be classed with the above, because when a husband predeceased his spouse the distribution of real property was withheld until the wife's death. Two houses were occupied by women who had received them from deceased husbands. Presumably, these would pass to sons on the death of the mothers. There were four cases in which men had inherited houses from their in-laws; and one each of inheritance from a brother, a grandmother, and an uncle. The uncle had no male issue [6, 18].

To summarize, patrilineal bias was indicated in forty of forty-eight cases of house inheritance. Of the remaining eight, there were six instances in which daughters inherited from fathers, two in which the property passed from mothers to daughters [23, 36, 72]. Unfortunately, in these latter eight cases, it was not ascertained whether potential male heirs were present or not. Primogeniture was not a consideration in house inheritance. In fact, younger sons were more apt to inherit as older ones were already established [6, 23].

Less frequently, the Spanish-American pattern of house inheritance was followed, with rooms or parts of rooms being left to individual heirs. The obvious disadvantages of this procedure appeared to have prevented its general adoption. "If there were not enough rooms, the house would be divided according to the number of *vigas.* One person might get a space of five *vigas,* the next, five, and so on" [68].

Occasionally, presumptive heirs were disregarded and a house was left to the moiety or to a society for ceremonial use. This was true of one informant [15], who willed one of his houses to the Winter moiety as a storehouse for kachina masks. According to another man [73], there had been several examples of this.

The pattern of land inheritance differed in several respects from that in force for houses. Usually surviving spouses inherited, and on their death the farm was divided equally among the children regardless of sex. This was a reflection of Spanish-American practice. However, there was nothing to prevent a testator or testatrix from dividing the property unequally or disinheriting individuals. Both were done. After the death of parents, the legatees often made adjustments and transfers of land on the basis of need [36, 44, 62]. Actually acquisition of land through heirship was not crucial, since a surplus was commonly available for assignment.

Orchards were divided equally among the children. Each received the same number of trees. If an equal distribution was impossible, the parent willed the extra trees to the child he or she liked best [27].

4

Agricultural

Economy

SUBSISTENCE

There is ample evidence that the relative roles of various economic endeavors at Santa Clara have varied throughout the historic period. Aboriginally agriculture and hunting were the most important subsistence activities, providing for the support of the population about equally. With the arrival of the Spanish and the introduction of new plants, new mechanical techniques, and draft animals, farming began to gain ascendency, and hunting declined correspondingly. Finally with increasing colonization and settlement of the area by Europeans and Americans, hunting became obsolescent.

Less important economic pursuits, that contributed in varying degree over time, included gathering, fishing, warfare, pastoralism, trade, handicrafts, and wagework. Perhaps because of a well-developed agriculture, gathering was consistently a minor venture. It was associated with therapeutics and curing rather than with food production. Fishing was carried on seasonally. Presumably this was an aboriginal trait and general for the area. Warfare, before its disappearance, contributed some economic goods in the form of booty. It is difficult to evaluate the role of pastoralism. Historic ac-

counts suggest that it may have been more important earlier than in the recent period. Certainly during the last hundred years, it has been a desultory pursuit, and domesticated animals other than sheep and goats were used primarily for purposes of draft and transport. The sale of handicrafts to non-Indians began as early as 1890 and, with the increase of tourist travel in the last four decades, has substantially augmented the income of some families. The trend in wagework has paralleled that of handicraft in recent years. It was relatively unimportant until the establishment of the Los Alamos research center in 1943, when it began to dominate the subsistence scene. Following this development, many families ceased farming and shifted to a cash economy.

The primary unit of production and consumption was the patrilineal extended family. These units were quite variable as to composition, and for obvious reasons the economic efficiency of a particular group was in part dependent upon its size. However, the disadvantages inherent in the inability to command a large labor force were mitigated by informal reciprocal assistance between friends and relatives outside the extended family group. Furthermore there were formalized village-wide communal obligations which were related to subsistence. These were associated primarily with agriculture and involved the maintenance of the irrigation system, but also occurred with regard to fishing and religion. In the latter case, the activities could be classed as pragmatic only in that they furnished psychological sustenance.

Agriculture

Until recent years agriculture was one of the most important economic endeavors at Santa Clara Pueblo. Aboriginally the staple products were maize, beans, and pumpkins. Nonfood plants included cotton, gourds, and tobacco. Planting and cultivation were formerly accomplished with simple wooden implements: two kinds of digging stick and two varieties of hoe. Irrigation was practiced and was characterized by considerable mechanical ingenuity.

The arrival of the Spanish brought the introduction of new plants and techniques at Santa Clara. The most important introduced plant was wheat, which soon rivaled maize as a staple and surpassed it as a trade product. Barley was less popular. Watermelons and muskmelons were accepted and became so well integrated into the agricultural economy that the Indian considered them as native plants. It has been suggested that they may have diffused to the Tewa on the aboriginal level. Of a number of vegetables and fruits, chili, onions, peaches, apricots, and apples were and still are the most important, the last three as trade items especially. While gardens were common, vegetable crops seemed never to have been popular and their cultivation was desultory at best.

More far-reaching in effect than the introduction of new plants by the Spanish was the introduction of new implements, new mechanical techniques, and draft animals. These included such items as the metal hoe, the wooden rake, fork, and shovel; the plow, the *carreta;* and horses, donkeys, and oxen. While these improvements were crude judged by modern standards, they were infinitely superior to aboriginal implements and techniques, and allowed some expansion in the acreage cultivated, increased trans-portation possibilities, and led to the enlargement of irrigation systems.

It is probable that the acceptance of these innovations was a slow and gradual process. Early *entradas* were poorly equipped to serve the purpose of material diffusion. In addition the political unrest which led to the Pueblo Revolt of 1680 and the rejection of foreign culture, as well as the population dislocation during the Reconquest, must have acted as a deterrent to diffusion.

Contemporary and late historic accounts have indicated that deficiencies in agricultural techniques and equipment continued to exist until recent times. According to one informant [23], "There was little farming in those days [circa 1870, WWH]. We had to buy corn from the Mexicans. Most of the people made their living trading with the Comanches. Oxen were borrowed from the Mexicans. There were only five teams in the pueblo at this time." Another [62] stated, "Before 1870 the farm plots were small due to the lack of equipment and the poor quality of the native tools." Poore (1894:427), in his 1890 report, commented as follows: "There are 22 horses, 4 oxen, and 30 burros in the pueblo. Some who have horses have no harness and no money to purchase. The agency granted two plows for the village, which are used by lot."

Farming was almost exclusively a male pursuit. A rather rigid occupational dichotomy, based on sex, existed at Santa Clara. "The woman's place is in the home, the men do the farm work" [27]. "The women did not help in farming, that was purely a man's job" [44]. With few exceptions, female participation in agriculture consisted of occasional help in planting and such marginal aspects of harvesting as husking and winnowing.

Much emphasis has been placed upon the numerous communal aspects and controls associated with Pueblo agriculture, and these features have been strongly manifested at Santa Clara Pueblo. These must, however, be accepted with caution. The basic factors in the agricultural process were essentially controlled by the individual and/or the patrilineal extended family. Considerable range of expression was possible within the boundaries of the culture pattern. Whether a man farmed or not, what and how much he planted, and how well he attended his crops were matters of personal concern subject only to the individual's sensitivity to the coercive effects of public opinion. Likewise the use and disposal of the fruits of his labor were almost entirely a matter of personal choice. With these items in mind, the more complex communal agricultural factors fall into their proper perspective.

Agriculture brought into action several complex types of communal action and control. While the majority of these were fixed, a few were informal. Of the informal ones, the most important were connected with the labor of clearing the fields, planting, and harvesting. It was customary for relatives and friends to render mutual assistance in these types of field work. Participation was entirely optional and voluntary, although the obligations of kinship were recognized as an important factor. Moiety affiliation was not involved, and there was no rendering of joint help on the basis of society membership as in some western pueblos. No payment was made for this help, as it was undertaken on a reciprocal basis. It was, however, incumbent upon the individual whose farm was worked to furnish food to those who labored.

The governor received no community assistance other than the informal help of kin and friends. Definite communal obligations were formerly recognized in connection with the religious heads (caciques) of each moiety, and members of the village assisted them in planting and harvesting. While not all members of the pueblo participated at any one time, the work was formally organized. This usage lapsed many years ago, presumably the victim of factionalism. Robbins, Harrington, and Freire-Marreco (1916:83), in referring to planting in 1912, stated that ". . . this has not been done in the last fifty years."

Another communal aspect developed with the establishment of the Catholic church at Santa Clara Pueblo. The church was assigned a certain acreage which was tilled and harvested by members of the community. "This was in exchange for the services of the priest at baptisms, marriage, and funerals." Such practice was consistent with the native pattern of relieving those with ritual obligations of a certain amount of economic responsibility. Again, this type of work received formal recognition, although the total population was not involved at any one time. Each year the governor designated certain individuals to perform this duty [44, 62, 64].

The communal phases of agriculture were best developed where the native religion impinged and also in connection with irrigation. Greater detail on the relationship between religion and farming is given in Chapter 10. Suffice it to say here that every ceremony was considered to incorporate features relevant to fertility, rain-getting, purification, and general economic welfare. While the activities of agriculture and religion were functionally linked in the minds of the people, there was almost no temporal coincidence between ceremony and practical activity.

This lack of correlation was particularly striking to the author after having engaged in fieldwork among the Navajo, where every step of the agricultural process was accompanied by more or less religious behavior on the part of the individual. At Santa Clara little ritual of any kind was connected per se with clearing, planting, cultivation, and harvesting. An exhaustive inquiry elicited only the following meager details: the first, from a highly acculturated Indian [52], "After plowing, the owner would say a prayer for the good of the crop"; the second, from a conservative member of the pueblo [65], "You go to the priest and get Holy Water and sprinkle it over your seed to insure fertility and a good crop. I do not do this; I only invoke the name of the Lord, then go ahead." The latter represented a practice taken from Spanish and Spanish-American neighbors; the former was under suspicion of Christian influence. The Santa Clara "man in the street" conducted the practical processes of farming complacent in the knowledge that religious acts had been and would be performed by the proper societies and ritual groups to which he might or might not belong.

The amount of agricultural religious participation on the part of the individual varied with the degree of his or her advancement in the moiety hierarchy, and membership in societies. The religious contribution of some consisted merely of taking part once or twice a year in ritual functions involving a whole moiety, while others, such as members of the Winter and Summer managing societies (Oyike and Pay-oj-ke, respectively), went into retreat at least every month for the purposes of the public weal. However, regardless of degree of participation, agricultural ritual was an enterprise in which the total population was an inseparable part.

There were two principal irrigation systems at Santa Clara Pueblo. Santa Clara Creek was the source of the first and older system. The inlet to this ditch was located approximately a mile and a quarter up the Santa Clara Canyon, north and west of the pueblo. Slightly downstream from this first ditch was an inlet to another, which furnished water to the Spanish-American village of Guachiponge (p'oci pa^{n}geh). This was of recent construction and furnished water to many Santa Claras who had recently purchased land in this community.

The other important system was the Rio Grande canal, the intake of which was about fifty yards north of the Española bridge. Water from this source was used to irrigate the cultivated acreage lying south of the pueblo to within a few hundred yards of the San Ildefonso Pueblo Grant. The irrigated area was roughly four to five miles long and varied in width from one hundred to five hundred yards. The Santa Clara Creek canal watered fields in the immediate vicinity of the pueblo and a few fields east and south of the pueblo. The water supply from the latter source was somewhat uncertain. At least once each year floods destroyed the inlet section and irrigation was temporarily interrupted until repairs were made. In late July and August the water supply was frequently so low that irrigation was irregular [18].

Hand irrigation was practiced, but only in cases of severe drought. It was confined to the small garden plots located in the vicinity of the pueblo [14].

The governor was responsible for the maintenance of the ditches and activities related to irrigation though he might, if he wished, delegate this authority to the lieute-nant governor. He issued a call sometime between late February and the middle of March for assistance in cleaning and repairing the ditches and laterals [14, 23]. All adult males of the village were expected to participate. After the political breakup, one party worked for one week, another for the next, and so on until the canals were in order [20, 43]. "More recently all parties have met with the council, and the council has decided who was to work" [43].

The formal opening of the ditches was always preceded by religious observances. The night before, representatives of the two Bear societies, curing societies, walked the length of the system and purified it. The following morning the water was released, and a member of the Winter and Summer societies, each appointed by the caciques, walked ahead of the flow, singing, and deposited prayer plumes at intervals. More recently this rite has been performed by two members of the Pay-oj-ke.

Requests for water were made to the governor. Petitions were granted according to the order they were received. If a person failed to take advantage of water at his allotted time, he forfeited his rights and had to wait until all others had been served [20, 27]. Permission was required only in the case of water from Santa Clara Creek, not from the Rio Grande [27].

Field Location

The selection of an agricultural plot was determined by several factors. One of the primary considerations was its location with regard to water resources. Earlier (before 1870), fields were located in the vicinity of Santa Clara Creek. Later, with the construction of the Rio Grande ditch, there was a gradual shifting of land holdings to the river bottom, and farms were irrigated by laterals from that canal. It was not uncommon for a man to have three agricultural plots: one along the river bottom, another in the mountains along the valley of the Santa Clara Creek, the third a small garden plot near the pueblo. A few families lived at their mountain farms during the summer, returning to the village after the harvest [62]. The fields in the mountain area were often dry-farmed as rainfall was heavier at that elevation.

The Santa Clara Indians were also concerned with soil composition. If possible, a locality with sandy loam was selected. Land with too much sand was avoided, as was clayey soil, the latter being too difficult to work with primitive tools. Alakline soil was recognized by color and shunned. Possible land productivity was judged by the amount of brush and weed growth. However, another criterion of land selection was relative freedom from such natural encumbrances as stones, brush, and trees [14, 23].

Land title or usufruct was acquired in a variety of ways: assignment, inheritance, purchase, exchange, and loan (see Chapter 3). Farm size was quite variable. Poore (1894:247), as of 1890, stated that:

> Below the village on the right bank lies most of the tilled land. Three hundred and fifty acres are here devoted to corn, wheat, alfalfa, and a variety of vegetables. There are but few orchards. The largest plot owned by one man is thirty acres. From this the holdings decrease in size to 3 and 2 acres... In the pueblito, or little village of the canyon live five families... They farm small patches here and there, in all about forty acres.

According to informants, the average farm for this period and later approximated six acres of lowland and highland holdings combined. This plus other sources of income was deemed sufficient to support a normal family under ordinary conditions. This acreage was comparable to that reported for the area by the Soil Conservation Service in 1936.

It is doubtful whether the above data had much meaning, except in the most general terms. Both in the past and at present, the amount of cultivated land varied with the individual's need, equipment, and ability to enlist assistance from relatives and friends. While better farming methods and machinery have increased productivity, there has been a definite decline in agricultural activity since the 1940s due to the competition of wagework and crafts. During this period some families did not farm at all, subsisting entirely on these other sources of revenue.

Once acquired, a field was differentiated from other such plots by a variety of devices. Wooden stakes were sometimes placed at the corners, or rows of stones placed along boundary lines [23]. When domesticated animals became available, loads of cedar branches were transported from the mountains, and fences were constructed. These consisted of erect poles secured by either rawhide or buffalo hide thongs [14].

Preparatory to planting, the land was cleared. If acreage were being brought under cultivation for the first time, this involved removing the small stones, felling the smaller trees, and either pulling the weeds by hand or burning them. Large trees and boulders were allowed to remain in the field. In the case of a new field, this work was extensive enough so that a man, even with the help of friends and relatives, was seldom able to clear more than a small portion of his holding and prepare it for planting the first year. Additions were made each year until the whole was under cultivation [27, 44].

The use of fertilizer appears to have been unknown in aboriginal times. "The land did not wear out." In recent years, however, manure has been worked into land on which alkali appeared. Crop rotation is another recent innovation. It applied only to the alternation of corn and wheat [23, 27].

Planting

Late January or early February was a period of intensive ritual activity during which all societies worked. The Winter people held the Ka-ve-Na Ceremony; the Summer people, the Edge of Spring Ceremony. These signalled the transfer of religious responsibility from the Winter to the Summer moiety and ushered in a new agricultural cycle. Both rites, among other things, were concerned with agricultural fertility. This concept of fertility was also a prominent feature of ceremonial shinny, a component and terminal aspect of the Edge of Spring performance. Formerly, the two clown societies, as custodians of the sacred seed, played important roles in the ritual.

Jeançon's comments illustrate the symbolism behind these activities. He stated (1904–30):

When the corn was husked after harvest particular attention was paid to the perfect ears, those completely covered with grains, and these were laid aside for ceremonial use exclusively. The summer and winter priests went about and gathered these, the white ones going to the winter priest and the blue ones to the summer priest. White is the winter color—snow; and blue is the summer color—blue sky and green fields. Perfect ears of corn of other colors were reserved for first planting and given into custody of the winter clowns— Quarrano [Kwirana] to pray over and vitalize during the winter ceremonies. In the spring it was turned over to the summer clowns—Kossa [K'osa] who made the necessary magic for it to grow before it was taken to the fields and planted. After wheat and other European grains were introduced, perfect heads were sought for after the same manner as the perfect ears of corn. In fact all seeds and grains were selected in this way for ceremonial planting that preceded the regular one. Corn, wheat and other things selected in this way were called "kaye" meaning: "the spirit of" or "spirit thing." Thus a perfect ear of corn was known as "kung-kaye" meaning "corn spirit" or "spirit of corn." This does not mean that the physical ear of corn was spiritual but that it contained the spirit or vital principal of life of the corn which could be filled with strength and power by praying over it. Only the perfect ear of corn contained this spirit or life principal, and after it was placed in the ground or on it in a field, it impregnated all the other grains with its powers. Other grains or seeds would not grow unless the ground was impregnated with the kaye's power. It was the duties of both the winter and summer priests to keep it alive and functioning properly. The grain of corn represented the male element in Nature, the Earth-mother, the female element, and by bringing them together they produced new life and multiplied.

Once the special plot of "kachina corn" was sown and subsequent to the shinny game, anyone who wished could begin preparations for planting. Actually, because of climatic conditions, sowing the fields was not done until April or May. May was known as "corn planting month."

The increased factionalism which began just before the turn of the century gradually resulted in some impairment of the religious routine. The Ka-ve-Na and Edge of Spring rites occurred only sporadically or without the cooperation of the opposite moiety. The last performance of ceremonial shinny was held in 1906. These changes were accompanied by the assumption of former religious prerequisites by the secular arm of the government. Included was transfer to the governor of the responsibility of setting the time of planting. This dignitary (probably at the direction of the Summer cacique) consulted with the council, and the date was set. No one was allowed to plant before the specified time. "When the ice was off the land and the ground was not frozen, the governor knew it was time to plant." When the day arrived, all were expected to participate, even though some made only a token effort. After this each person conducted his agricultural activities as he saw fit [14, 23, 29].

More recently even this modified form of control has been lifted. As one informant [20] stated in 1948, "You planted without being told" (see also Robbins, Harrington, and Freire-Marreco 1916:108).

Harvesting

Controls over harvesting seem to have paralleled those over planting. Earlier the two caciques designated the day when the village could begin the harvest. Later the governor assumed this prerogative and, after meeting with the council, set the time. The official announcement was made in the evening, and the following morning families began gathering the crop. Actually the date was usually known a week in advance. This gave the women an opportunity to prepare food for relatives and friends who would help with the work [14, 64]. Farms along Santa Clara Creek were harvested first [64].

Violation of the harvesting edict, as in the case of planting, was formerly considered a major crime and the guilty person was whipped or placed in stocks. Today these restrictions have disappeared, and each individual follows his own volition [64].

Pest Control

Crops were subject to periodic inroads by insect and animal pests, and a variety of devices were developed to control them. Most farmers, before planting, treated their seed with a solution which consisted of a plant called "blue stone" *(osa pu),* ground up and mixed with other wild species. This was believed to protect the plants from insects and worms and to encourage growth. Pumpkins were reported to be the most vulnerable to damage from these sources. One informant [65], "had tried everything" without success; another [62], however, sprinkled ashes around the pumpkin plants and claimed this afforded protection.

Infestations by grasshoppers were frequent. Damage from this source varied, in some years slight, in others heavy. On one occasion, "only one field was saved" [65]. There appeared to be no practical safeguards against their inroads; however, attempts at control by religious rites may be inferred since at one "large treatment," or curing rite, the witch dolls were stuffed with grasshoppers (see Chapter 10).

Birds and animals were reported to have menaced the maturing crops. Crows, magpies, and jays were the most troublesome birds. Scarecrows were placed in fields to frighten them, and watchers with slings, bows and arrows, or guns frightened them away or killed them. Similar methods were used against gophers, squirrels, skunks, porcupines, coyotes, and bears [23, 27].

ABORIGINAL PLANTS

Corn

Corn was the most important aboriginal plant, both economically and religiously. Six principal varieties were distinguished on the basis of color, and each was associated with a cardinal direction and a mythological figure: blue (xuŋca^{n}wa^m?i?) north, Blue Corn Maiden; yellow (xuŋc'ezhi?), west, Yellow Corn Maiden; red (xuŋp'i?i), south, Red Corn Maiden; white (xuŋc'e^n?i?), east, White Corn Maiden; variegated (xuŋ$t$hu wi?), zenith, Variegated Corn Maiden; black (xuŋ $t$heŋdi?), nadir, Black Corn Maiden (see also Robbins, Harrington, Freire-Marreco 1916: 81). Besides the above, there was a variety of white dwarf corn with very small ears (xuŋ $t$hinini). This was associated with Dwarf Corn Maiden. In addition, popcorn was occasionally grown. While native to the area, it was thought to have been recently introduced [14, 23].

A series of corn specimens was collected in 1946. These specimens were identified and described by Dr. Edward F. Castetter as follows:

White:
Typical Pueblo Indian corn, flour type. Colorless pericarp. Colorless endosperm. Colorless cob. Only untypical characteristic: a little long. 14 rowed.
Variegated:
Typical Pueblo Indian corn. Flour type. Red pericarp. White endosperm except some grains have purple aleurone. 14 rowed.
All colors:
Typical Pueblo Indian corn. Flour corn except there are some flinty grains. A good deal of segregation. Pericarp is white, but some grains have purple, some red aleurone; some grains have colorless aleurone. 12 rowed.
All colors:
Typical Pueblo Indian corn. Flour type. Colorless pericarp. Some grains have red, some have purple aleurone, others colorless. 14 rowed.
Variegated:
Typical Pueblo Indian corn, except a bit slender. Flour type. Red pericarp. Colorless endosperm. 10 rowed.

Blue and white:
> Typical Pueblo Indian corn. A mixture of flour and flinty grains. Pericarp colorless; some grains white, others with purple aleurone. 18 rowed.

All colors:
> Typical Pueblo Indian corn. Flour type. Colorless pericarp. Some segregation in endosperm. Most grains have red aleurone, but some have purple and some are colorless. Some grains are flinty. 14 rowed.

Purple:
> Typical Pueblo Indian corn. Flour type. Colorless pericarp. Purple aleurone. 12 rowed.

Variegated—all colors:
> Typical Pueblo Indian corn. Flour type. Colorless pericarp. Considerable segregation as to endosperm color. Grains variable as to aleurone color intensity (shades of blue), some grains are white, some yellow. 14 rowed.

Brownish:
> Typical Pueblo Indian corn. Flour type. Some grains have purple, some colorless aleurone. 18 rowed.

Faded red:
> Typical Pueblo Indian corn. Flour type. Red pericarp. Colorless endosperm. 12 rowed.

All colors:
> Typical Pueblo Indian corn. Flour type. Colorless pericarp. Aleurone mostly purple of various shades, but a few grains with red aleurone and some colorless. 12 rowed.

Blue:
> Typical Pueblo Indian corn. Flour type. Colorless pericarp. Purple aleurone. 12 rowed.

The Santa Clara Indians differentiated between the seed of domesticated and wild plants. Any seed of a domesticated product was referred to as ko?zhi; that from a wild plant, "those which would not be planted," t'urg [18, 52]. Selection of seed corn was a matter of considerable moment. Some farmers raised a small plot of corn in the garden near their homes. The plants were carefully tended and when harvested were set aside for seed the following years [23].

The majority, however, selected seed corn during husking. The choice was made on the basis of size of the ear (especially its length), the straightness of the rows, and whether the kernels were well developed and extended to the tip of the cob. Only part of the husk was removed, and the remaining portion was braided to the husks of other such ears. These bunches were placed on the housetops to dry, then stored until needed.

Jeançon (1904-30) confirmed the above and added that:

> Formerly it was the custom to reserve from each crop enough corn to have seed for a second year in case the first year's crop failed. In fact corn kept until the second year was considered stronger and better for seed, just as a man in his twenties is supposed to be more robust and have more vitality than a younger boy.

Periodic famines were known to have occurred due to crop loss through drought, grasshoppers, and other causes. Traditional tales existed dealing with periods when in order to survive the villagers boiled the rawhide thongs used to secure the fence poles and the hides of buffalo, cattle, and sheep to make soup [18].

Before planting, it was customary, as noted earlier, to treat the seed with a solution made from a plant called "blue stone" (osa pu). This and several other wild forms were ground up and mixed together. It was believed that this prevented damage by worms. Seed was never soaked prior to planting to facilitate germination [27, 29, 44, 52].

Corn was planted during the latter part of April or the first part of May. Often a second planting was made two weeks after the first in order that the crop would mature at intervals [27, 44]. Unless it had rained recently, the field was irrigated before planting.

Formerly the digging stick, "sharp pointed stick" (fe K'eh), was used in planting. More recently, this implement was replaced by the plow, and corn was furrow planted. The farmer plowed five furrows, and the corn was dropped in the fifth, being covered by the subsequent round of the plow. This was continued until the entire field was seeded. A few people planted in the fourth furrow, but this was not considered good practice, as it crowded the plants. Clusters were planted about one pace apart. Two to five kernels were planted together [27], or five [65], unless worms were prevalent, in which case six or seven seeds were dropped. Formerly the depth of planting was about five inches. More recently, planting depth has depended upon the depth of the furrow and has normally been greater than five inches. The different colors of corn were planted in different sections of the field, and these sections were marked with stakes. According to one informant [65], this was to prevent the color varieties from mixing. Another informant [14] had no conception of cross-pollination. According to others [27, 44], no attention in planting was paid to corn color and directional association, and planting did not begin in any particular section of the field.

Irrigation began when the corn stalks reached a height of six to ten inches. As soon as the ground dried, it was cultivated. The field was hoed to remove the weeds and the clusters thinned and hilled. Hills were thinned to two or three stalks. "If you leave too many stalks you do not get many ears in the fall" [27]. Formerly wooden and shoulder-blade hoes were used; later the metal hoes of the Spanish and Americans were introduced. After hilling, corn was irrigated whenever the need arose, possibly as many as five times during the season if water were available. The last irrigation normally took place just as the corn began to mature.

Various stages of corn growth were recognized and named:

Na ci yo pu mu, "sharpening out from the root." This referred to the first emergence of the plant from the soil, "like a knife coming out."

Na we^n mu, "second set of leaves appearing to be a ring around it." This referred to the appearance of four leaves on the stalk. The same term was used for subsequent stages, i.e., when the second, third, etc., sets of leaves have come out.

Na kaŋ po', "to be blossoms it happened," referred to the corn in blossom.

Na se^n po', "to be ears it happened," referred to the appearance of ears on the stalk.

Na xuŋ he po', "to be kernels it happened," referred to the forming of the kernels on the cob.

Na xuŋ ke'po', "to be kernels hard it happened," referred to the corn when it matured [27]. (For names of various parts of the corn plant, see Robbins, Harrington, and Freire-Marreco 1916:80.)

Green corn was available for eating from the latter part of July through August, but the main crop was not ready for harvest until September [27]. As this time approached, older men went to the fields, selected one or two mature ears, chewed some of the kernels and spit them out. This was believed to cause the remainder of the crop to mature [25].

Relatives and friends cooperated in the harvesting on a reciprocal basis. Each worker selected a row, stripped the ears from the stalks, and placed them in conveniently located piles. Earlier the harvest was transported to the homes in sacks, blankets, and other containers. Subsequent to the arrival of the Spanish, carretas lined with rawhide were used when available. More recently wagons and trucks were used for transport. Once the corn was picked, the stalks were cut and brought to the corrals to be used for winter fodder.

Women began husking the corn as soon as it arrived from the fields. This was done by hand or with the help of a knife-like pointed wooden tool. In the latter case, the point was inserted in the husk, the husk ripped open, and then removed by hand [18]. If immature ears were encountered during husking or ears whose maturation had been interrupted by an early frost, the soft kernels were salvaged by scraping them from the cob and placing them to dry [25]. Again, relatives and friends assisted. Husking bees were frequently occasions for social interplay, the tedium being enlivened by gossip and story-telling.

Once husked, the ears were placed in a crib or on the ramada to dry. When dry, and if time permitted, kernels were removed from the cob; otherwise whole ears were stored. Storage facilities included back rooms, inside bins, or roof bins.

The butt of a cob was used to loosen or dislodge the kernels from an ear. The ear was then wrung in the hands to remove those kernels that remained.

While the most immediate use of corn was for food (see Chapter 5) and trade (see Chapter 6), secondary utilizations of the plant and its by-products also played an important role. Corn pollen was believed to possess medicinal properties, and was mixed with water and drunk to alleviate pain. Both pollen and meal were used as offerings during ceremonials and rituals. Women gathered the pollen; they placed baskets under the plant and shook or struck the stalk to dislodge the pollen. Corn smut was used by mid-wives to assist in birth (see Chapter 8).

Double and triple ears of corn were saved and fed to stock in the belief that they would increase the fecundity of the animals. It was said that a woman who saw a double ear of corn would give birth to twins. This statement, however, was not taken seriously. In this same semihumorous vein was the following: if a worker during husking encountered an ear devoid of kernels, it was thought to indicate that the individual was lazy, and a coworker would strike her on the back with the cob (see also Robbins, Harrington, and Freire-Marreco 1916:83).

The corn stalks and portions of the husks were saved for fodder. The finer portions of the husks were utilized as cigarette paper. Cobs were used for fuel [27].

Beans

Beans were considered almost as important economically as corn, not only because of their food value, but because they constituted an important item of trade with local Spanish-Americans. For this reason farmers attempted to raise a surplus. Several varieties of beans were grown, some of which represented recent introductions. The most highly considered, and according to informants, indigenous, was a "yellowish-white" type called tewa tu, "Tewa Bean." Another, somewhat lighter in color, was also designated as "Tewa Bean," or tsa tse dji. Recently, pinto beans have also been cultivated. These were called thun we tu, "spotted bean."

Beans were the last crop to be planted, usually in May. Preferably, they were grown on the mountain farms, as the cooler climate

at this higher elevation was believed to produce a heavier yield, and irrigation was unnecessary. It was also said that loss from insect pests was less in that area. When they were grown in the valley, the plot was given a pre-planting irrigation.

Formerly beans were planted with a digging stick; more recently they were furrow planted. Rows were spaced about three furrows apart, seed clusters about a foot apart. Four to six seeds were dropped at each interval, depending upon the prevalence of worms. After planting, the field was dragged with a log drag. Beans were never planted between rows of corn.

When the plants appeared, the clusters were thinned to encourage a heavier yield. Next they were hilled to protect them from the wind. The use of low, brush windbreaks of the type found among the Hopi was denied.

When the crop matured and dried, the whole plants were pulled and placed in piles in the field. They remained there from three days to a week and were then brought to the homes. Normally, they were threshed by women with the aid of a wooden flail. Less frequently, a threshing floor was prepared in the field, or the beans were taken by men to the one used for wheat. Cattle, horses, or sheep were then driven over the plants to dislodge the beans from the pods. Winnowing was accomplished with the aid of a shovel, fork, or basket. Beans were not screened as wheat and barley were.

When harvested, the crop was spread inside the house to dry. The dry beans were placed in rawhide sacks or pots and stored in storage bins on the roof or inside the house [13, 20, 25, 44, 62].

Pumpkins

The pumpkin was the least important of the aboriginal food plants and, according to informants, the most difficult to grow because of its vulnerability to insects and disease. The indigenous type was pear-shaped and green with white stripes, and was called po'fu wi, "spotted pumpkin." This grew to a length of about two feet. An introduced species was also raised, which was round and yellow (po c'ezhi?, "yellow

1. *Santa Clara Pueblo, vertical air photograph as of about 1950. The paved road (State Highway 30) at the bottom of the photograph is on a north-south axis.*

2. *Santa Clara Pueblo, oblique air photograph looking northward toward Española (Spence Air Photos [E-9996], 10-11-39). In the intervening decades, the areas north of the pueblo on either side of the highway have been filled in with modern housing.*

3. Santa Clara Pueblo, oblique air photograph looking westward toward the Jemez Mountains (Spence Air Photos [E-9995], 10-11-39).

4. *View across Santa Clara Pueblo, looking southsoutheast toward Black Mesa (1879 photograph by J. K. Hillers, Bureau of American Ethnology, Smithsonian Institution, #1981-C).*

5. *View of Santa Clara Pueblo, looking to the southwest; kiva in plaza, left center of picture (1879 photograph by J.K. Hillers, Bureau of American Ethnology, Smithsonian Institution, #1986-E-2).*

6. *Santa Clara Pueblo, view to the northwest from roof of the church (1900 photograph by A.C. Vroman. Bureau of American Ethnology, Smithsonian Institution, #1977). The tall wicker basket, right center, was a cage, or house, for chickens.*

7. *Santa Clara Pueblo, view to the southwest from roof of the church. Kiva in plaza, left center (1900 photograph by A.C. Vroman, Bureau of American Ethnology, Smithsonian Institution, #1980).*

8. *Santa Clara Pueblo: two-storied house; also baking ovens and ramada (Museum of New Mexico, #1401.2).*

9. *Santa Clara Pueblo: architectural details—two-storied house, ramada, and fenced porch (Museum of New Mexico, #1401.4).*

10. *Santa Clara Pueblo: corn, squash, chili, and hay drying on ramadas (Museum of New Mexico, #1401.8).*

11. *Santa Clara Pueblo: view to the north of harvested crops drying on roof-tops and ramadas (Museum of New Mexico, #1401.11).*

12. *Santa Clara Pueblo: view to the northwest, close-up of drying corn, squash, and chili (Museum of New Mexico, #1401.9).*

13. *Santa Clara Pueblo: threshing floor being used with horses (Museum of New Mexico, #1401.5).*

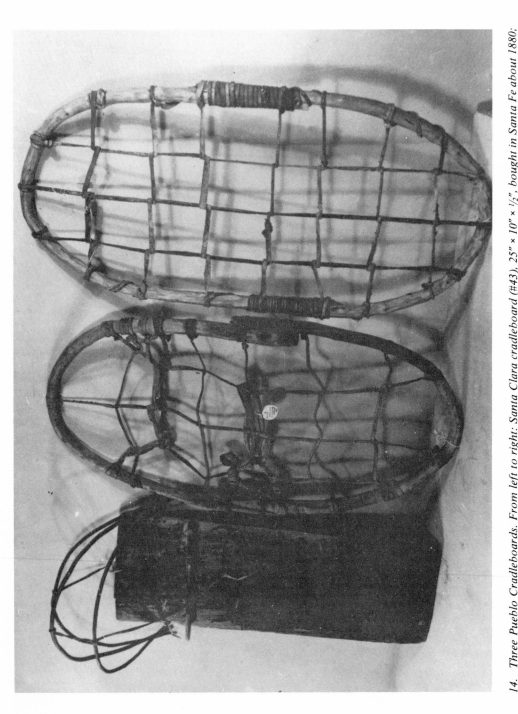

14. *Three Pueblo Cradleboards. From left to right: Santa Clara cradleboard (#43), 25″ × 10″ × ½″, bought in Santa Fe about 1880; Santo Domingo swinging cradle platform (#52), 29″ × 16″, 1957; and Santo Domingo swinging cradle platform (#51), 30.5″ × 14″, 1957 (Museum of New Mexico Collections).*

15. *Santa Clara Men at Omaha Exposition, 1898. From left to right: Cajete, Guadalupe, Dolores, Bonifacio, Governor Diego Naranjo, Geronimo, Ex-Governor José Jesus Naranjo, and Casimiro (photo by F.A. Rinehart for the Bureau of American Ethnology, Smithsonian Institution, #1970).*

16. *Santa Clara Men at Omaha Exposition, 1898. From left to right: Santiago, San José, Agustín, Pedro Baca, David Tafoya, Juan Diego, Albino (photograph by F.A. Rinehart for the Bureau of American Ethnology, Smithsonian Institution. #1971).*

pumpkin"). Nonindigenous species of squash were imported around the turn of the century [9, 23].

Pumpkins were grown in separate plots in either the mountains or the valley. The mountains were preferred because of the cooler climate, and because insect pests were not so numerous in that area. Planting took place in May. Formerly a digging stick was used; later, fields were plowed and several seeds dropped in the furrows at irregular intervals [23]. The rationalization against row planting was that should rodents attack, they would follow a straight line, whereas if the plants occurred irregularly, they would be confused [14]. Ample distance was left between clusters to allow the vines to spread. The field was dragged after seeding.

Pumpkins were irrigated in the lowlands, but not in the mountains. Cultivation began when two leaves appeared, and was continued at intervals until the pumpkin began to form. The vines were never pinched back to prevent excess growth.

Some of the crop was harvested and eaten when the product reached a diameter of about five inches, but the bulk of the crop was allowed to mature. Degree of maturity was judged by pressing a fingernail into the rind to test its hardness.

Pumpkins were stored whole or in dried strips. In the former case, three beams were suspended from the rafters, or vigas, lashed together, and the pumpkins placed on this shelf. They were said to keep all winter. In the latter instance, the rind was first removed, the pumpkin cut spirally, and placed on the roof to dry. When dried it was stored, sometimes tied in hanks [14, 25, 50, 64, 65].

Squash were grown and treated in the same manner as pumpkins.

NONFOOD PLANTS

Cotton

Cotton (se xe^m? povi) has not been grown at Santa Clara Pueblo for over sixty years. This was confirmed by Robbins, Harrington, and Freire-Marreco 1916: 103), "...and a man who died in 1909 used to raise a small quantity of cotton, probably to provide cotton string for tying prayer-feathers and for other ceremonial uses." Only a few remembered details of its cultivation.

According to one informant [23], cotton was planted about May 15. Only a row or two, "not too much." Twine was made from it, being twisted by hand. Others were of the opinion that fairly extensive plots were formerly planted along the base of the hills southwest and northwest of the village. Planting took place early in the spring, "just before the salt bush flowered." The land was plowed before irrigating and again before planting. The plants were hoed.

Both men and women engaged in harvesting the crop. The cotton seeds were removed by hand, and most were discarded [14, 27, 62].

Tobacco

Tobacco (t'owa sa, "people's tobacco," or tewa sa, "Tewa tobacco") has not been grown at Santa Clara since about 1930. It was planted in garden plots, approximately sixty by eighty feet in size, located in the vicinity of the village. Two methods of planting appear to have prevailed. Some saved seed for the following year's crop at the time of harvest [20, 64]; others tossed the stalks and pods in the corner of the field and the following spring transplanted the plants that had sprouted in these refuse heaps [27, 44, 65].

Moist soil was essential for both planting and transplanting. Seeds or plants were spaced about a foot apart. The earth was always pressed firmly around the stems of the plants which were moved. Holes were dug with a spatulate-bladed digging stick. Most of this work was done by men, though women did participate. The garden was irrigated immediately on completion of the planting.

Plots were irrigated and cultivated whenever the need arose. Weeding was done by hand or with a hoe, and the plants were hilled. After the leaves appeared, any auxiliary buds which grew at the base of the leaf stem were removed in order to promote growth.

While the leaves were still green, the plants were cut, tied in bundles, and brought to the home. If seed for the coming year was to be saved, the pods were removed and then the stalk was stripped. The leaves were first spread singly to dry, either in a room or outside. Usually drying was accomplished inside, as it was said that if dried outside the tobacco became strong. When the leaves turned yellow, they were placed in piles until the curing was completed. These stacks were continually examined to prevent sweating and subsequent mildew, which would cause the tobacco to turn black and become overly strong. No preparation was used to facilitate the drying process. When the leaves were completely cured, they were bundled together, tied with yucca, and stored in the house until needed [20, 30, 62].

Gourds

Some gourds (k'e re, "ladle") were raised by Santa Clara farmers, but their cultivation was sporadic. This was due to a prevalence of diseases which were credited with attacking the vines, and the difficulty of getting the seeds to germinate, which contributed to the uncertainty of the crop. Most individuals preferred to obtain gourds through trade from Santo Domingo and other southern pueblos.

Gourds were always planted in the lowlands. They were planted at the same time as pumpkins (early May), "when the salt bush was beginning to blossom." Only a few hills were planted, since yields were heavy if the crop was successful. Holes were made with a sharp-pointed digging stick and two or three seeds inserted and covered by hand. The plants were subsequently irrigated and cultivated whenever the need arose.

Plants whose products were destined for use as ladles, dippers, or round rattles were located near a fence, in order that the vines might climb and the mature gourds retain their natural form. Occasionally, trellises were built or stakes set up if a fence were lacking. If flat-sided rattles were desired, vines were allowed to run along the ground and flat rocks were placed under and over the maturing gourds to insure the desired shape. There were three species of gourds, one for dippers, one for rattles, and another for canteens [30].

When the gourds were thoroughly mature, and had turned yellow and hardened, they were picked and placed on the roof tops for additional drying. After this they were used to construct ladles, canteens, pottery smoothers, rattles, and other ceremonial items [23, 51, 64, 69].

INTRODUCED FOOD PLANTS

Watermelon

In recent years several varieties of watermelon have been current. Earlier, only one kind, a large round dark variety (thu wi?, "spotted"; also called po be' or more commonly by the Spanish name, sandía) was grown. All varieties were said to be subject to disease and were considered difficult to grow successfully.

Separate plots, usually in valleys, were designed for melons. This minimized the danger of destruction by the coyotes that were numerous in the mountain areas. The planting occurred immediately following that of corn in April [23] or May [62]. Plantings were often repeated after an interval of two weeks so that mature melons would be available over a longer period. The plot was given a preplanting irrigation. The seed was broadcast sown, but handfuls were thrown toward certain points in order that the plants would sprout in clusters. Some farmers planted in rows, others irregularly across the field. Sowing was followed by plowing and dragging to cover the seed.

When the plants appeared above the surface of the ground, the field was hoed and irrigated. This and subsequent irrigations were followed by hoeing. Normally, there were four irrigations. By the fourth, the melons had formed, and it was thought that future inundation would damage the crop.

The first melons ripened about the middle of August, supposedly by August 12, Santa Clara Day. The harvest was completed by the first of September. Although most melons were red when mature, some were yellow. The older type of watermelon was about the size of muskmelons [23, 44, 50, 69]. A portion of the crop was consumed at the time of harvest; the remainder was stored. The melons were placed in yucca-leaf slings and suspended from beams in the house. In this way, they kept through the winter and occasionally until spring.

A secondary utilization of watermelons was in connection with curing. The leaves of the plant were ground, mixed with water, and used for washing sore eyes. They were also rubbed on the head to alleviate headache. The blossoms were not used, and no melons were ever utilized in a green state [23, 50, 62].

Muskmelon

The oldest variety of muskmelon (be nunde, from Spanish?) was relatively smooth skinned, but regularly corrugated or ridged longitudinally. A smaller round species (cantaloupe?) was a recent introduction.

Muskmelon culture and its utilization for food were identical to the practices in connection with watermelons except for an additional method of preservation. A portion of the crop was selected, the rind removed, and then the melons were cut in halves. These were inverted over poles or twigs to dry. When partially dry, they were cut spirally, arranged in hanks, and thoroughly dried. They were stored in this condition for winter use.

Muskmelons which were stored whole kept until November. No attempt was made to ripen green melons in storage [14, 25].

Chili

Chili (cidi se^{n}i?, a version of the Spanish word "chile" plus the Tewa word for bitter) was grown in garden plots fifty to seventy-five yards square. It was usually planted in May. Before planting, the plot was plowed and dragged. A pointed digging stick was used to make trenches two inches deep and two feet apart, the length of the garden. The seed was sown in the trenches and covered by hand. An effort was made to space the plants at approximately one-foot intervals.

Chili was usually irrigated four times during the season; however, an additional inundation and cultivation would be given if the weed growth was excessive. The first took

place immediately after planting, the second and third when the plants reached a height of about two and four inches, respectively. The fourth took place when the chili was six or seven inches high and after the rows had been thinned. The plants removed in thinning were transplanted to fill bare areas in the garden. After each irrigation, with the exception of the first, the plot was weeded. Plants were hilled after the final inundation.

Green chili was picked in July, roasted on the coals, peeled, and eaten, often mixed with other foods. The mature red chili was harvested in August. Both green and red were picked, strung on yucca, and hung outside to dry. When dried, they were stored in the house to be used as the occasion demanded.

No medicinal value was attributed to chili [14, 23].

Wheat and Barley

Similar methods were practiced in growing spring wheat (ta taŋ c'e^n?i?, "white wheat"), winter wheat (tenuyii ta taŋ), and barley (sonyo nerd, "bearded wheat," Tewa name—ta Ooi?, "hairy hay"). In recent years, winter wheat has not been grown. No informants mentioned oats, though they must have been aware of the existence of that crop. Spring wheat and barley were the first crops sown, usually in March. Formerly the seed was mixed with a solution prepared by grinding several wild plants; today, the plant "blue stone" (osa pu) in water is sprinkled over the seed. These treatments were performed as protection against the inroads of insects.

The field was given a pre-planting irrigation and allowed to dry for about a week. One half of the field was planted at a time. First the seed was broadcast. Next a furrow was plowed down the center of this acreage, and plowing continued around the central furrow until all seeds were covered. The field was then dragged with a log drag to break up any clods that remained. When this was completed, a ditch was constructed by hand, along the high side, and a check dam or ridge run through the center of the field to facilitate irrigation and drainage.

Wheat and barley were irrigated either

four or five times during the season. The first irrigation occurred when the plants reached a height of about four inches; a second when they began to head; a third when the heads began to open. A fourth irrigation usually brought the wheat to maturity, but a fifth was given if it was necessary. Weeding was accomplished by hand. Normally one or two weedings were sufficient; wild sunflower was the worst pest.

Maturation began in the latter part of July and was complete in August. Wheat and barley were generally harvested immediately after Santa Clara Day, August 12th. The plants were cut with an iron sickle, or wooden scythe, or the axe-like type of wooden hoe. Lacking these the whole plant was pulled. The stalks were piled conveniently for the worker and later tied in sheaves, using the plant tse djo as a binding. The sheaves were transported to the threshing floor on the backs of men or burros. If the yield was small, the threshing was accomplished with a wooden flail; if large, the grain was trampled out by stock animals. The sheaves were piled in the center of the threshing floor; the stock was driven onto the floor and kept moving over the pile by shifts of men and boys. After an interval the stock was removed, and the scattered wheat and straw again piled in the center. Then the stock was reintroduced, and the process continued until the threshing was completed. (See Plate 13.)

Winnowing and cleaning were done in three steps. A wooden fork was used to remove the larger pieces of straw. Next the grain was thrown into the air with wooden shovels or slowly poured from baskets to allow the chaff to blow away. Finally it was sifted several times through a handled sieve—a box with a perforated rawhide or tin bottom, to remove any remaining impurities. The cleaned grain was placed to dry in a well-swept corner of a room. When thoroughly dry, it was deposited in rooftop bins or in oven-shaped storehouses on the ground [27, 44, 52,].

Sorghum

Sorghum was grown at Santa Clara and used in the production of sirup [18, 50]. According to Robbins, Harrington, and Freire-Marreco (1916:110),

> Sirup...was made at Santa Clara within living memory. The cane stalks were squeezed into a large wooden press, and the juice running into a wooden trough (?) which had formerly served as a canoa on the Rio Grande. As it was necessary to boil the juice immediately after pressing, a large party of men, women and children would assemble to do the work, keeping up the fires all night, with singing, drumming, and dancing. [While Robbins referred to sirup made from sugar cane, he must have been in error since there is no evidence that cane was grown at Santa Clara or that it would grow at that altitude. WWH]

Peaches

Both cling (tucivei?, "flesh sticks to nut") and freestone (tucivepi?i?, "flesh not sticking to nut") peaches were grown. Orchards were located along Santa Clara Creek, preferably against a hillside to protect the trees from frost. All trees were seedlings; the seeds were planted and when they sprouted, transplanted. The orchards began to bear at the age of five or six years.

Peaches matured in late August after Santa Clara Day.

Some of the crop was eaten fresh; the remainder was dried for winter use. This product was popular as a filler for pies [14, 27].

Apples

Apple (be) culture was similar to that of peaches, as was the utilization of the crop. There was evidence (Robbins, Harrington, and Freire-Marreco 1916:114–15) that in some instances apples were an important trade item between the Santa Clara Indians and the Apache.

Apricots

Apricots were grown at Santa Clara. Presumably their culture and utilization paralleled that of peaches.

Vegetables

It is apparent from the Spanish sources and from more recent studies that the Santa Clara Indians were aware of the existence of a large number of vegetables and plants of European provenience. However, with the exception of those mentioned above, there is little evidence that these were cultivated except sporadically. Only one informant [45] volunteered information on this subject. According to her, string beans were sometimes grown, and onions were frequently included in the garden plots. In the latter case the villagers were familiar with the wild form, which may explain their semipopularity.

ANIMAL HUSBANDRY

The practice of animal husbandry at Santa Clara could best be described as desultory. Informants viewed the pursuit with a marked lack of enthusiasm, and there was every reason to believe that this attitude prevailed in the past also. Livestock was relatively unimportant economically except in a few individual cases in recent times. Domesticated animals played only a small role in the overall subsistence picture. Their principal importance was in draft and travel.

With the possible exception of the dog, all domesticated animals were introduced. The Santa Clara Indians were undoubtedly familiar with livestock from conquest times. However, because of their relative scarcity during the colonial period, such animals were probably not available in quantity until comparatively recent periods. While initially derived from Spanish sources, later sources, particularly of cattle, horses, and to a lesser extent, sheep, were the Plains and Marginal Plains tribes.

Dogs were kept as pets and used in hunting (see also Henderson and Harring-ton 1914:28). They frequently occupied outside ovens as kennels when these were not in use. Pets other than dogs included an occasional rabbit, fawn, duck, or magpie [62].

Sheep and goats were never numerous, and only a few families possessed them [9, 23]. Another [30] stated that they were not raised at Santa Clara at all and that wool was imported. These opinions were confirmed by Henderson and Harrington (1914:15) who, referring to the Tewa generally, stated that very few owned sheep or goats. They added that sheep were never milked, although goats were. While informants made no mention of swine, Henderson and Harrington (1914:32) indicated that they were kept in limited numbers by the Tewa.

Cattle and horses were more prevalent than sheep, although never numerous. Each family had a few head of cattle, and at about the turn of the century one or two individuals owned as many as sixty. Cattle were primarily used for draft purposes rather than food [6]. Oxen were utilized with carretas to transport produce from the fields and products of the hunt from the Plains [9].

By the twentieth century, horses had become the general purpose draft animals. Prior to that time, they had been almost exclusively for riding and were the principal means of transportation when extensive journeys were involved in connection with trade, hunting, and warfare. Donkeys, while never numerous, were used on shorter journeys. They were both ridden and packed [9, 14, 20, 29, 30].

Some families had poultry in 1896. Chickens, however, were few in number. They were kept in pens made of stone or in willow cages [50]. One such cage, made of interlaced willow withes, appears in the right foreground of the plaza in a photograph by Vroman taken in 1900 (Plate 7). No domesticated turkeys were raised at Santa Clara Pueblo [65].

5

Preparation of Food and Diet

FOOD AND COOKING

The Santa Clara Indians classified most foods, as well as some other materials, as either hot or cold, a concept undoubtedly borrowed from the Spanish (see Foster 1953; 1960:6, 14–15, 20n, 61; Ortiz 1969: 113–14, 118, 128, 178–79n24). There appeared to be no logical or consistent basis for assignment to one or the other of these categories. Furthermore, informants differed in detail on some of the designations. According to Jeançon (1904–30),

> When certain foods are cooked they are considered hot or cold without respect to their temperature. They are by nature agents which produce hot and cold conditions. Thus, certain meats are cold even though served in boiling condition, the belief being that they will produce cold results after consumption. The same applies to hot substances in like manner. They (foods) are associated with all that is hot or cold in song and story.

Jeançon's informants assigned to the hot category: beef, mutton, rabbit, corn, raisins, prunes, as well as buckskin and wool. They placed in the cold division: beans, piñon nuts, apples, grapes, lemons and other modern fruits, and cotton cloth. Rock, iron, pine, and scrub oak were thought of as hard substances; all other woods were soft (Jeançon 1904–30). Hot foods included deer, buffalo, rabbit, game in general, sheep, cattle, corn, beans, wheat, canteloupe, beeweed, and tortoise. In the cold group were pork, goat, fish, pumpkin, watermelon, piñon nuts, and all sweets. Steel was in the cold category, but water, wool, and cotton were in a neutral grouping [14].

Individuals were prohibited from eating cold foods during illnesses. This tabu was extended to include women during pregnancy. Fish, beans (?), piñon nuts, and sweets of any kind were thought to accelerate infections and were denied patients [14, 27].

The concept of hot and cold foods did not seem to have invaded the more esoteric religious aspects of the culture. There the distinction was made on the basis of aboriginal versus nonaboriginal foods. Those actively participating in rituals were prohibited from eating any foods but native ones. These consisted of game and corn products. Paramount among foods for ceremonial occasions were those derived from blue corn. All canned foods were banned, as was seasoning; specifically mentioned were salt, pepper, sugar, cinnamon, garlic, and onions [14, 27, 50, 61, 72].

Other potential foods considered inedible included wolf, fox, coyote, eagle, and hawk. Marrow was eaten only by adults. If children ate it, it was believed they would develop arthritis [27, 30].

Most cooking, other than baking, was done in the home except in summer. During the warm season this activity was often transferred to a ramada; there windbreaks of adobe brick were frequently erected to shield the outdoor fires [62]. There was no communal cooking; each family or consumption group prepared food for its own members. Ordinarily sufficient food for a day or more was cooked at any one time [62], and in the case of baked foods usually a week's supply was finished at a particular baking [29].

On "baking day" the whole female segment of the family participated in the preparations and work. This activity had certain social overtones. Children habitually gathered and watched a woman remove bread from the oven. They were silent, but it was understood that they expected a gift. Additional "pies" or bu ci ("vagabond") were made by the baker, and these were tendered to the children. This custom was called parᵑ kʼa "bread watch" [56, 72].

A similar convention was associated with the return of villagers from a shopping or extended trip. Children called at the home and welcomed them back. Usually candy or some other delicacy was distributed to these children. This was known as the aⁿ pʼo kʼa, "sugar watch," or "candy watch" [72].

Prior to a feast day or ceremonial, cooking activities were greatly increased. Preparations began at least two days before the event, and large food surpluses were accumulated. Not only was there a religious obligation to feed relatives who were performing rites, but also to feed moiety or society members similarly engaged. Hospitality also demanded that relatives and friends who came from other villages to witness the performances be entertained and fed. Even under normal circumstances, offering food to a guest or visitor was a recognized obligation [13, 18].

While many dishes were aboriginal, others were obviously derived from Mexican and Spanish-American sources. These included tortillas, tacos, sopaipillas, tamales, and posole. Most cereals were baked, boiled, or fried—often in combination with meat. Wild plants and vegetables were usually eaten fresh or boiled. Meat foods were most often prepared in stews or in the form of baked or fried "pies." Birds and small mammals, and occasionally the meat of larger animals, was spitted and broiled [27, 29, 52, 61]. No stone boiling was practiced; one informant [30] considered the idea bizarre.

Several types of seasoning were utilized. Of these salt was considered most desirable. "Salt is important in the Tewa diet. Meat without salt is not considered fit to eat" [4]. Before the commercial product became available, salt was obtained from deposits in the Estancia Valley. It had religious as well as utilitarian importance.

When salt was lacking, "rock ash" (ku nu, "lye") was used as a substitute. This mineral was obtained in trade from the Spanish-Americans or from deposits in the mountains. Before being used, it was reduced to powder. The mineral was placed between two flat rocks. Slabs of rock were placed on edge around these two. The whole was then covered with large hunks of dry manure, and a fire was lighted. This was kept burning for four days and nights. At the end of this time the "rock ash" was reduced to powder [25, 35].

Wood ash [25] and another mineral, na a ("epsom salts"?) [35], were occasionally used for flavoring in lieu of the above. Plant seasonings included green squash blossoms, chili [56], mint (?) (povi warᵑ), and mountain flower (piᵑ povi) [44]. In recent years pepper, sugar, cinnamon, onions, and garlic have been added to the list of condiments.

Water for cooking and domestic purposes was obtained by the women. The principal source of supply was Santa Clara Creek, immediately north of the village. When this dried up or was muddied by flood, water was secured from one of four other localities. One was the Rio Grande, although this was normally dry during July and August. Other sources were three springs: one about three or four miles southeast of the village; another, P'o ci be?, about a mile or mile and a half west on Santa Clara Creek, and a third, P'o ci pa^{ge}, about a mile north of the pueblo. The greater part of the day was often consumed carrying water from these more distant locations, and in such instances every drop was carefully handled [29].

The first wells were dug about the beginning of the century. At that time a pronounced schism existed between the two moieties, and each dug its own well. These were on the banks of Santa Clara Creek, about fifty feet apart.

About 1920, the government drilled a well in the northwest plaza and installed a hand pump. The hand pump was replaced by a windmill, and a horse trough added, about 1925. In 1938 a reservoir was built in the foothills west of the village, and water was piped to within a few feet of each home [18, 72].

According to one woman [38], windmills were not built until 1914. Before that water came from a spring, wa *ch*upange, and also from a mile up Santa Clara Canyon where there was another spring. Still another spring was located a mile east of Santa Clara.

Women placed large water jars on their heads and took gourd ladles. They went in groups either in early morning or early evening; women of all ages went. They asked each other and arranged to go in groups, never alone. Sometimes they carried an extra jar in their hands; sometimes they carried babies on their backs if necessary. Rainwater could be gotten from pools that formed on hard ground. The women were afraid to go alone because of fear of attack by pueblo men or strangers.

The women wore a shawl on their head and placed the jar on top. The ladle was placed in the jar when it was full. A jar had better balance after being filled. Water was strained through a cloth (earlier, a horsehair strainer) as the jar was filled.

At home the jars were either placed on the floor or in the branches of a small tree trunk buried upright in the dirt floor by the door.

During the summer they got water from irrigation ditches.

Quantities of water were stored in large jars on pads and in tubs. The jars were covered by anything at all, a basket, cloth, or whatever. Thus they did not have to get water every day. In the old days they either licked eating dishes dry or washed them in hot water poured into a tub. There was no soap for dishes [10, 38].

Wood for cooking and heating was supplied by the men. There was some evidence that this task was formerly assigned to women. Robbins, Harrington, and Freire-Marreco (1916:24n) stated,

> The acquisition of donkeys, and subsequently of horses and wagons, with iron tools, by the men, has removed woodcutting from the woman's sphere of labor. Occasionally an old widow, or woman whose husband is an invalid, may be seen chopping wood or gathering branches.

Elsewhere (pp. 23–24) they noted,

> A few billets of firewood, carried by means of a cord on a man's shoulder and thrown down beside a woman's door, is considered an appropriate present. When a woman is about to be confined, her husband's father often brings her firewood.

Piñon was preferred for firewood. It was said to burn slowly and produce a better bed of coals [20, 23]. After piñon, juniper and pine were selected in that order. A tree struck by lightning could not be used for firewood, "because it will crackle as you burn it." Coal was never used for cooking [20].

Formerly fire was made with a drill. The drill was of oak and one piece. The hearth was of feK*e* (osage orange?). Depressions were made in the hearth for the tip of the drill, but no channels were cut to lead the hot dust to the tinder. Cedar bark was used as tinder. Drills have been obsolete for a considerable time [44].

The flint and steel replaced the drill [42, 44]. This consisted of a piece of flint and small iron file [42]. Wool, cotton [44], or a piece of cloth [42] served as tinder.

Before matches were introduced, each family bedded the coals at night. If the fire went out, fire was borrowed from a neighbor. "In the morning after waking see where smoke is rising. Go into the house and say 'I am coming for fire' (o fa ke nea). The answer, 'take it' (ma Ke). Fires were started in this manner when there were no matches" [42].

Stone axes were used earlier for cutting timber and firewood. According to descriptions these were chipped from obsidian or chert. A few were double bladed. Both full and three-quarter groove types existed. The grooves were made by abrasion. Axes were hafted in two ways. In one a piece of oak was split, the axe inserted in the cleft, and the haft wrapped and tied with rawhide, immediately above and below the head. For the full-grooved type the end of a length of oak was tapered, soaked in water, heated over the fire, and then bent around the head. It was secured below the base of the head with a sinew wrapping [20, 23, 27, 36]. During the Mexican period the village was given four metal axes by the government. These were used in turn by each family as needed [6].

Corn was the staple food, and a great variety of dishes was prepared from it or in combination with it and other foods. Ears of green corn were boiled or roasted (peXo Kwa). All but two or three husks were removed, and the ears were placed in boiling water and boiled to produce pe tsi wi, "fresh corn fried." Green ears were also treated and stored for winter use. The unhusked ears were put in a preheated outdoor oven. The opening was closed and water was poured through the vent. The vent was closed and the corn steam cooked. It would keep in this condition until needed [24, 45].

Most mature corn was converted into meal (agen). The kernels were removed from the cob and then ground. Of the foods produced from meal, the most highly regarded was bu wa (piki, or wafer bread), which was an adjunct of any ritual occasion.

Piki was always made from blue corn. The kernels were put in a pottery bowl and placed on a bed of coals. They were stirred with a stick until they turned yellow, and were then allowed to cool. When cool they were ground on the metate. After grinding, the meal was sifted through a horsehair sieve. Next it was placed in boiling water and cooked until a thin batter was produced. While cooking, it was continually stirred in order that it would be of uniform consistency. After boiling, the batter was poured into a bowl; water, meal, and "rock ash" were added, and the mixture kneaded. The "rock ash" insured that the final product would be a rich blue. The thick paste was then ready to cook [25, 27, 42, 45, 70].

The griddle was placed on four stones over a bed of hot coals and preheated. When very hot, it was greased. The woman took a ladle full of batter from the bowl, dipped her hand in the ladle, and with her hand spread a thin smear of paste on the griddle. The thin sheets of bread cooked immediately and were removed and stacked near the fire [25, 42, 51].

A kind of tortilla (bu wa k'a r a) was also made from blue cornmeal. The meal was prepared in the same manner as for piki except that the batter was thicker. Enough batter to produce a tortilla, hot-cake sized, was poured on a heated ungreased griddle. These were cooked on both sides, being turned with the hands [42, 45].

The ordinary tortilla (ota bu wa) was made from any variety of corn. The kernels were boiled with "rock ash" to remove or loosen the hulls. Cottonwood ash was used if "rock ash" was not available [42]. Next the kernels were rubbed gently over a slab or rough stone to remove any of the hulls that still adhered. After this they were winnowed to remove the "chaff." The corn was then ground and dough prepared, which was patted between the hands to produce the tortillas. These were about a quarter of an inch thick. While working, the operator continually moistened her hands to prevent the dough from sticking. Tortillas were cooked on a griddle [25, 42, 51].

Two types of tamales, "tamande" (from Spanish), were made using corn as a base. Kernels from green corn were ground, mixed with chili and meat, wrapped in corn husks, and boiled. In the more common form, meat and chili were placed on a tortilla and the tortilla folded over. This was encased in corn husks, the ends tied, and boiled [45].

Pies (parg sito, "bread stuffing") were made from cornmeal, wheat, and barley flour; recently almost exclusively from wheat flour. The dough was kneaded and lard, sugar, and cinnamon added. "In the old days, we ground cinnamon ourselves" [25]. A section of dough about an inch thick and the size of a pie crust was rolled out with a corncob rolling pin. On one half of this was put fresh or dried fruit, or dried and pounded meat. The other half of the crust was folded over the filling and the edges of the crust pinched together and sealed. Pies were placed on corn husks, put in the oven, and baked [25, 27, 42, 52, 68, 72].

Any remaining dough was made into small cakes, bu ci ("vagabond"), and baked with the pies. These were given to the children who gathered around the oven while baking was in process, as noted earlier [18, 25].

Less elaborate dishes prepared from corn included bread, mush, hominy, tacos, and parched corn. Bread made from wheat flour has almost entirely replaced the earlier corn bread, although this was still made on occasion. White cornmeal was preferred for bread. In fact one informant [62] stated that it was used exclusively for this purpose.

Cornmeal mush (sa ke we) was formerly a common food. "It was a substitute for bread" [19]. The meal was cooked in boiling water. Several types of mush were recognized, depending upon their consistency.

When hominy was made, the kernels were first boiled with cottonwood or "rock ash" to remove the hulls. They were then drained and reboiled. Meat was occasionally added to make posole [19, 51].

Tacos were made with meat or fruit. The meat or fruit was placed on either corn or wheat tortillas, the tortilla folded over and dropped in boiling grease [19].

Parched corn was also eaten at Santa Clara. The kernels and hot coals were placed in a twilled yucca basket, whose interior was coated with clay. The kernels were stirred with a corn cob until they were done [19].

Corn stalks were not eaten; they were used only for forage.

The preparation of native foods other than corn was not elaborate. Beans (tu sa^{n}) were usually boiled. They were placed in a pot of water; the pot was covered with a slab of flat rock, buried in a bed of hot coals, and allowed to remain there overnight. "If the rock was properly placed the water would not evaporate" [45]. Beans were seasoned with salt or mint. Occasionally pork or ears of corn were included [45, 68].

Squash and pumpkins were prepared in several ways. The mature fruits were often boiled (po xo ki) or baked (po xo to). In the latter case they were placed in the outdoor oven, the opening and vent were sealed, and they were left there overnight. Small squash or pumpkins the size of baseballs, or dried chunks of the mature fruit were boiled. When cooked they were drained; cheese, milk, and occasionally onions were added, and they were reboiled. This dish was called "small squash meal" (po e sa^{n}). "They got rennet from the stomach of sheep" [25]. Pumpkin seeds were parched and eaten. At other times they were ground, and a thin gruel or mush was made from them. The blossoms were used for seasoning pies [14].

Wheat was the most important economically of the introduced plants, and during the later historic period wheat flour was preferred for bread (parg, from Spanish). Before grinding, the kernels were placed in a yucca basket and taken to the stream and washed. "The water was run through the basket like a sieve." When clean it was dried, ground, and sifted [25].

Earlier sourdough bread was made. Recently yeast has been increasingly used for leavening. In the former case a portion of the dough was set aside at each baking to be used as leaven or "starter" (o wa si, "bread spoiled") [19, 25]. "You always keep a starter in the house. If you run out, you can borrow from another family" [25].

On baking day women arose early, mixed the dough and leaven, and placed it by the fire to rise. This was occasionally done the night before [19]. Then the fire was kindled in the oven. At least an hour was required to heat the oven, and about three armloads of wood were consumed. From time to time the coals were leveled and distributed with a poker to insure that the floor was evenly heated. While this preparation was in progress a space was cleared on the house floor, a cloth laid down, and the dough kneaded and made into loaves. The finished loaves were carried to the oven on a flat board [25, 29, 42, 61].

The coals were swept from the oven with a wet rag on the end of a stick and its temperature tested. A corn husk was thrown in, and if it burst into flame, it was too hot; if so, the oven was swept again with the wet rag to cool it. Correct temperature was indicated when the husk turned yellow or barley smoldered. The loaves were placed on the wooden paddle and put in the oven. A wet cloth was hung over the opening, and a board or flat rock put against this to keep it in place and close up the aperture. The wet rag on the end of the pole was placed over the vent [45, 52, 72].

The baker examined the bread at intervals; if it was baking too rapidly, the oven was opened and allowed to cool. When done the loaves were removed with the paddle and stored in baskets, jars, or bins until needed [19, 29, 45, 52].

Tortillas were also made from raised bread dough (bu wa *thi thi*). They were rolled out with a corn cob, placed on a hot griddle, and fried on both sides. When finished they were stacked in a basket. "They were about a quarter of an inch thick" [25], "like tortillas only thicker" [42].

The same dough was used to make sopaipillas or the so-called "squaw bread" (Ka p'o wenu, "grease liquid dip"). Chunks were dropped in a container of boiling grease. When they became swollen and light brown in color, they were removed with a sharp pointed stick [25].

A highly regarded bread or "pudding" (bu wa Xo, "bread roasted") was made from germinated wheat. It was popular for ritual occasions, and large quantities were baked during the period between Palm Sunday and Easter. Because it was sweet it was also a favorite food for hunting trips [18, 25].

The wheat was washed and placed in a jar near the fire. When it germinated it was packed tightly in a sack and the mouth of the container securely tied. A heavy stone was placed on the sack to increase the pressure. If it was a calm day, it was placed in the open to dry; if not, it was left in the house. When dry it was ground on the metate, and the

flour sifted. This was placed in a pot of boiling water and stirred as it cooked. In the meantime, the outdoor oven was preheated. When the oven was hot, the uncovered pot was transferred to it and the opening and vent closed and sealed. "This keeps the pot from boiling over." It was left there overnight. The cooked product resembled a very thick mush and had about an inch of crust [25].

The most important of the earlier introduced plants, aside from wheat, were melons, chili, and fruit. Melons had been a part of the economy so long that they were accorded aboriginal status and were among the foods distributed by the kachina impersonators as gifts. Both watermelons and muskmelons were eaten fresh or stored whole for later use. Muskmelons were also dried and later boiled and eaten like any other dried fruit [25].

Chili was used primarily for seasoning. The mature pods were dried for this purpose. In its green state chili was roasted on the coals, peeled, and eaten [14].

There was evidence that many families in the past maintained orchards and that a few had vineyards. Apricots, peaches, and apples were the most popular crops. These were eaten fresh and also used both fresh and dried as filler for pies. Grapes were eaten when ripe or made into jelly [45, 62].

Few vegetables were grown. Of those mentioned, only onions and string beans (ta whi sa^n, "ragged bean food") seemed to have been important. The former were eaten raw and used as seasoning. The latter were boiled or added to stew [45].

While a large number of wild plants were utilized, only a few added materially to the food resources. These included yucca baccata, prickly pear, beeweed, and piñon nuts.

The fruit of the yucca baccata (fa fu p'o, "mountain amole") was picked, boiled, and spread on a sheepskin to dry. When dried it was stored for winter use. Small pieces were cut and soaked in water and eaten. "It was sweet and used for dessert" [23].

The fruit of the prickly pear (se^n be) was gathered and placed on hot coals to remove the spines. It was then eaten, either without further preparation or after boiling [23, 25].

Leaves of the beeweed (xwaⁿ) were gathered and boiled like spinach [23, 25, 29]. Other plants utilized in the same manner were amaranth, or pigweed (ki'su, prairie dog arrow) [25], lambs-quarters, which was also dried for winter use [23], prairie clover (Xwire *the*) [19, 25] and several unidentified species: K'e aⁿ *the*, K'o wi arᵹfe, and te ogo [19].

Piñon nuts were gathered in large quantities if the harvest was abundant, roasted in the oven and stored for winter. "They were eaten in the winter while telling stories" [23, 29, 52].

Of marginal significance was a whole array of other plants. The chokecherry (ave) and gooseberry (tsi fu) were eaten both fresh and cooked. When cooked they were sometimes stored for winter [56, 65]. The fruit of "Tewa fruit" (snowberry?)—(Sericotheca dumosa) was eaten fresh. However, if the harvest was abundant, the small fruits were baked in the oven to remove the skins and then stored for winter [45]. The leaves and roots of the "wild celery" (ci ma ha, Spanish *chimaha)* were eaten fresh [23]. The groundcherry (ci go *the*) was boiled [45]. The wild onion (ahkonsi) was eaten fresh or used as seasoning, either fresh or dried [23]. Wild strawberries (piᵹ pu pa, "mountain wrinkled base") were eaten fresh [23]. The roots of the shield fern (Xarᵹ arᵹ *the*, "mountain lion foot plant") were chewed and sucked [45, 65]. Acorns were cut in small pieces and used as pie filler. A few were eaten raw [25]. Mushrooms (te) were formerly eaten, but seldom in recent years.

Few distinctions were made in the preparation of meat of wild and domesticated animals; special observances were accorded only to the bear and mountain lion. Those who ate bear meat had a ceremony performed over them [15, 20, 52, 72]. Mountain lion meat was shared only by relatives [15, 30]. Prohibited for food purposes were the coyote [20, 27], wolf [27], and fox [27, 30]. Skunk meat was eaten, but only for medicinal purposes [27, 30].

The principal big game hunted was buffalo, deer, antelope, elk, mountain sheep, mountain goat, bear, mountain lion, wildcat, and beaver [6, 18, 20, 23, 40, 61, 62].

Fresh meat was usually prepared in stews or broiled over the coals. It was rarely roasted or fried. The meat of most small animals was utilized in stews. Most dried, or jerked meat, other than that from domesticated animals, was derived from larger animals. Usually these were species that ranged at a considerable distance from the village. This factor made it necessary to preserve the meat in some manner to prevent spoilage in returning to the pueblo. Included in this category were buffalo, deer on occasion, and elk and mountain sheep on those rare instances when they were found and killed. One informant [64] denied that antelope meat was jerked.

Dried or jerked meat was later pounded or ground and used in stews or pies, less frequently in tamales or posole [25]. Blood sausage and also sausage stuffed with lung were made [14].

Most important of the smaller animals were the rabbit and wood rat. These were not only utilized in ordinary stews but in a special meat and cornmeal stew considered a delicacy. Wood rats were also spitted and broiled [20, 27, 36, 61, 72, 76].

The wild turkey was the most highly considered bird. It was fried or boiled. Similarly treated were ducks, geese, sandhill cranes, and grouse. Smaller birds were usually spitted and broiled. The most important of these were the dove, quail, and band-tailed pigeon [23, 30].

Eggs of the wild turkey and quail were eaten, but not those of the eagle [14].

Fish were usually broiled on the coals but were also fried or cut in chunks, mixed with chili, and made into soup [13, 18]. When more were caught than could be immediately consumed, they were baked and dried. "This way they keep a long time" [20]. Later chili was added, and they were boiled.

Locusts and grasshoppers were the only insects eaten. They were parched or fried. "They have a high oil content" [78].

6

Nonagricultural Economy

As noted earlier, agricultural pursuits provided the principal basis of the economy, or subsistence, of Santa Clara Pueblo; however, this was by no means an exclusive dominance. Nonagricultural activities provided a significant portion of the overall economy. As indicated in Chapter 4, various economic endeavors at the pueblo had shifted in relative importance over the years. It was not until later historic times that agriculture assumed obvious dominance. Going back in time, to the earlier historic period and on into prehistory, hunting and also such activities as gathering and warfare were relatively more important. The significance of trading is more difficult to assess; the acquisition of improved means of travel and transportation would appear to have facilitated and encouraged contacts with other tribes and communities. However, in more recent decades the increased mobility of the Santa Clara Indians and their increased participation in wage-earning opportunities have led to a growing patronage of stores and various commercial outlets in the neighboring communities, as well as expanded trading ventures of a more traditional nature [CHL].

HUNTING

Hunting formerly occupied a more important position as an occupational pursuit and economic base. While it never approached the significance of agriculture, a substantial percentage of Santa Clara subsistence was derived from game resources. The principal animals hunted were deer, buffalo, antelope, and rabbit. These furnished the bulk of the meat supply as well as hides for clothing and other purposes. Playing a minor role in the hunting economy were bear, mountain sheep, several species of cats and rodents, and various birds.

A number of historical factors have combined to lessen the importance of hunting. The settlement of the area by the Spanish and later the Americans, and the introduction of modern firearms, led to the virtual extinction of such animals as the buffalo and antelope, and reduced other species to a minimum. The availability of livestock furthered the decline, as it made possible the replacing of wild game as a food staple. While hunting has become submerged economically, it has still survived as an important factor in the social and religious life of Santa Clara Pueblo. The social features have paralleled those in our own culture. It was a recognized sport and those participating in it successfully enhanced their individual prestige. It represented an approved vehicle for individual expression. In the religous field hunting was an indispensable adjunct of kachina performances and initiations. This association more than any other was responsible for keeping alive the techniques and behaviors that were once a part of a more vital pursuit.

The composition of a hunting party was variable, depending on the animal hunted and whether the venture was primarily economic or ceremonial. Ceremonial hunts preliminary to kachina dances and initiations included most of the male personnel of the moiety involved in the rituals. Antelope, buffalo, and rabbit hunts that were held for economic purposes were communal to a lesser degree. The hunting of most large animals absorbed the efforts of several individuals. Normally the hunting parties, when not communal in nature, consisted of three or four men, and were made up of related individuals from a single household. There was also individual hunting.

The practical aspects of hunting were poorly developed at Santa Clara. The techniques employed were few in number and exhibited little of the ingenuity characteristic of the southern Athapaskan and Plains tribes. When parties were small or when an individual hunted alone, the most common procedure was to track the animal and bring it to bay or to tree it. This was often done with the assistance of dogs. The surround was practiced in conjunction with communal hunts. The chute and pound, running over cliffs, stalking with disguise, and flagging methods of hunting were denied by all informants, as was the pit trapping of eagles.

Most hunts were accompanied by prescribed types of behavior and varying amounts of ritual visits and gifts to the head of the hunt society—who "works for your success." The degree of participation in this pattern was somewhat optional, but minimum requirements included bathing before leaving, the adoption of a serious mien during the conduct of the hunt, and some

ritual act accompanying the disposal of the entrails.

Ritual was most elaborate in connection with bear hunting. In general, there was a positive correlation between the size and danger of the animal hunted and the amount of ritual associated with the hunt.

As in the case of hunting techniques, individual ceremonialism was poorly developed compared to that practiced by the Plains and southern Athapaskan tribes. This was explained in the following terms: "The Plains Indians must live on meat, and they have to use a lot of medicine in their hunts. We are farmers and do not have so much meat, so we do not have to have so much medicine" [20].

Santa Clara Indians shared certain beliefs and practices of wide distribution in North America. Among them was the conviction that the animals controlled the success or failure of the hunting venture; any deviation from the prescribed type of behavior would result in lack of success, i.e., the game would not allow itself to be killed. This was associated with the doctrine that game that was slain did not die but "was reborn," thus assuring the continuity of nature, or a constant supply of food. Much of the ritual attending the disposal of entrails and other bodily parts of the animals stemmed from this belief.

Tabus of various kinds were extant. One was the prohibition against cooking the meat of wild and domesticated animals at the same time. Another was concerned with the treatment of albino animals. At Santa Clara, "these albinos are the leaders and caretakers of the animals and you do not shoot them. We try not to harm them" [20].

It was also tabu to hunt during the period of the winter solstice. In this "closed" season not only was hunting prohibited, but it was believed that all weapons were rendered ineffectual [9, 13]. "If a deer walked into the plaza during this time, your arrows or bullets would not harm him" [18].

A related account was also recorded by Jeançon (1904–30). According to him,

> Stories of ghost animals are very common. There is one interesting tale about the giant ghost deer that frequents the

country in the neighborhood of Puye. Many have tried to kill this animal but none have been successful. In fact no one seems to be able to get close enough to it to even get a shot. They say it is often seen but when any one attempts to approach it it dissolves into the air. It is most often seen at the time when the animals are in retreat in their kiva (Winter solstice) and therefore is a sort of guardian of all the rest of the animals.

Most tales told by the older men imagine that they really have experiences of this kind. They do not tell the stories with any intention of lying but may have dreamed something of the kind or experienced a vision of similar events during a ceremonial fast and by dwelling upon this and by telling the tale over and over again they become firmly convinced that they really have had the experience.

According to Jeançon's informants,

The animals go into their kivas on the sixth of December and make very strong magic. They remain here until the end of the month. During this period, you cannot kill them even if you try; they are too powerful. One informant stated that he had attempted to hunt during the interval. He said that he shot a deer through the head, and the animal charged him and knocked him over. When he got up, the animal was grazing nearby. He shot it again, and it fell. He went over to it and cut its throat from ear to ear, and the deer got up and knocked him down again. He was not able to get up for some time. The deer stayed near him and ready to charge when he arose. Its throat had closed up; there was no mark or cut. The third time, the man shot the deer and thought it was dead. However, when he approached it, the deer caught him on its antlers, ran a short distance with him, and threw him over a cliff into the canyon below. He never saw the deer again.

A boy's first kill was accorded particular recognition. If the animal was a deer, his mother prepared a feast to which all relatives were invited. If a coyote or fox was killed, the boy was thereafter allowed to smoke [20].

Today hunting ritual is an individual activity and limited in extent. Formerly a hunt society, headed by a priestly official, the p'inghengzho, existed at Santa Clara. The leader and members of this organization acted as directors during the ritual and some communal hunts, and the society as a whole functioned ritually at stated intervals. However, it has been obsolescent for some time, and the exact nature of the former duties has been lost for the most part. A person approached the group with a request for ritual assistance in the chase, and it is probable that, as in the case of agriculture, the hunter rested secure in the belief that the necessary rituals for success would be taken care of by esoteric groups with which he need not necessarily be affiliated.

ANIMALS HUNTED

Deer.

Two varieties of deer (pe') were distinguished at Santa Clara: a grey (pe' ho wi?, "greyish deer") and a red (pe' p'i i, "reddish deer"). Deer hunts usually took place in the fall. The animals were in better condition during that season, and it was a period in which the pressure of other economic activities was at a minimum.

Deer hunting parties of a nonceremonial nature were comprised of from two to four men. These were usually related individuals representing a single household. Some days prior to the hunt, equipment was examined and mended, and the women prepared food for the journey. Parties left early in the morning, stopping to bathe either in the Rio Grande or Santa Clara Creek. According to informants, this gave them the man strength to pursue the deer and to follow it through brush or whatever natural obstacles were encountered.

The journey to the environs of the hunt

was made on horseback. It was reported that deer were formerly plentiful in Santa Clara Canyon and in the vicinity of Puyé. On arrival at the campsite, the horses were left, and the party set out on foot and endeavored to locate game. Hunters followed a spoor and attempted to approach and kill the animal without being sighted. If this failed and the deer was flushed, it was pursued until exhausted and brought within range of a bow and arrow.

When a kill was made, some of the blood was drunk and some preserved to cure women who suffered from stomach disorders. The hunt was considered successful if two deer were killed. If more than this fell prey to the hunters, the meat was cached until horses could be brought to pack it out. All participants shared alike in the spoils.

According to Parsons (1929:135), the surround was utilized in hunting deer:

> Formerly, when there were deer drives ("two wings would spread out and then close in, and the men from behind would come up slowly"), the Outside chief would come on ahead of the successful hunters to announce their return to the "oldest man or the chief *(tunjo),*" who would build a fire in the kiva. They got a pipe and all the hunters smoked. They had to relate all that had happened from the time they left until the time they got back. Then all the people were told to bring bowls to get meat. Of the quarry the killer got the hide and horns and the backbone.

Butchering followed the same procedure as that employed on sheep. The head was left attached to the hide. The stomach was carefully examined for gastroliths. These were highly prized as hunting charms. It was believed that anyone possessing one was assured of continued success in the chase and would be successful on every hunting venture. This was confirmed by Jeançon (1904–30). The intestines were eaten in the field, either cooked or raw. The remainder of the entrails were placed in a pile and covered with boughs from a Douglas spruce. Before the men left, an offering of feathers wrapped in corn husks was placed on this, and a prayer was said. This included a request for "those in charge to help the hunter," and it was believed that the action "caused the animals to come alive again."

According to Jeançon (1904–30), if a hunter killed a doe in January that contained twin fetuses, he placed their heads to the north. Next he drained the blood and water from the womb onto the earth, and rolled the resulting mud into a ball which he rubbed on the noses of the fetuses. The ball was then placed in the shade to dry. This was carried on subsequent hunts and was believed to insure success.

Whatever portion of the venison was not consumed in the field was packed back to the pueblo. This included prenatal fawns, which were considered a delicacy. When the deer was brought into the house, the women sprinkled cornmeal upon it, after which it could be utilized. The greater portion of the venison was consumed fresh. However if a hunting party was fortunate and a surplus of meat accrued, it was jerked and stored for future use. A tabu existed against cooking mutton and venison together.

Occasionally deer were also pit-trapped. A deep pit was dug in a trail and then covered with small twigs and earth. Sharpened stakes were never placed in the pit.

Deer were sometimes run down, but this was rare. In such cases, the deer would run until exhausted, "one was stabbed with an arrow" [14].

Hides were dressed and used in the production of clothing and for other purposes. Antlers were utilized in making tools and also for dance costumes. They were placed on the roof of the successful hunter's house and at shrines in the vicinity of the village. Offerings were made at these locations for success in hunting [13, 18, 20, 27, 40, 44].

Buffalo

Buffalo (Ko?o) hunts were conducted during the fall. As in the case of deer, the reasons given for the choice of this season were that the animals were in prime condition, that the weather was cold and the meat kept better, and that the men were free from other economic occupations. Hunting parties composed of from six to ten persons were organized. These bands were informally selected and were not led either by a war captain or hunt society chief. They journeyed to the Plains for the hunt. One of the favored locations was a place known as Lake Palicarnua, where the buffalo came to drink. Frequently Santa Clara hunters joined bands of Comanche or Kiowa, or groups from San Juan and San Ildefonso, and in the later period, Spanish-Americans.

Expeditions of this type necessitated extensive preparations, as the party was often absent from the pueblo for a period of two or three months. Clothing and weapons were made or repaired. The women ground corn and prepared food. The men accumulated fodder for livestock that would be taken along. As both trip and hunt were made on horseback, the best animals were selected. A carreta was occasionally included to facilitate return transportation.

On arrival at the hunting locale, a permanent camp was established, and hunts proceeded from this base. When a herd was sighted, each man selected an animal and rode in as close as possible to it. As he drew his bow, he attempted to brace his foot against the buffalo in order to get the maximum velocity into the shot. If possible the arrow was placed in the soft area between the ribs and the hip, "in the kidneys." At times the missile went completely through the animal; if not, it worked its way into the body as the buffalo ran. The hunter was sure of a kill when he saw blood gush from the mouth. Some men preferred the lance to the bow and arrow; a lance was aimed just above flank. The consensus of opinion was, however, that the danger of being dislodged from the saddle by the handle of the lance when the animal was speared added too much hazard to an already dangerous pursuit [23, 30, 40].

Some men in each party were assigned the duty of butchering. These followed the hunt, skinned and cut up the kill, and transported the meat to the camp. The expiring buffalo fell on its knees generally, and as it was too heavy to turn, a longitudinal incision was made in the hide along the back. The skin

was removed downward from this starting point. When this was completed, the quarters were detached first, and then other sections of the animal. These were tied together and placed on horses for transport. The head skin was not removed unless needed for a dance costume. Tongues were saved, dried, and hung outside the houses as an indication of hunting prowess. At the completion of the butchering the entrails were placed in a pile "in order that the animal might live again."

The meat was jerked on return to camp. It was first removed from the bones, then cut in thin strips. The hide of the animal was laid hair side to the ground, and on it were spread the meat strips. These were flattened by stamping upon them, which aided in quickening the drying process. The bones were dried and used for fuel, a rare commodity in the Plains area. Horns and hooves were utilized in the same manner.

When ten or fifteen buffalo had been killed, at least one or two for each member of the party, the group prepared to break camp and return to the pueblo. The jerked meat was put in sacks about 4′ × 5′, fashioned from the hides. These were placed on the backs of horses or in the carreta, and the homeward journey begun.

At the pueblo the meat was stored for future use. Besides storage containers, buffalo hides were used for moccasin soles, cordage, and robes. The fat was prized for frying and carefully stored in pots [20, 23, 40, 62].

Antelope

Antelope (ta‘) were formerly hunted in the plains and foothill areas. These hunts were communal and held under the auspices and direction of the war captain (p’ing xaṇ io) and two of his assistants. This official announced a projected hunt three days before it was to take place, and requested that moccasins and weapons be examined and put in good repair and that food for the trip be gathered. Women prepared enough food to support the hunters for a period of three days to a week.

On the fourth day the party left for the location where the hunt was to take place. A permanent camp was made and used for a base. The surround technique was employed in hunting. The principal war captain divided the group and directed each half to encompass an area in a huge semicircle. When the leading men of each party made contact and a circle was completed, the group converged toward the center and shot the enclosed animals. Not all the trapped antelopes were killed; a few were allowed to escape. "This was in order that there would be more the next time the hunters came. This was a way of getting more food. You kill only what you need" [30].

The game was transported to the base camp. Here the animals were eviscerated and the hides removed, leaving the head attached to the skin. The carcasses were hung outside the shelters until the party was ready to leave. Only intestines and internal organs were eaten, as the remainder of the meat had to be left untouched until arrival at the pueblo.

A successful hunt produced thirty to fifty antelope. These were packed home on horses to the house of the principal war captain. This official called the people and apportioned the meat in equal shares. When this was completed, the hides were distributed as far as they would go. If there were not sufficient to go around, those who got only one, or none, would be the first to receive a hide at a subsequent distribution.

Antelope meat appears not to have been jerked. The bones were saved; dogs had to be prevented from getting them; and when the meat was consumed, they were taken and deposited in the river. Horns were used on dance costumes and for making tools. Hides were utilized in the fabrication of clothing [30, 64].

Rabbit

Cottontail (pu) and jackrabbits (kwang) were secured in a variety of ways. Most complex were the rabbit hunts which occurred in conjunction with the masked dances, such as the Summer kachina initiations. These were communal in scope and under the direction of the head of the hunt society (p'irg he^{n}rg zho), more recently the war captain. A surround method similar to that employed in hunting antelope was used. Clubs replaced bows and arrows as weapons, however. The products of these endeavors comprised a portion of the gifts presented by the kachina and k'osa during the dances. Because of this religious association, rabbit hunts of this type had greater cultural significance than was justified by their economic importance. Hunts of this kind were also held for purely economic, or subsistence, purposes. Women as well as men were allowed to participate in these. According to Jeançon (1904–30), it was believed that if parched corn was placed on a rabbit trail, the animal would double back a step and you could kill it.

Individuals commonly hunted rabbits in the vicinity of the pueblo. They used dogs trained for that purpose, bows and arrows, clubs, or more recently, firearms. Rabbits were also tracked in the snow. Cottontail rabbits were removed from burrows by flooding or with sticks. In the latter case, a pliable sapling was roughened at the end, inserted into the burrow, and twisted into the rabbit's fur. The ensnared rabbit was then pulled out. Today barbed wire is used for this same purpose. No attempt was made to dislodge rabbits from their burrows by means of fire or smoke [18, 23, 36, 61, 64].

The use of rabbit-skin nets was denied. However, shinny balls were stuffed with rabbit skin or fur; although there were no woven blankets of rabbit skins, blankets or robes were made by sewing rabbit skins together [23, 44].

Bear

The people of Santa Clara distinguished three species of bear (ke): black (ke fe^{n}di?), yellow (ke c'ezhi?) and white (ke c'e^{n}i?). The third was obviously of rather recent acquaintance, unless it referred to the occasional albino.

Some bear hunts were premeditated, or specifically planned. The animal was tracked by trained dogs, brought to bay, and killed. All informants stressed the fact that several arrows were invariably necessary to dispatch the quarry. Besides this organized type of hunt, bears were killed whenever encountered. If a party did not consider itself of sufficient strength, word was sent to the pueblo for assistance. All able-bodied males usually responded. When the reinforcements arrived, the group "sang a song," then surrounded the animal and attacked with bows, arrows, and clubs. Hibernating bears were not killed, as the period of hibernation normally coincided with the "closed," or ritual, season.

Butchering was done at the site of the kill. The intestines were removed and branches placed upon them as in cases previously cited. The hunters then blackened their faces or the area below their eyes. This was confirmed by Parsons (1929:135). This was said to protect them from attack by bears on the homeward journey. However as all those who subsequently ate the meat performed the same act, it seems probable that this ritual practice had broader connotations than the protection of those who took part in the hunt.

Consistent with general western North American Indian practices, Santa Clara bear hunts were surrounded with more ritual than was accorded the capture of any other animal. An anthropomorphic attitude toward the bear was pronounced, and behavior corresponding to warfare practices occurred, both on the return journey and on entering the pueblo. The transportation of the bear homeward was accompanied by song. Women met the successful party at the outskirts of the village and sang songs expressing joy at the return and success. The men entered the pueblo as if carrying a scalp, dancing and shouting; however, no scalp pole was used.

Distribution of the meat varied with the type of hunt. If it had been an organized venture including only members of one or of related families, only relatives participated in the feast at the termination of the hunt. If the hunt included the pueblo as a whole, a distribution of the meat was made at the conclusion of the ritual, and all shared alike. Bear hides were used for robes, bedding, and rugs. Claws were made into wristlets or worn on shirts. They were thought to give the individual "power to fight like a bear." Paws were contributed to members of the curing societies for containers and as ceremonial equipment, gauntlets, or "paws"

[15, 30, 52, 72].

Mountain Sheep

Rocky Mountain Sheep (P'irg K'u'wa) were hunted by the same methods as were deer. One to three hunters formed the normal party. In historic times, hunts have taken place in the vicinity of Cochiti Pueblo. The meat and hides were utilized in the same manner as venison and buckskin [20, 64].

Elk

Elk did not occur in the normal hunting range of the Santa Clara Indians. When in rare cases they were encountered, they were killed and utilized in the same way as deer [20, 64]. Another informant [23] claimed that elk were not hunted as far as he knew.

Mountain Lion

A mountain lion (xarg) hunt was considered a dangerous undertaking, and the successful accomplishment of such a venture was rewarded by a corresponding amount of prestige. Because of the risk, it was rarely attempted by a single individual. Usually several men, household heads, accompanied by dogs, trailed, treed, and killed the lions.

Before butchering was begun, the head of the lion was oriented toward the pueblo. Skinning followed the pattern employed on sheep and goats. The intestines were placed in a pile at the site of the kill and covered with boughs. "This is because the animal comes alive again" [20].

A distribution of the meat was made when the butchering was completed. All in the party shared alike. The skin fell to the lot of the hunter who was responsible for the mortal wound. This was determined by an examination of the location of the arrows at the time the kill was made. Mountain lion skins were highly prized for quivers, also for robes. Fat was rubbed on shields to give them power [20, 64].

A subsequent distribution of the meat was made when the party returned to the pueblo. The head of each household issued invitations to a feast; only close relatives were included. Female guests contributed flour and food for the banquet, and at its termination were presented with portions of lion meat [20, 36].

Wildcat

The wildcat (harg c̓e^n, "lion" [bob cat?]) was treed by dogs and shot. The flesh was eaten and relished. Hides were used for quivers, robes, and clothing; they were also used for dance costumes and hats [20, 23, 44].

Wolf

The wolf (xurgzho) was trailed with dogs, brought to bay, and shot. A difference of opinion existed as to whether the flesh might be used for food. According to one [20], it was eaten, a statement denied by another [14]. The skin of the wolf was used in the construction of quivers [20, 27].

Fox

The fox was not used for food, but it was important because the skins served as a necessary element in ceremonial costumes. Foxes were shot or trapped; dogs aided in the hunting of foxes [20]. Many hides were also secured from outside sources. Two species were recognized: the blue fox (de tsa wa) and the Plains fox (akon de) [14, 30, 72].

Wood Rat

Wood rats or pack rats (xwan) were hunted by building fires and smoking them out of their nests in rock crevices. They were often given by the kachinas as gifts. They were utilized as food in the same way as were rabbits [12, 14, 20].

Others

Other animals were also hunted by the Santa Clara Indians, but their economic importance, individually and collectively, was slight. Included among these were [9, 13, 14, 18, 20, 29]:

badger (ke̓a) [44].

beaver (ozho): were eaten; the skins were used for head bands, hats, hair ties, and dance costumes [65]. Beavers were either trapped or shot [64]; they were also killed by clubbing by hunters wading in the ponds [65].

chipmunk (ko wizhi): claws were rubbed on children to prevent their falling when climbing ladders [44].

coyote (de, p̓osa xwa, culture hero term): not hunted to any extent [44].

gopher (churggi) [44].

porcupine (song): quills used as needles; also used in embroidery on shirts, leggings, moccasins, anklets, belts, robes [27, 30, 64].

otter: fur used for headbands, collars [27].

prairie dog (ki̓) [44].

skunk (sa^n): hunted in winter when fur was prime; used as anklets in ceremonial costumes [44]. Eaten, but primarily for medicinal purposes [65].

rock squirrel (xwargzho, or c̓e tha) and tree squirrel (sa^n we^n): skins were used to make dolls for children [44].

small weasel chipmunk (bena): hair ties [44].

weasel (dzherg): hair ties, wraps for braids [44].

BIRDS

Hunting of birds at Santa Clara Pueblo was fostered by both economic and ceremonial considerations. Their economic importance was not great, however, and there was little to suggest that their utilitarian role was much larger in aboriginal times than in recent years.

Ducks, geese, grouse, quail, and wild turkey were the principal species secured to augment the food supply. The eggs of quail and wild turkey were eaten. The feathers of all these birds, as well as those of several other species, were used in fletching arrows. As in the case of other animals, game birds have diminished in quantity in the face of increasing settlement and the introduction of more proficient weapons.

Feathers were necessary ingredients for most offerings and also for the fabrication of ceremonial paraphernalia. Most hunting was with this goal in mind, and it was in this secondary ritual association that birds were actually more important. There was a definite association of specific species with cardinal directions; correlations with colors and deities were similarly important. The correct performance of many rituals was dependent upon the presence of specific feathers from particular birds.

The securing of birds was primarily an individual endeavor. Hunts were planned, but chance encounter was the more usual pattern. The prey was normally shot, either with bow and arrow or gun. However rabbit clubs and various traps and snares were employed to secure some species. Little ceremony appears to have been associated with the hunting of birds. The only indications of religious elements in this respect were the customs of placing unused feathers at various shrines near the village and of depositing carcasses of some species in the Rio Grande. This was presumably done with an idea of reincarnation, although some vagueness on this point existed in the minds of informants.

Ducks

The people of Santa Clara were familiar with the bluewinged teal, cinnamon teal, mallard, and canvasback ducks. Only the canvasback was designated by a specific term (fu wi?, "high"), however; the remainder were referred to as o uiŋ. All were hunted whenever the opportunity presented itself. The meat was consumed; the feathers were used in fletching, on ceremonial paraphernalia and costumes, and, more recently, for stuffing pillows [65].

Geese

The wild goose (ka^n gi) was highly valued as food. Only one species, the Canada goose, was recognized by informants. Hunters crawled within range while the birds were feeding and dispatched them with bow and arrow. The feathers were used in fletching [65].

Herons

The great blue heron (p'o K'e peŋ, "water Adam's apple") was a fairly constant visitor

in the vicinity of Santa Clara Pueblo. It was not considered edible, but was killed on occasion for its feathers, which were used in fletching [65].

Cranes

The sandhill crane (pu ga·, "from the sound it makes") was hunted and utilized in the same way as geese [65].

Coots

The American coot (axa wae) was well known, but informants denied that it was used [65, 72].

Sandpipers

Birds of this family were termed p o *the*n. No use was made of them [65].

Plovers

The killdeer (po te dji) was well known, but not utilized in any way [23, 65].

Woodpeckers

All species of woodpeckers were normally designated "woodeaters" (fe koi), with the exception of the hairy woodpecker, termed "corn-eating woodeater" (xuŋ fe koi) and the red-shafted flicker (fi o), named after its cry. In addition the western red-headed woodpecker and Lewis woodpecker were recognized. None was utilized, according to informants [23, 29, 65].

Goatsuckers

The nighthawk (aga p'i) and a smaller relative, "one who sleeps a lot" (*zho* ho i, possibly the whippoorwill), were recognized but not used [65].

Hummingbirds

Both the black-chinned and rufous hummingbirds were called Xo he. They were not used [44, 65].

Turkey

The wild turkey (piṇ di) was hunted with bow and arrow. It was highly valued as food. Its feathers were used extensively on dance costumes, in ceremonial equipment, and for fletching [65].

Grouse

The dusky grouse (caⁿ?) was hunted in the mountain regions. They were described as easy to kill during the nesting period, because they habitually pretended to be wounded in an endeavor to decoy the hunter away from the eggs or young. The meat was used for food; the feathers were used on dance costumes and for ceremonial purposes [65].

Quail

The scaled quail (to tan) was hunted with bow and arrow for food. The feathers were not used. The Gambel quail carried the same designation; it was said to be a recent introduction in the area [44, 65].

Pigeons

The band-tailed pigeon (piṇ paloma, Tewa mountain, plus Spanish dove, i.e., mountain dove) was hunted with bow and arrow for food. The feathers were not used [65].

Doves

The mourning dove (k'o wi) was killed with arrows and occasionally rocks. It was used for food [65].

Parrots and Macaws

The range of these birds was outside the usual areas of Santa Clara contact. However their feathers were highly prized and essential for certain ceremonies and paraphernalia [44, 65].

Eagle

The eagle held the preeminent position among birds in Santa Clara ideology. This was the consequence of its connection with religious beliefs and the use of its feathers for ceremonial purposes. Both the golden eagle (ce') and the bald eagle (p'o ce, "water eagle") were known, though the latter was of rare occurrence.

Eagles were shot, clubbed, and removed from aeries. There was considerable trade in eagle feathers between Santa Clara and the Comanche, and also between Santa Clara and other pueblos for both feathers and live eagles. Pit trapping was not engaged in, although all informants were aware of this practice among the Indians of Jemez Pueblo. Occasionally the hunter lay hidden near a dead animal until the bird had gorged itself. Then he rushed from his hiding place, and before the heavily laden eagle could take flight, it was dispatched with a rabbit club or arrow.

Robbing aeries necessitated the cooperation of at least two, generally three, men. When a nest was located, the nearly grown birds were removed in one of two ways. In the first method, two men were stationed on the cliff above the nest. One protected the other from attacks by the parent eagles. The third man took his place at the base of the cliff. A chicken, either alive or dead, was lowered on a line to the edge of the nest just beyond reach of the eaglets. They were lured over the nest's edge in an attempt to get the bait, and were caught by the man stationed below.

Hunters were also lowered to the nest by ropes. A man tied the eaglets to a line that was hauled up by another man above. One such hunt was reported from a locality called "rocks loose gap" (kiv uhu) in the Santa Clara Canyon.

The legs of the captured eagle were tied to prevent clawing, and the bird was wrapped in a blanket with the head protruding to allow for breathing. On arrival at the pueblo, it was placed in a cage.

Cages were made of split pine. They were of cribwork construction. The cribbing was secured with wet rawhide that contracted as it dried and gave stability to the structure. Cages were equipped with perches. Captive eagles were fed fresh and jerked meat. In the latter case the meat was softened by soaking in water before feeding.

The plumes from beneath the tail and wings, and the tail and wing feathers (kung) were the principal ones used. The plumes were worn on dance costumes; the tail feathers went into the construction of headdresses and Sun Dance symbols; wing feathers were used on costumes worn by the eagle dancers; all three types went into the fabrication of ceremonial equipment. Wing and tail feathers were also used for fletching.

Captive eagles were plucked every three months [15, 40], every spring according to another [50]. One man held the head and neck of the eagle, a second the feet, and a third pulled out the feathers. "The eagle did not like it." After plucking, cornmeal was sprinkled on the areas from which the feathers were removed. "This made them grow back faster." When a captive eagle died, the feathers were removed and the carcass was deposited in the Rio Grande.

Many items of the eagle complex present among other Southwestern peoples were lacking at Santa Clara Pueblo. The flesh, claws, and eggs were not utilized; the use of wing bones in making whistles was denied. Ownership of aeries, individual or otherwise, was unknown. No offerings were placed in the nests when they were robbed [9, 15, 30, 36, 44, 50, 65].

Hawks

Of the various hawks, the western redtailed (xwang p'i, "red tail") was the most sought after. These were hunted with bow and arrow. The wing and tail feathers were used for fletching and on dance costumes. The feathers of the Cooper and sharpshinned hawk (both termed xwang fu, "spotted tail") and the sparrow hawk (t'ing) were utilized on arrows [65].

Vultures

The feathers of the turkey vulture (o kawae) were used in fletching [65].

Owls

With few exceptions, members of this family were referred to by a single generic term (ma hung). Those recognized were the American barn owl (ma hung); screech owl (fiu', after its sound), and burrowing owl (ki mahung, "prairie dog owl"). All informants denied that these birds were utilized in any way! They were considered birds of evil and were associated with the practice of witchcraft [29, 44, 65, 72].

Roadrunners

The roadrunner (ogo wi) was important in religious phases of the culture. Feathers of this bird were utilized in dances and in ceremonials [65].

Kingfishers

The belted kingfisher (p'o cire, "water bird") was known at Santa Clara but was not used [65].

Flycatchers

From the flycatcher family, the Say's phoebe was known, designated po jung. The kingbird was called si han. The Say's phoebe was the only one of this group used. It was eaten, and the feathers were a necessary part of certain ceremonial articles [18, 23, 29, 65].

Larks

The western horned lark (ko i) was recognized but not used [65].

Crows

The western crow (odo) was known, but it was not used [65].

Jays

The long-crested jay (c'e K'wee, "Douglas spruce magpie") and piñon jay (xae) were known in the vicinity of Santa Clara Pueblo. The feathers of these birds were worn as hair ornaments during dances. They were eaten in earlier times; they were hunted with bow and arrow [65].

Magpies

The American magpie (kwae) was hunted,

as were jays. The tail feathers were worn in dances. They were not eaten [65].

Titmice

The Bushtit was known, but there was no record of its use [65].

Meadowlarks

The meadowlark (p'o c'e, "yellow water") was known, but no use of it was reported. It was frequently and jokingly called "yellow water Jew spilled the chili preparation" ("p'o c'e xorio i cidi p'o deṇg") as its song sounded similar to that phrase as spoken in Tewa [65].

Blackbirds

The red-winged blackbird (a nu k'uṇg pi?i, "red-winged young lady") and the yellow-headed blackbird (a nu k'e ce zhi, "yellow-necked young lady") were used for food. They were hunted with the bow and arrow and also caught by horsehair snares [52, 61, 65].

Orioles

The Scott oriole (huṇg te ce', "juniper cottonwood eagle") and bullock oriole (te ce', "cottonwood eagle") were eaten, and the feathers were used ceremonially. The birds were both shot and trapped [23, 65].

Sparrows

All sparrows were termed ci i. Occasionally those having distinctive white markings on the head were designated tsi pon ta, "sparrow striped head," to differentiate them. The English sparrow was known by a number of nicknames, and it was known to be of rather recent introduction. None of the sparrow family appears to have been used [65].

Finches

The house finch (wï wï) was well known at Santa Clara, though no use was made of it [65].

Grosbeaks

The Arizona blue grosbeak (weṇg se, "pine bluebird") was known but not used [65].

Crossbills

The Bendire Crossbill (piṇg cire, "mountain bird") was known. Informants denied that it was used [23, 29, 65, 72].

Buntings

The lazuli bunting (huṇg se) was eaten [65].

Juncos

The gray-headed junco (tsi k'e feṇg, "tsi," the sound it makes plus "black neck") was caught in snares and used for food [52, 61, 65].

Tanagers

The Louisiana or western tanager (huṇg te ce p'o p'i?i, "juniper cottonwood eagle redhead") and the Arizona hepatic tanager (cire p'i?i) were known. Their feathers were utilized in the same manner as those of the oriole [65, 72].

Swallows

The American barn swallow (kwe^n xwere) and the cliff or bank Swallow (kaṇg ozho, "beaver tassel"—"tassel" referring to a botanical tassel, as of corn) were known but not used [65].

Shrikes

The white-rumped shrike was known but not used in any way [65].

Warblers

The western yellow warbler and Grace warbler were distinguished at Santa Clara. These and other unidentified forms were all designated as ka cire, "leaf bird". They were important birds ceremonially. Their feathers were in great demand for ritual purposes; they were also eaten. Most were secured by snares [65, 68]. Another warbler, the long-tailed chat, was recognized by the Santa Clara Indians, who called it po jung, the same name they used for the Say's phoebe, as noted earlier.

Wrens

The rock wren (sawa di, "cooking rock," di, for the sound it makes) was known but unused [65].

Mockingbirds

The western mockingbird was occasionally captured and kept as a pet. "They provided music" [65].

Bluebirds

The mountain bluebird (tse) and the chestnut-backed bluebird (warg tse, "pine bluebird") were trapped by snares for food and also for their feathers, important in rituals [23, 65].

Robins

The western robin (se wae) was hunted with a bow and arrow and used for food [65].

REPTILES

Turtles

"In old days," most turtles were traded in from the Comanche [65].

Snakes

"Medicine" was formerly carried to ward off snakes [65].

Lizards

Lizards were not used. "There is one kind that, if it spits on you, it will cause sores" [65].

Frogs

No frogs (o Kwarg) were used [65].

INSECTS

Bees

The hives of wild bees were robbed whenever found. "Snake weed" was burned in front of the hive, scattered about it, and chewed and spat in the direction of the hive to drive away the bees. The honey was used in conjunction with several foods [39, 65]. It was also used medicinally [65].

Locusts

Gathered in a bowl filled with water. The locusts were picked off plants and dropped in the water. Parched and eaten [39].

Grasshoppers

Parched and eaten [65].

FISHING

Fishing played an unexpectedly large part in the Santa Clara economy. The streams and river appear to have been well stocked in aboriginal times, and the Indians capitalized upon this fact. Several species of fish, including carp (pa tue, "fish large"), sucker (tse wudge, "yellow to separate," "has mouth which opens low down"), catfish (pa cizho, "fish knife"), and the eel (pa owhi, "slimy fish") were obtained from the Rio Grande. Carp and catfish were the most numerous. The mountain streams furnished varieties of trout (pa pi whan, "fish red stripes"; pi pa, "mountain fish"; kum p'fa pa, "fish fins red on spread").

Hooks and lines, nets, and bow and arrows were employed to secure fish. Shooting fish was, however, a rare practice except when they appeared in large schools. Individual anglers worked the nearby streams and the Rio Grande. This type of endeavor furnished no important amount of food and was relegated to the role of sport. Occasionally during low water, barriers were thrown up along the river course, artificial lagoons were formed, and the impounded fish were captured. However the only substantial supplies of fish were procured by seining in the Rio Grande.

Seining was a communal endeavor, and nets were communally made and owned. When not in use, they were cared for and stored by the head of the hunt society (p'irg harg *zho*) or, in more recent years, by the war captain or the governor.

A projected seining was announced by the governor or the "town crier." Formerly all available boys and men repaired to the river at the time designated. In recent years, since the political schism, only one moiety at a time has fished. If possible at least one representative from each household was present. The work was directed and supervised by the head of the hunt society or, since the demise of that office, by the war captain. Operations might continue for two or three days; the seining began near Ranchito, in the vicinity of San Juan Pueblo, and ended several miles downstream near the pueblo of San Ildefonso.

The net, which in storage was rolled around a log like a coil of wire, was carried by four men to the river and unrolled. Two to four men worked each end of the net, and others grasped the top and guided the central portions. The men at one end waded into the river and were followed by the rest. When they arrived at a sufficient distance from the bank, the seine was dragged shoreward, the ends somewhat ahead of the center. When the bank of the river was neared, those along the center reached down and lifted the bottom of the net, enclosing the fish in the trough. The catch was tossed to those waiting along the shore. Eels were given an especially strong toss so they could not get back to the water. Those on shore strung the fish on sticks, passing the stick through the gills. In this manner they were easily transported.

Each time the net was removed any necessary repairs were made. The described process was then repeated working down the river. Seining continued until enough fish had been caught or until night fell. If the catch was sufficient, the net was dried, rolled, and stored; if not, it was left on the bank, and the next day operations were begun at that point.

All present shared in the catch. The head of the hunt society received first choice of the fish. Next choice went to those who worked the ends of the net, next to those who worked the center. Finally fish were distributed to the remainder of the participants. Each individual commonly received from five to twenty fish.

Fish were utilized only as food. If a surplus accrued they were baked in an oven and then dried. In this condition they could be stored without danger of spoiling.

Little information was forthcoming on the association of ritual with fishing. It can be presumed that the head of the hunt society formerly performed certain religious acts to insure the success of the communal fishing endeavor, but since the disappearance of that office such behavior has lapsed and been lost. All that remained were simple acts patterned after the behavior associated with hunting. When the fish were gutted, the entrails were thrown back into the stream. "This was so the next time you went fishing there would be fish there."

Several folk sayings referred to fish but these were in no way considered in a serious vein. If a child dawdled over its food an elder would say, "What are you doing, picking the bones out of the fish?" If a group of children were fishing and one could not swim but wished to learn, one of the group would tell him, "Catch a small fish and swallow it alive; then you will learn to swim quickly" [9, 13, 14, 15, 18, 20, 52].

To close this discussion of fishing at Santa Clara Pueblo, the following comment on "Rio Grande Indian Fishermen" by Spinden (1914) is of interest.

> Most of the Southwestern Indians will not eat fish, but the tribes along the Rio Grande have gotten over this prejudice if they ever had it. An explanation for the former non-use of fish is as follows: When the people came up out of the underworld through a lake in the north they wandered about looking for good places to live. When they came to the Rio Grande the leader made a bridge of Guacamayo feathers. Those persons who refused to cross are now nomadic Indians, those who crossed safely are the Pueblo Indians, and those who fell in are the fish.

The methods of fishing are various, although snares and traps seem to be the most ancient. The snare is made of a horsehair loop tied to the end of a short stick. Lying on the bank, the fisherman maneuvers this snare till it is directly in front of the fish, and then draws it up with a jerk. The fish, startled, shoots straight ahead and is caught. The Indians of Taos Pueblo are very skillful at fishing in this manner. The fish-hook has been acquired from the white man and is called a "pointed fish snare." Bone ones are sometimes made.

GATHERING

Wild Food Plants

The floral resources of Santa Clara and vicinity were ample and varied. However the emphasis on agriculture and the increasing availability of commercial products, at least in recent times, have militated against a full utilization of these natural resources. Evidence points toward a gradual decline in gathering activity. While many individuals possessed an extensive knowledge of the botany of the area, these persons were concerned primarily with plants which had real or supposed medicinal properties. Gathering at Santa Clara Pueblo was a highly desultory pursuit. The piñon nut, Rocky Mountain bee plant, and prickly pear were the principal products secured for food purposes; the importance of other flora was negligible in this regard.

Securing piñon nuts (t'o) was a household enterprise. Families journeyed to productive areas and camped; three days to a week would be spent in gathering. A blanket or canvas was placed under a tree, and the nuts dislodged by shaking the limbs or striking them with a stick. Nuts were separated from dirt, leaves, etc., by sifting them through a screen of the type employed in cleaning wheat [13, 18, 29, 44].

The Rocky Mountain bee plant (xwa[n]) grew abundantly in the vicinity of Santa Clara Pueblo. The leaves were and are collected and used for greens; they were also used for making black paint for pottery.

Other plants utilized as greens, but of minor importance, included amaranth (pigweed, ki·su, "prairie dog arrow"), and prairie clover (xwire fe). The latter frequently constituted the gift given by men to their partners at the termination of a dance [25, 44].

The fruit of the prickly pear (se[n] be) was picked and the spines removed by placing the fruit on hot coals. The fruit of the yucca baccata (mountain amole, fa fu p'o) was gathered for winter use. Other fruits and berries that were utilized were the wild strawberry (pirg pu pa, "mountain wrinkled base"), ground tomato or ground cherry (ci go fe), chokecherry (ave), gooseberry (tsi fu), and snowberry (Sericotheca dumosa) [25, 44].

Minor use was made of wild onions (akhorg si) which were picked and eaten when found and the roots of the shield fern (xarg arg fi "mountain lion foot plant") which were chewed and sucked. Mushrooms (te) were formerly eaten but have not been used in recent years. Mint was occasionally utilized for flavoring. Acorns were little used [25, 44, 45].

Salt

Salt (a[n] ne[n]) was considered essential in the preparation of food and also ranked high among the elements which possessed curative and purifactory properties. The source of this commodity in aboriginal times was the saline deposits of the Estancia Valley, ninety miles south of Santa Clara and east of the Rio Grande. Trips were made periodically to this region, and supplies of this commodity were transported to the pueblo on the backs of persons or burros.

No information was available as to whether or not these expeditions and the gathering of salt were ritualized procedures. Presumably the ritual pattern prevalent in the remainder of the Southwest was in force at Santa Clara; at least the myth of Salt Woman was current in the pueblo. Disrobing before gathering salt was considered essential, and expeditions were looked upon as religious pilgrimages with both restorative and healthful consequences.

TRADING

It has been difficult to evaluate the importance of trading at Santa Clara Pueblo. Certainly it was never a major pursuit and until the development of the tourist market, could have contributed relatively little in terms of the overall economy. This was due in part to a normal lack of surplus quantities at both Santa Clara Pueblo and among neighboring groups, and in part because many articles traded fell into the category of ceremonial or luxury items. There was no thought of gaining a livelihood in the commercial field until very recent times. A few individuals made yearly trips to barter with surrounding groups, but these were exceptions. Sporadic participation at irregular intervals was the rule, and there were many who had never engaged in trade beyond the village or with adjacent Tewa pueblos.

More important than the economic factor was the dynamic effect of trading contacts. While there were shifts in trade interests and trade products throughout the centuries, there was ample evidence that this pursuit had contributed substantially to the enrichment of Santa Clara culture. Travelers from Santa Clara had opportunity to observe diverse cultures. They were able to exercise selectivity both in terms of material items and intangibles; many cultural borrowings can be attributed to this activity.

There is evidence, however, that trade in its formalized aspects was a religious as well as an economic experience, and this in itself was important. Trading ventures were frequently headed by religious leaders, and trading party members engaged in religious rites under their direction. Trade was also important in terms of derived status. Many items obtained fell into either the ceremonial class or the luxury-prestige category, and as such were badges indicative of an enhanced status. Furthermore, those who made extensive journeys embellished their reputations through the recounting of their experiences.

The most sustained and important trade relations of Santa Clara Pueblo were those with other Pueblo villages. Close and frequent contacts existed with Tewa linguistic affiliates in the northern Rio Grande area, particularly with the pueblos of San Juan and San Ildefonso [20, 23, 64].

Considerable trade was also carried on between Santa Clara and the Towa pueblo of Jemez. This trade prevailed in spite of the fact that relations between the two villages were said to have been intermittently strained during the middle historic period [20, 23, 64]. Possibly this relationship was a corollary of the close connection which existed between Jemez Pueblo and the Navajo.

Trade contacts with the Tiwa pueblos of Taos, Picuris, Sandia, and Isleta, were characterized as minimal or nonexistent [20, 62, 65]. "Sandia and Isleta had little to trade, and Taos and Picuris had the same things as Santa Clara, and there was no use to trade" [20].

From among the Keres, Santo Domingo and Cochiti played the most important commercial roles [20, 23, 50, 62]. Less frequently, Santa Clara Indians traded with those of San Felipe, Santa Ana, and Zia. San Felipe and Zia were "poor and had little to trade" [20]. Of the Western Keres, Acoma received slight mention, and Laguna no mention at all in terms of Santa Clara trading relations.

Commercial interchanges also flourished between Santa Clara and the western pueblos of Zuñi and Hopi, especially during the later historic period [20, 23, 40]. In the case of the Hopi these contacts were undoubtedly stimulated following the establishment of the Tewa village of Hano on First Mesa subsequent to the Pueblo Revolt of 1680 and the Reconquest Period, 1692–96.

Aside from these other Pueblo tribes, trading was conducted with Plains and marginal Plains groups. The most important of these were the Southern Ute, Jicarilla Apache, and Comanche. Friendly relations were described as essentially stable between the Southern Ute and Santa Clara; relations with the Jicarilla Apache and Comanche, however, were somewhat less stable. Some trade was also engaged in with the Kiowa during periods when the two tribes were at peace. However, these contacts under the best circumstances were characterized by an atmosphere of mutual distrust. The Arapaho and Cheyenne were also known to the Santa Clara Indians but were considered enemies and, hence, were avoided. Commercial intercourse with the Navajo was likewise denied [20, 27, 44]. This was confirmed in part by data from the Navajo (Hill 1948: 374) and was also consistent with the feeling of traditional enmity that existed between the two peoples. Navajo items reached Santa Clara, but invariably through middlemen.

The importance of trade between the Spanish and Santa Clara is difficult to assess, although its historic depth can unquestionably be accepted. That it flourished during the colonial period is readily apparent from an examination of the culture of both groups. Better documentation was available for trade relations during the Mexican period and later with Spanish-Americans or Hispanos. Trade between Anglo-Americans and Santa Clara developed shortly after 1850. However it was not until the twentieth century, with the increase of the tourist business, that its impact on the Santa Clara economy became apparent.

Intravillage trade was minimal and tended to operate on a gift exchange basis, rather than on a commercial level.

Trade with neighboring Pueblo Indians and Spanish-Americans was informal, unorganized, and primarily on an individual basis. It was part of the normal social intercourse between the villages, intensified during periods of ceremonials and at the times of saint's day feasts. "They would make large quantities of pottery before feast days to trade with visitors" [11]. Women as well as men participated in intervillage trade. The Santa Clara acted in the capacity of both travelers and hosts [4, 19, 42].

Relations with distant Pueblo tribes were only slightly more formalized. Where the Santa Clara assumed the role of travelers, groups of males traveled together, presumably for mutual protection, especially in "the old days." Reciprocal visits were normal and common. Primary exceptions to this reciprocity were in the cases of Santo Domingo and the Hopi. The Santo Domingo usually operated as

travelers [11, 51, 64], as did the Santa Clara in their trade with the Hopi [22, 31]. There was, of course, less contact with the more distant villages. It was reported that an individual would visit Hopi or Zuñi, for example, on trading trips only once or twice in a lifetime [30].

Formal and organized trade existed only between Santa Clara and the Plains and marginal Plains tribes. Such ventures were of considerable duration. "They required two months, at least. You had to find the Comanche" [23]. While much trading was done during the summer, it was not uncommon for a party to leave for the plains in the spring; another favorite time was in the fall. "A few might go every year" [23]. Occasionally a group spent the winter in the plains [22]. Parties left after harvest and some individuals remained with the Comanche as long as three months to a year [14].

Groups were usually composed of older men rather than youths. They frequently contained personnel from several pueblos and local Mexican or Spanish-American villages. Women were never included. The party leader was a religious official who was responsible for the enactment of the proper rituals and who directed practical procedures [23, 30]. In some instances at least, rendezvous were prearranged.

Normally the Santa Clara acted in the role of travelers in trading contacts with Comanche and Kiowa, although occasionally Comanche visited the pueblo. Trading relations with Jicarilla Apache and Southern Ute entailed reciprocal visits. At least in recent years, the Santa Clara have attended Ute and Apache ceremonies and vice versa [14, 23, 30, 31, 72]. Language barriers were no problem. Some Santa Clara were familiar with sign language; others through the years had acquired a basic knowledge of Comanche. Since the Comanche frequently had captives of Mexican or Spanish-American descent, these acted as interpreters for the bilingual Tewa or local Spanish-Americans who had accompanied the Pueblo traders [23, 44].

The principal commercial items produced by the Santa Clara in historic times were cornmeal, wheat and barley flour, and foodstuffs derived from these. Their reputation as potters was well known, and a substantial amount of this commodity was traded within a restricted geographical area. Presumably, difficulty of transport, danger of breakage, and the nomadic character of Plains cultures precluded a wider trade in this item. Because of the advantage of their peripheral location and rather regular contact with the Plains, Santa Clara Indians commonly acted as middlemen in the distribution of buffalo robes, buckskin, and deer hides to the more internally located Pueblo villages. Retrading of articles essential for ceremonials, generally obtained from the Keres, Zuñi, and Hopi, was also practiced.

Data on exchange standards, or equivalencies, were difficult to obtain. "There was no standard price; you got what you could get" [44]. Informants were unwilling to quote prices or, if they did, indicated that they applied only to a single transaction. All were well aware of the law of supply and demand. While some men were recognized as shrewd businessmen, favorable margins of success in trade were usually attributed to the efficacy of the religious leadership or a reward for conscientious participation in ceremonials.

When dealing with the central and western pueblos, a Santa Clara trader could expect to receive either a kilt, belt, manta, or Navajo blanket for one or two buckskins or a buckskin and a rawhide. In one instance at Zuñi, a Santa Clara traded five sheep for three mantas [71]. Favorable balance of trade opportunities for Santa Clara Indians were much greater when dealing with Plains and marginal Plains tribes. Informants agreed that a small amount of cornmeal or flour or a few loaves of bread were generally equivalent in trade to a buckskin, an item of buckskin clothing, a bow and arrows, several baskets, a buffalo robe, or a head of livestock. All agreed that the most lucrative transactions were with the Kiowa and Comanche [14, 27, 30, 44, 72]. This was confirmed by Robbins, Harrington, and Freire-Marreco (1916: 109), who stated: "[in the Comanche country] . . . a sack of hard-baked bread would buy a good pony."

The general self-sufficiency of Pueblo culture militated against extensive trade relations between Santa Clara Pueblo and other villages. However, in spite of this, enough local specialization and individual virtuosity in handicraft existed in the various towns to insure a relatively steady interchange of goods. Where raw materials were involved, the question of surpluses or lack of the same was a determining factor controlling commercial relations at any given time. Among the Tewa towns generally, there was considerable exchange of farm products, particularly corn and wheat. Depending upon the supply, corn was traded for wheat or vice versa, or for other products [44, 65]. Well-known craftsmen were frequently approached and requested to make a specific article. "He would do that, and then you would give some flour for it. In the old days, we used to help each other more. It was really not a trade" [20].

Specifically mentioned among the Tewa villages in trading discussions were San Ildefonso and San Juan pueblos. From San Ildefonso, Santa Clara obtained willow wicker baskets [14, 44] and pottery destined for ceremonial use (Jeançon 1904–30). Wicker baskets were also obtained from San Juan. Two-way exchanges existed among San Ildefonso, San Juan, and Santa Clara in corn and wheat. People fortunate enough to possess oxen were able to cultivate larger acreages, and yields beyond their needs created surpluses that were traded. The same reciprocal arrangements frequently involved trading foodstuffs for clothing or buffalo hides [23, 30].

The only references to trade with the Tiwa were with Indians of Picuris Pueblo. It was stated that some micaceous clay was obtained from that pueblo [20], and also that cooking pots, typically of micaceous clay, were derived from the same tribe in recent years [27].

With the obsolescence of basket making at Santa Clara, twilled yucca baskets were acquired from Jemez Pueblo, a specialty of that village [30, 44, 62; see also Robbins, Harrington, and Freire-Marreco 1916: 52]. Jemez Indians also acted in the capacity of middlemen and were the source of many of the Navajo blankets in the Tewa area [23,

30]. According to the publication just cited (p. 103), cottonseed for medical purposes was also imported from Jemez Pueblo; specifically, cottonseed was "used as a remedy for baldness in children," being crushed, chewed, and applied to the child's head.

Santo Domingo's preeminence in the trading field appears to have been established early. Following the Pueblo Revolt, weaving and belt making became obsolescent among the Tewa, and Santa Clara secured many woven kilts and plaited belts (both essentials for ceremonial costume) from Santo Domingo. This Keresan village was also one of the principal sources of turquoise necklaces. In most cases, the Santa Clara traded buckskins for the finished product. However, turquoise was occasionally mined in the vicinity of Cerrillos, New Mexico, by Santa Clara Indians, who took it to Santo Domingo. The Santo Domingo manufactured the beads, keeping half in payment for their work [14, 64, 65]. Other commodities traded by the Santo Domingo to the Santa Clara included materials used in producing a red pottery slip [11], Navajo blankets [14], gourds, cotton shirts, and cotton trousers [44], and on at least one occasion, macaw feathers [9].

Commercial relations between Santa Clara and Cochiti were almost as frequent as with Santo Domingo. Trade articles and trading arrangements were similar to those with Santo Domingo [23, 30, 62]. A few kilts and belts were also obtained from the pueblos of San Felipe and Acoma [30].

The antiquity of trade relations between Santa Clara and the Hopi and Zuñi is difficult to determine. The establishment of the Tewa village of Hano on First Mesa undoubtedly promoted the relations, as did the need for woven products with the decline of Santa Clara weaving following the Pueblo Revolt. During the later historic period, most black mantas used for ceremonial dress were obtained from Zuñi and Hopi, either directly or through middlemen [20, 27, 44, 68, 71; see also, Robbins, Harrington, and Freire-Marreco 1916: 97]. These two groups were also a source of belts, kilts, and dance paraphernalia in general. Both acted as middlemen in the distribution

of Navajo blankets [20, 23]. The Hopi also traded baskets [20, 23] and were the main source of parrot and macaw feathers for Santa Clara [20]. In return the Santa Clara brought the Zuñi and Hopi buckskins and buffalo robes and occasionally sheep, captured en route, from the Navajo.

Farm derived products, particularly cornmeal and wheat flour as well as bread, were traded by Santa Clara to the Southern Ute and Jicarilla Apache. Robbins, Harrington, and Freire-Marreco (1916: 115) also cited an instance in which two burro-loads of apples were taken to the Jicarilla for exchange purposes. In return the Santa Clara acquired much of their buckskin, undressed deer hide, and buckskin clothing from these tribes [23, 29, 30, 62]. Elkhorn bows were secured from the Ute, and bows, arrows, and arrowheads from the Jicarilla [23]. Navajo blankets were also obtained from the Ute [30], and considerable basketry from the Jicarilla [30, 44, 62]. In later years, sheep were acquired from the Ute and Jicarilla [9, 23, 30]. It is probable that the Ute and Jicarilla Apache were also among the main sources of horses for Santa Clara (see also Henderson and Harrington 1914: 31).

In spite of intermittent hostilities, trade between Santa Clara and the Comanche appeared to have flourished during the latter part of the eighteenth and the first half of the nineteenth centuries. This was indicated by informants and also by Robbins, Harrington, and Freire-Marreco (1916:97), who stated that, "...Santa Clara... became a depot for trade in woolen goods and buffalo hides between the Hopi and Comanche."

Large quantities of meal, flour, and bread were traded by the Santa Clara to the Comanche, as noted earlier. The Comanche were said to be particularly fond of wheat flour and wheat bread, and during the latter periods more wheat than corn was grown to satisfy this desire [65]. As indicated, woven materials were also in demand. In return the Santa Clara received jerked meat and pemmican, buffalo robes often painted or ornamented with quill embroidery, pipe pouches, some tortoise shells, parfleches, and some lances used in buffalo hunting and warfare [20, 23, 29, 40]. It is probable that most of the Osage orange, highly prized for making bows, came from the Comanche (see Robbins, Harrington, Freire-Marreco 1916: 68). The Comanche were also a principal source of Santa Clara livestock, including cattle, horses, mules, and burros (p. 109). Many of these animals had been captured in raids to the south, often as far away as Texas, and the Comanche were anxious to dispose of them as quickly as possible [23, 29, 30].

During periods of uneasy truce, the Santa Clara traded with the Kiowa. The goods exchanged were the same as in the case of the Comanche, but the extent of these relations was somewhat limited [23, 30].

Commercial relations between Santa Clara and the Spanish-Americans were probably inhibited by the relative paucity of items available in their respective material cultures. In the early period the Santa Clara found a ready market for war captives among the more wealthy Spanish and Mexican farmers. These captives consisted primarily of women and children, usually Navajo. They were normally disposed of immediately to prevent their escape, although younger children were occasionally kept for a while to "fatten them up" [14, 15]. Pottery, particularly the tub-like forms used for bread mixing and washing clothing, was another commodity in demand by the Spanish population [12]. Depending upon the existence of surpluses, there was considerable interchange of agricultural products [12, 14, 23]. Beans, especially, were traded to the European villages by Santa Clara [12]. In return, besides agricultural products, the Santa Clara received rock ash (see also Robbins, Harrington, and Freire-Marreco 1916: 93n3), micaceous clay, selenite, and some livestock, principally sheep [12, 23]. In recent years Chimayo rugs have been imported from that Hispanic village, east of Española [29]. Santa Clara Indians formerly accompanied the Spanish to Chihuahua, Mexico, to work, and on such occasions obtained macaw feathers [20].

With the occupation of the Territory of New Mexico by the United States, trading posts became more numerous. One of the earliest was Gold's Old Curiosity Shop in Santa Fe; it was located on the corner of Burro Alley and San Francisco Street and was founded in 1859, according to T.S. Dozier in his pamphlet, "Statement to the Trade for 1907." Such stores began to serve as outlets for Santa Clara products, particularly pottery. By 1893 pottery was also being sold at the railroad station in Española [12]. From this small beginning there eventually developed a flourishing tourist trade.

The first decade of the twentieth century saw this trade firmly established, in part due to the efforts of Kenneth M. Chapman and the Indian Arts Fund of Santa Fe. Initially monetary returns for the Indians were slight. In 1906–07 a barrel containing twenty-four pieces of assorted Pueblo pottery sold for approximately four dollars and fifty cents, F.O.B., Española or Santa Fe (T.S. Dozier, *About Indian Pottery*). However, by the early 1940s it was reported that four families at Santa Clara derived most of their income, aside from desultory agriculture, from the sale of pottery, and that two others gained a considerable amount of their support from this endeavor. It was estimated that some families realized a cash income of as much as a thousand dollars a year from this pursuit. In several instances men ceased farming in order to assist their wives in making and selling pottery [11, 12]. The establishment of the community of Los Alamos and opportunities for wage work reversed this trend for awhile, but it was subsequently reestablished. A gauge of the importance of this craft was that during the period under discussion, Maria Martinez, the famous potter in the neighboring village of San Ildefonso, unable to meet the demands of the tourist trade, imported substantial quantities of dried but unfired pottery from Santa Clara. She then decorated, signed, and fired these and then disposed of them to tourists as her own [4, 11, 18, 29, 42, 45, 54, 72].

Actual conditions under which commercial relations were conducted are illustrated in the following accounts of two trading trips, one to the Ute [30], another to the Kiowa [40].

Six men with three burros went through

the Apache country. We went to the Durango-Cortez [Colorado, WWH] area. There was a regular trading center at the headwaters of the San Juan River between Pagosa Springs and Durango. The various Tewa and the Ute, Taos, as well as the Jicarilla Apache, would gather there in the fall for trading purposes. We were lost for several weeks. Finally we met some Ute who told us where to go. We found the Ute leader. We said that we heard they had a lot of buckskins. This was true. The Ute women were dressing the skins. Finally we arranged a trade. We used Spanish and sign language, also Ute and Tewa until we got the idea over. We traded with both men and women. The Ute preferred cornmeal to wheat flour. I got six buckskins for a sack of meal about the size of a barley sack. In all we got fifteen buckskins and fifteen undressed deer hides. I traded a rifle scabbard for a pair of buckskin leggings with beaded panels and fringe. The Utes gave us a feast as they had lots of meat [30].

One year a party of Taos Indians went to the Kiowa country. The Kiowa asked the Taos to take a message to the four pueblos: Santa Clara, Nambé, San Juan, and San Ildefonso. They said they wished to make friends with those pueblos and wished to meet them either in September or October near Rocky Ford, Colorado. The pueblos chose September. They gathered about one hundred and twenty-five men to represent the four pueblos. José Pablo Moquino was governor at this time. He was half Hopi. This happened about 1860.

Before they left for Rocky Ford, all the men met at Taos. Some Taos went with them. Not only the Kiowa but other tribes as well were at Rocky Ford. It happened that one of the Kiowa chiefs was riding a beautiful blue roan. He rode back and forth and spoke to his tribesmen saying that the Pueblos were here in peace to trade with them. One of the Taos headmen was riding back and forth on a white horse and telling his

people the same thing. Some of the men noticed that several of the horses the Kiowa were riding had been stolen from the pueblos.

The Kiowa chief wished to trade horses with the Taos headman. He offered the blue roan and a mule, but the Taos headman refused to trade his horse. The Kiowa chief threatened the Pueblos. There was a Mexican interpreter with the Kiowa. The chief told him to tell the Pueblos that if the Taos did not trade horses, the Kiowa would attack the Pueblos. The Pueblos said that they did not have their wives and children with them as did the Kiowa and Comanche. They told the Mexican interpreter to tell them that they would kill some of their wives and take others and their children as their slaves. One of the men who had been in the fight the year before lifted the piece of scalp they had taken and said, "We won the last fight and will probably do worse to you this time." The man who lifted the scalp was called Earthcolored, i.e., white man.

The Kiowa and Pueblos were lined up ready to fight. The Pueblos knew that the Kiowa could not do much, as the Comanche sided with the Pueblos. The Comanche said that the Pueblos need not fight, that if the Kiowa wanted to fight, the Comanche would fight them. While the talk was going on, the women and children fled in every direction.

The Kiowa chiefs decided they would not have war. They told the warriors to go and get their women and children. When they were brought back they were told they could go on trading, which they did. They traded buffalo hides, pipe pouches, and blankets for the flour and bread that the Pueblos had brought. The Kiowa also traded meat and beaded moccasins.

The Pueblos got suspicious when the Kiowa women and children began to pack up. The Pueblos likewise packed. The Kiowa chief said, "Why do you do this; come in pairs to the tepees and have dinner." The Tewa leader told them it would be too easy to be killed if they did that. They did not go to the tepees to eat.

The Pueblos started for home that night. It was late and they wished to hurry. The next morning they arrived at Menton. They stopped there, cooked, and ate. A few Comanche were following them to protect them. After eating and smoking they formed a semicircle. Each Pueblo gave the Comanche a bullet, arrow, or gun powder for helping them.

After this the Pueblos left for home, and the Comanche told them to travel day and night. In a day and a night they reached Trinidad. From Trinidad to Taos was another day and a half. The next morning they went to their various villages. They were happy that nothing had happened to them and they had traded successfully [40].

WARFARE

The various ramifications of warfare were integrated with so many parts of Santa Clara life that it is difficult to confine its discussion to any particular segment of the culture. However, in spite of an unconscious sublimation, economic factors were the primary consideration in determining most offensive actions, and for this reason the major discussion of the subject has been included in this chapter. A considerable amount of property in goods was acquired through military efforts. The plunder varied, but in historic times, at least, livestock, jewelry, and captives (to be sold as slaves to the Mexicans) were the principal objectives of every raid.

Other and more overt explanations for making war included the desire for revenge and the inclination to enhance individual prestige. Prestige resulted not only from prowess on the field of battle, but also from the ceremonial distinction that accompanied membership in the war society (c'e o?ke).

Warfare as a functioning element in Santa Clara culture began to disappear in the period from about 1860 to 1870. Only a few of the oldest inhabitants of the pueblo remembered incidents concerning this pursuit, and these were too young at the time to have participated in war ventures. Accounts were, therefore, fragmentary.

Defensive Warfare

Defensive and offensive operations were engaged in against the Navajo, Jicarilla Apache, Comanche, and Kiowa. Traditional enmity focused on the Navajo, and the majority of the hostilities occurred between Santa Clara and this group.

There was little elaboration of defensive tactics. Guards were kept regularly posted to warn the village against marauding bands, and news of an approaching enemy party was sent by runners to neighboring Tewa villages. This often resulted in the arrival of reinforcements from other pueblos who argued with some validity that their safety lay in repulsing the attack before it might reach their own territory.

Guard and defensive operations were in the hands of the "outside chief" (akongei tunzhorg, "head outside the village"), more recently designated as capitan major, capitán de guerra, or, most commonly, war captain, and his assistants (his right and left-hand men [23]; or his five capitanes [14]. Once the enemy was discovered, these officials organized against the attack. Usually the outside chief led a party against the enemy in an attempt to disperse them before they reached the pueblo proper, or at least to delay them until proper defensive preparations could be completed. This tactic was frequently successful, and more often than not hostilities were confined to minor skirmishes in the outlying fields.

Offensive Warfare

Motives for offensive action, the desire for plunder, revenge, and prestige, have already been cited. These appear to have been strong enough to have overcome a sense of military inferiority that was current in the minds of most tribal members. What individual or body was responsible for leading offensive actions is obscure. Announcement of and the destination of the projected raid was given by the outside chief or governor, and it is probable that these two were most prominent in determining the decision.

The announcement preceded the departure by several days to allow for preparations. Much of the able-bodied adult male population made up the party. These were often joined by individuals from other Tewa towns and occasionally by neighboring Mexicans. The size of such composite groups varied considerably. A contingent numbering two hundred seems not to have been unusual and one party, augmented by Zuñi, was said to have totaled four hundred [40].

Practical preparations (for details of spiritual preparation, see War Society, Chapter 10) consisted in constructing, repairing, or testing the armament, including bows, arrows, stone-headed clubs, lances, shields, and in more recent times, firearms. If horses were to be used, these were selected with care. The women ground cornmeal for food. As much meal as possible was carried, since trips of a month's duration or more were not unusual. While traveling the party foraged and hunted to augment these slender resources [15, 27, 35].

When the designated day arrived, the fully armed group moved out of the pueblo. War ventures were considered critical endeavors, and the uncertainties engendered considerable anxiety. Women customarily wailed as the group departed, and fear concerning the outcome was a constant topic of discussion. Casualties actually were, as a rule, extremely light, although traditional accounts existed of parties that were decimated, and of parties that never returned [4].

Field strategy varied according to circumstance. The party might work as a unit or deploy in smaller groups. There appears to have been some attempt to conform to the fighting pattern of the tribe attacked. The Tewa, once enemy territory was reached, endeavored to keep well out of sight. Scouts were dispatched to locate the enemy, and if conditions were favorable, a surprise attack was made. However, chance encounters were frequent and resulted in numerous unplanned engagements. Evidence of formalized warfare is absent for the most part, except with the Plains tribes, where

occasional challenges and combats between individual champions occurred [14, 15].

Surprise raids usually took place early in the morning. An attempt was made to engulf the settlement or encampment and to kill or drive off the male population. Scalps were secured. These were large, or full; incisions were made along the lower portion of the forehead and around the head just above the ears. No trophies other than scalps were taken. Whenever possible, the women and children were taken captive. These were disposed of to neighboring Mexicans soon after the war party returned to the village. Slavery as an institution did not exist at Santa Clara Pueblo, and every man attempted to make a quick sale to avoid loss through escape.

Livestock was driven off en masse and was subject to division at a later time. While sheep and horses were the principal plunder, the warriors systematically looted the defeated for any equipment that could be easily transported and also for jewelry [14, 15, 27].

War parties began the return journey to Santa Clara Pueblo as soon as the plunder was organized. Immediate departure was essential, since captured livestock, particularly sheep, handicapped the speed of movement, and unless considerable distance could be covered soon after the fight, the danger of the enemy organizing a successful pursuit and reprisal was increased. Rear guards on horseback were positioned to warn against the contingency of a counterattack; food was consumed in relays, one section eating while the other stood watch. Vigilance continued until the group was well out of enemy territory.

When still some distance from the pueblo, one or two men were sent ahead to announce the return. These reported on the success of the venture and made a request for food if the supplies had dwindled. The pueblo immediately selected and dispatched a welcoming party. This official contingent was joined by any who wished, and all left carrying food and gifts for the returning warriors. When contact was made, songs expressing joy at the safe return and of victory were begun. The war party was escorted to the pueblo amid shouts, singing, and dancing to begin the Scalp Dance and ritual purification [14, 15, 27].

Peace

There is some evidence that formal peace negotiations occasionally took place between Santa Clara and enemy groups. One such instance was described by Benavides (Hodge, Hammond, and Rey 1945: 85–87) in September 1629. On this occasion a delegation of Santa Clara Indians approached a Navajo settlement. While still at a distance the leader of the Santa Clara shot an arrow into the Navajo encampment; the stone point had been replaced by a feather. This indicated that their intent was peaceful. The groups met, a cane cigarette was smoked, and amicable relationships were established.

Another account from a war tale deals with Santa Clara–Comanche relations. On this occasion delegations from each group met. The groups sat facing each other: a Pueblo opposite each Comanche. They used sign language, promising that hostilities between them would cease. While conversing they smoked cornhusk cigarettes, and each man dug a small hole in front of him. When an agreement was reached, each placed a cigarette butt in the hole [15].

WAR TALES

Encounter with the Kiowa and Comanche.

A group from Santa Clara, Nambé, San Juan, and San Ildefonso started on a buffalo hunt. As they traveled they passed through Springer, New Mexico. They stopped that night at Springer. The next day, they stopped at a place called kureimpa posa. They stopped for the night. They allowed their horses to graze. There was a river nearby.

At dawn they noticed a group of Indians approaching: Kiowa and Comanche. When they saw them the Pueblo men ran as fast as they could and hid behind some sandstone outcroppings. From this position they shot at the enemy. The enemy would dance for a while, then attack, and then return and dance again.

There were four brothers. One of the brothers spoke Kiowa; he had been married to a Kiowa girl. He talked to the enemy and explained to them that the Pueblos were hunting and did not wish to fight. As the Kiowa rushed forward, they shot one down. The others rushed forward to get the horses.

A governor from San Ildefonso was the leader of the Pueblo party. He told them to be brave and to fight—not to give up. The enemy secured the horses, however, and took them across the river. They also destroyed all the Tewa supplies that they could. After this the enemy did not return.

The Tewa did not know what to do without their burros and horses. Some took what horses were left and pursued the enemy. The San Ildefonso governor issued a challenge to the Kiowa leader to come and fight him. Both were armed. The Kiowa had only a small shield. As they came close, they began to shoot with bow and arrow. Then they closed. The Tewa had a knife. He had said to his people, "We must take something back to show we have fought." The Tewa killed the Kiowa and took his scalp. He held up the scalp and asked if anyone else wished to fight, but no one did. After that the Kiowa retreated and did not bother the Tewa again.

The Pueblos were proud to have taken the enemy chief's scalp. They started for home; they had to return on foot. The sun was beginning to set. They saw a light early in the morning. It was the ranch house of a Mexican. They ate there and rested until noon. They then set out again and reached Moriarty that night. In order that each pueblo would know that they had fought, the scalp was divided into four parts, and each pueblo held a scalp dance on their return [15, 40].

Encounter with the Kiowa

A trading party consisting of about ten Santa Clarans and a few San Juan

Indians lost their way, and Kiowa attacked them. They killed several Kiowa, but no Santa Clara were killed. The Kiowa leader wore a distinctive war headdress of eagle feathers and carried a shield. After the fight the Santa Clara returned home. Later they went back with a larger group that included some Mexicans. They went to where they had encountered the Kiowa before; the Kiowa were there. The Santa Clara leader wore the headdress and carried the shield that had been captured earlier. He said to the Kiowa, "You recognize this headdress and shield, don't you?" The Kiowa remembered and wanted friendship. They laid down their weapons even though they outnumbered the Santa Clara [44, 65].

Encounter with the Comanche

This I have not seen, but it was told to me. There is a place this side of Española. The Tewa heard that the Comanche were coming. Two men put on shirts made of two thicknesses of buffalo hide and went to meet them. The Comanche shot with bows and arrows, but the two men were protected. Arrows were sticking all over their shirts.

More men came from Santa Clara. The Comanche retreated toward the east. They sank into the quicksand and could not turn back. They were caught and killed. This place is called p'o ci pa^{n}ge, ("quicksand bottom").

A few Comanche escaped, but most were killed. The Comanche had their camp and families at a place called Yellow Cedar near San Juan Pueblo. The survivors went back to their families. They decided they wished peace. The men from Santa Clara pursued them. The Comanche came to meet them on horses, but without their fighting equipment. They met the Santa Clara and took them into their camp. They wished to make peace and did [71].

Encounter with the Navajo

The Navajo were damaging the Rio Grande pueblos. The Tewa banded together to fight the Navajo. When the Tewa arrived near Zuñi, they saw arrows sticking in the trees and in the ground; the Zuñi and Navajo had fought. The Zuñi were also enemies of the Navajo. They joined the Tewa to hunt for the Navajo. When they got near the band of Navajo, they stopped for the night. There was a Navajo boy among the Zuñi. This boy sang and spoke in Navajo. The Navajo leader told this boy that they would come the next day and fight the Pueblos. The boy said, "The Pueblos will fight if the Navajo ever come to the Rio Grande again." The Navajo said, "We are brave enough to fight." The Navajo leader said, "Whoever is brave [i.e., could kill him WWH], can have my beads and silver bridle."

The next morning a few Pueblos went to meet the Navajo. They led the Navajo into the main band of Pueblos. Then they fought, and a Mexican killed the Navajo leader. The Pueblos asked, "What has become of the Navajo chief?" The Mexicans said, "We have not seen him." The Pueblos said, "If you do not tell, we will take you prisoner." The two Mexicans had the Navajo leader's coral beads and large turquoise earrings. The Pueblos wanted them. They questioned the Mexicans, but they would not tell what they had done with the jewelry so the Pueblos took them prisoner and went back to camp.

The Tewa had taken the saddle and blankets that belonged to the Navajo chief. The two Mexicans were questioned again at the camp. After three or four hours had passed, one denied that he had taken part of the beads. The other was questioned, but he did not answer. He had the larger beads from the lower portion of the string. Finally both confessed that they had taken the beads. The beads were taken to be divided among the party.

The next thing to decide was who had

gotten the bridle, blankets, and martingale, and also whether the Tewa who had captured them should be allowed to keep them. Another question was who was to get the horse; a Tewa had it. All four of the Tewa groups voted to see which of the Pueblo leaders should get the horse. They even considered whether or not the Navajo boy should get the horse. They wished to be fair to each leader. One of the Pueblo leaders thought of an idea for distributing the property. He asked who in the group had a pair of moccasins that had not been worn. One man said, "I have a pair." The leader took the moccasins and hid a stick in one of them and placed them face down on the ground. The leader said, "In order to be fair, either the Navajo or one of the Mexicans should get the horse." The Mexican was asked to choose a shoe. There was no stick in it.

The Navajo boy told the party to split up in three parts. There were about two hundred men from Zuñi and two hundred from the Rio Grande. One party was to go to Gallup, one to Shiprock, and one north of Shiprock. The second group located the Navajo; they sent word to one of the parties to join them. They arranged to surprise the Navajo at midnight. The Navajo were all sleeping. They killed what Navajo fought back, and they got most of the Navajo sheep. They started back to the base camp with the sheep. Some Navajo

followed them. When they got near the sheep, they gave a call and the rear guard of the sheep turned back. The Pueblos could not keep them from turning back. When they arrived at the base camp, some of the Pueblos had left for home. They left a sign that they had left for Zuñi. The rest started for Zuñi. They caught up with the first group about midnight the next night.

Most of the Pueblos were on foot driving the sheep. Some were on horseback watching for the enemy. One group ate while the others watched. Then they exchanged places. Then they went on again. Finally they arrived at Zuñi. They had the sheep. They had brought no prisoners because of the difficulty of getting away from the Navajo country. They were raiding rather than attempting to capture slaves.

The Tewa were admired because they had captured sheep. The Tewa wished to go home. The Zuñi asked them to stay for four days to make sure that they would be safe from attack. They planned to leave on the fifth day. They made plans for the journey and for their protection on the way home. The sheep were divided. Each man got five sheep. Some Tewa traded their sheep for mantas. My great uncle got three mantas for his sheep; not all traded their sheep. The fifth day they started home. They arrived home safely, but the journey took twenty-two days [15, 40].

7

Material Culture

The subject of material culture continued to hold a rather unusual fascination for W.W. Hill throughout his anthropological career. His Santa Clara Pueblo study was no exception, and the present chapter is an obvious reflection of that interest. (Further evidence of his interest came to light in a number of publications, perhaps most clearly in Hill's final publication, *Navaho Material Culture,* coauthored with Clyde and Lucy Wales Kluckhohn [1971].)

In the course of the editorial preparation of the present volume, the persistent focus on material culture has been something of a problem. In addition to this chapter as originally written, additional data were found here and there in a number of other chapters, a dramatic demonstration of the inherent interrelatedness of the parts of any culture. With the aim of greater convenience and perhaps improved readability, some gathering and reordering of these scattered segments has occurred.

The inventory of material items, the processing involved, and related topics have been integrated with the available information regarding variations in form, the making or manufacture, the makers, and the use made of each item. This consolidated approach seemed to provide more coherent discussion of each subject. However it should be noted that there are still additional material culture data in other chapters, most of these being well embedded in the closing chapter concerning the religious, or ceremonial, life of Santa Clara Pueblo. These and other discussions can be located by consulting the index [CHL].

STRUCTURES

House Building

House construction was a male occupation. Men cut the timbers, prepared and laid the adobes, etc. Only the plastering was done by women. The magnitude of the task varied. Sometimes a new house was built; at other times an old home would be torn down and rebuilt with the same materials. Occasionally a new room was added or an old one repaired. It was normally a cooperative endeavor. The group of cooperators was variable in its makeup, depending upon the owner's age and the kind and number of his existing relatives. Commonly a father and his sons, or a group of brothers, occasionally augmented by cousins, worked together [21, 52, 61]. At other times the affinal relatives of a husband

and wife combined their efforts [21, 30]. If hardship cases were involved, the governor might assign the task to the village, or a cacique, to the male membership of a moiety [23, 50]. One instance was cited where the moiety affiliates of a man with a protracted illness dismantled his home in the mountains and rebuilt it for him in the village [9].

Helpers received no pay except food, although reciprocal obligations were recognized. House building ordinarily represented an interrupted rather than a sustained effort.

In recent years, with advances in technology, the presence of modern tools, and better transportation facilities, Santa Clara dwellings have expanded in size. Correspondingly the number of rooms, room size, and ceiling height have increased. As will be noted many modern structural features have been incorporated.

While most buildings were one story high, the multistory and terraced "typical pueblo" structures were formerly common. Several two-story houses were present during the time of the fieldwork (see also Stubbs 1950: Fig. 9), and a few remain today. An older informant [65] did not remember having seen a house of more than two stories; however, according to another [20], three-story dwellings were occasionally built. This latter opinion is probably an exaggeration, since the photographs of Hillers (1879) and Vroman (1900) show no houses of more than two stories (Plates 4, 5, 6, and 7), and such forms were denied by Bourke (Bloom 1936: 256).

At the turn of the century, the ordinary home consisted of two or three rooms, seldom more. One informant [21] was able to name about ten families who occupied two rooms and indicated that this was overwhelmingly the case. "Houses usually had two rooms" [52, 61]. Three and four-room houses typically resulted from a father either enlarging his house upon the marriage of his sons or allocating them a section of his home [52].

When the home included three rooms, one was used for a kitchen, another as a combination living room and bedroom and for entertaining guests. The third was used for storage [23, 30]. When a fourth room existed, it functioned as a bedroom for the family or a sleeping place for unmarried male guests [20]. In multistoried, terraced houses, the back ground-floor rooms were inevitably used for storage [20].

Rooms in the older homes were smaller. According to one informant [20], interior dimensions of a three-room house were about eighteen by twenty feet; according to another [65], twenty-five by fourteen. A room six or seven feet by twelve was formerly considered large [20]. These estimates were confirmed by examination of several older homes. Ceilings were low in these older homes, some barely six feet. Recently as noted, modern tools and practices have made possible an increase in all dimensions.

House foundations were of rock and adobe; the walls, of adobe brick. The major roof supports, vigas, or rafters, were variously covered with smaller rafters, willows, tule, and earth. Houses have always been made of adobe, at least during one informant's life time [23]. According to another [20], stone and adobe were used earlier; this was not confirmed.

Plans for building were begun six months or a year in advance of actual construction. If the location selected for the house was on tribal land, the individual petitioned the governor for permission to build [13]. If the land was privately owned, the site was purchased [13, 52].

When the house location was secured, the builder and helpers went to the mountains and cut the large vigas (pe so) and the smaller crossvigas (fe e). These might be of aspen, fir, or pine. When felled the bark was removed, and they were usually left to season for several months [20, 29, 30, 52, 61].

The adobe bricks were next prepared. These were approximately twelve by eighteen inches and four inches thick. Formerly they were larger, and older house walls were correspondingly thicker. Informants estimated that three thousand adobes were needed to construct a house. Three to seven days were required to make these bricks if a large number of people cooperated [29, 30, 52, 61].

Formerly the earth was brought to the

house site, and the bricks were mixed on location. Earth was transported in large sack-like parfleches on the backs of men or burros [30]; wheelbarrows were later used [29]. More recently bricks have been made at sites where desirable material existed, and the finished product brought to the pueblo in wagons or trucks [13, 18, 29]. One of these favored sites was near a small creek west of the railroad [52]; another was in the uncultivated area north of the pueblo [29].

A hole or basin was dug, and water and adobe were poured in it. Straw was added as a binder, and the materials thoroughly mixed with a shovel and hoe. When the mixture reached the right consistency, it was poured in a mold and carried to one side to dry. Recently bottomless forms with several compartments have been used. The adobe is poured into the frame, allowed to set, and the frame then lifted from the bricks [13, 29]. Bricks were usually left in their original position for two or three days before being turned [13]. Some, however, preferred to place the bricks on edge to dry after this initial period [29]. Bricks were allowed to season for at least two weeks; when dry they were stacked in tiers until needed [13, 29].

When construction was ready to begin, the vigas were brought from the mountains. Earlier, *carretas* were used for this purpose, or lines were tied to them, and they were dragged down by burros [30]. More recently wagons, and, when feasible, trucks have been used.

The builder outlined the area to be covered by the exterior walls. The positions of the room partitions were marked next. A trench approximately three feet deep and eighteen inches wide was dug where the walls would rest. The bottom of the trench was tamped with a tamp, wooden sledge, or heavy rock to insure it was solid. The tamp consisted of a flat section of wood with a handle fixed to the center. A layer of wet adobe and small boulders was then placed in the trench and tamped down. This process was repeated until the foundation reached ground level, or in some cases, as much as a foot above the ground. It was then capped with adobe. Soil with a high "lime" content was occasionally used in the foundation and capping for added strength [29, 52]. Foun-

dations were allowed to settle and dry for at least two weeks before actual construction was begun [52].

Adobe bricks for the walls were laid in courses. Adobe mortar was placed between each brick and each course. Building usually began at the corners. When the courses met near the center of a wall, bricks were broken to the proper size to fill the space. The corners were bonded, and the joints of alternating courses of bricks were broken. There was some doubt as to whether this was always done. Some houses had buttresses at the corners, composed of stones and adobe; in others, additional support was given to walls by timbers. Openings were left for doors and windows. Board or split-log lintels were inserted over the openings to carry the higher courses [29, 52].

Framing was completed at a later time. While doorways were in common use by 1879 (see Hillers' photographs), informants [20, 27] stated that formerly one-story houses were without doors, and that entrance was gained through a hatchway in the center of the roof. This opening also served as an outlet for smoke. Access to and from the ground-floor rooms was by means of ladders. One type of ladder was a notched log. The other consisted of two vertical poles in which holes were bored at intervals to receive the rungs. Ladders of more modern type were still in use to enable persons to reach roofs and the tops of *ramadas* [20].

Doorways in the older houses were smaller than those built more recently. The jambs were not flush with the ground, but rested on the foundation. Since this might be as much as a foot above the surface, it was necessary to step up and over to enter the room. Doorways between interior rooms were similarly elevated. The old doors were unframed and more like gates than doors [13].

While casement windows were in use during the time of Hillers (1879), those in the older houses were much smaller than modern types. Evidence of the earlier type of window was still to be seen in several of the older houses, and "selenite windows are not too far back" [14]. This aboriginal form consisted of a round opening about eight inches in diameter left in the wall of the house.

Sometimes a piece of selenite, worked thin, was placed in the opening [13, 20, 23, 27]. On other occasions, a cloth was placed over or in the opening to keep out wind and cold [20, 23].

In many houses tiers of adobe bricks, two to two and one-half feet high, were laid along one or two of the interior walls [14]. These served as benches for the occupants. They were still present in some of the older homes.

When the walls reached ceiling height, the major vigas or rafters were set in place. These were spaced one to two feet apart and rested on slabs of wood set on top of the wall. Ends of the vigas normally extended beyond the wall for several feet. When they were in position, the intervals between them were filled with adobe bricks. The walls were then continued above the beams from two to six courses—creating a low "fire wall" [18, 52].

Split lengths of cedar, piñon, or pine were laid on and at right angles to the vigas. These were set as close together as the conformity of the wood would allow. On these, again at right angles, was placed a layer of apache plume or green willow with leaves on, and frequently transversely to this was a layer of tule. Next, several inches of adobe were spread over this base and tamped down. Finally loose dirt to a depth of several inches was scattered on top of the adobe. The adobe and earth occasionally reached a foot in thickness [13, 29, 30, 64].

An attempt was made to graduate the adobe and earth covering from front to back to facilitate drainage. Log or board troughs or a flat rock were inserted through a hole in the "fire wall" to carry off the water. These drains, or *canales,* extended outward from the wall on the side least exposed to public view and most "out of the way." A flat rock was placed on the ground where the water fell from the troughs. This was inclined so that it guided the water away from the wall and into a drainage trench dug for that purpose. Recently modern roofing materials have been used [13, 29].

Inside the house the floor area was first tamped solid, covered with about three inches of wet adobe, and smoothed with the hands. When thoroughly dry another layer, sometimes mixed with blood, was added and smoothed. Recently trowels have been used for this smoothing [13]. Many families used earth from the floors of Puyé ruins. "This was a black dirt and made a harder floor" [64]. Earth floors were still the common type at the time of the fieldwork.

Construction of second-story rooms in most instances was similar to that just described. However one informant [65] stated that upper-story walls were frequently of coursed, or puddled, adobe, not adobe brick. The wall was built up in adobe layers, and each layer held in place by lengths of split cottonwood until it dried. Then another layer was added until the desired height was reached.

Houses were plastered inside and out by the women [65]. Soil with "lime," or caliche, in it was often selected for plastering [30, 52]. A rough coat of plaster was applied to the exterior walls and smoothed with the hands or, more recently, with trowels. Wheat chaff was mixed with the initial coat for better binding. The final coat was put on after the first had dried for three or four days. Finely textured soil was selected for this, and in recent years has been screened before it was mixed.

Colored plaster was often used in room interiors; red, yellow, white, and, according to Jeançon (1904–30), pinkish and blue. "You plaster with whatever color you like" [64]. In many of the older homes, the lower third of the wall was yellow, and the remainder white or red [72]. According to one informant [72], kaolin was often used; according to another [64], gypsum was used, secured from a site north of the Ghost Ranch, northwest of Abiquiu. Gypsum was baked in the oven and then ground to powder before it was mixed.

Rooms were commonly decorated with religious lithographs, santos, and photographs of relatives. Jeançon (1904–30) stated,

> Every house has its quota of cheap lithographs of the saints, our Savior, and the Virgin Mary, as well as cheap plaster statues of the Holy Ones decorated with tinsel and rosaries. Personal photographs and cheap post cards of

views of places which the owner has visited all have an important place on the wall.

House exteriors were frequently replastered. This was done whenever the need arose, in preparation for major ceremonies, feast days, or when a "general clean up" of the pueblo was ordered.

According to tradition aboriginal fireplaces consisted of a fire pit located below the hatchway in the roof. No examples of these existed in the pueblo with the exception of those in the kivas, and it was doubtful if any informant was familiar with the oldest domestic type. Hooded fireplaces as introduced by the Spanish were still present in kitchens in the 1940s, although many homes were equipped with modern wood-burning stoves.

Nearly all rooms had fireplaces, and their installation was an integral part of house construction. Fireplaces seem invariably to have been situated in room corners, a location which minimized the structural difficulties. All had raised hearths of adobe brick. Those used for cooking were often four or five feet in diameter and frequently had a raised ledge or bench running along the two walls at the back. The hood rested on two transverse beams. In some instances one end of the beams was inserted in the wall structure and the other rested on a post located at the front angle of the fireplace. The two faces of the hood sloped gradually toward the walls. The hood was constructed of horizontally laid willow withes, which were covered with a thick coating of plaster on both the interior and exterior surfaces [13, 18, 20].

In some cases the flue of the chimney extended into the room for a short distance; in others it began at ceiling height. Chimneys extended several feet above the roof and firewall. One or two bottomless pots were added to the top to increase the drawing capacity [13, 18, 20].

Fireplaces for heating were smaller in all dimensions than those for cooking. While usually in room corners, some were erected near the outside doorway or midway in the room. In the former case a low wall was often built, extending from the doorway into the room, to form the angle for the fireplace. The hood rested on a piece of wood or metal placed transversely in the wall angle. The chimney extended farther into the room than in the case of the kitchen type [13, 18, 20].

Fireplaces were plastered to conform to the interiors and exteriors of the houses when completed.

Among orthodox families when a house was completed, one of the Bear Societies was requested to "bless or cure" it. For a description of the ceremony, see Chapter 10.

In addition to houses there were a number of lesser, or subsidiary, architectural forms. These included such structures as ovens, storage facilities and granaries, ramadas, threshing floors, corrals and pens, and hunting shelters.

Ovens

Almost every household possessed a semi-spherical Spanish-type oven. These were located either on the ground in close proximity to the owner's house or on the roof. The 1879 photographs by Hillers show several of the rooftop type. When a family lacked an oven, that of a close relative was used.

Ovens were made by men. The ground was first leveled, and the area to be covered marked off. Oven hearths were always raised, usually about a foot in height. The builder first laid the circular exterior foundation wall. This consisted of adobe and small boulders. When this had set, the interior of the circle was filled with wet adobe, and the surface was smoothed. Small stones were occasionally added to the adobe [13].

The walls of the oven were of adobe bricks. Dry bricks were cut in keystone shape. They were never poured in that form. Each succeeding circular course of adobe bricks contained one less brick than the previous one. This produced the desired construction and the semispherical shape. When the top was reached, two crossed pieces of wood or iron were laid over the opening, and odd pieces of adobe brick and mortar were used to close the aperture. No keystone was used.

Courses were interrupted in the front of

the oven to produce the opening. When the desired height was reached, a board or strip of iron was laid over the top as a lintel to carry the succeeding course. Openings were closed with gunny sacks, cloth-covered boards, or stone slabs.

A stoop was usually constructed at one side or extending outward from the opening. Bread and other foods were placed on this platform prior to or after baking. A small vent, two to three inches in diameter, was left in the side wall near the top of the oven.

When the structure was completed, it was given a rough coat of plaster both inside and out. When this had dried for a day or more, a finer coat of plaster was applied. The plaster in both instances was smoothed with the hands or, more recently, a trowel. When the oven was finally thoroughly dry, a fire was built to "try it out" [13].

Each oven was equipped with a poker, "mop," and "wooden shovel." The poker was any convenient length of wood. This was used to break up the coals and distribute them so that the hearth would preheat evenly over its entire surface. The "mop" consisted of a pole with rags attached at one end. The rags were wet and the mop used to sweep out the coals prior to baking. When the oven was in use, the mop was leaned against it so that the rags closed the vent. The wooden flat-bladed shovel was used to place the bread in the oven and also to remove it when it had baked [13].

Storage Facilities and Granaries

Beside the secondary storage discussed under household equipment, there were two independent structures used for this purpose. One was a rectangular bin utilized primarily for food stuffs; the other, an oven-like granary for wheat.

The walls of the bin were constructed of adobe bricks. The roof consisted of pole stringers covered with a transverse layer of willow, tule, or both. On these was placed wet adobe. Access was through an opening in one corner. This was covered with a panel and sealed to protect the stored items from rodents and inclement weather [13, 50]. The size of the bin was determined by the needs of the family, but averaged about four by six feet in width and length and four feet in height.

Such bins were usually located on the roof. Two may be seen in the 1879 photograph by Hillers: one in the left foreground, the other in the right background. A bin in bad repair was examined in the course of fieldwork at Santa Clara Pueblo in 1941. Such bins occasionally occurred in rooms of larger houses. However demands for living space normally precluded this location.

Granaries used primarily for wheat were constructed in the same manner as ovens, but were larger. Access was by a framed opening located midway in one side. One in partial disrepair is pictured in the foreground of Vroman's photograph of 1900.

Ramadas

Ramadas served a variety of purposes. The roofs of those adjacent to houses were often used as front porches, particularly if the houses possessed a second story. During the harvest, crops were placed there to dry. During the summer members of the household sat in the shade under the ramada and cooked, worked, or visited (see Plates 8 and 9). Those located in the corrals served to protect the stock from the weather. Forage was stacked on their roofs, where it was readily available when needed (see Plates 10, 11, and 12). The principal purpose of independently located ramadas was for drying produce, especially corn, but also squash, pumpkins, melons, and fruit. These were erected in the fields or plazas. Secondarily they furnished shade for workers. Such drying stages, some of which were adjuncts to homes, were often equipped with walls. In these instances one angle of the fork of the main support posts extended beyond the other. Poles were lashed to these at right angles, a foot or so above the roof. The intervening space was filled with interlaced willows (see Plate 10). More recently boards have been used.

Threshing Floors

Threshing floors (erra) were constructed and commonly used by families and near relatives (Plate 13). When such a facility was needed, members of the group went to localities where alkali soil (lime?) was plentiful and brought it to the pueblo. This was spread on the site selected for the floor, sprinkled first with water, and then with dry earth. Next this surface covering was tramped by driving sheep and goats over it. At times horses were used for this purpose. Finally it was smoothed and allowed to dry. Threshing floors were always surrounded by a fence, the area enclosed being thirty to forty feet in diameter. Once constructed they were repaired or renewed and used year after year [18, 27].

A comparable description for the Tewa generally was given by Robbins, Harrington, and Freire-Marreco (1916: 108). According to them an American threshing machine was used for the first time at Santa Clara Pueblo in 1912.

Corrals and Pens

Corrals and pens for livestock were usually located on the peripheries of the village; their construction was simple. The fences were made of closely placed posts or stakes set or driven into the ground. Near the top of the fence transversely placed poles were lashed to the uprights, formerly with rawhide, and more recently with wire (see Vroman photograph, Plate 7). As mentioned above ramadas were often built in the corrals, and log watering troughs were occasionally used.

A specialized pen was sometimes built for chickens. This was a conical structure produced by interlacing willow withes. One was shown in the right foreground of Vroman's photograph (Plate 7).

Hunting Shelters

Facilities associated with hunting were not great in number; the Santa Clara structures have been reported widely distributed not only in the Southwest but throughout western North America as well.

Hunting shelters were erected at the base camps associated with buffalo and antelope hunts. Their ground plan was semicircular. At each point of the semicircle was placed a forked pole. A rafter was strung connecting the two poles. Stringers were run from the rafter to the ground toward the back, the central stringers being longer than those on the side, forming a half circle (Figure 1). These were covered with brush to complete the structure. The opening always faced east. "This was because it was warmer." On buffalo hunts the brush covering was often replaced by a covering of buffalo hide, because of the shortage of tree and brush growth in the Plains area. In this case the shelters were of necessity smaller. The number of windbreaks constructed depended on the size of the party [20, 64].

FURNITURE AND HOUSEHOLD EQUIPMENT

Until commercial products became readily available, furniture and household equipment tended to be meager. Recently and especially since the shift toward a wage economy and the introduction of electricity through the federal Rural Electrification Administration, many Santa Clara homes have acquired the standard conveniences of any rural community. Beds, tables, chairs, and even a variety of electrical appliances have become fairly common.

Earlier floors were of dirt and covered only by an occasional sheepskin or buffalo robe. At a somewhat later date, rag rugs and a few woven blankets acquired from Chimayo, New Mexico, were used for floor covering. During the period of the fieldwork, while most floors were of dirt, many were covered with linoleum. Only a few modern homes were floored with wood. Regardless of the type of floor, most homes were kept scrupulously clean and formerly were swept every morning with a broom composed of stalks from the Apache plume [6].

Prior to the introduction of beds, the family slept on the floor. Pelts, robes, and blankets were added to the floor coverings for comfort and warmth. Bedding was usually rolled up each morning and placed along the walls. These rolls served as seats [18]. Lacking these occupants sat on sheepskins or robes, or if the house contained interior benches, on those. A three-legged

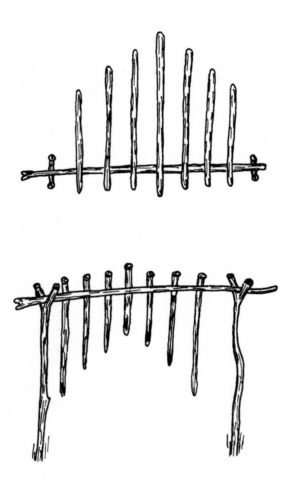

Figure 1. Hunting shelter: basic pole framework.

stool was occasionally used. These were most commonly of pine, and sheepskin was usually put over the top [64]. Members of the family knelt on one knee around a common pot or pots when eating, and selected food with their fingers or ladled it into individual bowls [64]. What light there was drifted through the windows or the doors or was furnished by the fire. After Spanish contacts crude candles were made. A number of strings were suspended from a horizontal stick; sheep or beef fat was melted and slowly poured over the stick at the junctures where the strings were tied. It dripped down and adhered to the string and slowly built up the candles. "Candles were highly considered. They were used only for special occasions or for church. Lamps came later" [19].

Most homes were formerly equipped with a bank, or series, of two to four metates. It was usually located in the living room but occasionally in a separate room or the kitchen [19, 20]. The few families that lacked this facility went to neighbors and did their grinding there. By 1940 manos and metates were used for grinding only in conjunction with religion. Hand-ground meal and flour for food had been completely replaced by commercially milled products. The obsolescence of metates began with the establishment of a water-powered mill in the pueblo about 1885 [19].

Men made the metates and manos and

constructed the banks; within a bank, the metates were typically graded in terms of the coarseness of the surface. Any hard stone was utilized; there was no preference for one type over another. Some were made of visicular lava [21]. Blanks roughly the size of the metate or mano were selected in the field, brought to the pueblo, and shaped with stone and iron tools. This was a slow and arduous process, and metates in particular were never manufactured in quantity. From time to time a lucky person would find a metate on the surface of an archeological, prehistoric or historic, site; these were brought home as valued treasures. More manos were made since they were easily broken. Both passed from generation to generation, normally the oldest daughter inheriting from the mother. It was believed that metates and manos improved with use through time.

Metates were approximately eighteen inches long, ten to twelve inches wide, and five to eight inches thick. The bottoms were rounded, the grinding surface flat when new. Depending on the location and number of metates in the bank, the cutting or grinding surface varied as to texture, as noted. The first metate had a coarse, rough surface; the next metates were graduated in refinement. When the surfaces became smooth, they were "sharpened" by pecking with a hard stone. Manos were about ten inches long and three to four inches in width and thickness when new.

Metate banks were usually located in the corner of a room. A rectangular frame of split log planks was made first. Three sides were about eight inches in height; the fourth, about a foot and a half. One of the low sides was placed close to or against the house wall. The high panel was located far enough from the other wall to allow ample room for the operators. This arrangement conserved space yet allowed easy access to the metates from three sides.

Next the frame was divided into compartments, one for each metate, by inserting plank partitions. For a bank of two metates the outer frame was approximately five feet by three feet; for four metates, ten feet by three feet. When this was installed a floor of adobe and ash was added to the interior. The edges of this floor extended up the sides of the frame and held it in place.

Finally a metate was centered in each compartment. They rested on a stone and adobe foundation. The upper ends were elevated several inches above the floor of the bank and almost touched the high wall of the frame. The lower ends were raised somewhat less from the floor.

When ready to work the operators knelt behind the high wall of the bank. A quantity of unground kernels or partially ground meal was placed on either side of the metate where it could be conveniently reached by the operator. The mano was gripped with both hands. Starting the stroke at the bottom, the operator lifted the near side of the mano and in this manner controlled the amount of corn or wheat to be worked. The grinding motion was back and forth. The ground meal was pushed from the lower end of the metate onto the floor of the compartment.

It was necessary to repeat the grinding process several times before the meal attained the proper consistency. Fresh kernels were easier to grind than older ones. In the initial operation the kernels were placed on the metate with the coarse cutting surface and partially reduced. At this stage the meal was moist and was put in a pottery bowl about two feet in diameter and four inches deep. This was placed on a bed of coals in the fireplace to dry the meal. "It took about a half hour to dry. You could tell when it was dry by the odor" [42]. When dry it was allowed to cool for about half an hour and then reground on the metate or metates with more refined surfaces until the desired consistency was achieved. When the grinding was completed, both metates and manos were swept clean with a stiff grass brush or broom [19, 29].

Corn grinding was one of the more important and highly considered women's tasks. While commonly described as laborious, it often had social as well as practical significance. Some families ground corn each day to meet their needs. Ideally, however, surpluses were produced through concentrated periodic efforts.

Grinding was most actively engaged in during the winter months. This was a time when economic pressures were at a minimum. December in particular was designated for this work [42, 64].

> Women got up at one or two in the morning and ground until dawn. It was very hard work and seldom did one woman attempt the job alone. The men got up at the same time to gather wood. The grinding sound carried to the neighbors, and the people sleeping on the floors would often be disturbed. They did not object to this, because this was the season (December) and the time for grinding, and they should be at work even if their men were not gathering wood [42].

Two women working from one or two o'clock until dawn produced enough meal to fill a twenty-pound lard bucket. Surplus beyond immediate needs was stored in large pottery ollas and the openings sealed with adobe [19].

On other occasions four to six unmarried girls would gather at a home early in the evening, and a number of young men, both married and unmarried, would join them. The men sang as the girls ground corn. Older men might also join the singers. Some of the songs were standard; others were composed on the spot. "The songs often had words which would make the girls laugh" [42]. As the evening progressed, food was prepared by the family, and there was feasting and social interchange until late at night or early morning [19, 29].

Stone mortars and pestles were also used for grinding. These were relatively small and produced by abrading and chipping [14, 23, 36]. They were used for grinding herbs [14] and jerky [23, 36]. One informant [36] claimed to have owned a mortar and pestle "years back."

Backrooms and upper-story rooms, as noted, were used for storage purposes if not otherwise occupied. These were often stacked with pots, parfleches, buffalo and cowhide storage bags, baskets, and, more recently, modern containers like boxes and trunks in which food, personal effects, tools, ceremonial equipment, and any materials not required regularly or in the near future were kept.

Many storage rooms had shelving. Before lumber became available, however, these and other rooms were equipped with poles suspended horizontally from the vigas by rawhide thongs. Clothing and other materials were hung over the poles. Shelves were similarly suspended from the ceiling. These consisted of poles or split poles placed side by side and held in place by crosspieces at either end. These were lashed to the poles with rawhide [36, 64].

All rooms were equipped with wooden pegs and hooks conveniently located for hanging. Depending on the room these might be for everyday use or storage.

Cradles were of two types; both operated as swings and were suspended horizontally from the vigas by four lengths of rawhide or rope. Some near relative made the cradle, usually the father or a grandfather [45].

One type consisted of a flat board covered by a sheepskin or other convenient material. A shaped stick of wood was attached, transversely, to the cradleboard near the bases of the canopy frame elements. Holes were drilled through the board for the thongs. Four holes, two pairs, were also drilled on each side of the cradleboard for the wrappings and to secure the baby. The hood foundation was formed of three withes [45]; four were used according to another [5]. These were covered with a cloth. The withes were bent in semicircular form, then loosely tied together at their bases, and attached on either side near the upper end of the board. A buckskin thong ran from the top to the foot of the cradle, and was tied at the top of the arc of each withe in turn, leaving a space of about six inches between withes. This kept the hood foundation spread out—a better frame for the covering cloth. When not in use the cloth was removed, the bottom end of the thong was untied, and the foundation was collapsed and pushed back at the head of the cradle [5].

The second type of swing cradle was elliptical in shape, the head being somewhat wider than the foot. A willow or cottonwood branch approximately an inch in diameter and slightly over six feet long was secured, and the bark removed. This was heated over the fire and bent in the shape of an ellipse. Next the two ends were beveled, fitted together, and tied with a buckskin thong. Transverse and longitudinal rawhide thongs were strung across this frame at intervals of about three inches. Thongs were secured at the edges and knotted at their intersections. A cloth pad was placed on the cradle on which the baby rested [52].

Swing cradles of both types were still in use by some families as late as 1941 (see Plate 14). (Dennis and Dennis [1940: 107–15] in their paper "Cradles and Cradling Practices of the Pueblo Indians," have presented a detailed study of this topic with data from various pueblos.)

Pottery

Until recent times most household utensils were pottery vessels. During the historic period the principal pottery types were a culinary ware of unpainted micaceous clay, and polished black and red wares produced in recent years primarily for sale to tourists.

There is little evidence that decorated, whether painted or polychrome, pottery was ever made in quantity until relatively recent times. According to Jeançon (1904–30) a few Santa Clara potters had made a ware with a white or cream colored slip and polychrome decoration, but had discontinued it prior to the turn of the century. A contemporary informant [11] indicated that some of the stepped-edge polychrome vessels used ceremonially were made by female affiliates of the pondjo oke society. This presumably applied to the members of other societies as well. T.S. Dozier, in his pamphlet *About Indian Pottery* (n.d.: 8–9), stated

Of late years [circa 1906 or before WWH], Santa Clara women are making a decorated ware, using aniline dyes. Now these garish things should not be tolerated; for the decorations are put on to please often even after the pieces have been baked; the figures will not fade, but they can be easily rubbed off. No one should buy a piece of pottery decorated by the San Juan or Santa Clara Indians.

Apparently this represented a short-lived commercial experiment by these potters.

In more recent years, however, Santa Clara potterymaking has become an important commercial enterprise. When it was formerly produced mostly for utilitarian purposes, it was entirely the preoccupation of women. Since demands for the tourist trade have increased, a few men have been making it, and others have assisted their wives. It has represented in many families a joint effort, and no stigma was attached to males who participated. "Earlier there was one man who made pottery figures. He was thought to be somewhat queer at the time" [11]. This vocational change has had repercussions in the general area of economics, and also in the status of women.

Every family formerly made pottery, though not in great quantity. Jeançon (1904–30) indicated that it continued to be used for domestic purposes until about 1870. Earlier several types of clay were used. Two of these, a bluish-white (grey) and a reddish, were available in Santa Clara Canyon and were particularly prevalent in the vicinity of the "amphitheater." A third type, micaceous, was derived from the Chimayo Valley. Some villagers journeyed to the sites; others obtained it from neighboring Spanish-Americans who came to the pueblo to trade [11].

Few descriptions of Santa Clara pottery making have been found. The most comprehensive is a four-page leaflet by Jeançon (1931a), entitled "Santa Clara and San Juan Pottery." It contains most of the material in his field notes between 1904 and 1908. Short descriptions were also provided by James Stevenson (1883: 330–31) and T.S. Dozier *(About Indian Pottery)*. The latter is a brochure published in 1906 or earlier, containing a general description of pottery making presumably based on Santa Clara, with which he was most familiar. It also contains specific references to several other pueblos. [These remarks should be somewhat revised in view of the more detailed study, *Santa Clara Pottery Today,* by Betty LeFree, that was published in 1975. CHL]

Pottery clays formerly occurred near Santa Clara Pueblo, but the beds were covered through flood action and Santa

Clara potters subsequently obtained it from the Picurís Indians. This clay was used in making cooking wares. During the period of the fieldwork, only the reddish clay was being utilized [51].

Clay was selected on the basis of its purity, i.e., freedom from foreign material. If the resulting pottery was good, the potter returned to the same area for another supply. Until recently women secured the clay; at present men sometimes assist. According to Jeançon (1904–30)

> The gathering of clay and sand was often an excuse for a sort of picnic. More often than not several families would combine their efforts, or a group of friends would get together, or several women cronies would join in a party. All of them would start early in the morning, taking food for the noon meal. The babies, if there were any, would be bedded down on shawls and blankets with one of the children, or an old man or woman, to keep an eye on them. The women would scatter and search for the best deposits; the men would saunter off to gather medicine herbs, sticks for arrows or bows, bright stones, or sit in the shade of a tree and meditate. Perhaps the man had brought a shoe to be mended, or a piece of broken harness that needed attention or some other light task...
>
> The noon meal is an occasion of mirth and joking. Should there be a girl in the party who is being courted by some boy, she is teased at great length, sometimes this becomes so personal as to be embarrassing, but it is all done in the spirit of fun and without any malice. A short rest followed after the meal, and then the work was resumed. Very often yellow ochre beds, kaolin or white earth beds, are in the same neighborhood as the clay and sand beds, and when this is the case all these are gathered at the same time...When sufficient material of all kinds had been gathered the party returned (in their wagons) to the village.

Formerly clay was dug from the beds with stone or hand-wrought iron axes; more recently with picks. It was carried to the village in the women's loosely woven cotton shawls. More modern forms of transport have now replaced this older method.

While pottery making was not rationalized in the mythology, clay was referred to as "mother clay." "It was believed to have soul or deity" [51]. For this reason gathering it involved ritual. (Jeançon [1904–30], however, stated that while he accompanied many clay-gathering parties, he saw no ritual. [It may be that it occurred out of his view and hence escaped his attention. CHL]) Sacred meal was always scattered over the site. "You must treat the clay right; if you do, it will treat you right" [51]. Illness was believed to result if the proscriptions in gathering were ignored. Curiously if the pottery cracked during drying or firing, this mishap was attributed to technical ineptitude rather than ritual breach.

Some potters practiced geophagy while making pottery. "They form the habit when they are making pottery and can not break it. When they smell the odor of clay, they want some. One woman would go out to get clay just to satisfy this desire. She had a desire for this as a child" [51].

Pottery was sand tempered. Tempering material was available in Santa Clara Canyon, along the Rio Grande, and in the vicinity of both Chamita and Pojoaque Pueblo. Material from the Pojoaque site was said to produce a pot with a smoother finish and a higher polish than ordinary temper. During his residence, according to Jeançon (1904–30), a few of the older women still used sherd temper.

When the clay was first dug it was often damp, and on arrival in the village was placed on the rooftop until thoroughly dry. Then it was put on a large flat rock and pounded and ground until reduced to dust. Discarded manos and metates were often used for this purpose. Any foreign material was removed during this process. According to Jeançon (1931a), it was also sifted. When reduced to an even texture, the clay was placed in a container, water poured over it, and it was allowed to soak overnight.

In the meantime the tempering material was placed in a sack and pounded. According to Jeançon (1931a), it was first washed and dried on a cloth. After being pounded it was sifted to ensure a uniform consistency. Before the introduction of modern forms, horsehair sieves were used. They consisted of a split-oak, circular frame and horsehair mesh.

The following morning the soaked clay was placed on the inside of a sheepskin or cloth, dry tempering material was added, and the two materials kneaded together with the fingers and palms of the hands. The amount of tempering material was not measured; the potter knew from experience when the clay had reached the right consistency. Jeançon (1931a) estimated two parts of clay to one of sand. Water was added as needed. In past years a coarser temper was used, and less moisture was required. Since the introduction of Pojoaque temper, coils have been made from clay about the consistency of heavy cake batter. When large amounts of clay were prepared, it was kneaded with the feet. Men have recently performed this operation. Again experience determined the amount of clay prepared. The potter knew the approximate quantity needed to produce a given number of pots. Any surplus clay was stored for future use.

The first step in the construction of a pot was molding the base. Each potter possessed a set of saucer-like base forms. These were of pottery and of varying sizes and shapes to meet the requirements for all the standard pottery types. Those for water jars had welled bottoms. Many of these form sets were old, having been passed down within the family for generations. Those used by one informant [51] had belonged to her great-grandmother.

The potter took a lump of clay and by working it between the palms of the hands produced a sausage-like fillet for the first coil. Beginning clockwise or counterclockwise, as the operator preferred, the coil was placed on the lower inside of the base. It was pressed to the base with the thumb on the outside and the index, middle, and ring fingers on the inside. At the same time the coil was reduced to uniform thickness and width. The top of the coil was flattened to facilitate the attachment of the subsequent one. When this was completed the interior

and then the exterior were smoothed with a moistened piece of gourd to obliterate all joints and also to remove the thumb and finger marks.

The above process was repeated with subsequent coils until the pot was finished. If a coil was too short, a piece was spliced to the end. There was a correlation between the size of the pot and the width of the coil; the larger the pot, the greater the coil width [51].

When completed the pot was set aside to dry. Two stages of drying were involved. When it had dried sufficiently to be handled, it was removed from the base and again smoothed both inside and out. Following this it was allowed to dry thoroughly. If good weather prevailed, it was placed outside in the sun for two or three days. If not it remained in the house for a week.

When thoroughly dry it was scraped with an old knife, a piece of glass, or rubbed with coarse sandpaper (Jeançon 1931a). According to T.S. Dozier *(About Indian Pottery),* a piece of bone or sharp stone was formerly used to smooth the surface.

The pot was next slipped. Red ocher imported from Santo Domingo has been used for the slip in recent years. Potters formerly obtained this product in the vicinity of Santa Clara Pueblo. The vessel was moistened and the ocher was applied with a brush. Commercial brushes have been used for this in recent years. Before these were available, the base of a yucca leaf was chewed until it was frayed, and this utilized as a brush. Sometimes a rag was used to apply the slip. As many as ten coats were applied. "The potter knew from experience when she had enough" [51].

Following each application the vessel was polished with a stone. Polishing stones were of varying sizes and, like base forms, were passed down within the family. Earlier marrow was used in the polishing process; more recently, lard purchased at the store has been used. After polishing the pot was "warmed up" in the stove, formerly in the corner fireplace. Less attention was given to the finish and polish on utilitarian pieces than on those destined for commercial marketing.

Pots were fired in the open. The number fired at any one time obviously depended upon size; if large, only two; if medium in range, six to eight; if small pieces like ashtrays, a dozen or more. A bed of coals was first prepared. A piece of galvanized iron, often the end of a gasoline drum, a piece of tin, or a grid was placed on the coals. Flat rocks were formerly used. Dry kindling, usually cedar, was added and on top of this, burro dung. The pots were inverted on this base.

When red ware was desired, large chips of cow dung were piled around and over the pots. Sheep manure could also be used if large chunks were available in the corrals. More recently pine cones have been used for fuel or added to the dung. The coals were next fanned into flames, and firing began. Fuel was added from time to time if needed.

When pots turned a deep red, the chips were brushed aside, the pots pushed on their sides, and lifted from the fire with a length of iron. "If they were lifted from the fire with a pole, it would smudge the red ware" [51]. It took at least an hour with a hot fire to fire red ware. After firing pots were allowed to cool and then polished with a rag.

Black ware was fired in much the same manner as red with the following exceptions. Pulverized and often moistened cow dung was used for fuel instead of large chips. This created an oxidizing atmosphere. The black pottery was removed from the fire with a wooden pole. The firing period was longer, averaging between two and three hours. Red and black ware were occasionally fired at the same time. In these instances the red ware was removed when fired, and the remaining pots were covered with chips. Pulverized cow dung was poured over these, and the firing continued.

The current decorated forms of the old black and red polished ware began to be made about 1932-33. These embellishments were achieved by incising, painting, and by depressing the soft clay with the fingers. Many designs were old ones, transferred to this new medium; such designs included the bear paw, hand, cantaloupe, and horned serpent (avenu). Other designs were recent (Figures 2 and 3).

Designs created by indenting, or depressing, the clay were made as soon as the coiling and smoothing were completed and before

the pot was placed to dry. Incising was done after the pot had dried overnight.

Painted designs were applied after the pot was slipped and polished. A paint composed of grayish clay was used to draw figures on red pottery. The firing produced a tan design on a polished, red background. The paint used on black pottery was derived from Rocky Mountain beeweed. The plants were boiled until concentrated, "almost carbonized" [51]. "They were boiled until they reached the consistency of molasses, run through a sieve, and worked into a brick with the hands. This hardened like clay" [65]. A piece was broken off when needed and mixed with water. After firing the design element emerged in dull grayish-black on a lustrous black background. Paint was allowed to dry for an hour to an hour and a half before firing [51, 65]. Beeweed was also used formerly as a substitute for ink [65].

According to Jeançon (1904-30) the micaceous ware continued in use for cooking purposes until about 1880. However a few women were still making an occasional pot of this ware in the 1940s [64]. The construction of this type of pottery followed the general pattern of that described for black and red wares. The micaceous clay did not require the addition of temper, however. According to informants [11, 13] this clay was "stronger" and kept its form better during the coiling process. For the same reason pots of the material were constructed of coarser paste, and the walls were thinner. Accordingly they dried more rapidly than other wares. Comments by Jeançon (1904-30) do not agree with the above. He stated that, "This pottery was not only carelessly made but it was friable, easily broken and seemingly disintegrated with continued use." [This was not confirmed by my own observations. WWH]

When dried the pots were smoothed both inside and out with a wet corncob. They were then fired for about one hour. This produced a yellow ware; if overfired, reddish. These culinary wares were normally pinkish yellow before they became smudged from use in the open fire. Some potters rubbed piñon pitch on the pots immediately after firing. This was said to strengthen

Figure 2. Examples of pottery from Santa Clara Pueblo.

Figure 3. Examples of pottery from Santa Clara Pueblo.

them.

Pottery was assigned to one of five categories on the basis of its use: (1) cooking vessels; (2) storage pots; (3) culinary wares; (4) ceremonial vessels; (5) pottery destined for commercial purposes. Some overlaps occurred between various categories, as will be noted later. Some dozen standard forms were recognized among the three utilitarian divisions, although there was some deviation in shape and considerable variation in size within each form. Commercial wares were characterized by greater variability in form and constant innovation. (A monograph could and should be written dealing with the variations of Santa Clara pottery sizes and forms. This presentation touches on these problems only in the most general terms. WWH [As noted earlier considerable additional detail on Santa Clara pottery making appeared in the 1975 study by Le Free. CHL]) For some ideas of these formal and dimensional deviations, see the descriptions and figures in the papers by James Stevenson (1883a: 415–16) and (1883b: 443–49), and the illustrations in Jeançon (1931a).

There was very little variation in the micaceous cooking vessels (se' be) except in size. They were globular in shape with modified rims. They averaged between ten to fourteen inches in height and eight to ten in diameter. The size of the opening was also variable. Occasionally these so-called "bean pots" were equipped with handles.

The classical storage vessels were the "large round pots" (pom be fu?). They averaged thirty-two inches in height and slightly less in diameter. According to Jeançon (1931a) larger examples of these were as much as four feet in height and diameter; T.S. Dozier (About Indian Pottery, p. 4) reported some having a capacity of twenty-five gallons. Openings were about ten inches in diameter, and rims were not pronounced. According to Jeançon (1931a) some were equipped with lids. Storage jars were usually black ware, occasionally red. They were used to store water, meal, flour, wheat, barley, corn, and bread. When flour was stored the opening was sealed with adobe; if bread, a basket was placed over the top [51].

Culinary wares included a wide variety of shapes and sizes. The term tub (natu) was applied to two somewhat different forms. One was a vessel averaging eight to ten inches in height and fourteen to eighteen inches in width. It had a pronounced shoulder and a large opening. Its primary use was for the temporary storage of meal, although it was also used for kneading dough and washing clothes. The other type, often alluded to as a "dough-making tub," was of the same dimensions, either with slight shoulders or without them, and more bowl-like in form. Nests of these were among the early items traded to Spanish-Americans. Both groups used them for mixing dough and washing clothes. Both types were polished black ware [51].

The "flared plates" were basket-like bowls with flattened rims. They were made in both red and black. They averaged about seven and a half inches in depth and fifteen in diameter, although dimensions were variable. They were predominantly used as food containers, especially for dry foods. Shallower forms were used to dry meal after the preliminary grinding. They were also used for popping corn. Tempering sand was placed in the bottom of the bowl. This heated rapidly and made the corn pop quickly [70].

The term "soup bowl" was applied to two different forms of black ware. The first averaged fourteen inches in height and twelve in diameter. It was globular in shape, with a pronounced shoulder and a rounded, incurving rim. It was primarily used in the home as a container for semiliquid foods such as stews and mushes [51].

The dimensions of the second type averaged fourteen by fourteen inches. It had a narrower base than the first and a straight neck, but also a pronounced shoulder. It was equipped with handles. A rawhide thong was tied to the handles for purposes of transport; it was used to carry semiliquid foods to the field [51].

"Water jars" averaged fifteen inches in height and ten inches in diameter. The sides and shoulders were rounded. The neck was approximately one-third of the length and terminated in a lip. Formerly the bottoms were welled so that they could conveniently be carried on the head, both to and from the river or creek. Water jars were produced in both polished black and red [51].

Pottery of this type without the welled bottom and reduced in size has recently been made for the tourist trade. The necks were often ornamented, and the designs drawn or pressed in by the fingers while the clay was still wet [51].

There were several types of pottery designated categorically or in part for ceremonial use. One of these was the so-called wedding vase, "branched or two-necked bowl." It was normally rather small, about seven inches in height and five in width. The base portion was globular. From it extended two opposing spouts which terminated in lips. The inner sides of the spouts were joined by a handle. These pots were produced in both polished black and red [51].

The use of these vessels for ritual purposes was probably greater than indicated by the data. According to Jeançon (1904-30) the bride and groom drank from one of these during a part of the marriage ceremony. Also according to him, at the induction rites of an oyike, this principal was presented with one of these jars containing water from the four sacred lakes. They were also occasionally carried by "pour-water-on-the-head old woman," one of the savadjo characters (see Chapter 10).

Another ceremonial container was stirrup shaped. This consisted of two globular bases with long necks extending upward, joining, and terminating in one short-rimmed spout. The bases were joined just above the bottoms by a strip. Jugs of this type averaged about ten inches in height. They were either red or black in color. They were used by "pour-water-on-the-head-old-woman" and presumably enjoyed greater ritual use in former times. Both this and the wedding-vase type have recently been made for commercial purposes, where they have been popular forms [51].

A third ritual container consisted of two small bowls, approximately four inches high and three wide, joined at the bases by a three-inch strip. A handle extended upward in an arch. They occurred in both polished red and black ware. Some houses lacked

wall niches in which sacred meal was stored. In these instances, vessels of this type were used for meal. They also have recently been made available for sale to tourists [51].

Stepped-edged polychrome ceremonial bowls were known to have been used on the altars of the Winter and Bear Societies (see Chapter 10), and were undoubtedly used by other esoteric groups as well. James Stevenson (1883b: 446-47) illustrated a bowl of this type and another probable ceremonial container. While some polychrome ware for ritual purposes was made [51], most was acquired from outside sources. Jeançon (1904-30) indicated that the bulk of it came from San Ildefonso Pueblo; cream-colored wares with red and black designs were produced there for this purpose. No description of the construction of terraced ceremonial containers, either round or rectangular, was available from Santa Clara informants.

After pottery became important commercially, many utilitarian and ceremonial wares that were on the verge of obsolescence began to be produced for sale. The instances of the water and stirrup-shaped jars were mentioned above. Tub forms, semiliquid food containers, and a great variety of bowls, often reduced in size, were likewise popular pieces [51].

In addition new styles were created. One was the "lamp bowl." These were made in either polished red or black. They were about ten inches in height, with a long neck. The bowl-like bodies were incised. Other similarly ornamental forms included bowl-like vessels, about six by six inches with four-inch openings.

Many small, frequently exotic, pieces were also produced; these included a great variety of ashtrays and figurines. The latter depicted a wide range of zoomorphic figures [51]. Stubbs (1950: 46) wrote, "... the commonest pieces now seen for sale in the pueblo are the little animal figures of polished black pottery—horses, cows, pigs, alligators, skunks, and birds."

While pottery vessels were the most common container form numerically, other forms existed. These included stone and wooden bowls, baskets, parfleches, and gourds.

Stone Containers

Stone bowls were rare. However a few families made and used them as food containers. They were produced by pecking and abrading with hard-textured stones [44]. The slight use of stone mortars and pestles has already been commented upon.

Wooden Containers

Wooden vessels were more numerous. Most were basin or bowl shaped. The interiors were formed by burning and chipping. The wood was charred with hot coals, and the charcoal then removed with chert scrapers. This process was repeated until the desired shape was achieved. The exteriors were fashioned with a knife, axe, or rough stone.

Large bowls were used for kneading dough or for water storage. In the latter case the interior was coated with pitch. Small bowls averaging six to eight inches in diameter and four inches deep were used for food. Holes were often bored in the rim and a string inserted so that they could be hung on the wall when not in use. One informant [64] still had one of these bowls that had belonged to his mother.

Basketry

Baskets were used for both utilitarian and ceremonial purposes. With few exceptions, however, they were imported from other tribes. One older informant [65] stated that he had never seen a basket made in the village, and that they were all obtained from the Hopi, Apache, or Navajo. All available evidence indicates that the art had been obsolete for a considerable period. The craft seems never to have been a flourishing one, and only those baskets needed for local consumption were produced [64].

According to Jeançon (1904–30),

Basket making was also unknown excepting a large open weave basket, the technique of which was learned from Mexican neighbors. This is a recent thing and no one at Santa Clara does this work. There is an old man at San Juan who weaves this type of basket. [These baskets were often used for washing grain. CHL]

Because of the above factors, descriptions of the processes of basket making are fragmentary. According to one informant [68] they were made by men; according to another [64] women did the coiled, and men, the twilled and wicker, or twined-wicker work. The production of pitch-coated baskets for carrying water, "canteens," as made by various Apaches and Utes, was specifically denied [30, 64].

Several variations of the coiling process were practiced. In one a bundle foundation was used. Bundles were of dry grass about an inch in diameter. The stitching was widely spaced and the weft passed over the upper bundle and then through the center of the lower bundle. [A portion of a basket of this type was found in a deserted home and examined. WWH]

Circular coiled-basket trays were also made. These ranged from six inches to two and one-half feet in diameter and from three to five inches in depth. Either two or three rod foundations were used. Rods were usually of willow, occasionally sumac. When rods were joined the ends were tapered to produce a perfect junction [30, 64]. The weft element was sumac. The new spring growth was preferred, as it was more pliable. "Now you have to get them in the hills; formerly they grew along the river" [64]. After the materials were gathered, they were placed on the roof to dry.

When the weaver was ready to work, the sumac was buried in moist earth until it became flexible. Next the withes were split into two or three lengths. Each length was scraped with a piece of chert until reduced to the thickness of rawhide. The sewing was then begun, aided by a bone awl. One basket of this type, alleged to have been made at Santa Clara, had a chevron finish and an inconsistent split-coil stitch [30].

Awls were made of deer bone or antler [27]. Antler was generally considered too porous, however, and was used only for hafting iron tools. It was boiled until soft, when the end of the tool was inserted in the horn. Bones of the forelegs, especially the ulna, were preferred for awls. They were shaped by rubbing on sandstone. The preliminary work was accomplished by a rough stone; a finer textured one was used for finishing. Those used for basket making were about the size of a pencil. "You have to resharpen them, and they finally wear out" [65].

Most baskets of the tray type were ornamented with a geometric design, usually black and red. This was achieved by introducing dyed weft elements. Black dyes were derived from Rocky Mountain beeweed, and red, from the root of an unidentified plant, possibly dock or sorrel. The weft elements were boiled in solutions prepared from these plants. One popular design was a stepped line representing mountains. Another was stepped but composed of alternating squares of red and black. This denoted cloud flowers [64].

Basket trays served a variety of purposes. They were used as bread and meal containers, "one basket would be used for each kind of bread" [64]. They were employed for winnowing wheat. Formerly women carried them on their heads to transport goods from one place to another. They were also used in a ceremonial capacity as containers for ritual items, sacred meal, and food. They were utilized as sounding boards for the musical rasps, and were carried by participants in the Basket Dances [55, 64].

In recent years all twilled yucca baskets have been imported from Jemez. The last person known to have made them at Santa Clara Pueblo was Toribio Ortiz, who died during the middle 1940s. He had not made any for many years before his death. According to descriptions the technique was the same as employed at Jemez (see Williamson 1937a or 1937b).

Yucca baskets were used as bread and meal containers. Wheat was placed in them after winnowing and washed, and the remaining chaff that floated to the top was skimmed off. Occasionally these baskets were used for washing clothes. They were also used as measuring units in trading. "Ortiz made them the same size for this purpose" [64].

Wicker baskets were made from willow. Weft elements were inserted over and under alternating warps, or a simple twine technique was employed. New warps were added as the body of the basket was enlarged. When the basket was completed, the ends of the warps were bent over the last weft and inserted downward between the alternating wefts. Each succeeding warp was bent so that it served to keep the preceding one in place [40, 64].

Baskets of this type were used for storage purposes and for transporting food to men in the fields. This type of basket and the technique were said to have been borrowed from the Spanish [40, 64].

Parfleches

Parfleches were made for use in transport and also storage. The most common form was a large, rawhide sack. These were made from cowhide, formerly buffalo hide. The hides were trimmed, moistened to make them flexible, folded once, and the edges sewn together on the bottom and side. They were then filled with sand or earth and allowed to dry. When dry the contents were removed, and the rigid rawhide retained its shape. These were used for storing commodities and personal effects, for transporting adobe, as noted, and other materials, and for carrying breadstuffs to the Plains area for trade [44, 64, 68].

Cylindrical forms were also made. They were manufactured in the same manner as described above. These were equipped with buckskin covers secured by two buckskin hinges and a tie. They were used to store ground and pounded jerky [44].

Smaller rawhide envelopes were made of parfleche for the storage of personal effects, such as papers. A rectangular piece of hide was cut with a flap at one end. The piece was folded longitudinally to the base of the flap and sewn along the sides. The flap was secured with a buckskin tie [68].

A variant of this envelope had a top which was fitted or telescoped over the base [68]. A specimen of this type observed in the Peabody Museum, Harvard University, had a thong attached to the top of the base at the sides and running through the upper corners of the top, serving as a handle.

So far as could be ascertained, parfleches were not decorated at Santa Clara Pueblo.

Canteens and Ladles

Unusually large gourds, some two feet in length, were saved, dried, small openings cut in the tops or ends, and the insides cleaned out. These gourds were covered with rawhide, or in lieu of this, a cord or buckskin netting. A thong was attached for a handle. The opening was closed with a wooden plug, corncob, or piece of cloth. These gourds served as water containers and as canteens on trips [44, 64].

Ladles were also made from gourds, usually by men, rarely by women. The larger ones were used as dippers and for drinking; the smaller, for eating. Several small holes were punched longitudinally in the dry gourd, slightly above the midpoint along the body. This was accomplished either with a bone or iron awl. The top section was then removed with a knife and discarded. The edges of the lower section, the ladle, were smoothed. It was next soaked in a solution of "rock ash" (ku nu) to remove the bitter taste and also any fibers still adhering to the interior [12, 14].

Less frequently ladles were made of wood or horn. The technique employed in the production of wooden ladles was the same as that for wooden bowls [48, 64]. Buffalo or cow horns were boiled until soft and then cut and bent to ladle shape [65]. According to one informant [51] pottery ladles were never made. According to another [62] abalone shells were also used for drinking ladles.

Other Culinary Equipment

Much of the energy of women was devoted to the preparation of food. Some of the equipment used for converting raw materials, their storage, and cooking have already been described. There were a number of other specialized appliances, however, located in the kitchen and utilized in the cooking process. These included such items as pot rests, griddles, stirring sticks, pokers, grindstones, and knives.

Pot rests were of several types. One consisted of braided rings of corn husks or cloth. These were made by the women with three-ply braids. The bases of pots were placed in these to prevent them from tipping. Women also wore the rings on their heads for the same purpose when transporting water from the springs [51].

Stones, usually three, were used in the fireplaces to brace and stabilize pots during the cooking operation. A more modern version consisted of an iron tripod surmounted by a ring in which the pot rested. This had the further advantage of lifting the pot above the coals [62, 64].

Most kitchens were equipped with griddles (bu wa ku, "flat rock for making piki bread"). While these were primarily used for making blue-corn wafer-bread, they were also employed for cooking other foods. In one type the base of the griddle was stone, and the cooking surface, pottery. They were oval in shape and about two to two and one-half inches thick.

A "black rock," presumably volcanic and the approximate size of the griddle, was selected; the surface was smoothed with an old axe no longer fit for wood cutting. A smooth layer of pottery clay about the thickness of a finger was spread over the surface. This was allowed to dry and then slipped. When the slip dried it was given a high polish and then fired. Hard chunks of manure from the corrals were used for fuel. The firing period was twenty-four hours [25].

Another type of griddle lacked the pottery surface. Possibly this represented an earlier form. This type again consisted of an oval flat rock; a rock about one inch thick was selected and its surface smoothed. It was utilized in much the same manner as a frying pan [25].

Stirring sticks and pokers were usually made from oak, although any wood could serve. No particular care was taken in their manufacture. Stirring sticks were used singly, never in bunches. A stick was assigned to each container [62, 64]. Sharp pointed sticks served as forks for removing food from boiling grease or water.

A grindstone, usually a piece of sandstone, was conveniently located near the hearth for sharpening utensils [68]. While steel knives have been in use for many years, chipped stone knives were formerly used. These were unhafted. Knives were also made from mountain mahogany wood, or of deer, elk, or buffalo bone [27, 62]. This tool was a generalized one, employed also in various capacities outside the kitchen.

DRESS AND ADORNMENT

Most activities concerned with the production of clothing and ornaments took place in or near the home. Those associated with the processing of raw materials, previously discussed, were predominantly male occupations. Most sewing involving buckskin was done by men; that of textiles, by women.

Data on dress and adornment are meager except as they pertain to modern forms and materials. Traditional and semi-traditional items still existed, however, and were worn on formal and religious occasions. Most of these items were heirlooms, and the majority had been secured through trade from the Central and Western Pueblo tribes. Aboriginally men's clothing was made of dressed skin with only an occasional item woven from cotton. After the introduction of sheep and goats by the Spanish, wool replaced cotton as the principal textile source. With the establishment of the Santa Fe and the Denver and Rio Grande railroads in the 1880s, commercial clothing and materials became available throughout the area (see Douglas 1940: 175). From that time on the Santa Clara Indians began acquiring clothing from local sources or producing garments from commercially woven textiles. Items representing several eras were often combined in a person's attire, and earlier forms were frequently made from new materials. Modern forms have essentially superseded older types for everyday wear in recent years.

Men's Clothing

Formerly men's clothing consisted of a shirt, leggings, breechclout, belt, and moccasins. Robes or blankets were worn as the occasion demanded.

The common type of men's shirt (sergto, "man to cover") resembled those of the Plains and was made of dressed skin. This appears to have been standard for the area at the time of European contact. It was current in Oñate's time (Hammond and Rey 1953: 624, 645) and was still utilized for everyday wear by a few at the turn of the century (see Plates 14 and 15). They continue to be worn by some principals on ceremonial occasions, especially members of the chorus in outside dances. An older informant [68] stated that they had been worn as long as he could remember. The one he owned he made in 1925 from an elk hide given him by Frederic Douglas.

The most frequently used material was buckskin; however, dressed skins of mountain sheep, elk, antelope, and wildcat were also utilized [20, 23, 52]. At least two skins were necessary to produce a shirt. These were trimmed along the edges and sewn together along the sides and over the shoulders with sinew. A running stitch was used. The sleeves consisted of separate pieces and were fitted and sewn in the armholes [6, 14, 23]. Some shirts opened down the front; however, the majority were slipped on over the head [14].

The hair was not removed from shirts made of wildcat skin. Several hides were trimmed and sewn together. Such shirts were lined with buckskin, and during cold weather they were reversed and worn with the fur inside [20].

Shirts were ornamented in a variety of ways (see Plates 15 and 16). Many, though not all, were fringed around the armholes or along sleeve or shoulder seams. A separate piece forming a tippet was often added to the front. Formerly panels of porcupine quill embroidery, more recently of beading, were added to the shoulders and along the sleeves. Shirts were commonly dyed with yellow ocher or coloring derived from chamisa or rabbitbush blossoms. Designs were formerly painted on the front and back of the shirt in yellow, white, and turquoise [14].

Traditionally a few men's shirts were woven of cotton, later of wool. These appear never to have been numerous; they were poncho-like and without sleeves. Two woven panels were sewn together along the sides and over the shoulders, leaving openings for the head and arms [23]. Some were equipped with elbow-length sleeves; the sleeves were woven separately and attached to the arm holes [14]. Shirts of this type were never embroidered or brocaded [23].

A shirt with full-length sleeves, purportedly of the type woven at Santa Clara, was illustrated by Douglas (1939: 157–60).

Cotton shirts obtained from commercial sources or made from commercial materials were in common everyday use before the turn of the century (see Plates 15 and 16). The shirts made in the village were long-tailed and fitted at the sides. The collars were made separately and attached (Figure 4). While many shirts were white, others were made from figured, striped, or solid-colored material, depending upon individual prefer-

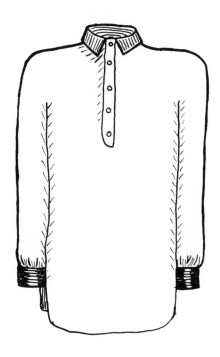

Figure 4. Men's shirt (serg to).

ences (see Plates 15, 16, and 17). Shirts were worn outside the leggings or trousers, with the tails hanging down [29, 52].

White cotton shirts of the above styles, but with ruffled fronts, were used on formal and ceremonial occasions. These shirts were usually secured through trade with the Keres, especially with Santo Domingo Pueblo [23].

Buckskin leggings (K'o) continued in everyday use until relatively recent times (see Plates 14, 15, and 16). One informant [13] stated that the standard costume until 1900 consisted of leggings, a cotton shirt, and breechclout, and that, for example, the grandfather of informant 72 was wearing leggings still in 1920. Another man [64] gave a vivid description of the difficulties he had putting on his first pair of trousers, as he had always worn leggings. Leggings have continued to be worn by some men during ceremonial occasions and at outside dances [23, 30, 61, 62].

Leggings were usually made from dressed deerskin [30, 52, 62], less frequently of mountain sheep, elk, and antelope hide [30]. They were full-length, extending from the hip to the ankle (Figure 5). Some were narrow and tight fitting (see Plates 15, 16, and 17); others were wide. Presumably this simply depended on the material available. One buckskin was used for each leg. Leggings were seamed on the outside with sinew, using a running stitch. A strap or strip extended under the instep, and they were

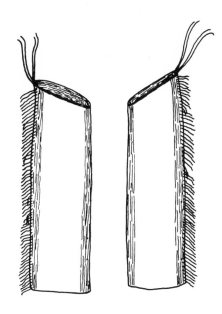

Figure 5. Men's leggings.

secured by thongs tied to the belt on the outside at the hip [30].

Most leggings were ornamented. Frequently they were dyed yellow, using a dye prepared from yellow ocher or chamisa blossoms [13]. The sides along the seam and bottoms of the legs were commonly fringed. In more recent years panels of porcupine embroidery or beadwork have been added to the sides (see Plates 15, 16, and 17) [30, 52, 62]. In those instances where leggings were undecorated, white clay was rubbed into the hide. This type was periodically cleaned by subsequent applications of white clay or tufa [30, 52].

A pair of Santa Clara leggings in the Peabody Museum, Harvard University, collected in 1912, was examined; there were beaded panels sewn to the outside of the legs and others encircling the leg near the bottoms. The designs were geometric. The lower portion of the legging sides was fringed, as were the sections above the bottoms of the legs. Between the beaded panels and the fringes there were several beaded flower-like designs. A series of circular openings had been cut immediately above the bottoms of the legs.

About the turn of the century, flannel began to be substituted for buckskin in the making of leggings. These were similar in pattern but much wider than the older forms (see Plates 15, 16, and 17). Like the older type they were ornamented with panels of porcupine quill embroidery or beadwork and, in more recent years, ribbon appliqué.

Knee-length leggings were made by both men and women and were worn by both sexes for additional warmth. In recent years they have been seen only at formal and ceremonial occasions. They were of two types. One was of white cotton knitted or crocheted in open-work pattern (see Douglas 1939: 157-60). Many were fringed, either up the front or on the side. A strap passed under the instep, and they were secured at the top by a woven tie or garter. A few of this type reached above the knee. An older informant [23] had made these.

The other type was solid and knitted from blue or black dyed woolen yarn. As in the case of the first type, they were equipped with an instep strap and secured by ties

below the knee [23].

Cotton trousers were formerly popular as a substitute for leggings. These, plus cotton shirts, with or without breechclouts, constituted the everyday costume—especially during the summer. This garment was in fact widely used by all tribes in the Southwest. While their ultimate derivation remains in some doubt, they are Spanish Colonial in style and were presumably adopted from that source. Those at Santa Clara Pueblo were loose fitting and slashed or open from below the knees down on the outside of the legs [44, 52]. Many were obtained from the Keres, particularly from Santo Domingo Pueblo [44].

Traditionally breechclouts (puzha Xwe, "to tie in between the root") were made of buckskin or woven from cotton or wool. More recently they have been made of commercial materials, cotton or flannel. They were placed between the legs and over the belt both in front and back. Cotton ones were for everyday wear, and as late as 1942 they were still worn by some of the older men in lieu of underwear [13]. The flannel ones, either red or dark blue, were saved for formal occasions, and were sometimes decorated with beads, panels, or edged with ribbon appliqué [14, 36, 52].

Men's belts were about four inches wide, and of buckskin [6, 14] or dressed buffalo hide [14]. Most were natural color, but some were dyed red, yellow, or turquoise. More recently they have been ornamented with quill embroidery or beadwork [6, 14]. A few men owned silver concho belts that they wore on formal occasions. Undoubtedly these had been derived from outside sources. Men also wore the women's type of woven belt. This however appeared to have been limited to individuals who were participants during ceremonials.

Men's moccasins consisted of four pieces: a vamp with tongue, two side pieces, and a sole (Figure 6). The uppers were of buckskin, the sole of rawhide, formerly of buffalo skin, more recently of cow or horsehide [13, 14, 64].

A section of rawhide was buried in moist earth overnight. The next morning it was removed, rolled up, placed on a log and beaten with a foot-long club to soften it. The

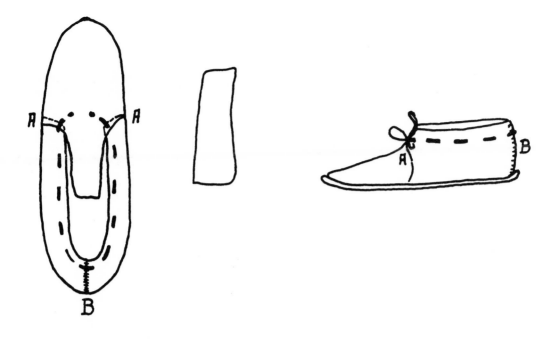

Figure 6. Men's moccasins.

hair was removed or not, depending upon the desire of the maker. To remove it the worker rubbed the hide with a rough stone or a piece of wood. Gravel was used as an abrasive. The foot was next placed on the sole, and it was cut to measure, leaving an excess of a quarter to one-half inch around the foot. The sole was then reburied in moist earth until needed.

Before attaching the upper elements, the sides of the sole were bent upward and puckered at the heel and toe area. The vamp was inserted inside and sewn. The side pieces were then secured to the sole and vamp. The side pieces were next sewn together at the heel. The uppers extended up to the ankle or slightly above. A drawstring, a buckskin thong, was inserted near the top and tied in front to secure the moccasin to the foot [13, 14].

Sewing was done with sinew, and several types of stitches were employed. The one most frequently used was a whip or overcast stitch. When a finer product was desired, the sewing element was passed through the sections of the upper but only partway through the interior of the sole near the upper edge

and pulled tight. In this way the stitching was not visible from the outside. In a less frequently used type, the sewing element was double and pushed through the sole and upper from the outside. A sinew thread was then inserted in the loops formed by this operation to secure the elements (Figure 7) [13, 14].

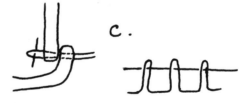

Figure 7. Sinew stitching for men's moccasins.

Moccasins worn on formal occasions were often ornamented with porcupine quill or bead embroidery. Sometimes the decorative elements completely covered the moccasin; usually, however, they were limited to the area of the instep and junction of the sole and upper [20, 23].

It is doubtful whether the Santa Clara ever made snowshoes, per se. One informant

[27] denied it. Another [30] however stated that four pieces of oak, the length of the moccasin, laid parallel and held together by strips of hide passing over and under the elements, were sometimes tied to the moccasins. "You did not sink into the snow with these sticks."

Men's robes and blankets served a variety of purposes and were made from a variety of materials. They were worn for warmth, used as bedding, and occasionally as rugs. When not in use for these purposes, they were rolled up or folded and placed along the walls to sit on. Traditionally they were woven of cotton, later of wool, or made from hides, or, more recently, of flannel. There is no record of men's woven robes being produced in recent years. Those that existed were obtained through trade with Pueblo or Navajo sources and were predominantly Navajo in provenience. One such, a Navajo "chief" blanket, was illustrated in a Hillers photograph of 1880 (Plate 18). Pueblo-woven men's robes were plain, not ornamented with brocade or embroidery.

Hide robes were made from the dressed skins of buffalo, mountain lion, deer, bear, and rabbit. Buffalo robes were formerly quite common. Some were secured through trade from Plains tribes; others were made by Santa Clara from skins obtained during their own periodic hunts. The halves of the hides were first dressed. As described under hunting, buffalo, when killed, normally fell forward on their bellies. Incisions were then made along the back and the hide and meat removed from each side. When dressed, the two sections of hide were sewn back together. There is evidence of this procedure in two Chicago Natural History Museum [Field Museum CHL] photographs (Plates 19 and 20).

The interior surfaces of buffalo robes were usually painted. Designs were variable. Some were geometric after the types in vogue in the Plains (see Plates 19 and 20; also Plates 21 and 22). Naturalistic representations were also common, and included figures of deer, buffalo, horses, birds, bows and arrows, the sun, the moon, and stars. Symbolic representations including clouds and lightning were similarly utilized [14, 20,

44]. Panels of porcupine quill embroidery were also used for decoration [20, 44]. Buckskin robes were ornamented in the same manner as those made from buffalo hide. Bearskin robes consisted of two hides, but no other details were uncovered. Two skins were also necessary to make a robe of mountain lion skin. These were trimmed along the edges and sewn together with sinew. They were considered prestige items. "They lent distinction to the man who owned them" [20]. When not worn they were sometimes placed over the saddle as an ornament.

Rabbitskin blankets or robes were made from a number of hides which were dressed, trimmed, and then sewn together. The existence of woven rabbitskin blankets at Santa Clara was denied [14, 35].

In recent times the older types of robes have been replaced by flannel ones of the familiar Plains type, or by the "Pendleton" blanket. Flannel ones were usually dark blue. They were frequently ornamented with panels of beadwork and the edges were bound with ribbon. Sometimes the binding was scalloped.

Vests were also worn for additional warmth in lieu of robes. The derivation of this trait is uncertain. Tailored men's suits were extant in the village before the turn of the century, and they may have come from this source (see Plates 15 and 16). It is also possible that they were borrowed as a result of contacts with the Plains. Some worn on formal occasions were ornamented with typical Plains beadwork; regardless of their source, their popularity was evidenced by their frequent occurrence in early photographs.

Men's types of headgear were made from a variety of dressed skins including elk, buffalo, deer, beaver, fox, wildcat, otter, and skunk [15, 27, 36, 64]. Various kinds of headgear were utilized only in conjunction with warfare [15]. However other informants [27, 36, 64] indicated that they were worn both on formal and informal occasions, though particularly during ceremonials.

In their simplest form, they were merely fillets. On others a crown or occasionally a bill of the same or other material was added (Figure 8). Often feathers, feather rosettes, and other decorative items were included,

Figure 8. War cap assemblage, with crown and bill.

frequently creating a bizarre effect (see Plate 23). Simple fillets were usually made of dressed beaver or otter skin or dyed buckskin [6, 14, 44]. More elaborate forms were constructed from the cased hides of beaver and fox, or halves of skunk hide. The skins were placed around the head, fitted, and sewn together at the back. The head, tail, and legs were allowed to hang down the back for added decorative effect [14]. Fox-skin hats of this type frequently served a dual purpose. The stitching was removed and the hides suspended from the belts of dancers during ceremonies. Wildcat-skin hats, lined with buckskin, were used in cold weather. They were reversible and equipped with ear flaps [30].

The Santa Clara Indians also wore eagle feather headdresses on formal and ceremonial occasions. These were undoubtedly copied from those in the Plains, but without the significance attributed to them in that area. There was no reflection of coup counting or similar honors at Santa Clara. A skull-cap of two sections of buffalo hide formed the base, and the feathers were attached to this and to a panel down the back [14]. Strips of weasel, rabbit, or squirrel skin were suspended from the crown for additional ornamentation.

Most headgear were held in place by thongs tied under the chin.

During the last fifty years, these earlier forms of headdress have largely disappeared. They have been replaced by hats of various styles or handkerchiefs and headbands obtained from commercial sources.

Women's Clothing

During the Spanish Colonial Period (Hammond and Rey 1953: 626, 645) the standard items of women's clothing in the Tewa area were the *manta,* hip-length buckskin leggings, buffalo hide moccasins worn with the hair inside, and blankets worn around the shoulders. These last items were described as ornamented with mask or face-like designs. With the exception of the hip-length leggings, these styles have persisted at Santa Clara into the twentieth century, although the materials used in their production have changed.

The cotton or wool *manta* (se *zh*a mu′a) was a woven rectangle, blue-black or black in color. This was folded and stitched or laced up the right side and over the right shoulder, leaving an opening for the right arm. The garment was worn over the right shoulder and under the left arm (Figure 9). Initially it was of cotton, and later, after the introduction of livestock, of wool. It has continued to be used for formal and ceremonial occasions. However none has been woven at Santa Clara Pueblo since about 1890. Those that have survived are heirlooms or have been secured through trade with the Western Pueblos. A daughter usually inherited the manta of her mother unless the mother was a society member, in which case she was buried in it.

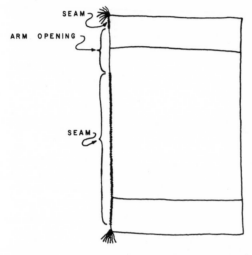

Figure 9. Women's manta, cotton or woolen.

Historic specimens in museum collections were often ornamented with brocade or embroidery at the bottom or top, or at both the top and bottom (see Plate 24). Frequently the edges were also embroidered and tassels added at the corners.

A specimen in the Southwest Museum (see Plate 24), collected at Santa Clara, but possibly of Hopi origin, was three and a half feet in length. The weft was native material. It was embroidered at the top and bottom with green and red Germantown yarn. The edges were ornamented with an embroidered running, spiral design, and there were red tassels at the four corners. The right side was sewn together with yellow yarn, and there was a lacing of the same material at the right shoulder.

With the introduction of commercial fabrics about 1870, mantas began to be made from these materials. While the style remained the same, they were designated *nu a* to distinguish them from the earlier forms woven from cotton and wool. Flannel or cotton, more recently some silk for dance costumes, was purchased at nearby stores, and by the turn of the century garments of these materials had become the standard everyday dress in the village. Commenting on this period Jeançon [1904–30] said, "Most women make their own calico dresses and shawls from materials purchased at the stores."

Some of these mantas were of solid color; others, particularly of cotton, were of figured materials. Bands of contrasting color were frequently sewn around the bottom [13, 18].

Modern mantas were worn over a one-piece dress, or a blouse, or blouse and underskirt. These were of cotton. Dresses were of solid colors or figured materials. Women's blouses (kwi to) were usually white although some used figured materials. Usually an old blouse was used as a pattern. In general they resembled the shirts of the men except in the following details: they were gathered about the collar and cuffs, had more buttons than men's shirts, and were not fitted at the sides (Figure 10). As

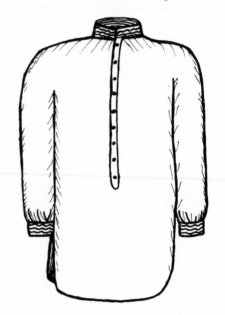

Figure 10. Women's blouse (kwi to).

mentioned they were worn under the manta, often with an underskirt. In this latter case the tails were tucked inside the underskirt. Underskirts were modern in design. Those for ceremonial occasions frequently had lace sewn around the bottom. This edge came just below the manta for deocrative purposes.

There is no account in the more recent historical sources of women wearing full-length buckskin leggings as mentioned in accounts of the Colonial Period. Some of the principals, however, on ceremonial occasions, wore the knee-length knitted or crocheted types worn by men.

Belts (b a? a), woven of cotton or wool, were worn with all the above costumes. They were still being made until recently. Those for everyday use were red and blue. Those worn on formal occasions were woven in a variety of colors and geometric designs [14, 30, 52] (see also Douglas 1939: 160; Aitken 1949: 37). Narrow and shorter versions of the belts served as garters to secure knitted and crocheted leggings and also as hair ties.

The earliest type of women's moccasin in the area was described as being made of buffalo hide with the hair inside (Hammond and Rey 1953: 645). More recently other styles have been in vogue. How old these were could not be ascertained, but it seems safe to assume that they have considerable antiquity.

Moccasin soles were of rawhide. Buffalo hide was formerly used; more recently, cow or horsehide. Uppers were of buckskin; less frequently of dressed antelope skin [13, 20].

The type of moccasin used most frequently for everyday wear by the women consisted of two pieces, a sole and upper (Figure 11). The sole was prepared in the same manner as those for men. The exterior was usually dyed black. The upper was sewn to the sole with sinew, normally employing a whip or overcast stitch, although the variants used on men's moccasins were also utilized. After the upper was attached to the sole it was seamed up the back (Figure 12). If the area over the toe or instep did not fit properly, a separate piece was inserted to correct this discrepancy. Similarly, if the upper lacked sufficient height, a section was added. The top of the moccasin was secured with a thong; the area around the ankle, with a drawstring, as noted previously [13, 14].

There were two pairs of moccasins of this type in the collections of the Museum of New Mexico, Santa Fe, acquired in 1949 (see Plates 25 and 26). Both pairs had sections added to the top to increase their height. They were equipped with thongs to secure the tops and with drawstrings to secure the ankle areas. Both had panels of beadwork added to the backs, starting at the heels; the designs were geometric. One pair (specimen 24525/12) had blue and black

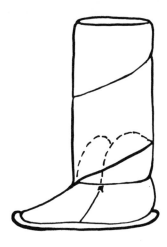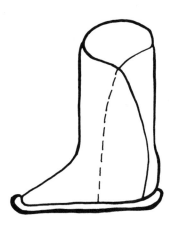

Figure 11. Women's two-piece moccasins.

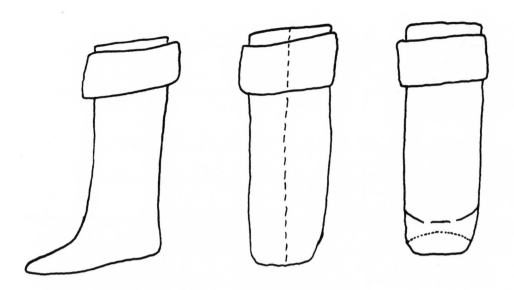

Figure 12. Women's moccasins: variant type.

beads on a white background; the other pair (specimen 36583/12), two shades of blue and red on a white background.

Another style of women's moccasin was also two-piece, but was short-topped. In this form the upper was sewn to the sole, and the ends were overlapped on the outside, where they were secured with a buckskin tie or button. This type was sometimes also worn by men in the Buffalo or Deer Dances [61].

A final type was the familiar Pueblo, wrapped form. This was usually reserved for formal occasions. It normally consisted of four pieces: sole, a two-piece upper sewn together at the sides, and the wrap. Half a buckskin was used for each wrap. Usually one end was attached at about ankle height, midway on the outside of the upper. Less frequently it was actually a separate piece. Occasionally the wrap formed the upper as well, reducing the moccasin to two pieces. The wrap was secured by a buckskin tie at the top [61]. Moccasins were cleaned with tufa [13, 14].

Women's woven woolen blankets were variously designated as blankets, robes, and shawls. None has been produced at Santa Clara since before the turn of the century. Informants described these late historic types as like mantas but smaller in size, bluish or black in color, and without orna-

mentation (see Plate 23). They were worn over the shoulder, or tied in front. According to one of the oldest informants [78], a few were made in poncho form.

Douglas (1939: 160) illustrated and attributed a striped woolen blanket to this era. He also stated that maiden shawls (white with red and blue stripes) and embroidered shawls were made of imported cotton. The latter type were worn during ceremonies as mantas, and were covered by shawls made of commercial silk.

In recent years a variety of commercial products has become increasingly common. These included shawls designated by their Spanish term, and the ubiquitous Pendleton blanket [13, 18]. Inferentially, dressed skin robes were also utilized by women.

There are no descriptions of women's headgear. Presumably if the occasion demanded, they covered their heads with a blanket or shawl. The only exception to this was an eye shade and head protection used when working in the hot sun. A slender cottonwood twig, with the leaves on it, was selected. A circle was formed and the remainder of the twig wound around itself. Similar twigs were added in the same manner, creating a kind of bird's nest. "The wider the covering the better the leaves protected the wearer from the sun" [51].

Children's Clothing

Infants were wrapped in blankets as long as they remained in the cradle. Once they began to toddle about, the amount of clothing depended upon weather conditions. On warm summer days they wore no clothing at all or only abbreviated shirts. At about the age of eight they were dressed in breechclouts as well. Shortly after this age, they assumed adult-style clothing appropriate to their sex.

Children went barefoot most of the time, but moccasins were available when needed [18, 19]. One child's pair in the Peabody Museum, collected in 1912, was a three-piece type (Plates 25 and 26). It consisted of a sole, vamp with tongue, and heel section. The flap of the heel section extended around the outside and was tied on the side. A drawstring secured the moccasin at the ankle.

Personal Adornment

A multiplicity of ornaments and jewelry existed at Santa Clara Pueblo. This was worn on formal and ceremonial occasions, and much of it was considered ceremonial paraphernalia. It included necklaces of coral, turquoise, shell, silver, and commercial beads; beaded and hide collars and yokes; hide and beaded fillets; turquoise and silver earrings; silver rings, bracelets, and concho belts.

There is little evidence that the type of craftsmanship necessary for production of these items ever flourished at Santa Clara Pueblo, at least in recent years. Many were heirlooms and the majority, according to informants, were derived through trade.

Formerly turquoise earrings and beads of turquoise, coral, and shell were made in the pueblo [27, 30]. Both informants were familiar with the pumpdrill (mi mi fe be, "boring stick") used for this purpose. The pumpdrill was equipped with a chert drill point [14]; according to another [64] the tip was of metal. An example of this type of drill from Santa Clara Pueblo was found in the collections of the Museum of New Mexico (specimen 26040/12); the drill point, however, was missing (see Plate 27).

Two informants [44, 64] denied that sil-versmithing was ever practiced at Santa Clara. According to Adair (1945: 187–88), however,

> Silversmithing goes back to the 1880s at Santa Clara. At that time a Mexican *platero,* who had been living near San Ildefonso, where he made silver for the members of that pueblo, came up to Santa Clara. Three men of that village picked up the art from him, and they made silver jewelry up to the turn of the century, when the art seems to have died out in the pueblo. There are three younger men, brothers, who work at the art today [1940, WWH]. They picked up a knowledge of silversmithing from their Navajo brother-in-law.

Skin Dressing

Skin dressing at Santa Clara Pueblo conformed in most respects to the general pattern found throughout North America. The dressing was done by men. Hides utilized included those of deer, antelope, elk, mountain sheep, mountain lion, bear, buffalo, wildcat, wolf, fox, weasel, beaver, skunk, otter, and rabbit.

Deer, antelope, and elk were the principal sources of buckskin. The hide was first soaked in water. It was then placed around two poles and tied at one side. A wringing stick was then inserted in the loop formed between the two poles and twisted to wring out as much moisture as possible. After this one portion of the hide was placed over the end of a beaming pole, and the top of the pole was leaned against a wall or fence. The operator then began to dehair the skin with a beaming tool, shifting the hide as the occasion demanded. If rough or resistant spots were encountered, they were rubbed with tufa or a sandstone rubbing stone to soften them. Any meat or fat adhering to the inside of the hide was also removed at this time (Figure 13).

Beaming was always done at some distance from the home, since the hair was thought to be potentially dangerous to women and children. In winter a warm place in the corral was selected for work; in summer any suitable location was used.

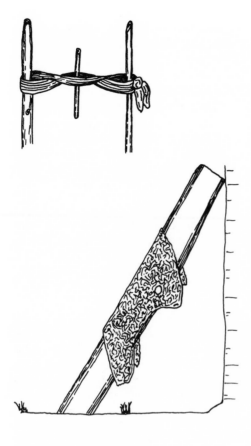

Figure 13. Skin dressing.

The elbow-handled type was made from either bone or antler. The blades were either beveled or serrated. Frequently however, a chert, obsidian, chalcedony, or, recently, a metal blade was lashed to the handle. This produced a superior implement. One example in the Laboratory of Anthropology (Nat Stern Collection), Santa Fe, was of elk horn, ten and a quarter inches long, with a chalcedony blade secured to the handle with rawhide (Plates 28 and 29).

The beamer, operated on spokeshave principle, was made from a rib or a foreleg bone. The angles of the bones were sharpened or intensified to produce a better cutting or scraping edge. With the introduction of metal tools some men used scythe blades. Recently modern spokeshaves have been employed [44, 61, 64].

Depending upon the thickness of the hide, the beaming process consumed from two hours to half a day. When dehaired the hide was allowed to dry thoroughly. When it was dry, brains were rubbed into the outer surface. "The brain goes into the hide more smoothly if the hide is dry" [61]. "After this the pelt was put in the sun to dry, for three to five days" [64].

Following this the skin dresser soaked the hide in water, wrung it out, and began to work it with his hands and stretch it to soften it. This process, depending upon the thickness of the hide, might be repeated two to four times before the desired result was achieved and the buckskin was finished. It was never smoked as a part of the curing process [61, 64].

Not all hides were dehaired as a part of the dressing process. Specifically mentioned in this regard were buffalo, bear, mountain lion, wildcat, fox, beaver, weasel, and rabbit [61]. In many cases these skins were destined for use as robes, ornamentation, or ceremonial purposes, and the dressing process varied from that used in the production of buckskin.

One informant [79] gave a detailed description of the preparation of a mountain lion skin that he had used to make a quiver (Plate 30). While not specifically confirmed in other instances it can be assumed that this account represents a general pattern.

When the hide was brought into the

After the hair was removed it was gathered and deposited in the river or on top of a ridge.

Several types of beaming tools existed. One was end-bladed, another had an elbow handle and was operated like a small hoe, a third like a drawknife or spokeshave. These were made of deer or elk antler or bone. Formerly the bones of buffalo, elk, or deer were used; later those of domesticated animals were included. Bones included the ulna, radius, scapula, and rib [44, 61, 64]. In recent years metal tools have been added to the inventory.

The cutting or scraping surface of the end-bladed tool was either beveled or serrated. Bone and antler tools of this type deteriorated rapidly [64]. In recent years a metal blade with a wooden haft has been substituted.

home, it was first stretched. This was accomplished by placing it against the wall and driving pegs into the adobe to hold it in place. It was allowed to dry in this position for about four days.

Next the skin was removed and buried in damp earth to soften it. After this it was placed on a beaming pole, and any traces of fat or meat were removed with a beaming tool. Following this tufa was rubbed on the interior of the hide "to smooth it." "No brains were applied" [64]. The dresser then began to manipulate the skin with his hands to soften it. This was continued periodically whenever there was leisure time. If hard spots were encountered, they were softened with a rubbing stone. "It would take about a week to complete the job" [64].

Another variant was described for the treatment of buffalo hide destined for use as moccasin soles, thongs, or ties. When still in the field the hides were cut in long strips. These were rolled on sections of wood and allowed to dry in that position; a section of the appropriate length was cut and the hair removed whenever needed. It was then pounded with a rock or club to soften it, or occasionally rubbed with grease or brains.

Goatskins were accorded no special treatment. They were merely soaked in water, rinsed, and then worked with the hands until pliable [61].

Weaving

Historical sources indicate that weaving was a well-established craft prior to arrival of Europeans in the Tewa area. During the early Spanish Colonial regime, woven mantas and blankets were among the principal items of tribute demanded by the conquerors. According to Oñate (Hammond and Rey 1953: 630), a quota of two thousand was set for the province. Whether this ever materialized is very doubtful. Reaction soon mounted against this unreasonable requirement and other forms of oppression, however, and there is evidence that the Rio Grande pueblos essentially ceased weaving thereafter. Jeançon (1904–30) believed that weaving was not done to any extent after the arrival of the Spanish. This seems an accurate assumption, since later references

to the craft in the area are, at best, sporadic.

Data on weaving derived from Santa Clara informants is accordingly scanty. The final obsolescence of the craft began in 1870, with the completion of the railroads and the introduction of commercial fabrics. Jeançon (1904–30) stated that,

Twenty years ago (circa 1870) one might find, here and there, in a Tewa village, a belt weaver. Such a man was Aniceto Swazo of Santa Clara. He also understood weaving the ceremonial kilts but as far as is known he did not attempt to weave blankets. His belts, the broad ones worn by women, were very well done. He learned the art from an old man while he was still a young man but did not make use of it.

Essentially this was confirmed by elderly informants. According to one [65] a few men were still weaving when he was a small boy (circa 1870). "It was hard work and only a few wove." Another [64] stated that he remembered a man named Xavier who used to weave mantas. Another informant [71] said that José Pelado (deceased) formerly wove mantas; "He got his ideas from San Juan and several Santa Clara began weaving." According to still another [62], this activity constituted a revival of the old art. He did however say that mantas and kilts were formerly woven. As of 1941 there was no one alive who knew how to weave mantas [68]. There was general agreement that most of the traditional forms of clothing and ceremonial costumes extant in the village were secured through trade from the Central and Western pueblos during the last hundred years.

A fragmentary description of the loom and its accessories was obtained. Weaving was done by men during the winter months. Looms, "manta makers," were located in the kivas, or rooms reserved for ceremonial purposes, or a specially designated room in a house. Women and children were prohibited from entering these areas [44].

The loom was suspended from a beam lashed to the vigas of the room, and the bottom was secured to the floor by a series of pegs. Loom bars were located at the top and bottom. A second bar was placed above the upper loom bar for the purpose of regulating tension. The warp was wound around from top to bottom, not crossed at the center. Two shed rods, "manta sticks," were used. These were not tied to the warp, but were simply inserted between alternate strands. A small stick, or bobbin, "manta string weaver," was used to complete the last six inches of the blanket, when it became difficult to operate the shed rods. A loom baton, "manta to hit," was used to tamp down the weft. The weaving area averaged a little more than four feet in width. The products were coarser and more loosely woven than those produced by the Navajo [44].

While the above description is sketchy, it appears that the Santa Clara loom conformed to that used at Zuñi (see Spier 1924: 66–69). An upright loom similar to those of the Navajo was occasionally utilized. However no details on their construction could be learned [71].

Hand-carved, wooden combs were used for carding wool [64, 65]; when carded, wool was spun on a spindle equipped with a whorl [61, 62]. Spindles were about sixteen inches in length; the whorl, four and one-half inches in diameter [65]. Spinning was accomplished by twirling the spindle along the thigh; it was usually done by men, although occasionally women helped [62].

Belt weaving persisted until recent times. It was mentioned that Juan J. Gutierrez and Cándido Tafoya had both woven belts, and that a Santa Clara woman, formerly married to a Jemez Indian, had learned from her husband.

Cándido Tafoya was still weaving in 1913, and Barbara Aitken (1949: 37) published a short, illustrated account of his activities.

At Santa Clara, New Mexico, a Tewa man (Cándido Tafoya) was weaving women's waistbands on a circular horizontal warp running from a miniature beam pegged to the floor to another which was attached to a strap passing around his waist; the weaver sat on his heels on the floor and wove with stick-and-string pseudo-heddles and alternat-

ing rod, supplemented by selection with his fingers (see Plate Ee, f, and fig. 1)...

It was stated that one end of the belt-loom work was hooked over the end of a viga, and the operator sat on the other end. He said that the loom arrangement was similar to that at Hopi and Santo Domingo [65]. Another [62] believed that there were still (1941) men in the village capable of weaving women's belts of either wool or cotton. According to several [18, 27, 52], cotton hairties were also woven on the belt loom.

Embroidery

Information on embroidery is meager. Formerly it was done by both men and women and applied to mantas and kilts. It presumably disappeared with the cessation of weaving. What may have been a partial revival of the art was noted by Jeançon (1904–30) shortly after the turn of the century (circa 1906). According to him, "School girls are making some embroidery with colored yarns on coarse commercial cotton fabrics. This has been taught them in the schools they attend."

Porcupine quill embroidery was used to ornament many items of men's clothing. These included robes, moccasins, buckskin shirts and leggings, and skunk-skin anklets.

This work was done by men, and two techniques were employed. In one the point of the quill was removed, and the quill threaded on sinew. The quill was then flattened and held in place by stitching it to the buckskin with the sinew thread. In the second type the point of the quill was pushed through the buckskin from the inside leaving a segment of the butt projecting. It was then flattened on the surface and the point passed through to the inside where the butt and point were secured with sinew (Figure 14) [23, 27, 30].

Dyeing

There is little evidence of native dyes being used in recent years. Formerly buckskin shirts and leggings were often dyed yellow. Yellow ocher [61, 62, 64, 68], chamisa blossoms and some other plant [61], or

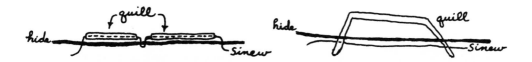

Figure 14. Sinew stitching with quill work.

crushed blossoms of the rabbitbrush (Jeançon 1904–30) were boiled to produce the color.

Red was derived from a plant called chung fe [65], or mock orange [64]. It was used for dyeing moccasins or wool.

The root of a plant was used to produce green. The informant [65] could not remember its name. He said it was secured at some distance from Santa Clara, some of it from as far away as the Hopi territory. A purplish dye was made from lichens [61]. Black was derived from the Rocky Mountain bee plant. Boiling water was added to it, and wool was dipped in this solution [64; Jeançon 1904–30].

Sewing

As mentioned previously, most sewing involving buckskin was done by men; that involving textiles, by women. A few women made moccasins, but this was unusual.

Formerly the principal sewing implement was the bone or antler awl, which also was used in basket weaving. Bones of the forelegs of deer were preferred and thought to be strongest. Rib bones were used but were less desirable. Sections were split from the bone or antler and the point sharpened by rubbing on a rough stone. The broad end functioned as a haft. Recently metal-pointed awls with wooden hafts have been utilized [61, 64].

Needles were also used. One type consisted of a slender awl with a hole bored at one end to form the eye [64]; another was made from quills from the feathers of large birds [62]; a third, from porcupine quills. In this last type the butt of the quill was bent back on itself to form the eye [65].

Jeançon (1904–30), commenting on the period immediately after the turn of the century, stated that, "Now and then one sees a sewing machine but they are not plentiful. The girls and younger women who have learned to use these at schools are the only ones who sew on them."

Sinew was formerly the principal material used in sewing. That from deer was preferred, as it was said to produce the finest thread. Next in popularity was sinew from buffalo and cattle. It was taken from the back of the animals and dried. When needed, two or three strands were removed and rolled on the thigh to produce the thread. In lieu of this, buckskin thongs or yarn might be used [64].

Men's Hairdress

Men's hairdress has varied considerably through time and according to individual preference and the demands of the specific occasion. Formerly the front was banged at eyebrow level, the sides bobbed at shoulder length, and the back left long and arranged in a club, secured with a woven wool or cotton hair-tie or a piece of cordage. This was the "typical Pueblo style" [27]. Cutting was done with a piece of chert or other type of stone [27]. Some men wore their hair long, parted in the middle, and allowed it to hang loose (Plate 31); others tied it at the sides with hanks of yarn (Plate 18). These styles appear to have prevailed in everyday, informal situations.

According to several [27, 52, 61], after contacts increased with Plains tribes, particularly the Comanche, the Plains type of hairdress became common. The hair was parted down the middle and three-ply braids arranged on either side (Plates 15, 16, and 17). On formal occasions it was customary to wrap the braids with strips of hide with the fur on, strips of flannel, or, more recently, ribbons. Weasel and beaver skins were preferred [61, 65, 72]. When flannel and ribbons were used, the strips were frequently of different colors. These wraps were crossed in opposite directions, creating a diamond-shaped design. Normally the wrap completely covered the braid (see Plates 15, 16, 17, and 23). The chorus and drummers who took part in the outside dances usually dressed their hair in this manner [61, 72].

When engaged in work men often constrained their hair with a piece of cloth or a handkerchief, or at formal occasions with a piece of silk or a silk scarf, and more recently with a beaded fillet.

From the turn of the century, felt hats of sombrero type have come into vogue. As of the post-World War II period, almost all except the older men wear their hair cut short.

Women's Hairdress

Women's hair style appears to have remained unchanged until about 1930. About that time the younger members of the village began to adopt the prevailing styles current in the adjacent towns. Formerly the hair was banged at eyebrow length in front and bobbed level with the mouth on the sides. The remainder of the hair was left long. This was separated from the side hair by a transverse part, folded in a club, and secured with a tie woven of cotton or wool or a woolen cord [27, 29, 52].

General Hair Care

Both men and women used a brush for grooming the hair. This consisted of a loosely tied bundle of grass stems called "tassel grass," or "broom grass," ta fe ni [27, 51, 52]. Marrow or fat from buffalo or cattle was rubbed in the hair. These products derived from deer were never used "because the strength they contained would cause the hair to turn grey" [27].

Both sexes washed their hair frequently. Since hair washing was prerequisite to ceremonial participation, it assumed an added importance as one of several preliminary rites of purification.

Yucca root was used as soap. Large unblemished plants were selected, dug up,

and the leaves removed. "If you brought the leaves in and they got near water, you would have them sprouting from your head" [51]. The roots were usually dried on the roof-tops. When needed they were first placed on a flat rock and pounded with a stone. Next they were put in a container of warm water and stirred until suds about eight inches in depth were produced. The roots were then removed and hair was washed in the "washing bowl" (na t u n). Then it was rinsed in clear, cold water and dried in the sun [50, 51, 52, 62, 73]. "There is a saying that washing the hair in yucca strengthens it and prevents it from falling out" [51]. Formerly commercial soaps were never used for washing hair [69].

Men customarily plucked their beards and eyebrows. Earlier this was accomplished with the fingernails; now tweezers are used. Body hair was not removed [62].

Both sexes appeared to have bathed rather frequently, weather and available water permitting. There were no specially designated places for this purpose. Santa Clara Creek, the Rio Grande, and, in summer, irrigation ditches were used. Cold water was always utilized. Neither yucca nor commercial soaps were used on the body. The latter were believed to cause the skin to wrinkle.

Women usually bathed in the middle of the day, men in the early morning or early evening. Boys were encouraged to bathe frequently, especially in the winter, as it was believed that this strengthened them and tested their fortitude. Frequent baths were also taken prior to Saint John's Day in June. This saint was believed to have placed "medicine" in the streams, and it was thought that benefits could be derived from this source [69].

As in the case with hair washing, bathing was intimately associated with religion. All the principals in any ceremony purified themselves by bathing prior to the rite. This was repeated at the termination of the ceremony. It was obligatory that they remove paint as well as paraphernalia before returning to their homes. For example kachina impersonators went to the river to wash at the end of their performance [43, 73].

AGRICULTURAL IMPLEMENTS

Digging Sticks

Aboriginal planting was accomplished by means of a digging stick. The widespread use of this implement seems to have continued into the middle of the nineteenth century, when it was finally superseded by the plow and hoe. As of the 1940s the digging stick survived solely in connection with the cultivation of tobacco and chili, or as an adjunct to gathering.

Digging sticks were manufactured from hardwood, preferably oak. Their average length was about three feet; their diameter varied with the personal preference of the maker. Two varieties were in vogue, one with a beveled spatulate blade, the other with a simple point. Formerly stone knives and abrasion were employed to shape the tool. The finished product was placed in hot coals to dry and harden. This increased not only the life of the implement, but also its efficiency.

Digging sticks were often equipped with foot rests. When this was the case, a tree limb was selected with a branch located near, and more or less at a right angle to, the distal section. This increased the effectiveness of the tool and lessened the labor involved, as the implement could be propelled into the soil by placing the foot on the projection. A digging stick with a side notch on which to rest the foot was also described by one informant [6]. Judging from the absence of reported occurrences of this type from other Southwestern groups, however, it seems likely that it was an innovation inspired by familiarity with the modern shovel or spade [23, 27, 36, 68].

Plows

The introduction of the plow at Santa Clara Pueblo was coincidental with the advent of draft animals. While the crude wooden Spanish plow barely scratched the surface of the ground and was no more effective than the digging stick, it was more efficient in that it lessened the amount of time and labor necessary to prepare the field, and allowed larger acreages to be brought under cultivation.

The body of the plow was constructed of oak, cottonwood, or piñon; the share was always of oak. If possible a tree was selected that had a branch projecting from the trunk at approximately a forty-five degree angle. The tree was cut and the trunk furnished with what corresponded to the moldboard of the modern plow; the branch was used as the handle. If no tree was available with a branch at the desired angle, a hole was bored in the "moldboard" and a handle inserted. The beam was a single piece of wood about two and a half to three inches in diameter. It was affixed to the handle and "moldboard" as follows: a hole was bored partway through the base of the handle, and the butt of the beam was fitted into this. Then holes were bored through the beam, about two feet from the butt, and through the "moldboard" near the center of its length, and the two parts were fastened. Occasionally the beam and "moldboard" were merely tied together with rawhide, but this was not as satisfactory as the above type of bracing. The oak share was fitted to the end of the "moldboard" and secured with hide. Customarily hide wrappings were used to reinforce all parts of the plow. They were applied after moistening and allowed to dry. The contraction during drying assured a tight binding. This material deteriorated quickly with use, however, particularly the share binding, which was subjected to the greatest strain and wear. For this reason, workers always carried a supply for replacement.

Two methods of hitching the plow to oxen were employed. In one method the end of the beam was bored transversely, and a section of wood about six feet long was run through the hole and secured with hide. The ends of this were then tied to the horns of the oxen. This was the earliest method. Later, neck yokes were made. These were cut to fit the animal and held in place by a U-shaped piece of wood which passed under the neck and through holes in the yoke. The beam was attached to a rawhide loop tied to a groove at the center of the yoke.

Some oxen were trained to respond to commands; others necessitated an extra workman, who led them or prodded them with a stick when he desired them to turn on the furrow. When work was completed the plow was reversed end for end on the yoke and dragged home on its beam [23, 36, 62].

Hoes

Hoes, "weed cutters," were of two principal types. Both were made of fire-hardened oak. The first and presumably the older, was a sword-like implement about three feet long and three inches wide. It was made from a single piece of wood shaped by abrasion with stone, and later with iron tools. The cutting edge was beveled (Figure 15B). The worker knelt and removed the weeds with a swinging, sidearm motion. Presumably this was aboriginal. A mace-like tool of this type was mentioned in the Oñate report (Hammond and Rey 1953: 660). A modification of this was a shorter type which resembled an axe, and was probably suggested by the modern implement (Figure 15C). It was used in the same manner as the first, and was also employed in cutting wheat and barley.

The second variety of hoe was shaped like a straight-handled shovel, with a blade eight to twelve inches wide. It was manufactured in the same way as the first. Both the front and sides were beveled, and it was pushed ahead of the worker as well as swung to the side. It is possible that this form was suggested by the shoulder-blade hoe, which was also in use. Shoulder-blade hoes were made by attaching the scapula of an elk or buffalo to a wooden handle. The shoulder blade was in a vertical plane with the handle, joined and secured by a rawhide wrap (Figure 15D) [6, 14, 27, 44].

The modern iron hoe was in use in the pueblo at least seventy years ago. One informant [68] claimed that the angled shoulder-blade hoes were patterned after the iron type. Presumably he was in error, since small hoes were mentioned in the Oñate report (Hammond and Rey 1953: 660).

Rakes

Rakes were usually made of juniper. A limb was selected which terminated in several branches. This was cut and the branches trimmed evenly to form the teeth. No set number of prongs was necessary— the usual number was three or four (Figure 15E). In order that they present an even dragging plane, they were heated over a fire, bent to a common level, and tied in position to dry. Once cooled the cordage was removed, and the wood held its shape.

Rakes were used for breaking clods in the fields and gardens, removing weeds, and gathering straw. In the first case it was customary to place a rock or some heavy object at the fork of the branches. This added weight facilitated the leveling process.

In more recent times a wooden rake of modern design was made. This consisted of a series of wooden teeth placed between two blocks of wood and lashed in place with rawhide. A handle was then secured, its length varying with the size of the user [23, 36, 68].

Forks

Forks were a comparatively recent innovation. They were made of the same materials and in the same manner as rakes, the tines being horizontal instead of at an angle to the handle (Figure 15E). Four tines were considered a minimum. Forks were used for removing weeds from the fields and for handling hay and straw [6, 14].

Drags

Logs were dragged over plowed fields in lieu of harrows to break the clods and level the soil [27, 44].

Sickles

Sickles patterned after the European type were formerly made of oak. The blades were beveled to produce a cutting edge [23]. As long as another informant could remember, the Santa Clara possessed saw-toothed iron-bladed sickles. Both were used in harvesting wheat and barley. Scythes were employed for the same purpose. There were no data available on the date of their introduction [20].

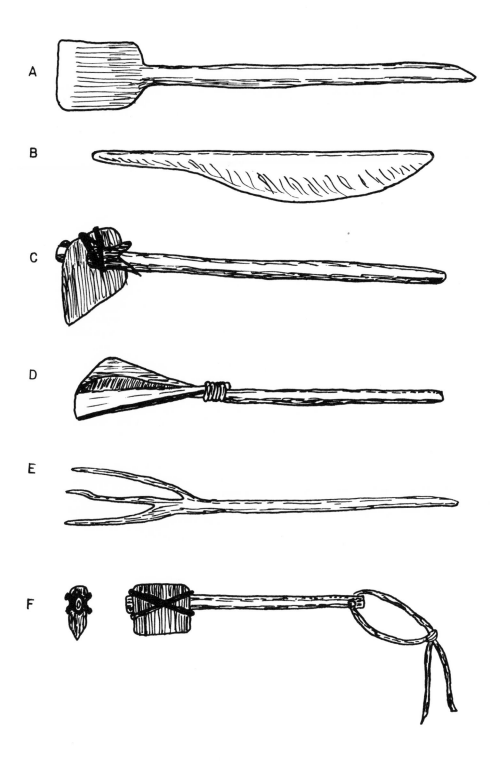

Figure 15. Agricultural implements of wood, bone, and stone (pre-metal): A. Straight shovel, or spade, of wood; B. "Sword" hoe of wood; C. Hoe with blade of wood, bone, or stone; D. Scapula hoe; E. Wooden rake or fork; and F. Stone axe.

Cornhuskers

The cornhusker consisted of a wooden knife-like blade with a pointed end. A buckskin loop was tied near the butt end. The operator placed her thumb in the loop, forced the point into the husk, and ripped it open [29].

Flails

Threshing flails were made of cottonwood and occasionally of oak. Their average length was about six feet, with a diameter of two and one-half inches. With use the flail acquired a slight upturn at the end, which increased its striking surface and, coincidentally, its effectiveness [14, 25, 36].

Shovels

Shovels were made of fire-hardened oak. They were shaped with iron tools and presumably were post-Spanish. Their form was that of a straight-handled spade (Figure 15A). Shovels were used for planting and winnowing wheat, but more frequently for cleaning and digging ditches [23, 36, 62].

Wheat Cleaners

This implement was of Spanish derivation. It consisted of a handled wooden frame about three feet wide and five feet long. To this was affixed a perforated, rawhide bottom, later one of metal. An operator grasped the handles at each end and the cleaner was moved backward and forward. In this manner the wheat was sifted through the perforations, and the chaff was screened out [14, 52, 72].

HUNTING AND WAR EQUIPMENT

Bows

Self, sinew-backed, trussed, and elk-horn bows were known at Santa Clara Pueblo. Both straight and recurved forms were made. The simple bow was presumed by informants to be the oldest, the sinew-backed, the most prevalent, and the elk-horn bow, the most highly considered. According to one informant [50], the sinew-backed bow was introduced at Santa Clara by the Jicarilla Apache—the time was not known.

Self-bows were made of wood from the three-leaved sumac, black locust, osage orange (this imported), oak, and juniper. Straight-grained, mature wood was selected. It was cut during the fall to avoid the sap and thus facilitate the curing process. The bow was first roughly shaped and then carefully scraped to achieve the final, desired dimensions. In length, bows averaged from three to three and one-half feet, although some were four feet or more. Their width at the back and belly varied from an inch and a quarter to an inch and a half, diminishing toward the wing ends to three-quarters of an inch. The depth at the grip was an inch to an inch and a quarter, tapering toward the wing ends to five-eighths or one-quarter of an inch. The ends were notched to take the bowstring. Bows made for children were relatively smaller in all dimensions.

When shaped the bow was allowed to dry or cure for some time before using. Each day during this period it was strung and flexed several times. "This was to prevent it from breaking when it was used." Finally the bow was greased. If available, bear or mountain lion fat was used for this purpose. "The spirit of these animals enters the weapon. It is as if you had the power of these animals to fight and kill."

The preliminary steps in the construction of the sinew-backed bow were similar to those in the fabrication of the self-bow. Once shaped, however, it was placed on a flat piece of wood, and wooden cylinders were put under the wing areas. The bow was then tied to the board at the grip and tips of the wings, and allowed to cure and dry in this position. This produced the recurved form present in most sinew-backed bows and occasionally in self-bows.

The sinew backing, or lining, was affixed after the bow had set. Sinews, preferably those from the back, of deer, buffalo, and cattle were used. Those from deer and buffalo were considered best. Boiled pine pitch was used for glue.

The trussed bow was made in the same manner as the self-bow. Sinew trusses were usually applied and secured at four points [44].

In constructing an elk-horn bow, the horn was split, then boiled until pliable, and bent to the desired shape. When it had set a sinew backing was applied [62, 69].

Bowstrings

Bowstrings were of sinew. Formerly sinew from deer and buffalo was used; more recently that of cattle was utilized. The sinew was soaked until soft and the fibers separated. These were then rolled on the thigh to produce cordage. Bowstrings were of two or three-ply cord according to one [69], four to six-ply cord according to another [62]. The string was tied to the base of the bow at the notch, and a loop at the other end of the bowstring was slipped over and into the notch at the top of the bow. Bows were unstrung when not in use. "This gives the bow a rest" [62, 64, 69].

Bowguards

Bowguards were made of rawhide. They were about three inches in width and long enough to encircle the wrist with an overlap for tying. The guard was secured by a thong. In recent times ornamental guards of leather, decorated with silver and occasionally set stones, have been worn as bracelets only [62].

Arrows

Arrows were made from mountain mahogany, Apache plume, and cane. Apache plume was preferred. When manufacturing other than cane arrows, small branches of approximately the desired diameter and length were cut, and the bark was removed by scraping. These were tied in a bundle, placed above the fireplace hood against the chimney, and allowed to dry.

When entirely dry the shafts were sized and straightened. This was usually done with an arrow wrench (see Plate 32). Lack-

ing this the worker employed an arrow plane, known more commonly to archaeologists as an arrow straightener (see Plate 33), or used his hands and teeth.

The shafts were smoothed after straightening. Smoothing was formerly accomplished with a single or double arrow plane. In recent years the preliminary stages of this process were facilitated by employing a piece of perforated tin. Nails were driven through the tin until one side resembled a grater. This was wrapped about the shaft and worked back and forth to remove major protuberances before the final surfacing with the plane.

After the arrow was smoothed, incised markings were made the length of the shaft. These rills were either two or three in number and might be straight, zigzag, or both. This was done with any sharp implement. In recent times a knife or a sheet of tin with a nail driven through it was used. Formerly a portion of the shaft was painted in one or more of the "kachina colors": blue, north; yellow, west; red, south; white, east; black, down; varied colors, up. Ocher and other earth paints were used for coloring material. These were chewed with piñon gum and the resulting mixture rubbed on the shaft. "The reason that you put on the kachina colors was that the kachinas would help you in war or hunting. It was like putting animal fat on your bow. You would be afraid of nothing" [9].

The feathers of ducks, geese, herons, cranes, eagles, hawks, vultures, and turkeys were used for fletching. The outside portion of the quill was scraped; then the feather was split in half by pounding the inside of the quill with some heavy object. When a sufficient number of halves had been accumulated, they were placed on a board and cut to identical lengths and widths. Finally some material was removed from the upper and lower portions of the quill, and it was ready to fasten to the shaft. The quill was laid flat, parallel to the shaft, and held at the top and bottom by sinew wrapping. Three feathers were placed on each arrow; they were never spiraled.

Cane arrows were cut to size and equipped with a foreshaft. Their fletching was similar to that described above [62, 69].

Arrow Wrench

The arrow wrench (see Plate 32) was made of horn, preferably that of a female mountain sheep, although other types of horn were also used. Four to eight holes of varying sizes were bored to accommodate shafts of different diameters. Formerly a flint-pointed pump drill (mi ni fe, "boring stick") was used to make the holes. Recently perforations were made with a hot iron [62, 69].

Arrow Planes

The arrow plane (see Plate 33) was made from a small, flat stone. A straight, half-round groove was abraded in the center, the length of the stone. Arrow planes were usually used in pairs, a top and bottom [62, 69].

Arrowheads

Arrowheads of iron were in use for many years at Santa Clara Pueblo, and only a few of the older residents could recall having made and used stone points. Those who did agreed that obsidian was preferred and most easily worked. Pink and white flint points occurred, but the texture of this material made the manufacture of points difficult and uncertain. Pressure chipping was employed. Pressure was applied with a deer, antelope, or elkhorn flaking tool. A buckskin pad was held in the hand to protect the palm.

Wooden-pointed arrows were used in archery practice, and the arrows used in some games were tipped with corncobs. There was no development of specialized point forms for hunting birds or shooting fish, however.

Stone points which were found were kept and tied either to the bow or quiver—"this was done to protect the person from being struck by lightning" [50, 62, 68].

Quivers

Quivers were made from the skins of mountain lions, wildcats, or wolves. Mountain lion skins were considered most desirable, not only because of their size, but also because their ownership was a symbol of prestige. Certain individuals were known for their abilities as quiver makers, and these specialists were hired by less proficient workmen. Payment for services was usually made in flour or dressed skins.

After the skin was dressed, it was folded lengthwise and cut (Figure 16). Section A was utilized for the quiver proper. The tail end of the hide formed the mouth of the quiver. The tail was allowed to hang down at the back for ornamentation. A cup-shaped piece of rawhide was inserted in the bottom of the quiver, and a length of wood was

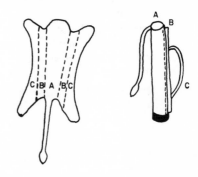

Figure 16. Construction of a mountain lion skin quiver; A. Quiver proper; BB. Bow case; and CC. Carrying strap.

placed along the inside of the seam. These kept the container extended, and prevented the mouth from folding over and obscuring the arrows. The stick also served both as a reinforcement for the assembled quiver and an anchor to which the bow case and carrying strap were lashed.

The bow case was constructed from sections B,B. They were measured to fit the bow which they would enclose. The carrying strap was made from sections C,C. One end was attached to the quiver and case, at a point a third of the length down from the top; the other end, a third of the length from the bottom. All sewing on the sides and bottoms of the quiver and case was done with sinew. A simple running stitch was used. Lashings which held the three elements of the quiver together were of buckskin, and the bottoms and tops of the quiver and bow case were fringed.

Several wildcat skins were necessary to make a quiver. They were pieced together to attain the requisite size. The same was sometimes done when wolf skins were used.

The completed quiver was rubbed with the fat of mountain lion or bear, to give the owner prowess in hunting and fishing. Arrowheads were tied to it as a protection against lightning and for luck in hunting. Formerly when a quiver was completed, it was blessed. This ceremony was presumably similar in basic ideology to that performed by members of one of the Bear Societies when a house was completed [62, 64, 69].

Quivers were carried on the back. The carrying strap passed over the left shoulder and under the right arm, if the individual was right handed (see Plate 30). When the weapon was needed, the quiver was pulled over the shoulder to a position in front of and at right angles to the man. The bow and an arrow were extracted, the quiver was pushed back to its former position, and the hunter was free to shoot. This was repeated each time an arrow was removed. While this procedure appears complicated and time-consuming, informants exhibited remarkable celerity in clearing themselves and getting into action.

In shooting the bow could be held in a vertical plane, horizontally, or transversely, at the preference of the archer [50, 62].

Lances

Lances were used occasionally for hunting buffalo (Figure 17). Some believed these had been taken over from the Spaniards [30, 40, 64]; however, others said they may have come from the Comanche [44, 65]. The heads were sometimes fashioned from bayonets obtained from soldiers [30].

The shaft was about six feet in length; the wood usually came from the Plains area; the iron points came most often from the Comanche who, in turn, obtained them from Mexico. A hole in the end of the shaft was made to receive the butt of the blade. This area was then wrapped with raw buffalo sinew, which tightened as it dried. Eagle feathers were often attached at the junction of shaft and blade. Blades were occasionally made from bone or antler [44, 65].

Firearms

The modern rifle and shotgun for all practical purposes have entirely replaced the bow and arrow in hunting in Santa Clara Pueblo. That this replacement process began some time ago is evidenced by the presence in the village of several smooth-bore, muzzle-loading rifles. These antiques have been relegated to the ceremonial category, and continue to be used in con-

Figure 17. Buffalo hunting on horseback with the lance.

junction with the Roman Catholic communion. One of the native church officials is stationed outside the door of the church; each time the host is elevated before the altar, this individual fires the gun.

Powder Containers

Powder horns were made from the horn of buffalo and cattle (see Plate 32). The core was first removed from the horn, which was then scraped, leaving a collar at a distance of three or four inches from the tip. The tip was then removed, and the hole at this end enlarged. A willow plug was carved and inserted in the opening. It was secured by a buckskin thong running through the stopper and tied below the collar on the horn. The base of the horn was plugged with a willow disk about an eighth of an inch thick. This was held in place by three thongs running through the plug and the disk. Two of the thongs were set close together, and acted as a hinge when the horn was opened for refilling; the third was opposite the other two, and functioned as a hasp. A staple was driven into the center of the disk for the attachment of one end of the carrying strap. The other end of the strap was tied at the collar. A small wooden measuring cup tied to the horn completed the equipment. The horn was worn at the right side, the carrying strap passing over the left shoulder and under the right arm.

Another type of container resembled a powder flask (see Plate 34). This was made of either cow or deer rawhide. It was stoppered by a willow plug, secured to the neck of the container by a strip of buckskin. These receptacles were occasionally used for tobacco as well as powder [64].

Slings

Slings were made of buckskin (Figure 18). They consisted of three pieces: A, the pocket which held the missile; and the strings, B and C. The string B was released when the missile was thrown; C was retained in the hand. A loop at the end of C was passed over the thumb to prevent its slipping [44, 64].

Clubs

Rabbit clubs (pu fe) were made of wild cherry, oak, or cedar. Clubs ranged from a flat, angled variety (Figure 19) to a knobbed, or ball-headed type. The latter were manu-

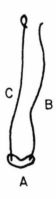

Figure 18. Sling, used primarily in hunting.

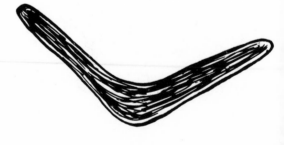

Figure 19. Rabbit club—flat, angled type.

factured from tree roots or from sections of wood which had a knot at one end. Clubs for women were of lighter weight than those used by men (Figure 20). About two feet in overall length, these weapons were thrown with a sidearm motion [30, 36, 52, 65].

Traps and Snares

Traps and snares were most frequently employed in the capture of birds, only secondarily in obtaining rabbits and other small game. Warblers, juncos, blackbirds, and bluebirds were the principal birds secured by this method.

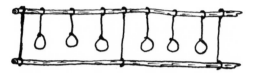

Figure 21. Warbler trap.

Warbler traps were hung in willows beside streams or the Rio Grande. To construct the trap, two twigs of equal length were tied together, one above the other and approximately four inches apart. Horsehair nooses were suspended from the upper stick and hung in the interval between the twigs (Figure 21). When the birds perched on the lower twig, they became entangled and were caught [65].

Juncos were trapped during the winter. These birds travel in flocks and are fond of congregating on patches of earth exposed by

Figure 20. Rabbit clubs with heads of wooden knots—female and male types (see also Plate 32, a,b).

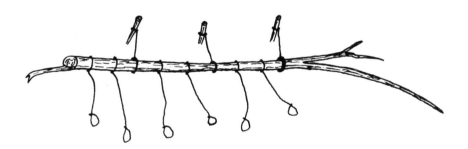

Figure 22. Junco trap.

melting snow. Snares were set at these locations. The trap consisted of a tree branch, on the ground, with horsehair nooses attached. The branch was anchored to stakes (Figure 22). "When one bird was caught, it acted as a decoy and brought others" [52].

A trap similar to that employed by the Navajo (see Franciscan Fathers 1910: 323; Hill 1938: 175) was used to capture bluebirds. Its mechanical aspects were much more ingenious than those of the foregoing types (Figure 23). A hollowed sunflower stalk (A) was the main element; perforations were made in it about two inches (B) and eighteen inches (C) from the top. The butt of a pliant twig (D) was placed in the lower hole and acted as the trap spring. A twisted horsehair terminating in a sliding loop was tied to the twig end and passed through the upper opening. The noose rested on the stalk's upper edge (E). Tension was sustained by a small piece of wood (F) tied just below the noose and set delicately across the stalk opening.

These traps were set in cornfields. When the bluebird alighted on the end of the stalk, its weight dislodged the stick (F); the spring tightened the noose about its leg and drew it into the stalk—securing the bird [52].

Cottontail rabbits were sometimes snared in noose traps. Two methods of setting the traps were used. In one the noose was placed flat in the mouth of a burrow and covered with leaves. Its end was anchored to a stake, log, or tree. When the animal entered or left the burrow, it became entangled.

The noose in the second type of trap was placed around the sides of the burrow and held by a twig (Figure 24). The twig was so placed that it would be dislocated by the entrance or exit of the animal, allowing the noose to encompass and catch the rabbit. This type of trap was also used to capture foxes [50, 52].

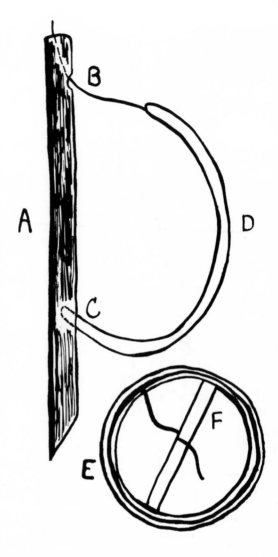

Figure 23. Bluebird trap.

Figure 24. Rabbit and fox trap.

FIGHTING EQUIPMENT

The weapons used in offensive warfare included bows and arrows, clubs, lances, and, in more recent times, firearms. With the exception of clubs, all weapons were of the same type and manufacture as those used in hunting. According to one informant [9], the points of war arrows were occasionally dipped in rattlesnake venom to make them more deadly. This statement, however, was not confirmed by other accounts.

War Clubs

War clubs were of two kinds. Both were rigid but the head of one was oval, or axe-shaped; the other was ball-headed. The head of the oval type was grooved. The haft consisted of the tail of a buffalo or cow, from which all but the terminal hair had been removed. In some cases several of the vertebrae were removed from the upper end of the tail; the remaining ones were allowed to dry, forming the handle; in others, all verte-brae were removed and replaced with a piece of wood to lend rigidity to the haft. In either case part of the hide at the upper end was cut away, leaving two flaps. These were fitted around the groove of the head and sewn together at the top of the club. The weapon was then allowed to dry, the shrinking that resulted from this process assuring that the head was firmly seated.

Ball-headed clubs were constructed in the same manner, except that the round stone chosen for the head was completely encased in the rawhide. The handles of both types were usually equipped with wrist thongs near the base. The hafts were commonly painted, and the feathers of eagles, night-hawks, or other birds were attached to the top or butt. These feathers were believed to confer a supernatural potency to the weapon [27, 50, 52].

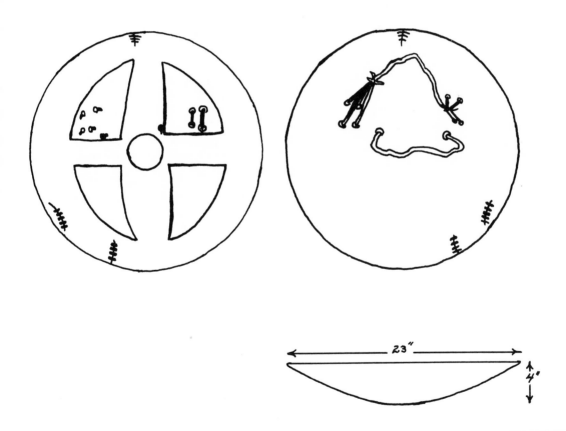

Figure 25. Hide shield.

Shields

The principal item of defensive equipment was the circular, hide shield. These appear to have been designed for use on foot, and were fairly large, about two feet in diameter (Figure 25). They could be made by anyone who desired them and knew the technique for their manufacture. Formerly buffalo hide was used, more recently cowhide. The skin from the neck and shoulder of an old animal was preferred because of its toughness. The hair was removed and the hide cut in circular form, somewhat larger than was desired for the finished product. The worker then dug a round, shallow depression in the ground, the approximate size and shape desired for the shield. The circle of skin was fitted into this and glowing hot corncobs were heaped upon it. This process shrank, thickened, and hardened the hide. It was repeated until the shield was thoroughly dried and shaped [27, 50].

The hair was then removed and the rawhide cut to size. A mound of dirt was made, and the hide placed over it with its edges pegged to the floor and weighted down with rocks. This created a convex shape when dry. Finally boiling pitch was rubbed into the skin to shrink and dry it. "Pitch will deflect even bullets, as it has a smooth shiny surface" [23].

Thongs were attached for carrying the shield. These were inserted at either side of the center about midway from the edge, the distance depending upon the length of the owner's forearm. The strap nearest the elbow was allowed considerable play; that passing around the wrist fitted snugly, to steady the shield and prevent it from interfering with the discharge of weapons. When not actually in use, shields were carried on the back, suspended from the neck. A thong was placed near the periphery for this purpose.

All shields were decorated by painting the face and the occasional application of a piece of red cloth and feathers along the upper periphery. Designs were usually in red, yellow, blue, or black, and personal whim governed the choice of pattern. Geometric motifs prevailed, although zoomorphic figures, the deer, elk, and "sun bear," and representations of cosmic phenomena, the sun, moon, and stars, were not uncommon. These symbols were considered the most significant part of the shield, in that they were believed to possess and impart power; such power was transferred to the user, and not only protected him, but made him more formidable as a warrior. Mountain lion fat applied to the shield was thought to endow it with the same qualities as the designs [27, 44, 50].

On return from a raid, the shield was covered and hung in the house of the owner. The cover was of buckskin, which fitted over the exterior and was secured in back by a drawstring. Covers were undecorated except for occasional fringe or pendant feathers [15, 27, 65]. These same shields were carried during the Comanche Dances [64].

Armor

According to tradition corselets were sometimes worn when combat was anticipated. These consisted of double thicknesses of buffalo or cowhide. They were sleeveless and reached from the neck to the waist. Occasionally a buckskin shirt was added. Normally warriors wore no clothing above the waist, however. In these instances the chest, back, and face were painted. "Each individual was free to choose his own designs, just as in the relay race." Presumably as in the case of the shields, the body paintings protected the individual and increased his effectiveness in battle. Less frequently buckskin shirts were worn [15, 27].

FISHING EQUIPMENT

Hooks

As of the early 1940s, commercially acquired hooks, lines, and nets were being used for fishing. Formerly wire was bent to hook shape. Before the introduction of wire, there is some doubt as to whether angling was practiced, although one informant [30] suggested the possibility that bone hooks had been used in earlier times.

Nets

When nets became so worn that their repair was impractical, they were discarded and new ones made. This involved the co-operative efforts of a large number of people. Informants varied as to the composition of the work party and its leadership. According to one [30] each household was represented by at least one male member; according to another [40] members of the kachina societies were selected for the work, but it was not known how or by whom the selection was made. (This is not a real discrepancy, as under normal conditions all adult males were members of the kachina societies, and most families would therefore be represented.)

The work group went to the mountains to gather yucca. On their return, it was apportioned to every family in the pueblo for the production of cordage. The women boiled the yucca, sometimes with cornmeal. The leaves were then chewed by various members of the household to further loosen the fibers, which were then stripped and twisted into two or four-ply cord by rolling them on the thigh. Short lengths were tied together to form a continuous strand, and wound in a ball.

Two or three days were usually spent in preparing cordage. When it was finished it was distributed to members of the kachina societies [40], or household representatives [30], who gathered in Plaza Three and began the fabrication of the net. Two systems of net manufacture prevailed. In one system two long lengths of cordage were laid parallel to each other, two to three finger widths apart, and were tied together at intervals by shorter pieces. When this had been done, other lengths were placed parallel to the first two. The process was repeated until the net attained the desired width and length [40]. In the second method each person took a ball of the yucca twine, doubled back one end, formed a double loop, and secured it with a knot. The double loop was spread, and three additional loops were tied (Figure 26). These were placed over stakes. The operator then began tying loops similar to the last three at the base of the five original ones. Subsequent ones were added to these, the work progressing back and forth until a length of five feet was achieved. A continuous line was used in the netting. These completed sections were tied together to make the net [30].

A uniformity in mesh size was considered desirable, although no gauge other than the

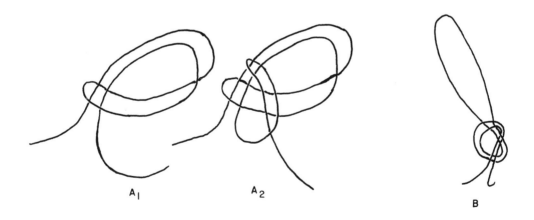

Figure 26. Knots used in making fish nets.

fingers was used. Sizes varied from two to three finger widths. Nets were from five to six feet in width, and up to seventy-five yards in length. Guide ropes of yucca fiber, two inches in diameter, were attached to the top, bottom, and ends of the net. More recently rawhide replaced the yucca. To the upper line were tied a series of gourd floats; to the bottom rope were attached grooved stone sinkers. No nets were made for purposes other than fishing [30, 40].

8

Life Cycle and Social Organization

INDIVIDUAL DEVELOPMENT

Crisis situations and shifts from one status category to another at Santa Clara Pueblo were not signalized by complicated religious rites and observances. In general they were met in a thoroughly practical manner and with a somewhat disinterested, if not fatalistic attitude, except as they concerned individuals or the immediate in-group. Only in connection with the initiation of males into the kachina cult, the fertility rite for girls, or during kachina performances was there a real approach to a rite of passage.

Indicative of the lack of religious concern with these areas of culture was the number of borrowed elements associated but not integrated with those of native provenience. While the bulk of the culture remained relatively impervious to outside influence, the impact of Western European beliefs, both religious and secular, was apparent in the behavior surrounding birth, marriage, and death. Here more than in any other compartment were seen the effects of Christianity. [A definitive discussion of the concept of compartmentalization as a characteristic of Eastern Puebloan culture was presented by Spicer (1954: 665–70), along with com-

mentaries by Ellis (1954: 678–80) and Dozier (1954: 680–83). Further and more detailed discussion of this topic was subsequently provided by Dozier (1961). CHL]

While the stages of growth, maturation, and degeneration might be said to be under-ritualized, this does not mean that Santa Clara culture lacked well-developed mechanisms for socialization. On the contrary, practical and often formalized processes existed for education, implanting goals and attitudes, and fitting individuals for life roles.

While there was a general continuity in culture conditioning and in the processes for educational development, certain shifts in emphasis and in attitude toward the individual took place from time to time. However the age at which these changes occurred was variable, and appeared to be determined both by the rate of physiological development in the individual and by personal circumstances in the particular family.

For the first two or three years, the principal concern was with the physical needs of the infant; these were given almost constant attention by the immediate family. The individual was subjected to few frustrations besides cradling, and these were accomplished with a minimum of pressure and interference. Relatively optimum conditions for adjustment were maintained, and the child developed in a warm, sympathetic environment with a tremendous feeling of security within the ingroup. In initial years of life, the infant acquired a few motor skills, the most important being facility in walking. Its cultural inventory included a rudimentary knowledge of the language, some slight knowledge of social relationships, and possibly some comprehension or feeling of religious sentiment or awe. The acquisition of any skill or knowledge was rewarded by constant encouragement and attention.

At about the age of two or three years, a new educational pattern was gradually inaugurated; this pattern was designed to carry the child through the age of six to eight years. It included a shift in emphasis from concern with physical needs to one with cultural needs. In this period contact with the outside world was extended, and responsibility for supervision was shifted to a wider circle of persons. Frustrations were increased in number. The child was weaned at the beginning of the period; at a later time, it was subjected to toilet training and introduced to the concept of modesty. The child was expected to undertake small tasks and to assume certain responsibilities. More emphasis was placed upon acquisition of skills and knowledge designed to fit the individual for his or her cultural role. Education was, however, unformalized. While all accomplishments were encouraged and rewarded, goals and expectations were reinforced. The child was confronted for the first time with a rigid disciplinary pattern that included not only scolding but corporal punishment and also threat of supernatural retribution. Usually at the end of the six to eight-year period, the child was affiliated with one or the other moiety and underwent what might be its first conscious, personal religious experience. This in a sense marked the transition to the next period, that of preadolescence/adolescence.

The principal difference between the preadolescent/adolescent period and the previous one was in the character of the educational mechanisms. Instruction had been informal; it next became relatively formalized and much more intensified. Stress was placed upon the acquisiton of specialized skills and knowledge, and the individual began to be forced into relatively rigid patterns of the culture. In many respects this period was the crucial one in the life of the person, since it was during this time that he or she developed those practical specialized skills and acquired those approved attitudes that would determine his or her success or failure as an adult in the community. For boys this period can be said to have ended with the initiation into the kachina cult; for girls, with physiological maturity.

Education did not terminate with the arrival of adult status. It might be said, however, to have become somewhat optional from this point on. By this time the individual had sufficient knowledge to function effectively in the culture. Depending upon individual temperament, persons could choose between living a life of standardized mediocrity or achieving prestige or esteemed status. If they chose the latter, several approved paths were open. For males these involved the attainment of virtuosity in any number of practical fields, or gradual advancement in secular politics or in the religious hierarchy. Opportunities for women were more limited in scope, but again were along lines either of technical proficiency or modified religious advancement.

The final recognizable role period for the individual was that of old age. Once a person passed the age of effective economic participation, he or she assumed a dependent role. There was some evidence that this "retired" status was not accepted with equanimity. However the culture was geared to cushion the shock of the transition as much as possible. Elders were accorded unlimited respect and care; many acted in advisory and teaching capacities or held high religious offices. This in part compensated for losses in other areas.

The entire socialization process, or enculturative experience, was designed to foster the idea of "social selection," rewarding those traits of personality of which the culture approved and inhibiting the undesirable qualities.

Childbirth

Large families represented one of the goals or ideals of Santa Clara culture. This attitude was exemplified in religious terms in the ritualistic impregnation of pubescent girls and adult females which was part of the overall fertility concept of kachina enactments (see Chapter 10). An impending birth was usually anticipated with pleasure by both parents. "They have a general desire for and a pride in large families. The culture admires large families" [25]. There was evidence that childless couples were looked upon with disapproval and were even suspect—possibly of human sacrifice in connection with witchcraft. "They seem to shun people who do not have children" [25].

The Santa Clara Indians were fully aware of the physiological aspects of conception. During the childbearing span of a woman's life, children were born at intervals of approximately a year and a half [4, 19]. That the goal of large families was not always achieved was due to the high rate of infant mortality that existed prior to the introduction of modern medical concepts and practices.

Consistent with the ideal, barrenness was a matter of grave concern; knowledge and use of contraceptives were generally denied [4, 13, 52], and abortions unknown [42, 45, 76].

Several methods for curing sterility were reported. The barren woman might go to a midwife for treatment [45, 52]. This practitioner bathed the patient in a solution derived from boiled Osage orange and an unidentified plant. This was said to induce sweating and result in recovery. The patient remained in bed eight days after the medication [45].

If this procedure proved unsuccessful, the woman joined one or another of the secret societies. Initiation into one of these groups constituted a curing rite and was believed to make it possible for her to conceive—"to make sure she would have children." Similarly if several children were stillborn or died in infancy, parents would vow or dedicate the next one to one of the societies. "This was done just before it was born. This was to insure its health" [21, 50].

Only one informant [56] admitted knowledge of a contraceptive. According to her conception could be prevented by drinking a boiled solution made from Osage orange once a day for twelve days. It is doubtful that this treatment was frequently employed, since its administration was believed to cause permanent sterility.

Related to the theory of contraceptives but of a different nature were several types of behavior associated with multiple births. For example double ears of corn were not eaten by women, as a preventive measure against twins. Other negative acts of this type were recorded by Parsons (1924b: 148):

> There is at Santa Clara a prophylaxis against twins. A girl who passes by a dog lying down in the house or by a bow and arrow laid on the floor or a gun, will have twins; and so, as the twins are not desired, the thing to do is to chase the dog out or go around him, and to go around carelessly dropped weapons.

According to two informants [35, 42], twins were often witches. "If you urinate on twins at the time of their birth, they will grow up to be ordinary children." The fact that twins were generally considered undesirable appears to stem from the additional responsibility involved in their care and feeding, and because it was believed that they often became witches in later life [25, 35, 42].

As mentioned earlier, abortion was denied. Miscarriages were rare [4, 19]. When they occurred or when a child was stillborn, it was explained either on the basis of lack of regular exercise and work on the part of the expectant mother [25], too heavy work immediately prior to the time of delivery, or too vigorous a massage by the midwife during parturition [4, 19]. It was stated that unmarried girls frequently overworked just prior to delivery, in the hope that the child would be stillborn [4, 19].

Prenatal Behavior and Beliefs

There was a minimum of prenatal restrictions and beliefs. Jeançon (1904 and 1906) also commented on the simplicity and paucity of ceremony attending birth, and it can be presumed that the current condition has existed for some time. What restrictions existed were primarily concerned with the protection of the unborn infant and its welfare following birth, rather than with the well-being of the mother. No limitations other than that of cohabitation were placed on the father during the prenatal period, and there was little evidence of even a limited couvade following birth [25, 35, 40, 42].

The expectant mother usually sought advice from an older woman or midwife relative as to dietary considerations and work activities. Food tabus were few, and the woman was allowed essentially a normal diet [25]. It was recommended, however, that a ground and boiled plant, ie to wo (like groundsel), and cartilage be eaten. The former was thought to strengthen the child; the latter to insure it having a light complexion [29, 52].

Throughout the prenatal period women were urged to carry on with essentially their normal work routine. Exercise was thought to facilitate delivery [25], and only the heavier forms of manual labor and such occupations as house plastering were prohibited [35, 42]. Some pursuits were thought to be particularly efficacious. Among these was water carrying. It was believed that if the mother made frequent visits to the spring or creek for water, the child would be born without defects [25]. Another approved activity was corn grinding. This was highly recommended as the woman approached the period of labor. It was thought that the movements involved in grinding loosened the placenta and eased the birth [35, 42]. According to Parsons (1924b: 148), "eight or nine times before the birth of the child the Tewa mother bathed every four days."

It was considered inadvisable for a woman to stand in the threshold of the house or to look out the window for any length of time. Such action was thought to indicate anxiety and fear and a desire to delay the delivery. It was also believed to result in protracted labor [25]. Again according to Parsons (1924b: 148), "were the prospective mother to peep out of the door or window the baby would 'look out [on the world, WWH] and go back.'"

Birthmarks were thought to result from eclipses occurring during the period of the pregnancy. Such phenomena were particularly dangerous when they occurred during the month in which the child was to be born. Preventative measures included wearing a chert or steel knife or a key next to the body [4, 29, 42, 52]. A similar device, a key or ring worn in the belt, was cited by Parsons (1924b: 149). According to her it was worn on the night of the eclipse as protection for the foetus against physical deformities. Informants [35, 42] stated that they had seen no birthmarks on visible portions of the body of any member of the tribe for over sixty years.

Care was also taken to shield pregnant women from persons or animals that had physical or other abnormalities. It was thought that if expectant mothers encountered such peculiarities in others, they would be transferred to the unborn child [25].

Parturition

There were several acceptable alternatives in behavior during and immediately after parturition. Change was apparent, however, in this area of the culture. The more orthodox families still (1941) adhered to much of the old pattern, but many younger and educated individuals had discarded all or part of it, and depended when possible upon modern medical science. More and more in recent years, members of the latter group have gone to Santa Fe to the Indian Hospital for confinement. This tendency was deplored by the more conservative element in the village, and it was said that the younger girls had more difficulty in delivery than earlier generations. This was attributed to their mental attitude and to readily accessible medical facilities [25, 56].

The room in which the confinement was to take place was prepared in advance of the event. One that was warm and easily heated was always selected. All informants stressed the necessity of warmth and protection against wind and drafts during confinement. Buffalo robes or blankets were draped around the bed or the blankets upon which the parturient woman knelt [25, 35, 42]. "This was done even if there was no wind outside" [35, 42]. Other blankets and robes were collected and stacked along the wall or on the bed (if one existed), where they would be available when needed [25].

The midwife was not summoned until labor was well advanced [25, 35, 42]. "The expectant mother is up on her feet and about the village until the labor pains have become so severe that she has to lie down. When this time arrives, word is sent to two women, not necessarily belonging to any healing society or related to her. These two are the godmother and the midwife" (Jeançon 1904 and 1906). Some child in the family was usually sent to bring the midwife and her assistant. Frequently the baby was born before their arrival [25].

An older sister or maternal aunt often functioned in the capacity of assistant, although this was not obligatory [25]. The assistant acted under the direction of the midwife, brought various articles as needed, and supported and lifted the mother during labor. Because of this latter duty, a woman of considerable physical strength was chosen [35, 42].

Male relatives including the husband were excluded from the house, according to several informants [25, 35, 42, 76]. Jeançon (1904 and 1906) stated that the husband might assist, however. A similar contradiction existed in regard to the functions of the Bear Society. According to an informant [25], they did not officiate at the time of birth, although they might be called in at a later date if the mother suffered from postnatal complications. According to Jeançon (1904 and 1906), however, "if the case was too serious for the ordinary attendants, a member of the Bear Society was called."

Immediately upon arrival of the midwife, the woman was made as comfortable as possible. "Formerly the patient was couched upon a bed of fine sand covered with a blanket, but now she may lie on a mattress on the floor, or, in some of the houses where they have beds, she lies on one of them" (Jeançon 1904 and 1906). Recently women have either occupied a bed or a stack of blankets in the center of the floor.

When the woman was settled, the midwife prepared a solution from boiled juniper berries and gave it to her to drink. This was believed to facilitate and shorten the period of labor [25]. For similar reasons pine twigs or cones were burnt in a container. The bowl was placed near the patient's feet, "so that it would warm her and she would absorb some of the smoke into her limbs" [35, 42]. Jeançon (1904 and 1906) augmented the above list of plants used as aids to birth. According to him the parturient woman was given "tea" made from the flowers of a plant called koyaya, malva leaves, or pounded cedar limbs.

The woman usually rested her weight on her knees and elbows and parturition took place in this position [25, 35, 42], although occasionally in a lying or semisitting position [25]. "The woman usually is, or was, delivered on her hands and knees with her feet pressed against a wall or some heavy object to give purchase for pressure. During the labor pains, she may get up and walk about supported by her attendants or by her husband" (Jeançon 1904 and 1906).

As labor progressed the assistant passed her arms around the upper abdomen of the woman, held her tightly, and exerted a downward pressure on the belly while lifting her up and down (see Jeançon 1904 and 1906). Simultaneously the midwife massaged the lower abdomen. These movements were continued until the birth took place [25, 35, 42]. "Labor contractions resulted from the fact that the child was trying to crawl upward toward the chest. That is what they say" [35, 42].

When labor was protracted or the midwife was confronted with a breech birth, she first attempted to force the birth or correct the position with increased massage [35, 42]. If this was unsuccessful, several alternatives were possible. The midwife might reach into the uterus and attempt to dislodge or right the child [25, 35, 42]. As Jeançon (1904 and 1906) observed, this procedure often resulted in severe damage to the uterus and other organs, and led to complications, such as infection and displacements. Another option cited by Jeançon was to summon a member of the Bear Society, "who resorted to incantations and magic."

The third alternative involved the administration of herbal treatments. According to Jeançon (1904 and 1906), the patient was given "an infusion of rabbit-bush tops or peacock feathers, burned and steeped in water. The latter is supposed to be a Mexican remedy." Rabbitbush was a rare commodity, obtained from the leader of the Bear Society, who made a special trip to Jemez Pueblo each year to obtain it. "You would have to give the leader a large amount of cornmeal and buckskins in return" [25].

This plant was put in a bowl of water and placed on the fire to boil. Hot coals were then added to a bowl of ground rabbitbush and juniper berries. This container was placed near the patient, who inhaled the smoke and absorbed the heat. Theoretically this caused the woman to perspire and righted the fetus. If birth did not ensue, liquid derived from the boiled herb was administered. This was given only in crisis situations, since it reportedly induced very hard, rapid labor and almost immediate birth—often resulting in the death of the mother from hemorrhage, but more frequently in the death of the child [25].

Apparently death as a result of childbirth was formerly rather common. Two informants [35, 42] were able to remember several cases of women who had succumbed in this manner. Both denied any knowledge of postnatal insanity, however.

Postnatal Care of the Mother

The postparturient woman was formerly subjected to special care and restrictions for a considerable time span; however, the number of restrictions has recently been lessened and their severity relaxed. The first four days following a birth were and still are envisaged as a critical period, and the woman was not freed of all restraint until a month had passed. The special behavior was evidently primarily related to the physical recovery of the individual. The concept of birth as a crisis situation which exposed the person unduly to malignant influences or rendered her impure was present, but definitely secondary.

Parsons' and Jeançon's data, cited later, tend not to substantiate this view. Both viewpoints are probably correct, the apparent inconsistencies reflecting the progressive secularization of this area of the culture over a period of about fifty years.

Immediately after the birth, the mother's stomach was massaged to assist her in discharging the placenta [25]. When this was accomplished, several woven belts were wrapped about her abdomen, and she was put to bed [35, 42]. She remained in bed for four days [25, 35, 42]; see also Jeançon (1904 and 1906) and Parsons (1924b: 148). According to Jeançon this practice was not always strictly adhered to. He reported seeing women up and about, doing housework twelve hours after confinement.

During this four-day interval, the woman was cared for by female relatives, usually assisted by the "umbilical cord cutter." The mother must never be left alone, "a person was in the room at all times guarding her" [35, 42]. (This same pattern was also followed after a funeral.)

Jeançon's comments (1904 and 1906) at this point are of interest, since they give evidence of changing conditions:

> For four days the mother is attended by some member of her family, and one or two women, usually the god-mother of the child is one of these. In former times the husband was the only male permitted in the room during this period excepting her nurse, but now anyone of the family, and sometimes even friends are permitted to come and see her during the four day period.

As soon as the mother was put to bed, she was fed. Her initial food consisted of beef, mutton, or venison broth [35, 42], beef broth and corn meal gruel (Jeançon 1904 and 1906), gruel and blue cornmeal mush [25]. The woman was under dietary restrictions for thirty days. "She was given only good food, beef, mutton, venison, beef or mutton broth, no pork" [35, 42]. According to Jeançon (1904 and 1906), tabued meats during this period were pork, venison, and goat meat:

> They are considered "cold substances." She may eat beef, mutton, and rabbit as "hot" substances, although there are two concepts about rabbits. One is that if the mother eats this flesh this baby

will be a good runner like a rabbit; on the other hand there is danger that the child will be timid like a rabbit and so this meat is not often eaten by a new mother.

Parsons (1924b: 148) speaking of the Tewa generally, commented:

During the first half of the month after birth some women drink water that has been boiled; then, during the second half water that has been warmed only. Other women drink cold water only. During this time watermelon and peaches are not eaten "because, they say, they are cold."

According to Jeançon (1904 and 1906), a hot fire was kept burning in the room throughout the four days. "This partakes of the nature of a purifying rite." My own informants [29, 42] confirmed the presence of the fire, but only in the case of male children. According to them, "men spend much of their time hunting and out-of-doors and need fire wherever they may be. This was done so that when they became adult, they would never want for fire."

At the end of four days, unless there were postnatal complications, there was a partial resumption of the normal routine of life. The mother was allowed to get up and to leave the house. She was expected to participate in the naming rite and to be responsible for the child's care, since the "umbilical cord cutter" was dismissed following the ceremony. She was not supposed to engage in activities of a too rigorous nature [35, 42].

While the fourth day marked the end of the critical period, complete freedom of action was not achieved for a month. Restrictions other than those concerned with diet were enforced during the longer time. These included, according to Jeançon (1904 and 1906), a prohibition against leaving the village, making pottery, or handling clay or other "cold" substances. Violation of these prescriptions was said to result in the woman "having cold bowels and lots of pain," and in a softening of the bone structure in the child. According to Parsons (1924b: 148), the Tewa mother bathed "on

the fourth, eighth, twelfth, etc., days" after the birth of the child. Jeançon (1904 and 1906) mentioned that a hot bath was taken and cedar tea drunk on the morning of the fourth day. The mother was not supposed to have sexual relations until thirty days after the birth of a daughter, forty days after the birth of a son (Parsons 1924b: 148).

If the mother suffered from postnatal complications, she was treated either by one of the Bear societies or by the midwife. In the latter case, dried and ground yucca fruit ("mountain amole") was mixed with water and given to the patient to drink. Seeds of the same plant were put in a buckskin sack and worn by the woman as an amulet. If the cure was not effected in four days, it was continued for four more days. When she recovered the mother went to the river, accompanied by the midwife, and was immersed four times. On the fourth immersion, the amulet was allowed to drift downstream with the current [25].

Care of the Newborn

For four days following a birth, those intimately concerned were intensely preoccupied with activities believed to relate to the future welfare and development of the child. In these activities the major role was usually played by the umbilical cord cutter. The naming rite at which the infant was formally "presented" to the village was the terminal feature of this critical period, and marked the resumption of a relatively normal routine of life.

Accounts of treatment of the infant at the moment of delivery are variable. According to one [25], "it was not slapped or spanked; it was usually breathing when born." Others [35, 42] stated that the infant was made to cough, since it may have swallowed fluid or blood and not be able to cry." If it gave no sign of life, the midwife attempted to revive it. She first breathed on its forehead, then wrapped it in a blanket to produce perspiration. "This opened all the passages, and it began breathing" [25]. No data were available on the efficacy of this procedure.

Once it was determined that the child was alive, the woman selected to name it and conduct the naming rite was notified and came to the house. She was responsible for cutting the umbilical cord, and was designated as the "vessel (vein) cut mother" (si ca zhia) or "umbilical cord cutter" [35, 42]. This operation was formerly accomplished with a stone knife, more recently with a scissors [25, 35, 42]. Occasionally a burning corncob was substituted (Jeançon 1904 and 1906).

Meanwhile a corncob was placed in the fire, and the umbilicus cauterized with this by the umbilical cord cutter [25]. A hot coal was sometimes substituted for the corncob [40]. This operation might also be performed by the midwife or assistant if necessary [35, 40]. The remainder of the cord was detached from the placenta, and either burned in the fireplace or deposited with the placenta in the Rio Grande at a later time [35, 42].

According to Jeançon (1904 and 1906), when that segment of the umbilicus attached to the child dried and fell off, it was covered with meal, wrapped in a cloth, and buried under the sill of the door, "where the child and mother passed out to the offering of the sun." Parsons (1924b: 149) speaking of the Tewa in general, stated that in the case of a girl, it was buried near the grinding stone, "so when she grows up she will not be lazy"; in the case of a boy, in the field, "so he could work."

Parsons (1924b: 149) again referring to the Tewa generally, stated that, "if the navel 'waters' (after the cord comes off) dust from rafters is rubbed on. The mother of an infant with a sore navel will not eat eggs or beans."

"The placenta drainage is allowed to accumulate in the sand on the floor and when completely discharged is gathered up and thrown in the river. Every drop must be gathered up and thrown away" (Jeançon 1904 and 1906; see also Parsons 1924b: 149). The umbilical cord cutter usually performed this function, although it might be done by the midwife, assistant, or the woman's mother. The placenta and the umbilical cord, if it was included, were sprinkled with meal before they were deposited in the river [35, 42]. There were no beliefs associated with the amniotic fluid [25, 45, 56].

After the cord was severed, the infant was cleansed. Formerly this was accomplished by rubbing the child with cedar ashes. It was not bathed in water until after the fourth day (Jeançon 1904 and 1906). More recently the umbilical cord cutter has first bathed the infant in lukewarm water, dried it with a soft cloth, and then rubbed its body with cedar ash. The application of the ashes was believed to prevent the growth of body hair and to strengthen the child [5, 7, 25, 35, 42]; see also Jeançon (1904 and 1906). Lately this custom has been ignored by many families. "This is why people in those days did not have as much hair on their bodies as they do now" [48].

There is evidence that activities immediately after delivery were further complicated if multiple births had occurred. As indicated earlier, twins were not considered desirable, and at least two informants stated that unless remedial measures were taken, twins might become witches. The prophylactic action against this eventuality consisted of urinating on the newborn infants. "If this was done, they grow up to be ordinary children" [35, 42].

Several alternatives were possible in the treatment of the child subsequent to its cleansing. Recent standard practice seems to have been as follows: the infant was given a minute portion of blue cornmeal mush [25], a cloth or scarf was tied around its head, its arms were straightened and put by its sides, it was wrapped tightly in a blanket to prevent movement of its extremities, and it was then placed with the mother [29, 35, 42]. Thus the child suffered its first major frustration immediately after birth. What in all probability was an earlier usage was reported by two informants [45, 48]. According to them the infant was not swathed, but was given immediately to the mother and shared whatever covering blankets the mother used. Only after the fourth day was it wrapped and its movements restricted. "After four days, a loosely woven cloth, 'savana,' bought in Santa Fe, was wrapped about the child. Cloth was scarce in those days. If you had enough, you might make it a shirt" [48].

The baby might also be swathed and placed on the cradle, but this was recognized as unusual procedure. As soon as the child was put to rest, the umbilical cord cutter arranged an ear of blue corn on either side of it and placed a bowl of "sacred" water, containing ground shell, at the right of its head. The ears were kept in this position whenever the child was at rest, for a period of from fifteen to thirty days. After this time they were hung in the room until the spring planting, when they were used for seed [18, 19, 29]. This custom was unconfirmed by other informants, and appears to be related to parts of the naming rite.

Inconsistencies were also present in accounts dealing with the initial feeding of the infant. According to two informants [35, 42], the child was given to the mother to nurse shortly after its birth; a wet nurse was employed only if the mother lacked milk. This was confirmed by Jeançon (1904 and 1906). Another informant [25] stated, however, that a wet nurse was always present, and that the mother was not allowed to nurse the child for the first two days.

When the mother's milk was slow to come, she was given a brew of milkweed to start the flow [25] (Jeançon 1904 and 1906). When twins were born, the mother's milk was supplemented by that of sheep and goats. "This was before canned milk" [25].

Following the initial feeding, the child was nursed whenever it cried. Nursing the child was the mother's only responsibility for the first four days. All other duties associated with its care were performed by the umbilical cord cutter.

Naming

The average person at Santa Clara Pueblo received several names during the course of a lifetime. The first of these was acquired at the naming ceremony, four days after birth. This name and others received immediately subsequent to that ceremony were Tewa names. Later, if the Catholic baptismal rite was performed, the child acquired a Spanish given name and patronymic. Finally another Tewa appellation was received at the "water immersion" (po ku) ceremony.

Names among the Santa Clara lacked the significance generally attributed to them by most Indian groups. For instance the Santa Clara had an almost cavalier attitude toward their names as compared to the Navajo. Names were freely used, and the one of several selected to designate the person rested upon individual whim or family preference. "As a rule, the baby received many names—the prettiest being retained by the mother or family" [29]. "You get a name four days after birth; you get another at the poku. Use whichever one sticks" [22]. "They may give the child any name they like. The child may have a dozen names. The parents choose the one they like best" [51].

Nicknames occurred, but their use was infrequent. Such appellations were not used in face-to-face situations. In my own name list, only three cases of nicknames, all males, are noted; Parsons (1929: 22–25) recorded none.

Any tendency toward teknonymy was denied [25, 44]. There was no tabu on the reuse of names of the deceased.

There is ample evidence that Tewa names were being supplanted by Spanish patronymics and given names. In a sampling of eighty-seven individuals, mostly household heads, three male informants [29, 50, 52] were able to give, in addition to Spanish appellations, the Tewa names in only fifty-two instances (males: forty-five, including three nicknames; females: seven). Twenty-six males and nine females, a total of thirty-five, were known only by Spanish names or the Tewa-influenced variant of Spanish names. In the latter case, twelve were males and one female. In working with informants, use was made of Genealogy III and the accompanying table provided by Parsons (1929: 22–23); Tewa names were recorded by Parsons for forty of the fifty-seven alive. (Genealogy IV was not used, because the family did not appear on the 1940 census.) [For Hill's genealogies, see Appendix A. CHL] Of the remaining seventeen, only eight were adults, seven were fifteen years or younger, and two, presumably so. If children are excluded from consideration (according to informants [29, 50, 52], the names of young children were rarely known outside the immediate family), forty-eight adults are left, approximately eighty-three percent of whom were known by their Tewa names. In 1941 this was true of approximately sixty percent.

Tewa names referring to flowers were preferred for females, animal and mountain names for boys [25, 48]. However there was no rigid adherence to this pattern [48, 49]. "Names do not belong to one or another sex" [48]. This is evident from both my own and Parsons's lists. Qualifying adjectives were commonly used.

According to Jeançon (1904), if the child was born in winter or fall it was given a winter name like "white snow" or "ice," a "cold" name that fitted the season. If born in summer, it received a name which referred to flowers, trees, green mountains, rain, or clouds, i.e., a "warm" name. This was confirmed by one informant [51], who stated, "They were usually named after the season they were born; if in the fall, yellow after fall colors, if in the winter, after snow, etc."

Family preferences for particular categories of names were denied [25, 50, 51]. This was substantiated by Parsons's data (1929: 22–25). There was no feeling that particular names were owned by or associated with either moiety [5, 48].

The following is a list of translatable Tewa names collected in 1941.

Males

Obsidian Mountain	Dew on Flower	Turtle
Grass Mountain	Dew on Leaf	Fox (??)
Fir Mountain	Lake Leaf	White Bear
Turtle Mountain	Mountain Lion Stalk	Wolf
Mountain Ridge	Bird Leaf	Fawn
Fog Mountain	White Flower	Blue Bird
Obsidian Colored	Tree	Little Bird
Gleaming Stone	Evergreen Tree	Aspen Bird
Dew	Fir Wood	Red Bird
Fog	Blue	Down (Feathers)
Sound Made by Water	Squash Man	Yellow Cloud
Rippling Lake		

Female

Mother Deer	Leaf Edge Design	Fir Blossom
Male Deer		

Naming Ceremony

The naming ceremony, "to awaken from sleep to go out" (djo wo wa pi dje), was held the morning of the fourth day following the birth of the child. If the child was born in a hospital, away from the village, this ceremony was deferred until its return [51]. While designated as a naming ceremony, the

rite was of greater consequence than is indicated by the title. It marked the end of a critical period in the individual's existence, a lifting of tabus, and the transition from the newborn to infant category. It terminated the services of the umbilical cord cutter, and shifted the responsibility for the infant's welfare to the individual's ingroup. In the ceremony the infant was presented to the pueblo for the first time, and became a legal entity and reality in the eyes of the village, i.e., achieved the status of a unique personality. The acquisition of the name was actually a secondary consideration.

Accounts of the naming ceremony, from several sources, vary in details and richness. These disparities reflect the processes of change and breakdown attending this segment of the culture. Although the rite was still in force and conducted by most families, its content had diminished, and alternative behavior was becoming acceptable.

The person who acted as umbilical cord cutter usually conducted the ceremony and named the infant [25]; see also Jeançon (1904 and 1906). There was no firm rule, however, and the office might be performed by any female relative of the mother [72], or by a woman selected by the mother from among family friends who might or might not have volunteered their services [58, 70, 72]; see Jeançon (1904 and 1906).

Jeançon's account of the ceremony is as follows:

On the fourth day, before the sun is up, the god-mother and sometimes a friend (female) take the mother and child outside the house. The god-mother carried the child and two ears of blue corn. The mother carries a slab of bark on which is a glowing charcoal. While standing with her face to the east, the mother is turned, by the god-mother, four times, to the north, west, south, and east. Another informant says four times to the left, finishing with her back to the sun and facing west. The writer has seen it done both ways. By the time this is done the sun is just beginning to come up, and all stand with their backs to it, as it rises over the horizon the mother takes the bark with the glowing charcoal on it and throws it over her right shoulder towards the east.

Here again fire is a purifying power, and she throws away from her, by means of the fire (live charcoal), all sickness, bad luck, and evil. The god-mother then gives the baby a "baby name."

Recent descriptions confirmed the general pattern outlined by Jeançon, although there were variations in detail. It was stated that early on the morning of the fourth day, the umbilical cord cutter substitute came to the child's home, took the child, and accompanied by the mother went to the adjacent plaza. The umbilical cord cutter carried hot coals secured from the fireplace. When they were several hundred feet from the house, the coals were given to the mother, who threw them over her shoulder [35, 42].

According to another informant [25], the umbilical cord cutter carried instead of coals, two ears of corn, either white or blue, and a bowl of "sacred water." "The child's face was revealed to indicate that it belonged to the village." The two ears of corn were later placed on either side of the child when it was put to bed. According to Parsons (1924b: 149), they remained there for four days.

After the child was presented to the village or the coals tossed over the mother's shoulder, the trio (or quartet) returned to the house. The umbilical cord cutter obtained a piece of white shell, rubbed it against a rough stone, and mixed the resulting powder with the sacred water. She then poured or asperged some of this mixture into the mouth of the child and gave it a name. Finally she turned to any relatives or friends who were present and said, "I have given the baby a name; now you may give it a name if you desire" [35, 42, 51].

When the official naming ceremony was completed, it was customary for any or all of those present to repeat the above rite and bestow names on the child [25, 35, 42, 49, 51]. "Relatives or friends may take the baby out and in a similar manner give the child another name of their own liking" [72]. The family selected from among this aggregate of names the one that they preferred, and the child was thereafter designated by that. (See Parsons [1924b: 148–49] for a somewhat similar account of a naming ceremony at San Juan Pueblo.)

When the newborn had been dedicated by its parents prior to birth to one or another of the secret societies, additional proceedings were included in the naming rite. Jeançon (1904 and 1906), who witnessed them, reported as follows:

Sometimes, among the older people who persist in more of the older customs, a small basket containing meal and fetishes is placed at the head of the child. One such basket, seen by the writer, contained sacred meal, a fine long spear point of obsidian, a piece of crystal, a mountain lion figurine, and several other stone objects of indeterminate nature. This basket was for a boy who was pledged to the warrior society, and the objects were arranged by that society. I was told that had the infant been a girl, a round piece of quartz crystal would have been substituted for the spear point as this is an emblem of the womb and a prayer that the girl, upon attaining proper age, would bear many children. Other objects would also have been substituted for the mountain lion figurine. These fetish baskets and their contents remained with the child for four days after which they were removed.

A child pledged to the Summer or Winter society was taken to the headquarters of that group four days after the naming ceremony. There it was given a drink of sacred water [43, 50]. The vowing of children to a society prior to birth was also confirmed by Parsons (1924b: 150).

The convention of visiting newborn infants prior to and at the time of the naming rite appears well established, especially in recent years. Visitors customarily approached the child, ran their hands gently over its body, then spread their hands toward the west, saying, "I have cleansed you of crying. Cry, go and live among the Navajo" [29, 42].

Such contacts with outsiders were not,

however, without the possibility of dangerous consequences, and the attitude toward visitors was one of ambivalence. Parsons (1924b: 149–50), speaking of the Tewa generally, noted that were a menstruating woman to hold the baby, it would make its skin rough and spotty and the child irritable. It must also be remembered that infants were believed to be particularly susceptible to witchcraft, especially the "evil eye," and were therefore guarded against outsiders, or strangers. For this reason babies were almost never left alone at this, or even later periods of their lives. If it were necessary for the mother to leave the room, she placed a broom next to the child for its protection. "This guarded it from witchcraft" [29, 52]

Baptism

Baptism was an alternative available to the "devout" members of the village. The mother and father of the child selected the godparents. These were usually a husband and wife, although occasionally a brother and sister were chosen. Either friends or relatives were eligible to serve [29, 48].

Children were baptized when they were about three weeks old [48]. The time interval was variable, since in recent years mass was held at Santa Clara Pueblo only on the first Thursday of the month. Those who wished to avoid delay had the child baptized at the Spanish village of Santa Cruz (five miles away and east of the Rio Grande), where regular masses were held.

The godparents called for the child and carried it to the church or, if the baptism was at Santa Cruz, used a wagon or car. They chose the name that was given. When the ritual was completed by the priest, the child was returned to its home. Parents could attend the rite, but not in company with the godparents or in the same conveyance [29, 72]. A feast was occasionally held following the ceremony, although this was unusual [48].

According to Parsons (1924b: 149),

In all the towns there is also a Catholic Christening. Within a week or two of the birth the infant is taken to the church "for his Mexican name," by his madrenha [madrina] or popoyiya (wet head mother) and his padrenho [padrino] or popotara (wet head father). The same persons continue to serve as Catholic god-parents to a family unless a god-child dies, when new god-parents are called for. Possibly a like rule holds for the "navel mother" in native ritual.

When it was obvious at the time of birth that the child would not live, baptism could be performed by the mother or any close friend. The choice was made among the individuals who were closely enough associated with the Catholic Church to have learned the broad outlines of the ritual from the priests or nuns or had become familiar with it at parochial schools. These took salt acquired from visiting nuns or a Catholic school, placed it in water, poured it on the infant's head, and recited the baptismal rite. (Sister Mary Henry, of Rosary College, informed me that baptism by lay members was an unusual Roman Catholic custom; when done, only ordinary water was used. WWH)

Care and Socialization

Once the infant was named and "presented" to the village, a pattern of care and socialization was inaugurated designed to carry the individual through the first twelve to fourteen years of life. The pattern was a flexible one and allowed for certain additions and shifts in emphasis—adjustments necessary to compensate for physical maturity and the progressive acquisition of motor habits, skills, and attitudes in the individual.

In the early years of helplessness and dependency, primary emphasis was upon physical needs and care. During this period the major responsibility for welfare and training rested in the immediate family, and contacts with the outside world were minimal. As the child matured, increased its cultural inventory, and attained some degree of independence, greater weight was given to the socialization processes. Not only was there more emphasis on these processes, but their number was greater, and they were applied with more severity. Concurrently with this shift, there was a delegation of responsibility for care and training to a wider circle of relatives and an increased contact with the outside world. This whole period was one of gradual conditioning, one in which the basic foundations for future development were laid. When it ended the individual was ready and equipped to assume an adult role in the community.

Feeding

As noted earlier the mother normally began to nurse the infant shortly after its birth. No attempt was made to develop a feeding schedule, and the baby was put to the breast whenever it cried [29, 35, 42, 48]. "Crying seems to be the natural sign that the baby wants to be fed" [35, 42]. If crying continued after feeding, an effort was made to discover other sources of discomfiture [29, 42].

Children were usually removed from the cradle when nursed. The head of the infant was rested against the upper arm and the body supported in a position midway between vertical and horizontal. Alternation of the breast varied with the whim or belief of the mother; it was not conventionalized. The infant was allowed to fully satisfy its hunger [35, 42].

According to one informant [25], the infant was not permitted to sleep immediately after it was fed. However, others [29, 42, 52] stated that some mothers nursed the baby on the swing cradle and, when it had been satisfied, swung the cradle to put it to sleep (see also Dennis and Dennis 1940: 115). No attempt was made to make the infant burp by patting it on the back after nursing [25]. If it developed colic, the grandmother or some other woman was called and relieved the condition by massage [25].

No food other than the mother's milk was given the infant for the first month. After that time supplementary items were introduced. Those included meat soups and blue cornmeal gruel (agerg). The latter was prepared by mixing finely ground meal with warm water and creating a paste. The paste

was then put in boiling water, thoroughly stirred, set aside until lukewarm, and then fed to the infant [48].

The above diet was adhered to for the first eight [48] or nine [25] months of the individual's life. After this, solid foods were added. The infant was first given bread or pieces of meat to chew [25, 48]. From this time on, its menu became more diversified until by the age of a year and a half to two years, it had access, with only a few exceptions, to a complete range of adult foods.

Included in the exceptions were "hot and bitter foods, onions, and chili," also marrow. "If the child was fed hot and bitter foods, it would grow up to be p o k e, hardheaded," i.e., stupid and disobedient. "If marrow was given the child, it was believed it would cause ill health in later life—have rheumatism, etc. The child would give the marrow to the mother or father" [29, 52].

Informants differed on whether or not thumbsucking was controlled. According to one [48] no attempt was made to break the child of this habit; others [29, 42] stated that the practice was discouraged, and that a cloth was tied over the child's hand to prevent it. Actually, since the child was confined to the cradle with its arms restricted for the first months, the problem seldom if ever arose, and was seemingly never acute.

Weaning

The age at which children were weaned depended upon several factors, and varied in time from one and one-half to three years. When another child was expected, the previous one was weaned just prior to its arrival [35, 42]. When no other children were born to the mother, it was not uncommon for the infant to be nursed until it attained the age of two or three years. In such cases the time of weaning was determined by the ability of the individual to adjust to and consume the normal adult diet [25, 48]. "The child was weaned whenever it showed signs of wanting to assist itself in getting food" [25]. "After a child has learned to eat almost everything, it is weaned" [48].

Jeançon's observations (1904–30) confirm my own:

Some mothers nurse their children until the next one arrives, and when there are no other children, the mother has been known to nurse her youngest one for two and a half to three years. Such a case occurred in 1930. In that year a young mother, who had lost her husband by death, was nursing a child thirty-one months old and made no effort to wean it.

Weaning was accomplished in an abrupt manner [25, 35, 42].

Cleanliness

Responsibility for the cleanliness of the infant was shifted from the umbilical cord cutter to the family after the fourth day. The baby was usually bathed by the mother each morning, although this duty could be and was delegated to older children in the family [25, 35, 42].

The baby was changed and cleansed whenever necessary, or when it indicated discomfiture that could not be attributed to a desire for food [29, 42]. If the anal-genital region became inflamed, grease or tallow was applied [29, 35] (see also Parsons 1924b: 150).

As the baby grew older and learned to walk, it was sent to the river or creek to wash and bathe. Bathing in itself was considered a highly beneficial pursuit and was believed to condition and strengthen an individual; emphasis placed upon it derived as much from this motive as from any idea of sanitation. Particular advantages were thought to stem from washing and bathing in icy water during the winter. Formerly there was pressure placed upon children to rise early in the morning to avail themselves of this opportunity [30] (see Parsons 1924b: 150).

Toilet training was not inaugurated until the baby was able to walk and had mastered the rudiments of the language. "When they began to understand, you told them to go outside" [48]. Training was a gradual process, not abrupt; ridicule was the principal coercive weapon.

Modesty was not inculcated until a much later date. During the summer months, it was not uncommon for children of eight years or under to play in the plazas with no covering at all, or only an abbreviated shirt [29, 42].

Cradling

Cradling constituted a continuation of the interference to motor differentiation and experiment initiated shortly after birth when the infant was tightly swathed in a blanket and put to bed. Informants differed on the time when the cradle was first used. According to two [29, 42], it was immediately after birth; according to others [25, 48], not until the eighth day. Jeançon (1904 and 1906) gives it as the fourth day; Dennis and Dennis (1940: 115) as about two weeks. As noted earlier, a near relative, generally the father or grandfather, made the cradle [45].

Cradles were used only during the day. The infant slept with the mother at night. Before being placed on a swing cradle, the infant was wrapped snugly in a blanket. It was next placed on the sheepskin or pad and secured there by a strip of cloth or buckskin. In the case of the board cradle, the wrapping went entirely around the board; in the rawhide type, it was placed around the baby and pad and threaded through the interstices [29, 42]. Household members gently swung the cradle from time to time as they passed it in the course of the general household routine.

Once accustomed to the cradle, the baby apparently preferred it to the bed. Instances were reported where a baby put in bed at night cried until one or the other parent placed it back in the swing [29, 42].

Cradles were not used to transport babies from place to place. When the mother, father, brothers, sisters, or some other relative took the infant visiting or into the plaza, they placed it on their backs and secured it there by wrapping a blanket about their shoulders [29, 42].

The baby was broken of the cradle habit at about the age of one year, or nine to twelve months according to Jeançon (1904 and 1906), shortly after it began to creep. Babies who desired to remain on the cradle beyond this period were ridiculed and teased by relatives and visitors [29, 42].

Swing cradles of both types continued to

be used at Santa Clara Pueblo as late as 1941.

Sitting, Creeping, and Walking

Between the ages of eight and ten months, infants began to creep and to sit up. Both activities were encouraged by the parents, who assisted the baby in its efforts [25, 48]. Creeping in particular was believed to strengthen the body and limbs. Once the infant became adept at creeping, it was clothed in aprons, one in front and one in back [48].

Once the baby was able to toddle about, much of the responsibility for its supervision was delegated to older children in the family, particularly girls, if there were any. These, when not otherwise occupied, played in the plaza adjacent to the home, and the baby accompanied them. As it grew older, it was included in the informalized play activities and became a member of one or another of the children's groups.

Santa Clara babies learned to walk between the ages of nine and thirteen months [25, 48]. This falls within the range reported by Dennis and Dennis (1940: 107) for the Tewa, but is somewhat earlier than the average age reported by them. It was said that males learned to walk earlier than females [25].

As in the case of other accomplishments, the acquisition of this skill was accompanied by constant encouragement and assistance from relatives. "The infant was held by the hands, instructed in how to take steps, and praised for its success" [25, 48]. When it achieved some facility, moccasins were made for it if it was a girl, moccasins and leggings if a boy [48].

According to two informants [29, 35], a red ant (spider) was tied to the leg of the child to make it walk early.

Talking

Almost inordinate effort was expended by parents and grandparents in teaching the infant to talk. A conscious attempt was made to familiarize the individual with the world and the nuclear group of persons upon whom he could depend and with whom he was expected to cooperate. Objects were pointed out and named, and persons were designated by their kinship term [25, 48]. "They usually learn the terms for maternal uncle and aunt first" [25]. "When they seem to catch a word, you repeat that over and over to them" [48]. Stress was placed upon correct grammar and pronunciation. "When a child is learning to speak, he is told when he does wrong not to do it" [48]. "They correct pronunciation and grammar in children. They prevent baby talk when it occurs" [25].

Some children were able to say a word or two as early as nine months [25], but the time that they begin to acquire real facility was between the ages of one year and eighteen months [48]. According to Parsons (1924b: 150), "Children could be made to talk early by placing a stirring stick, still warm from use, in the child's mouth and stirring it around."

Play

There was little that could be designated as play during the first year of the child's life, and certainly nothing of an organized nature. While members of the immediate family, when not otherwise occupied, might talk to, fondle, or otherwise attempt to entertain the infant, it was usually left to its own devices. Once broken of the cradle, its horizons increased, and it might amuse itself by observing the antics of older children and exploring the room.

Toys were not numerous. Occasionally the child was given one of the household implements and amused itself with that. Dolls were made for small girls. These were of two types: rag dolls and the cased skins of tree squirrels stuffed with cotton. A few had ladder-like swingcradles in which they placed the dolls [36, 51].

Playthings of a more complicated nature were presented to the child as it grew older. Among these were stilts and gourd "buzzers." The latter consisted of a gourd disc perforated in two places near its center. A continuous cord was threaded through the perforations and twisted. The loops were then placed on the fingers. By contracting and expanding the distance between the hands, the disc was whirled, giving a roaring sound [65].

Another toy, devised to test skill and coordination, consisted of a hollow cane tube and a bean. The child placed the bean with its long axis horizontal to the end of the tube and attempted to shift the axis to a vertical position by blowing in the other end. "They did not have pea shooters" [65].

As soon as the child began to toddle or walk, its opportunities for entertainment were greatly increased. When weather permitted, it was allowed outside, and was included in one of the informally organized neighborhood groups. These indulged in both organized and unorganized forms of amusement. Group leadership appeared to rest primarily on age.

One of the favorite unorganized games was "playing house." This was indulged in by children of both sexes, who imitated the actions of elders. Making "mud pies" was another popular amusement. This was often combined with the above, and mud houses and household utensils were made [23, 65].

Hide-and-seek ranked high in the category of organized children's games, and was played by mixed groups of girls and boys. Another favorite was the so-called "arrow game" (mi i). In this a number of corn cobs were placed upright in the earth. Participants threw corncobs at these and attempted to knock down as many as possible [23, 65].

A correlate of the above, but played with arrows, was described by T.S. Dozier (Culin 1907: 395):

> On the bringing in of the corn and after the dance in honor of that event the first games of the season begin. Then the boys, from the smallest tot able to walk to well grown up ones, and the younger men may be seen at different places about the pueblo with the ah (bow) and tsu (arrow). As you go by you ask: "Humbi-o" (What are you doing?), and they reply, "I-vi-tsu-ah-wa" (Playing the arrow). The game is a very simple one, as played by the Tewa, the bows not being the stronger ones formerly used, nor the very excellent ones now made by the Apache, Navaho, and Ute. A ring, vary-

ing in diameter from 5 to 6 inches to 2 or 3 feet is made on the ground, and the arrows are placed upright in the earth. The players take their places around the ring and shoot for position. The ones coming nearest the place, generally marked by a stone or a piece of wood, from which the arrows will be shot at, will shoot first in their order. The shooting then begins, and in order to win, the arrow must be thrown entirely from the ring, and the ones winning the most arrows take positions in the next shooting and go until the arrows in the ring are exhausted.

Boys practiced with a bow and arrow from a very early age in order to perfect their marksmanship [23].

Another organized game reported by Dozier (Culin 1907: 643) was shinny. The competing teams were made up of individuals of the same sex and approximate age. When played by children the game was purely for amusement, and lacked the ceremonial association present when adult males competed.

What was said to be a relatively recent introduction for the amusement of boys was tops. These were shaped like modern tops, fashioned from piñon, and were spun with a buckskin string [43, 50]. According to T.S. Dozier (Culin 1907: 748),

> The Tewa of Santa Clara call a top pfet-e-ne; playing a top, i-vi-pfet-e-ne-o-a-rai-mai. This no doubt is of modern date, but the small boys are the most expert top spinners I ever saw. It is played without gain, but in the old way, where the other fellow may have his top ruined by being knocked out of the ring.

A still more recent introduction has been the game of marbles, played by both sexes and all ages [43, 50].

Acquisitions of Skills

During early childhood the foundations were laid for the development of many skills that would later determine the individual's success in the role of male or female in the culture. This early period was one of indoctrination by indirect methods. Much knowledge was imparted through play or acquired by imitation. At no time in the early years was there a great deal of pressure placed upon the child. "You teach the child more through play at first. They learn things from watching their elders. Girls volunteer to grind. They are corrected" [48]. "Learning to make pottery was left up to the child. The mother would be making pottery, the child would be given a piece of clay. It would imitate the mother, the mother would correct it" [51]. "Some daughters began fooling with pottery when they were only about five" [29].

Girls learned many skills, in rudimentary form, by marginal participation in the routine duties and activities of the household. This participation was encouraged by the mother and other relatives. "As they get older, they really begin to be some help" [48]. Young boys similarly accompanied male relatives on work trips and learned, by observation and by play participation, the techniques relevant to their spheres of life. It was the men's job to educate the boys. Girls were educated by the women [65].

Once the child reached the age of six to eight years, the earlier attitude of tolerance began to change. From that time on, the individual was expected to assume increasing responsibility and to acquire a specialized knowledge of skills. Coincidentally the processes of education became more formalized than previously, and the boy or girl began to be forced into the traditional pattern of Pueblo culture.

This era was really the crucial one in the life of the individual, since success in an adult role and in attendant personal adjustments depended to a large extent on how well he or she mastered the techniques of living. While it was a period of intensive learning, it was one into which the child entered with a minimum of uncertainty. In the previous years, a pattern of rewards and punishments had been created which made later acquisition of the culture easier. There was also ample motivation, since the value and desirability of knowledge and virtuosity in skills was immediately apparent and observable in the successes and failures in

the village. Parsons (1924b: 151) summed up the educational methodology as follows: "In craftmanship, as in education at large, the Pueblo way is the way of apprenticeship."

Mothers or other female relatives, as noted, proceeded in a practical manner to teach girls. Much of the care for younger children was delegated to them under supervision. They were expected to engage in general household duties, and were taught how to prepare foods, care for the house, clean, plaster, etc. Pressure was applied upon them not only to learn, but also to perform their allotted share of work.

In recent years pottery making has been the principal medium through which women can achieve individual prominence. If a girl showed aptitude in this art, she was encouraged to pursue it. Instruction might be given by the mother, if she was an adept potter; if not, by any relative or a friend. "My friend [70] learned to make pottery at about the age of ten; her daughter learned from her" [29]. "In another case... this woman, now middle-aged, had learned as a girl to make pottery from her aunt who was a particularly good potter. This girl would visit her aunt and work with her" (Parsons 1924b: 151).

Male roles were more diversified than those of women, and the education of boys was correspondingly broader. Fathers or other male relatives normally acted as instructors. Boys, as they grew older, accompanied them to the fields and learned through observation and participation, as well as by direct instruction, the fundamental knowledge of agricultural processes.

Education in hunting was complicated by the necessity of ceremonial knowledge. Some of this was taught to the boy before he joined a hunt party. "You tell him the ritual to perform before he leaves and what to do in the field, how to dispose of the intestines, how to place the boughs, etc." [64]. Once in the field, practical instruction took place.

Any organized work party also functioned as an educational medium for young males. This was especially true of groups organized for hunting or wood cutting. These parties ordinarily remained away from the village for several days. At night around the campfire, it was customary for the elders to discuss any and all subjects with the conscious goal of teaching the young men [43].

Education of this same sort, applied to both boys and girls, was also carried on in the village. Elders, past their peak of economic usefulness, acted as instructors, lecturing to the youth of the village as opportunities arose. Much of this instruction was conveyed in story form, both through the use of folktales and by reference to actual situations of the past [29, 72].

Games also had their educational role. Through participation, boys acquired proficiency in handling weapons. They likewise had their value in perfecting coordination and individual conditioning.

Values and Their Acquisition

A variety of related but somewhat intangible items of culture, such as approved attitudes, goals, ideals, and ethics have been grouped under the heading of values. In their totality they constituted an important part of the world outlook of Santa Clara Indians. In a real sense they represented phrasings and emphases that produced the unique character of the culture of that pueblo specifically, and of the Tewa culture generally. These values were the principal criteria of prestige and esteemed status among adults, and the degree to which they were ultimately exemplified in the individual was a partial gauge of the person's standing in the community.

Information concerning the acquisition of values was difficult to obtain. First, many of the concepts were not tangible; accordingly, this was not the type of information readily volunteered by informants or easily expressed by them when questioned. Second, many were traits that were rarely, if ever, at the conscious level.

Because of the above reasons, and for the sake of objectivity, discussion of value acquisition will be limited to those for which specific information was available, and to those whose attributes were objectified in concrete or observable behavior. While the author is aware that the following roster is incomplete, he believes that it includes most of the important concepts that acted as

motivating forces for approved behavior and which resulted in the formation of compatible personality traits.

Among these ideals were industry, respect for old age, courtesy, conservatism, secretiveness, cooperation, generosity, and conformity. Many of these were, of course, interrelated. For example the ideal of universal courtesy was in part an extension of attitudes associated with the aged; conservatism was a partial reflection of the regard in which the aged were held; secretiveness was part of the mechanics of enforcing conservatism; and generosity was in part an outgrowth of the emphasis on cooperation.

The mechanisms by which values were introduced to the child were usually indirect and unformalized. Much of this knowledge was absorbed tangentially, as part of more specific instruction in specialized skills and routine attainments necessary for the proper performance of everyday roles. Other learning came through observation and imitation of behavior of those with whom there was daily contact. When formal teaching was involved, it served mainly to reinforce and permanently fix the approved concepts rather than to institute them.

Industry was considered one of the most esteemed personal characteristics. Exemplification of this virtue was usually present in the home, and the child could not fail to be impressed by constant example. This was fortified by direct reference and encouragement to emulate persons in the family or village who possessed this trait in high degree. The subject was also a part of any formalized lecture given by elders at gatherings, whether these were social in nature or groups assembled for the performance of specific tasks either secular or religious [29, 43]. When example and instruction proved insufficient, disciplinary measures were employed to stimulate conformance [49].

Some specific attitudes involved and the methods used in conveying this principle were expressed by informants as follows: "When I was a boy, work and bathing were emphasized. You had to get up early and bathe, think good thoughts, and work hard in the fields" [64]. "The ideal woman, among other things, was one who was industrious"

[65]. "Some children, when they reach the age of ten, are whipped if they will not work. All Pueblo people work. It is only the evil who do not work. Idleness is evil" [77]; deviants in this respect would commonly be suspected of witchcraft, i.e., nonconformists. "They would say, mind your grandparents, keep busy all the time, be industrious" [44].

An objectification of the attitude toward industry was also to be found in customs following birth. When that section of the umbilical cord attached to the baby dried and fell off, it was buried near the grinding stones if the baby was a girl, "so when she grows up, she may not be lazy"; if a boy, in the field, "so he could work" (Parsons 1924b: 149).

The pattern of religious and political authority at Santa Clara Pueblo could be termed a gerontocratic theocracy. Early in life the individual was introduced to this system and its concomitant, a respect for seniority. As in the case of industry, much of this respect was engendered through observation of examples at home, as well as by direct reference. Approved attitudes toward the aged were also conveyed to a child as it was taught kinship terms and the reciprocal obligations inherent in the kinship system. As the social contacts of an individual increased, this early pattern was extended to include more distant relatives and nonrelatives. At the same time, coercive measures were applied to insure high conformance to the pattern.

This attitude of respect, almost approaching veneration in some instances, was objectified in various ways. It was apparent, for example, in the behavior of all of my interpreters in dealing with older informants. It was expressed in such concrete terms as: "When I was a boy, the old people were the best. My grandfather was one" [64]. Younger men followed the admonitions of the old. "You did as the elders told you. In the old days they respected grandfathers and older men and listened to what they said. That was why things were better in the old days. I tried to make myself like my grandfathers and granduncles" [65]. This attitude became explicit in the constant attention and care bestowed upon the aged,

whether related or not [29, 64]. It was exemplified in numerous small deferences. For example, "Whenever you give something to elders, such as a drink of water, you fold your arms while they are drinking. You do not say anything until they finish. This is a mark of respect" [61].

Emphasis on seniority was also reflected in the kinship structure. Siblings were differentiated on the basis of younger or elder. Special terms were applied to the mother's (and father's) sisters, depending upon their age relative to that of the parents. Grandparental terms were applied to nonrelatives in the elder category as a form of courtesy. In a similar manner, "pet names," such as "my old mother," were used as forms of daily address.

Courtesy in dealing with others in face-to-face situations was a highly considered personal quality. This was impressed upon the child early in life, and he or she was constantly kept aware of it. "They were taught to greet one another and be respectful. They used to address people by relationship terms even if they were not related" [64]. My own observations confirmed this attitude as one of the most obvious adult personality traits. Throughout my fieldwork, overt behavior toward me was uniformly gracious and tolerant; this continued to be true even in the face of situations that in many instances must have been repugnant to the individuals with whom I was dealing. For example, on several occasions informants denied knowledge of certain areas of the culture with which they were commonly recognized to be familiar. This recourse allowed them to preserve their own integrity without violating the dictates of good manners through direct refusal.

As was true of most things acquired as part of the socialization process, this form of approved behavior was not taught as an isolated fragment, but was tied in with learning in general. Examples have already been cited, and it was implicit in the data on kinship, discipline, and especially attitudes toward seniority. That individuals were tested from time to time is obvious. "There was emphasis on courtesy. Older men would tease or ridicule younger men while working. It helped pass the time. No one got mad. The young men did not answer back. Women did the same" [64].

Oldsters represent the conservative element in any population. At Santa Clara Pueblo, the stress placed upon this segment of the local group and the amount of power vested in them resulted in a reinforcement and an implementation of these conservative tendencies to a degree rarely encountered among other societies. The elders were literally "the books," and there was a general belief that there was a great good inherent in the practice of the "old ways" they advocated. This accent on the maintenance of the established order was one of the most characteristic traits of Santa Clara culture, and one that made possible the continuation of a high degree of cultural integrity in the face of over four hundred years of European contact. While it applied most strongly in the religious and social fields, it was extended to include the most mundane subjects.

Children, at an early period in their development, were imbued with confidence in the established order, as well as with the necessity for maintaining it. Instruction on these subjects tended to be more formalized than most. Some was imparted by the parents to the child; other teaching came through the "story-lectures" given by the grandparental generation. But the most effective devices were those highly formal lectures usually preceding and following religious ceremonies. Probably the best examples of these are the talks given by the cacique or other religious officials at the time of a kachina ceremony. On such occasions the benefits to be derived from conservative behavior and adherence to the old patterns were pronounced, and there were also reminders of the dangers inherent in deviance from them, both supernatural and secular.

Behavior and beliefs objectifying this principle were numerous, and only a few will be given as examples. Formerly lack of conformity in both children and adults was handled by stern coercive measures: in the case of children, by whipping; in the case of adults, either by whipping or by tying to a tree in the plaza, or in extreme cases by banishment from the pueblo. These measures were fortified by a firm belief that illness and accident were often the supernatural consequences of such transgressions.

Secretiveness was one of the principal mechanisms employed in the preservation of the conservative ideal. While in theory secretiveness applied primarily to relations with outsiders, it actually went beyond this and permeated everyday relationships within the village as well. So thoroughgoing were its effects that Santa Clara Pueblo represented a somewhat anomalous situation among nonliterate peoples; i.e., Santa Clara Indians lacked the usual homogeneity of such groups, since much of the cultural knowledge, especially in the area of religion, was restricted to a minor segment of the population.

The same system of indoctrination and the same controls and punishments employed to engender conservatism were used to insure secretiveness. The degree to which the desired results were achieved and some appreciation of this value in terms of Santa Clara culture were apparent in numerous incidents occurring during the course of my field research.

The following episode illustrates the depth of this principle in connection with mundane aspects of life. On this occasion the author was discussing basketry with an informant [64] at the home of his daughter. In order to clarify a technical point, the informant volunteered to go to his house across the plaza and bring a basket. When he returned it was nowhere visible; I asked if he had been unable to find it. He then removed it from where he had hidden it under his shirt. He had been unwilling to cross the plaza carrying the basket openly, since it might arouse curiosity, cause gossip, and result in criticism.

This behavior was later described to another informant [50]. He found it neither inconsistent nor surprising. His comment was, "They hide everything, if they can hide it," thus expressing concisely one of the most powerful themes in Santa Clara culture, one which was continually exemplified by interpreters and informants.

During 1941 the author lived in the pueblo, and much of the fieldwork was done in the room that he occupied. Throughout the period interpreters and informants never arrived together. Each came alone and by a different route. One interpreter was unwilling to walk past the house of the Winter cacique with me, and was obviously ill at ease on the few occasions when it could not be avoided.

One informant [55] refused to work except at night. The two sessions he worked lasted from 8:00 P.M. to 2:00 A.M. A few days later, the author offered him a ride to Española. He accepted but he absolutely ignored the fact that he had served as an informant or that we had even seen each other before. [Here Hill had written in this comment concerning another informant, "(71) has decided to die with knowledge of K'osa rather than to pass it on." It is unclear whether this referred to other Santa Clara Indians, even K'osa members, or only to Hill. CHL]

The gravity of the violation of secrecy was increased if matters concerning religion were involved. This stemmed not only from the belief that those who transgressed would be subjected to divine retribution in the form of illness, but also from the conviction that retailing religious information weakened its supernatural potency [65]. Care was taken to screen the audience before any esoteric religious performance; outsiders and those suspect were denied admission [61, 72]. Furthermore, psychic powers were attributed to religious performers, enabling them to tell whether there were nonbelievers in the audience, and whether such people intended to reveal secrets. In the case of the Bear societies, these individuals would be slapped with bear paws by society members [61].

Two other examples will suffice to illustrate the intensity of the sentiment associated with secrecy. During the course of the fieldwork, the author had occasion to show a conservative informant, heir apparent at that time to the Winter caciqueship, a copy of Parsons' *Social Organization of the Tewa.* This resulted in one of the few instances of overt anger I witnessed in an adult. The informant vilified Parsons's informant. He then lectured the interpreter on the danger and disadvantages of allowing information except on the most mundane things to be divulged to outsiders. He finished this tirade by pointing out the consequences of such acts in terms of jeopardizing the well-being of the village, and then by reciting the concluding statement given at a kachina performance: "Hide it in your crotch, under your arm pits, etc." Incidentally his lecture revealed much information that was needed for clarifying the religious picture.

At a later date, an attempt was made to secure one of Parsons's informants [80] as an informant for my work. The man, since deceased, knew he was suspect, having previously been subjected to criticism. He informed the interpreter that no one ever gave such information; confronting him with Parsons' book almost resulted in a case of shock—the man turned pale, shook, and was unable to speak.

Early in its life, a child was imbued with the ideal of cooperation. This feature was initially limited to the activities of the family and/or ingroup. Loyalties were directed toward this social segment, and children were expected to assist and share in the responsibilities and duties, which included production, maintenance of the household, and care of its membership, to the limits of their capabilities. Evidence of the individual's efforts toward the achievement of this goal was apparent in all aspects of the socialization process.

Once ingrained the extension of the pattern of cooperation expected of adults, from the smaller social grouping to include the moiety or village, was a simple matter. Verification of this value is apparent in the data pertaining to the family, community work, religious participation, and the care of the aged and indigents, and will not be repeated here. What is involved here is a unanimity so important, especially in religion, that it extends beyond the usual meaning of cooperation. This unanimity embraces ideas and beliefs as expressed in ceremonies.

The culture of Santa Clara was so oriented that generosity was an obligation expected of all village members. This was expressed both in material ways and through personal service. It did not necessarily represent a spontaneous action on an individual basis, but instead was predominantly a matter of habit.

The accumulation of economic surpluses, or hoarding, was foreign to the cultural ideology. Fortunate or wealthy individuals were expected to use, and usually did use any economic excess for the benefit of others. Only through the distribution of goods could one of the factors leading to an enhanced status be achieved. "A man did not get respect by sheer wealth only. He should hire people to help him and distribute the goods. Generosity would elevate a man" [65]. Here again was a pattern reminiscent of the Plains tribes.

The ultimate manifestations of generosity in terms of personal service included placing the general welfare of the community or larger group above that of the individual. In the ideal person, it resulted in the development of an attitude of selflessness, and in extensive participation in various civic enterprises, both secular and religious.

Generosity was closely related to the ideal of cooperation, and was in part an extension of it. The sharing of responsibility and activities in the home included the sharing of goods; a child had this specific trait impressed upon it as part of a larger complex. Beyond this immediate group, the developing individual could observe and participate in the application of this principle in situations as it applied to the care of the indigent and aged, and also to hospitality both within and outside the village.

From the viewpoint of a Santa Clara Indian, conformity represented a summation of all values and all desirable personality traits. A conformist was one who conducted life's activities according to the traditional patterns, and implemented them by expressions of personality that fell within the approved boundaries of the culture. To say a man was a conformist was, in the Santa Clara sense, to say he had integrity. The stress placed upon this concept elevated it to the position of the most all-pervasive theme in Santa Clara culture.

Since conformity was inherent in all values, children were instructed in this paramount virtue as part of the general socialization process. Two concerns, both important in the formation of personality, were peculiar to this value area. One was the stress placed upon relative anonymity; the second was the curbing and discouraging of idiosyncratic tendencies in a child. In early life the same techniques of education and enforcement were used as in other value areas. As the individual matured, the mechanics of enforcement applied to adults—gossip, threats of accusation of withcraft, and direct coercive action—were used to insure social normality and conformity.

In the eyes of a Santa Clara Indian, a nonconformist was a person without integrity. This is implicit in several examples already used to illustrate other values. However, the depth of this all-pervading principle, as well as the attitude toward the violation of secrecy, is perhaps best summarized in a statement by Aitken (1930). Regarding the political schism of the nineteenth century at Santa Clara Pueblo, Aitken (p. 386) wrote:

> The offence against co-operation, against unanimity, against solidarity was deeply felt. In 1815 Antonio Canjuebe had denounced the "customs" to the Spaniards as "diabolical rites"; his spiritual successors in 1897 repeated the same phrase, and before a lawyer in Santa Fé made accusations of human sacrifice and "things that cannot be said." This breach of solidarity hurt worse than mere heresy. "If *you* were to abandon the Christian religion," the Summer Side governor remarked, "I think you would have more decency than to disclose what you know about it!"

Religious Awe

Contact with formalized religious phases of the culture was established early in the life of an individual. While there is no reason to believe that the transmission of religious concepts as such took place as early as two or three years of age, it can be assumed that the child of this age was already aware of the cultural reality of the supernatural, and already possessed some feelings of religious awe or sentiment.

The impact of the supernatural on the

individual was experienced in several ways. Parents customarily brought infants to kachina performances, and it would have been surprising if the one or two-year-old did not experience some reaction from witnessing the antics of the masked impersonators. Reactions of a similar nature could be expected from attendance at other rites, for example those of the several secret societies, particularly of the curing groups, whose medical exercises and purification ceremonies were usually held in the homes. The child might even have acted in the capacity of patient in one of these. Another means, and perhaps the most effective, was the use of the concept of supernatural bogies for purposes of discipline.

The effectiveness of all these agencies was accentuated as a child became older. What might be called the culmination of religious education in childhood was the "Water Immersion" (Po ku) ceremony. In this ceremony, a child underwent the first personalized religious experience of which it was conscious, aside from possible curing rites. This ceremony was also important in that it marked to some extent the transition from childhood to preadolescence and adolescence.

As will be seen later, purposeful and organized religious training, for both men and women, was associated with adult development rather than with childhood.

Rewards

The ages of infancy and early childhood comprised a period in which the individual was constantly rewarded in the form of various kinds of attention. This is particularly true of the infant stage. During this helpless period, he or she was almost never out of sight or hearing of the mother or some other relative. The slightest indication of distress was an occasion for action on the part of some member of the family. When the infant cried, it was nursed. If it continued to cry, it was changed or an attempt was made to discover other sources for its discomfiture. Parents, grandparents, and siblings talked to the baby and fondled and coddled it. It was constantly encouraged and praised for its achievements, and subjected

to a minimum of frustration. Every effort was made to create an atmosphere of warmth and affection in the home. As the child matured, material awards in the form of gifts were added. Whether consciously or not, these practices set the pattern for strong family solidarity so characteristic of Santa Clara culture.

Punishment and Prohibitions

Contrary to popular belief, the Tewa child did not grow up in a free, uninhibited manner, but was subjected to a variety of cultural controls and disciplinary measures. Since children were not considered responsible beings, some reprehensible actions were excused on this basis—especially in the early years. However, from infancy on, a certain, definite code of behavior was expected; penalties were applied to those who were disobedient or indolent, cried inordinately, had tantrums, frequently lost their tempers, lacked respect for elders, or otherwise failed to conform [58, 64, 65].

One to three-year-olds were subjected to a minimum of punishments or prohibitions. Little or no corporal punishment was administered during this period of an individual's life. Occasionally the infant was scolded, but the scoldings were never severe. If, when it began to creep and toddle about, a child approached things that might endanger it or that it might damage, the customary procedure was to remove the object if possible, and if not, to take the child to another area of the room or house and distract its attention [48, 58].

From this time on, there was a gradual increase in the variety and severity of disciplinary measures. Scoldings increased in frequency and severity, and were bolstered by corporal punishment. "Some families had to whip their children; in others, the children behaved themselves" [64]. Parsons (1924b: 150), speaking of the Tewa generally, gave the following confirmatory incidents:

Parents may punish directly too. "Do what the old people tell you, else I will beat you," a mother might say to a child. And formerly no child would ever think of saying as children say today, "What you pay me?" to a senior asking service. I heard of a man who did whip his two little boys when they had been "mean" to their sister. She and her brothers would be sent to the river, as used to be the practice, to wash their face, in winter through the ice, and on their way the brothers would tease—"boys are mean to girls."

When the refractory activities of the child impinged upon persons outside the relationship, village authorities might administer the punishment. For example, "If children drove cattle into the fields, members of the governing body would visit and whip the children. Parents in the old days would say, 'That is right'" [64].

Unsanctioned behavior was also controlled by means of ridicule and teasing. Those who performed in an undesirable manner were subjected to odious comparisons and teased by both elders and near age-mates [59, 64, 72, 77].

The "bogey" concept was another practice used to induce obedience. The effectiveness of this increased in direct proportion as the child gained in comprehension. The principal "bogey" characters were the masked impersonators, the savadjo, and related members of that group, and the coyote. When a child was insubordinate or cried inordinately, the mother or some other relative threatened to call one of these supernaturals, who were believed to punish and to kidnap. Much of the potency of this form of control derived from the fact that impersonators of these characters appeared intermittently in the village, and sometimes actually administered corporal punishment. Details of the activities and descriptions of bogies are given in the section on clowns (Chapter 10) and will not be repeated here.

In like manner the kachinas themselves might be used as a threat. Details of this tool of supernatural control occur in the discussion of kachinas, the organization, and the ceremonies (Chapter 10).

Occasionally actual people were substituted for supernaturals. Parents would tell untractable children that they would give them to such and such a person if they did

not behave. The person selected was usually one whom the child disliked or feared, or who was a stranger [49, 59, 73]. On several occasions when children interrupted the fieldwork, the parent threatened to give a child to the interpreter or myself to take to Albuquerque. This was usually sufficient to control the situation.

As children advanced in age, outsiders might be called in for disciplinary assistance. There were always several elderly men who were held in high esteem by the whole village. Frequently parents sent disobedient children for advice and admonition to such an individual, and this action was said to produce highly successful results. The method of these men was one of gentle counsel. "They never laid a hand on the child, yet because the words of these men were so respected, their advice was usually carried out." "Children would also go to them of their own accord when they had been bad; in late years for moral reasons. Sometimes adults too" [18, 72].

Major responsibility for discipline, however, rested with the parents. In the early years of a child's life, the brunt was borne by the mother, since the father was occupied away from home for a large part of the day [45, 48]. Retaliation on the part of the child was unthinkable in view of the culture's stress on respect for seniority. It was believed that should a child strike its mother, its hand would shrivel [29, 52].

Corporal punishment was administered with a cowhide whip. The lash was of dressed hide and usually three-ply braid. This was attached to a wooden stick, or handle [48].

Social Controls

Santa Clara Pueblo lacked a legal code in a modern sense, and it operated under a system of customary law. Within this framework, however, different degrees of criminality were recognized. An important distinction was made between major crimes, antisocial actions which were believed to jeopardize the welfare of the state, and minor crimes, infringements which violated the rights of or threatened the individual. In effect there existed a body of "public law" and a body of "private, or personal law."

"Public law," while not comparable in terms of specifics, was similar to Catholic canon or English ecclesiastical law, whose objective was "concern with the health of the soul." Most violations of "public law," major crimes, represented cases of religious defection, i.e., they were acts of heresy. They included all behavior deemed offensive to supernatural agencies, that consequently might endanger the success, well-being, and general health of the community. Since, in a theocratic state, almost any action is capable of religious interpretation, "public law" was broad in scope. It was in this area that legal thinking was best organized.

Some examples of the violation of "public law" and resultant punishments are cited in the discussion of political factionalism (Chapter 9). In every case the situation was interpreted as an instance of religious nonconformity. Proper intent was always assumed in cases involving adult males, since they had undergone the kachina initiation and were, therefore, cognizant of right and wrong.

The category of major crimes encompassed the following types of antisocial behavior: failure to perform religious obligations, i.e., take part in a dance or ritual, to help in cleaning the ditch or village, failure to participate in reconditioning the church or kiva, or to do any type of cooperative project designated by the cacique through the agencies of the outside chief or governor. If a man did not wish to dance, he would be whipped. Other actions designated as major crimes were leaving the pueblo for an extended period without permission from the cacique or governor (in the case of society members, absences of this type affected religious continuity and effectiveness); harvesting or planting prior to the day appointed by the caciques; practicing witchcraft; and giving information to outsiders on religion or other aspects of Santa Clara culture.

"Private, or personal law" dealt with misconduct of lesser magnitude. In minor crimes religious involvement was lacking or less pronounced. These were deviations which primarily concerned individuals. Public welfare was not endangered. They in-cluded cases of personal injury and infringement, and breach of contract. Cited as minor crimes were various types of assault, malicious gossip, nagging, slovenliness, lewdness, adultery, fornication, drunkenness, and conflicts involving damages and ownership.

Within the legal framework there were a number of recognized agents and agencies, as well as cultural mechanisms, which were invoked for purposes of social control. Of these mechanisms, some were formalized and operated as direct instruments; others, while unformalized, indirect, and often subtle, were equally effective.

Preeminent among the direct agents were the caciques who, in their capacity as theocratic arbitrators and interpreters, either personally or through the outside chief or war captain and the governor and their aides, meted out the punishments, enforced compliance, and made adjudications. Within this hierarchy, the caciques had almost unlimited power. As indicated in Chapter 9, the outside chief was primarily concerned with transgressions of a religious nature, and the governor, with secular ones. To what extent these two officials held authority to operate independently of the caciques is not clear. Presumably, in situations for which there were precedents, they could act without referral.

Prior to 1936 the council also functioned as an agency of the caciques. The extent to which these religious officials dominated this agency concerned with major crimes is illustrated by this statement by an informant [81]:

> Cases were referred to the council, not for the purpose of determining the guilt or innocence of the accused, but rather to mete out a sentence. It was assumed that the defendant was guilty when he was brought before the council. Long lectures were delivered to the accused by the older members. The conventional manner of behavior was praised, and the accused reproved and made to realize that what was important was not so much the offense itself, but deviation from the conventional way of behaving. Under the conservatives, council meet-

ings were really courts of inquisition. Punishments were meted out rather than holding a disinterested trial. Violators of tradition were always suspected of an attempt to overthrow the ideals handed down through the years, and there was little mercy shown them.

Besides dealing with major crimes, the council could and did sit on cases of land assignment, land and water disputes, and personal injury or infringement.

The constitution of 1935 gave the council a certain degree of autonomy, and released it in part from the domination of the religious hierarchy. Since that time it has functioned more in the capacity of a legislative and judicial body.

While their major focus was in other directions, the Clown and Bear societies acted in part as formalized agencies for social control (see discussions of these groups in Chapter 10). The principal weapon of the clowns was sanctioned public ridicule. When acting in their official capacity, they were given unlimited license and were extremely effective.

They were particularly concerned, however, with minor crimes—especially moral lapses and abnormal natural and social behavior; secondarily, with blocking innovation. Their lampooning of Anglo and Spanish-American behavior and custom was an effective deterrent to acculturation. While their chief coercive weapon was ridicule, they were privileged to attack a person bodily and destroy the property of a transgressor. On ceremonial occasions they also acted as informal police.

The unaffiliated clown figures of the savadjo group focused on the deviations of children and juveniles. Their roles in this connection have already been mentioned.

The Bear societies, in their part-time capacity as social control agencies, operated in a more subtle and indirect manner than the clowns. Their primary concern was with religious defection. In their capacity as diagnosticians, they were instrumental in publicizing supernatural retributions resulting from a breach of tabu. As the front line of defense against witchcraft, they were responsible for publicizing the penalties of that crime. In the main, however, they acted as deterrent rather than as a positive legal arm of the government.

Besides the regularly constituted legal figures and agencies, there were a number of men of prestige and esteemed status who, though lacking in coercive powers, acted in instances of deviation. Normally their sphere of influence was in the area of "personal, or private" law, and was limited to their extended families or other relatives. Occasionally, however, such a figure would act for an entire moiety. Within this restricted segment of the population, they functioned as admonishers and legal advisors. They were especially concerned with juvenile and family problems. Delinquents were often sent to them rather than to the caciques.

These practices do not imply that the kin group could in any sense be construed as a legal unit; it definitely was not. Furthermore, any idea of collective responsibility, in a legal sense, was lacking.

There were two principal, unformalized mechanisms for the enforcement of social norms. One stemmed from a conviction of the reality of divine retribution. The other was the power of public opinion. One or both often operated in conjunction with coercive measures to assure compliance.

The consequences of divine retribution are detailed in the section on disease, medicine, and curing societies. Any breach of tabu or law placed the individual in the category of sinner as well as that of criminal. It was believed that even though a person escaped the notice of and punishment by human agencies, supernatural agencies would eventually manifest themselves, and retribution in the form of illness, accident, or some other misfortune would be visited on the individual. Such punishments were often combined. This teleological factor in the diagnosis of disease resulted in constant self-analysis, and also in the development of considerable anxiety. This awareness of conscience was a major factor in cultural stabilization.

Besides general approbation or censure, public opinion employed a number of specific devices to safeguard the mandates of society. These were brought into play as soon as deviations occurred or were suspected. They included ridicule, social ostracism, gossip, rumor, and accusation of witchcraft. Since the population was small and in an almost constant state of interaction, the impact of these weapons was enormous. Once mobilized against a wrongdoer, they were extremely potent forces for conformity.

Ridicule, besides the sanctioned religious kind occurring during ceremonies, was common. Much of this took place "behind the back" of the recipient. But it was not uncommon for social deviants to be publicly rebuked and ridiculed by villagemates. Often this pressure, exerted over a period of time, was so great that persistent nonconformists left the pueblo. "Those who can't take it, leave" [52].

Another effective punishment where adults were concerned was social ostracism. Errant individuals were systematically avoided and shunned, and slighted on public occasions. As in the case of ridicule, the prolonged application of ostracism often led to the departure of the person from the village.

The egocentric character of the village furnished fertile soil for gossip. This practice, as in most small towns, was one of the most vicious of Santa Clara traits and a favorite preoccupation. It encompassed almost any subject, from the most trivial to those of vital concern to the whole village. Even the most insensitive were aware of its existence and potency. As one informant [81] expressed it:

They gossip about anything or anyone who violates a rule of the pueblo. Even if they get only a little hint, they enlarge upon it. They gossip about girls having affairs. If an unmarried girl becomes pregnant, they gossip about who is the father. There would be gossip about letting secret information out of the pueblo.

Rumor was closely related and often went hand in hand with gossip. Any suspected or imagined violation was immediately publicized. According to an informant [82]:

A rumor would spread through the whole village in about fifteen minutes. Children would be sent to other houses by their mothers to spread them. Some women are regular newspapers. As soon as they hear something, they go right out. [He named several women, including one of his aunts. WWH] Rumor that someone had done wrong would also spread. A rumor that a society was "working" would spread. They see several in a group going into a house, and they think they are "working." If they see someone carrying food, it is a sure sign.

According to another informant [61], on each occasion the author visited Santa Clara, word of my arrival immediately spread through the village, and speculation regarding my activities began. "This would take fifteen minutes."

The wealthy, the too skillful, the too fortunate, and those who departed from customary norms were open to accusations of witchcraft (see discussion of witchcraft in Chapter 10). This form of retaliation, with its social consequences, was an effective means of insuring conformity. For example many progressives of the 1894 schism were accused of practicing witchcraft. While most accusations were leveled by persons seeking a release for aggression or acting out of jealousy, this did not detract from its efficacy as a coercive threat.

Direct punishment varied according to the magnitude of the offense. Whipping was one of the common penalties for major crimes. The culprit was tied to a post or tree and whipped by the governor, sheriff, one of the war captains, or a man appointed by the governor. No one questioned the governor's authority. From one to twenty strokes were administered. Whips were made of braided rawhide with the lashes inserted at the ends. When not in use they were stored at the governor's home.

Another prevalent form of punishment for major defections was placing the individual in "stocks." He or she might be tied either to a post in the kiva or to a tree in the plaza. In other instances the wrists and ankles of a malefactor were tied together, the arms forced over the knees, and a pole inserted above the arms and below the knees. This effectively immobilized the person, and he was then placed either in the kiva or the plaza. In some instances the person was released at night and allowed to return to his home until the next morning. This prevented any release under cover of darkness, and it also provided the greatest public exposure.

Those in the "stocks" were questioned periodically by the governor or other officials. When they convincingly agreed to conform and had apologized to the governor for their behavior, they were released. Those tied or left in the plaza were, of course, subjected to public ridicule.

A less frequently employed form of punishment consisted of standing the wrongdoer in a circle drawn on the kiva floor. The person was then lectured and questioned for a long period of time, concerning his defection. If the individual became exhausted and stepped out of the circle, he or she was beaten. This was continued until a promise of compliance was extracted. [For a recent, public administration of such punishment at Zia Pueblo, see Lange 1952. CHL]

Another alternative, somewhat more violent, was to bind the person securely and drop him or her through the hatchway of the kiva onto the floor. This was repeated until acquiescence was promised.

Those judged guilty of major crimes might also be penalized by having their property confiscated and distributed to members of the village. The amount of property involved varied with the degree of the infraction. In cases where the fields were harvested prior to the date set by the cacique, for example, only the crop was taken; in instances of exaggerated and continued disobedience, however, not only the real estate and foodstuffs but the personal property was appropriated. Such action usually resulted in banishment. This was an extremely serious penalty because of the difficulties of survival outside the confines of the village. Some individuals remained in exile for the duration of their lives. Others drifted back to the village after indeterminate periods and were able to

reestablish themselves as law-abiding members of the community. A gauge of the thoroughgoing effectiveness, as well as the oppressive nature of the mechanism of social control is to be seen in the fact that numerous individuals had chosen self-exile rather than conformity.

This discussion has covered the principal penalties assessed for major crimes. It must be borne in mind, however, that infractions of this magnitude inevitably placed the guilty person in double jeopardy. Not only was he subject to the physical and other punishments just described, but he could also expect divine retribution in the form of illness, accident, or other misfortune.

In the case of witchcraft, divine retribution seems to have been the only penalty. Informants denied that witches were ever "smelled out." They were discovered after the fact, namely, when the power or "wisdom" used for evil boomeranged and caused their demise.

Murder was not included in the list of major crimes, because there was no record of a murder ever having been committed in the village. Informants also denied any incidence of murder involving a member of Santa Clara and some other pueblo, such as San Juan, or San Ildefonso. Cases of suicide were also denied.

"Personal law" covering minor crimes came under the jurisdiction of a number of agencies; penalties were variable, although whipping was the most frequent punishment. Instances of theft were extremely rare. "A person might take a melon from a field, not his own, and no one would say anything because he had probably helped with the work. No one would steal from a home" [52]. Stealing of farm produce by children was handled by the savadjo. In those infrequent cases of theft that reached official channels, restitution was enforced and the culprit was whipped by the governor or his agents. More recently the council has assessed a fine and enforced restitution.

Assault of various kinds was punished by whipping and, more recently, by fines. Penalties were designated by the governor, the council, or both. If both participants were judged guilty, both were punished. Cases were cited resulting from disputes over a woman, disagreements between two women, and friction which developed during the course of communal work. Instances of wife beating were often settled by elders within the family; when official notice was taken of them, the husband was whipped. In addition brawling of any kind was censored by means of gossip, ridicule, or the clown societies.

Rape as a legalistic concept did not exist at Santa Clara. The occurrence of sexual deviants was denied. Cases of adultery, fornication, or lewdness were usually punished by whipping. Both principals normally suffered the same penalty. In addition the guilty were ridiculed, and their crime publicized through the mechanisms of public opinion and the clown societies.

Slovenliness was punished by the clowns, during the course of ceremonies. They entered the home of a disorderly housewife and overturned furniture and personal effects, or threw them into the plaza. Nagging women were brought before the council, and a whipping penalty was assessed.

Drunkards were whipped in past times; more recently they have been fined.

Cases involving malicious gossip or libel were under the jurisdiction of the governor, the council, or both. Earlier the guilty person was tied up or whipped; more recently, fined. The individual at fault was also forced to apologize to the person who had been maligned. Shortly after the constitution of 1935 was adopted, a young man was brought before the council for slander and fined five dollars. Since libel was one of the favorite pastimes at Santa Clara, this action precipitated an avalanche of similar cases. The docket was so heavy that the council had little time for other business. Finally a particularly insignificant example of this type came up for judgment, and the council solved the dilemma by fining both parties. The governor announced to the village that this precedent would be followed in future cases.

Disputes over water rights and land ownership were passed on by the governor or council. Cases involving crop damage by cattle were usually settled "out of court." If the two litigants were unable to reach an agreement, the case was taken to the governor, who often appointed a committee to determine the amount of the damage. Restitution was usually in kind; less frequently a cash settlement was made.

Adolescent Rites

Adolescent rites as such were not stressed, and they did not occur as isolated events. They were worked into and formed a part of some broader calendrical ceremonial effort. For this reason the age at which an individual underwent the rite varied. There was no necessary coincidence between arrival at pubescence and the public, religious recognition of the fact.

Induction into one or the other of the kachina societies constituted the adolescent rite for boys. At this time the boy received his first organized religious instruction. The details of this experience are outlined under the heading of kachina initiations (see Chapter 10). The successful completion of this ceremony not only conferred adult status on the individual, but obligated him with the responsibilities of an adult role.

The traumatic consequences which have been attributed by some to this experience are difficult to assess. Certainly the rite was impressive and frightening, as indicated by several descriptions and accounts of individual reactions. In some cases there was partial disillusionment in connection with the revealing of the kachinas as masked relatives, friends, and other townsmen.

Recognition of all these factors was implicit in the treatment of initiates immediately following the ceremony. The older members attempted to make the boys feel at ease by joking with them, etc. The negative effects were also cushioned by compensation in the form of increased responsibility and privilege. In recent years at least, the amount of disillusionment has been minimal, since most individuals of adolescent age have already been aware of kachina impersonation. How true this would have been in earlier times is unknown.

My own impression is that while the rite may have constituted an ordeal at the time, its psychic consequences for the individual were not lasting. As noted by one man [37],

"If kachina initiates have good reasons to be frightened, then they are (i.e., if they were in need of discipline); but in most cases, they are not."

The occurrence of the first menses was not signalized by any special event. The mother normally counseled the girl concerning her future behavior, but other than this the circumstance went almost unmarked. "There is no ceremony when she menstruates. The mother simply gives good advice; tells her not to chase around with boys or stay out late at night" [56].

The only religious incident approaching an adolescent rite for girls was the ritual impregnation in the kachina enactment (see Chapter 10). Pubescent girls were selected to play the role opposite the "hunter." However, even here the emphasis was on the generalized concept of fertility rather than carrying specific, or personalized, significance.

Consistent with the above remarks, there were few menstrual tabus; the occurrence of menstruation interfered little, if at all, with the normal routine of life. Parsons (1924b: 149–50), speaking of the Tewa generally, indicated that menstruating women must not carry infants, since it was believed that it would make their skin rough and spotty, and the baby irritable. My own inquiries revealed no tabus.

The general lack of concern with this area of the culture was illustrated by an incident in the summer of 1941. On the occasion of Santa Clara Day, August 12, the Kwitara was danced. The daughter of one of my informants [70] was making her initial appearance as a dancer. On the morning of the event, she menstruated for the first time. She was neither barred from the dance nor from the kiva. The only concern expressed by her mother was that the girl did not feel well.

MARRIAGE AND ADULTHOOD

There were several alternative procedures involving the selection of mates and the customs surrounding marriage. The most highly considered practices, and those which carried the greatest prestige, were those that conformed most closely to the old patterns.

Deviance from the ideal was subject to little criticism or social pressure. Like birth and naming, marriage rites exhibited borrowings from European sources. Where these foreign influences appeared, however, they tended to be additions rather than integrations. For example the Christian marriage service, or some part of it, might or might not be performed depending upon the orthodoxy of the contracting parties. Details on alternatives will be included under the various topics relating to marriage.

Premarital Relationships and Illegitimacy

The period immediately following adolescence was one in which sexual experiment was prevalent. Estimates by several informants [13, 29, 52, 72] of the numbers or the proportion of girls who had had premarital relationships were high. This was confirmed by Jeançon (1904–30), who commented as follows:

While there was formerly, and probably still is, a lot of promiscuous sexual intercourse, this was confined to the natives themselves,...and as no particular stigma is attached to sexual intercourse, it is quite natural for them to do as they do.

While the desirability of virtue in girls was recognized (they were warned and lectured by their mothers when they reached puberty), the stigma attached to its loss was not great. Even less concern was shown with boys [45, 56].

As might be expected, the percentage of illegitimate children was high. Data from five genealogical tables showed that roughly 4.5 percent of the persons listed were known to be illegitimate. The real percentage was probably considerably greater, since marriages to the father or another male often took place following the birth of a child, and conferred post facto legitimacy on the offspring. One informant [72] estimated that twenty-five percent of the women at Santa Clara Pueblo had borne children before they married. This opinion agrees with Jeançon's remarks (1904–30) to the effect that, "Young girls often have a child or two before marriage, but this may be laid to the general rule that illegitimacy carries no stigma for the mother or child."

While the attitude toward failure to conform to the ideal was certainly one of tolerance, there is evidence that Jeançon's statement should not be accepted too literally. The fact that a lack of virtue and pregnancy out of wedlock carried some social disapproval was shown in several ways. Specific criticism was leveled at individuals by the clowns during kachina ceremonies (see Chapter 10). Pressure was often brought to bear on the boy to marry the girl. "In recent years, he may even be brought before the village council" [68]. As mentioned earlier, girls frequently did heavy work just prior to the birth of a child, in hopes that it would be stillborn. There are also indications that the marriageability of the girl was affected. One informant [72] estimated that while ninety-nine percent later married, "they usually married widowers, and a few married single men." There were two cases of illegitimate pregnancy observed during the course of the fieldwork. In both instances sympathetic comments were made concerning "the trouble" in the families, and there was evidence that the situation was a source of embarrassment.

The possibility that the current attitude represents a gradual recent development and a partial acceptance of European tenets of morality must be considered. Lack of virtue in women offered little or no barrier to advancement in prestige-earning areas of the culture. In two cases reported during the fieldwork, both women held ceremonial offices. In fact the more flagrant transgressor, mentioned below, held the highest ritual position in her moiety.

Only in cases of pronounced violation of the code did the village exert real censure. In one such instance the woman was a widow who had had three children prior to the death of her husband. She subsequently had three more: one by an Indian, one by a Spanish-American, and a third by an Anglo. Even in this case, however, criticism was directed primarily at the fact that her relations had been with non-Indians.

Furthermore, she had received these suitors openly. The grounds of immorality, per se, were not considered significant. This illustrates Jeançon's statement (1904-30):

> There is no such thing as a public prostitute at Santa Clara. Some of the women have lewd tendencies but do not permit these to get the better of their judgment. Americans and Mexicans as lovers are taboo, and such amours as they have are carried on with their own people.

As in the case of virtue, there was inconsistency in the attitude displayed toward illegitimate children. According to the official version, no stigma was attached to illegitimacy [61, 72]; see Jeançon (1904-30). However, statements referring to the subject usually contained some explanatory or qualifying element. For example Jeançon commented: "A child born out of wed-lock is treated the same as any other child, and some of the finest minds and characters amongst these Indians have been the result of an unlawful union." Two informants [52, 72] stated that there was no stigma associated with illegitimacy, and that illegitimate children "seem to do better than legitimate ones." One of the same informants [72], on another occasion, however, referred to a successful woman who was illegitimate and said, "She worked harder to get ahead because of her background."

My own impressions are that "the lady doth protest too much," and that the consistent reference to the success of illegitimate children was an attempt to compensate for recognition of a separate status, if not an actual handicap. In the case of an adult with whom I had several interviews, there was considerable evidence that she was aware of her irregular antecedents. Again, however, the possibility of changing attitudes and a growing tendency to conform to Christian tenets must be taken into account.

Adoption

The care of illegitimate or orphaned children was not a problem, since adoption was prevalent. Parsons (1929: 30), speaking of the Tewa generally, stated that, "As elsewhere the practice of adopting children, more particularly of kindred, is very general." My data for Santa Clara confirm this. Adoption of orphaned and illegitimate children by relatives was the most common form [37, 49]; see also Jeançon (1904–30). However, they might be absorbed into families of nonrelatives as well. Furthermore it was not unusual for childless couples to adopt children of those who had large families [65, 68].

There was no formalized procedure or ceremony of adoption. "In the old days, you just took the child in" [68]. According to Parsons (1929: 30):

> The widow of house 56, Santa Clara, has been "given" two grandchildren by her daughter, and a grandchild has been "given" the couple in house 58. When Genealogy III, 8, a widower, was dying, he gave his three children to a couple that were unrelated to him and of the other moiety.

Selection of Mates

Several considerations entered into the choice of a mate. These included, among other things, mutual attraction, possession of culturally approved personality traits, economic considerations, current attitudes toward village, tribal, cultural, and racial exogamy, and real or assumed nearness of relationship.

Boys and girls were considered marriageable when they reached adolescence, and formerly, in the case of boys, were initiated into the kachina society. Early marriages were advocated, a point confirmed by Jeançon (1904–30) for his day. Courtship was informal and mutual attraction appeared to be the dominating factor in bringing couples together. What constituted physical attractiveness is difficult to define, since it varied with the individual; informants were unable to give a cultural stereotype for beauty in either men or women. According to two informants [59, 77], "Beauty and property were not essential for marriage. Simply liking one another was the main thing." Many lasting attachments resulted from the period of sexual

experiment. Jeançon (1914) commented on this as follows: "When a young man takes a notion to marry, he has usually been courting the girl for sometime, occasionally having gone so far as to have sexual intercourse with her."

There is evidence that personality traits and status, as defined in terms of achievement of values, dictated to some extent the selection of a wife or husband. But whether these arose on a conscious level or not, it is questionable as it is in our own culture. Persons of even and amiable disposition were highly considered. Industry was an essential quality in both men and women. Status or prospect of status in the politico-religious field was a desirable quality in men. Virtue was to be looked for in women.

In recent years couples have tended to be approximately the same age. Formerly, however, marriages between older men and young girls, and between young men and older women were frequent. The explanation of these unions involving disparity in age was basically economic. "The older men and women have a great deal of property" [59, 77]. Jeançon (1904–30) noted the same phenomena for an earlier period. According to him:

> Another interesting thing of past generations, although not so common now, is the marrying of old women by young men, and young women by old men. The boys or young men who have married or gone to live with an old woman say that she has a house, some money, knows how to cook and look after a man, makes good pottery and hence earns money, and last, but not least, is not likely to have affairs with other men. On the other hand, the young girls make the same claims for the old men, excepting in sex matters. They say that an old man is easily satisfied sexually, and that there is not much danger of them becoming pregnant, and is therefore more inclined to give them more liberty in sex matters with younger men.

While alternatives in the form of exogamic marriages were allowed, each varied in degree of prestige depending upon the prevailing attitude toward outside groups, both Indian and non-Indian. The most highly approved union in the past was within the village. Considered almost as desirable was a wife or husband selected from any of the other Tewa villages. "This was considered as good as a marriage within the village" [65]. Next in order of prestige were the members of other Pueblo villages.

Where exogamy involved Indians other than Pueblos, the desirability of the marriage appeared to rest upon the degree of cultural differences and the current degree of intercultural amicability. The traditional enmity between Santa Clara and the Navajo relegated the latter to an undesirable or even prohibited category. "There was real objection to Navajo only" [65]. Formerly individuals from the Comanche, and by implication the Kiowa and other Plains tribes, were not considered acceptable as mates. "Marriages were forbidden with Comanche as well as with all warring tribes" [65]. According to another [62], these included Kiowa, Comanche, Ute, Apache, and Navajo. "The least desirable unions were those with persons of European antecedents, i.e., Spanish-Americans and Anglos. Marriages with Mexicans were forbidden" [65].

Evidence that ideals have been ignored and that attitudes have fluctuated in the past fifty or sixty years is provided by the actual marriage data. Jeançon (1904–30) commented as follows:

While at present there are no other Indians than Tewa themselves living at Santa Clara [sic, WWH], yet, they are far from being pure bloods as in the past they have intermarried extensively with other Indians, more especially with the Utes. There are several Santa Clara girls living in Dulce, New Mexico, who are married to Jicarilla Apaches, and one or two girls are married to Utes at Ignacio, Colorado. In addition to the above there are several Santa Clara girls married into several of the Lower Rio Grande villages. It is the custom, quite often, that when a young man does not meet the girl of his heart in his own village he seeks her elsewhere. Some-

times he brings her back to his own home and again he stays in the new country or village where he is married. There are a number of Santa Clara boys who are married to girls in Oklahoma, and one is married to a white girl in Detroit.

As late as 1847, at the time of the occupation of the country by the United States, it was customary to keep captive women and children, and to incorporate them into the tribe. The women were sometimes married to the man who captured them or were given to a friend as wife. In this way much foreign blood was introduced into the village. As there has been no war of any importance since that time the custom has been to seek these outsiders by more peaceful means.

Parsons (1929: 31-32) also gave data concerning exogamous marriages in terms of village, tribe, or race. In some instances her data are not clear as to residence, but her information may nonetheless be summarized. She listed twenty-four exogamous unions. In thirteen of these the spouses resided in Santa Clara. These included eleven Santa Clara men, three of whom were married to Tesuque women and two to San Ildefonso women. The wives of the remaining six were respectively San Juan, Zia, Laguna, Osage, half-Pojoaque–half-Spanish-American, and Spanish-American. Of the two Santa Clara women whose husbands had come to reside in the village, one was a Tewa-Hopi and the other, a Zuñi.

In exogamous marriages listed by Parsons in which Santa Clara spouses had taken up residence elsewhere, four men and seven women were represented. The men were were married to San Juan, Ute, Navajo, and Anglo women; the women, to men from San Juan, Tesuque, Jemez (2), and Jicarilla Apache.

My own data of 1941, based on one hundred families for which marriage information was available, show seventy-one cases of village endogamy as against twenty-nine cases of exogamy. In twelve of the instances representing village exogamy, the spouses resided with their Santa Clara mates in the village. These included four women: one married to a San Juan man, one to a Tewa-Hopi, and two to Navajo. In the cases of the eight men, the provenience of the wives was San Ildefonso, Pojoaque, Nambé, Tesuque (2), "Navajo or Apache," Spanish-American, and Anglo.

The seventeen cases of village exogamy in which Santa Clara spouses had taken up residence elsewhere involved nine women and eight men. The women had selected mates from Isleta, Laguna (2), Jicarilla Apache (2), White Mountain Apache, Chippewa, "another tribe," and Anglo. In the cases of the eight men, one was married to a Jicarilla Apache, one to an Oklahoma Indian, a third to a Spanish-American, and five to Anglos.

Statistically these data are not significant. However, certain trends and changes in attitude can be detected over the interval between Jeançon's and Parsons' fieldwork and my own. First, there has been an increase in the number of marriages to persons other than Tewa and Pueblo, i.e., to individuals of tribes or races who were formerly considered least desirable. Second, as a result of the above, there are a greater number of non-Tewa spouses who have taken up residence in the village. This has occurred in spite of the fact that when marriages took place between Santa Clara and non-Tewa, and also non-Pueblo peoples, the tendency was to establish residence elsewhere than at Santa Clara.

In part these changes are understandable, since in recent years a greater number of children have gone to school at Santa Fe and elsewhere; they have had more opportunity to meet people from other groups, and because of better education they have been able to compete in the economic world outside the pueblo. A continuation of these trends is to be expected because of increased opportunities for wage work, resulting from the Los Alamos development and an influx of Anglos in and around Santa Clara.

When the choice of mate was made within the village, closeness of relationship was a primary factor for consideration. Parsons (1929: 32) made the following statement for the Tewa generally:

Within the recognized blood ties between collateral relations, maternal and paternal, there is considerable restriction in marriage. Descendants of the same grandparents or even great-grandparents may not marry. In the latter degree of collateral kinship, test cases show irregularity of ruling or uncertainty and self-contradiction in the mind of the informant. In some cases marriage of descendants of the same great-grandparents was accounted proper, in some cases, improper.

For Santa Clara, Parsons (1929: 33) cited specific instances in which marriages were disallowed; one involved a paternal cross-cousin, and three cases, second cousins, i.e., descendants of grandparental siblings.

My own data substantiates those of Parsons in the main. In the incest categories were placed unions between parent and child, uncle and niece, aunt and nephew, and parallel and cross-cousins [56, 64]. Incestuous marriages of the above type were alleged to produce offspring who were deficient physically and mentally [45, 56].

Marriages between second cousins (descendants of grandparental siblings) were also prohibited; here, however, inconsistencies in the data were apparent, and transgressions of the rule were recognized. "Second cousins were forbidden to marry in the old days, but they are doing it now" [70]. "Second cousins are barred from marriage. It doesn't turn out right" [49, 59]. Third cousins were stated to be acceptable mates by some [56, 70], but not by others [49, 59].

In actuality adherence to the conventional rules of incest regarding second and third cousins was theoretical rather than real, and Santa Clara represented a highly inbred community. Two factors, unrecognized by the people, contributed to this. The first was the high percentage of illegitimate members resulting from illicit unions within the pueblo. Second, an analysis of genealogies showed that only five (possibly six) lines of descent were represented (see Appendix A). [Here there was a note, "Include analysis after checking data in the field," but there is no evidence that Hill had an opportunity to follow through on this. CHL]

Since Santa Clara unions were monogamous, this precluded the most common type of sororate. The rare form, marriage to the deceased wife's sister, was formerly prohibited [56]. "Marriage to a dead wife's sister was not done at Santa Clara" [49, 59]. "However, this is being done at the present time" [56]. This informant also stated that the wife-stepdaughter sororate was permissible in case of the wife's death, but was unable to cite any case in which it had occurred.

The levirate appeared to be foreign to Santa Clara thought. "This does not happen at Santa Clara" [49, 59].

On the positive side, marriages between a brother and sister of one family with those of another family were thought to be highly desirable. "This was recommended whenever possible. It strengthens the bond between the two families" [65].

Marriage Arrangements

The following accounts of marriage arrangements and ceremonies deal with alternative but standardized procedures. Some deviations from the generalized pattern did occur, but they were rare. For example there were occasional elopements, usually the result of strong parental objections [71]. There were also instances where couples were married by a justice of the peace, circumventing both native and Christian rites. However, in the overall picture, the number of such cases was negligible.

In standard practice the responsibility for initiating arrangements preliminary to marriage rested with the boy. He announced his desires to his parents, who then called a meeting of his relatives [40, 42, 61, 72]. If the parents were dead, the maternal uncle might substitute for them [61, 72], or lacking this relative, the god-parents served [61, 72; also, Jeançon (1919)].

There is evidence that until thirty-five or forty years ago, the godparents, padrinho-madrinha (padrino-madrina), played a much greater role in marriages than at present. Formerly they acted as the sponsors for the couple [49, 59], and many times they were responsible for all aspects of the wedding. This was the case in the marriages of several informants [69, 70, 78]. As of the 1940s, this introduced Spanish-American convention has almost ceased to exist. Its discontinuance appears to be part of the general withdrawal from and change in attitude toward Spanish-Americans, which has become increasingly apparent in recent times.

The boy's relatives discussed the projected union, and if there were no objections, several persons were selected to negotiate with the girl's family. According to one informant [40], the negotiating party consisted of two relatives; according to another [54], the boy's father, his godfather, and a third relative; and according to Jeançon (1919), negotiating was done by the parents and a "go-between," the latter being responsible for all subsequent arrangements.

The negotiating party went to the girl's home and made the proposal. This was followed by a lengthy discussion dealing with the personalities of the principals and the amount of property to be given the girl and her parents. If both parties were favorably inclined toward the union, it was assumed that the marriage would take place. However, custom dictated that additional time for consideration be requested by the family of the girl. This gave them an opportunity to prepare for the marriage feast, and to discuss the proposal with relatives and with the girl, since the ultimate decision of acceptance or rejection rested in her hands [40, 61, 72]. The delay gave the boy's parents an opportunity to gather and prepare food and to enlist the help of relatives in amassing the gift property [40, 41]. Formerly an interval of eight days intervened between the visit of the boy's delegates and the return visit of the girl's representatives bringing the answer [42, 54].

The procedure and speeches of these preliminary negotiations were highly stylized. Jeançon (1919), who was present at one such negotiation and the subsequent marriage, reported as follows:

> Should the girl's parents be willing to consider the matter, there is a lot of talking; the girl's parents first saying that the child is not old enough to marry, does not know how to cook, is of unset-

tled mind and other remarks of the similar nature, all depreciating their daughter. The boy's parents follow with similar remarks about him, until the girl's parents begin to praise the boy, and are succeeded by his parents in praising the girl.

All of these things are only preliminary. After all have agreed that the boy and girl are everything that they should be, her parents begin to wail about the loss of their daughter. "What will they do without her; she is such a good girl, so obedient, and such a good cook, and, etc. etc." Some compensation must be made them for their loss. Should she be a widow with children the matter is even more complex for usually she has her own home, some cattle, and other things that help establish a home. After much wrangling and talk, the boy's parents suggest that the girl's parents, with their relatives, should attend a feast at his home. At this time all the relatives from both sides will be present, and the matter more fully discussed by all. This is agreed to and after ample time has been given to prepare the feast (a week is usually sufficient) all parties interested gather at the boy's home.

In most cases the preliminary features were a mere formality, since the principals had usually reached an understanding and the parents had consulted each other unofficially [29, 40, 42, 52]. Formerly protocol demanded that if the suit was rejected, the boy's family should be notified on the fourth day; acceptance was announced on the eighth [42]. Recently, however, rejections have been given at the time of the first contacts of the two parties. Both acceptances and refusals were couched in formal terms. In the former instance, the girl's negotiating party, father, godfather, and other relatives, came to the boy's home and announced, "You have a child (daughter) to command" [29, 42]. In cases of negative decisions, the spokesman for the party said, "*Zhosi* (Jesus) had not deemed it fit that these two should marry" [29, 42]. Such a refusal was termed being given a pumpkin: "O po me^n ge, he has been given a pumpkin" [29, 42, 52]. Both conventions associated with rejection of the suit represent borrowings from Spanish-American sources.

Once begun negotiations seldom bogged down, but situations occasionally arose in which the wedding was called off at the last moment. One such instance was cited by an informant [83]; it concerned her grandfather, Juan Ventura Silva, and occurred as nearly as she could ascertain about 1820. All arrangements had been completed and the marriage feast prepared; the boy's relatives had arrived at the girl's home and had presented the gifts. "The girl's mother asked her, as she stood loaded with gifts but in tears, whether she really wanted to marry Juan Ventura. She said, "No!" Juan Ventura heard her and in anger picked up his own gifts and those of his relatives and returned home. Apparently this had been a marriage plotted by the parents and relatives without the approval of the bride, and at the last minute the mother became sympathetic and "let the chicken out of the coop."

Jeançon's material (1919) supplements the above. According to him, "Up to the day before the actual ceremony the girl has the right to drop the whole matter, and upon informing her parents of this fact, all arrangements are cancelled. This has actually occurred within the writer's knowledge."

Formerly a period of trial marriage existed, extending from the time when negotiations were begun until the ceremony was completed. According to Jeançon (1919),

> If, after the first visit of the boy's parents the girl's parents agree to consider the wedding, the boy goes to her house every night and sleeps and cohabits with her. This is usually during a period of three or four weeks. In case the negotiations fail, or for some reason the marriage does not take place, then his visits cease.

At the end of the eight-day interval (a week, according to Jeançon), the girl's delegation arrived at the home of the boy. Accounts of proceedings immediately following their arrival varied. Probably all were correct and represented alternative choices dictated by family circumstance, whether the native or Catholic elements of the marriage ceremony were emphasized, and which of the rites was held first.

According to Jeançon, as noted, the girl and her relatives arrived and were feasted, the invitation having been issued by the boy's party at the time of the preliminary negotiations. Elsewhere, Jeançon commented:

> The feast is spread. After all have partaken of the good things, the nearest relatives gather in a room and discuss the wedding and particularly the gift to the girl's parents. After much argument an agreement is reached and the date for the ceremony is set, when the boy's god-father (sponsor) in clan or society must give a feast at the girl's house on the wedding day to all who care to come, even including strangers in the village at the time. [It is obvious throughout Jeançon's manuscript that he was confused on the subjects of clan, moiety, and society. It is possible in this instance that god-father referred either to a society sponsor or the moiety sponsor of the Water Immersion ceremony. Since the ceremony he described emphasized Catholic elements, however, it is most probable that the god-father was one in the Christian sense, i.e., the boy's padrinho. WWH]

In the rite witnessed by Jeançon, the native ceremony was presumably held subsequent to the Catholic one (he cited a case in which this happened). According to my informants, this was the reverse of the usual procedure. One [40] stated that the girl's group reported their decision to the boy's, and if it was in the affirmative, a date was set for the native wedding. At this time the groom's relatives assembled at his home, collected the gifts, and made their way to the bride's house, where they were given a feast furnished by her people. Later the groom's family, occasionally that of the bride, arranged a marriage in the church. The accounts of others [29, 42, 54] parallel the above except that, according to them, the wedding and feast were held on the day the acceptance was tendered.

The Native Wedding

On the wedding day the groom's relatives and the guests were notified and gathered at his home. When all had assembled, the party left in a body for the home of the bride. Parents and near relatives led the procession, while the groom brought up the rear and lagged behind [29, 42].

Each individual carried a gift or gifts to be presented to the bride and her parents. The parents and near relatives gave the richest and most pretentious gifts [29, 42]. These included prepared food of various types [29, 40, 52]: cornmeal [40], flour [40], corn [29, 40, 52], jewelry [40]; also, woven garments, mantas, belts, blankets, and trunks or containers for storing them; kitchen utensils and household articles, and any items the couple "would need to use in their married life" [29, 42].

The bride stood in the doorway of one of the inner rooms, and beyond her were her parents or several other relatives. As each person arrived, he or she embraced the bride and presented her with the gift or gifts. She passed these to the person behind her, who in turn passed it on to the next, and so on, until it reached the last in line, who stacked the articles in the room.

Accounts of the actual marriage rite are fairly consistent as to content, but they differ regarding the order in which certain parts were performed. According to one version [40], as soon as gifts were distributed those present sat down and were given food prepared by the bride's family. When all had eaten, the parents of the couple arose and gave a series of talks, advising the pair as to their future conduct. When they were finished, any relative who wished came forward and gave a similar lecture. This completed the ceremony, and the groom's relatives left for home unless one of the godparents (madrinha or padrinho) of the girl or boy was present. In this case he or she told the boy and girl to kneel, took their rosaries, placed that of the bride around the neck of the groom, and that of the groom around the neck of the bride. After this the parents knelt and prayed.

On the evening of the ceremony, it was customary to hold a "prisoner's dance" (Parg *share*) for general entertainment [40].

According to two accounts [29, 42], after the presentation of the gifts, all stood and were silent. An older man finally addressed the bride and groom. "He admonished them. He emphasized the hardships of married life. He told them that marriage was for life and not to listen to others when once married; that some people might wish to have them separated." When he finished talking, he exchanged the rosaries. Following this the older male relatives made speeches directed to the couple. When all who wished had talked, those present seated themselves, and all were fed except the newlyweds and their parents. This completed the rite proper, which was designated as "daughter-in-law feast" (sa e puwe) [29, 42].

A native marriage ceremony witnessed by Jeançon in 1906 conformed to none of the previous accounts. On that occasion the rite followed a Catholic one held at the church in the Spanish-American village of Santa Cruz.

> Upon arrival of the bridal pair at the edge of the village, after the Roman Catholic service which took place at Santa Cruz, they were met by the god-mothers of the pair, who placed two fingers of the boy and the girl in openings in a small piece of pottery with four holes in its top. They then went, on foot, to the girl's house, and at the door were again met by the god-mothers and also the god-fathers. They were presented with a double-necked jar, or one with two spouts, containing water from a sacred spring. The girl first drank from her side, and the boy next from his side. This concluded the native rites (Jeançon 1906).

I was unable to verify the information contained in Jeançon's account. Two of my informants [40, 42] were approximately fifty-four and thirty years old, respectively, at the time Jeançon witnessed the ceremony—yet neither mentioned it. That a part of it might have represented a recent innovation was suggested by a description of a staged wedding, given as an example of a humorous incident [84].

> Filaro Tafoya was getting married in Manitou, Colorado. Mrs. Allison, who owned the Cliff Dwelling, wanted publicity for the place. She asked me to think up an idea. They had a wedding jar (two spouts) made for the occasion. There was much publicity about the couple getting married in old Indian style. They wanted to bring trade to the hotel. They charged a dollar to see the ceremony, and a big crowd came. The groom drank out of one spout, the bride out of the other. They auctioned off the vase. It sold for thirty dollars. Since that time they have been making those pots at Santa Clara.

The Catholic Marriage Ceremony

Depending upon individual preference, the couple might or might not have the Catholic marriage service performed. In most cases, this was held subsequent to the native rite, and usually after an interval of three weeks or a month. This time lapse allowed for posting of the bans on three consecutive Sundays and preparing for the wedding feast. The date for the church wedding was usually set at the time the girl's representatives indicated their final acceptance [40, 42, 72]; see Jeançon (1919).

On the eve of the wedding, it was customary for the groom to kill a calf or sheep in front of the bride's home. He took a portion of the meat to his home, and the remainder was given to the bride's parents. According to Jeançon (1919),

> On the morning of the wedding, the bride presented her future mother-in-law a basket of cornmeal or wheat flour. On this occasion the groom presented the bride a buckskin and any other gift he could afford, usually Navaho silver, turquoise, and shell beads.

The couple were accompanied to the church by their parents and witnesses. The witnesses were usually a man and wife. They

17. *Santa Clara Men at Omaha Exposition, 1898. From left to right: Cajete, Geronimo, and Dolores (photograph by F.A. Rinehart for the Bureau of American Ethnology, Smithsonian Institution, #1965).*

18. *The Governor of Santa Clara Pueblo (1880 photograph by J.K. Hillers, Bureau of American Ethnology, Smithsonian Institution, #1973).*

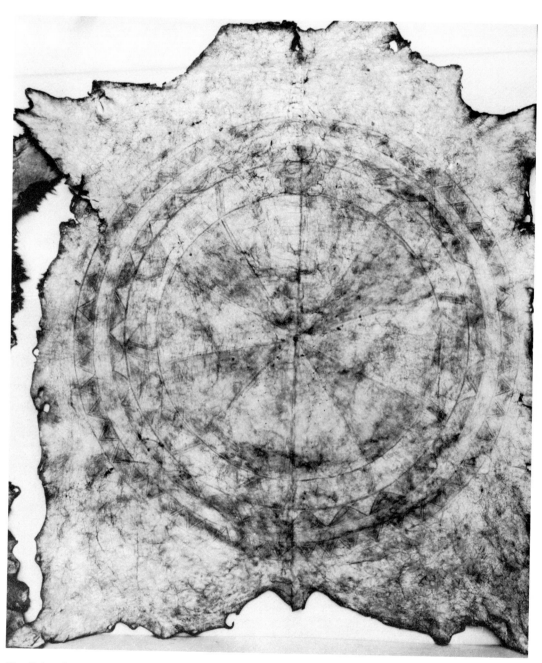

19. *Painted Buffalo Robe, Santa Clara Pueblo (Chicago Natural History Museum [Field Museum of Natural History], #92400).*

20. *Painted Buffalo Robe, Santa Clara Pueblo (Chicago Natural History Museum* [*Field Museum of Natural History*], *#92399).*

21. *Painted Buffalo Robe, Santa Clara Pueblo (Chicago Natural History Museum [Field Museum of Natural History], #86219).*

22. *Painted Buffalo Robe, Santa Clara Pueblo (Chicago Natural History Museum [Field Museum of Natural History], #86220).*

23. *Santa Clara Indians (Denver Art Museum, 1906 photograph, possibly by J.A. Jeançon).*

24. *Santa Clara Woman's Embroidered Dress, or* Manta *(Southwest Museum, Highland Park, Los Angeles).*

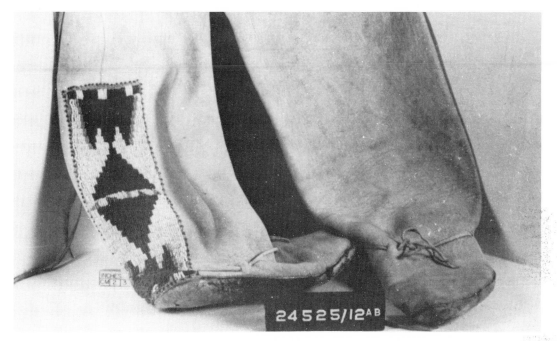

25. *Beaded Moccasins, Santa Clara Pueblo (Museum of New Mexico, #(24525/12ᴬᴮ; photograph probably by W.W. Hill).*

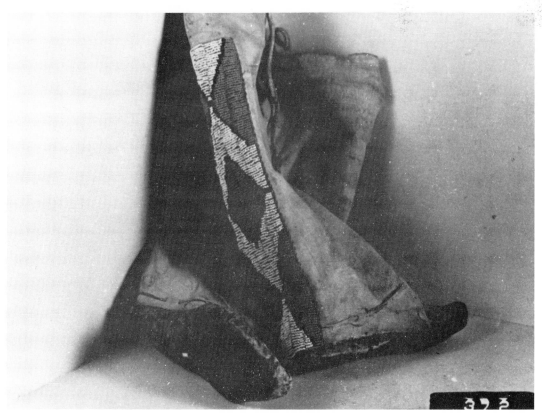

26. *Beaded Moccasins, Santa Clara Pueblo (Museum of New Mexico, #36583/12ᴬᴮ; photograph probably by W.W. Hill).*

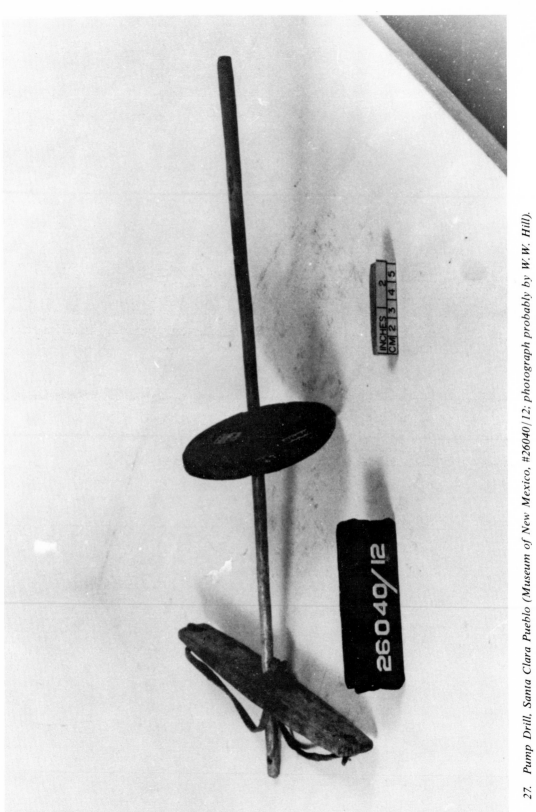

27. *Pump Drill, Santa Clara Pueblo (Museum of New Mexico, #26040/12: photograph probably by by W.W. Hill).*

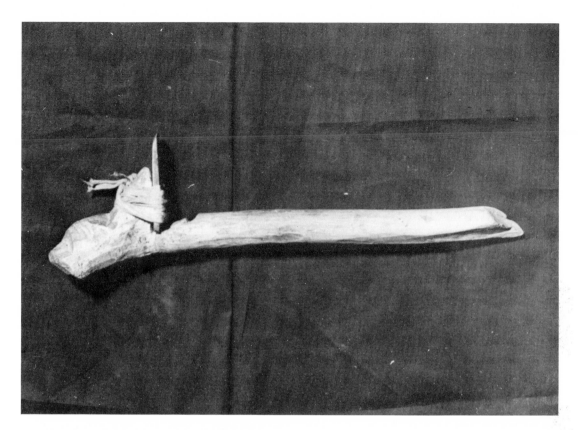

28. *Elk Horn Fleshing Tool, Santa Clara Pueblo (Laboratory of Anthropology, Museum of New Mexico; photograph probably by W.W. Hill).*

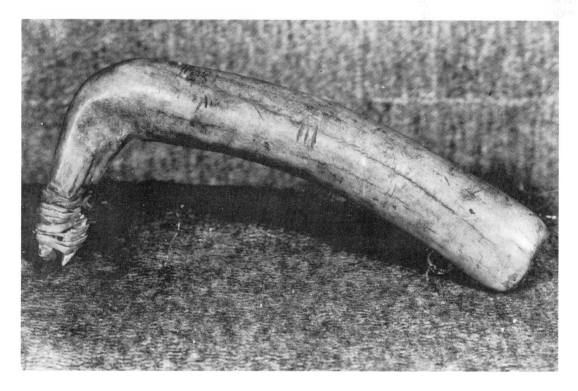

29. *Elk Horn Fleshing Tool, Santa Clara Pueblo (Nat Stern Collection, Laboratory of Anthropology, Museum of New Mexico).*

30. *Quiver of Mountain Lion Skin, Santa Clara Pueblo (photographed about 1940, probably by W.W. Hill).*

31. *José Leandro Tafoya, Governor of Santa Clara Pueblo (1900 photograph by J.K. Hillers, Bureau of American Ethnology, Smithsonian Institution, #1959b).*

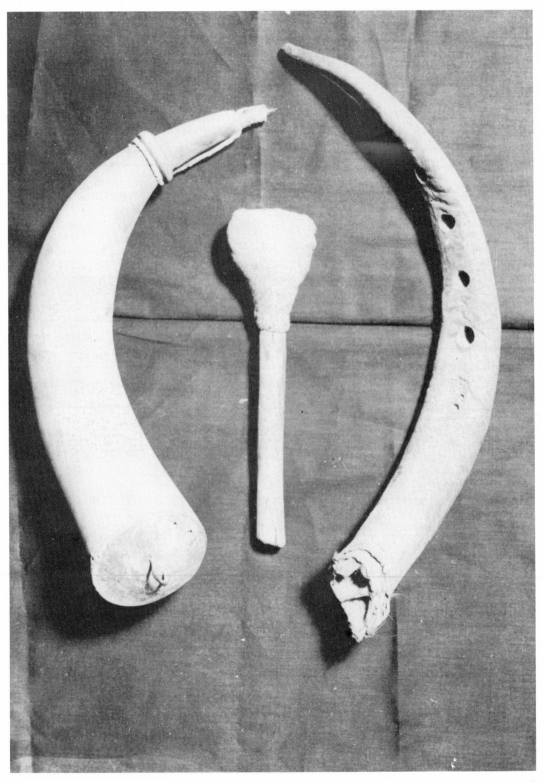

32. *Powder Horn, Child's Rattle, and Arrow Wrench, Santa Clara Pueblo (1941 photograph, probably by W.W. Hill).*

33. *Arrow Shaft Smoother, Bone Pipe and Pottery Rest, and Clay Pipe, Santa Clara Pueblo (1941 photograph, probably by W.W. Hill).*

34.   *Pipe and Tobacco Bag, Gunpowder Container, Santa Clara Pueblo (1941 photograph, probably by W.W. Hill).*

were known as the "grasping of arms father and mother" (to ca *zh*ia, "marriage mother," and xo ca tara, "marriage father"). These two and the fathers of the couple occupied chairs near the altar [29, 42].

Following the ceremony a marriage feast was held. This event was formerly attended by the whole village. "Elaborate preparations were made. All kinds of pies and breads were baked in outdoor ovens. Even a calf or sheep was killed for the occasion" [29, 42]. According to these informants, food was served at the homes of the bride, groom, and witnesses; members of the village ate at all three places. According to Jeançon (1919), however, the wedding banquet was given by the boy's godfather (padrinho).

Residence

Marriage was followed by a period of temporary matrilocal residence. Jeançon (1919) said that this extended over a period of a year. My own informants [29, 40, 42, 61] stated that the matrilocal residence terminated after a period of two or three weeks. At the end of this time, the couple moved to the home of the boy's parents, where they occupied one of the existing rooms or an additional room built especially for them.

While exceptions dictated by unusual circumstances did occur, permanent residence within the village was overwhelmingly patrilocal in former times [29, 40, 42, 61]. Exceptions included cases where the bride's parents were indigent, or where she was a widow with her own establishment. There has been a growing tendency recently toward separate residence, particularly among younger and better-educated couples. These have built homes across Santa Clara Creek, north of the village proper. The beginnings of this trend were noted by Jeançon as early as 1919. This is one of several symptoms indicating the gradual weakening of the extended patrilineal family and its gradual replacement by the conjugal type.

In cases of interpueblo marriages, the Santa Clara man normally lived in his wife's village for a time, but eventually returned to his own. Women normally established permanent residence in the home of their

husbands [29, 42]. Exogamous marriages involving other than Pueblo Indians adhered to no consistent rule of residence.

Divorce

Divorces were recognized, but were subject to social disapproval. How much of this disfavor resulted from Catholic Church attitudes and how much was indigenous is difficult to judge. However, its reality was vouched for by several [61, 65, 72]. It was also obvious, in one instance at least, in the reticent attitude and sensitive reaction on the part of one of my informants [65], whose daughter had recently been divorced.

Perhaps the above reasons explain why divorces were relatively rare. Incompatibility was the principal cause [61, 72]. More specific causes were the interest of one of the spouses in another man or woman, and disagreements over property [35, 49]. Wife beating, nagging, and adultery were not considered valid reasons for separation. These and other disputes were brought before the council, and while guilty parties were whipped, the council did not grant divorces [40, 68]. According to Jeançon (1904–30),

> Divorce was an easy matter for the woman; all she had to do was to set the man's personal belongings outside the door and that was the end of the matter. [This seems incompatible with strong patrilocal residence. WWH] In the case of the man wishing a divorce, he often had to give back to the girl's family a part or all, or its equivalent, of what she had brought with her. This was not always the case, however. Divorces were and still are very rare.

Divorced persons usually remarried. If small children were involved, they stayed with the mother. Older children chose the parent with whom they wished to live [68].

Adulthood

Admission to adult status and role was usually coincidental with marriage in the case of women, with initiation into a kachina society in the case of men. The transition was marked by two things: the assumption of obligations and responsibilities, mainly in the practical areas of the culture allocated to adults; and the beginning of active involvement in principally nonmaterial endeavors that were vehicles for prestige and esteem. Participation in the latter was, however, prevailingly optional.

In the practical fields, the person was given an opportunity to test the adequacy of his or her accumulated knowledge in role performance. The change from dependence to complete self-sufficiency was a gradual rather than an abrupt process. Under the extended family system, the boy or the newly-weds were part of an already established unit of production. As members of this unit, they served first in apprentice capacity, sharpening and perfecting their technical knowledge under the supervision of elders, until the time they were called upon to assume leadership in the unit.

Optional avenues leading to personal advancement included, among others, virtuosity along technical and practical lines or, more importantly, acquisition of knowledge leading to advancement in the religious hierarchy. Those who chose to satisfy personal ambition in any of these ways embarked upon courses of specialized study which often continued past middle age. Their success and achievement depended upon both ability and personality factors which, in turn, were measured in terms of cultural values.

Opportunities for diversified activity were greater for men than for women. This was especially noticeable in the field of religion and was consistent with the strong patrilineal bias of the culture, further strengthened by the influence of the Roman Catholic Church.

A fairly rigid dichotomy of activities existed on the basis of sex. In the practical and economic fields, particularly, the efforts of males and females seldom overlapped. Few if any individuals were capable of performing or were wholly aware of the refinements of the role of the opposite sex.

Role of Men

As a minimum, men were expected to be conversant with a variety of fields of production; the creation or securing of the bulk of the raw economic goods was a male prerequisite and obligation. Agriculture, formerly the single most important subsistence pursuit, was almost entirely in male hands. "The fields are the men's job" [65]. "The men tend the fields. They cleared the land and did most of the planting. They cultivated, irrigated, and performed the heavy labor connected with harvesting the crops" [62]. Agriculture was considered a most honorable occupation, and outstanding farmers were looked upon with respect.

Hunting and fishing, before their virtual disappearance, were almost entirely male prerogatives. The same was true of warfare. Women shared in this only vicariously and as custodians of the symbols of victory, the scalps. All three of these pursuits offered avenues for personal advancement. In part this resulted from the danger involved, in part because they necessitated travel in foreign territories, itself a dangerous undertaking, and finally because they were often associated with a religious experience. The ability to recount one's adventures, the mountain lion skin quiver worn by a successful hunter, the buffalo robe which hung in the house, and membership in the War Society as a result of scalping were all measurable symbols of a separate, honored status.

Most craftsmanship was carried on by men. They produced the weapons, and the majority of the implements and tools, as well as many household utensils. Formerly the bulk of the weaving, all dress and most belts, was performed by men. The manufacture of many miscellaneous items like ceremonial equipment and musical instruments also fell into their sphere of work [64, 65].

As one might expect, the importance of craftsmanship has greatly diminished in recent years. There is ample evidence, however, that excellence in this area was formerly highly regarded. Several informants [64, 65, 68] who showed samples of their handiwork did so with obvious pride. Appreciation of the work of others was also evident in conversation.

The substitution of modern, manufactured articles for native ones was generally deplored by the older generation. One informant [64] made the following nostalgic statement: "In those days all men knew how to make things. Today they do not know how."

While trading was participated in by both sexes, that requiring contacts outside the village, or outside other Pueblo Indian villages, was carried on mainly by men. The acquired items again served as badges of status. The mere fact that this activity often necessitated visits to unfamiliar regions added to personal stature. This was summed up by one informant [44] as follows: "Traders enjoyed high prestige. People would go to them for stories."

With the exception of plastering, the construction of houses, storehouses, and ovens was the responsibility of men. They cut, seasoned, and hauled the vigas, made the adobes and laid the walls, placed the vigas and built the roofs. Once the house was completed, however, their responsibility for its maintenance and for the activities taking place in it were minor. While they occasionally helped with the heavier chores, the only duty for which they were strictly accountable was cutting and furnishing firewood. The erection of ramadas and the building of corrals were also tasks for males [64].

Of the two major introduced areas of production, pastoralism and wage work, the former has been carried on entirely by males, and the latter, predominantly so. Pastoralism appears never to have offered real competition to other subsistence endeavors, and has been indulged in by only a small percentage of the population. Since it has never been an integrated part of the culture, its status rewards have been limited.

Wage work has only recently become important in the overall economy. The attitudes toward this endeavor were mixed, and no appraisal of it in terms of status was possible. Its increase has resulted in a gradual shift in the economic base, and repercussions from it were being felt in the social and religious areas of the culture. A gradual evolution in old subsistence patterns, as well as in other aspects of the culture, was still in progress.

Once outside the practical fields of subsistence production and handicrafts, participation tended to become permissive rather than mandatory. A few things such as the instruction of boys in male roles, were expected of all men. However, as in the case of counseling, whether an individual did more than meet the minimum requirements or was an outstanding instructor and advisor to many was a matter of personal inclination and aptitude.

Secular politics was exclusively a male pursuit, and all offices were held by men. The relationship between this branch and the religious hierarchy is discussed elsewhere (Chapter 10). How active a person was in the secular, political phases of the village was dictated in part by individual predilection. Since it was one of the approved avenues for personal advancement, it was fairly popular; because the duties of the office demanded implementation of existing policy, the derived status was clearly one of prestige, but rarely, if ever, of the esteemed category.

The field of religion, while not exclusively a male prerogative, was dominated by men. Men held most of the religious offices, which were political as well, and were responsible for initiating and carrying out most religious activities. Beyond membership in a kachina society, vowed or dedicated membership in one of the secret societies, and participation, often marginal, in moiety-sponsored religios affairs, further religious activity was optional.

Religious activity did offer the surest medium for satisfying personal ambition, however. Those who were willing to sacrifice the time and make the effort progressed through the various stages of the hierarchy. Their status increased in direct proportion to their acquisition of "wisdom," knowledge of ceremonials and the supernatural. As will be seen later, this area of achievement was critical for ultimate status recognition.

Role of Women

While women played subsidiary roles at Santa Clara Pueblo, outlets for their energies were fairly numerous. The bulk of their activity took place in and around the home. Once the raw materials of the farm or chase were turned over to them, they were solely responsible for converting them into food. Grinding, cooking, water carrying, etc. fell in their sphere. They were also responsible for the general house work and cleaning. Plastering newly built homes and replastering old ones were also among their duties [62, 64, 65].

In the general area of agricultural production, they were allotted the less arduous tasks. They helped occasionally in planting. They assisted in the cotton harvest, gathered pollen, husked most of the corn, and helped tend the gardens.

Their participation in handicraft work was limited primarily to pottery making. This, however, was important, both in the past and at present, because of its relationship to status. There were definite distinctions made between those who produced only mediocre pots and those who exhibited virtuosity in construction and art form. In recent years another factor, that of commercial income from the sale of pottery, has entered the picture.

Trading was done by women to a limited extent. Most of this activity was formerly centered in the village; to a lesser extent, it was interpueblo.

Very recently women have also engaged in wage work. While this has been limited, its repercussions were already being felt and have been noted in the discussion of the family.

In the nonmaterial secular fields of the culture, one of the major responsibilities of women was the care, discipline, and education of younger children, as well as the education of older girls.

Some specialized secular occupations were also open to women. These included the roles of midwife, masseuse, and herbalist, all recognized avenues to prestige.

While women played subsidiary roles in religion, it was, as in the case of men, the optional area of participation that was the principal avenue for status. The only exclusively female organization was the Scalp Society. Women functioned as ancillaries in the Bear and Clown societies and also in the Summer and Winter societies (see Chapter 10). A woman from each of the latter two organizations was responsible for leading in the kachina performers at ceremonies of those groups. Implicitly women were eligible also for membership in the Hunt Society.

Status

During the course of the fieldwork, seeming inconsistencies developed relative to the status of contemporary and past personnel of the village. It was not until the appearance of Bienenstok's article on the Jewish shtetl community (1950) that it was realized that what had seemed antithetical attitudes were merely expressions of two kinds of status, and that a situation comparable to that found in the shtetl existed at Santa Clara Pueblo, i.e., prestige and esteemed status. While the bases for achieving prestige and esteemed status are not identical in the two instances, the end results are analogous. Distinctions in both cultures rested upon the way in which a person used his or her natural endowments and acquired attributes.

Status in terms of prestige and esteem at Santa Clara was based on several criteria: performance in mandatory roles, performance in optional roles, and personality and character factors. Professions in a conventional sense did not determine status. What stratifications existed in the society occurred on the basis of achievement in other areas. Nor could social position be inherited, though for obvious reasons children of those families that had achieved it enjoyed more advantageous situations than those where it was lacking.

Creditable performance in mandatory roles offered a minimal foundation upon which personal aggrandizement might be built. Competency in these instances was expected as a matter of course, and unless this was forthcoming no man or woman could expect to advance far in the good graces of the community.

Virtuosity or success above the average in one or several of those fields carried with it rewards in terms of public recognition. Thus, the man who excelled in farming, was a famous hunter, or a well-known craftsman, or the woman who was a noted potter, a good mother, or an excellent housekeeper, reached the first rung of the ladder of social hierarchy. It was taken for granted that achievement in these roles would be effected through means consistent and compatible with established cultural patterns. For example, success in farming or the acquisition of wealth had to have resulted from individual industry—never from lucky accident or through circumstances that could be interpreted as suspicious.

Excellence in the performance of mandatory roles was not, however, a major criterion. It operated primarily in a negative sense; unless capability in this area was demonstrated, further advancement was impossible.

Participation in permissive or optional roles, on the other hand, raised the individual above the category of mediocrity. Thus, men who indulged actively in secular politics or who gave unstintingly of their time in religious affairs could achieve prestige or esteemed status if they possessed the proper character and personality traits. While women could never gain esteemed status, for reasons indicated later, they could, through similar performances in the optional area, arrive at positions of prestige.

While both types of role performance played their part in a person's ultimate status, factors of individual character and personality were even more crucial.

Aitken (1930) and Lowie (1937: 266–67, 276), among others, have commented on the problem of the social selection of personalities. Both concluded that, in the main, there are two types of societies: one in which the tone is set by individual temperament, the other in which individuals yield to social precedence. Both placed Pueblo Indian cultures in the latter group. The data from my research confirm this premise, and an attempt was made to arrive at some of the specific components leading to the social selection of personalities in Santa Clara culture.

The problem was approached in the following manner. Santa Clara values were analyzed with the hope of isolating those character and personality traits which appear necessary or compatible for the realization of status under this system. Next, data on the socialization process, religion, and folklore were examined for clues regarding what the culture considered desirable in the individual. These produced mainly positive features, the presence of which was considered essential in the individual.

Data from Aitken and Lowie were then tested against volunteered statements and observed reactions to specific character and personality manifestations by informants. This yielded principally those factors to which the culture reacted negatively, i.e., their occurrence was seen as a barrier to advancement. Since in most cases they were contrapositive, however, they confirmed the data above.

Finally informants were asked to list those whom they considered outstanding men and women of their own and past generations. An effort was made to ascertain reasons for these choices. The names were then checked with other informants, and where possible, the roles of the candidates were analyzed.

From this process there emerged an assemblage of personality factors on which the selective mechanisms of Santa Clara culture operated either positively or negatively. While they undoubtedly do not represent the full complement upon which social selection for purposes of status was based, they do include most of the important ones. None of these features is unique in itself. What is unique is the peculiar phrasing by Santa Clara culture and the effect of this on individual behavior.

In order to avoid needless repetition, material upon which the following conclusions were based and which occurs elsewhere in the volume will not be specifically cited. The reader is particularly referred to those sections in Chapter 10, and elsewhere, dealing with roles, goals, witchcraft, and descriptions of cacique, Bear, and clown activities, as well as the attitudes inherent in the operation of secret societies.

Consistent with the emphasis on industry, one of the most highly desirable, if not required, personal qualities was individual enterprise. Associated with this quality was a strong sentiment for, or admiration of, success through adversity, i.e., the idea that adverse conditions created a testing ground for advancement. This Horatio Alger theme was amply illustrated in mythological material and also confirmed by informants [50, 65, 69].

While the culture placed a premium on enterprise, it also defined the channels within which it could operate. While diversity of activity was expected, its direction was controlled. Phrased in these terms, enterprise was largely divorced from its usual concomitants of initiative and originality. This factor was exemplified in part in the tendency toward "thinking by analogy," or "like causes like," one of the typical Pueblo attributes noted by Parsons (1939: 76, 88–97, passim) many years ago. In Santa Clara it was demonstrated in such instances as the bifurcation of the clown and curing societies.

The negative reaction toward initiative and originality is in harmony with the whole attitude toward idiosyncratic behavior. Any marked tendency toward this was viewed with suspicion. From the Santa Clara point of view, idiosyncratic behavior, including uncontrolled initiative and originality, was looked upon as a potential threat to the culture. It violated the major precepts of conservatism, unanimity, and conformity, and it immediately invoked mechanisms of social control. Pronounced proclivities in these directions were definitely detrimental to one's advancement, except in those areas of the culture where it could be seen as a return to tradition, in essence an involution. Here individual compensations were available. For example, in "song writing," those with a propensity for any of the characteristics under discussion could indulge in almost unlimited individual expression, so long as this took place within the major pattern structure.

Opposition to idiosyncratic behavior and pressure for secrecy, conservatism, and conformity created an atmosphere congenial to persons with an inclination toward anonymity. Those who accomplished such ends without being obvious possessed a socially approved attribute. Modesty in achievement was insisted upon, at least publicly. Boastfulness was looked upon as a violation of the principle of anonymity. Those who indulged in it lost stature.

"A person who boasted was not sought out for advice" [44]. "A person who talks too much, boasts about his achievements, is the most disliked person, and though he may possess wealth, be a good farmer, a good hunter, or a good athlete, he is still not held in high esteem. Such a person never achieves a position of respect, is not sought after for advice, and children are not brought to him for discipline" [50].

Overt aggressive tendencies of any sort were also blocks to advancement; overt expressions were penalized. Those who held positions of religious and political responsibility were expected to accomplish their office without obvious coercive measures, and to approach their duties with a high sense of humility.

While overt anger was recognized as occurring in the adult pattern, it was not approved of. "You are not acting like a man if you lose your temper" [20]. This does not mean that disagreements were not possible, merely that in public interpersonal relations an individual should control himself. Those of placid temperament benefited by this endowment, since they achieved the goals of anonymity and courtesy with little effort; persons of irascible disposition were avoided and criticized [30, 65]. This last observation was verified in several instances during the course of the fieldwork.

Acquisitiveness was also looked upon as a form of aggression and carried the same type of public censure. Any attempt to amass material goods, to hoard, or to use wealth as a means of personal advancement was in direct conflict with the principles of cooperation and generosity. Any one of these would bar an individual from status consideration. Avarice was looked upon as a mortal sin.

The gerontocratic stress at Santa Clara Pueblo led the culture to place the stamp of approval on those easily reconciled to a social system in which seniority prevailed, and on those willing, overtly, to accept the domination of entrenched authority. This included an uncritical acceptance of the ethos and satisfaction in the status quo. In other words, this system worked most easily, or best, for those personalities with a well-developed feeling of dependency. It also called for an individual endowed with sufficient patience to advance slowly toward the realization of personal goals. Again, both qualities were implicit in and also in harmony with a positive attitude toward anonymity and a negative one toward aggression.

Finally the all-pervading concept of secrecy created a climate hospitable to those with strong introspective and introverted tendencies.

From the foregoing discussion can be derived some of the components leading to status. These included competency in all, and virtuosity in some mandatory roles, and an extensive participation in optional roles. The accomplishment of these goals had to be accompanied by at least outward manifestations of industry, respect for age, courtesy, conservatism, secretiveness, cooperation, generosity, anonymity, and conformity. This fostered the social selection of individuals who possessed certain personality and temperamental predispositions. These included enterprise, but no great degree of initiative, originality, or idiosyncratic tendencies. It included those in whom aggression and acquisitiveness were minimally expressed or at least not externalized, who were placid and patient, who were inclined to be introspective and introverted, and in whom the desire for anonymity and a feeling of dependency were well developed.

While informants were by no means conscious of the total range of criteria upon which status rested, they were remarkably consistent in their designations of persons or kinds of persons who occupied the two status categories. In all instances, men who achieved positions of "prestige" or "esteem" were mature or elderly individuals who showed to a high degree many of the personality traits upon which the culture placed a premium. They were also prominent in optional role performances.

Those specified for prestige were invariably persons who by choice or accident were preeminent in secular affairs. They were men who occupied or had occupied executive and administrative positions, such as governor or war captain. In such a capacity they implemented policies laid down by others. This involved positive action, often accompanied by coercive or punitive measures. Since it was impossible for them to remain anonymous or nonaggressive under these circumstances, they inevitably fell outside the pattern of ideal behavior for the culture. Such men were respected for the power they wielded, but the attitude toward them was quite different from that associated with esteemed status. In part this reaction may have come from a lack of complete integration in the culture. While the secular governmental offices had been introduced several hundred years ago, there was some suggestion that sentiment against their foreign provenience still existed.

Another attribute usually associated with those who held prestige ranking was superior economic position. Granted that this was arrived at through prescribed cultural means, it nonetheless had social consequences. As in the case of secular office, wealth commanded respect because of the power it gave the individual. It did not assure unqualified admiration, however.

Finally, in all cases on which data were available, those receiving a prestige rating exhibited some progressive tendencies. In part this resulted from the very nature of their political roles, and from the fact that they were negotiators with outsiders. It did, however, mark them as potential nonconformists.

Prestige status did not act as a permanent barrier against advancement to the esteemed category. Analysis of the background of those of esteemed rank indicated that they had formerly operated at the prestige level. Presumably this was the normal course expected of those who succeeded to the ultimate, or esteemed, status.

Esteemed Status

A description of qualifications leading to the achievement of esteemed status is complicated by the contrapositive attitudes and beliefs associated with the position. Minimally, it includes all those culturally desirable attributes in the prestige category. In addition, however, it depends upon the acquisition of "wisdom," or supernatural power, by the person. Reference to the concept of "wisdom" has already been made in connection with induction into the kachina societies. On this occasion, its concomitants were explained for the first time to the candidates. This power was not associated with a specific being or class of beings. It was thought of as an impersonal potency whose embodiment might be recognized in humans and supernaturals. In a restricted sense, it operated in the same manner as mana.

It is obvious from various accounts that all persons possessed "wisdom" to a greater or lesser degree. For example, it was a largess distributed to the audience by the principals in most ceremonies, and to patients during curing rites. However, its acquisition in other than negligible quantities resulted from joining religious societies and intensive preoccupation with matters of a religious nature. If such a course was pursued, an individual eventually became qualified for esteemed status. These men were believed to possess an inordinate amount of "wisdom." Ideally they used this potential in a selfless manner for good and the common weal [29, 40, 43, 50].

A summarization of the attitudes and factors operating for selectivity in the esteemed category derives from several sources. Some insights on this problem were noted by Freire-Marreco (1911: 327):

> If you were to ask a Pueblo Indian about morals, he would say, that all people are good, "because they keep the customs." He might confess that some few men are not good; but they are regrettable exceptions. If you press him about himself, he will admit that he is a good man, like all the rest of the people; but not so good a man as his father. He knows how he ought to act in every relation of life, and every action is hedged with responsibilities, to the pueblo as a whole, and to various

groups in it. To these every private advantage ought to be sacrificed.

A more specific expression of Freire-Marreco's statement was given by an informant [69]:

> The primary desire of the villagers was to be free from illness, to be happy, and to be free from fear. The ones who contributed the maximum to this were the most admired and respected. There was little credit or admiration given to one who was fleet of foot or a good farmer, or even a good hunter. "Wisdom" was the most admired trait, and the two caciques and the members of the Bear societies bear this trait. They were sought after for advice, and disobedient children were sent to them for counseling and admonishing.

This was corroborated by another [65]:

> There were always a relatively few old people who did not have wealth, but who had lived well; they had "wisdom." Many people went to them for advice. They might not like the criticism, but they went for it. The ability to speak well and truthfully was an important thing in building up a man.

There were never more than three or four persons who occupied the esteemed category at any one time. Informants had no difficulty in identifying them, and the criteria of selection were consistently those of "wisdom," supernatural power, and counseling roles. Almost invariably they included one or both caciques and the heads of secret societies. In cases where selectees lacked unanimous backing, this could usually be attributed to schisms existing between the moieties. Of former holders of the positions, one was a cacique and another was the head of one of the Bear societies. One informant [65] characterized his father and grandfather as esteemed, but would not divulge their ceremonial affiliations.

During the course of the fieldwork, three members of the esteemed group were personally known by the author; two served as informants on secular matters. All three were intellectually superior. As far as could be ascertained, their lives had been characterized by unusual participation in optional roles, particularly in the field of religion. While they were persons in comfortable economic circumstances, none was ostensibly wealthy.

It is obvious from data on government and religion that those members of the religious hierarchy who achieved the esteemed category wielded tremendous power in the village. They were able to do this without suffering most of the disabilities inherent in the prestige status group. First, their positions marked them as guardians of traditional cultural values. They had religious sanction for their acts, functioning merely as liaison agents between the supernatural and secular worlds.

Second, in cases where coercive or punitive actions were involved, the task of implementing such measures was usually delegated to secular officials. Accordingly they shifted the onus of their duties to others. They were safe even in their capacities as counselors and advisors, since requests for these services were always initiated by others.

In spite of the uniformity of the data praising esteemed persons, there is ample evidence that the general attitude toward them was ambivalent, and they were both feared and mistrusted. This characteristic is a Pueblo-wide phenomenon, and often included other members of the priestly hierarchy in addition to the esteemed (see also Hoebel 1960). In part the ambivalence resulted from authoritarian roles played by these religious officials. In addition, all possessed ample "wisdom," capable of being used for antisocial purposes as well as good. This generated an atmosphere conducive to the growth of anxiety, insecurity, and suspicion, all prominent features of Santa Clara personality. In order to ameliorate these conditions and establish an equilibrium, the Santa Clara and neighboring Pueblo Indians developed practices of surveillance, warnings, checks, and punishments for deviations. Examples of these are described in the discussions elsewhere dealing with

witchcraft, government, social control, and the operations of the secret societies.

Status of Women

Women were considered second-class citizens at Santa Clara Pueblo. This resulted from a variety of factors. First, they were not initiates of the kachina organizations. This precluded their having the concept of "wisdom" revealed to them, which deficiency was believed to prevent them from actually distinguishing between right and wrong. For this reason they were potentially dangerous and inadvertently the cause of many breaches of tabu. "They do not know what to avoid" [65]. It obviously disqualified them from esteemed status. It also limited their participation in most spheres of religion other than in some ancillary capacity. Another factor having restrictive consequences affecting women's activities was the strong patrilineal bias which characterized the culture. This was most pronounced in the area of government and politics, where all offices were held by males [65].

While women suffered from these culturally defined disabilities, this did not preclude their achievement of prestige status within their own spheres of endeavor. Since the bulk of their activities were centered in and around the home, many judgments used in rating individuals were derived from their role performance in that area. Several informants [23, 50, 66] stated that the ideal woman was one who had raised a large family, "who was attentive to her children," and whose children were respected by the community. Wives were expected to be subservient to their husbands and to avoid public embroilments.

Industry and efficiency in the performance of household duties were highly considered. Stress was placed upon being a good housekeeper, and women who were slovenly were publicly criticized by clowns and other religious officials.

Pottery making was one of the few handicrafts dominated by women. Within this pursuit, excellency of product and art form were recognized. Superior potters in the village were well known and enjoyed enhanced status in the community. This has further increased during the last sixty years because of the commercial demand for their products. Many women periodically augment the family income through the sale of pottery.

Another outlet open to women was the practice of therapeutics. Many illnesses were treated with herbal remedies and by massage. Both sexes engaged in this. Where the patients were relatives, the efforts were considered secular in nature. If outsiders were treated, elements of religion were frequently present. Adequately trained and experienced women were often as highly thought of as their male counterparts. Related to these skills was the vocation of midwife. This was exclusively a female profession; it also was one which led to an advancement in status.

While women were downgraded in the field of religion, they were by no means excluded, and their participation opened another avenue for derived prestige. The best example of this is the Women's Scalp Society. This organization functioned on a par with other secret societies, conducted initiation and cures, "worked" in monthly retreats, and cooperated with other secret organizations when its services were deemed essential. Women were also initiated members of other secret societies. While their participation in these was marginal, membership nevertheless added to their standing in the community.

It is obvious from the foregoing data that a female elite existed at Santa Clara Pueblo. This was the result of status derived from one or more of the criteria listed above. While differently based, the women's derived status was roughly comparable to the men's prestige group, and its existence was acknowledged by the village.

Old Age

Emphasis on seniority and respect for elders had practical consequences in the care and treatment accorded the aged. The shift from the adult category to the role of elderly person was a gradual rather than an abrupt one. Furthermore, the culture was so organized that when the infirmities and

disabilities of advanced years precluded active participation in economic fields, other segments of the culture not only remained open but were extended to absorb the energies of these individuals. In fact, old age was attended with many compensations, and many status positions were open only to elderly persons. Total retirement for men and women who were not senescent and actually handicapped was unknown at Santa Clara Pueblo. This tended to lessen or cushion the psychological repercussions that are often associated with this shift in role in other cultures.

Numerous compensations and outlets for the aged have been discussed in other connections and therefore will not be repeated in detail here. They included the inordinate respect for elders as a widely recognized cultural value; the connection between age and the prestige and esteemed status categories; and the association of age with religious office, political office, and social controls. In short, age was a prime prerequisite for participation in the more highly considered areas of the culture. Those so inclined could channel all their energies into the fields of religion, teaching, counseling, and directing, or combinations of these activities.

External expression of this respect, if not reverence, for age was to be found in daily interpersonal relations whenever the aged were involved. Elderly persons were always addressed by the terms "tara," father, or "zia," mother, as a mark of deference, whether or not they were relatives [20, 29]. If elders ventured unassisted into the plaza, parents delegated children to help them if there was need. Again, this concern applied to all old people, whether related or not. Elderly visitors were welcome in any home, and special efforts were directed to their comfort and entertainment. They were given a seat near the fireplace in winter or against a sunny wall in summer [29, 72]. In another sphere, that of religion, elderly men were always seated nearest the altars and received the prayer plumes representing the more important supernaturals [9].

While the bulk of the care of the aged, physically incapacitated, and indigent population was assumed by relatives, the whole village or any individual came to their aid whenever necessary. This might involve small tasks, such as concern with their personal appearance, or the washing and mending of their clothing; visiting the blind or bedridden and requesting them to tell stories to sustain their ego were also common activities.

There were also more formalized mechanisms for the support of the helpless. If a person was unable to harvest his or her crop, the governor appointed men to accomplish this [23]. The whole village contributed to the support of indigents [23, 27]. A small amount of produce was given to the governor by every family that was able, and this was distributed to any members of the community who were in need [27, 62].

There was no change in the status of women following menopause, as in some societies. The occurrence of psychological disturbance attending the male climacteric was similarly denied [22, 31].

Death and Burial

The various agencies and factors leading to death are covered in the section on curing and illness (Chapter 10). They included breech of tabu, witchcraft, accident, and old age. According to informants, actual death took place when the ha, "breath," left the body [9, 43, 50].

Consistent with the general tenor of the culture, the attitude toward death was relatively fatalistic and outwardly unemotional—with the exception of certain rigidly patterned mourning procedures. At Santa Clara Pueblo there was none of the generalized hysteria which has characterized the Navajo and other Athapascans. This was commented upon earlier by Jeançon, who was familiar with both groups, and it was particularly apparent where adults were involved. According to Jeançon (1904), "With adults, especially when a person has attained a fairly good old age, they often say, 'Well, he or she has lived a long time it is alright for them to go now and rest.'"

A more recent manifestation of this attitude was encountered when an attempt was made to institute a medical research program in the village. The comment of those with whom the project was discussed was "We know we are all going to die, but we would rather not know what we are going to die of."

Such an attitude does not mean that near relatives of the deceased did not feel or express grief. They did, and this was especially apparent in cases of the death of children. As will be seen later, death was surrounded by various tabus and purificatory rites. However, compared with most cultures, this crisis was underplayed at Santa Clara Pueblo, and as Jeançon (1904) remarked,

> [Mourning] has all the appearance of being perfunctory and ritualistic. While there is much wailing and crying, some of this is exaggerated by mourners who are not really paid for their services, but hope to partake of the funeral feasts.

As in the case of other crisis stages, many Western European cultural influences were apparent in the behavior associated with death and burial—both during Jeançon's residence and in the 1940s. In most instances these manifestations were superimpositions rather than true integrations; their inclusion tended to be optional and depended upon the conservatism of the particular family.

Many of the "aboriginal" funeral and mourning patterns recorded by Jeançon (1904) were still in force in 1946 among the conservative element. According to him,

> Immediately after death the body is washed by female relatives. (There is a question as to whether this is not a custom acquired from Christians.) Amongst the more conservative members of the Santa Claras, the body is then wrapped in a blanket which is sewed up to the neck. In the blanket are placed the fetishes of the person; and, in the case of a man, his bow and arrows; in the case of a woman, her tools for making pottery. The body is laid on the floor with an adobe brick for a pillow. The body is not dressed prior to sewing

it up. Sometimes the face is whitened with meal and at other times not. No reason could be found for this.

Additional details of activities preliminary to burial were contributed by contemporary informants [29, 50, 52]. A cloth was placed under the jaw and tied over the head of the deceased to close the mouth, and the corpse was always laid out in the house, with the head toward the east. "Otherwise, it might come back." These informants also stated that female relatives prepared the body of a female, and males, the body of a male, except in cases where the deceased was a member of one of the societies.

There was evidence that many of the older funeral procedures have survived among the population at large because of their maintenance by the secret societies. Jeançon (1904) stated that, "In many cases the Kossa prepares the body, especially if it is that of a member of their society." It is not clear from his statement, however, how far they acted as undertakers for the village as a whole.

According to recent informants [29, 40, 43, 52], "the societies took care of their dead." In the instance of the Tesuque Bear Society at Santa Clara, members laid out the corpse and conducted the funeral. The deceased was sewn in a blanket, never placed in a coffin, never wore shoes, and was carried to the cemetery on a ladder. The ceremonial paraphernalia of the individual remained in the society. The kaje [amulets or fetishes, CHL] of the dead were taken to a shrine and "sent away." A purification ritual was also enacted by the society. This and the terminal feast on the fourth day were apart from and in addition to the one held by the family [29, 52]. According to another informant [43], when a Bear Society member (possibly Jemez Bear) died, he was wrapped in a blanket, his moccasins were reversed on his feet, and his kaje were placed under his head. The remainder of his ceremonial equipment was taken to the hills and buried. Caciques were given the same type of burial as society members [29, 43, 52]. Inferentially, the membership of either the Summer Society or the Winter Society conducted the rites.

A modified version of this conservative laying out and burial pattern has been practiced by progressive groups in recent years, and was also in force even during Jeançon's residence. This procedure also included optional European elements. The body was washed and prepared by the godfather or godmother, if such existed, otherwise by relatives. The eyes were closed, and the hands were crossed on the breast. The clothes removed from the deceased were tied in a bundle and placed on the roof of the house. They remained there until four days after the burial, when they were washed and given to unrelated individuals. Jewelry, on the other hand, was removed and kept by relatives. Instead of being sewn in a blanket, the deceased was dressed in his or her best clothes. However, the clothing was reversed; that of a man were put on backwards; the manta of a woman, normally secured at the right shoulder, was tied over the left. Footgear was placed on the wrong feet. "If a living person does this, they say you are putting on a dead man's shoes" [29, 40, 52].

When prepared, the body was laid on the floor, a platform, table, or two chairs, with the head oriented to the east, and any clothing or personal effects which were to go in the grave were put beside it. Coffins were optional. Candles were next placed at intervals around the body. These were kept lighted during the period of mourning in the house. Finally a bowl was put near the foot on the left side of the corpse. In this the mourners put money to be used to pay for additional candles or masses [29, 52].

After the body was laid out, mourners began to arrive. According to Jeançon (1904),

All visitors touch the forehead, hands and feet of the corpse, telling it that they forgave all wrongs done by the person deceased and in turn ask to be forgiven any wrongs they may have done it. So the spirit of the dead leaves in peace, and when met in the spirit world is friendly. The writer [Jeançon, WWH] believes that this is a custom acquired from the Mexicans.

The somewhat perfunctory character of the mourning behavior of visitors has already been noted.

Formerly it was customary for the cacique of the appropriate moiety to come to the home and perform a ceremony over the deceased. It was not ascertained whether or not this convention was still in force. According to Jeançon (1904), this rite was conducted in secret, and this dignitary remained alone with the corpse. "The object of this is to lay the spirit of the dead and keep it from coming back and annoying the living. It is also to open the trail to the Sibobe or Place of Emergence, so that the spirit will not get lost on its way to the underworld." When members of the Bear societies were present, they sang four songs. These described the journey to the afterworld.

Mourners as well as relatives said prayers, both native and/or Christian, formerly and also at present. If the family was Catholic in persuasion a *veloria* might be held in the home, or lacking this, friends and relatives could sing Christian hymns [29, 52]; see Jeançon (1904).

Burial was normally held the morning following a death. Since the establishment of the mission church at Santa Clara (1526? WWH), interments have presumably taken place in the cemetery, or *campo santo*. One informant [62] "guessed" that before that time they were made in arroyos.

According to Jeançon (1904),

Amongst the conservatives the blanket is covered over the face just before leaving the house for interment. Also with these people [conservatives, WWH] children as well as adults do not have a coffin, but are placed in the earth wrapped only in the blanket with an adobe brick for a pillow. This is the same brick that was used at the house for the same purpose. As was said before the more progressive people use coffins and dress the corpse. Both parties use many Roman Catholic prayers as well as native ones.

Clothes and other articles belonging to the deceased are buried with the body. The toys of a child are placed on the grave. A favorite piece of pottery was formerly "killed," that is, broken on her grave [in the case of a dead woman, WWH]. When not wrapped with the body, the bow and arrows or rifle of a man were placed on the grave. Now these things are usually interred with the body. Prayer and food offerings are also made at the grave.

Contemporary accounts of burials of progressives other than those of society members reflect the influence of Catholicism. The church warders (pi?ka) were in charge of proceedings. Among other things, they designated certain people of the village to dig the grave, and it was the pi?ka who carried the corpse from the house to the cemetery. For this and other work, they might receive gifts; ordinarily, however, their duties were considered community obligations.

The funeral procession followed the deceased. It was made up of relatives and any friends who wished to take part, "mostly women." There was no order of march [15, 29, 52].

The deceased was taken first to the church. Throughout the journey, the church bell was tolled, three strokes, then an interval of about thirty seconds, and three more strokes, etc. This tolling continued until the body was lowered into the grave. It was also customary to toll the bell in this manner for about ten minutes to announce to the village that a death had occurred.

If a priest was present and the family desired, a mass was said in the church; if not, those present prayed. The body was next removed to the graveside. Again, if a priest was present, hymns were sung while the deceased was carried to the cemetery and prayers led by the preist were said at the grave. Otherwise, those who wished prayed as food was placed in the clothing of the deceased and the body and personal effects were lowered into the grave. "The land of dead was a four-days' journey, hence the food" [29, 52]. The head was always oriented toward the east.

Finally the grave was covered. The priest, if present, threw in the first shovelful of earth. In turn, those present threw in a handful. Those who had dug the grave then completed the operation. Usually a wooden cross with name and dates was erected [29, 40, 50, 52].

Following the ceremony the mourners returned to their homes. Each, however, washed his hands before entering the house [29, 52].

An exception to normal funeral custom occurred in connection with miscarriages and stillborn infants. These were disposed of under the floor of the room in which the birth took place and, apparently, without ceremony [56]. It was stated that witches were accorded the same type of burial as that given more desirable villagers [29, 52].

Mourning activities continued actively in force for a four-day period following a death. During this time it was mandatory that someone remain at all times in the house or room where the person had died. Various rationalizations were given for this behavior. Some stated that the spirit of the dead remained around the house for four days; others believed that if no one were in the house, someone else in the family might die, or that the spirit might return and cause the surviving relatives harm; still others thought that it took the deceased four days to reach the afterworld [29, 52, 73]. "The soul stays around the house four days, even if the person who died died away from home and was buried somewhere else" [73].

According to Jeançon (1904),

> The spirit of the dead is supposed to linger, in the neighborhood of the house where the person died, for four days after death. The whole family remains in the house during this time, on guard against its return to the place where it formerly lived. The head of the house or some older member of the family sits in the place or lies on the bedding that the deceased occupied when alive, so that, should the spirit succeed in entering the house it will find its place filled.

Any dances or major ceremonies were canceled when a death took place, and were rescheduled at a later date [18, 19].

What could be considered the terminal mourning rite was held on the fourth night following a death. This appears to have had the dual purpose of honoring the dead and safeguarding the living. It was described in its essentials by Jeançon and also by several of my informants [29, 72]. In 1946 the grandson of an oyike member, the great-grandson of the right arm of the Winter cacique, died. It was pertinent in this case that, while the family was nominally Catholic and the death took place in Santa Fe, neither the *veloria* or *descanso* was held—only this native mourning rite.

About five or six in the evening, relatives and friends brought food to the house of the deceased. This food was conveyed by the senior woman of each household, and theoretically at least, every extended family in the village was represented. "It is said that all households must take food, because wherever the souls of the dead are gathered, only those souls whose relatives brought food to the recently deceased person will share in the feast. Those whose living relatives failed to bring food go begging, and none of the other souls will give them food" [29]. Formerly native foods were brought; more recently canned foods and candy have been added, "anything the deceased might have liked when alive" [29]. Usually each donor brought enough to feed three or four people. The food was received by the head of the household or some elderly male relative, who placed the containers in a line on the floor. This man later conducted the ceremony. In the 1946 case, the grandfather of the deceased performed this office.

By eight or nine o'clock, all relatives and friends had assembled, and the ceremony began. The household head or his substitute came forward and took a small pinch of food from each container and placed it in a bowl for the dead. It was believed that when the dead received this offering, the food multiplied and enabled all Santa Clara dead to feast to their satisfaction [29, 43, 52, 71].

The leader next rolled two cornhusk cigarettes, using "people's tobacco" (towa tsa, "Indian tobacco"). One he placed in the bowl, and the other he smoked. Then he took charcoal from the fire, broke some into the bowl, put some in his mouth, and departed for the cemetery. (He also drew crosses on the sole of each moccasin with charcoal [43].) Normally the leader went alone, although occasionally he was accompanied by another man who was learning the rite. Talking was prohibited on the journey to and from the house, and the leader did not look behind him or to either side. On arrival at the cemetery, he went first to the grave and said a prayer, then to the northeast corner of the cemetery, where he deposited the food and broke the bowl. Jeançon (1904) reported that he sat down at the grave facing west and prayed, then took the bowl, which must be carried in the left hand, and broke it with his left foot. In the 1946 instance, the leader approached the cemetery backward, and when he reached the fence, threw the bowl over his left shoulder and shattered it. This was standard procedure [43].

On the return trip to the house, the principal must not look back. "If he did, he would see a skeleton coming to eat the food, hear someone calling, or feel someone tugging at him" [29, 52]. According to Jeançon (1904), he should also make four parallel lines in the earth with his left foot ["cutting the trail," i.e., transverse to the trail, most likely, CHL].

When the leader reached the house, he circled it [in Chapter 10, Hill notes, "the ceremonial circuit is counterclockwise." CHL] and spit chewed charcoal on all doors, windows, and about the wall. Then as he came through the doorway, he made an announcement of the following kind: "That you may live"; "All of you will live" [29, 52], or "You may live longer" (Jeançon 1904), and those inside answered, "Yes."

The leader then rinsed the charcoal from his mouth and, according to Jeançon, fumigated the interior of the house with burning cedar boughs. When this was completed, he signaled the relatives, and they began the feast. When they finished, all present who had brought food ate. During the feasting there was much joking and fun-making, and no mention was made of the deceased. When all had finished, the surplus food (and a considerable quantity usually remained) was divided among the visitors and relatives [29, 52].

According to Jeançon (1904), it was customary four days after the interment for the relatives and friends of the deceased to visit the cemetery and make final offerings of food and say prayers at the grave.

Native prayers to the dead are of many kinds. They ask the spirit to bear greetings to their friends and relatives who have gone through the Cebobe [Place of Emergence, CHL]; ask them to stay where they are and not come back and annoy the living and to be happy in their new condition. Requests are made that the newly dead will intercede with the cloud people for them that they may have lots of rain, and good weather for their crops. They ask that the dead be good and not come back in the form of witches, and to help them to make their hearts good. The food offerings are made directly to the spirit of the dead, with instructions that the living are feeding them and that they must appreciate the food and the kind thoughts of the living. The dead are also asked to make the magic of the living stronger.

No account of this action was obtained during the time my fieldwork was in progress, but this could well have been an oversight. Presumably this rite took place the morning after the purificatory ceremony and signalized the termination of mourning proper.

Beside traditional native observances, several mourning features of Spanish-American derivation were occasionally invoked; these were entirely optional. One was the *veloria,* or wake, which coincided with the aboriginal rites at the home. Its performance depended in part upon whether there was a villager available who knew the ceremony, or whether a neighboring penitente could be hired to conduct it.

When a *veloria* was held, visitors as they arrived knelt before the deceased, said prayers, made the sign of the cross over the body, and placed an offering in the bowl. They then seated themselves and remained quiet or communicated in whispers. When sufficient mourners had gathered, the leader began the rite. This consisted of hymns and prayers in Spanish, initiated by the leader, but in which the group participated. "They may sing three or four songs and then pray." This continued, often interspersed with native observances, until about eleven o'clock in the evening. At this time a rosary was recited, and then food was served in a separate room. The men ate first and then the women. Normally one or two hours was spent in eating, after which hymns and prayers were resumed. Another rosary was said about three or four o'clock in the morning. Breakfast was served at five or six o'clock. "There would be only a few left at that time." Hymns and prayers were then continued until the body was removed from the house [29, 42, 52, 62]; see Jeançon (1904).

A fire was always built in front of the house when a *veloria* was in progress, and around this a crowd gathered, composed mostly of the youths of the village. "These joke, tell stories, and think about the food which will be served later. They are interested in the feast. The tales dealt with the dead and the dead coming back. If a person had an itching shoulder they said, 'That is the dead person scratching you,' and all laughed [29, 52]. This casual behavior was another manifestation of the detached attitude toward death.

Velorias were also held at the time a new house was dedicated, as fulfillment of a vow, or for some favor that had been granted after planting and occasionally during the winter, "just for the general good." Again, their occurrence depended upon the existence of trained local leaders, the availability of neighboring penitentes, and the degree of Hispanicization of the particular family [29, 42, 52].

Another Spanish-American rite, the *descanso,* was sometimes performed when a death took place away from the village. This ceremony was appropriate whether or not the body was returned for burial. In either case the deceased was "met," and the funeral procession returned slowly to the pueblo, "even if in cars." "Mourners sang rather than reciting the rosary." A halt was made midway in the trip, and a cairn of stones was erected. Each mourner contributed at least one stone to the pile. Finally a cross was placed on top of the cairn. According to two nominal Catholics, "They believe that the dead have gone on a journey, and the cairn will rest their souls" [29,

52]. It was customary for persons traveling to or from the village and town to add stones to these cairns. "This was like saying a prayer" [29, 52].

While rites of the foregoing types terminated the mourning proper, other acts honoring the dead were engaged in periodically. One of the most common was a food offering prior to meals. Each person took a pinch of food and tossed it behind him. This was considered a gift to souls of the deceased, in general, and not to that of any specific person. An extension of this concept has recently developed. "Today, when drinking, a man takes a drink of whiskey and another says, 'Hey, you did not give some to the souls.' The man would offer some to the spirits" [43].

Another rite, predominantly native, was held on All Souls' Day. (Some confusion existed as to whether All Souls', All Saints' Day, or Halloween was the proper occasion.) This was performed by all households in which a death had occurred during the year. The ceremony duplicated the purificatory rite following burial. All relatives of the deceased contributed food. "The best of the summer crops were saved for this night." The household head selected a pinch of food from each container and placed it in a bowl. "Often the bowl was an old one which was partly broken." Two cigarettes were made; one was for the household head, and one for the deceased. "The dead's cigarette was not smoked, simply lit. If a man smoked the cigarette or ate the food for the dead, he would be just the same as dead." The food and cigarette were then deposited in the cemetery by the head of the household. On his return, he chewed charcoal and spat through the windows and other openings of the home. After this he washed his hands and mouth, and all present feasted [29, 42].

Eschatology

Santa Clara eschatology was poorly conceptualized. This was consistent with the casualness with which death was viewed and the general lack of interest in this area of culture. Ideas were vague concerning the soul, or spirit, the role played by the individual after death, and the character of the afterworld. Those accounts which were at all developed or relatively complete were, in most cases, tinged with European thinking or were combinations of native and Christian ideology.

This cultural blending is apparent in the only substantial account obtained dealing with the land of the dead [43, 50].

This happened at San Juan. A person had died and was dressed for burial. People were kneeling and saying prayers. The man's soul was wandering around, though his body was there. He saw people whose tongues had been placed in a split oak branch. Then their tongues were twisted. There were different stages of twisting. Their physical condition was determined by the number of twists. Some were dried up and ready to drop. These had been dead for years. Another spirit was leading the dead man around and telling him what these things meant. He told him that these men had not lived right. He saw others whose prayer plumes were small, worn out, and in small dusty piles. These had not worked well in the societies when they were alive. Others had large piles of glossy feathers. These had done their work well. The spirit told the spirit of the dead man that he was merely a visitor and that when he returned he could tell the living. He was shown some people who lived miserably and others who were well off and who had much produce. Some had good crops, large melons; everything was growing well. He was forbidden to eat or touch the crops because he did not yet belong there. Then he was brought back and saw his body lying there. He said, "That is a dead man there." The spirits leading him then pushed him, and his spirit entered his body again, and he asked for water. He had been told by the spirits that when he returned to life he would become Summer cacique. He was told to reveal what he had seen so that others would work well. He lived many years and was made cacique.

The idea of retribution was expressly denied by others [29, 52, 61]. In general the afterworld was envisaged as similar to the natural world, and existence there paralleled that of the living [27, 29, 52].

A distinction was made between supernaturals, those who had never been mortals (se t'a di mu pi?iŋ), and mortals (se^n ta). The souls, or spirits, or the ghost of a mortal, were designated as p'o wa^n ha^n. The orthodox version of a soul destination was probably the one given by Jeançon (1904). According to him, "Spirits of the dead go to the lake in the underworld through the place of Emergence, Cibobe, and there dwell forever."

Some believed that the dead became kachina, but this view was not universal. "When a person dies, he becomes ohua. These spirits bring rain. There was a woman whose children died. It was raining. She said, 'My children must be in the cloud bringing rain'" [69]. Jeançon (1904) stated, "The principal duties of the spirits are to help the cloud people in bringing rain and good crops to those living on earth. In fact there is a basis for the belief that the dead themselves become rain makers."

Spirits of the deceased were capable of returning to the natural world. However, there is no evidence that they constituted a real menace to the living, although the germ of this idea might certainly be inferred from the purification rites following death. Most returned souls were those of individuals who had suffered frustrations and had come back to accomplish something they had been unable to do when alive. Normally the presence of spirits or ghosts was regarded as semihumorous or at the most, was cause for annoyance or uneasiness. There was none of the hysteria typical of Navajo culture, and there was no tabu on the use or mention of the name of the dead.

If it was necessary for a person to visit the church or graveyard at night, he chewed charcoal. This prevented the souls of the deceased from bothering or frightening him. "They [the souls] would be rushing past" [43].

Other instances of soul return and attitudes associated with them were illustrated in the following account [43]:

It was believed that the spirit of the deceased would return if the house in which death took place was not occupied continuously for four days after the death. Such a house was referred to as na ha' po?. This also meant haunted, spoiled, or ruined.

The same term was applied to an intoxicated individual. The spirit essence was manifested by noises at the windows or in room corners. In such instances one of the Bear societies was engaged to purify the house [43].

Sometimes knocks were heard at the door of a house. If upon investigation no one was there, those inside said, "I forgive you." It was believed that a soul unable to reach the afterworld had returned to ask for assistance [29, 52].

Another brief account of spirit return was given by two informants [29, 52]. According to them, their grandmother went to town to sell pottery. One of their mothers, then a child, wished to accompany her, but was told to remain at home. She followed and thought she saw her mother in the distance, but the woman disappeared. "It was a woman who had died two or three years before, who had come back" [29].

[In concluding this chapter, it seems important to add some commentary concerning clans at Santa Clara Pueblo. The careful reader will undoubtedly note that Hill included no more than a few passing mentions and no extended discussion of this subject. The explanation for this omission can be found in the words of Parsons (1929: 82–83), writing as of the 1920s. Already weakened and of little, if any, social significance as of her time, the reasons for Hill's failure to include some discussion several decades later become readily apparent. Parsons wrote the following in regard to "Clanship":

Among the Tanoans at Taos, Picuris, and Isleta, there is no clan system; at the other limit of the Pueblo area, among the Hopi, clanship is highly developed. The clan system of Zuñi approximates the Hopi; the systems of the Keresan towns vary somewhat with their dis-

tribution west and east, the western Keres having a more pronounced system than the eastern Keres. (Mrs. Goldfrank refers to the "degeneration" of clanship at Cochiti...) At Jemez clanship is fairly insignificant. Among the Tewa, clanship is still more insignificant, functioning not even as an exogamous institution, and, as far as I could learn, devoid of ceremonial associations. It is merely a question of a name, which, to the younger people at least, may be even unknown. Even to the older people of San Juan and Santa Clara the clan affiliations of women or men marrying into the family are for the most part unknown, let alone the clan affiliations of neighbors....How far ignorance or indifference... in the matter of clan classification may go comes out plainly in the analysis of our genealogical tables. In few cases, if any, is the clan of an unrelated person known.

Kinship terms are not applied to those bearing the same clan name. In fact, given the prevailing ignorance of clan affiliation, the existence of unrelated clanspeople, i.e., mere clanspeople, is unknown....

San Juan, Santa Clara, and Nambé informants not only denied that marriage choice was in any way affected by clan, but they were even surprised by the suggestion that marriage within the clan might be questioned....

...the clan name descends unilaterally, sometimes through the maternal line, sometimes through the paternal. Two Santa Clara members of the family (Gen. III, 36, 38) posited clanship in the paternal line, "the father is stronger than the mother," (... "They follow their father's clan in Santa Clara," my First Mesa informant had been told by his ex-Hano friend.) and the clan name was compared to the Mexican patronymic as having neither more nor less significance. Specifically it would be said that two Badgers not genealogically connected were no more related than, let us say, two patronymically named Naranho or Tefoya [sic]. They might be related, they might not be. And just as you could take your mother's Mexican patronymic, if you preferred it to your father's, so you could take your mother's clan name. "If you don't like your father's *t'owa,* you can take your mother's." And this is what people sometimes do, i.e., they change their clan at pleasure! How frivolous this would seem to a Hopi!

Further on, Parsons (pp. 86–87) listed Santa Clara clans she found "Specifically represented, 1923," "Not specifically represented, 1923," and those that Hodge had recorded in 1895. These lists are interesting to compare with one compiled by Bourke in 1881 and which appears in Chapter 2 of this volume.

Clans Present, 1923	Clans Not Present, 1923	Clans Present, 1895
Red Stone		Coral
	Stick	Firewood
Badger		Badger
Corn		Corn

Clans Present, 1923	Clans Not Present, 1923	Clans Present, 1895
Sun		Sun
		Calabash
		Cloud
		Cottonwood (Squash)
		Deer
		Eagle
		Gopher (Weasel)
		Oak
		Willow

Clearly, from the observations by Bourke (1881) and by Hodge (1895), and the sharp decline noted by Parsons only a few decades later (1923), it is easily understood that in the period of Hill's fieldwork clans at Santa Clara Pueblo were of little, if any, consequence. It is quite likely that if Hill had been able to complete his discussion of social organization, he would have included comments of this nature. In terms of culture history, the demise of the clan system is unquestionably significant; in terms of mid-twentieth century Santa Clara culture, however, clanship obviously is no longer a meaningful factor. CHL]

9

Political
Organization

[This discussion of political organization as seen by the Santa Clara Indians involves one of the facets of culture specifically mentioned in the Preface. Major elements of this important aspect of Santa Clara life are included in this chapter, as one would expect. However, concepts of ownership and inheritance have been discussed in Chapter 3, and various aspects of social control, a facet of behavior often viewed as a prime concern of the governmental structure, appeared in Chapter 8 as part of the conditioning process experienced in individual development. Other aspects of politics and government may be found in the concluding chapter, Ceremonial Organization.

The placement of these discussions is, as noted earlier, largely a matter of an ethnographer's perception of a culture. As changes have occurred at Santa Clara, and continue to occur, it is clear that the power and influence of the traditional theocracy have been fading in recent times. Acculturation, wage earning in outside communities, internal factionalism, and a written constitution, adopted late in 1935 (see Appendix B), have been both the precipitants and the products of change.

The traditional organization and changes in it were the concerns of Hill as he attempted to gain insights into and understanding of the multiple factors interacting in complex and sometimes obscure fashion over the span of several decades. As of the years prior to and following World War II, Hill's discussion focused on the primary ingredients in this process. Needless to say, trends and factors were identified that have actively continued in subsequent years and will persist into the future. CHL]

Santa Clara, like the great majority of Pueblo Indian villages, was politically autonomous. Alliances and cooperative endeavors with linguistic affiliates or other towns were ephemeral. Most were for purposes of mutual defense; a few, the result of offensive military action. While cooperative ventures between villages for trading and hunting took place and reciprocal religious obligations were recognized, only a small and select segment of the population was involved in such matters.

The aboriginal political system can best be described as a centralized theocracy with gerontocratic overtones and autocratic tendencies. For governmental and religious purposes, the village was divided into moieties, Winter (kwere) and Summer (xazhe). A religious hierarchy existed in each moiety, the pinnacle of which was an esoteric religious society, often referred to as a managing society. The winter organization was called Oyike, or Ozhike, and the Summer, Pay-oj-ke, or Pa'zho o?ke. The two caciques, who were at the head of these two organizations, were responsible for the direction of internal secular affairs and religious proceedings. There was formerly constant cooperation between these two leaders, direct responsibility shifting seasonally for religious purposes, annually for secular ones.

[In this discussion of the two Santa Clara moieties, and also later in discussions of the related managing society and cacique affiliated with each moiety, it is of interest to recall comments by Bandelier (1890–92: I, 302–3) as he compared these data between the Tewa and the Keresan Pueblos.

Basing his remarks primarily upon data from Santa Clara and San Juan, Bandelier noted that the two caciques among the Tewa were "on the whole equal in power," and yet he indicated that the Summer cacique "enjoys a certain pre-eminence over his colleague." The detailed background for this situation, as Bandelier (p. 303) explained, lay in the distant past, from the time of emergence at "Ci-bo-be, now a lagune in southern Colorado..."

Among the Keresans, as at Cochiti Pueblo (see Lange 1959: 299, 309, 314, 324, 343), the Turquoise Kiva, or moiety (associated with winter), took procedural precedence, and as Bandelier worded it, "enjoys a certain pre-eminence" over the Pumpkin Moiety.

The Santa Clara structure, however, did not seem to have been so completely developed or, perhaps, as rigidly maintained. Data in Ortiz (1969: 15, 29, 63) and in E. Dozier (1970a: 169) indicated a slight, but inconsistent, Summer priority at the same time these authors were stating that equality between the Summer and Winter moieties was typical for the Tewa, a blend possibly of the seasonal alternation traditional among

the Tewa and the disruptive effects of long-term factional strife, as at Santa Clara Pueblo.

Hill's discussion of the moieties, their managing societies, and the caciques at Santa Clara gave little, if any, impression of pre-eminence of one moiety over the other. His sequences of discussion often place the Winter data first, although the data in Chapter 10, Ceremonial Organization, were presented, for the most part, with Summer first and Winter second. It is uncertain whether this situation resulted from the affiliations of Hill's informants or was otherwise purely accidental, or whether any idea of pre-eminence, formerly present, had faded, or was fading, from the cultural awareness. To what extent the alternation was derived from the "emic" views of informants or the "etic" views of Hill can not be ascertained. Sequences in the discussions of these chapters on the political and ceremonial organizations have remained as Hill wrote them, or if a change has been made, it is noted as such. CHL]

A third dignitary, the so-called outside chief, was concerned with all matters external to the pueblo or emanating from external sources. He also constituted the only effective check on the power of the caciques.

The roster of the Winter (Oyike) Society was composed of individuals who had acquired membership through dedication at birth, through a vow during illness, or through trespass, and who had subsequently served a probationary period and been initiated. All male initiates of the Winter kachina group, and both males and females were initiated members of the Winter Moiety. (For details of pledging, initiation, rites, etc., for both the Summer and Winter societies, see Chapter 10.)

The leader of the Oyike Society was the Oyike sendo: variously referred to as Winter cacique, Winter chief, or Winter priest. Next in rank, in descending order, were two officers: "the right on that side arm" (koring merg geri?i xo), and the "left on that side arm" (ye merg geri?i xo) [40, 50, 55].

The comparable organization in the Summer Moiety was the Pay-oj-ke Society.

This was headed by the Summer cacique (Po e tuŋ zhon), Summer chief, or Summer priest, and his two assistants, the right and left arms. The details of organization and qualifications for membership paralleled those of the Oyike Society.

The Winter and Summer caciques served for life. Theoretically impeachment was possible, but there is no record of such a case at Santa Clara. Three instances were reported for San Juan, however, two involving heads of the Summer Moiety and one the head of the Winter Moiety [50, 69].

Upon the death of a cacique, a temporary replacement, called an *interino,* was appointed to serve until a successor could be selected. This was necessary since the deliberations leading to the choice of a new cacique were often of considerable duration. Furthermore, installation rites for the new appointee could be held only during the winter solstice for an Oyike, and only at the summer solstice for a Po e tuŋ zhon; the *interino* was often the right arm, although this was not mandatory. Occasionally a cacique indicated to the right and left arm whom he desired for *interino* before his death, and his wishes were usually respected [31, 43, 71].

Depending upon the moiety in which the vacancy existed, a new cacique was selected from the male membership of the Winter or Summer Society. Since the composition of these organizations was based upon random factors (dedication, vow, trespass), the position was not an inherited one. For example, in 1923, the incumbent Summer cacique was unrelated to his predecessor. The Winter cacique had succeeded his paternal uncle, but his heir apparent was in no way related (Parsons 1929: 113–14). In 1941, neither the right nor the left arm of the Summer cacique was related to him or to the other [69].

Normally the right arm succeeded to office. This was true of Victoriano Sisneros, Summer cacique in the 1940s. The left arm moved to the position of right arm, and a new left arm was chosen from the remaining male personnel of the appropriate society. Often the *interino* was confirmed as cacique. However, if the right arm or *interino* lacked the requisite qualifications, the left arm or some other member of the group was chosen. This was the case of the predecessor of Victoriano Sisneros, who had been a member of the Summer Society, but neither right nor left arm [31, 50].

In theory the members of the society alone were responsible for making the selection. However, since their choice was of concern to the entire moiety, and to a certain extent to the pueblo as a whole, outside pressures presumably entered into the deliberations. The weight of such public opinion is, however, difficult to assess. According to Jeançon (1904–30),

> If either of the priests die, his successor is chosen by the heads of the people. Sometimes the colleague of the dead priest is called upon for assistance in determining the successor, although the deceased has more likely than not named a preference for his follower in office before his death, and the election is more or less influenced by this preference.

What Jeançon meant by the "heads of the people" is not clear. The suggestion that the moiety or pueblo at large was consulted was denied by one informant [31], himself a member of the Winter Society, and also by another [40]. If by "heads" Jeançon referred to the council, his statement is meaningless, since their confirmation of the appointee was automatic. That a deceased cacique often designated his successor before death was confirmed, as well as the fact that his wishes were usually honored by the society [55, 69].

In actuality, screening of potential candidates for caciqueship began many years before a vacancy existed. Young men who showed aptitude and interest were groomed for the position. In a sense they served an apprenticeship. This was considered desirable, since many years of training were necessary before a candidate became familiar with the enormous amount of ritual and administrative knowledge prerequisite to and required in the office [40, 55, 69].

Qualifications for caciqueship were high, and it is doubtful whether all expectations were ever realized in one individual. A candidate had to be an orthodox fundamentalist in religious matters. Constant adherence in this respect was watched for and demanded. Only those who exhibited intense preoccupation with religion and who participated extensively in religious rites over a long period could hope to be considered. Prolonged participation in ceremonials was necessary not only for the acquisition of knowledge, but because it was through this medium that an individual accumulated the supernatural power or "wisdom" basic to eligibility. Aspirants had also to exhibit in large measure those qualities of personality selected by the culture as criteria for esteemed status. This was associated with the idea of a "good heart," namely, the use of supernatural power in a selfless and beneficial sense. Finally, the candidate had to be a man with administrative talent [31, 50, 71]. The time involved in achieving the above qualities insured that an aspirant would be mature, if not past middle age, before he was selected.

If a man met the minimum requirements, he had also to be willing to dedicate his life to his position, to the general welfare, and to live in a separate status. Once the office was accepted, resignation was impossible. It will be obvious from the discussion of cacique functions that the position had advantages; however, the behavior and activities of a cacique were considerably curtailed. He was expected to devote his entire time to his office, and rewards in a material sense were slight. Formerly, the moiety planted and harvested for him, but these services were discontinued after the major factional split in the latter part of the last century. This prospect, plus demands upon time, have often made otherwise eligible men hesitate to accept the office [29, 50, 55].

These factors were noted by Jeançon (1904–30):

> Both of the offices of winter and summer priest entail many privations and much effort. They have served a long apprenticeship before beginning their duties, having so much to learn regarding seasonal changes, making of various "medicines" to control Nature,

the magic lore; and many other things that are connected and associated with the offices. During the term of office they were not able to do any kind of work outside on account of the time taken up in performing the duties required of them by their positions. In the old days a plot of ground was set aside and worked by all the men of the village for the benefit of the priest and his family, he also had some income from special prayers and offerings made for individuals or their families. At this time the working of a communal plot for his benefit has been discontinued and he has to depend upon anything he can make "on the side" for his living. Also the duties and requirements are not so strenuous as before and all his time is not necessary as in former days. So much of the old magic and medicine has been lost that he has much more leisure.

In 1912 the office of winter priest was offered to a friend of the writer [Jeançon, WWH] but had to be declined as the man did not have sufficient means to support himself and family, although he had prepared for the office for a long time.

Another detrimental facet of this esteemed position was that while a cacique had enormous power, he still might be subject to reprisal for unpopular action or the uncontrollable adversities of nature. Jeançon (1904–30) stated that, "Although the winter and summer priests have control of religious matters yet their persons are not invulnerable. There are cases on record where he has been attacked, beaten and put in stocks in the public square. These cases are exceedingly rare." Caciques were subject to check by the outside chief. He scrutinized their activities and behavior and not only advised but criticized them if they deviated too far from the expected norm. He might even inflict physical punishment in exaggerated situations. "Of course you cannot force people today" [69]. For example, if a cacique attempted to resign or to leave the pueblo, it was the duty of the outside chief and his assistants to beat him and force him to return. The Bear societies also acted in similar restraining capacity. Implicitly they operated in instances where insinuations of witchcraft were involved [69]. Furthermore, a cacique was not exempt from censure and ridicule by members of the clown societies.

Ceremonies surrounding the installation of a cacique were not well known, and information on them was difficult to obtain. Material on these rites is described under the ceremonies of the Winter and Summer societies. According to Jeançon (1904–30),

It is always customary to observe at least one year of mourning for the deceased priest, and sometimes the period extended over to two years. The newly elected priest functions during the period of mourning but is not officially inducted into office until the period of mourning is completed.

My own informants [50, 55, 69] indicated no such delay. According to them, installation took place at the end of the term or year of the deceased's tenure—referring either to the winter or summer solstice.

The functions of the caciques were extensive. They were charged with responsibility for the internal well-being of the village. This included not only the direction of spiritual affairs, but also the guidance of political and secular activities within Santa Clara Pueblo. Concern with political appointments alternated annually. Religious obligations alternated seasonally; the Summer cacique assumed responsibility for village religious welfare roughly from the vernal to the autumnal equinox, and the Winter cacique, from the autumnal to the vernal equinox. This does not mean that either principal was periodically relieved of authority, merely that direct responsibility shifted from one to the other. Actually, interaction between the two officials was expected to be close, and according to Jeançon (1904–30), "each one must assist his colleague four times during the period he was in office." Presumably this refers to ritual cooperation.

In former times there were elaborate ceremonies at the time of the equinoctial transfers but these have lapsed in recent years as a result of factional disputes. They had apparently existed in attenuated forms for a considerable period. According to Jeançon (1904–30),

Formerly there were elaborate ceremonies at the time when one priest turned over the duties of office to another. These have now been so abbreviated that they only consist of a sort of ceremonial visit of the retiring priest to his colleague; both are accompanied by their right and left hand men.

The specific activities of the caciques in the spiritual area are detailed in Chapter 10, Ceremonial Organization and will not be repeated here. Broadly speaking, they initiated or sanctioned and administered all ceremonies in which the whole village was involved, and also those specifically associated with the particular moiety of each. These included the large calendrically determined rites, for which they enlisted the cooperation of the curing, clown, hunt, war, and scalp societies, as the occasion demanded.

Within the moiety the caciques were concerned with moiety initiations, kachina performances and initiations, and ritual activities of the Winter or Summer society. Only the more specialized activities of secret societies, whose membership crosscut moiety lines, were beyond their immediate jurisdiction. It was their prerogative and duty either through cajolery or moral force to see that all those obligated performed their religious requirements. While much of the authority for the execution of these obligations was delegated to the right and left arms, other members of the Winter and Summer societies, the outside chief, war captains, and governor, the ultimate responsibility rested with the caciques.

In recent years factionalism has diminished the secular power of the caciques, and the constitution of 1935 (Appendix B) relieved them of much of their secular authority. From Spanish times until 1936, they had appointed the governor. Until the schisms interfered, this was done on an annual alternating basis; one year the appointment was made by the Winter cacique, the next by the Summer. Despite the adoption of the constitution, however, there is evidence that the caciques have continued to play a significant role in nominating candidates for this office and influencing their election [27, 31, 36, 40, 45, 50].

For a considerable part of the historic period, the selection of the outside chief or war captain was under jurisdiction of the caciques. Again, this was formerly on an annual, alternating basis [27, 31, 36, 40, 45, 50]. As will be seen later, the appointment of the outside chief and war captain by the caciques was of considerable consequence from the point of view of the consolidation of authority and power in the hands of these two priestly officials.

Other duties assigned to the caciques included designating the days on which planting and harvesting began. There was no office of "sun watcher" at Santa Clara; the determination of calendrical events was the task of the caciques [31, 40]. They were also expected to initiate and oversee all communal work. This involved cleaning and opening ditches, cleaning the village before major ceremonies and feast days, and any cooperative efforts to alleviate the hardship of individual moiety members. The direct supervision of communal projects was performed by the governor or war captain, but ultimate responsibility and authority were vested in the caciques. Each addressed his moiety before the work began, "telling them they should work hard and not cause trouble" [40]. "There was no special reward for communal work. Each in turn was supposed to do his share of work. There were no favorites played"[45].

The third member of the political hierarchy was "the head outside the village" (a korg gei tun zhorg), variously referred to as outside chief, war captain, capitán mayor, or capitán de guerra. There is evidence that the outside chief and his five assistants were at one time a politically autonomous unit, with a permanent and continuing membership that selected its own leader and replacements. This is consistent with the Santa Clara emphasis on balance, and would have

made this body a more effective check against the autocratic power of the caciques.

According to informants [30, 64], formerly when an outside chief died, or was incapacitated because of illness, or resigned his office, the "next on the tail" right arm assumed his position. At the end of the year, the five remaining war captains selected a new member to bring the organization to full strength. "Now men for this group are selected every year" [64].

At some later date, the right to appoint the outside chief, or war captain, was assumed by the caciques. This possibly coincided with the decrease in warfare and the corresponding deterioration of this officer's role as a defensive leader. In any event, for a considerable period of time the outside chief or war captain has been selected by the caciques on an alternating, yearly basis [31, 40, 44, 45, 50]. According to two [31, 45], the year the Winter cacique named the governor, the Summer cacique selected the outside chief. This was reversed the following year. Again, this was clearly in harmony with the Puebloan concept of balance, and furnished a check on the power of each moiety.

In recent years it has been customary for the outside chief and governor to visit the caciques four or eight days prior to the new year and tender their resignations. At this time they were told the names of their successors. On January first the two retiring officials presided at a meeting of the council. The caciques did not attend. At this time the names of the incoming outside chief and governor were presented. "This was the first time the names were known" [69]. Theoretically the nominations could be rejected by the council, but evidence indicates that confirmation was automatic.

The outside chief or war captain chose his right and left arms and three other assistants. Three of the six men were selected from each moiety [27, 45, 50]. In recent years deviations from this principle have occurred as the result of schisms.

It was the duty of the outside chief and his five war captains to protect the village from any dangers emanating from outside sources. This not only included physical dangers of enemy attack, but was interpreted and extended to include any outside contacts or ideological infiltrations which might jeopardize the status quo. Within this framework they furnished the defensive military leadership in former times, acted in part as an internal law-enforcement body, and were the administrative arm of the caciques, especially in the religious area. In all but their military capacity they worked in close cooperation with the caciques, secondarily with the governor.

In their authoritative capacity there is nothing to indicate that these dignitaries were religious officials in the sense of being religious practitioners. Rather, they were officials of the religious hierarchy and guardians of religion and "custom." This status was confirmed when the constitution of 1935 was adopted. Interestingly, the outside chief and assistants continued to be appointed, and were not included among those secular officers elected by popular vote.

Their role as guardians against outside attack lapsed after the 1860s and 1870s. Prior to that time they had maintained a sentry system to warn the village of the approach of marauding bands. When such were reported, the outside chief mobilized his forces and directed the defense of the pueblo. At least three war captains remained in the village at all times for the purpose of protection [27, 40, 76].

While there was nothing to prevent it, at least in recent years, the outside chief did not need to be a member of the War Society, much less leader of that organization, whose main concern was with therapeutics, purification, and protection through supernatural means [44]. The leaders of offensive war parties were persons other than the war captains. Presumably the defensive responsibilities of the war captains precluded their leaving the pueblo. However, they did announce a projected raid and assisted in preparing and organizing the party [27, 40, 76].

Within the pueblo the war captains functioned as mobilizers, overseers, disciplinarians, guardians, and administrators of most village religious affairs. They implemented the policies and desires of the caciques and the governor, and they saw that the edicts of these officials were properly carried out.

The outside chief and war captains were also guardians against ideological deviations. This included any deviation in thought or act from the traditional way of life, or any violation of the "customs," namely religious transgressions. In this role they operated as brakes against acculturation and as protectors against outsiders, especially the malignant influences of anthropologists and missionaries [45, 50].

The outside chief was the one person empowered to check the otherwise unlimited power of the caciques. He was expected to discuss village affairs with these officials. He acted in an advisory capacity, and if the occasion demanded he might even admonish a cacique or override his decision. Presumably these were cases where religious defection was involved. However, situations of this type rarely, if ever, developed [45, 50]. Should a cacique attempt to resign his position or leave the pueblo, it was the duty of the outside chief, using physical force if necessary, to persuade him to return and conform [50].

Within the aboriginal framework, headed by the hierarchy of the caciques and the outside chief, there developed one of the most autocratic states in North America. This was made possible by a variety of direct and indirect mechanisms for social control available to the leadership, and also because the leadership was acting in an intermediary capacity between the natural and supernatural world, supported in their actions by supernatural sanction.

Any direct coercive weapon, short of the power of life and death over subjects, was available to the caciques and outside chief. Recalcitrant members of the village had their property confiscated, and could be beaten, whipped, or tied up in the kiva or plaza until they expressed a desire to conform. If exaggerated cases of non-compliance developed, the deviant was banished [30, 40, 44, 72]. Particularly in earlier times, this was often tantamount to the death penalty, since survival outside the cooperative confines of the social group was a dubious undertaking.

Besides these direct mechanisms of enforcement, the caciques could and did invoke supernatural sanctions. Latitude in this area was enormous. "They worked in the background" [56], namely, through intermediaries—the outside chief and governor; as another [15] stated, "No one knows but the caciques what their real duties are." As theocratic heads they could claim any prerogative and interpret it in terms of religious obligation. Those who did not give whole-hearted support to their edicts were not only subject to direct reprisal, but were guilty of breach of tabu and liable to supernatural punishment as well. Furthermore, since all religious activity was directed toward village and individual welfare, any nonconformance jeopardized everyone. This conclusion resulted in the identification of public opinion with constituted authority.

There is no doubt but that caciques were feared. This was apparent from observation of behavioral patterns as late as 1948. This resulted partly from the political powers inherent in their position, and partly because of the enormous amount of "wisdom," or supernatural power, attributed to them. This commodity, while ideally used for beneficial purposes, could also be used to harm or injure individuals, and acted as a major deterrent against personal reprisal.

The battery of secular officials introduced during the Spanish regime, to be discussed shortly, enhanced rather than curtailed cacique power. In fact this innovation resulted in an extension and consolidation of theocratic authority. The outside chief or war captain and the governor were responsible more than any others for implementing cacique policy, dictates, and actions. Since they owed their offices to one or another of these religious officials, their loyalty and sympathetic cooperation could be assumed except in extreme circumstances. Even in cases where disagreements arose, the tenure of office (one year) of the outside chief and governor was too short to pose any effective threat to the vested interests of the religious hierarchy.

In the same way the tribal council, since it was composed of current political appointees in addition to exgovernors, acted as handmaiden to the entrenched authority.

Besides the aboriginal governmental officials just discussed, there were a number of secular officials introduced during the period of Spanish domination. These have been a part of Pueblo culture so long that few if any modern Indians were aware of their origin. They consisted of the governor, lieutenant governor, *alguacil* (sheriff), *pika* (church warders), the council, and the war captains. The latter, which early became identified with the outside chief and assistants, have already been discussed.

The governor (tung *zhong*, head), or *governador*, until 1936 when the constitution of 1935 took effect, was chosen by the caciques. As mentioned earlier, the selection was on an alternating basis. The Winter cacique made the appointment one year, and the Summer cacique, the next. While the term of office was for one year, there was nothing to prevent an exgovernor from serving again at a later date, and this has occurred in several instances. Caciques were not eligible for governorship, but an exgovernor could be chosen cacique. If a governor died in office an *interino* was appointed to serve the remainder of his term [27, 30, 31, 36, 40, 44, 50].

The duties of the governor were numerous and predominantly secular in nature, as opposed to those of the outside chief. Until recent years his actual power was slight. His role was that of an intermediary who primarily implemented decisions and policies of the caciques, secondarily those of the outside chief or war captain, and to a lesser extent those of the council.

The governor was the liaison between the religious hierarchy and village, and the outside agencies and individuals who wished to conduct business with the pueblo. Such business relations were variable in scope. They might include anything from negotiation for extensive projects of economic rehabilitation with the Bureau of Indian Affairs to issuing a permit to a tourist or visitor to photograph in the village. In this liaison capacity, he made no decisions of moment without first consulting the council and/or cacique. His decisions were invariably based on established precedent, or common law.

Within the village the governor functioned, often in conjunction with the war captain, as mobilizer, expeditor, and supervisor of projects originating with the caciques. In this connection he, with the council, enjoyed certain limited executive and judicial functions. The governor also had the privilege of appointing certain secular officials.

The governor formerly addressed the village from his housetop each day, disseminating information of interest to the pueblo, and announcing any contemplated communal work. If he was a man of advanced years, he delegated this duty of town crier to some younger man, selecting one with a clear, strong voice [27, 31, 40].

The most prominent of the governor's internal duties had to do with communal works, and the most important of these was the maintenance of the irrigation system. There was no office of "ditch boss" at Santa Clara Pueblo; early in the spring the governor organized work parties to clean the ditches and ready them for use. Once the irrigation season began, he arranged for ditch patrols. When breaks were reported, he recruited workers and directed repairs. He also allotted water to individual land holders and, with the council, settled disputes over water rights. Because of his manifold duties, the governor often appointed the lieutenant governor or some other person to assist him in irrigation management. Such individuals were directly responsible to him [25, 40, 64, 65]. "The governor is, of course, responsible to the cacique" [25].

The governor also supervised the cleaning of the village befor major ceremonials and feast days. This usually included the church as well, a task assigned to the church warders under the supervision of the governor [40, 64]. "Long ago the governor had charge of cleaning the pueblo. The men would clean, and the women carry the trash away. Now the women only calcimine the church and clean the altar. Trucks carry the trash away" [40].

Other administrative duties of the governor included patrolling the tribal area to prevent unauthorized outsiders from cutting wood [30], and arranging for the removal of livestock to the mountains in the spring. This last action was to prevent damage to the fields after the spring planting. "Since the constitution, there have been two fence riders to watch the cattle" [40]. The governor formerly designated the time for planting [27, 44].

Besides his many executive obligations, the governor served in a limited judicial capacity; some disputes were brought to him for adjustment rather than to the religious hierarchy. For example, he regularly acted in cases of land assignment and land disputes. When the controversies were of considerable magnitude, or when he was unable to reach a satisfactory agreement, the governor, in his position as chairman of the council, referred such matters to that body for final disposition.

Each incoming governor chose his own lietutenant-governor (*teniente,* or right arm) and sheriff (*alguacil,* or left arm). Since the activities of the governor were extensive, he delegated many responsibilities to the lieutenant-governor. He supervised much of the work connected with the maintenance of the irrigation system and its inherent problems [27, 30, 31, 36, 40, 44]. "He pays special attention to the ditch even if the governor is in the village" [40].

The sheriff also assisted the governor when and wherever needed. However, he was specifically concerned with the punishment of malefactors. It was he who usually administered whippings or other penalties decreed by the council or religious officials [27, 30, 31, 36, 40, 44]. "Now he takes care of the drunks. He can fine them without going to the council" [40].

The governor also appointed the principal church warder (pika), pika *mayor* or *fiscale,* who in turn selected three assistants. Unlike other officials, these tended to serve consecutive terms, or to be reappointed by each succeeding governor. Like the war captains, they were looked upon as religious officials, and were not included among the elective officers in the constitution of 1935. These four, subject to supervision by the governor, were responsible for all things associated with the church [40, 50, 64, 68]. They swept and decorated the church before a mass. They directed the laborers who periodically plastered the exterior walls and whitewashed the interior. "The girls of the pueblo helped with the cleaning, whitewashing, and making things for the church" [64].

The pika were also responsible for the organization of the Christian features of religious processions and saint's day feasts. They made funeral arrangements and conducted burials. By implication, they formerly directed the planting and harvesting on the plot of land assigned to the church for the support of the resident priest [29, 30, 36, 40, 50, 52].

In earlier times the pika served as catechists. They instructed the unmarried girls and boys in Christian religious doctrine, and taught them catechism and prayers. "They used to send the younger boys and girls over to the church to learn to say prayers, morning and evening. This was in the fall. There was not much to do in that season" [71].

Some general welfare elements were also under their jurisdiction. They were expected to care for hardship cases among the younger children and to prevent undue privations among the widowed of the tribe. Finally, the pika might be called upon by the governor to perform any type of work that was necessary [30, 31, 36, 50].

Beside the pika, two other individuals contributed services to the church. One acted as altar boy; the other discharged a rifle during the consecration of the mass in lieu of ringing a bell on the altar. Neither was necessarily pika. Formerly the head of one of the Bear societies had served consecutively as altar boy from the time of his appointment until his death. The "shooter" likewise served in a dual capacity, functioning as a substitute clown during native rites.

The council, or *junta general,* was composed of the governor, lieutenant-governor, sheriff, the six war captains, the four pika, and all the exgovernors (*principales*). Formerly only the governor could call meetings of the council—usually at the bidding of the caciques. Only the governor could initiate business, and nothing could be discussed unless he desired it. All decisions had to be unanimous [14, 36, 72]. This body also acted

as a limited legal and judicial agency. They heard requests for land and water assignments brought to them by the governor; they adjudicated disputes over land and water rights between members of the community and within families. They assessed penalties in cases of theft, damage, or other transgressions—either religious or secular. In these latter instances, they functioned more as a sentencing agency than as a deliberative judicial agency [36, 40, 62, 72]. With the adoption of the constitution of 1935, the rather tenuous powers of this political group were greatly extended.

FACTIONALISM

Santa Clara political history has been marked by turbulence. Over a period of four hundred years, recurrent dissension and the pressures of alien peoples have resulted in the alteration of several facets of the governmental system. Strangely, however, much of the aboriginal core, both structural and functional, has survived and has continued to operate in the present.

While many have considered Santa Clara factionalism a unique development, there is considerable evidence that the same types of change have occurred in other Pueblo villages. There is little doubt that these adjustments stemmed initially from acculturative factors. However, the form taken by these adjustments was peculiarly Puebloan. It has been stated elsewhere that Pueblo Indians typically suffered from "cabin fever." This created a hostile social environment and fostered an unusual number of personal animosities. While ideally aggressions could only be expressed covertly, feelings were invariably close to the surface, ready to erupt, and frequently manifested themselves in political factionalism. This tendency was further fostered by the autocratic inclinations of the theocratic hierarchy, which created a climate favorable to schism in an acculturative situation.

Since political and religious powers were vested in the same persons, political shifts have too often been interpreted in terms of a breakdown of native religious beliefs. Undoubtedly the impetus for dissent in individual cases has stemmed most commonly from Christian contacts. However, there is no evidence of the existence at any point in time of a Catholic party at Santa Clara Pueblo. I am more inclined to agree with Aitken (1930: 385) when she wrote, "I am convinced that the external conflict between Spanish and Native religion simply gave a rallying-ground to leaders whose temperament demanded a chance to express dissent." This view is further substantiated by an analysis of the composition of political parties. More often than not at Santa Clara Pueblo, the so-called "progressive" groups were in fact conservative reactionaries.

The first major political adjustment occurred shortly after the arrival of the Spanish. In 1620 the King of Spain decreed that on January first of each year an election of officers should be held in the pueblos of New Mexico (Bandelier 1890-92:(1): 220n.1). It is not known when this decree actually became effective, but the sanction for the current set of Spanish-type officials at Santa Clara dates from that time. Added to the indigenous political framework were the offices of governor, lieutenant-governor, sheriff, war captains, church warders, and councilmen.

There was, however, one important deviation from the decree; these new officials were not elected by popular vote but were, instead, appointed by the religious hierarchy. This probably explains in large measure the lack of recorded opposition to the innovation. The assumption of appointive power by the caciques not only preserved the vested interests of the theocracy, but as time went on, it actually extended their political control into new secular areas. Futhermore, in the instance of the war captains, the concept of stratified military leadership and responsibility was so nearly identical in both Pueblo and Spanish cultures that these dignitaries were easily absorbed into the existing framework embodied by the outside chief and his assistants.

While this initial change appears to have had little disruptive effect, later changes proved to have greater impact. Presumably the gradual infiltration of European ideas resulting from Spanish colonization and missionary activities following the Reconquest (1692-96) accentuated the ever-present tendency of the Pueblo Indian tribes toward factionalism. In any event, schismatic developments were reported as early as 1701 at Santa Clara, and they have continued in varying degrees of intensity to the present day. Aitken (1930: 385-87) commented on some major controversies between 1701 and 1913. Parsons (1939: 1137note) confirmed the continued existence of these earlier splits. According to her, "In 1926 the two moieties would not even work on the ditch or build roads or dig wells together. Nor would they look at a dance by the other moiety ('class'); 'they won't even peep outside,' said a Nambé visitor."

That the same situation existed in 1935 was apparent from the depositions and minutes of meetings recorded by Elizabeth Sergeant, David Dozier, and Edward Dozier, preliminary to a vote on the constitution; this information was confirmed by informants' accounts in the 1940s. Since Aitken's summary (1930: 385-87) is basic to an understanding of these developments, it is quoted here in full:

In the year 1701, in the troubled decade that followed the Spanish reconquest of New Mexico after the rebellion in which his people had played so large a part, a Tewa Indian of Santa Clara, called Francisco Canjuebe, began to buy up land from Spanish grantees, outside the communal village grant. In 1744, Roque Canjuebe, of the same pueblo, being rich in cattle and horses and resenting the "continual public works" imposed on him which prevented his giving attention to his business affairs (for in the Rio Grande pueblos the gay working parties of the Hopi were replaced by compulsory work for the priest-chief and on the communal irrigation ditch), petitioned the Spanish Governor for a separate grant of land, for which he surrendered the use of fields nearer the village. This was granted, on production of a certificate that he was instructed in the Christian religion; and there grew up, just inside the boundary of the village lands, a hamlet of nonconforming families—Canjuebes, Bacas, Pubijuas, and Cisneros—some of whose descendants are still leaders of the Winter "Liberal" Side. "They worked on the ditch but on no other public works; they were not obliged to dance, and only did so when they felt inclined"; so, at least, the inheritors of their tradition declared in 1913. In 1815 the governor and councillors of the village (bearing names still prominent on the Summer Side) brought suit to dispossess Roque Canjuebe's grandchildren of their grant; the Canjuebes and their friends seem to have won the last of their costly appeals to the Commandant-General at Durango (*Archives in the Office of the Surveyor-General of New Mexico, Santa Fé*, No. 213. *Letters in the Archive of the Pueblo of Santa Clara*, 1782–1911. *Field Notes, Santa Clara*, 1910, 1913), but the village had the best of it in fact; the nonconformist families drifted back to the village, there to form the political core of the Winter Party. Through the nineteenth century (under Spanish, under Mexican, and under American rule, if I understand the evidence right) there persisted on the Winter Side a thread of the Canjuebe principles; a claim for liberty to dance or not to dance; criticism of the customs by the standard of Catholic morality; and a general colour of approximation to Spanish Christianity. I am convinced that the external conflict between Spanish and Native religion simply gave a rallying-ground to leaders whose temperament demanded a chance to express dissent. They made their protest that unanimity is not the be-all and end-all of religion; that even "what all the people do," "what the ancestors have come along doing until now," is not beyond criticism. But, for the most part, both sides professed "to keep the customs." Each accused the other side of innovation. Each, when in control of the village government, used its power to make sick and bereaved persons on the other side take part in dances, refused them exemptions in old age,

beat them and tortured them to enforce conformity. There were secessions of families from side to side "because of a dance." To cut a long story short, in 1894, after a bitter struggle and a successful appeal to the American authority, the Summer Side secured the power to appoint governor and war-captain, and has held it ever since. Thereupon the Winter Side (led by an extremely able man, Francisco Naranjo) announced a definite schism; they could not secede and found a new village—though there was talk both of secession and of explusion—for there was no free land to go to; so, they would be *in* the pueblo but not *of* it. In certain public works they would share ("without your immoral customs"), but they would not attend the governor's council, or dance under the orders of the war-captain, or take part in ceremonies. "You say that we want to make changes in 'the customs'; we repeat that we reject 'the customs' altogether." Francisco had given his side a conscious, definite programme. For themselves, reform, education, modernization; towards the village, nonconformity. In part it was a political move, in part a genuine Puritan movement. Of course, it produced a schism within the schism; two of Francisco's own brothers could not forsake "the customs," and went over to the other side; the third, José Manuel—a conformist by temperament if ever I saw one—Francisco's overbearing influence carried with him into dissent.

So matters stood at Santa Clara in 1910, when the feeling between the parties was very acute. Ostensibly, the issue was the enforcement of the public works. But the real indignation felt by the Summer Side was because the Winter people would not dance. They had withdrawn their cooperation; the calendar was maimed by the absence of ceremonies which they alone could perform; the Summer Side were dancing and "thinking" to provide all the rain, and the other side were profiting by it! The offence against co-operation, against unanimity, against solidarity was deeply felt. In 1815 Antonio Canjebe had denounced the "the customs" to the Spaniards as "diabolical rites"; his spiritual successors in 1897 repeated the phrase, and before a lawyer in Santa Fé made accusations of human sacrifice and "things that cannot be said." This breach of solidarity hurt worse than mere heresy. "If *you* were to abandon the Christian religion," the Summer Side governor remarked, "I think you would have more decency than to disclose what you know about it!"

As a matter of fact, these Winter People, who are said by the Summer Side to have "renounced the Indian religion," believe themselves to be the preservers of that religion in its primitive form, free from superstition and abuses. By 1910, when I first knew them, the Puritan movement had partly spent its force; Francisco himself was old; there were distinct signs of an Oxford Movement in the Winter Party. About 1906 they had filled the vacant place of the Ice-Priest by appointing Francisco's brother, José Manuel; but the Summer People said that the appointment was secret and irregular, done without the concurrence of the war-captain; that his ritual acts were therefore invalid, and that he ought to be called out to work on the ditch like any other layman.

Now and then a threat from outside to the village lands drove the parties into temporary unanimity; and on those occasions the Winter Party brought out a dance as scrupulously correct as any other. I thought I perceived in them a difference of devotional tone; the Summer Side spoke of the Sun and Our Mother and the expected deliverer P'oseyemu with a more matter-of-fact reverence; it was on the Winter Side that I heard P'oseyemu's name spoken with love and with tears. But, then, all Indian religion at Santa Clara seems very serious, nurtured as it has been in past persecution, secrecy, and hard-learnt loyalty.

What can be designated as the second era of political change at Santa Clara began in 1701 and culminated in 1894. Many of the principals of the 1894 schism were still alive in 1935, 1940, and 1941. Data derived from them and their adherents amplify Aiken's statements and bring to light causal factors which explain the composition of the several parties. Further insights on the background of party alignments were also derived from an analysis of genealogies and societal affiliations. These more recent data indicate that earlier accounts tend to present the political situation in oversimplified form.

From Aitken's data (1930: 363–87) on schismatic incidents prior to 1894 substantiated by later informants, it can be inferred that in the main they involved individual instances of acculturation. The primary cause of dissent appears to have been enforced participation in communal work. Those who were landless, whose agricultural holdings were small, or whose livelihood was derived in whole or in part outside the village felt imposed upon. To a lesser extent, cases of actual religious defection were involved. However, since any deviation from custom was interpreted in terms of a religious violation, it is difficult to determine whether these were always defections in fact.

Some typical episodes which led to the original schism between the Winter and Summer moieties and the ultimate emergence of a progressive group within the village are the following:

First Deposition

Juan Ventura Silva was a great craftsman and one who would not take part in the pueblo customs. He was one of the first who was subjected to punishments, because of having "progressive" ideas and using "progressive" means to make a living.

In the Pueblo, Silva was known as a saddle maker, but his skill in making many other things in wood and iron was equally famous. His talent was in demand throughout this part of the country.

He was a born artist and worked for many years for the Catholic priests.

During this time, he made use of the opportunity to learn to use tools. He was always employed by rich settlers (Spanish settlers). As a result of his being a craftsman, he was well off during a period when there was a famine in the Pueblo, and Indians were dying of starvation. People came to his place and begged for food; others picked up the remains of food which was thrown out.

The Pueblo was jealous of this man's success, and as he would not adhere to the customs of the Pueblo, he was put under severe punishment of all sorts, but he never gave in. They tried to put him out of the Pueblo, but he would not go. After he made many brave stands against the ravaging Pueblo officials, he was finally stripped of all his belongings, land, money, etc.

Silva had five sons, who were also punished like their father, but through the advice of their father they moved out of the Pueblo while they still had a few of their things. Little is known of their history after they left the Pueblo. Most of them went to Abiquiu; one went to Galisteo. Many years later they came back when things were more peaceful in the Pueblo.

Juan Ventura, with one or two of the boys and a girl, even though they never submitted to the customs, remained in the Pueblo. After the boys came back, they were not bothered very much, but the family was never permitted to enjoy success (Deposition taken by David Dozier, August 18, 1935).

no avail. He then refused to turn over his find to the officials. The officials were determined to get the deer and held a short conference in which they agreed that the meat should be divided into four parts. After that, the men should all stand at a reasonable distance, and then all would run and get their share. This was done, even though the lad did not agree, as he knew he was yet too young to beat these men in a race. They ran, and the officials all got their unlawful share except the boy. But apparently, this was not enough punishment. When they came to the Pueblo, he was brought before the Pueblo Council, where it was decided that he should bring down from the mountains on his back three large loads of choice wood for the governor. The lad and his brothers on this occasion started a riot in the Pueblo, but were easily subdued, as they were alone against the whole Pueblo.

Somehow the Indian Agent, a Spaniard by the name of Sanchez, was notified and he came to the Pueblo. At a meeting held in the Pueblo, he saw the injustice being done to this boy and his family; he told the governor that he would pay a reasonable sum of money from his own pocket for the release of the boy. No sum of money, however, was accepted. Jesús, with some of his brothers, left the Pueblo after this because they would not take the unjust punishment (Deposition taken by David Dozier, August 18, 1935).

Second Deposition

During one autumn, one of these boys, Jesús, who was quite young, was bringing in wood for the family. While out gathering wood, he found a deer killed by someone who had lost it because it had strayed off while wounded. He was busily engaged butchering it when four officials of the Pueblo came and found him. They told him that the meat should have to be used by the Pueblo and that he had committed a grave wrong in killing the deer. He tried to explain but to

Third Deposition

Among those who revolted from the old Cacique rule to that of the Progressives were José Domingo Gutierrez (my grandfather), Pedro Cajete, Vidal Gutierrez, and several others whose names I cannot recall, but which are known to Uncle Vidal.

The real split occurred about fifty years ago. The unjust ways of the old customs had increased, and the Winter people, of which the Progressive Party is composed, resolved to put a stop to them. Uncle Vidal and a few others did not go out to assist in the Pueblo cleaning. To show his complete independence, Uncle Vidal, then still a young man, with a child in his arms, went up on top of his house and watched the cleaners. Seeing him there, the governor and the lieutenant-governor came and bade him come down and assist in the clean-up, as was his duty. Uncle increased their fury by laughing and refusing to come down. He further told them that he and the rest of the party would not assist in community work until a more just system was put out. The governor and his lieutenant attempted to force Uncle Vidal to assist in the work, but José Domingo Gutierrez, my grandfather and father of Uncle Vidal, chased the governor and lieutenant away, telling them that they had no right to trespass on his property.

The governor and lieutenant left; but before leaving, they assured grandfather and Uncle Vidal that they were going to take the matter to court.

The court trial was held several days later. Uncle Vidal and the group of Progressives saw a lawyer and gave him their cause. The Conservatives chose Crist as their lawyer.

In the court trial, Uncle Vidal was among those who were questioned. He related all the unjust rules of the old customs. He especially emphasized the fact that even women and children were compelled to assist in cleaning the village. He also stated that in the ditch work, all men and even young boys were forced to work, whether they possessed or did not possess land.

This information and the fact that there is no law in the United States which binds an Indian under any Pueblo rule, won the case of Uncle Vidal and the group of Progressives (Deposition taken by Edward Dozier, 1935).

This situation involving isolated instances of individual revolts described by Aitken (1930: 385–86) and others might have continued indefinitely except for a series of his-torical accidents occurring in the latter part of the nineteenth century, which in 1894 resulted in the emergence of four distinct political parties.

Before the late 1800s, there were too few dissenters within the village to threaten pueblo solidarity. Earlier the problem of nonconformists was effectively handled by a variety of mechanisms for social control. They were shamed, beaten, or tortured. In extreme cases, their property was confiscated, and they left the village of their own accord or were banished. Many were absorbed into neighboring Spanish-American settlements; others went to the refugee settlement of Abiquiu. This effectively syphoned off the idiosyncratic element, and a high degree of conformity within the resident population was maintained. As Dr. Edward P. Dozier (personal communication) has commented, this insistence on conformity, probably more than any other factor, has been responsible for the continuing conservatism of Pueblo culture.

By the latter part of the nineteenth century, population in the Territory of New Mexico had greatly increased, free agricultural land was no longer available, and as a result more and more dissenters were forced to remain in the village. As Aitken stated (1930: 386), "They would be *in* the pueblo but not *of* it." By 1894, there was a considerable number of nonconformists at Santa Clara, whose reasons for dissent differed, but who nevertheless felt a common bond. Since all were under pressure, tensions mounted.

By chance, the majority of the progressive element were affiliates of the Winter Moiety under the leadership of Francisco Naranjo (see also Aitken 1930: 386). The episode which led to his withdrawal was reported as follows:

Under the old customs, violation of the commands of the cacique merited grievous punishment. If an Indian refused to take part in a ceremonial dance, even in the case of an urgent agricultural necessity, he was taken by force, by men appointed by the cacique. He was taken to the kiva and was dropped from the opening on top of the roof to the floor of the kiva—a depth of about fifteen feet. He was asked then, if would take part in the ceremonial dance. If he consented, he was made to stand at the end of the dancers with the small children and was an object of ridicule.

If however, he did not consent to take part in the ceremonial dance after being thrown into the kiva, he was tied up. He was left in the kiva and questioned every so often if he will henceforth obey the order of the caciques. If he did not consent, he was left, tied up until fatigue, hunger, and darkness finally compelled him to consent.

Similar punishments were inflicted on those persons who violated the rules of the old customs in community work.

When these old customs were followed some years ago, all planting and harvesting were subject to them. The governor of the Pueblo announced when wheat or corn was to be gathered; if some person gathered his corn or wheat before the day appointed, he was guilty of violating the customs and hence subject to punishment.

An instance of this violation occurred about fifty years ago and was one of the incidents which led to the organization of the Progressive Party. Francisco Naranjo, the grandfather of Desidario Naranjo, was the violator. It was the period when corn was to be gathered and stored away. The governor had announced when the gathering was to start. The day before the corn was to be gathered, wandering cattle broke down the fence of Francisco Naranjo and entered his cornfield. The cattle destroyed a large amount of the corn, and Francisco in order to save it was obliged to carry in the corn that was knocked down by the cattle. When he was engaged in this work, the governor came and seeing Francisco gathering corn before the day appointed, he called his assistants and had him taken to the kiva. There they tied him securely as a punishment for gathering corn before time.

Francisco had five sons and when they came home in the evening and heard that their father was tied up, they immediately went to the governor's house. A nephew of Francisco was also with them.

When they saw their father tied up and in agony, they demanded his immediate release. When the governor and his assistants refused to release him, the sons and nephews prepared for a fight. A fierce and bloody struggle followed—one which ended in the release of Francisco.

From this day on, the old customs lost some of their power over the people, and the number of the Progressives steadily increased (Deposition by Vidal Gutierrez, taken by Edward Dozier, August 9, 1935).

The event which triggered the upheaval of 1894 was a political coup by the Summer Moiety. Prior to that time, according to informants, the Winter Moiety had dominated the political scene. However, that year the Summer Moiety, with the connivance of the United States government, reversed the situation, gaining control of the canes, and through this establishing their "right" to appoint the governor and war captain, which they continued to do until 1936.

[Canes were given to the various pueblos first by the Spanish, later by the Mexican government, and finally by the United States during President Lincoln's administration. Two of these canes exist in most villages today. They are the symbols of the governor's authority, and are transferred at the time a new governor takes office. Throughout the years they have assumed religious as well as symbolic significance, and unless they are in the actual possession of a governor, he cannot exercise his authority and is not recognized by the group.

Involved here is one of the numerous examples of thinking by analogy characteristic of the Pueblo. If the fetish is lacking, the ceremony is nullified; without the canes, an officer may not serve. This action by the Summer Moiety at Santa Clara has been duplicated at several other pueblos, and in every case it has successfully barred a segment of the population from participating in the secular government. (For details concerning the derivation of the canes, see Farris 1952 and Barton 1953.) WWH]

The usurping of secular power by the Summer Moiety, which caught the Winter group unaware, created a violent reaction. Latent schisms crystalized, and the political pattern which dominated Santa Clara from 1894 until 1936 emerged. Four parties came into existence that, for want of better designations, were called the Winter progressives, Winter conservatives, Summer conservatives, and Summer progressives.

The Winter progressives, the only genuine progressive group, since they were excluded from secular political appointments and had nothing further to lose, became ardent advocates of the earlier movement to separate the religious power from the secular. They renounced their native religion. They refused to do certain communal work or to do communal work in the company of the Summer Moiety. "In certain public works they would share ('without your immoral customs'), but they would not attend the governor's council, or dance under the orders of the war-captain, or take part in ceremonies" (Aitken 1930: 386). As a final act of revenge, the Winter progressives, who were at the moment numerically strong, forced their moiety to withdraw from cooperative religious activities with the Summer group. This was to have far-reaching consequences, as will be explained later.

The core of the Winter party was made up of idiosyncratic individuals, whose reasons for dissent differed. In the crisis of 1894 and for some period afterwards, under the leadership of Francisco Naranjo, they functioned effectively. However, unlike the three other groups, they lacked deep roots and a traditional program. By 1935, in line with Aitken's appraisal as of 1910 (Aitken 1930: 386), the movement of the Winter progressive group, the "Puritans," had run its course. Its effectiveness had dwindled with the death of Francisco Naranjo and the death, defection, and departure from the village of many of its members. In 1935 it was not even mentioned as a major party; its leaders and two other members were assigned to Vidal Gutierrez's splinter group

of Winter conservatives.

In 1941 only nine adult members of the progressives could be identified. They were from heterogeneous backgrounds, and ineffectual. Five held no societal memberships, and one of the five was a member of the Summer Moiety, a nephew of the group spokesman, José Felario Tafoya. Of the remaining four affiliates, one was a female Nambé K'osa, married to an Apache, and presumably inactive ceremonially; another, an inactive member of the Tesuque Bear Society. The remaining two were a wife and husband; she was a midwife, and he, a Summer Moiety member, but inactive [43, 61, 72].

Within the Winter Moiety, at the time of the 1894 schism, were numerous individuals, including two brothers of Francisco Naranjo, of orthodox religious persuasion. They refused to accept the liberal religious views advocated by Francisco. The result was the "schism within a schism" referred to by Aitken (1930: 386), and the Winter conservative party was born.

Some of the most conservative of this group solved their problem by leaving the Winter Moiety and joining the Summer [9]. The remainder, while they agreed to withdraw from village-wide religious cooperation, still continued to practice, often in isolation and under difficulties because of reduced manpower, their own religious rites. They advocated the separation of the secular from the religious, or else a return to the alternating appointment of secular officials by the caciques. They were for optional rather than compulsory participation in communal work and ceremonies, and would not take part in either activity in conjunction with the Summer Moiety.

This was the party of the Winter Society which included the Winter cacique, the right and the left arm, and the orthodox members of secret societies who had not defected to the Summer Moiety. In 1933 or 1934 the group underwent another schism and, in 1935, was represented by two splinter factions, one under the leadership of the Winter cacique and the other under the right arm.

The incident which led to this subsequent break was explained as follows: Severo Naranjo, the Winter cacique, became ill, and before leaving for the hospital, delegated his authority to Vidal Gutierrez, the right arm. This was consistent with proper procedures according to aboriginal custom. At a somewhat later date, Severo was visited in the hospital by a cousin, Nestor Naranjo. On this occasion Severo rescinded his earlier action and delegated his power to Nestor, a man with no reported ceremonial affiliations. This created a bitter dispute. Vidal persisted in carrying out the cacique's duties, and was supported by his adherents. With Severo's recovery and return to the pueblo, antagonisms, if anything, increased. Both principals insisted that the other was in the wrong and owed him an apology. In characteristic Pueblo fashion, each refused to compromise. The major result of this split was a further impairment of the religious activities of the Winter conservatives. Since unanimity was impossible, ceremonial cooperation ceased; the two groups either failed to perform rites or hobbled through their religious obligations with the aid of substitute personnel. Eventually Severo appears to have won, since on his death his son-in-law, Phillip Dasheno, a Hopi, became Winter cacique [43, 61, 72].

In 1941 the conservative subgroup of the Winter Moiety under the leadership of Vidal Gutierrez included twenty-nine articulate adults. Twelve of these were Vidal's relatives. Of the twenty-nine, twelve held societal positions, and seventeen were secular adherents. Ten of the religious belonged to the Winter Society. These included two who were vowed to the organization, but uninitiated. Other society affiliates were a Tesuque Bear, a San Juan K'osa, and two kachina leaders (se^n shu) [43, 61, 72].

In 1941 the conservative subgroup of the Winter Moiety under Severo Naranjo consisted of twelve articulate adults. They were equally divided between secular and religious. Four of the religious were Oyike members, including Severo Naranjo, the Winter cacique. One other was a Jemez Bear, and another, a substitute clown (pinini) [43, 61, 72].

The conservative party of the Summer Moiety consisted of some thirty-seven adult articulate members in 1941. This group represented the hard core of Santa Clara tradi-

tionalism. It was the party of Pay-oj-ke, the Summer "managing" society. It included not only the most conservative element of the Summer Moiety, but also some Winter conservatives who had switched moiety affiliation under the 1894 split. In 1941 the leadership of the party was in the hands of two extremely able men, Victoriano Sisneros, the Summer cacique, and John Naranjo, the right arm. Both are dead now. There is evidence that while Victoriano was religiously sincere, he was also a political opportunist. He was formerly a member of the Winter Moiety who had switched affiliations. John Naranjo was an example of characteristic Pueblo inconsistency. While a conservative in terms of native religion, he had earlier been married to an Osage, later to an Anglo. With money inherited from his first wife, he had bought an elaborate modern altar for the village Catholic church.

Sixteen members of the party belonged to religious organizations. Eight were Pay-oj-ke (Summer Society members). Included in these were John Naranjo, the right arm, and the cacique, Victoriano Sisneros, who was a member of the Nambé K'osa, and one member who was a se^n shu as well. It also included one Tesuque and three Jemez Bear members. One of the latter was vowed to membership, but not initiated; another was also a member of the Women's Scalp Society. Beside the above, there were two se^n shu, the only Kwirana member, a pinini (substitute clown), and two pika [43, 61, 72].

In 1941 the identifiable articulate membership of the progressive party of the Summer Moiety consisted of twenty-six persons, under the leadership of Santiago Naranjo. Twenty of this group were members of religious organizations. This was primarily the party of the Bear societies; the members were religiously conservative in spite of their "progressive" label. Santiago, head of the Tesuque Bears, had succeeded in attracting to his group five members of the Tesuque and seven members of the Jemez society. Beside these, there were five affiliates of the Pay-oj-ke, including the left arm, four Nambé K'osa, one San Juan K'osa, the head of the Women's Scalp Society, and a pika. Several of the above held dual memberships. One Pay-oj-ke was also a Tesuque Bear, another a Nambé K'osa. The head of the Women's Scalp Society was also an affiliate of the Jemez Bear and Nambé K'osa organizations.

When Aitken (1930: 386) spoke of a "schism within a schism" in the Winter Moiety in 1894, she failed to note that a similar division was under way in the Summer Moiety, and that the "progressive" designation was derived from their opposition to compulsory participation in ceremonials.

According to Santiago Naranjo, the incident which led to the original schism was as follows (Dr. Bertha P. Dutton: personal communication): José Naranjo, Santiago's father, was a prominent figure in secular government affairs, not particularly active religiously. Among his children was a sixteen-year-old daughter who was in poor health. On the occasion of a ceremony, the cacique came to her and told her that she should dance. José remonstrated with him and asked that the girl be excused. "The cacique said, 'No. Someone else will then want to be excused.'" The girl danced, subsequently caught pneumonia, and died. "José took his group out. They would not function in any pueblo business. He would say, 'Bring back my daughter, and I will bring back my group,'" i.e., engage in community affairs.

Temporary reconciliations took place between the two Summer parties from time to time for religious purposes. One such period, of short duration, existed in 1912–13, according to Dutton. However, starting about 1923 and continuing into 1935, Santiago Naranjo became involved in a series of incidents which not only created a permanent split between the two Summer factions, but also alienated further the conservative wing of the Winter Moiety.

The fieldwork by Parsons among the Tewa encompassed the period of 1923–26. Santiago was suspected of being one of her informants, which he was. This led to gossip and bitter recriminations. Finally the whole turmoil was brought to a head through a succession of events in 1934–35.

The initial difficulty began during an illness of the Summer cacique. At this time he delegated his authority to Santiago. In so doing, he bypassed his right arm. However,

this action was not totally inconsistent, since Santiago for all practical purposes was religiously orthodox. This action coincided in time with the appointment of new secular officials. Against the urging of several prominent figures, Santiago selected his brother Ologio for governor. Ologio was old, becoming senile, and lacked the education to discharge his office effectively. A storm ensued, but since Ologio had been appointed by traditional legal means, the opposition was powerless.

Ologio created a business committee, headed by José Felario Tafoya, former leader of the Winter progressives, to handle the affairs of the village. Since this represented an innovation, the conservative elements of both moieties reacted adversely and sabotaged committee actions.

To add insult to injury, Ologio, at the end of his term, refused to relinquish the canes and began serving for another year. This was illegal, of course, according to native procedure, as no governor served two consecutive years. However, the Summer cacique was helpless; without the canes he could not legally induct a successor. The situation was not without its humorous side. The Summer conservatives were, in a sense, hoisted on their own petards, as Ologio's coup was identical to the one executed by them in 1894, when they wrested power from the Winter moiety. Ologio's protagonists rationalized the situation, contending that since he had already begun to serve the term (his second one), he could rightfully continue it, since a governor once appointed remained in office until the end of the year. In so contending they, of course, ignored the impropriety of the second, or consecutive, term in office.

To add to the confusion, Ologio's appointees also continued in their offices. When the time arrived for planting, Ologio asked his lieutenant-governor, Epimenio Sisneros, to mark off the sections of ditch to be allocated to the several groups for cleaning and conditioning. Epimenio, who was nearly blind, asked Nestor Naranjo to perform the task for him. The Summer conservatives resisted violently, as according to them Nestor was not a regularly constituted officer of the village, and officially had no right to function in that capacity. As usual name calling ensued, and recrimination followed recrimination in which all parties participated. Some even went so far as to include accusations of theft by their opposition from the poor box in the church.

So stood the Santa Clara situation in the spring of 1935. The Winter progressives had almost disappeared, but an irreconcilable split had developed among the Winter conservatives; the old schism between the Summer conservatives had broadened and crystallized. While there is little reason to believe that this represented anything other than the normal chaotic state that had existed for almost two hundred and thirty-five years, Ologio's actions had created a favorable opportunity for the eruption of latent antagonisms and for the operation of the Pueblo genius for obstruction. Governmental functions were at a standstill.

By chance this crisis roughly coincided in time with the passage of the Indian Reorganization Act. The Indian Service was actively engaged in persuading various tribes to accept a constitutional form of self-government. Elizabeth Sergeant was sent to negotiate with Santa Clara Pueblo. A series of meetings was held with the several parties and groups during part of July and most of August. Sergeant, with the assistance of David and Edward Dozier, recorded a series of depositions and minutes.

Fortunately for the advocates of the constitution, because of the current political stalemate many of the villagers were receptive to the idea of some type of change. This does not necessarily mean that they desired a constitutional form of government, or that they actually knew what it involved. A large number are on record as favoring a return to the theocracy as it had once existed. Finally, however, on December 14, 1935, the constitution was voted upon and approved.

The data of Sergeant and the others show that all parties, insofar as they understood the real issue, reacted in an expectable manner. Severo Naranjo, because he was both Winter cacique and an arch conservative, was against the adoption of the constitution; it represented change, and his group supported him in this opposition. He still hoped that the old system of alternating appoint-

ments by the caciques might be re-established. Furthermore, since the other splinter party of the Winter Moiety favored some type of change, he automatically opposed it. Resorting to a familiar Pueblo tactic, he and his group withdrew entirely from the preliminary proceedings and refused to participate in the voting.

The other splinter group of the Winter conservatives, led by Vidal Gutierrez, came out in favor of the change and allied themselves with Santiago Naranjo's Summer progressives. This was consistent with their traditional stand against compulsory participation in communal work and ceremony. The reaction was one that could have been fully expected against the Summer conservatives, who had refused to relinquish political control after 1894. Vidal's group had nothing to lose politically, and saw in the constitution an opportunity to break the government monopoly of the Summer Moiety.

The few remaining members of the old Winter progressive party either joined Vidal's Winter conservatives or the uncommitted Summer Moiety affiliates, and voted in favor of the constitution.

In the Summer Moiety the conservatives led by Victoriano Sisneros, the cacique, were against the constitution. This was also to be expected. They had controlled all secular offices and officers since 1894, and were opposed to anything that would weaken the political power of the cacique. At one of the early hearings, Victoriano indicated his willingness to cooperate, if all parties would sign an agreement. He then presented a document which committed all to return to the old form of government as it had existed under the Summer cacique. The Winter Moiety and the Summer conservatives reacted vehemently, and Victoriano and his adherents left the meeting and took no further part in the discussions.

The Summer progressives under Santiago Naranjo, because they were traditionally against compulsory ritual participation, voted for the change. Their stand was influenced as well by current antagonisms within the Summer Moiety resulting from Ologio's actions.

In retrospect the acceptance of a constitution by Santa Clara Pueblo appears to have resulted partly from intent, partly through default (Severo Naranjo's opposition group did not vote), and partly through a misunderstanding of what was actually involved. Some were under the impression that by voting affirmatively they would wrest political control from Ologio's group and return it to the Summer cacique. Others believed that it entailed a return to power of both caciques. This was clear from Sergeant's report of July 26, 1935. "It seemed that the words 'new form of government' were not understood here as Vidal and the progressives understood them. What was really meant was *a new Governor under the old rules of Government* [italics Sergeant's, WWH]—by Cacique appointment.'"

In any event a fourth era was inaugurated at Santa Clara in 1936. The constitution of 1935 instituted several important departures from earlier practices. First, it provided for the election of secular officers by popular vote, thus divesting the caciques of their appointive rights. Second, it designated sixty-five as the upper age limit for holding office, councilmen excepted. This was a heavy blow to the gerontocratic foundations of the society (constitution of 1935, pp. 1–9; Appendix B).

While no age limit was placed on councilmen, this body was also to be elected by popular vote. It no longer necessarily included all exgovernors, the war captains, and pika—another check on theocratic power. Furthermore, the council, instead of functioning primarily as a sentencing agency as it had formerly done, was given broad executive and judicial powers. The war captains and pika were relegated to purely religious roles, and continued to be appointed by the caciques.

One final change under the constitution of 1935 was that those over seventy-five years of age were no longer compelled to engage in communal work.

How successful this attempt to separate church and state will be, only time will tell. Most of the principals of the 1930s and 1940s have died or become inactive, and leadership has passed into other hands. It may be that progressive elements have lost the battle, in spite of the constitution. During the 1940s, informants [43, 61, 72] observed that successful candidates for secular office were overwhelmingly nominees of the caciques or of religiously oriented groups.

More importantly, there is evidence of greater intermoiety religious cooperation and of a general religious resurgence, beginning shortly after 1936. The conservative segment of the Winter Moiety under Vidal Gutierrez shifted allegiance, and for ritual purposes were working with the Summer conservatives. In 1948 the Winter Moiety held its first kachina enactment in many years. Whether this was continued annually is not known, but another performance was reported to have been held in 1959. It may be that the old ceremonial calendar was being reactivated. This possibly represents a nativistic movement to combat the acculturative influences of Los Alamos (where numerous Santa Clara Indians had found employment). However, on the other hand, one of the evangelical Protestant sects has also been gaining converts.

If this last section has been unduly protracted, it is because the long-standing factionalism is a good example of the processes of acculturation, and because it involves some of the best-documented manifestations of Santa Clara Pueblo personality and culture.

10

Ceremonial

Organization

This chapter, as noted in the Preface, was the unit most nearly completed by Professor Hill. In the original plan it actually was to be a separate volume, the first of the several that Hill planned for his Santa Clara Pueblo study. In terms of detail, the discussion here is clearly the richest; this disparity may have been something that Hill would have rectified at least to some extent, had he been able to complete his study. Any of his preceding chapters could have been readily expanded with the aid of his informants.

However, as any knowledgeable Tewa would recognize, even Hill's discussion of ceremonialism cannot be considered complete. There is really no such thing as a complete study of any major facet of a culture; such a study can never be more than a theoretical, or idealistic goal. There can only be lesser degrees of incompleteness, and in that sense this chapter is relatively full of detail for numerous aspects of a very complex subject.

The abundance of Hill's ceremonial data may be taken as a measure of his interest in this subject, and of the degree of cooperation he obtained from numerous informants regarding this most sensitive topic. On the other hand, the abundance may also be taken as a reflection of the importance at-

tached to this phase of their culture by the Santa Clara Indians, and the elaboration and emphasis that have consequently developed in the ceremonial life of the pueblo. Both interpretations may be considered as essentially valid. [CHL]

MOIETY ORGANIZATION

While the dual religious organization, Summer and Winter, played an all important role in the political life of the pueblo, it was predominantly religious in its emphasis and connotation. Both groups functioned the year around, but direct responsibility for religious leadership was apportioned on a seasonal basis. In recent years the Summer Moiety has assumed jurisdiction from late February or early March to late October or early November; the Winter Moiety for the remaining period of the year [6, 9, 14, 25]. There is some evidence that formerly the shifts in responsibility coincided with the vernal and autumnal equinoxes, and this may well have been the case. It is quite possible that the general weakening of the Winter Moiety through recurrent schisms, plus the recent domination of the political scene by the Summer Moiety, have led to a corresponding domination in the religious area. The transfer of religious responsibility from one moiety to the other was formerly accompanied by elaborate rituals [6, 14] (confirmed by Jeançon). The Summer Moiety was thought of as personifying the feminine aspects in nature; the Winter, the masculine ones.

Associated with the moieties were two ceremonial structures, or kivas. In these were enacted many of the esoteric rituals which concerned the moiety as a whole. The Winter kiva was known as town kiva (bute te); the Summer kiva, as plaza kiva (buge te), also according to Parsons (1929: 99), "in a hole kiva." Formerly there was an underground, round kiva used by both moieties [9, 22] (also M.C. Stevenson 1912). According to an informant [15] who was born in 1903, this was still in use in his grandfather's time. As late as 1918, the current Summer kiva was built and was utilized by both moieties. Subsequent to that period, with the increase in factionalism, the Winter Moiety built their present kiva (M.C. Stevenson 1912) on the site of the former round kiva. "When they were building the new kiva they found it. It had caved in" [15, 40]. In 1928 an addition was made to the Summer kiva [40].

Both kivas were rectangular and were equipped with stepped benches, "cloud flowers" (ox uwa povi), located just below the hatchway. This area was also referred to as the altar or the wood box, "place where wood is kept" [9]. Fireplaces were on the north side, and each had a sipapu (si p'o fe ne), "out of the ground," "from the earth," or "place of emergence" [13, 21]. These openings extended above the floor and were plugged with bundles of religious materials [13]. Masks belonging to kachinas of the Summer Moiety were stored in the annex of that kiva. Those of the Winter kachinas were first kept in one house (#43) and then, more recently, moved to another house (#82). This latter structure was willed to the organization by Pedro Cajete.

While the two kivas were utilized for general moiety ritual purposes, and by the Winter and Summer managing societies, some of the more esoteric functions of these latter organizations were carried out at other locations. In the 1940s those of the

Winter took place in a house belonging to the Winter cacique. This was part of a row of contiguous houses on the west side of the plaza, which had originally been his home before he moved to the house of his daughter. The headquarters of the Summer Moiety was in the lower floor of a two-story house (#21). Both caciques, Severo Naranjo and Victoriano Sisneros, who were alive in 1940, have since died, and it is probable that the organizations are now quartered at locations belonging to their successors.

Jeançon in 1926 visited one of these rooms. According to informants, it was in the home of the Winter cacique who preceded Severo Naranjo. His description (Jeançon 1926: 133–34) was as follows:

It was the writer's good fortune in 1926 to have the privilege of visiting such a room in the pueblo of Santa Clara, New Mexico, and to be, possibly, one of the first white men to see and enjoy its sacred precincts. The room is situated back of a living room in the house occupied by a member of one of the sacred fraternities controlling its functions. Entry was gained through a low door in the east wall, and while there cannot be any doubt that some of the ceremonial objects were very old, yet they have been repainted, and some objects are of more recent date.

The house in which the room is located is one of the older ones of the village, with a beautiful old roof, and floors of mixed adobe and animal blood. The dimensions of the room are about 10 by 12 feet, and as the floor is pretty well taken up by the ceremonial paraphernalia, it is somewhat crowded, and would not hold over eight to ten persons during a ceremony. As can be seen from the ground-plan (Fig. 1/[Figure 27]), additional space is occupied by posts supporting the roof. These are not arranged in special manner, but are placed so as to best fulfill their function in the same way as they are in other secular rooms.

There are two windows in the east wall. The floor of the room being nearly three feet higher than that of the room

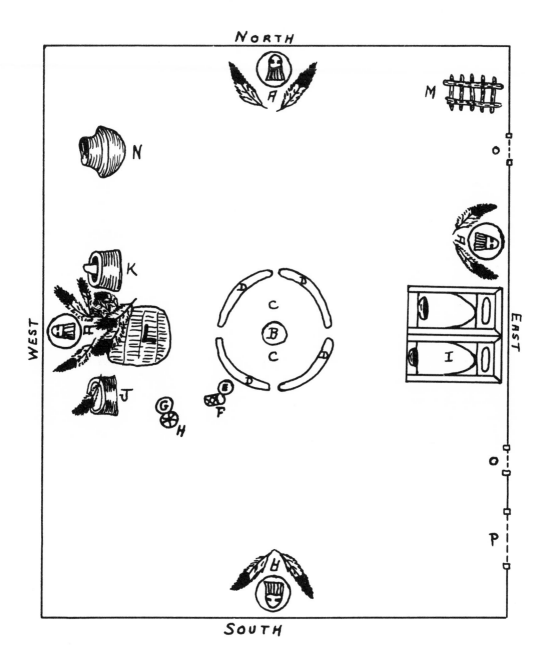

Figure 27. Jeançon's "Fig. 1," a drawing of a "Groundplan of a rectangular ceremonial room at Santa Clara Pueblo, New Mexico." This drawing was included in Jeançon's paper, "A Rectangular Ceremonial Room" (1926: 135). (See Jeançon's account, reproduced here [pp. 204–8], for identifications and descriptions of items in the room.)

through which one must pass to enter it, these windows look upon the roof of the lower one. The raising of floors in interior rooms, in consecutive levels, is a common feature in the Rio Grande pueblos, and occurs very often in prehistoric ruins of that section of the country. The rooms are usually built one back of the other, three deep, the front room having the lowest floor level and the rear one the highest. The front or exterior room is used as a sleeping room, the second one is used as a kitchen, and the rear one for storage purposes.

Upon entering the room one is struck by the fact that the main altar is against the west wall facing the east; this is strictly in accordance with tradition. There should be a door or other opening in the east wall directly in front of the altar, but owing to the manner in which the room is constructed, the door is a little south of east. The room was probably not intended, at the time it was built, for ceremonial purposes, and therefore the opening in the east wall is not quite in the place it should be with reference to the altar. There are no openings in the west wall.

The altar (Fig. 2 [Figure 28]) consists of a reredos, made by the wall of the room, upon which is painted a rainbow. In front of this is an elongated cone of sandstone, at the foot of which is a mass of feathers, hawk and eagle, lying upon a large fragment of buffalo hide. On the right and left of the hide are mortar-shaped sandstone vessels. On the north of the altar is a large jar containing a reserve stock of pollen or sacred meal. On the south of it is one of the posts supporting the roof; hanging from this is a shield upon the surface of which is painted a nondescript figure, of possible symbolic significance.

The colors of the rainbow begin with white at the top, red next, then blue, and then yellow. This sequence is according to the Rio Grande system of designating the colors of the cardinal points: beginning with white for the east, red for the north, blue for the west, and yellow for

the south. According to the information given the writer by various Pueblo Indians, they always turn, in their dances and ceremonies, in a left-handed or sinistral circuit, whereas the Navajo and related peoples always turn in a right-handed or dextral circuit, the Pueblos going against the sun circuit and the others going with it. [Jeançon was oversimplifying here regarding general Puebloan ceremonial circuits and color associations; for a more detailed discussion regarding cardinal directions and colors, see Riley 1963. CHL]

The conical stone is placed at the foot of the rainbow, and is dressed in a grass skirt which extends upward a little more than half of the figure. Eyes have been indicated by rectangular painted marks, but there is nothing to indicate a mouth or a nose. The upper part of the figure is not painted the proper color of the cardinal point, but in this case is colored yellow. In winter the grass skirt is replaced by one made of pine boughs. These stones are similar in form to those described by Dr. J. Walter Fewkes and called by him Corn Goddesses:

"In many Hopi altars the Hopi have a 'cone' made of wood or clay, . . . They represent Muyinwu, which appears to be another name for Alosaka, the Germ God. . . . They are survivals of very ancient idols, as several similar objects made of stone found in cliff ruins on the Mesa Verde are so similar in form that they have been regarded as practically the same" [Fewkes 1920: 602].

"Next in importance to the idol of the Sky god is that of Muyinwu, the Corn Mountain or Germ Goddess, which occupies a prominent place on the majority of Hopi altars. The archaic form is a conical stone or wooden object called the corn hill or corn mound" [Fewkes 1922: 388].

On the north and south of the cone are sandstone vessels about 18 inches in height and about the same diameter at

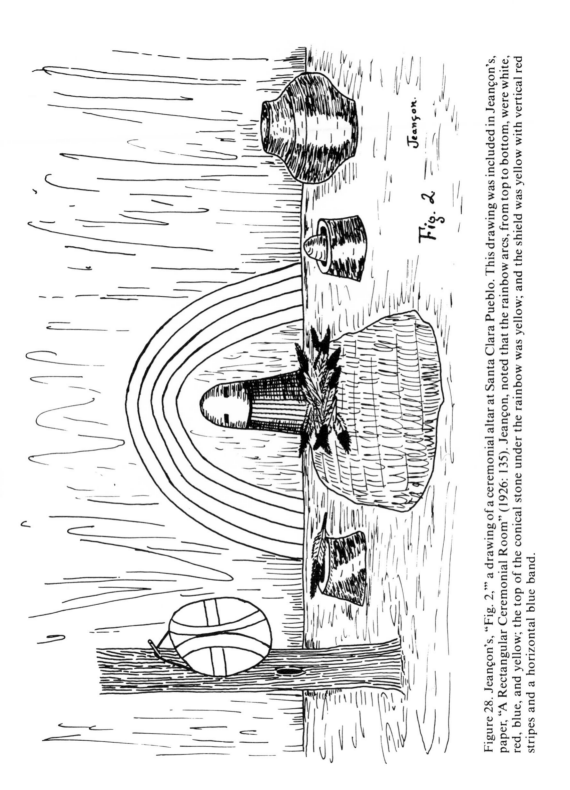

Figure 28. Jeançon's, "Fig. 2,'" a drawing of a ceremonial altar at Santa Clara Pueblo. This drawing was included in Jeançon's, paper, "A Rectangular Ceremonial Room" (1926: 135). Jeançon, noted that the rainbow arcs, from top to bottom, were white, red, blue, and yellow; the top of the conical stone under the rainbow was yellow; and the shield was yellow with vertical red stripes and a horizontal blue band.

the bottom and tapering somewhat as they rise from their base. The one on the south contains water from the first rainfall in the spring, and has an eagle wing tip feather with which to asperse. The container on the north has in it water from the first snowfall in the autumn, and also contains a large, cone-shaped stone painted white. In making the ceremonial aspersions during the summer the sprinkling is always done to the southeast. The fragment of buffalo hide in front of the altar is used to make burial moccasins for the custodian of the shrine.

The south altar is very simple, having only the cone, the upper part of which is painted red, and a single band of yellow in terraced form on the wall behind it. The east altar is equally simple, being located to the north of a couple of mealing bins containing two metates, some baskets with pollen or ceremonial meal, and the hand stones. The cone of the east altar is painted white, and on the wall back of it is a yellow disk representing the sun. At the north altar the cone is painted blue, and on the wall behind it is a single terraced line of red. Below this line is a crescent moon painted in yellow (Fig. 3[Figure 29]).

In the center of the room is a sort of "world shrine" with four ceremonial openings pointing northeast, northwest, southwest, and southeast. There is a low raised wall, not over three inches in height, making a circular inclosure broken by the ceremonial openings, and the whole inside of this space, not occupied by a post supporting the roof, is covered with white ceremonial meal. On another post close to the world shrine is hung a drum used in the rain ceremonies. In the northeast corner is a ladder leading to a hatchway in the roof, and formerly this was the only means of access to the ceremonial chamber.

Each moiety incorporated three groupings forming a hierarchy through which males might rise to high priestly office. In the Summer Moiety, in ascending order,

these were Summar (Xa zhe), a generic term referring to all who had undergone moiety initiation without regard to sex or their status in the hierarchy; the Summer kachina organization (Oxu wa); and the Summer managing society (Pay-oj-ke). In the Winter Moiety the equivalent groupings were Winter (Kwere); the Winter kachina organization (Oxu wa); and the Winter managing society (Oyike). (The unaffiliated and the uninitiated were referred to as punuɾgge?i.) All these units, with the exception of the first, were responsible for the performance of specific religious duties. Some of the rites were executed by the bodies acting as separate entities; others, particularly larger moiety ceremonies, entailed the cooperative efforts of the two higher groups and one or more of the nonmoiety secret societies.

Under aboriginal conditions, membership in either the Summer or Winter Moiety was a normal adjunct of the growth and development of every Santa Clara child. In affiliating themselves with a moiety, individuals assumed legal identity in the eyes of society, and males entered upon the threshold of the moiety hierarchy. These groupings were essentially informal, serving only to identify the population religiously and politically. The individual was merely attached to one or the other group, but did not necessarily assume obligations other than those of marginal participation in events of significance to the whole moiety.

Moiety membership showed a definite patrilineal bias. However, there was no rigid adherence to this principle. Parents belonging to opposite moieties often alternated their children, dedicating the first child to one moiety, the second to the other, and so on. Women often changed moieties upon marriage if their husband belonged to the other group, though this was not obligatory. Changes in moiety were also made if a person was dissatisfied or considered that he might better himself [6, 9, 15, 18]. "You take the side which you think will be best for you" [15]. The Summer cacique, who died in 1952, was a former Winter man who had switched his affiliation. Such changes were normally accompanied by reinitiation. For example, the mother of one informant [21] was Summer, but shifted to her husband's

Figure 29. Terraced "wood box" in kiva; these also serve as altars in certain circumstances and are referred to as such.

moiety. She underwent the Winter initiation ceremony and received a new name.

Formerly all males of the pueblo inevitably became members of the Summer or Winter kachina organizations. Membership in these organizations was referred to as "Summer or Winter, one step above." Undergoing the moiety "water immersion" (po ku) was prerequisite to becoming associated with a kachina organization. Initiation usually coincided with those of the other moiety divisions, but it might also be held independently, during the preliminary period of any "hidden dance" (nu xi). Boys were inducted between the ages of twelve and fifteen.

The ceremony of initiation into the kachina organization was referred to as a rite which "made the boys men." It incorporated many of the features of the classical adolescent rite. Novices were placed in limited seclusion. Food tabus and continence were enforced. The scratching stick was used by novices of the Summer kachina. During the ceremony the boys were whipped, purified, and supernatural power, "wisdom," was bestowed upon them. They received religious instruction, and the esoteric aspects of rituals were revealed to them for the first time. Coincidentally the responsibilities and obligations, "the right ways of life," were impressed upon them. Finally, they were sworn to secrecy and accorded adult status in the community [9, 13, 18, 21].

Girls were not "made women," i.e., initiated into the kachina cult, although there is evidence that female members of the Winter and Summer managing societies were whipped by the kachinas [25]. Details of these organizations were revealed to them at the time of their marriage [9, 13, 18, 21]. The fertility rite and symbolic impregnation of girls during a kachina enactment can, however, be considered a form of adolescent ceremony.

While the kachina groups were definite esoteric organizations with specific duties and prescribed ceremonies, they appeared to have functioned also as cooperating adjuncts to the managing societies, rather than as distinct entities. Each kachina society was under the direction and leadership of specially designated members of the two managing societies. Those from the Summer were called "the fathers of the kachina" (se^n su); those from the Winter, "the elders" (pa re), or "fathers of the kachina."

Ceremonial obligations of the Summer kachina included participation in the "hidden dances" (nu xi) held in early spring, on the night of Good Friday, and in the fall. They also played a prominent role at the "Edge of Spring" ceremony, and at the summer solstice when a new Summer cacique was inducted.

These ceremonies, with the exception of the "hidden dance in the hills," took place in the kiva. They were all aspects of larger moiety ceremonies in which several groups played roles. Dances were always preceded by retreats, during which the membership conducted esoteric rites, made preparations for the final rituals, and initiated and inducted new members. Retreats were held in the "kachina house," a room set aside for their exclusive use in the residence of the leader of the "fathers of the kachinas," or in the annex of the Summer kiva [13, 18, 52].

The roles of the individual members varied considerably. Depending upon experience and length of service, a member might be expected to take part as a masked impersonator, i.e., a kachina proper, or as a member of the chorus, or as a dancer. Individuals also acted as sponsors in the moiety initiation, and assisted at the pledging and possibly at the initiation of "the fathers of the kachina."

In general the duties of the Winter kachina group paralleled those of the Summer. Members participated in the now infrequent "hidden dances" of that moiety, and played their part in moiety initiations and inductions [14, 21].

As indicated earlier, the elite groups within the moieties were the Summer and Winter managing societies. These organizations contained the top echelon of the theocratic hierarchy which dominated the political scene, and were responsible for much of the spiritual well-being of the village, largely through the planning and execution of moiety ritual. These societies included the two caciques, and their right and left arms; the fathers of the kachina and elders; and the woman in each society who acted in a ceremonial capacity during kachina performances, as well as regular members.

In 1940 the membership of the Summer managing society, as nearly as could be learned, consisted of twelve males and four females. Five members were designated as "fathers of the kachina," one of whom was inactive [9, 13, 18]. According to Parsons (1929: 113), there were ten male and four female members in 1923.

As nearly as could be ascertained, the roster of the Winter managing society in 1940 included eleven males and four females. Two of these, a man and a woman, were vowed to the organization but had not undergone final initiation. Another woman was in inactive status. Three members were designated as elders. According to Parsons (1929: 113), there were eight male and six female members in 1923. In both cases the membership figures represent a minimum, since the esoteric nature of the managing societies precluded knowledge of the total personnel by other than the initiated.

Membership in both managing societies was acquired through dedication of a child by the parents at the time of its birth. Also, in both the Summer and Winter societies, membership could be the result of a vow during illness or subsequent to a cure, and by petitions and through trespass or trapping, definitely in the Winter Society, and probably also in the case of the Summer [9, 14, 25]. Prior initiation into the kachina organization was a prerequisite for all male candidates; membership in their respective moieties was sufficient for females.

The limited size of these organizations seems to have resulted from hesitancy on the part of most individuals to assume the heavy obligations attendant upon joining, rather than from any restrictive ruling from within the societies. Educational, or training requirements were high, ceremonial responsibilities numerous and confining, and personal ambition and religious drive had to be great to overcome the practical inconveniences.

Once having attained full membership in the Summer Society of the Summer Moiety, ambitious individuals were free to work their way up the hierarchical ladder. The accomplishments and attributes basic to achieving the high priestly rank of cacique, or right or left arm, have been detailed in the discussions of political organization and of status, and will not be repeated here.

Data bearing on the selection or appointment of the "fathers of the kachina" in the Summer Moiety are unfortunately limited. According to one informant [25], these positions were filled as the result of a vow made at the time a man joined the society. Within this group there were a "leader of the fathers of the kachina" and two principal assistants. As far as could be determined, these purely ceremonial offices were never held concurrently with the offices of cacique or the right or left arm [9, 25, 50].

Presumably, any female member of the Summer Society was eligible to function as "Summer Woman," i.e., to draw the line of meal and lead in the kachina at the time of a "hidden dance." According to an informant [85] who held this office, all members who functioned in this capacity had been subjected to the whipping rite of kachina initiation.

Aside from political operations, this group with its priestly heirarchy had manifold obligations in the spiritual area. From late February or early March to late October or early November, the Summer Society assumed direct responsibility for the internal and religious well-being of the village. While these functions shifted to the Winter Society during the winter, the Summer Society was still active in religious matters during the remainder of the year.

Ultimate responsibility for all Summer Moiety spiritual matters rested with the Summer cacique (po an turg zhorg). Broadly speaking, he initiated or sanctioned and administered all ceremonies specifically associated with his moiety, as well as those village-wide ones that fell under his jurisdiction. He was assisted in this by his right and left arm, the "fathers of the kachina," and the Summer women. In actual function this group was truly a managing society. Assistance was also available to the cacique, upon request, from the outside chief or war captain, the other war captains, the governor, lieutenant-governor, or from any secret society whose cooperation was deemed essential in the successful performance of an integrated ritual.

While factionalism and acculturation have taken their toll, it is still possible to reconstruct the ceremonial calendar within limits. This process gives some appreciation of the magnitude of religious undertakings involving the Summer cacique under aboriginal conditions.

Once each month the society went into retreat and "worked." A retreat of one day was also held prior to the opening of the ditch in the spring. Whether this coincided with the regular monthly meeting was not determined. Retreats and "work" of a higher order, that consumed from four to twelve days, were scheduled at the solstices. A retreat at the summer solstice might include the induction of a Summer cacique. Another was held prior to the "Edge of Spring" ceremony in January or February. This retreat included cooperation with the kachina, formerly the transfer of village religious authority from the Winter to the Summer Moiety, and ceremonial shinny. Another work period preceded the "big curing" in March or April, with or without the poje.

Finally, retreats were held in conjunction with the kachina enactments in January or on Good Friday, and the "hidden dance in the hills" in September or October. When the latter coincided with moiety and Summer managing initiations, it was held in the kiva. Formerly the transfer of village authority from Summer to Winter Moiety took place at this time. Terminal features of all these integrated rites were presided over by the Summer cacique, and the Summer managing society as a whole was actively engaged in them, as well as in any coincidental initiations and inductions taking place within their own organizations, that of the Summer kachina, or the Summer Moiety.

Added to the above functions, the Summer cacique and Summer Society were responsible for the organization and supervision of any "big outside" or "little outside" dances in which the moiety was involved. These normally followed kachina enactments, but also occurred on special occasions such as Santa Clara day and San Antonio day, and periodically during the Christmas season and on January 6, when secular officers were inducted. Furthermore, the society was subject to call at any time as a curing agency. Considering the workload, there is little wonder that individuals hesitated to obligate themselves to membership in the Summer Society.

The function of the "fathers of the kachina" group within the Summer managing society was limited to Summer religious matters. Their organizational framework duplicated that within the parent group. There was a "leader of the fathers of the kachina" and a right and left arm. These three and other members acted in liaison capacity between the Summer managing society and the kachina organization, and coordinated the activities of the two groups. They were actually the heads of the kachina organization. "The se su is a ceremonial father whose presence is very precious" [25]. They received requests for "hidden dances" and acted upon them in consultation with the Summer Society. They were specifically charged with the supervision of kachina initiations and enactments. They planned the ceremony, instructed the kachina members in their various parts, helped direct the construction of the altars in the kiva and the preparation of prayer plumes, saw that the latter were properly deposited, and were directly responsible for the correct performance of the kachina rituals [9, 18, 21, 25].

Consistent with the general attitude at Santa Clara Pueblo toward women, the religious roles of female members of the Summer Society were somewhat restricted. Women were present during retreats but took little part in the rites. On these occasions, they secured and prepared food for the ceremonially engaged members. Their religious participation appears to have been restricted to kachina enactments, when they prepared the trail of meal and "led in the kachina," and when they acted as sponsors at Summer Society or Moiety initiations [9, 18, 21, 25, 50].

Organizationally the Winter Society paralleled the Summer. The head of the society was the Winter cacique (Oyike sendo), who was assisted by his right and left arm. The counterparts of the "fathers of the kachina" were the "elders" (pa re), with a designated leader and two principal assistants. The Winter women had the same roles as those of the female Summer Society members. General requirements for religious advancement were also the same. The induction of a Winter cacique, however, was held on or about the time of the Winter solstice.

As in the case of his Summer equivalent, the Winter cacique was ultimately responsible for all spiritual matters associated with his moiety, and was specifically charged with the well-being of the community during his "half" of the year, from November to February.

There is every evidence that before the moiety schism the Winter ritual calendar was an analogue of the Summer. Even in recent years the Winter Society, while its functions were impaired, was still active. The membership "worked" each month. It held retreats at the solstice periods, prior to the Ka-ve-Na ceremony in the early spring that formerly included the transfer of authority to the Summer Moiety. Other "work" periods preceded the November appearance of the kachina and at any coincident initiations and inductions taking place within the Winter Society, the Winter kachina, or Winter Moiety. Similarly, they were responsible for "bringing out" "little and big" outside dances on specific occasions, whenever sufficient unanimity existed within the moiety. They could and did act as a curing organization also. Organizationally and functionally, the "elders" and the Winter women were similar to their counterparts in the Summer Society [14, 21, 25].

MOIETY INITIATIONS
AND INDUCTIONS

Moiety intiations and inductions occurred at several levels. First there was the "water immersion" ceremony. This was designated as "becoming Summer, or Winter, one step above" and resulted in the individual's affiliation with one or the other moiety. The second was the initiation of males into the Summer or Winter kachina organizations. The third was the induction and initiation of members into the Summer Society or the Winter Society. Finally there were the ceremonies attending the induction of a Summer or Winter cacique.

Children were usually inducted or initiated into the moieties, i.e., "become Summer or Winter," between the ages of six or seven. Younger children and infants, however, could be dedicated to either group. In these instances they were taken or carried by their parents to the kiva and underwent the initial portions of the rite. The final initiation was completed at the next recurrence of the ceremony.

Moiety initiations were held ideally about every six or seven years. However, this interval has been extended in recent times. This has been the result of the general effects of acculturation and other specific causes. Inter- and intramoiety conflicts have been frequent during the historic period. Since amicable relationships are prerequisite to the performance of the rite, initiations were consequently delayed. Furthermore, a "water immersion" could be held only when a new member was inducted into the Summer or Winter Society. Since there have recently been few candidates for these positions, especially among the Winter people, moiety initiations have been correspondingly infrequent [9, 15, 18, 21].

Initiation into the kachina organizations has occurred more frequently. These rites could and did form a preliminary feature of the first day of a retreat prior to any kachina enactment.

Initiation Ceremony of the Summer Moiety

The performance of the "water immersion" (po'ku) initiation ceremony, by which children were "made Summer," involved the cooperation of several religious organizations and their personnel. These included the Summer Society, the Summer kachina organization, the Women's Scalp Society, and, according to one informant [61], one of the Bear societies. Prominent roles were performed by the Summer cacique, the "fathers of the kachina," the governor, and the war captain (outside chief) and his assistants.

Initiations were held in September or October. The decision to hold them, however, was made the previous spring at the time of the "Edge of Spring" ceremony. What body or individual determined the date has not been ascertained. Presumably it was the Summer cacique and the Summer Society, since these ceremonies could be held only when a Summer person was undergoing initiation.

Prior to the rite, two sponsors were chosen for each candidate. If the child was old enough, he or she selected these persons; if not, the selection was made by the parents. Boys were compelled to choose one sponsor from the male membership of the Summer Society, the other from the Summer kachina group. The latter could not be a member of the Summer Society. Girls chose as sponsors a female member of the Summer Society, and a woman who was a member of the Summer Moiety, but not of the Summer Society. These were referred to as "water immersion father," or "water immersion mother." In turn, they addressed the novice as "water immersion child." Sponsors were frequently relatives of the novices.

Of the two male sponsors, the kachina member played the more important role. While the Summer members presented the initiate with a bow and arrow, it was the kachina member who spent the most time with him during the course of the initiation, who guided and watched over him, and who finally presented him with substantial gifts of food, clothing, or other articles.

The initiation ceremony lasted twelve days. The actual rite encompassed ten days;

the other two involved purification of the principals prior to going into retreat, and subsequent to the kachina enactment. The first day both the Summer and kachina groups went into retreat and remained in seclusion until the fourth night. The Summer group then repaired to a room in the home of the Summer cacique, where the officers and the "fathers of the kachina" and other members planned the details of the initiation program. This included "work": the preparation of prayer plumes and their deposition at the shrines, and the manufacture of articles to be used in the ceremony and on the altar.

The kachina held their retreat in a house adjacent to the Summer kiva. Their "work" consisted of repainting and preparing the masks, gathering the evergreens to be worn by the dancers, and engaging in ceremonial hunts. When the occasion demanded, candidates of the society were initiated on the first day of the retreat [9, 21, 43].

According to one informant [61], candidates for initiation formerly went into retreat in the kiva the first day of the preliminary activities and remained there for four days. He said, "You followed a Bear Society member in his steps to a certain place in the kiva where your sponsor was." He also stated that as the neophite entered the kiva, a duck feather was tied in his hair, and he was presented with a scratching stick by the Bear Society member. Candidates were allowed to leave the kiva periodically, but had to return at night. They were supposed to answer the calls of nature only at night. When away from the kiva, they were always accompanied by a sponsor. The above account is at variance with later descriptions; perhaps the discrepancies are the result of changes over time, rather than errors.

During retreats food was prepared for and furnished to the societies by the Summer women, the wives of the "fathers of the kachina," and any other women of the moiety who wished to contribute food and service.

The climax of the first part of the moiety initiation ritual occurred on the fourth night. By this time all preparations and preliminary ceremonies had been com-

pleted; the kachina were ready for their appearance and the Summer Society had erected an altar in the kiva. Word was circulated through the pueblo that the ceremony was to begin, and the novices were ordered to report. They arrived at the kiva accompanied by their families. Small children who were to undergo only the first part of the rite were carried by their mothers. When all had assembled, the ceremony began.

First, a series of preliminary rites were performed by the Summer Society. The male members (Summer women were already in the kiva) of this organization entered the kiva in two lines, one led by the Summer cacique, and the other by "the right-arm man." Each of the leaders carried a "lightning stick," one of eagle feathers, the other made from feathers of the western red-tailed hawk. They manipulated these sticks with both hands as they led the swaying and zigzagging lines of men across the center of the kiva floor to the altar. When the altar was reached one line formed on either side, and the cacique and "right-arm man" manipulated the "lightning sticks" toward the four directions and "purified" the kiva. After this they seated themselves, the cacique in the center, the right arm on the right side of the altar, the left arm on the left side. The remainder of the Summer men filed out of the kiva.

Soon after this group departed, two of the members returned, attired in white shirts and white cotton trousers. Over their trousers were kilts held in place by sashes tied at the back. On their lower legs they wore red garters, and around their ankles, skunkskin anklets. They were barefoot. In their hair, which hung loose, they wore the plume of an eagle. Each carried in his hand a bouquet-like bundle of evergreens. They came to the center of the kiva and, beginning with the east, shook the bouquets toward each of the four cardinal points. As they were shaken, the seeds of various agricultural products (corn, beans, wheat, melons, and pumpkins) that had been concealed in the bouquets, spilled out upon the kiva floor.

These two were replaced almost immediately by two others, similarly attired, but carrying evergreen wreaths. They repeated the previous performance. In this case, however, water concealed in the wreaths was sprinkled over the seeds on the floor.

This fertility rite was followed by the ceremony of "water immersion." At a given signal all novices left their places and rushed to their Summer "water immersion fathers" or "mothers," who were assembled along the north wall of the kiva. Some sponsors had several initiates, others only one. Each sponsor in turn drank from a "sacred" bowl and aspersed the water into the mouth of the pledge. Boys then went to their kachina sponsors, girls to their moiety sponsors, who had formed along the south wall of the kiva, and the same performance was repeated.

Following the aspersing, a scratching stick was tied with a string around the neck of the initiates, and feathers from a yellow warbler and a roadrunner were placed in their hair. Finally a prayer was said, and a new name was bestowed on the initiate.

When the rite of aspersing was completed, the men of the Summer Society arranged themselves on either side of the altar and began a chant. During the singing, members of the kachina society, many of whom acted as sponsors, left by ones and twos to costume themselves for the coming dance or to assist in it. The songs were timed to terminate as the last kachina member departed from the kiva [9, 69].

When the singing stopped, a member of the Summer Society began the rite, describing the emergence of the kachina in the north and their progress to the pueblo. When the kachina arrived, they performed the regular Summer "hidden dance." The only two divergences from the normal performance were that a Summer member substituted for the clowns and songs replaced the clowns' buffoonery.

When the kachina left after their second appearance, the food which they had brought was distributed to the spectators. The Summer cacique then instructed the initiates. Instructions dealt with the use of the scratching stick, food tabus, and the general behavior pattern to be adhered to for the next four days. Only aboriginal foods could be eaten. "Food consisted of cornmeal gruel eaten and prepared at the sponsor's home"

[52]. Salt, sugar, or any other type of seasoning was forbidden. Canned goods and sweets were particularly avoided [9, 13]. No water from wells could be drunk, only water from mountain springs transported to the pueblo in jars [13, 52].

It was believed that a person who failed to use the scratching stick would suffer a cut or broken finger. Scratching sticks were used only by the Summer Moiety, not by the Winter [22]. Boys were instructed to have contacts only with male members of their families; girls, only with female members [9, 13]. When the cacique finished his lecture to the initiates, he gave another one on conformity and secrecy, leveled at the general population. This completed the ceremony, and all left [9, 69].

The next morning the initiates went either to the houses of their sponsors or else the sponsors came to get them. They were fed and then returned home. Sponsors alternated, the Summer Society furnishing one meal, and the kachina or the moiety sponsor, the next. This routine and the instructions as outlined by the cacique were followed for the next four days.

On the night of the eighth day, another ceremony was held in the kiva, in which the "fathers of the kachina" and the kachina replaced the Summer Society proper in the dominant role. An altar was erected, and this group took their positions in the kiva. The leader of "the fathers of the kachina" sat in the center with the altar in front of him, his right and left-arm men on either side. The kachina arranged themselves on either side, and were divided on the basis of their ability to sing. Members of the Summer Society distributed themselves about the altar, at the foot of the ladder, and at the entrance to the kiva, ready to assist.

When all was ready the initiates and their relatives were summoned and arranged themselves in semicircles on the north side of the kiva and in front of the fireplace. Men and women occupied separate areas. The cacique first addressed and admonished the people. When he finished, the leader of the "fathers of the kachina" struck the "kiva bells."

[These were actually long (8"–10"), narrow (1"–2") stones, K'utiti, or Kotiti, that were struck against one another. The ringing sound that resulted gave rise to the name "bells." They have also been reported from the excavation, particularly of kivas, of numerous upper Rio Grande sites. The stones varied from an essentially natural form to some shaping; in somewhat rare instances, for example, a large spear point. Stones shaped in such fashion are similar to weights attached to the ends of thongs and twirled about one's head, a bull-roarer. (See Parsons 1929: 250; see also Lambert 1954: 132–33, Pl. XXVIII.) CHL]

This was the signal to begin the four songs which "belonged" to the kachina. Then the leader of "fathers of the kachina" gave the "bells" to his right arm, and went through the routine of calling, watching, and reporting on the emergence and the progress of the kachina to the pueblo (note that the leader of the "fathers of the kachina" replaced the member of the Summer Society who played this role in the previous kachina appearance). The regular kachina performance then ensued.

With the departure of the kachina, the initiates were told to go to the house of the cacique (or to their own homes; the informant [9] could not remember which) and await their sponsors. Each sponsor met his novice or novices, and all left in a body for the river. The location chosen was the south bank of Santa Clara Creek, where it entered the Rio Grande. Each initiate stripped, and they were led into the stream until the water reached their waists. Each novice immersed himself in the water four times. Each held his scratching sticks in his hand, and the fourth time he disappeared beneath the water, he pushed the stick into the mud of the river bottom. This completed the rite at the river, and the party dressed and prepared to return to the pueblo. Part of the return trip was through a willow thicket, in which a tunnel had been formed by tying together the upper portions of the branches; this formed a winding path, with an arch low enough to force those who traversed it to stoop [9, 50].

The party arrived in the pueblo before dawn—about two or three in the morning. Initiates went first to the homes of their Summer sponsors. The food tabus were lifted, and they were feasted and given bows

and arrows and other gifts. After being welcomed by the Summer Society they went to their kachina or their moiety sponsors, were feasted again, and received more gifts, especially clothing. "Boys would get bows and arrows, and girls, buckskin shoes or something else buckskin" [22]. Food was prepared by members of the Summer Moiety, and the Winter Moiety members were guests. It was served until all had eaten their fill. When this occurred, all new moiety members returned to their homes.

No ceremonies were held during the day or night on the ninth day. This period was used for a much-needed rest. On the tenth night a "hidden dance" was held. K'osa replaced the Summer Society and "fathers of the kachina" in visualizing the emergence of the kachina. Guests from other villages also attended this dance [9].

Initiation Ceremony of the Winter Moiety

Detailed accounts of the Winter "water immersion" (po'ku) ceremony were unobtainable. From the limited information available, the rite appears to have had many elements featured in the Summer initiation. However, some differences in patterning existed, and certain omissions were apparent. The latter were probably attributable to the general weakening of the Winter group resulting from continued intramoiety disagreements.

"Becoming Winter" required the cooperative efforts of several units within the moiety, including the Winter Society, which dominated the program, and the Winter kachina.

Initiations were held either in November or December, and under normal conditions occurred at intervals of five to seven years. In recent years, however, this schedule has been disrupted. One rite was held in 1928 or 1929 [18], and another was reported in 1948 [21]. According to other informants [25, 43], they always coincided with the induction of members into the Winter Society and kachina organization.

The ceremony was twelve days in length. On the first day the Winter Society went into retreat to prepare equipment and to "work" for the welfare of their own initiates and those who were to undergo the "water immersion" ceremony. On the first day the principal act of this society was the planting of the "sacred corn" (or wheat), the sprouts of which would be used on the final night in the initiation of the novices. A rectangular pot with terraced edges, about two feet in length, was filled with soil and manure, and the seed planted in this. It was kept in a warm place; this heat, plus that generated by the manure, forced the germination and growth of the plants. According to native theory, growth was also accelerated by the songs, prayers, and chants which occupied most of the time of the members. This activity, or "work," was referred to as "making wisdom." "This in turn means making the corn grow" [21].

Eight days later the Winter kachina began their retreat and "work" (preparation). By eleven o'clock of the evening of the twelfth day, all preparations were completed. Members of the Winter kachina who were not impersonating and therefore not under ritual prescriptions, cleaned the kiva and heated it. Often fires were kept burning for two days to attain sufficient warmth. Guards were placed at all roads entering the pueblo. A guard was also placed at the entrance of the kiva. Among other duties, he collected food brought by the spectators. Other men directed the spectators to their places in the northwest section of the kiva as they arrived. No Summer people were allowed to witness the Winter "water immersion," and vice versa.

When preparations were completed, word was sent to the novices to report to the kiva. When all were present and in their places, the Winter Society entered. With them was an individual who was undergoing initiation. He was naked and painted with chalk (clay). He did not sit, but stood to one side. The Winter Society constructed an altar in the center of the kiva facing south, supervised by the Winter cacique's right arm. On it was placed the bowl of sprouted corn essential to the "water immersion" rite. The Winter cacique and his left arm stood to one side of the altar. The rest of the members formed balanced rows on either side. The women members, with the exception of the Winter Society women, formed a line back of the men. The Winter Society women sat on the north side between this section and the fireplace. The east end of the kiva was reserved for the Winter kachina.

When the altar was completed, a few prayers were said by the society. The Winter initiate then left with his sponsor. He returned in a few moments clad in a kilt, with bells about his waist, and carrying a bowl of sacred water. He placed the bowl on the altar and took his place among the rest of the Winter Society members, whereupon the "water immersion" began.

The first step was the choosing of sponsors. Unlike the Summer, the novice of the Winter Moiety had only one sponsor, not two, to guide him through the rite. Sponsors came from the Winter Society, the sex of the sponsor corresponding to that of the initiate. The relationship entered into at this time was continued throughout life; each individual obligated himself to render assistance to the other, should future need arise [21].

When the choices had been made, each "water immersion" child stood before its "water immersion father" or "mother." The Winter initiate handed the bowl of sacred water to one of the sponsors. The sponsor drank from the bowl and aspersed the water into the mouth of his protégé. He was next given a small piece of sprouted corn, which he chewed and disposed of in the same manner. He then said a prayer over the child and gave it a new name, which appears to have been used only by the sponsor. This completed the rite, and the child returned to his or her place in the kiva. This was repeated until all the candidates were inducted.

Following this, the right and left arms came forward and said a prayer. Next they began to visualize and describe the progress of the Winter kachina from the place of emergence to the pueblo. When a "water immersion" was held, these two dignitaries substituted for the clowns who ordinarily acted in this capacity at "hidden dances." They did not joke as the clowns did, but gave wolf calls.

Finally the kachina arrived, entered the kiva, and performed. The rite was similar to that given at ordinary "hidden dances," except that they made four appearances instead of the usual two, and enacted the complete routine four times at each appearance instead of twice. When the kachina left for the fourth time, everyone departed for their homes, with the exception of the Winter Society members. They remained in the kiva and enacted a short ritual, the details of which could not be learned. This terminated the ceremony. Winter initiates were not forced to use the scratching stick, bathe ceremonially, or conform to the other restrictions inforced by the Summer Moiety [21, 73].

The Initiation Ceremony of the Summer Kachina

The initiation ceremony of the Summer kachina was an esoteric rite. Only those males who had previously undergone the ritual, those who "had been made men," were privileged to take part and observe. The ceremony took place in the kachina house on the first night of the four-day period of retreat preliminary to a kachina "hidden dance." Seldom were more than two boys inducted at a time.

Candidates for initiation were selected during a meeting at the Summer cacique's house, attended by members of the kachina and Summer Society groups. The name of each boy was presented by the father or by a "guardian" if he had no father or if the parent belonged to the opposite moiety. Induction into this group usually occurred between the age of twelve and fourteen years.

Preparation for the initiation began immediately after the society went into retreat. The man who was chosen to act as leader in the coming dance donned his costume and mask and was led outside by the leader of the "fathers of the kachina," around the corner of the house to the west. The duty of initiation was his. By this time it was quite dark, and the fathers or "guardians" left the house to bring the candidates.

Those who had obligated themselves to impersonate the kachina at the coming dance removed their clothing, covered their bodies with blankets, and seated themselves in a semicircle in the western section of the room. Their masks were placed behind them

and out of sight. The remainder of the kachina membership found places in back of this group. Visibility in the room was intentionally poor, in order that the candidates would be impressed by the seriousness of the proceedings. Occasionally one lamp was lit, but normally all light was derived from the fire in the fireplace. The eerie quality was further enhanced by excessive smoking.

Upon arrival the initiate was led to his station near the north wall and opposite the doorway. He was told to remove his clothing, wrap himself in a blanket, and be seated. Shortly after this, a stomping of feet and a rattling of sleigh bells were heard, and the masked kachina leader entered, carrying yucca whips. He walked about, peered into the faces of those who were seated, and finally came to a halt west of the fireplace.

A Summer Moiety member of a clown society arose and addressed the leader saying, "Where do you come from?" The kachina gestured, indicating that he had come from the mountains. He was then asked, "Why have you come?" The kachina answered in pantomime, indicating small children and a desire to see them. The clown then led him to one of the kachina impersonators, who arose and dropped his blanket. The clown said, "Was this the one you wanted?" The leader replied in the negative by waving his yucca whips back and forth. Then he swung the whips at the kachina twice from each side, as if he were whipping him. Actually he stood at a distance, and no contact was made.

Finally the kachina leader moved to the center of the room and inhaled from the six directions, simultaneously making in-drawing motions with his hands. Then he repeated the pantomime of in-drawing, this time the hands being directed to the body, "as if to say, all this I have with me." This was followed by gestures indicating an antlered buck and conveying power to kill such animals upon the kachina. The leader pushed the power toward the man, and the kachina member drew it in. The kachina then returned to his place and sat down.

The clown walked to the novice and asked him to arise. The boy got up, placed his blanket where he had been sitting, came forward to the center of the room, and stood before the kachina leader. The clown asked, "Was this the child that you wanted?" The kachina nodded his head in assent. The clown told the boy to lean forward, and all the other dignitaries, the Summer cacique and "fathers of the kachina," simultaneously said, "bend down our child." The kachina lifted his whips and struck the back of the child four times with considerable force. The clown told the novice to stand erect, and the kachina leader reenacted the pantomime of deriving and bestowing power, "wisdom," this time with the initiate. The clown then told the boy to resume his seat. The kachina leader departed and joined the "father of the kachina," who had previously left, taking the leader's blanket. The kachina leader removed his mask outside the house, put on his blanket, and reentered with the leader of the "fathers of the kachina," carrying his mask in his hand. As they entered, all the kachina arose, and the initiate saw the masks for the first time.

This completed the initiation proper. During the remainder of the retreat, the initiate was instructed in the role of a kachina and was expected to adhere to all the prescriptions. He could not be said to have completed the initiation until after the "water immersion" ceremony. A member donned the mask that the boy would wear in the coming dance, and went through the routine. Then, in turn, the boy was masked and coached in his part. Newly inducted members were always given the simpler roles of the chorus or dancers to impersonate, never the role of the leading, or individual, kachina proper.

Initiation Ceremony of the Winter Kachina Society

Initiation into the Winter kachina society, as in the case of Winter Moiety induction, followed the same basic pattern as that of the Summer. However, enough variations occurred to justify a detailed account. Initiations were held either in November or December, and were coincidental with inductions into the Winter Moiety and the Winter Society.

The initiation proper took place on the first night of the four-day retreat prior to the kachina dance; however, initiates could not be recognized as full members until the end of the "water immersion," and until they had participated in the kachina performance of that ritual.

Initiations into both Winter and Summer kachina societies were incidental adjuncts to major ceremonial performances. The rite was held in the house of the Winter kachina. Candidates were selected or "trapped" during the solstice. The basis of choice was not discovered.

On the first day of the retreat, candidates for initiation were taken by their parents, or some member of the kachina organization, to the home of one of the clowns. Upon their arrival they were told they were about to enter a four-day retreat. They were instructed to bathe and then don a breechclout and blanket. Members who took part in the retreat also bathed. They waited there until called. During this interval, they were instructed by older men. "They were told stories to pass the time." They were told, "You are going to a pueblo in another world and will eat corn and wild game. You should eat all the apples you wish, since you will get none where you are going." (Both initiates and kachinas were under food tabus and could eat nothing but aboriginal foods, i.e., corn products and wild game. They were also to remain continent [43].)

The boys were delayed at the clown's house for a period of about two hours. During this time the members of the society made preparations for their induction. The masks were stacked in one corner of the kachina house, and two members held a blanket before them. The kachina leader who would perform the initiation ceremony was costumed and concealed behind a screen.

When all was ready, about 10:30 P.M., two older members of the society came to take the novice or novices to the kachina house. When they entered, the novices were told to strip and were seated on their blankets in the section of the room opposite the masks. When all were in their places, a prayer was said. This was followed by a series of ethical talks by older members of the society, who impressed upon the candidates the seriousness of the step that they were about to take and its religious significance. "They said, 'This is not a joke. This is life. You are here for four days. You are here to be made men. You are to keep secret what you see. The secrets of the old religion will be revealed to you. You will see how we as people do.'" [73].

At the termination of these moral lectures, the masked kachina leader appeared from behind the screen and danced toward the initiates. He carried a willow whip in each hand. He was met by the clown who said, "Here are your children." The clown was not in costume, but carried a bowl of sacred water. Simultaneously with the appearance of the kachina, the blankets were removed from the masks, and the novices saw them for the first time. An old member of the society led each candidate forward and gave him cornmeal to sprinkle on the masked leader. The clown then said, "Here he is standing," and the leader struck the initiate four blows with the willow whips, first on the right shoulder, then on the left, next on the right leg, finally on the left leg. Following this the leader pointed to the cardinal points and "breathed out, gave life." The candidate was next instructed by the clown to take a bite from the willow whip, chew it, and rub it on his body. He stated, "This will give you life and goodness of life."

If there were several candidates, the boys were whipped in turn, after which they resumed their places. The leader then disappeared again behind the screen, where his costume and mask were placed in the corner with the other paraphernalia. In 1948 there were twelve initiates, and these were presented to the leader of the "elders," or "fathers of the kachina," in groups of four. Prayers were said. ("These prayers were in archaic Tewa and not understandable to the majority of the group.") Then the boys were allowed to replace their breech clouts. Several more lectures were given, outlining ethical precepts and impressing the newly initiated with the secret character of what they had seen and were about to see. "They say that you are now a man, that now you know everything, and that all that you see and hear must be kept secret." Each boy was given a drink of sacred water, and this terminated the initiation proper.

"When you join the kachina and are made a man, good and evil are revealed to you. You have learned prayers and the right way of life. Kachina initiates have been instructed and cautioned and therefore are prepared to fight evil" [9]. Initiates were taught to behave in the right way and to pray in the right way. Violation would cause supernatural punishment, through illness or accident.

New members were then told to relax; they were allowed to smoke and talk. The older group joked with the initiates, told them stories, made them laugh, and endeavored in every way to make them feel at ease. "This made you feel better." Finally one of the leaders of the society announced that it was late and that practice should begin. Those who were to dance in the coming "hidden dance" associated with the "water immersion" stripped to their breech clouts, donned their masks, and rehearsed their parts. The newly inducted members were assigned parts, and various individuals in the society coached and instructed them. From this point on they participated and conducted themselves for the remainder of the retreat in the same manner as the older members of the group [21].

According to one informant [43], the initiation was formerly a more traumatic experience, and the restrictions more severe. He stated, "In the old days, the whipping was harder. Also the boys had to sit in a certain fashion. Today they can lie around. Young boys were shocked in the old days. Today they are more curious. Today they know what to expect."

Pledging and Initiation Ceremonies of the Summer Society

Membership in the Summer Society was acquired through dedication at birth, as a result of a vow during illness, by petition, and probably through trespass or trapping during the solstice periods, at the Edge of Spring ceremony, and other retreats [9, 14, 21, 25]. Minimum requirements of male candidates included affiliation with the Summer Moiety and membership in the Summer kachina organization; for females, only affiliation with the Summer Moiety. All potential members served a year's novitiate prior to initiation.

Dedication of a child to the Summer Society resulted from the following circumstances. When a couple had had several stillborn children, or children who had died in early infancy, and wished to insure the health of a subsequent child, they dedicated it to one of the secret societies. If the society selected was the Summer, a basket of meal containing fetishes appropriate to the organization was placed beside the head of the infant after its birth. Four days after the naming rite, the child was taken to the headquarters of the Summer Society. There it received a drink of sacred water from one of the principals and was given a "religious" name. If the person desired, this could be used in lieu of the given name. According to an informant [25], the names were usually archaic. When the individual reached adulthood, he or she was obligated to undergo the probationary period and initiation into the society [9, 21, 25].

Recruitment of members through illness involved the following procedures. A person suffering from ill health often solicited the society to effect a cure. Upon recovery they usually vowed to join the organization. Selection of the particular society, in this case the Summer, was often determined by a dream or visionary experience. "The first act occurs during sickness. The person has visions or dreams of ceremonial people, i.e., of a particular society. That is what decides you; that determines what group you join. These dreams recur. You get no rest. Even while you are awake, you are conscious of being watched by the ceremonial people. You call a relative or a friend who is a member. He arranges it [the cure, WWH]. He petitions by carrying meal and feathers to the head of the society" [25].

The pledging ceremony of the Summer Society was, in actuality, a curing rite. The same ritual applied to both men and women. When the patient had determined through visionary experience that the Summer Society was indicated, he contacted a relative or friend who was a member. This person acted as his sponsor. He prepared meal and feathers, presented them to the Summer cacique, and requested the cure.

The cacique called a meeting of the society at the organization's headquarters. Members removed their clothing, wearing only breech clouts. An altar was erected, with the assistance and under the direction of the cacique. At one side of the altar was a basket of sacred meal, on the other a bowl of sacred water. In front of the altar was a circle outlined in cornmeal.

When all was ready, the cacique inquired of the sponsor whether the patient was physically able to appear before the society. If he was too ill, the membership visited him at his home; usually, however, the ailing individual was brought before the society. On arrival, he was seated in the meal circle before the altar. The cacique then dipped two eagle feathers in sacred water, placed the tips in the mouth of the pledge, and permitted him to swallow some of the water. Then the feathers were redipped and passed over the head and down either side of the body. As they met at the feet, they were scraped or snapped across each other four times. The cacique next drank of the sacred water and aspersed the top of the pledge's head, hands, knees, and feet. Finally he took the "kiva bells" and beater, dipped them in water, rubbed them together, and passed them over the body as he had the feathers. Again, he completed the act by scraping the objects across each other four times. The snapping or scraping motion was called "blow it away" (fere), and had purificatory and curative significance. Following this, a new name was bestowed on the candidate.

When the cacique finished his rites, each member of the "fathers of the kachina" and any kachina members who were present duplicated his procedure. Following this, prayer plumes were made from the feathers which had been brought by each member of the society. Members were given sacred meal and prayer plumes, which they deposited on the shrines at the four directions. Meal was sprinkled on the prayer plume at the time the deposit was made. This terminated the ritual.

Following the ceremony, the patient returned to his or her home. From time to time, society members went to the mountains, gathered medicinal herbs, and administered them to the pledge. This procedure continued until the recovery was complete.

In cases where infants and young children were involved, the father sat in the meal circle and held the child in his lap during the ceremony. When the individual matured, he indicated his intention of fulfilling the vow, and underwent the regular novitiate [9, 25].

When fully recovered, candidates were summoned before a full meeting of the society and impressed with the importance of the obligations and duties they were about to assume. "They must look out for the welfare of the pueblo and must follow the ritual of the group. They must have in their hearts the good of all the children in the village" [25].

Following this meeting the individual began a year's novitiate. During this period he attended the monthly meetings of the society and other retreats. On such occasions he underwent intensive training in the ritual of the organization. During the novitiate candidates were not allowed to "leave the village," i.e., be absent overnight, since they were obligated to perform daily duties. These included the recitation of prayers each morning and the offering of meal. They were also responsible for the frequent production of prayer plumes and their deposit at village shrines and, on occasion, at the shrines of other villages as well. Male novices hunted frequently in order to obtain buckskin [25]. It is doubtful whether female novices underwent the stringent training imposed upon males, since female participation in the religious activities was restricted.

Final initiation took place at the end of the year, at the time of the "water immersion." Data concerning these activities are lacking; presumably they followed the general pattern of the Winter Society. Female novices and the other women members prepared food for the society membership. They were not allowed to use utensils for stirring the food, but used their hands. During the terminal ceremony in the kiva, they made the meal trail and led in the kachina. If there were several initiates, several trails were made [25].

Following the "water immersion" ceremony, both male and female members assumed full status in the society.

Pledging and Initiation Ceremonies of the Winter Society

The acquisition of members by the Winter Society, as well as their pledging and initiation, followed the general patterns described for the Summer Society. Children were dedicated by parents at the time of their birth for the same reasons cited for the Summer Society. The desires of the parents appear to have been binding, since failures to honor the commitment were remarkably few. During the period of fieldwork, only one case of defection was known, that of [21]. Recruitment through vow during illness was common. Again, the selection of the society was determined by vision or dream [9, 14, 21, 22, 25]. "They know which society to join. They would dream it, or they would concentrate very deeply, and it would come to them which society to join" [22].

Members were also secured through trespass or trapping. Trespass or trapping occurred during the performance of the Ka-ve-Na ceremony [22] and presumably on other "occasions when the society was in retreat and 'working.'" During the Ka-ve-Na, if a nonmember "inadvertently" crossed the meal line dividing the spectators from the society or entered the room where the Winter Society members were performing, they were considered to have trespassed or to have been trapped, and were accordingly obligated to join [9, 14, 21].

The minimum prerequisites for membership (moiety affiliation, and in the case of males, initiation into the kachina organization) were the same in the Winter groups as for the Summer. However, according to one informant [21], the selection of Winter women was limited to those who had never given birth to a female child. This is consistent with the idea that the Winter Moiety and the Winter Society exemplified the male component in nature. The same informant stated that no such restriction regarding the bearing of male children was placed upon Summer women.

Like that of the Summer Society, the pledging ceremony of the Winter Society was a curing rite. Whenever possible the patient was brought to the headquarters of the society where an altar was erected prior to his arrival. Male members wore only breech clouts; they had eagle down in their hair. Females wore mantas and were barefoot. The room was without furniture.

The winter cacique sat in the altar with his fetish by his side. When the patient arrived he was seated within a circle outlined in cornmeal on a white manta. He faced the cacique and wore only a breech clout. The cacique took two wing feathers of an eagle, stood up, and presented their tips to the patient. The patient grasped the tips of the feathers and was "lifted up." If too weak to stand, he was assisted or held up by members of the society.

Next, one of the "elders" ("fathers of the kachina") and a female member came forward. The "elder" removed the bowl of sacred water from the altar. The woman dipped some of the liquid from the container with a gourd ladle and presented it to the "elder." He in turn took a mouthful, aspersed the patient, and gave him a religious or ceremonial name. All members then duplicated this performance, the men first, then the women. This terminated the pledging ceremony. The Winter cacique addressed the patient saying, "It is completed. You are now a member of the ceremonial people. All you lack is the final ceremony." Following this the patient went home and, upon recovery, began a year's novitiate [25].

(It should be noted that the Summer and Winter societies engaged in general medical practice in the same manner as the Bear societies, and that such treatments did not necessarily obligate the patient to join the society. House calls were made by various members; specifically, the Winter Society members were mentioned in connection with curing stomach disorders, asthma, rheumatism, and illness resulting from witchcraft. They also set broken bones. Cures were effected by massage and the use of medicinal herbs [21]. They were also noted for their treatment of burns. In such instances, they utilized a white clay called "winter clay" [9]. WWH)

During the novitiate, candidates, including those dedicated and trapped as well as those vowed during illness, were under the same restrictions, engaged in the same general activities, and engaged in the same course of intensive study as previously indicated for Summer candidates [25].

At the end of the novitiate, the final rites of initiation were held. These took place preliminary to and in conjunction with the general moiety ceremony, the "water immersion" rite, and the induction of boys into the Winter kachina cult [22, 25].

The Winter Society went into retreat at their headquarters twelve days prior to the final "water immersion" rites. An altar was erected, and in the center of the room was placed a basket of prayer plumes and a "medicine" bowl. Candidates for initiation were then brought in. Frequently, a man and woman were initiated at the same time. Males were dressed in white buckskin, and their bodies painted with white clay. Bells were attached to the ends of their breechclouts, the upper portion of which carried an embroidered serpent design. Females were also painted with white clay; they wore blue mantas and white buckskin boots. The tail feather of an eagle was tied to the hair of the novices. "If the person has joined the society in good faith, the feather will remain tied; if not, it will fall off" [25].

An "elder" took a clay pipe filled with "mountain tobacco," lit it, and blew smoke into the medicine bowl. This act was duplicated by the Winter cacique, followed by the rest of the membership. "This should cause a fog or cloud to form. It usually brings an actual fog or rain outside" [25]. After this two members sang, accompanying themselves with "kiva bells." Then the initiates danced. Following this, food was served, and chanting and dancing continued until about three o'clock in the morning. At this time two men were designated to take baskets containing meal and prayer plumes and deposit them at the "south mountain shrine." This shrine was located opposite Black Mesa on the west side of the Rio Grande.

When the men left for the shrine, the initiates were taken to separate inner rooms, where they remained until the terminal rites of the twelfth night. Each occupied a corner of the room, and was supervised and visited periodically by the sponsors. A rectangular, earth-filled pottery vessel was placed before each candidate. In these were planted corn and wheat. "If the candidates had joined the society in good faith, the plants ripened by the twelfth night" [25]. These vessels were brought to the kiva at the time of the "water immersion" ceremony and exhibited. The cacique gave a grain of corn or kernel of wheat to each family. These were planted with other seeds to insure good crops, or used to "anoint" bodies [25]. During the retreat, initiates remained continent, and their diet was restricted. According to one informant [25], they were fed only native food, cornmeal, and wild game. According to another [21], their food consisted of a single blue cornmeal wafer each day. The first day this was approximately the size of a silver dollar. As time passed it was increased in size, until by the evening of the twelfth night, the wafer was as large as a hand. On the final night candidates were allowed to leave their corners and were given a roasted ear of corn to eat, in order to strengthen them for their roles in the kiva [21].

During the course of the retreat, the novices underwent intensive instruction, and females assisted in the preparation of food. As in the case of the Summer Society, they were prohibited from using utensils, and stirred food with their fingers [25].

On the evening of the twelfth night, just prior to the beginning of the "water immersion" ceremony, the male Winter novices were conducted to the unlighted kiva by their sponsors. They were naked, but painted with white clay. They stood before the altar while prayers were said. Following this, they returned to the society headquarters and attired themselves in a breechclout, kilt, and belt. Presumably, female candidates did not undergo this rite. According to one informant [25], however, all had previously undergone the whipping ceremony of the kachina initiates. When the males were dressed, each was given a bowl of sacred water and, accompanied by the society membership, returned to the kiva. The bowls were placed on the altar, both male and female candidates took their places with the rest of the society, and the "water immersion" was ready to begin.

During the ceremony, male initiates assisted the Winter cacique in visualizing the coming of the kachina—replacing the clowns who normally performed this function. Females drew the cornmeal trail. If there were several initiates, several meal trails were drawn [21, 25]. The day following the ceremony, gift exchanges took place between sponsors and novices [25].

Jeançon (1931b: 41–43) also described a Winter Society induction. (Jeançon, in his manuscript, used the terms clan, moiety, and society interchangeably, and it is sometimes difficult to distinguish what he meant in terms of modern usage. This account, however, was vouched for by an informant [24] who was a Winter Society member. WWH) This account is somewhat more comprehensive than the one above. According to Jeançon:

When the proper time for initiating children into their proper groups arrives, unless the child has been pledged at birth or after a sickness, there is a council of the father, mother, and close relatives. Here the matter is talked over and a gift—usually of meal, other foods, turkey feathers, tobacco, and perhaps buckskin and calico—prepared and sent to the head of the society in which it is desired to enter the child. One of the child's uncles takes the gift, in a basket, over to where the head of the society lives, early in the morning before the sun is up. The latter then calls the members of the society together and they talk it over. If all is satisfactory and agreed to, the same evening the head man takes the answer back to the parents and within four days, the candidate enters upon the initiation ceremonies for adoption. A boy has a chief male sponsor and a girl, a chief female sponsor. There may be others who act more or less as honorary sponsors, but these are not important. Tradition says that in the past there had to be four sponsors, two male and two female, perhaps the honorary sponsors of today are remnants of that practice.

In the case of a boy, he remains in his own home, in seclusion, for twelve days. [Note that later Jeançon states that the last four days of the retreat were in the kiva. WWH] During this period he is taught the secrets of the clan [sic, WWH] or society, such folklore as is still known to them and many other matters pertinent to his life and actions. Corn is sprouted during this period in the house of the initiate and made into medicine which is the only drink of the candidate during his retreat. He partakes only of native foods and no salt. During this period the boy sits nude in a corner walled off with a line of ashes which is a barrier to keep off evil from attacking him. The chief of his sponsors smokes all the time. The boy must sit with his knees drawn up and is not permitted to extend his legs during instruction. This position becomes terribly tiresome and often so painful that the candidate weeps. He is permitted to rise and stretch after a tale of instruction has been finished, and a short interval elapses before new instructions are begun. Functions of the bowel and bladder must wait until nightfall and only during the dark hours is he permitted to leave the room and relieve himself. At such times he is always accompanied by his attendants, and is not permitted to see or speak to a woman. Should he do this all the benefit so far secured would be nullified. His mother or godmother may visit him during his retreat to bring his food and talk to him when he is not occupied with his instructors. They usually do this early in the morning.

On the ninth day all the boys are gathered, before the sun is up, and they go into the kiva. From now on all ceremonies are conducted in that place. What these consist of the writer has not been able to learn. It is known, however, that the candidate usually receives a new name or perhaps his old name is given to him a second time. He is also flogged with yucca whips by impersonators of the Kachinas. During the four days of the culmination of the ceremony, he and his attendants must fast from sun up to sun down and when they do eat, at night, they indulge in a very limited amount of native food and drink, again no salt is used.

Plate 2 shows the final ending of the ceremony. The anthropomorphic figurine seated on a mound of green leaves and sprouts represents the Earth-mother and Sun-father; this hermorphoditic [sic, WWH] figurine is one of the most sacred fetishes in the village and belongs to the society or clean [sic, WWH] carrying on the ceremony. Most of them are very old and have been handed down for many generations. A mound of earth with corn sprouts growing in it and with the sun rising out of it is another representation of the Earth-mother and the Sun-father. The sun is made of buckskin—stretched over a hoop of willow withe. Each society has its own flute which is in the nature of a palladium or safeguarder of the songs. (As these flutes are not bored scientifically as to distance between holes, no set melody can be played on them.) In front of the anthropomorphic figurine is a "corn-mother" trimmed with blue parrot feathers; from this a line of meal extends to where a blue feather is lying. A miniature green field has a picture of lightning extending from it along the floor. The picture is painted with corn pollen and meal as is the snake between the black and blue birds. The basket of turkey feathers is a gift to be given to the boy's sponsors later at the finish of the ceremony. No sand paintings are made or used at Santa Clara.

At this time in the initiation the boy is no longer nude but wears a breech clout. In his right hand he carries a lightning stick and in his left, two eagle wing tips. At the finish of all the initiation, he is presented with a fetish or tiponi made of an ear of corn wrapped with twine and trimmed with feathers. This is given to him by one of the girls [a Winter woman (24), WWH]. It is to be his own special medicine and to be kept as long as he lives.

Induction Ceremony of the Summer Cacique

Information concerning the procedures accompanying the installation of a Summer cacique is meager. Presumably they followed the general pattern described in greater detail in the following section regarding the Winter cacique. Inductions took place at the time of the summer solstice. It was known that the Summer Society went into retreat and "worked" for twelve days prior to the terminal rite, but details of the ritual were unobtainable. On the final evening a kachina ceremony was held, and the masked impersonators "greeted" the inductee and "wished him well" [22, 25]. On this occasion Summer Society members replaced the k'osa and "called" the kachinas. [This discussion was moved ahead of the comparable account describing the induction of the Winter cacique to conform to the Summer-Winter pattern followed in this portion of the chapter. CHL]

Induction Ceremony of the Winter Cacique

The induction of a Winter cacique always took place at or about the time of the winter solstice. According to contemporary accounts, this was preceded by a twelve-day retreat, during which the Winter Society "worked." It terminated with a kachina performance, at which the kachina greeted the new cacique and "wished him well." Members of the Winter Society replaced the k'osa and "called" or visualized the coming of the kachina [22]. Parsons (1929: 114) stated that when Severo Naranjo was inducted as Winter cacique, the Winter Society was in retreat for twelve days in the Winter kiva; that a kachina ceremony was presumably held; and that everyone feasted.

Jeançon (1904–30) stated:

> Not much information could be obtained as to the ceremonies attending upon the induction into office of either summer or winter priest. When the time of mourning has elapsed, and the newly elected winter priest has been properly ratified, the men [presumably the Winter Society, WWH] make a four day retreat [probably 12 days, WWH] in the winter kiva. Fasting and continence are required during this time. Much smoking is done and magic medicine prepared. Prayers and incantations

are frequent, all for the purpose of creating a "good heart" in the new priest, and that his powers may not wane or be corrupted by misuse.

During the preliminary proceedings of the four-day retreat, the candidate must demonstrate his powers in several ways amongst which he must handle fire and hot ashes [used so-called Winter clay to protect him? WWH] without burning himself to show that he is really an "ice" man, and, therefore, invulnerable to fire. He submits to ceremonial flogging with yucca switches, but this is only a form and the blows are not severe.—He must also spend four days and nights of the retreat in a room without fires; being an "ice" man, cold cannot injure him.

While there are certain fetishes and other objects that were used by his predecessor, and which have come down to him, yet the new man must bring most of these things himself, as he does not inherit with the office anything other than the communal ceremonial objects belonging to the party he represents. If the former priest has left any so-called "tobacco," it automatically goes to his successor and is supposed to have special power and efficacy. The remnant of tobacco of his predecessor is better for all uses. The katchina chief presents him with old and new tobacco. This is a certificate of his election.

When the proper time arrives in the ceremonies of inducting a new Winter priest, the people have gathered in the kiva to witness it. The Katchina Chief, O-kuwa-tse-tung [oxuwa c'ethurg, "yellow-spotted body cloud person" (55), WWH] advances toward the priest who is nude excepting a brown apron in front and back and who is standing before a painting of meal [altar (55), WWH] representing clouds and red lightning. The designs on the floor are made of white cornmeal, also red and blue. The bear fetish is white. He has painted on his legs, arms, and breasts lightning designs in black [painted with naposhune (55), WWH].

As the katchina advances, the candidate stands and waits for him to approach. He holds in his left hand two turkey feathers, which he will trade for the corn-mother represented by an ear of blue corn carried in the right hand of the katchina. After this exchange, the katchina delivers to him a small double-necked jar, commonly called a "loving jar" or a "wedding jar." This contains water from the four sacred lakes and is accompanied by a piece of yucca. Then a child appears carrying a rainbow of tule painted in symbolic colors, red, green, yellow, blue, purple [Jeançon doubted whether purple should be included. WWH]. This child represents the winter clouds and winter magic in its highest form, and will appear only to the winter priest if his heart is "good." If his heart is good, the child comes to him as a messenger to signify that his people will increase at the same time that the katchina comes to him. While a human being represents this "power" at the time, yet it is only the presentation of one of the great things in their mystical world by human means. From all information obtainable by the writer this ceremony concludes the induction of the winter priest.

CALENDRICAL CEREMONIES OF THE SUMMER AND WINTER MOIETIES

Besides the intermittent ceremonies of initiation and induction, there were calendrically scheduled rites associated with each moiety. Some, on occasion, formed parts of larger integrated religious efforts; at other times they occurred as separate entities. The complexity of this series of rites varied. The one-day monthly retreats were relatively simple; others, however, were complex, extensive, and of considerable duration.

Those associated with the Summer Moiety included kachina performances, the "Edge of Spring" ceremony, ceremonial shinny, solstice ceremonies, marginal participation in the Sori wokan ["large treatment," curing ceremony, CHL] and salt-gathering expeditions, the opening of the irrigation ditch in the spring, monthly

retreats by the Summer Society, and the performance of "big" and "little" outside dances.

Those associated with the Winter Moiety were kachina performances, the Ka-ve-Na, probably former participation in the Sori wokan and salt-gathering expeditions, monthly retreats by the Winter Society, and the performance of "big" and "little" outside dances.

The Good Friday "Hidden Dance" (ivaxi) of the Summer Kachina

Hidden dances, directed by the Summer Society, were held by the Summer kachina in late January or early February, on the night of Good Friday, and in late September or early October. In recent years the January-February enactments have been sporadic.

Similar performances occurred in adjacent villages. According to one informant [43], they were still being held at San Ildefonso and San Juan. The San Juan rites have been reported on by Laski (1958). While her interpretations are suspect, the work contains a good description of the ceremony. According to my informant, kachina dances at Nambé lapsed sometime between 1914 and 1924. He stated, "Nambé once had a lot of 'wisdom.' According to the story, they decided to try it against one another. They did, and one would die. They killed off half the pueblo and stopped." [This reference to Nambé would appear to be to the series of witchcraft cases and trials that plagued that pueblo in the mid-nineteenth century. These cases were noted by Bandelier in his journal entries and were reported on by him in an article (1889) written in German. (See Lange, Riley, and Lange 1975: 385n253.) It is interesting that Hill's informant should have referred to these Nambé incidents in this conversation dealing with seemingly rather different subject matter; obviously, to the informant, there was relevance in the "wisdom," "power," or "magic" employed in both. CHL]

According to one informant [50], a man in his seventies, the Good Friday rites were held every year as long as he could remember, except in 1952. On that occasion the illness of the cacique prevented their performance. In 1948 the dance was held on the Wednesday before Good Friday, two days before that of the Winter Moiety. Appearances of the kachina in September and October have been intermittent in recent years, and presumably only in conjunction with the po'ku, or moiety initiation. Formerly, unless the rite coincided with a moiety initiation, it was held not in the kiva but in the mountains. The last recorded performance of a "hidden dance" in the hills, however, was between 1920 and 1925 [50, 72]. Essentially the same patterns were followed in all "hidden dances," although there were seasonal variations in detail. These and other discrepancies are noted in the text.

The overall purpose of the kachina ceremonies was to promote the general well-being of the village, and to insure the continuity of nature. They contained special fertility features applicable to humans, livestock, and crops. There were also rain-bringing rituals and harvest and thanksgiving festivals [29, 50, 52].

Any member of the kachina organization might initiate a hidden dance. The request to hold the dance was made to the leader of the "fathers of the kachina." The petition was accompanied by a gift of sacred meal, tobacco, and feathers. While a member had to make the request before the rite could be held, it was equally true that once made, it could not be refused.

When the petition was received, the leader of the "fathers of the kachina" instructed either his right or left arm to notify all those "who are made men" (di se ne? pa? niŋ) to report to his house that evening. When the time arrived, all assembled, and those who wished to participate in the dance were told to arise early the next morning, bathe in the creek, and then go to their "mother," the Summer cacique. Members of the Summer Society attended this gathering.

Early the next morning, the Summer cacique and Summer Society members erected a small altar in the cacique's house. The central portion of the altar consisted of a corn "mother" (zhia), an ear of corn surrounded by feathers held in place at the base by a twine wrapping. [These objects would appear to have been similar to a mili, the decorated ear of corn pictured, in color, by M.C. Stevenson (1904: Pl. CI). CHL] In front of the altar was an empty basket; beside it were the feathers given by the petitioner. Close to the first basket was another containing sacred meal. Part of the meal was that presented by the person requesting the "hidden dance." To this had been added meal from other sources.

The petitioner arrived before the other kachina members; they appeared after they had bathed. Each carried a bundle of feathers. They entered, stripped to their breechclouts, went to the altar, breathed upon their bundles, and placed them in the empty basket before the altar.

When all were present and had taken their places, the members of the Summer Society, including the "fathers of the kachina," began working (di vi t'o?o) under the supervision of the Summer cacique. The work consisted of preparing prayer plumes to be deposited at various shrines. Four cornhusks were spread on the floor. The bundles of feathers in the basket were untied and separated, and feathers were selected and placed on the cornhusks. Next the petitioner's bundle was untied, and feathers were chosen to be incorporated in each prayer plume.

The cacique then said a prayer, asking for "good living, rain, and better crops." The wrapping and tying of the prayer plumes began. This was accompanied by four songs referring to the preparation of the plumes; two of these were called "We are preparing feathers," and "We are offering feathers." At the conclusion of the songs, all present breathed on the completed plumes, "threw their breath ('power') on them" [50]. Following this the cacique selected two men to deposit plumes at the north and west shrines of the village. Those chosen were always men who would impersonate kachina in the coming dance. These came forward and the cacique handed each a plume, which they wrapped. Next a Summer Society member was selected to make the deposit at the south shrine, and a "father of the kachina," at the shrine in the east. (Note that the ceremonial circuit is counterclockwise. WWH) These men then received and wrapped their plumes. On some occasions at least two other principals were assigned to make deposits at shrines associated with zenith and nadir [50].

Finally a terrace-sided bowl of sacred water (wo'po) was passed counterclockwise to all present. Those who were to participate in any ritual capacity in the coming dance drank from the bowl. Those who did not wish to take part passed the bowl to the next man. Men who partook obligated themselves to observe the ritual tabus, and were so informed by the cacique. These obligations included abstaining from certain foods, including onions, garlic, cinnamon, and pepper, and remaining continent.

No active participant was allowed to touch a woman or to approach a woman, for fear her breath might touch the individual. The single exception was the leader of the "father of the kachina," who might receive food from women, and whose ritual efficacy was not believed to be impaired by their breath. If a kachina came close to a woman or felt her breathe, his mask would stick to his head. A long time ago a Santa Clara man violated this rule, and his mask stuck. They worked for four days trying to remove the mask. Finally he was carried to a spring about a mile west of the village, where they again attempted to remove the mask. It was thought that the kachina took him with them, since he never returned to the village [9, 19].

Following this, the cacique admonished the group and emphasized the seriousness of the undertaking. He then dismissed them. Those chosen to make the deposits left for the shrines. The remainder of the Kachina Society returned to their homes, prepared to observe the imposed restrictions.

That evening after dark, all those who had drunk the sacred water went to the kachina house. This included all participants—not only the kachina, but also members of the Summer Society, including the Summer cacique. The kachina house was located close to the kiva; it consisted of a large room ventilated by one very small window. Members brought with them one or more sheepskins or blankets, depending upon the season.

When novices were to be initiated, this rite was performed first. If no initiation was held, those who were to impersonate rehearsed their parts. The Summer cacique and the leader of the "fathers of the kachina" selected the individuals who would play the various characters. At the conclusion of the rehearsal, the masks were removed and placed at the back of the room. Members were then free to sleep. Those who had not been given parts went to their homes. The remainder of the group rolled up in their blankets and/or sheepskins and slept on the floor. They were told "to go to bed" (de po tsandi, literally, "to close all openings"). This was accomplished by rotating a yucca whip in front of the fireplace, ventilator, and door, which act completed the first day of the retreat.

If necessary, kachina members might visit their homes momentarily, if they observed all restrictions. Calls of nature might be answered, but a member always accompanied a person who left the kachina house.

Early the next morning, all those who would wear masks in the ensuing ceremony left, going some distance from the village and purifying themselves by vomiting. This was said to be optional; however, most members conformed. Vomiting was induced by drinking quantities of warm water or some other emetic, or by running a feather down the throat.

Shortly after their return, the Summer Society woman (who ushered the kachina into the kiva along the trail of cornmeal) knocked at the door. She brought food and water. She might be accompanied by other women who desired to contribute food to the dancers. These women were subject to the same restrictions and tabus as the kachina [25, 45]. The contributions were received by a kachina member who had not drunk of the sacred water, or by the leader of the "fathers of the kachina." The latter was accorded this special privilege because the breath of a woman did not endanger him. "If enough people were interested, the kachina were well fed" [50].

When the meal was finished, the Summer cacique asked for volunteers to gather yucca whips and ties, and Douglas spruce for the collars of the dancers. "Usually about four persons volunteered." These went first to the home of the Summer cacique and obtained feathers and deer fat. Spruce was gathered in the mountains west of the pueblo, yucca southwest of the pueblo. When limbs were cut from the trees or leaves from the yucca, deer fat was rubbed on the resulting scar. Feathers were deposited as offerings in the general vicinity where the material was collected. The spines at the ends of the yucca leaves were removed by burning at the time they were picked. "There is a belief that when the first kachina leader came to visit Santa Clara he, in anger, broke off the spiny ends of the yucca whips on the bodies of the people. That is why they are burnt off today" [9, 18].

On the return trip, all kept a sharp lookout for game. Hunting was prohibited until their mission was completed, but after that it was mandatory. The party could not enter the village until nightfall; if they returned early, they remained hidden on the hill behind the town. They often slept there until dark, one of their number acting as guard or watchman.

On arrival they placed their burdens along the west wall of the kachina house and entered. If there was food in sufficient quantity, they ate; if not, they went to their homes and obtained food. Only novices were forbidden to go to their homes.

When candidates were being inducted into the organization, they engaged in a series of ceremonial hunts each day for four days prior to the kiva ritual, and these presumably replaced the hunting activities described above. Rabbits were the principal game, although deer, pack rats, and quail were also killed. This activity was under the supervision of the war captain (p'ing xangzho, formerly) assisted by men of the Summer Moiety who were not otherwise occupied.

Beginning in the east, the group hunted in a different direction each day. When the hunting area was reached, the men divided into two groups, each led by a man armed with bow and arrow. Next the war captain lighted a "smoke fire." From this starting point, the leaders ran in wide semicircles, followed at intervals by other members of their party. Eventually a circle was formed, and the men forming its circumference converged toward the center, killing the game caught in the surround. In recent times the use of horses and modern weapons has been optional, except in the case of the leaders, who always proceeded on foot and carried traditional weapons. When firearms became the prevailing weapon, one semicircle was omitted, to prevent endangering the lives of the hunters. Several surrounds (probably four) were accomplished each day. The leaders "crossed over" upon the completion of each circle, i.e., reversed the positions of their parties on the semicircles of the surround.

The hunt was completed in the late afternoon. The game was collected and given to the war captain who, upon arrival at the pueblo, presented it to the Summer Society. The women of this group dressed, prepared, and cooked the meat, which was fed to the novices by members of the organization [9].

All gathered again in the kachina house for evening practice. Those who remained there during the day had scraped the old paint from the masks, and the masks were worn in that condition during the rehearsal. Sleeping in the kachina house during the day was forbidden. This and other violations were punished by the leader of the "fathers of the kachina," who whipped any offenders.

The general tempo of activity increased on the third day. Again all arose early in the morning. The man who was to impersonate "the hunter" (zheng sendo) and two or three companions left for a hunt. They were often joined by outsiders who knew of the coming ceremony and volunteered to assist. Any kind of game was killed—deer, rabbit, and pack rat. If the bag was more than was necessary for the bundles of "the hunter," the surplus was given to the kachina. Like the party of the previous day, the hunters were not permitted to return until nightfall; some slept while others watched. "When it begins to get dark, they come down lower. When it is dark, they enter the village." The products of the hunt were placed outside, along the west wall of the house.

Those who remained spent their time repainting the masks. As on the previous evening, a rehearsal was held. After the rehearsal, "the hunter" instructed the kachina to carry in the bundles of yucca and spruce, and the game. These were placed in the center of the room. The Summer cacique rolled a cigarette, lit it, reversed the end in his mouth, and blew smoke over the pile. He next took meal from a bowl at his side and sprinkled it over the bundles, "fed them." Finally he stood over them and recited a prayer. When this was completed, the cacique described the coming ceremony and spoke to the group of its import. "Then he spoke to the bundles and to their kind in the mountains. He spoke to them as if they were people."

The cacique then returned to his seat, and the leader of the "fathers of the kachina" and those kachina members who would wear masks stepped forward. Each in turn sprinkled meal on the bundles. As they "fed" them, they took bits of Douglas spruce, chewed some of it, and rubbed it on their bodies. This was repeated by all those present who were not actively engaged in the ceremony, i.e., not under ceremonial restrictions. They did not strip as did the active participants; they wore no shoes, but were otherwise clothed.

When they had reseated themselves, those who had gathered the materials came forward and untied the bundles. "The hunter" arranged the yucca and spruce for distribution. When he finished, he was approached by the leader of the kachina. The leader bent forward, and "the hunter" selected the two best whips, struck the leader once with each, and handed them to him. Then half the kachina "at the edge" came forward, and the above was repeated with each in turn. These were followed by the "chorus" and "the dancers," who were given spruce branches. They, however, were not whipped. Finally the remainder of the kachina "at the edge" were whipped and received whips. Materials were distributed according to the order in which the impersonators would enter the kiva: the leaders, the "kachina at the edge," the men's chorus, and the dancers (women impersonated by men; "not all nuxi have men impersonating women") [9].

After the distribution, those who were not participants left the house. The remainder came forward, selected additional yucca leaves for tying, and began to construct the

spruce collars. Upon completion they were tied in pairs and hung over a pole in a small chamber adjacent to the main room. Bundles of food to be carried by the kachina, and any remaining spruce boughs, were likewise stored. This terminated the activity of the third day, and all went to sleep.

During the fourth day the war captain and his assistants were busy preparing the kiva. The floor was swept, lights were prepared, wood was brought, and if necessary a fire was built.

Activity at the house of the kachina commenced about two o'clock in the afternoon. The collars were taken down and given a final checking. The various parts of the costumes were examined and laid out. Nonparticipants brought in native foods— melons, corn, etc.—which were arranged in bundles, tied, and placed beside the costumes. By dusk these preparations were completed, and activity ceased until about nine o'clock, painting of the kachina began. This occupied from an hour to an hour and a half. By ten-thirty or eleven [9] (nine-thirty [13, 18]), the participants were ready to costume themselves; word was circulated through the village by the nonparticipating kachina members and the war captain and his assistants that it was time to go to the kiva. Announcements were made at all homes in which lights burned [13, 18]. Formerly the invitation was accorded the whole village, but now only to Summer Moiety members [9, 69]. (According to others, however, Winter Moiety members attended the "hidden dance" in the spring of 1941.) Those of the opposite moiety went to the homes of relatives and friends of the Summer group to await the announcement.

All adults were aware of the coming ceremony, and those who wished to attend were prepared. Blankets were worn over regular attire. Moccasins replaced shoes. "Until quite recently, those in tailored shoes were not permitted to enter the kiva. Even now only a few wear shoes to the ceremony" [13, 18].

Those who wished to obtain choice positions from which to view the ceremony gravitated to houses near the kiva. Those who went to the kiva early were turned back by the guards stationed there earlier in the evening. They were told to wait in nearby houses until called. Great care was taken to give an impression of normality. Adults went from place to place singly, to avoid arousing the curiosity of strangers or creating an atmosphere of the unusual. Even the kiva guards kept in the shadows and made themselves as inconspicuous as possible [13, 18, 52].

When the announcement was made, all rushed to the foot of the outside kiva ladder. Here each one was examined and identified by a guard, to insure that no unwanted individual gained access to the ceremony. If Indians from other villages wished to attend, they had to be sponsored by a Santa Clara member, who confirmed their adherence to conservative Pueblo faith [13, 18].

When passed by the outer guards, individuals climbed the ladder, walked across the roof to the entrance ladder, and descended to the kiva. Here they were examined and again identified, before they were turned over to ushers, who seated them [13, 18].

Seating was in accordance with ceremonial rank. Initiates of both kachina societies were permitted to sit and range just below the entrance in the desirable eastern section. Summer members joined this group in order to be readily available for any assistance that might be demanded of them. The Winter members also sat in this eastern section. They were not obligated to assist, but might voluntarily do so. All women, children, and the uninitiated were seated huddled together in the northwest corner.

At approximately ten-thirty, kachina members arose and formed a curtain of blankets masking the ladder, entrance, and terraced "wood box" (sipapu) (Figure 29). From behind the curtain, the hooting of owls was heard [9, 50], as well as the sounds of sheep and doves [13, 18]. Gradually the blankets were removed to reveal two clowns sitting on the benches of the wood box.

After sitting for some time, they slowly descended to the floor, one step at a time. They proceeded along the edge of the audience, blinked, peered into faces, and began a dialogue [13, 18].

The clowns always address each other

as younger and elder brother. They pantomime as well as converse. They may imitate a boy or girl making love; a priest saying mass; they may bring a newspaper, one will read in Spanish, and the other interpret in Tewa. The content is always ridiculous. They make fun of each other. One would say, "I saw you with someone the other day. Your wife was looking for you and you were with some other woman." They make fun of the younger girls saying, "You have been going out with some married man." They criticize people who are slovenly or who have done things which are not approved by the pueblo. For example, X was criticized for lewdness and because she had illegitimate children.

The following is a description of the action and a partial transcript of the conversation during the 1941 rite. The clowns (pinini, in that case) wandered about the kiva, stopping from time to time to enact roles which lent emphasis to and augmented the histrionic effect. This preliminary rite was known as "song making" (xapa?). Those who were butts for the performance were believed to benefit supernaturally. No redress was sanctioned, and it was expected that no reference to the personal gibes would be made after the ceremony.

After peering into the faces of the crowd, one clown, showing great surprise, turned to the other and said, "Where have we dropped? What are these things huddled together?" They then proceeded to the west wall, placed their sheepskin-wrapped bundles in front of a seated boy, and said, "Do not watch these." [Most examples of such "contrary" behavior have been associated with the Plains tribes, but there are additional cases from the Pueblos as well. CHL]

They walked on and one selected a young girl, lifted her blanket, and peered at her face. He turned to his companion, and they indulged in the following conversation. "This one has red paint all over her face, elder brother." "The younger people are doing many strange things these days, younger brother." "Why they now even color their noses, lips, and even their toes." "Ho wa xi *zho* [exclamation]! Is that true, elder brother! "Do the women color their vulvas and the men their penises?" "It could be, younger brother [spoken very seriously]."

They began walking back and forth again, conversing. "True, they do strange things now, elder brother." "The people in our pueblo are in great hunger (i.e., have great desire for sexual relations)." "Have you heard of X [naming a man in the audience] and what he has been up to, elder brother?" "No, tell me, younger brother." They stopped, facing each other; one exhibited surprise, and the other, seriousness. "Well, I saw him in the store a few nights ago with a girl, and, older brother, he was attempting to seduce her against the counter and came around like this" (the clown demonstrated, using his companion as a foil). "Is that so, younger brother!" "Why, to see the boy one would never imagine that!" (They resumed their walk, still talking.) "True, you speak then, younger brother." "Our people cannot be surpassed."

"Oh! did I tell you about Y, elder brother?" (again a member of the audience was named). "No, younger brother!" "The other day I heard Y calling and whistling. I was on the roof of my house, so I turned to see who he was calling, as the call was not directed to me. No one was about but my wife. My wife is so old that I could not imagine anyone desiring an affair with her (Y's age was about fifty years, the clown's wife, seventy to seventy-five years), but I looked at Y and then at my wife, and surprisingly enough he was calling her. I made myself known and asked Y what he wanted. I said, 'If you want my wife, you may have her.' He stuttered, 'Oh, nothing,' and left the place greatly embarrassed."

"The old man cacique has been hunting skunks near the river's edge, younger brother." (Sa^n wo *zhi?*, "hunting skunks," was also applied to a person seeking someone to seduce.) When the cacique was mentioned, the audience all turned to look at him where he was seated by the fire. "Is that so, elder brother! Over by the bridge?" "Yes, younger brother, over near Z's."

"Elder brother, I am surprised that an old man would be doing such a thing."

"All these girls (gesturing to include all the girls, but referring specifically to those attending the Santa Fe Indian School) have been having relations with Navajo boys, elder brother." [The Navajo are despised by Santa Claras, and are traditional enemies.] "Now that they have come home, and our young men are in training in the army, the older men in the pueblo are getting their share of intercourse."

"Oh yes, younger brother, the two cousins, A and B, are fighting over a Navajo penis." "Is that so, elder brother!" "Yes; it seems, however, that A won, and now B is brooding over it and has gone to South Carolina. Shortly before she left, I saw her going over to C's house. B, as you know, is C's best friend. C came out to meet her, and they talked for some time in front of the house. I saw them wiping their eyes, and I could hear unmistakable sounds of their weeping. They went inside and I, wondering what the trouble was, went toward the house. As I approached, I heard sobbing and muffled talk." (At this point the clown imitated the weeping to his companion, and the audience burst out laughing.)

"Thinking I might be of some help, I opened the door and entered. Immediately they stopped weeping. What is the trouble, I asked. Oh, nothing, they said. We were playing, and she struck me across the eyes. The other quickly interrupted and said, yes, and she struck me across the eyes too. Then, through their tears, they pretended to be laughing. I looked from one to the other, and realizing the reason for their discomfort, left the house. And now, elder brother (shaking his head), C has gone to South Carolina to forget the Navajo penis!"

Buffoonery of the above type was continued for about an hour. Finally the clowns retrieved their bundles, which they had left in care of the boy. Taking them, they said, "I do not want this." They accused the boy of tampering with them, but gave him an apple for his trouble. They returned to the center of the kiva, sat on the floor, opened the bundles, and began eating. They commented upon the bad table manners of those present. From time to time they teased each other. They ate a small portion, gave food to the children, and returned. As they ate, their conversation gradually became muffled [13, 18].

It was almost midnight when the meal was completed. The clowns arose. One went to the fireplace and returned with a handful of ashes, which he deposited in a pile on the floor to the south of one of the center support posts [over the sipapu? WWH].

One clown said to the other, "Try and see if you can make out anything." The clown addressed took a pinch of the ashes, placed it in the palm of one hand, and slapped it smartly with the other, asking, "Which way, younger brother?" His companion replied, "To the west, elder brother." The first turned toward the west, pivoted, shaded his eyes with his hand, and gazed intently in the opposite direction. After some time, he lowered his hand and said, "Younger brother, everything is tightly enclosed; now you try if you can make out anything." The other clown inquired in which direction to look, was told the east, gazed toward the west, and repeated the previous performance. This routine was gone through four times by each actor.

Subsequent acts were also duplicated; the second clown confirmed the impressions and descriptions of the first, and often added slightly to the description. [Note that during the Summer "water immersion," these dual roles were played by a single pondjo oke, or kachina member, eliminating the duplication. Such introductions were therefore not as protracted as those occurring in the regular "hidden dances." WWH]

On the fifth occasion, the first clown was requested to look toward the northeast. He gazed in the opposite direction, the southwest, and reported, "I see a ripple of waters, through mist and fog, in the middle of the lake, located in unbelievable space. Look, younger brother, see if you can see as much."

The second clown confirmed the observation of the first, saying, "True you speak, older brother; way out in the middle of the lake, they come out one after another through the mist and fog from the ripples in the water" [13, 18].

A slightly variant account of this step was recorded from another informant [50]. According to his version: "Looking to the southwest, the clown reported that he saw faint signs of something moving at 'the place of emergence'" [a lake near the present pueblo of Laguna (13, 18)]. Next he said, "I see thick fog and light arising from the lake"; then, "I see fog swirling out of the middle of the lake"; third, "I see one peeping out"; finally, "They are coming out! They are coming out from all regions of the lake!"

Once the kachina had emerged, the reporters described in a most dramatic manner their progress toward the pueblo. References were made to geographical locations. The general pattern of the oratory was as follows: "They have placed their path made from a cloud and are coming along it"; "they place their path on (citing the name of a geographical region), and there they come again; they bring melons, wheat, pumpkins, and other foods"; (the informant [50] said that in the last ceremony he witnessed, a bottle of whiskey was added to the list of foodstuffs). "One ("the hunter," *zheng sendo*) is heavily loaded and is lagging behind." (When members of the clown society described the emergence, they joked about the actions and activities of "the hunter." When this rite was performed by the "leader of the fathers of the kachina," or a member of the Summer Society, such levity did not occur [13].) At every stop a description of the location was given [50].

The impression created by the clowns of the progress of the kachina was one of terrific confusion and commotion. They were described as sweeping everything before them, uprooting trees, and causing floods as they passed through bodies of water. "Nothing can stop them" [52].

Each geographical point named was nearer to the pueblo. The informant [50] did not remember the more distant locations (many place names, as well as the language, were archaic [13, 18]; stations near Santa Clara were:

"Head Waters"—p'o twiwi
"Pack Rat Excrement Wet"—xwang sa p'o
"Canoe to Cut Place of"—ko fe ca i we
"Warm High Bank Place of"—su wa kong ge

"Wide Cattail (leaves) Growing Place of"—awa fa sa kimu
"Oak Root Water"—kwe^n pu p'o
"Lake Small Place of"—p'o kwiŋ ege
"Earth Black Enclosure"—naŋ feŋ buge
(some kind of tree)—te *zhe*re
"Pumpkin Hollow (depression)"—pobege
"Water Muddy Corner"—p'o ci be? [50]

The above all referred to lakes or supposed locations of lakes; the remaining were shrines located near or in the pueblo.

"Wild Rose Growing Near Water"—xa p'o ge? ka' po ge
("the hunter" finally overtook the rest of the kachina at this point)
"Fetish Home of"—xa *zhe* fa *zhi*we
"The First Entrance (i.e., to village)"—p'o
   aŋ xwa wige
"The First Entrance to Middle Plaza"—p'o aŋ bu piŋge
"Kiva Ladder Foot"—te *she*?e hu?ge
"Top of Kiva"—te xwa ge [50]

Finally a stamping of feet was heard on the roof; piñon nuts and the seeds of various agricultural products showered down from the roof onto the floor; and the cry peculiar to the kachina was heard. Women spread shawls to catch the seed. Women, children, and the uninitiated took cornmeal, brought it to their mouths, and tossed it with a prayer in the direction from which the kachina would come. "They said to the kachina, be brave!" The clowns hurriedly secured the sheep or goatskins which had covered their bundles, and tied them around their bodies. These skins extended from under the arms to the knees, and protected the clowns from the whips. They said, "Someone is coming, get ready!" They told the kachina to be brave.

Meanwhile the kachina members screened off the ladder and entrance with blankets, and the Summer woman seated herself on the right side of the bench. The Summer cacique came forward and ordered all mothers to cover their children with blankets. The clowns repeated these instructions. "They are on the housetop, cover your children, for our old men are enraged at children, cover them well" [42]. All children were supposed to remain covered while the kachina were in the kiva. However, mothers permitted them to peer out occasionally, being careful lest they be caught by the impersonators, clowns, or cacique. Theoretically women were not allowed to uncover their heads during a kachina ceremony until they had had a child. "In the old days, the kachina would throw an ear of corn at them if they saw them uncovered" [42].

When all was in readiness, the clowns said, "Come warm yourselves, our old men." The blankets were gradually lowered and the kachina revealed.

The Summer woman, carrying a basket of meal, approached the group from the north. She began making a trail of cornmeal and "led" the impersonators to their places along the south wall. They appeared in the following order: the leader of the kachina; the kachina proper; at-the-edge cloud persons (oxuwa kiŋge), "edge" referring to the edge of spring [18]; the chorus, "young men cloud persons" (oxuwa e?nuŋ); "young women cloud persons" (oxuwa a?nuŋ). These last were men impersonating the women who would perform the basket dance. The names above refer not to individual characters, but to groups occupying certain positions and performing certain duties. At the 1941 rite, there were the leader, six kachina proper, six in the chorus, and four basket dancers [13, 18].

As the kachina entered, they created a tumult. "They give their cry. It makes you feel queer" [18]. The typical cry of the kachina was a shrill sound. This was produced by a bone or cane whistle. Some also emitted a low rasping or grinding sound and imitated the growl of a bear. A drum was beaten to add to the confusion.

The kachina shuffled in and across the center of the kiva. Occasionally they stopped and peered at the audience. At such times mothers covered their children's eyes so that they would not look upon the kachina. When they reached the south wall, the chorus formed a line, with the "women"

Figure 30. Man dressed as woman—part of the chorus in Easter Kachina Dance of the Summer Moiety. These also appeared in the Basket Dance held in the kiva in 1941.

in front (Figure 30). Some of the kachina proper kept time with their feet, others ran back and forth giving their shrill cry.

The clowns stood near the center of the room. As each kachina passed, they relieved him of the food he carried and piled it beside one of the posts. When all were in place, the clowns disappeared behind a blanket screen and emerged carrying a deer (1941). They were followed by the shuffling and dejected figure of "the hunter," heavily laden with food. Around his waist were tied rabbits, ducks, and fish. "The hunter" was unloaded by the clowns and other volunteers, and the food was stacked by a post. "This produce was considered sacred and highly valued because it was brought by the gods" [13, 18].

During the "water immersion" ceremony, the Summer Society members, replacing the clowns, collected the produce and stacked it. The amount on such occasions was considerable, since this dance was held in September when the crops were maturing.

The clowns then mingled with the kachina. They made fun of the impersonators, saying such things as, "What is this little thing doing here?" When they made these derogatory remarks, the dancers lashed them with the yucca whips. They in turn cursed their attackers, often in English and Spanish, and received further whippings. They also questioned the kachina, asking what kind of place they had come from, if the snow was deep there, etc.

Finally all reached their assigned locations, and the dance (oxuwa *sha*re, "kachina dance") was begun. The chorus accompanied it in high-pitched, feminine or falsetto voices. The troop performing the basket dance kept time with the singing. The basket dance performed in the kiva was identical to the exoteric one in the plaza, except that women actually participated in the latter. The kachina proper ignored the music in their performance, and "characteristically ran back and forth." They pretended to be angry with children whom they detected peeping from behind their blankets, and rushed toward them, slapping the house posts with their whips.

The song and dance consisted of eight parts. Part one was called "song root" (xa?pu) and was rendered softly. Part two was known as "loud song" (xa?keg). This portion was given twice, and the second rendition was louder and in a higher tone than the first. Part three consisted of a repetition of parts one and two. Part four was called xa?pe ue, and was a short verse. The fifth part consisted of part two; the sixth, of parts four and two; and the seventh, parts one and two. Part eight was called "shortening" (xirg nye^n irg), the finish. This song pattern was characteristic of all dances designated "kachina dances."

When the song ended, the leader of the kachina gave a signal, and the blankets were raised to obscure the exit. The complete routine consumed from half an hour [18], to an hour [9]. The clowns instructed the kachina to leave and warm themselves at a nearby house. The Summer woman came forward and again led them, this time toward the right side of the blankets. The basket dancers left first, the chorus next. The kachina proper lingered after the rest had departed. The clowns mingled with them, making disparaging remarks about their appearance and costumes. In retaliation the kachina whipped them, but this they ignored, continuing their jokes without interruption. Finally the kachina shuffled toward the blankets. Each disappeared and reappeared several times before finally leaving.

The dejected, humpbacked "hunter" alone remained. The clowns pretended to see him for the first time. "They said, 'What the hell are you doing here?'" One clown walked on either side of him, imitated his shuffling walk, and peered into his face. They made derogatory remarks about his character. They asked him what he was tracking; by pantomime he indicated a deer. They expressed unbelieving amazement at his prowess in killing the large deer brought to the ceremony. He was also asked about the conditions of the locality from which he had come, what kind of terrain existed, what were the climatic conditions, etc. Since the kachina do not talk, all questions were phrased so that they could be answered by gestures or a nod of the head [9, 13, 18].

Finally he was asked what he was tracking besides deer, what he desired? The hunter in pantomime indicated a woman's breasts. One of the clowns waved his arm over the audience and said, "Our old man, which of these girls suits your taste?" [9]. "Look at all these beautiful girls. Which one do you want?" [19]. The two took him by the arms and guided him along the edge of the blanket-wrapped audience, stopping from time to time to look at a member. At last a girl was selected. "The clowns elaborated on the beauty of the girl and her attributes as a cook, etc." [19].

Formerly, older girls or married women were chosen; more recently, a relative of the impersonator [9] or of the clowns has been selected [13, 18], usually a child about the age of twelve. The girl was always an initiated moiety member. She stepped forward into the center of the kiva and faced "the hunter" from a distance of four to six feet.

"The hunter" was asked, "Do you like this one?" He nodded his head, and indicated that he desired her to spread her shawl or blanket. One of the clowns parted the garment, while his companion ridiculed "the hunter" for his choice, and made disparaging remarks about the characters of both "hunter" and girl.

"The hunter" turned, shuffled about the kiva, and finally came back. A clown asked what he was prepared to give the girl. He signified venison, by pantomiming the action and antlers of a deer. Tied to his waist or inside his shirt was a spruce-bough-wrapped package which contained rabbit, duck, woodrat, or venison. He presented this to the clowns, who made lewd remarks as to its possible content. One gave it to the girl and asked whether she liked it. She nodded in assent, and the clown informed "the hunter," "She likes it, and you may reveal your 'wisdom'" ("oseŋ p'o e^n piŋ na pa"). (Revealing "wisdom" was explained as a metaphorical statement alluding to the concept of fertility, but with particular reference to increase in the human population [9]. WWH). According to others [13, 18], "the hunter" was asked to confer his "blessing or supernatural power" upon the girl.

Turning to the girl, one of the clowns said, "Now then, our old man desires you. Stand facing our old man. Spread your legs wide." The girl complied with these requests and stood facing, but at a distance from the impersonator (a kachina may not touch women). In his right hand he held a yucca whip, in his left a bow and arrow. These he placed on the floor. Then with his hands he drew "power" from the six directions. Next with his arms at his sides, slightly bent at the elbow, he simulated the sexual act, making a single thrust with his hips. As soon as this was accomplished, a boy or two boys rushed forward, picked up the bow and arrows from behind the clown, and returned to their former positions.

The girl returned to her former place. "The hunter" shuffled about, and was joined by the clowns, who asked, "How many have you made for her?" He nodded or motioned with his hands. Each movement was indicative of ten children [9]. "The clowns counted by ones in Tewa until they reached a hundred; then they switched to English and counted by hundreds" [13, 18]. One clown said, "My, that is too many! My, he must be a powerful man." At this juncture "the hunter" struck him with the whip. Finally they halted, and the other remarked with a startled expression, stamping his feet, "Cabrón! Son of a bitch! You are unbeatable, our old man! How do you do it? Caramba! This one is so strong" [13, 18]. Discussion of this type was continued for a time until one clown told "the hunter" that he might leave, "since his children were way

ahead of him," i.e., the population increase of the pueblo was assured [9]. He then went to the curtained area and, after several feints, disappeared behind the blankets. Occasionally the above rite was reenacted with a second girl [13, 18].

As soon as "the hunter" departed, the clowns began to distribute the food that had been brought by the kachina. In the 1941 ceremony, a doe was dragged to the middle of the floor, and the clowns, assisted by the Summer Society members, skinned and butchered it. The presence of the deer was said to have been somewhat unusual, though desirable. Quite often the hunting party had poor luck and rabbits were substituted [13, 18]. The bundled ears of corn and other agricultural produce were distributed first. The clowns called the names of all family heads in the pueblo and presented each with his allotment. If the head was absent, some relative was given the portion. Following this, the meat was distributed in the same manner.

These products were believed to have a special potency. They were stored (hung) in the house, and this seed, together with that obtained just prior to the kachina's arrival, was mixed with ordinary seed to insure successful crops.

After the distribution the blankets were again raised, the emergence of the kachina visualized, and a performance identical to the first, with two exceptions, was enacted.

One variation was as follows: the kachina, instead of leaving immediately, lingered in the kiva. The chorus and basket dancers were addressed by the two clowns in turn and thanked for coming. The address was highly stylized, and much of the language was archaic or unintelligible to most listeners [13, 18]. The speeches dealt with the general behavior of the people in the pueblo since the last appearance of the kachina. Deviations from accepted pueblo standards were specifically cited.

Apologies were made for deviations; "They told the kachina that they would understand these errors." Each clown said a few sentences and then paused in order that the impersonators might have an opportunity to express their approval. This they signified by shaking their rattles and giving their cry [13, 18].

Next the clowns went before the basket dancers and chorus and expressed appreciation and friendship to them. They made various requests of the kachina, asked them not to return to their country but to remain in an area northwest of the pueblo. "There you will find others who are similar to you and who are watching. You will ally yourselves with them, and working with them make smaller the hearts of our enemies and discourage any harm that might come to the village." There were many requests of this type. After each request the speaker said, "Now give a sign of your friendship to your children," and paused. The kachina shook their rattles four times and gave their call following each such interval. The clowns then asked that this sign of friendship be repeated four times, and the kachina complied. When all requests were made and answered, the chorus and basket dancers left the kiva, the kachina "at the edge" remained to perform in the next part of the ceremony. As the former left, they threw "their power" to the audience, who caught it and put it in their mouths.

With the departure of the chorus and basket dancers, four dignitaries stepped forward and faced the kachina proper. These were the Summer cacique, the war captain, the head of the Women's Scalp Society, and the governor. When the governor was one of the wrong moiety, i.e., the Winter, a substitute from the Summer group acted for him. One of the clowns led the kachina leader before the Summer cacique. The kachina leader presented his yucca whips, the Summer cacique grasped their ends, and swinging their arms in unison, the two defined an arc. Next the kachina removed an ear of corn from his belt, and presented it to the cacique. This rite, "to make friends," was repeated in turn with the governor, war captain, the head of the Women's Scalp Society, and the three members of the Kachina Society who ranked next to the leader. Since a kachina may have no contact with women, the head of the Scalp Society did not grasp the whips, but stood at a distance and went through the motions. The ear of corn was given to the cacique, who passed it to the woman.

Next the Summer cacique came forward and addressed the kachina leader and those of the kachina that remained. This talk was couched in archaic terms and not translatable. Finally the kachina indicated that the others were far along their homeward way; in order that they might overtake them, they would like permission to depart. The request was granted by the cacique, and they left one by one, after throwing power to the assembled group [9].

During the 1941 "hidden dance," the head of the Women's Scalp Society did not participate in this terminal rite, but the clowns did. This official may only have taken part during the fall rites associated with moiety initiations. It was not possible to discover the organizational affiliation of the two men who participated with the Summer cacique in 1941. Whether these were the war captain and governor, or substitutes, was not ascertained.

When the kachina had departed, only "the hunter" remained; the second variation involved his leaving after the completion of the fertility rite.

After he was informed that the population increase was assured, he was told to go to p'otsi, a spring about a mile west of Santa Clara, and there make his home [9].

A further modification occurred in 1941. After the ritual impregnation, each clown linked arms with "the hunter"; as they walked up and down the floor of the kiva at a fast pace, they sang the following song:

> Our old man!
> You have many women,
> One you have just made,
> One you have made pregnant,
> One is now with child,
> One is just giving birth.
> Our old man!
> You are so strong.

When "the hunter" had departed and food was distributed for the second time, the Summer cacique came forward and admonished the group. Again the language was archaic. The cacique commented upon the behavior of people in the pueblo. He stressed the advisability of conforming to traditional, conservative patterns in order that the blessings conferred by the kachina would continue to be bestowed on the village. "He told how the kachinas came. He told the people to be careful of their crops, not to waste food, and that all things would be right." Other officials spoke in the same vein. Correct behavior by children was also stressed.

Finally the cacique spoke briefly, requesting that nothing seen or heard in the kiva be revealed or repeated. "All seen should be forgotten as far as others are concerned." When these speeches were terminated, the audience rushed to the ladder and departed silently for their homes. The 1941 rite did not finish until two in the morning.

After the dance the leader of "the fathers of the kachina" and his right and left arms joined the kachina. The leader commented upon the performance of the ritual. If the ceremony had gone well, he told them, "You have earned a long life." However, if discrepancies or errors had occurred during the performance, if a feather had been dropped, part of a costume lost, or one of the participants had turned in such a way as to be recognized by the group, they were reprimanded. Following this the impersonators removed their costumes and masks [9].

Infractions during the ceremony were punished at the time they occurred, by the leader of "the fathers of the kachina." If an impersonator dropped part of his costume or committed an error, that dignitary whipped the offender and chased him from the kiva. If the lapse took place during the first performance, the guilty member might return for the later performance; if not, he waited at the kachina house until the termination. Errors of the above type were believed to result from, or be an indication of, a breech of tabu [9].

The "Hidden Dance" in the Hills of the Summer Kachina

Another "hidden dance" of the Summer kachina (K'u pu nye^n bu oxuwa, "amphitheater kachina goodwill ceremony") was held in late September. This coincided with the maturation of the crops, and was a harvest, or thanksgiving ritual. If it did not coincide with a moiety initiation, it was not performed in the kiva, but in a large natural amphitheater located west of the pueblo. In general pattern, it conformed to the Good Friday rite, although its location necessitated some alterations. According to informants [9, 18], it was last performed sometime between 1920 and 1925. No reason was given for the lapse in recent years.

Announcement of a coming "hidden dance in the hills" was made four days prior to the ceremony by the war captain, in the plazas of the pueblo. This dignitary informed the people that a hunt would be held on the morning of the fourth day. This clue was sufficient warning of the impending event. Since the rite entailed a general feast, those not directly involved began gathering and preparing food for themselves and the kachina. Those who would act as impersonators (oxuwa) went into retreat, observed ritual prescriptions, and rehearsed.

At daybreak on the fourth day, the kachina left for the hills. They wore their masks "on the backs of their heads," and carried as much of their costume and equipment as they were able. Surplus paraphernalia was packed on horses and burros. Masks and costumes were similar to those used in the Good Friday ceremony. Wagons for transport were outlawed, since no wheel tracks were allowed in the area where the dance was held. When the amphitheater was reached, they cleared and cleaned an area behind a ridge, unpacked the equipment, donned their costumes, and remained in hiding until time for their appearance.

The individuals who played the parts of the clown (k'osa) and "the hunter" sequestered themselves in suitable locations, part way up the alluvial fan at the base of the cliff.

After the sun had risen (seven or eight o'clock) the war captain, formerly the ping xarɐjo, announced in the plazas that the hunt was to begin. He went approximately an eighth of a mile away from the village, and built a fire. Those who planned to attend the ceremony gravitated to this point, laden with food. The party often included guests from other pueblos. All were dressed in their best clothing.

When the group was assembled, the war

captain chose two boys to act as the hunt leaders. They ran in wide semicircles, followed at intervals by horsemen, young men, young girls, and finally by the older members of the pueblo, in that order. The leaders ran until they met and formed a complete circle. The people on the circumference then converged toward the center, killing whatever game was caught in the surround. As soon as an animal was dispatched, it was picked up by a woman. "Sometimes the girls fight over the game" [9]. A man could not keep his kill. Five surrounds were held before the party reached the amphitheater. A sixth was completed on the return trip. The leaders reversed their positions after each surround.

A lookout reported the progress of the hunt and warned the kachina of the approach of the party. Guards were stationed in the surrounding area to prevent trespass by non-Indians. Others protected the dressing place of the kachina from uninitiated intruders. The first comers waited at the mouth of the amphitheater for all to arrive. Finally a signal to enter was given, and the younger boys, mounted on horses, raced forward to secure choice places in the shade for relatives and friends. Food was unpacked and everyone made themselves as comfortable as possible. Horses were picketed, seats were constructed of rock and wood, ramadas were erected from limbs and brush. When this was complete, a dance plaza was cleared for the kachina.

When all the preliminaries were accomplished, the audience relaxed to await the arrival of the impersonators. The clowns came first, noisily descending the alluvial fan, hooting like owls and bleating like sheep. They reached the dance place and began their joking. After some interval, "the hunter" appeared without prior announcement. In this ceremony the kachina were not called or visualized; they had been told the previous spring to establish residence in the northwest. The clowns appeared to notice "the hunter" for the first time, and began questioning him. Questions were again worded in a form that could be answered by gestures.

They said, "Where have you come from, our old man?" "Why have you come here?"

"The hunter" indicated that he had come so that they might have an opportunity to meet each other's children. The clowns inquired whether he was sure that he was telling the truth. "How are you going to bring your children when they are so far away?" "The hunter" indicated that he was not lying. The clowns said, "We will see if you are telling the truth. If you speak truthfully, our spittle will not dry before you have brought your children." The clowns then spat on the ground.

"The hunter" trotted around the corner of the hill and returned in a few moments, preceded by the kachina. The Summer woman made a trail of cornmeal and led them into the dance area. The clowns collected and stacked the food which the impersonators brought. The standard kachina ceremony was then enacted with only one or two minor variations, as follows: at their departure the kachina were given food which the people had brought, and after the symbolic impregnation of the girl, the clowns left with "the hunter."

When all impersonators had departed, everyone feasted. A considerable time was consumed in eating, and the second appearance of the kachina did not take place until late in the afternoon.

The clowns arrived first. They mocked the actions of the kachina and imitated their cries. They joked with the audience. Finally the kachina appeared, went through their routine, and left. The food was distributed, and the Summer cacique exhorted the people, impressing upon them the necessity of secretiveness and the conservative way of life. After that the group left for the pueblo. During the return the sixth hunting surround was accomplished [9, 69].

The Winter "Hidden Dance" of the Summer Kachina

The first "hidden dance" of the year, by the Summer kachina, took place in January or February. Its formal aspects coincided with those of the two ceremonies already described, but the masked characters differed radically.

The kachina which came in January were known as the "winter angry kachina." The troupe consisted of six different, matched pairs of impersonators, two "hunters," and the "kachina mother" (oxuwa *zhi*a). The last was a man dressed as a woman. There was no chorus or dancers. Rattles were absent, the kachina carrying a yucca whip in each hand. They danced in time with the singing. Clowns performed and visualized the coming of the kachina; in this case, they were described as emerging from a draw (pi hodji) northeast of the Hopi village of Walpi. When they arrived at the kiva, the Summer woman made a trail of meal, duplicated by the "kachina mother," who formally ushered them in.

They entered in single file, then formed the matched pairs. The tempo of the first part of the dance was rapid. Following each song, the performers skipped and hurdled back and forth in every direction, emitting their cries. As in previous dances, two entrances were made. After each exit, "the hunters" remained and executed the fertility rite—each with a different girl. The finale was identical to other performances. Various dignitaries described arcs ("made friends"), holding the ends of the yucca whips; the Summer cacique thanked the kachina and admonished the audience [9].

The "Hidden Dances" of the Winter Kachina

The functions of the Winter kachina organization have been badly impaired by intramoiety factionalism. Dances were formerly given in January or February, at Easter, and in the fall. At an earlier period, according to an informant [73], one was held in the hills instead of the kiva. A performance and initiation took place in the kiva in 1929 [9, 21]. Following this, however, activities lapsed, and no "hidden dance" was held by the Winter Moiety until Good Friday, 1948. On this occasion one of the factions succeeded in recruiting sufficient personnel for a performance, and twelve candidates were inducted. This enactment was attended not only by Santa Clara Indians, but by visitors from San Juan, San Ildefonso, and Tesuque, as well.

The standard procedure for initiating a Winter "hidden dance" was as follows. Older members of the kachina cult petitioned the "elders" or "fathers of the kachina" of the Winter Society. In turn these solicited the Winter cacique and the Winter Society women; their requests were accompanied by a gift of meal. The Winter cacique next asked aid of the Clown and Bear societies and alerted the songmakers. These applications for assistance were again accompanied by a gift, in this case meal and tobacco. Since none of the individuals or groups could refuse the petitions, word filtered back through the various channels to the Winter kachina confirming the request. The date for the performance was set [9, 21].

A four-day retreat by active participants preceded the dance. After bathing in the river, members gathered in the evening at the house of the Winter kachina. They were under no food tabus, unless the retreat was associated with a forthcoming moiety initiation. In such case only aboriginal foods, corn and corn products and game, could be eaten. However, strict continence was required of all those who were to impersonate kachina, and such individuals were not supposed to look at a woman. Should an impersonator require something from his home, he might obtain it—but only late at night, and if accompanied by another member. Participants were allowed to urinate in the house. Defecation took place outside, and a man who left for that purpose was accompanied by another member.

The period of retreat was one of preparation and practice for the coming ceremonial. If initiation was coincident with the rite, this was accomplished prior to practice. If not, the members lounged about until late in the evening, when finally one of "the elders" announced that it was getting late and that practice should begin. Impersonators stripped to their breechclouts, and one by one they were instructed in their roles. Once the mask had been donned, the wearer could not speak; he replied to questions by nodding or by pantomime. Practice was under the supervision of the "kachina leader," the "leader of the elders." It included instruction in specific roles and song and dance practice. Usually an hour and a half to two hours were consumed in this manner. The masks were then removed, placed in a corner of the house, a few prayers were said, and cornmeal was sprinkled on the masks. After this, members were allowed to roll up in a blanket or sheep pelt and sleep. This practice routine was repeated each night for the three nights prior to the ceremony.

On the first morning, members were awakened early, and a selected group was sent hunting. This contingent left before sunrise and remained after dark with the game. Similar parties were dispatched on the second and third days. Newly initiated members were not included in the hunt party on the first day, but participated in subsequent ones, under the guidance of an experienced leader. Those who remained in seclusion occupied themselves with minor preparations of equipment or slept.

On the second day, those in retreat began preparing the paraphernalia. If the masks were too dry or did not fit, they were packed with wet earth and stretched. Other members were sent to gather evergreens.

The third day and night saw an increase in the tempo of preparation. Hunting continued, and parties were dispatched in the evening for more evergreens and to gather yucca and black "paint" from the bottom of a swamp. All journeys were on foot, as riding was not allowed; all materials were transported on the backs of the searchers. On their return members busied themselves preparing evergreen collars, yucca whips, and the bundles to be carried by "the hunters." Following this, a dress rehearsal was held. The costumes were complete, except that the masks and bodies of the dancers were not painted, and no feathers were worn.

The fourth day was spent in scraping and painting the masks, preparing the feathers, and, toward evening, painting the bodies of the impersonators. Members not taking part in the dance were delegated to clean and heat the kiva. (In 1948, the kiva caught fire prior to the dance.) Others acted as guards and directed the spectators.

While it was explicit in accounts of the Winter "water immersion" rite that the Winter Society built an altar, it was not ascertained whether this was true for the usual Winter "hidden dance." Presumably they did not build an altar then, but functioned in the same way as did the Summer Society in the Summer "hidden dances."

When preliminaries were completed, moiety members were notified and gathered in the kiva. Soon after that, two members of the Clown Society made their appearance; they had prepared and costumed themselves at the headquarters of their organization. In 1948, one San Juan kosa functioned, and selected a pinini to assist him. When they arrived at the hatchway of the kiva, kachina members hung or held blankets to screen their entrance. The pair descended on either side of the ladder, one step at a time, hooting like owls. From time to time they parted the blankets and peered out, or looked around the edges, indicating surprise and amazement at the surroundings. Finally they stepped onto the "wood box" (xane'djo, "where wood is kept") and down its terraced sides into the kiva. Each went to a spectator, placed his bundle before him, and told him *not* to guard it. "They talked backwards."

Next the clowns began their stylized routine. They made derogatory remarks and indicated great surprise at what they saw. "They said, 'Is this place hell?' or said anything else that they pleased." They commented unfavorably upon recent happenings in the pueblo, and criticized the behavior of specific individuals. These humorous dialogues continued until a man stationed at the kiva vent gave the signal that the kachina were ready and that it was time to execute the next portion of the rite. In 1948 the signal consisted of dimming the kerosene lamp used to light the kiva. At this point the kachina members in the kiva left unobtrusively to assist in bringing the dancers from the kachina house.

This was a signal for the clowns to begin visualizing the emergence of the kachina and their progress to the village. It was a highly dramatic recital. Each kachina was characterized as it emerged. Those who emerged first were described as dancing about the lake while waiting for the remainder. When all were assembled, they began their journey toward the pueblo. A vivid portrayal of their progress from place to place was reported. "They tear all obstacles away; mountains were flattened into plains; trees were torn up, and so forth."

The following is an abbreviated account of this procedure. One clown turned to the other and said, "Shall we make magical beginning or first-man magic?" The other answered, "All right, we shall, younger elder brother. Do not ask the Summer [inverted reference] cacique that we shall make beginning-man magic." The younger clown walked to the cacique by the fireplace and said, "Our old man, we shall not make beginning-man magic?" The cacique replied in the affirmative, and the clown took ashes from the fireplace and went to the center of the kiva. His counterpart said, "Do the four-time one, our younger elder brother, do as a man." The clown leveled the pile of ashes, took a pinch, and rubbed it on his left palm, saying to the other, "Younger elder brother, which way?" The other answered, "Toward the heavens" (zenith). The clown slapped his palm, looked up, then down toward the nadir, shading his eyes, and said, "I have looked into the sky and there have seen dense fog, and that is all I have seen. Now do as a man, younger elder brother." The other clown took a pinch of ashes and said, "Younger elder brother, which way?" The other answered, "Down to the nadir." The former took ashes, slapped his palm, looked down and then up to the zenith, and said, "Down at the nadir I see nothing but dense fog."

This routine was then repeated in the east, west, south, and north, the clowns alternating roles in turn. [Here one would expect a counterclockwise progression, but there was no mention or indication of it. CHL] Finally, when the north was mentioned, one asked of the other, "Which way, younger elder brother?"; he was answered, "The same way, younger elder brother!"

The elder clown peered toward the north, and for the first time a place name was mentioned. Then the actual visualization and emergence of the kachina began. Again each alternated in the visualizing role. A free, condensed version of their conversation is as follows:

Elder: "Toward the north a lake (to ca'). From the lake, fog rolling,

cloud-flower rolling, that is all I saw, younger brother. Do as a man."

Younger: "Toward the lake, from the lake fog rolling, from the cloud-flower rolling, that is all you saw. So you said, did you not? Now way out in the midst of the lake something is peering out. That is all I saw. Elder brother, do as a man."

Elder: "Now way out in the midst of the lake something is peering out. That was all you saw, so you said, did you not? Away out in the midst of the lake; from there they come out, they come out. And then they lift their path, on top of which is their ceremonial paraphernalia, consisting of the feathers from various species of birds and also melons and fruit. Then from the lake they lift their path and bring it over to Sand Lake [near Alamosa, Colorado] and there they let it down."

At this juncture the clowns took turns describing the lifting of the path and its contents from one site to another, each time progressively closer to the village. When "Flint-Covered-Mountain Lake" was reached, "the hunter" was described. He was not mentioned by name, but his somewhat humorous characteristics were detailed. He was said to be lagging behind, heavily loaded with gifts for the pueblo. At "Cactus Place Lake" he finally succeeded in joining the rest of the kachina.

The progression of the kachina was as follows: from "Sand Lake" to "Warm Lake"; from "Warm Lake" to "Cliff Canyon Lake"; from "Cliff Canyon Lake" to "Flint-Covered Mountain Lake"; from "Flint-Covered Mountain Lake" to "Liquid Rat Dung Lake"; from "Liquid Rat Dung Lake" to "Amphitheater Lake"; from "Amphitheater Lake" to "Marshy Place Lake"; from "Marshy Place Lake" to "Cactus Place Lake"; from "Cactus Place Lake" to "Green Water Place Lake"; from "Green Water Place Lake" to "Terraced Water Lake"; from "Terraced Water Lake" to "Santa Clara Fetish Living Place"; from "Santa Clara Fetish Living Place" to "The Original Santa Clara Plaza"; from "The Original Santa Clara Plaza" to "The Foot of the Original

Kiva Ladder"; from "The Foot of the Original Kiva Ladder" to "The Original Kiva Mouth Opening."

At this point the clowns tied buckskin about their shoulders and announced that the kachina had arrived at the kiva. Shouting and stamping were heard, and corn, beans, piñon nuts, etc., showered onto the kiva floor, thrown through a hole in the kiva roof a few feet from the hatchway. They were gathered by the women. Meanwhile the clowns urged the kachina to "come in and get warm."

Some kachina members held up blankets to screen the ladder and a portion of the kiva along the wall. Others (the guards) entered, carrying agricultural products and game. If deer had been killed, they were brought first, then rabbits, other game, and farm products. In 1948 only two ducks had been secured by the hunters; this was widely commented upon and considered a highly humorous incident. The kachina began coming down the ladder. Each took a deep breath at the top, since they were not permitted to breathe during the descent. When they reached the floor, they exhaled and were handed game or produce. They then took their places behind the curtain of blankets on the south side.

In the meantime the Winter woman was standing in the center of the kiva. When all the kachina had entered, the blankets were gradually removed and the impersonators revealed to the audience. All unmarried women covered their faces. The Winter woman made a "trail" of cornmeal, and the clowns began dancing along it—singing songs belonging to their society. The kachina followed, and as they passed the "altar," they piled the game and produce on it.

Returning to the south wall, the impersonators began their routine. Four groups were represented: the chorus (xa uoŋ), the dancers, the whipping kachina, and the two "hunters." In 1948, because of lack of personnel, there was only one "hunter," and only one of the kachina was paired. Again because of lack of personnel, newly initiated members took the parts of impersonators, which was contrary to ordinary practice. The Zuñi basket dance was danced, but without baskets. The whipping group engaged in special steps that were not in time with the music. This contingent also threatened and frightened children who had been disobedient, stolen melons, etc. The routine was performed twice.

Upon the conclusion of the second routine, the clowns jokingly told the performers to go next door, that "there is an old woman there who has a lot of wood." The blankets were raised, and all departed except the two "hunters."

These had on their backs evergreen bundles tied with yucca and containing rabbits, ducks, quail, etc. The clowns pretended to notice the "hunters" for the first time. They said, "Who the hell are these? What are they doing here?" Conversation in this vein continued for some time. Finally the "hunters" lost their tempers and whipped the clowns once or twice with considerable force. The clowns, however, were protected by the buckskins which they had donned.

Next the clowns asked the "hunters" what was on their minds, what they desired? The hunters indicated breasts, in pantomime. One clown told the other to go and search for breasts. He departed, peered among the spectators, and finally returned with a girl. The girl opened her shawl, and the hunter was asked whether he approved of her. He nodded his head, and the clown inquired as to what he would give her. In pantomime the "hunter" indicated a deer. The clown said, "Give her the deer," and the "hunter" untied his bundle and handed the contents to the clown. The clown looked at it, remarking, "What the hell is this? My, what a large penis it has!" He took the venison to the girl and asked her approval. She approved, and was told to remain where she was until she was symbolically impregnated.

The clown informed the "hunter" of the girl's consent, and told him "to bless her from his position." The "hunter" laid his bow and arrows by his side; he drew in power from the four directions, clasped his hands in front of him as if holding his penis, took several short steps in the direction of the girl, and finally thrust forward and upward, as if completing coition. In 1948 the "hunter" made two mistakes, both of which were considered hilariously funny. First, he thrust forward before he was supposed to, "he was too anxious" [43]. The clown inquired of the "hunter" how many (i.e., children) he had made. Counting was begun, the hunter nodding his head as each number was called. Sometimes the count reached the thousands [43, 50].

According to Jeançon, the above ceremony was the terminal rite of a girl's initiation. He indicated that requirements during the retreat were not as rigid or exacting for girls as for boys, that the girls were not nude, and that the retreat was of only four days' duration. It can be inferred that a considerable number of candidates might undergo the rite on the same evening. There is no reason to doubt Jeançon's statement (1904–30). Presumably the absence of retreats in recent years and the latitude allowed in selecting candidates represents the general relaxation of ceremonial procedures.

His description of the rite is as follows:

The culmination of her initiation is when Yeen Sedo (lit., "he moves around all the time," or "restless going around old man") makes her his gifts. He is a sort of father of all the Katchinas....
The girl candidate has arrived in the kiva and is in charge of one of the 'kossa. Yeen Sedo enters through the hatchway and comes down the ladder. He peers around as though looking for something or someone. The 'kossa asks him where he came from (during the first part of the following Yeen uses pantomime and does not speak until later on). In answer to the question he gestures that he has come down from the mountains; 'kossa then asks if there is any snow on the ground up there; Yeen nods "Yes"; 'kossa asks "How much?" Yeen motions well up to his chest; 'kossa asks: "How did you get out and what are you tracking?" Yeen goes through a pantomime of wallowing in the snow, fighting his way out; showing how it first came to his chest, then to his waist, then to his knees, and finally to his ankles when he was able to move about easily. Then he makes the tracks of a deer on the kiva floor and shows it

to the 'kossa, who asks, "Is the deer here in the kiva?" Yeen nods; he then walks around as though tracking a deer. Yeen then begins to talk partly to himself and partly to the 'kossa. Then follows a play on words much of which is obscene, the 'kossa appearing to want to find out what the old man is looking for and the old man trying to put him off with word play; 'kossa makes all manner of fun of Yeen, prods him with an arrow, and pulls his rags. Finally 'kossa asks: "What are you looking for and what do you want?" Yeen says: "A doe and a young one at that," making a motion to represent the breasts of a woman, he looks around the crowd and finally points to the girl candidate. She comes to him; she is supposed to be very lucky by being picked out by Yeen Sedo. He stands in front of her and pretends to copulate with her. After this has been concluded, the 'kossa asks the old man how many children he has started; Yeen counts on his fingers and says that he has made many and that there will be lots of new babies come to the village. Then Yeen gives the girl a present of a rabbit and some spruce boughs. Each girl who has been initiated receives a similar present after going through the symbolic act of copulation with the old man. When the girls get home with their rabbits and spruce boughs, they sprinkle them with sacred meal. (White meal only is used by women and girls.) The boughs are tied with twine and hung up in the house and the rabbits cooked for a feast.

The girls to be initiated may wear dresses of any kind of gay colored cloth or calico. In the old days, they probably only wore a manta or very possibly were more or less nude, wearing only an apron. In this ceremony, as in all others, the main idea is fertilization and renewed life.

When two "hunters" were present, the fertility rite was repeated with the other impersonators and another girl. Following this, the clowns made fun of the "hunters," and finally told them to go to a place nearby to rest and warm themselves. They departed, and the game and produce which the kachina had brought were distributed to the married women. Children were given melons. The bows and arrows belonging to the "hunters" were given by the clowns to boys.

Following the distribution of food, the clowns again began joking. After an interval of this, the kachina were heard on the roof; they entered, repeated their performance, and departed. With the departure of the kachina, the Winter cacique came forward and admonished the audience, impressing upon them the need for secrecy and a conservative way of life. This speech was highly formalized. Its general vein is illustrated by the following fragment: "What you see and hear keep under your eyes, under your armpits, in your crotch, in the palms of your hands, and the soles of your feet. Nor should you take a step, nor two, nor three, nor four toward a revealing of what has occurred here tonight" [44]. In 1948 the role of the Winter cacique was performed by a member of the Winter Society and a "father of the kachina," because the Winter cacique was old and in poor health. Furthermore, he was not a member of the faction sponsoring the dance, although some of the members of his group helped with the performance.

This man in turn developed a sore throat on the final night, and the duty of admonishing the audience was performed by the clown. The clown, however, was faithful to his k'osa role, and delivered the routine in inverted speech [43].

Following the departure of the audience, a terminal rite was probably performed by the cacique; this is not clear from the accounts.

When the hidden dance was held in conjunction with moiety (piku) and Winter Society initiations, the kachina made four appearances instead of two. The right and left arms of the Winter Society performed a terminal rite as described in the section on initiations [43].

The Kachina

Descriptions of the various kachina were difficult to obtain. There was a general impression that traditional costuming of the various impersonators was rigidly adhered to in these performances. According to one informant [50], "Very strict attention was paid to conforming accurately to traditional standards in costuming."

Presumably this was an ideal which was seldom achieved. Actually costumes were not as standardized as they were assumed to have been, and there was considerable latitude in details. For example, the same informants [9, 13, 21, 43, 50, 52] over a period of years made alterations in and emendations to their original descriptions. Furthermore, descriptions by Parsons (1929: 158–62) and Jeançon (1904–30) showed discrepancies when these data were compared to more recent accounts. It should also be remembered that the numbers and varieties of kachina impersonated at any given performance were variable, since the overall performance depended upon the willingness of eligible personnel to participate. The following descriptions must therefore be viewed in terms of a generalized norm.

The "Edge of Spring" Ceremony of the Summer Society of the Summer Moiety

The "Edge of Spring" (Tong kegi) ceremony was performed by the Summer Society shortly after January 23, the Saint's Day of San Ildefonso Pueblo. It involved a four-day retreat, and presumably followed the "hidden dances," which were scheduled at this approximate time. Not only the Summer Society, but all other societies "worked" during this period, and produced prayer sticks that were deposited by their respective memberships at the shrines associated with the six cardinal points.

Formerly this ceremony signaled the transference of religious authority from the Winter to the Summer Moiety. Presumably, at one time similar rites were conducted in October or November, when the Summer Moiety relinquished its jurisdiction to the Winter Moiety. More importantly, the "Edge of Spring" ushered in the beginning of the new agricultural cycle. This and its terminal feature, the ceremonial shinny, represented distinct religious efforts apart from the "hidden dances."

The rationale for this ceremony and the corresponding rite of the Winter Society, Ka-ve-Na, were outlined by Jeançon:

It is a very serious thing when we wake up the Earth-mother. The winter and summer chiefs (priests) must get together with their right and left hands, (right and left hand assistants) and the 'Kossa and Quarrano, and all of them work hard to wake her up. Sometimes she don't seem to want to wake up and then we have lots of snow late in the Spring. After she wakes up, and about the last of January (sometimes a little later in February, the first week mostly) we have the Horse Dance (phallic in character, no full description could be obtained; most of it is done in the kiva). Now sometimes we do not have the horse dance any more. There are lots of other things that we have to do. The winter and summer chiefs get together and transfer the care of the people and magic from winter to summer. This used to be a fine ceremony, but now we don't do it any more. Just have the two chiefs and their right and left hand men get together and talk for a little while. [Jeançon quoting a member of the Winter Moiety, 1905. According to Jeançon, the transfer ceremony was abandoned about 1885. WWH]

The evening prior to the beginning of the ceremony, word was sent to all kachina members by the leader of "the fathers of the kachina" (se^n shu) to report to the kachina house early the next morning. This they did, after bathing in the river. Each member was accompanied by his "water immersion" son or sons. These might be true sons, or novices he had sponsored. They were always boys who had been initiated into the moiety but had not yet entered the kachina society.

Upon entering the kachina room, the men stripped to breechclouts and blankets. Clothes were piled in the corner. Each carried feathers. Some had large bundles, wrapped in buckskin, which were part of the ceremonial equipment regularly kept in the home. Others brought smaller packets of feathers, covered by cornhusks, procured for the occasion. Members breathed upon their bundles, sprinkled sacred meal on them, said a prayer, and placed them in a basket located near the site where the altar would be erected. Some also dropped tobacco in a nearby bowl.

When all had arrived, the leader and the "fathers of the kachina" began the construction of the altar. A grid of cornmeal was outlined on the floor, with a meal "trail" leading from it toward the door. The leader unwrapped his "mother" and placed it on the grid. This was considered the essential item; besides this the altar included a varying number of stone fetishes and a "kiva bell" stone. Nearby was a bowl of sacred water, one of sacred meal, a bowl for tobacco, and the basket containing feathers. Upon completion of the altar, those with feathers wrapped in buckskin came forward and deposited them in the same manner as their predecessors.

The leader removed the feathers from the basket and spread them on the floor by his side. He rolled a cigarette and blew smoke on them. Following this, he selected a number of feathers and prepared a prayer plume. This was presented to one of the kachina members who departed from the house, presumably to deposit the prayer plume at a shrine.

When the member returned, all present seated themselves on the floor, the older members and their novices concentrated near the altar, those newly affiliated on the periphery. Two songs were sung.

After the songs, the general preparation of prayer plumes was begun. All kachina members who were familiar with the procedure assisted. Feathers were first sorted, according to species and the relative importance of the deity with whom they were associated. The informant [50] was not sure of the order, but the following supernaturals were represented: Sun, Moon, Mother Earth, Big Snake (avanyu), Evening Star, Morning Star, and Ancestors of the War Captain (t'o wac). The Moon and owl [? WWH] feathers were associated, as were the Ancestors of the War Captain and eagle feathers. There were twelve Ancestors of the War Captain, so that twelve eagle feathers were necessary. "Usually there were more supernaturals represented by feathers than there were kachina present."

When the representative feathers were sorted, one was given to each kachina member. The elder men received those associated with the more important supernaturals. Each in turn came forward, took from the basket a yellow warbler's feather and either an oriole or Say's phoebe feather, and constructed the prayer plume. The deity feathers were placed on the bottom, the oriole or Say's phoebe feather in the center, the warbler on top, and the three were tied together with cord at the base. The man who was charged with constructing the offering associated with Mother Earth wrapped his plume with an unusually long cord. "A string long enough to reach around the entire room. This was so the coming year, the summer, might be a long one." Completed plumes were returned to the basket.

Next, prayer plumes which, later in the year, would be worn by participants in the ange *sha*re ("slow dance") were constructed. These were made by the "water immersion" sponsors, one for each novice. The procedure was the same, except that a roadrunner wing feather was substituted for that associated with the deity.

The final set of plumes was constructed by all those owning livestock. These sets consisted of bundles of turkey breast feathers and warbler tail and breast feathers. The number of plumes made depended on the needs of each individual.

The basket containing the finished prayer plumes was lifted up, and everyone attempted to place a hand on the rim. Those who were not able to reach the basket held the arm of someone who was. The leader of the "fathers of the kachina" held his "mother" (*zhi*a) slightly above the basket, and all began to chant. The men raised and lowered the basket, and the leader "danced" his "mother" in time with the song.

When the "basket blessing" was finished, sponsors presented the "slow dance" plumes to their "water immersion" sons. Livestock owners retrieved their plumes, which they later tied to the tails of their horses, cattle, or burros. The basket containing the deity plumes was presented at the altar to the leader of the "fathers of the kachina." He

and his assistants spread the plumes in a line in order of importance, the most important being nearest the altar. They were sprinkled with sacred meal and then with sacred water, as the group chanted. The song recounted the names and dealt with the various shrines at which the prayer plumes would be deposited. At the termination of the song, they were distributed to members. The older men received those of the more important deities. Each wrapped his bundle in cornhusks or buckskin.

A messenger was dispatched to the female relatives of the "fathers of the kachina" to request food. When the women arrived, they placed the food on the floor, drank from the bowl of sacred water at the direction of the leader of the "fathers of the kachina," and departed.

The leader took a small portion of each type of food, threw some in the fire, and some outside. Then each man came forward in turn and drank of the sacred water. As they drank, they were told to remain continent for four days (pi par̄ g yu). Following this, all partook of the food.

After eating, each rubbed himself with sacred meal, dressed, and left for home, carrying the bundles assigned to him. Upon his arrival there, all members of the household breathed on the plumes. The plumes intended for livestock and the "slow dance" were left in the house; the deity plumes were deposited at the proper shrine by the kachina member. The wrapping used to cover the plumes was brought back and placed in the vigas of the house. The above procedures engaged the energies of the society from early morning until three or three-thirty in the afternoon. At this time members were free until evening.

When night came (the informant [72] was not sure whether it was the first or second night), the kachina returned again to their house, but without their "water immersion" sons. As before, they removed their clothes and piled them in the corner. Each went to the fireplace and rubbed ashes on his hands and then his body. The leader and the "fathers of the kachina" again erected an altar, the "mother" forming the central portion. The best singers were selected by the leader; he seated them on either side of him and the other "fathers of the kachina." Two songs were sung, before each of which the leader struck the "bell stone."

When the singing ended, the leader arose, placed ashes in the palm of one hand, struck it with the other, and began to visualize the coming of the kachina. Two complete appearances of the kachina, lacking impersonators, were pantomimed. "The spirits of the kachina come to Santa Clara" [69]. The leader of the "fathers of the kachina" monologued his part, striking the "bell stone" from time to time, while the audience remained silent. This rite paralleled that of the "water immersion," except that the ritual impregnation and the masked characters were missing.

This completed all ritual until the night of the fourth day. At that time members went to the river and bathed, after which they were free to resume their normal roles.

Ceremonial Shinny

Ceremonial shinny (pu na be) was formerly an auxiliary and terminal performance in the "Edge of Spring" Ceremony. While shinny has been played in recent years, its ritualistic elements have been absent, and its character has been entirely secular and social (see also Parsons 1929: 230.) It is possible that at one time religious and secular forms of this game existed simultaneously, but evidence for this is lacking. Jeançon claimed to have witnessed the last occurrence in pure religious form in 1906, and it would appear from the 1896 account of T.S. Dozier (Culin 1907: 643) that even that occasion represented a revival. Jeançon's description is as follows:

The Summer cacique prepared the ball which contained all kinds of grain and seeds. The men (kossa and kwirena) [It is not clear from the account whether these two organizations formed the teams or not. WWH] assembled in the main plaza, all the women of the pueblo standing close by. The cacique sprinkled the players and the ball with sacred meal and tossed it between the two opposing lines of men. These drove it back and forth with their shinny sticks. From

time to time one of the men would deliver an unusually strong stroke, and the ball would fly to some distance. Immediately the women would pounce upon it and carry it into a house placing it consecutively in the north, west, south, and east corners of the room. The ball was then returned to the players, and the above was repeated until all houses of the village were visited. This was believed to insure abundant crops and plenty in each house.

After the houses were visited, the players drove the ball toward and into the fields. As many fields as possible were visited, the game continuing until the ball disintegrated. When this occurred, a runner was sent to the village for a drum. When he returned, the groups formed two files and, to the time of the drum, danced back to the village. On their arrival an announcement was made that the fields were in readiness for the general planting (Jeançon 1906).

Recent accounts have indicated a progressive dilution of the ritual adjuncts of shinny and its final emergence as a purely social event. No mention is made of the house blessing rite or the possibility of the clown societies forming teams. It has been claimed that the event was an intermoiety contest with evenly matched teams. The cacique or some older man constructed the ball, which the cacique sprinkled with cornmeal and blessed. The cacique then said a prayer for abundant crops, buried the ball in a mound of earth in the center of the plaza, and gave the signal for the game to commence. The ball was driven through each field [13, 18].

In its more modern form, or older secular form if such existed, contests were held between married and single men, intramoiety groups, and also in the plaza between women or small boys. The ball is no longer stuffed with seeds, but with deer or rabbit hair or, according to Parsons (1929: 231), rags. Bets are placed by both players and spectators. It is also customary for the losers to obligate themselves to dance during the Easter season [13, 18, 72].

Rules varied; on some occasions the team that succeeded in driving the ball the greatest distance in either a north or south direction was declared the winner. On other occasions a point was designated some distance from the village, and each team drove toward this goal. The winner was the team that retained possession of the ball for the greater length of time. The ball was kicked as well as struck with the shinny stick. No tripping or holding was allowed [13, 18, 72].

T.S. Dozier's account (Culin 1907: 643) conforms closely to the above, but adds some details:

> About the middle of January there is played a game that is to the Pueblos what baseball is to the Americans. It is nothing more or less than the old game of shinny played on the ice, as with us. The pu-mam-be, or ball, used is a soft, light affair, made of rags and buckskin or wholly of buckskin. The pu-mam-be pfe, stick, is generally of willow, with a curved end, and is about 3 feet long. Men, boys of all sizes, and girls of all ages, and now and then a married woman engage in this pastime. The sexes do not play together, nor the boys with men. Among the men wagers of every description are made. During the past winter [1895? WWH] a game between the men, which lasted nearly a whole day, the side that was beaten had to dance a solemn dance for a whole day. Quite a difficulty arose on account of it.

Subsequent to the shinny game, all persons were free to begin planting for the coming year [37, 50]; also Jeançon (1906). According to Jeançon, a special field was sown at this time for "kachina corn," presumably for use in ceremonies.

The Ka-Ve-Na Ceremony of the Winter Society

The Ka-ve-Na ceremony was the contribution of the Winter Society of the Winter Moiety to the "Edge of Spring" ceremonials held by all societies shortly after January 23. It was a four-day rite, held at the home of the Winter cacique. Formerly it was part of the procedure involving the transfer of religious responsibility from the Winter Moiety to the Summer Moiety. A Ka-ve-Na was held December 12, 1954; it was the first time in twenty or thirty years. The informant [73] was one of the guards. A similar ceremony of transference, the Ka-mi-na, was current at San Juan in the 1960s [9, 34].

It is possible that the term Ka-ve-Na was a generic one for any major retreat and "work" of the Winter Society. This same term was also applied to the Winter solstice ceremony [43], and there is a suggestion that retreats prior to a winter po'ku were designated by the same term as were the fall transference rites [45].

Only the last night of Ka-ve-Na was open to the public. Spectators crowded into the southeast section of one of the four rooms. (Other informants [13, 18] stated that Ka-ve-Na took place in four rooms. The Winter Society was in one, a central room with the Winter altar. Meal trails led from the altar to zigzag meal lines terminating in points formed by large arrowheads. Altars were cloud symbols about eight feet long, outlined in blue cornmeal. Outside was a bowl with sprouted corn and corn ornaments; also outside the altar were large black bowls. In the altar was a rectangular, terraced bowl with sacred water, WWH.) Those who were unable to find accommodations in the main room stayed in adjacent ones. The room in which the altar was located was divided by a line of cornmeal. According to the informant, the altar was of the type shown in Jeançon's pictures. Altar equipment was placed to one side when the dancing began. Any spectator who crossed the cornmeal line was considered "trapped," and was obligated to join the society. "It was believed that if you did not join, evil would befall you" [43].

The terminal ceremony began with prayers followed by songs. Each time a song slowed or finished, members howled like wolves. This sound was the peculiar property of the society. The songs were rendered by two chanters, who kept time with k'u titi. These bell stones were oval, flat, and about a foot long. One was black, one red; when struck, they gave off a ringing sound [73].

Following the songs, both society members and the audience danced. The Winter Society danced in a double line with alternating pairs of men and women. Spectators also formed a line, but the dancers in this case were nearly always women. After the dance all visitors were given a drink of sacred water, prayers were said, and they departed.

A guard was posted at the door and "work" was continued by the society (presumably the manufacture of prayer plumes). This, according to the informant [73], terminated the ritual obligations of the Winter Society until the following fall (October to November).

SOLSTICE CEREMONIES

Solstice ceremonies (pinge to, "half," or "central") were held on or very close to December 12 and June 15. In December the Winter Society had "a work for a termination of the whole year." There was no comparable ceremony in June, but Ka-ve-Na followed the December solstice ceremony.

Solstice Ceremonies of the Winter Society of the Winter Moiety and the Summer Society of the Summer Moiety

As indicated earlier, all societies "worked" at the solstice periods. In a sense, these were rites of world renewal, conceived of as insuring the continuity of nature. Those held during the winter solstice seem to have been greater in magnitude than those held during the summer. The Winter Society initiated the rites, beginning either December 6 or 12. This four-day retreat was followed by a corresponding one by the Summer Society [9]. The Winter Society held a retreat of this kind in 1954, the first one held by this organization for a period of twenty to thirty years [73].

The rationale for the ceremonies was recorded by Jeançon (1905), as given by one of his informants:

> The Santa Claras, like all Pueblo Indians, are agriculturalists, and their whole ceremonial philosophy is built upon prayers, magic and observances for rain, planting, growing and maturing the crops. Once the seed is planted in the ground, it must be nourished and brought to successful maturity by heat, moisture and care. The ordinary human effort used in hoeing and cultivating the crop is not sufficient to guarantee its successful growth. Before the ground is broken up for planting it must be prepared by the ceremony of waking up the Earth-mother, and throwing out her breast after her winter rest; the Sun-father must be set upon the right path again so that he knows how to go; and many other matters are to be attended to before the first planting can be done.
>
> ...this was accomplished in the following manner: About the sixth of December all the animals go into their kivas for a long retreat which lasts until the 24th or 25th of December. During this time you cannot kill them as their magic is too strong for a man to hurt them. About this same time the Sun-father goes as far north as he wants to go. Then when he gets there he does not know whether he wants to go north or south, and so when we watch him come up in the morning, he seems to hesitate which way he is to go; then we have to help him and we make medicine so that he knows how to go. Also about this time the Earth-mother is sound asleep and we must be very careful not to wake her up, so we don't sing or yell, or make any kind of noise. If anybody makes a noise by mistake, they ask her to forgive them. The women must not sweep the houses and we men don't chop any wood. Everybody stays in the house excepting when they have to go out. We are all as quiet as we can be. That is the time of the year to tell stories, and it is the best time of the year to tell stories because then the cloud-people, and all the other people above and in the underworld are asleep, and they don't get mad if you make a mistake in the stories. We make presents of tobacco to the men storytellers and wood to the women storytellers.

My informant [73] confirmed some of the details above and added others. According to him, all societies went into a four-day retreat. During this period the caciques watched the sun until it arrived at the winter solstice. "It stays at this point in the Sangre de Cristo range for from two to four days." They notified the war captains, who in turn announced the fact to the village.

During this period the village was under tabu. No uncooked corn could be touched or eaten. "Even if you feed corn to the stock, it must be cooked." Piñon pitch was placed on the forehead, chest (heart), shoulders and knees. "This means that you will stick on the sun, be carried on (live through) the following year." No one was allowed to bathe, comb their hair, or hunt during this period. "A man who hunted would have no luck. He might see game but could not hit it. The game would show up in great numbers as they knew that they were safe. These are free days for the animals." A breach of tabu was thought to result in death. "This would mean that a man had dropped away from the sun, would lose his life during the year."

As mentioned, this solstice rite was performed by the Winter Society in 1954. It was designated as a Ka-ve-Na, and available details indicate that it closely paralleled the ceremony designated by the same name executed by this organization at the "Edge of Spring." The informant [73] acted as one of the outside guards, so that his observations of esoteric features were minimal.

The rite was presumably held at the home of the Winter cacique. Four rooms were utilized. The society occupied the central room, which contained the altar and various items of ceremonial paraphernalia. Spectators, in this case limited to Winter Moiety members, were excluded from this room, but watched the rite from the doorways of an adjacent room. Entrance by an uninitiated person constituted trespass, and obligated the individual to join the society.

Terminal features of the last night of the retreat were predominantly intermittent singing, dancing, and praying. Singing was done by two "fathers of the kachina," or "elders," who wore only a breechclout and kilt. Tinklers were suspended from the latter. They accompanied themselves with k'utiti.

When the singing began, society members, both male and female, danced in a double row. Women wore the old style mantas. The Winter cacique and the right arm did not dance; the left arm danced only occasionally. After dancing, the society members sat about and "mumbled" prayers. The Winter cacique prayed first, then the right arm, the left, the remainder of the society, and finally the singers. This routine was continued all night.

Finally a bowl of sprouted corn was presented to the Winter cacique. He took the sprouts and mixed them in a bowl of sacred water, stirring the mixture with an obsidian blade taken from the altar. Next he dipped two eagle wing feathers in the mixture and sprinkled all members of the society in turn. The left arm then came forward and took the bowl; he went to the rooms occupied by the spectators and gave each a drink. This terminated the rite.

While no data were obtained on the Winter Moiety rites held at the summer solstice, or on the solstice rites of the Summer Moiety, other than that they existed and involved dancing, it can be inferred that they followed the same pattern [9, 50, 55]. According to informants, those held at the winter solstice by the Winter Moiety were more intensive than at the summer solstice, and the reverse was true of those held by the Summer Moiety.

OTHER CEREMONIES

Monthly Retreats of the Winter Society of the Winter Moiety and the Summer Society of the Summer Moiety

Both of these organizations went into retreat for one day each month and "worked" for the general welfare of the village. Retreats were ideally held on the 15th, but there was allowable latitude. At least in recent years, the societies have reached an accommodation with the economic commitments of their members. For example, the Winter Society worked on September 8, 1946, and on August 17 in 1948.

The ritual of the retreats was a modified version of those of greater magnitude. It consisted primarily of the preparation of prayer plumes, accompanied by songs and prayers, and their eventual depositing at the shrines in and surrounding the pueblo [9, 13, 25].

The following is an account of a monthly retreat of the Winter Society. The principal informant [73] was not a member of the society, but acted as a guard; he therefore knew the rite only from marginal participation.

The retreat was held at the home of the Winter cacique. Early in the morning the society members bathed. The male members then repaired to the society headquarters and began their fast and "work." Female members also fasted, but remained at their homes, preparing food for the organization.

Prior to the start of the ritual, guards, usually war captains, arrived at the Winter cacique's home with armloads of wood. This dignitary appeared, took the wood, and was informed by the donors that they were there for the purpose of guarding the rite against interruptions.

The ceremony then began. Society members stripped to their breechclouts and erected an altar. The cacique sat behind the altar at the center, his right and left arms and the remainder of the membership distributed on either side of him. The "work" consisted of preparing prayer plumes for depositing at shrines. This was accompanied by prayers and songs. "The series of songs which were sung determined the length of the work." When the "work" was accomplished, the Winter cacique instructed a society member to give the guard or guards a drink of sacred water from a bowl that rested on the altar. At this time the guards were warned to keep secret everything they had heard or seen.

Another man was sent to inform the female members that food was required. The women arrived with the food, barefoot and dressed in mantas. The baskets were deposited opposite the altar, along the wall. Prayers were said, and each woman was given a drink of sacred water and then departed. Women did not take part in the esoteric proceedings of the society.

Following the departure of the women, the guards were invited to eat; when they had finished, they were dismissed. Presumably, the society then ate, after which the plumes with meal were deposited at the various shrines [18, 25, 50, 73]. "They bury the feathers" [73].

No information was obtained on the corresponding retreats and "work" of the Summer Society.

Ditch Opening Ceremony of the Summer Society

The principal irrigation ditches were cleaned during the middle or latter part of March. When the work was completed, but before the water was released, the Summer Society went into retreat. Presumably this was a one-day retreat. It was not learned whether or not it coincided with the regular monthly retreat.

When all was ready, those who had worked on the ditch gathered at the headgate. Shortly afterward, two members of the Summer Society, selected by the cacique, arrived, wrapped in blankets. The water was released, and the members proceeded down the ditch ahead of the water, depositing prayer plumes at intervals [22, 50]. According to another informant [31], the plumes consisted of turkey feathers.

Salt Gathering Rites of the Summer and Winter Societies

Santa Clara behavior associated with salt gathering conformed to the general ritual pattern in the Southwest (see Hill 1940). The widespread myth accounting for the departure of Salt Old Woman (A[n]nekwizho) from the immediate vicinity of the pueblo was present and included the standard themes.

According to my informant [35], Salt Old Woman formerly lived at the site of the Spanish-American village of Guachupangue, adjacent to Santa Clara Pueblo. Once during a feast the people complained of a lack of salt. An old woman took the bowl and blew her nose in it. Those present refused to eat the food, whereupon the old woman claimed that she had supplied them with salt for many years. She became angry, left the village, took her salt, and went to Angue (a location in the Estancia Valley of

New Mexico). After she had gone, the villagers discovered that she was Salt Old Woman.

In another version, her departure was attributed to ceremonial breaches. According to another informant [45], a group of salt gatherers who were under tabu looked at and spoke to a woman, and on yet another occasion, the managing societies failed to conduct the associated ceremonies in their proper order.

An expedition to the Estancia Valley to gather salt was in the nature of a religious pilgrimage, and was believed to have restorative and healthful consequences [35, 51]. Salt itself was used as an agent of purification, and was rubbed and sprinkled on people for that purpose. It also had curative powers. It was rubbed on body sores and placed on top of an infant's head and on the roof of its mouth, to prevent the "root of its nose from dropping in." It was sprinkled outside houses during severe hail and electrical storms to avert danger from such storms.

Journeys for salt were normally planned to coincide with a "hidden dance," but this was not mandatory. Rites preliminary and subsequent to a trip were under the jurisdiction of the Winter and Summer societies. Usually four men were selected from each moiety to take part in the venture. They were under restrictions for eight days prior to their departure: they remained continent; they were prohibited from eating meat or salt; and their diet was limited to corn products and white clay. During this preliminary period, the Winter and Summer societies, in the course of their "work" for the coming "hidden dance," manufactured a series of special prayer plumes for deposit at the salt lake.

At their destination they camped a short distance from the lake, since their mission had to be accomplished before sunrise. The next morning all entered the lake naked, deposited the prayer plumes, and began to gather salt. During this interval they were not allowed to speak. When a sufficient quantity had been gathered, they left in a body singing a "special song." No one was allowed to look back once they left the lake [45].

The return to the pueblo was timed to coincide with the evening of the fourth day of the first four-day retreat of the managing societies. Upon arrival they presented the salt to their respective caciques and left to bathe in the Rio Grande. They were then "painted" with swamp mud—presumably from the lake.

Distribution of the salt took place the following day. During their absence the caciques had designated certain men to hunt and women to prepare food. The results of their efforts were given to the two caciques. When all was ready, a crier announced to the village that the distribution would take place. All went to the home of their respective cacique, the women carrying baskets or pots. Each family received its allotment of salt. Following this, all feasted on the accumulated food. This ended the ceremony. The gatherers then went into retreat at the headquarters of their kachina organizations to prepare for participation in the coming "hidden dances" [45].

Minor Individual Religious Rites

The emphasis on collective participation at Santa Clara Pueblo tended to suppress individual religious activities; the people could be said to have dealt indirectly with the supernatural. The priesthood acted in a liaison capacity between the people and their deities. Probably as a result of this, the deities were poorly conceptualized, and their attributes were poorly defined. It was difficult because of general reticence to get much information on the gods. However, it appears that devout individuals habitually engaged in rites of minor character, usually associated with the household.

One of the more frequent manifestations was a morning offering. Houses normally had a wall niche located near the entrance or in one or more inner rooms. In these were small stone animals, anthropomorphic figures, and cornmeal. These figures were called kue ("child rock," or "small rock"). The head of the household usually arose before sunrise. He went to the niche, took some of the cornmeal, went to the doorway, threw the meal toward the east, folded his arms, and said a prayer to the rising sun, "that the day may come out well, that I may have good health." The content of these prayers was variable, depending upon individual exigencies of the moment. They were directed to a supernatural or supernaturals (to wae), and most included thanks for protection during the coming day. Prayers were also directed to the full moon, morning star, and evening star. They were also petitions to Mother Earth for rain, good crops, and for the successful culmination of personal endeavors, and help in any specific need. It was also customary at this time to pray for the welfare of the village as a whole [31, 52].

A closely related rite was reported by an informant [35]. According to her, many homes possessed hand-carved wooden boxes which contained feathers and meal. Periodically, a household head arose early in the morning, took a few feathers and a pinch of cornmeal, walked to the nearest village shrine, and deposited the offering with a prayer.

Jeançon (1904–30) also reported on a series of religious acts associated with the household. He stated:

> Until about twenty years ago it was customary to have a bowl or basket of sacred meal near the doorway into the house, and those entering sprinkled the meal to the six sacred regions as an invocation to the gods for blessings on the house and its occupants. . . . After a cooking fire has been lit, it is the custom to throw a pinch of meal into it as an offering. . . . The same custom exists with regard to baking bread. After the oven has been heated and the coals cleaned out, a pinch of meal is thrown inside it. . . . Offerings of food other than meal, such as fragments of meat and any other food, are thrown into the cooking fire or thrown just outside the door. In many ceremonies which have a feast connected with them, food is placed in bowls and taken to the four cardinal points and left there, in this case to be consumed by the supernatural prey animals being invoked at the time of the rite.

CEREMONIAL DANCES

Participation in Dances

Participation in any dance was considered highly desirable, because of its religious connotation. By dancing, a person liquidated a public duty and a religious obligation. These rites offered a medium by which the individual could express thanks for supernatural benefits, both personal and for the community. Participation also created an atmosphere congenial to future gains from supernatural sources.

"You never get something for nothing. You ought to do something for what you get. You try to do something in return for what you have received, to expend some effort. You make an effort to do something beautiful. This is in the mind of all dancers" [21]. "Dances were given to establish good relationships with Indians, whites, and Plains Indians. For example, if I went to a Ute and wanted a blanket and got that blanket cheap, it would be because I earned it in a dance. Dances are prayers for success in any line. If all rules are observed and nothing is left out, if everything goes well, requests will be granted. They say we pay for what will come later" [50].

"A dance like the Zuñi Basket Dance would be given before planting. It was given as a prayer for the coming year" [43]. "Dances were for good days; for better crops; for hunting; for rain" [30]. "What you think about when you dance varies with the person. Many think about the benefits they will get, like better crops and weather" [37]. "All dances were for happiness and good crops. You were supposed to think of these things when you danced" [32].

Preparation for Dances

Theoretically a dance, like any other religious effort, could not be given unless complete harmony existed in the village. It is doubtful that such conditions prevailed in aboriginal times; certainly they have not obtained during the last forty years. As a result, adjustments and compromises have been made. These have allowed for the continuation of a rich ceremonial life, without impairing factional integrity. Where both moieties formerly participated in all dances [9, 18, 22, 52], now one moiety or a faction within it was in complete charge of a performance. Unanimity within such a segment was considered to meet ritual requirements. Accordingly, dances which once had broad participation have become restricted to a relative few, and the right of performance has come to be vested in a relatively small group. Over the years this has caused a general weakening of and some loss of ritual. Disharmony has often prevented a dance from being held when the appropriate time arose. Some rites have lapsed because schisms have prevented the cooperation of essential religious officials.

It should also be noted that recently some "little dances" have been performed on occasions when only "big dances" should have been held. It is possible that the Kwitara and Yan dewa, for example, may eventually achieve "big" status. As of 1961 this appears to have been effected. These substitutions are further evidence of disunity within the religious pattern.

Any dance required considerable planning and organization. First a request for a performance was made. This might originate in the religious hierarchy, or it could come from secular individuals. When the former considered a dance advisable, they consulted with their constituents. If unanimity existed, the performance was assured. Most important rituals originated in this manner. However, secular groups, if they wished, might petition the religious hierarchy for permission to perform a particular dance. Either the younger men, those who wished to take part in the chorus, or the song composer might request a particular dance [9]. This was indicative of an accord within the group, and there is no record of a request being refused [13, 20, 50]. When such a petition was made, the moiety or faction gathered in the kiva, where speeches were made commenting on the desirability of the dance, its purpose, and the benefits to be derived from its performance [50].

Once a decision to hold a dance was reached, the practical machinery of planning was put in operation. The song composer, or composers, were notified, participants were selected, practice was begun, and food for the participants was accumulated.

Song Composers

The office of song composer existed in both moieties. There is evidence that the position tended to be hereditary in the male line; the father chose as his successor the son whom he considered most talented, not necessarily the eldest. If the composer had no male issue, or if he believed his sons incapable of filling this office, he selected a successor from among near relatives [13, 21, 50].

Aspiring song composers underwent a probationary period. These candidates were selected as soon as their "voices changed." They were taught and trained for their role, and worked with their parent or near relative and older members of their group over a period of years. If they lacked the ability to compose verse or music, to detect mistakes in others, or had poor musical "ears," this soon became apparent. The candidacy was revoked, and another selection made [13, 18].

When the song composer was notified (in cases where he or his group had not made the request) that a dance (either "big" or "little") was to be held, he gathered a group, consisting of his successor and older members of the moiety or faction. Often this body consisted almost entirely of near relatives. These individuals recalled the former song versions associated with the particular dance, and sang them to the accompaniment of the slow beat of a drum. Once they had refreshed themselves, suggestions for changes in words or tone were in order, and were usually forthcoming. Additions and subtractions were discussed until a reformulation was agreed upon. The group then practiced until they had perfected the new version. When this was achieved, they taught the song to those who would form the chorus at the dance. It was stated that innovations in songs might come as frequently from members of the general group as from "song composers" [13, 18]. "Certain members of the moiety who have good memories and good ears assist the composer to bring out a song" [18]. This was the case in the Zuñi Basket Dance held March 17, 1946. [18].

The above has obvious implications with regard to cultural change. Certainly there is strong evidence against a static condition in this compartment of ritualism, and it is probable that the musical and textual content of songs has altered considerably over a period of decades. However, it was alleged that there was an irreducible core in all songs, that could not be tampered with. For example, especially in songs accompanying "big dances," certain references of a religious nature had to be made. Variations were possible only in terms of the "periphery" of the established pattern [29, 50].

Selection of Drummers

The selection of drummers was also of prime concern. As soon as a dance was scheduled, those in charge asked for volunteers for these positions. Those who offered their services underwent a tryout. If they were successful, they were appointed, and practiced with the chorus. Training for these posts was begun early in the life of the individual. Any child who showed ability and interest was trained and instructed by some relative.

Selection of Dancers

The personnel of "outside" dances might include society and nonsociety members, males and females. Selection of the dancers was made by whatever segment of the religious hierarchy was in charge of the particular event. Formerly this was on a moiety basis. War captains informed individuals that they had been chosen to participate. The announcement was formal. "It was almost prayer-like. 'You have been chosen,'" etc. "You may live well and long and do a good service" [21]. Men were selected first; if women were to take part, they were chosen and notified at a later date. The combination of public opinion, the power of the reli-

gious hierarchy, and a sense of moral obligation was normally sufficient to overcome any reluctance to participate; coercive action was seldom necessary [21, 52]. After all, failure to dance constituted a religious breach, and subjected the individual to the possibility of supernatural retribution.

Dance practice was begun as soon as the selection of participants was completed and songs were perfected. Male dancers were taught the steps, and singers and dancers practiced together for several days. [For definitive articles on Rio Grande Pueblo choreography, see Kurath (1958a; 1958b) and Kurath and Garcia (1970). WWH] Ordinary dress was worn until the final night of practice. On that occasion a "dress rehearsal" was held, and any women who were to participate practiced for the first time [13, 18]. Menstruating women were not barred from dancing or from the kiva, at least not in recent years [21, 50].

The first time a person participated in a "big dance" he or she was "tied" (xwian). This consisted of placing a ribbon or handkerchief about the dancer's neck or arm, or in the case of women, usually pinning the emblem on the shoulder. This obligated the person to sponsor or give a "little dance," almost always a Prisoner's Dance, at a later date [13, 18]. A non-Indian American folk dance was sometimes substituted for the Prisoner's Dance. "This dance was given as a kind of payment to the village for the privilege of dancing" [18].

On the other hand, dancers at the time of their initial appearances received gifts from members of the village. These presents might consist of money, clothing, or food. "They were given to show appreciation for the person having danced" [13].

As in the case of drummers, dance training began early in life. Children amused themselves by dancing at home. At such times they were usually instructed, corrected, and encouraged by their parents. Frequently children asked visiting relatives, especially their grandfathers and uncles, to sing for them, and executed dance steps to this accompaniment. Boys often went with their fathers to the practice sessions before a dance, and acquired additional instruction [13].

Food at Dances

Another preparatory feature of "big dances" was the accumulation of food; responsibility for this fell to the lot of the women of the moiety or moiety faction sponsoring the dance. Substantial supplies were gathered, prepared, and brought to the kiva or the house where the dancers originated. Food was served, usually about one o'clock in the afternoon, during the interval between the second and third appearances. All dancers and those who had aided in the dance, however slightly, sat and partook of the food. "At this time the dance was discussed, how it had been performed, the impression it had made on the village, etc." [18].

Dance Classification

Three categories of dances were recognized by the Santa Clara Indians. [See also Brown (1960) and Kurath and Garcia (1970: 24). WWH] The distinguishing basis was the degree, or level, of sacredness. The most sacrosanct were those esoteric performances, previously described, which were associated with kachina enactments in the kivas or in the hills, or with the functions of various societies at their headquarters.

The second and third categories were designated "big dances" and "little dances." "Big dances" included a large variety of performances of semiesoteric character, which usually took place in the plazas of the village. While these exhibitions had definite religious implications, the intensity of the association was not as great as in the kiva-society type, and they were recognized as belonging to a different order.

Included among "big dances" were the Basket Dance, Zuñi Basket Dance, Tablita or Corn Dance, Pogo *share*, Buffalo or Animal Dance, Tewa Buffalo Dance, Mountain Sheep Dance, Tewa Deer Dance, Horse Dance, and Relay Race. These normally followed a kachina enactment or were held at important periods in the ceremonial calendar, such as Santa Clara or San Antonio Day. They could not be performed during the Lenten season, between Ash Wednesday and Good Friday [9, 18].

"Big dances" were not duplications of dances performed in the kiva by the kachina, or maskless kachina dances, as Parsons implied (1929: 179–86), since the dance forms in most instances were different and the personnel variable. Furthermore, women did not perform in kachina dances. K'osa and kwirana often appeared in conjunction with "big dances," though this was not essential, since clowns might or might not be present at any type of dance [9, 13, 18].

The features distinguishing "big outside dances" from those of the "little" category were several religious adjuncts lacking in the latter [18, 21, 50]. For example, "big outside dances" usually meant the holding of a "slow dance" (ange *sh*are) prior to the major rite [29, 37] and, if women participated, the performance of a "center place dance" when the dance terminated. Both the "slow dance" and the "center place dance" were religiously significant [9].

The religious adjuncts also included a number of other items. Participants were blessed by the cacique before the dance. In 1941 this duty was performed by the k'osa, since the cacique was allied with the opposition faction and did not take part in the proceedings [21, 29]. A bowl of sacred water was kept in the moiety kiva (or a house of the sponsoring faction) for the duration of the dance [50]. Adherence to the ritual, sacred number was enforced; four appearances were made, and on each appearance the dance was performed in four plazas [13, 18]. One complete performance of the dance was also given in the moiety kiva or house of the sponsoring faction, when the dancers returned from their last appearance [29]. Finally, following the custom observed in most sacred rites, but not necessarily in all "little dances," all participants bathed when the performance was completed. Women washed only part of their bodies in Santa Clara Creek; men disrobed entirely and bathed in the Rio Grande. Evergreens worn as part of the dance costume, and cornmeal, were tossed into the water and allowed to float downstream [21, 29]. This was done after the Basket Dance in April 1941.

While the "slow dance" and "center place dance" were attributed to all "big dances" by informants [29, 37, 50, 52], references to specific cases of association with particular rites were forthcoming for the "slow dance" only in connection with Basket Dance, Zuñi Basket Dance, Corn Dance, and Pogo *share* [29, 37, 50, 52], and to the "center place" in connection with Pogo *Share* and Basket Dance (Tung *share*). The "slow dance" was observed in connection with the Basket Dance in 1941, and it can be implied from Freire-Marreco's account of the Pogo *Share* (Freire-Marreco 1911: 337).

"Slow dances" were performed in plazas one and four on the late evening and early morning prior to the "big dance." Only those males who were to participate in the coming event took part. Each wore in his hair a prayer plume prepared by the kachina society during the Edge of Spring ceremony. (This was a Summer Moiety ceremony. However, an informant [50] stated that the Winter group also danced the "slow dance," and therefore probably wore similar plumes.) These plumes were composed of a feather of a roadrunner, Say's phoebe or oriole, and yellow warbler. Mantas were worn instead of evergreens [29, 52].

The dancers arranged themselves close together and in single file. They flexed their knees four times, then slowly raised their right feet and brought them down, as each man in turn twisted his body to the right. This movement was then repeated twisting the body toward the left, then right, and so on. This created the impression of a rippling line from right to left, left to right, etc.

The dance was accompanied by a song. This had three parts, the first part or "root" (ha pu), the second (ha pe be), and the third, "smaller one," or "finish" (here ni). Each part was sung first in a soft, and then a loud tone. At the termination of each part, the file took three steps in one direction while shaking rattles, then turned and took three steps in the opposite direction before beginning the next movement. Each performance consumed approximately half an hour [29, 52].

The Pingge *shure share* was held after "big dances" in which both males and females took part. Those who had participated repaired to the kiva the evening following the dance. Two lines, one of men and one of

women, were formed, facing each other. The man and woman at the head of the line stepped forward and danced up and down twice between the two lines, then took places at the foot of the line. The next couple repeated this movement, and so on, until all had danced. The dance was accompanied by songs—in some cases the same songs used in the major rite [29, 37, 50].

This rite involved exchanges of gifts between partners, usually goods which had been accumulated prior to the dance. Formerly bread was given by women, and men gave a plant called ogo fe pu (whose roots were chewed and the juice sucked) or prairie clover (whiri fe). More recently introduced foods such as candy, cookies, peanuts, oranges, and bologna have since been substituted. Men usually presented their gifts before the dance; the women, at a later time [25, 50]. "This dance has religious implications" [9].

While the religious element was also present in varying degree in most dances designated "little dances," its importance was recognized as subordinated to social and entertainment features. Dances of this type were given to break the monotony of everyday life between gaps in major ceremonial activity and during periods of slackened economic pressure. They were held to honor and entertain visiting members of other tribes, and even for commercial purposes. "They might be held between Easter and San Antonio Day. They fill in" [43].

There were house-to-house dances of this kind on Christmas Eve by both moieties—the Ute Dance, Eagle Dance, Buffalo Dance, etc. "If a family liked a particular dance, they would request that it be given the next day or during the Christmas season" [50]. "Many were held on Kings' Day, when the new governor took office" [43]. "Small dances were also given to honor and to entertain visiting groups of Indians." (See Yan dewa for a specific instance. WWH) "These dances could be put on in emergencies, when the Harvey Tours ran through a large group of tourists. They were danced for pay, and in such cases were not religious" [61].

Many dances of the "little" type were obviously derived from foreign sources. Santa Clara has always been receptive to dance innovations, a proclivity recognized by informants [29, 43, 50], and also noted by Parsons (1929: 225). Since the vested interests of the religious hierarchy were minimal in the "little" type of dances, this category offered a convenient medium for expressing this propensity, ranging from wholesale borrowing, as in the case of the Hopi Buffalo Dance and Cow Dance, to lesser inclusions and innovations, as in the Eagle and Yan dewa performances.

"BIG DANCES" OF THE
SUMMER AND WINTER MOIETIES

Basket Dance

The Basket Dance (Tuŋ *sh*are) was performed sporadically, either in the spring prior to Ash Wednesday, or on Easter, following the Good Friday kachina performance, as it was on April 13, 1941. Freire-Marreco also witnessed a performance, October 21, 1912 (see Robbins, Harrington, and Freire-Marreco 1916: 42). After the pattern of other "big dances," it was formerly participated in by large segments of both moieties. There was no restriction as to the number of dancers, either male or female, though the sexes were kept approximately equal. The k'osa normally took part. It was one of the dances performed by the dancer group during a Summer kachina performance in the kiva [29, 50, 52, 72].

Factionalism had altered the recent composition of the dance, and in 1941 the dancers were members of the progressive and conservative groups. Since neither cacique was a member of these factions, they did not actively participate, and the use of the Summer and Winter kivas was denied performers. An ordinary dwelling (#103) was used for costuming, and the dancers emerged from and returned to it before and after each enactment. In the absence of the cacique or caciques, the rite was directed by the governor and three assistants. On this occasion twenty males and twenty-two females performed [29, 52].

Men wore dance kilts and carried gourd rattles. Women were attired in mantas and blankets, and carried baskets and musical rasps. Both sexes were adorned with fir (spruce?) twigs.

The governor and the three assistant dance directors wore moccasins, bright colored shirts, and neckerchiefs, and a blanket about their shoulders. Their faces were colored a faint red, not as pronounced as those of the dancers [29, 52]. Another informant [86] was of the opinion that once a line of paint had been placed under the eyes, the person actually represented a particular kachina.

Additional details of costume and equipment were given by Freire-Marreco (Robbins, Harrington, and Freire-Marreco 1916: 42–43):

> ...the male performers wore spruce branches hanging from their necks and waist-belts, while small twigs of spruce formed part of the headdress called *popobi*, "squash blossom." The female performers carried sprigs of spruce in their right hands, concealing their wooden rasps, ŋwaempé. On the afternoon of the day preceding the dance the five *capitanes* went to the forest, cut eight young spruce trees, and brought them, unobserved, to the village; and after midnight these were planted in the plazas, two at each dancing place. These were referred to in the song-phrase.... [No spruce trees were reported for the 1941 dance. WWH]

The 1941 dance began about ten in the morning. The dancers left the house in a double file, women in one, the men in another, and walked eastward along the road, entering plaza one from the west. Once in the plaza, the dance was begun.

The dance was in two movements. In the first, men and women danced side by side in two files. In the dance step of the men, the right foot was lifted and brought down; as it struck the ground, the heel of the left foot was elevated. According to informants [29, 52], this step was characteristic of all dances in which rattles rather than drums were used to keep time. Singing was in time with the rattles. This first movement of the dance consumed about seven and a half minutes.

At its conclusion there was a short intermission, during which the dance director and his assistants spread blankets, tied end to end, between the two rows of performers. The women knelt on the blankets, and each placed her basket face downward, with the upper portion of the rim resting on her knees, the lower on the blanket. One end of the notched stick of the musical rasp was placed in the center of the basket sounding board, while the unnotched stick was grasped in the right hand, and the group was ready to perform the second dance movement.

The men faced the women, and the dance was begun, accompanied by the musical rasps, rattles, and the song. The first part of the second movement was slow; in the second, the tempo was increased. During this phase, the rasp was given a short rapid stroke, and the gourd rattle a quick, short shake [29, 52].

The above performances were reenacted in turn in plazas two, three, and four. This completed one circuit or round, and the participants returned to house #103 to rest. During the course of the day four appearances were made in each of the four plazas. Behavior was the same in each case, with two exceptions. The rest period between appearances one and two, and three and four, was twenty to thirty minutes; the break between two and three was an hour to an hour and a half, to allow the dancers to eat [29, 52].

The second innovation was the inclusion of the k'osa during the first round at the second plaza, and the final round at the fourth plaza. A Nambé and a San Juan k'osa were participants. Both were old men and in poor physical condition. If such had not been the case, they presumably would have taken part at each performance.

They went through the characteristic K'osa motions, and gave the characteristic laugh. They mingled with the dancers, looked surprised, and inquired of each other the meaning of the dance and who and what the dancers were. They feigned astonishment and surprise at each other's answers. Finally they joined the dance, performing in approved K'osa fashion, motioning with arms upward, palms out, as if waiting to receive something. "This motion is associated with K'osa, a prayer motion" [29]. Both disappeared just before the completion of the round.

When the dance terminated, the participants again returned to the house, divested themselves of parts of their dance costumes, and then proceeded to the river to bathe [29, 52].

Zuñi Basket Dance

The Zuñi Basket Dance (Suni tung *share*) was formerly held in the spring or fall by either moiety [40]. Recently, it has become the "property" of the Winter group, and was danced by them on March 17, 1946 [18, 37, 50], and following the Easter kachina performance in 1948 [43]. According to two informants [29, 52], however, the Summer Moiety could perform it if they wished. According to Parsons (1929: 188–89), it was introduced from the south. This is partially substantiated by the fact that some archaic Hopi words were still retained in the songs [29]. It was one of the dances performed by the dance group during a Winter kachina performance in the kiva.

As was customary, the dancers made four appearances and danced in each of the four plazas. A separate song to the same melody was sung on each occasion. Songs referred to various shrines, the cardinal points, and to the coming of the kachina [29]. According to Parsons (1929: 189):

...The dancers stand in line and the little baskets, to which turkey feathers are attached, are raised and lowered by the women dancers as in the San Juan basket dance. The Nambé *kossa* in particular, come out for the dance at Santa Clara.

The dance principals consisted of two women and an indeterminate number of men. The men formed a single file. The position of the women was in front of the line, near the third and fourth man from either end. Each woman carried a basket with red-dyed goat hair and turkey feathers suspended from the rim. They were carried face outward and raised and lowered as the women danced. At certain times during the performance the women faced each other, danced forward and passed, and then went back to their original positions. All dancing and singing was done to the accompaniment of rattles; no drums were used [13, 27, 29].

Male dance costumes in the 1946 dance were somewhat variable. All wore dance kilts, some secured with belts to which sleigh bells were attached. A second standard item was moccasins, some beaded, some plain. Skunkskin guards were worn by all. Each wore a headband, beaded or plain, with an eagle feather projecting upward from a circular ornament at the front. A variety of bead, shell, or bone ornaments and/or bright-colored neckerchiefs were worn around the neck. Cinctures of yarn were tied around the leg below the knee, and in some cases sleigh bells were added to these. All wore arm bands, under which were inserted sprigs of evergreen. A gourd rattle was carried in the right hand; in the left, a half gourd attached to a wooden handle. Four eagle feathers were secured at intervals along the circumference of the half gourds. Further details on these items, said to represent the sun, were provided by Robbins, Harrington, and Freire-Marreco (1916: 102).

The women dancers wore mantas which were embroidered along the lower edges. Passing over the right shoulder and under the left, partially covering the mantas, were brightly covered silk shawls. Both women wore buckskin moccasins with wrapped tops and skunkskin guards. Cinctures of red-dyed goat hair were tied about the upper arm. Eagle plumes were worn in the hair. On the back, between the shoulders, was attached a rosette of feathers surmounted by macaw feathers which projected above the head of the dancer.

During a Zuñi basket dance any woman could place a basket containing a gift of bread or cornmeal before a dancer. This obligated the dancer to make a return gift; the basket was returned with the gift.

Tablita, or Corn Dance

[For a general discussion of this dance, particularly its occurrence among the Keres pueblos, see Lange (1957). WWH] The Tablita, or Corn Dance (Ho he je, a motion with the hand) might be performed following the "hidden dance" at Easter [50], and on Santa Clara or San Antonio days. Informants made a distinction between this and the Corn Dance, Kunɡ share, a "little dance" held during the Christmas season [14, 18, 21, 50, 52].

This "big dance" was formerly participated in by both moieties, who alternated appearances as was customary in other pueblos [14, 21, 50]. Recently, it has been designated as belonging to the Summer Moiety [29, 52]. Both men and women participated. The dancers formed two lines, a male paired with a female. According to two informants [21, 50], it was similar to the Santo Domingo Corn Dance.

Performance of this dance sems to have lapsed for a period of years. Parsons (1929: 193) stated that it was given by the Summer group at the Santa Fe Fiesta in 1927. It was almost certainly held in 1937 [see Keech 1937a (Appendix C), 1937b (Appendix D). Keech undoubtedly witnessed the Corn Dance; his descriptions indicate this, and were so identified by two informants [8, 9]. However, his references to Rainbow Women, sacred priestesses, etc., were pure fantasies. WWH] The Corn Dance was apparently not performed again until 1951, when it was presumably danced by the Summer Moiety. On this same occasion another group, probably a faction of the Winter Moiety, danced the Buffalo Dance. [I am indebted to Charles H. Lange for descriptions of both of the 1951 rites. WWH]

In 1951 the Tablita, or Corn Dance began about noon and lasted almost until dark. Preliminary to the performance, a pickup truck, equipped with a loud speaker, toured the pueblo, and a young announcer welcomed visitors to the village, encouraging them to enjoy themselves, but also stipulating that no drunkenness would be allowed. Those interested in photographing the events had already purchased "tickets" for this purpose, consisting of a short length of green yarn for one kiva group, red for the other. Prices for permission to photograph the Buffalo Dance were one dollar and twenty-five cents for still cameras and five dollars for movie cameras; for the Corn Dance, it was two dollars and five dollars, respectively.

There were two lines of dancers in the Corn Dance, each composed of about fifteen men and fifteen women. These were mostly young people; "there were no older people or children as is characteristic of Keresan dances of this type." The women were dressed essentially the same, except for differences in shoulder shawls or capes. They wore mantas over brightly colored dresses, woven sashes, modern silk shawls, and white wrapped moccasins. With minor exceptions, their *tablitas* were the same; the upper section was "pumpkin" yellow, the lower turquoise blue. Each had eagle down attached to the upper points of the terraces.

The men of one line had their upper bodies painted yellow; the other line, blue-grey. Both groups had a double row of white dots or short lines painted down across the chest to the waist, and extending around to the back and over the right shoulder, like a bandolier. Their hands were painted white, as were their legs above the knee. The costumes were essentially the same; white kilts bordered with variable embroidered geometric designs. These were secured with broad, woven white belts. A fox skin was inserted at the back. A few had bells around the waist. Arm bands were either blue or white, with sprigs of evergreen inserted in them. Garters were of yarn, and bells were attached at the back. Moccasins were equipped with skunkskin guards. Each dancer wore a silk handkerchief around the neck, and some augmented these with shell necklaces. On their heads were feather rosettes which included parrot feathers. Each individual carried a large flat gourd rattle in the right hand and evergreens in the left. The chorus and drummer wore ordinary modern costumes. The one large drum was painted yellow and black. There were about a dozen singers in the chorus.

The group made four appearances, and on each occasion danced in four locations:

(1) In front of the shrine at the west end of the kiva; (2) In the east or lower end of the plaza just north of the windmill; (3) Just west of the plaza on the other side of some houses; (4) West again in the area immediately south of the kiva. In the Tablita Dance, there was no sign of the pole which is so prominent in many Keresan Tablita dances. [It is difficult to correlate these locations with the four plazas indicated on Hill's map. CHL]

Pogo *Share*

The Pogo *share* normally occurred in the spring prior to Ash Wednesday or, according to Parsons (1929: 190), in December. Freire-Marreco saw it on February 9, 1911 (see Robbins, Harrington, and Freire-Marreco 1916: 42–43), and it was held Sunday, March 2, 1946 [18, 50]. The dance was thought to belong to the Summer Moiety [37, 45]; see also Parsons (1929: 190). The 1946 version was enacted by the cacique's faction within the Summer Moiety (see also Appendix D).

An indeterminate number of men and two women participated. Thirty men took part in 1911 (Freire-Marreco 1911: 334); twenty-four in 1946. Parsons (1929: 190) was apparently misinformed on this point, listing only two males and two females. In 1946 the same men participated throughout, whereas the female pairs were changed on each of the four appearances. A drummer accompanied the group, but there was no separate chorus; the male dancers furnished the songs to the time of the drum and gourd rattles [18]. No k'osa took part [50].

The 1946 dance consisted of three parts, each with its own song. The first part was enacted between the kiva and plaza. The dancers entered three abreast, dancing and singing. The women were stationed near the center of the file, flanked on either side by a male. Once in the plaza, the group assumed a V formation, "like geese in flight," [50], and finally as the song ended, reached a designated spot and fell into single file. The women occupied positions five stations in from either end of the line.

The second movement began as soon as the drummer reached his position at the right of the file. The dance step accompanying this interval consisted of raising the right foot and bringing it down hard, while simultaneously rocking the left.

Part three followed immediately on part two. The women came forward from their positions and danced, meeting at the center, in front of the group. Here they blocked each other momentarily, then passed, continuing to the end of the line. There they turned, danced back, met, passed, and took up their former positions. This coincided with the termination of the third song. Song one was then begun, and the group moved to the next plaza reenacting the complete routine.

Freire-Marreco's account of this dance in 1911 is exceptionally full. Because of its completeness and because it includes many preliminary and terminal features, as well as descriptions of costume, it has been quoted here in full (1911: 331–37).

Now let me try to tell you how things are in the Pueblo of Khapo, when the people are dancing to bring the early spring rain. Recall for a moment the scene in which the dance takes place; the compact little town above the river; the flat-roofed houses round the open *plaza;* the two large *estufas*—the dance-houses— with blank windowless walls and wide ladders for access. The dance I speak of "comes out" in late January or early February. And this dance, too, is supposed to be the outcome of an impulse: "the boys," it is said, "want to dance."

If I had been asked how such a dance would come about, I should have said, *a priori,* that it was founded on the general expectation of spring and the opening of the season for irrigation and planting, with all the community-work they entail; that this expectation of action in common favoured an access of social feeling which sought expression in the dance. And then comes in the effect of social habit, making the dance traditional and obligatory.

But this is too simple. I am talking as if the Pueblo Indians had developed agriculture and town life and yet had the social equipment of the Mohave-Apache. I was not allowing for an organisation to match the social morphology; and, in particular, I was not allowing for the organic specialisation of function by groups which is so marked in pueblo society. "The boys" (the unmarried men, that is) constitute an organ with functions, and apparently it is their function to feel the impulse to dance and communicate it to the rest of the body politic.

In winter "the boys" are more consciously an organ, and so, I suppose, more sensitive, than at other seasons. From March to November the fathers of families are in action, conducting farm work and irrigation; the boys are scattered, merged as their assistants. But from November to March the boys' functions come to the fore. Farm work is at a standstill. The only work is to bring firewood from the mountains, and by custom that is the boys' work: in former times they performed it more organically, so to speak, when all the boys brought wood for a common stock, not for their separate families. With the boys originates the impulse to play each of the winter games in turn; and as soon as the impulse reaches its height with them, it spreads from them upwards and downwards, to the young married men and to the children. So here, in the case of the dances, although there is undoubtedly a general emotional expectation of spring with its activities, yet it may well be true that the group of boys is the sensitive organ in which the impulse to dance for rain is first felt. "The boys want to dance." I knew some of the boys fairly well, but I never discovered who made the definite proposal; only, a boy would tell me as a valuable piece of news in advance, "They say that we are going to dance."—"When?"—"I don't know: maybe pretty soon."

Perhaps I am making too much of this. It may be said: Of course it is the boys who choose to dance, because they will have to do the actual dancing. But when one lives in a pueblo, it is hard to believe that anything is really spontaneous and unprescribed in the routine of society. However, such is the convention: no one in authority professes to order a dance, or to say when a dance will be, because "we cannot tell when the boys will want to dance." But there is a very general expectation that the boys will want to dance about the usual time.

This impulse to dance is very soon directed into orthodox channels. The boys go to the Captain of War and "take out a dance"; that is, they tell him of their wish and he reports it to the Council, who decide that there is no reason why the dance should not begin at once—this is called "giving a day"; and the proper authority decides what particular dance they shall take out. Of which high matters I know nothing.

The affair has passed out of the boys' hands into the hands of the war captains and the cacique. The captain counts up how many dancers he will want, and gives notice from house to house that he requires them to dance; and after "dispensing" a few whose parents make excuse for them and accepting some volunteers (married people, perhaps, who have a vow to dance), he completes his list.

After one or two evenings of informal singing and drumming in a private house, the dancers go to *estufa* for the formal practices. These practices extend over six, eight, even ten or eleven nights. They last from six or seven o'clock until long past midnight; and though they are genuine practices to learn the songs and dances, they are also important functions in themselves. In fact, the day when a dance "comes out" in public is only a part of the series of rites in the estufa. Sometimes the dancers sleep, eat, and spend the day in their homes; sometimes they stay in the estufa and have food brought to them there. The old men who know the dance teach the songs and the steps. It may be twenty years "since this dance came out," but the proper ornaments have all been laid up for it, even to the last feather. At the close of each meeting, the cacique and

other functionaries recite sacred formulas and preach to the dancers. When the girls begin to join in the practices, some old woman chaperones them in the estufa and takes them home again.

The cacique and the war captains are in charge—"the estufa is their house"—but the governor and all the high officers attend every practice and take part in the dancing. Once the series of practices has begun, they cannot leave the town, even if summoned to a general council of the league. It sounds a little like Mr. Marret's *genna: (The Birth of Humility,* pp. 22, 29) only I never had any feeling that the community was "on its spiritual sick-bed." On the contrary, the town never seems more alive than in those days of preparation. When the steady drum throbs half through the night, it is like the pulse of the town beating. Every morning there is a fresh rumour.

"We hear that the dance is to be *pogon shari.*" This is one of the dances in which the performers themselves sing, without a separate choir.

"Such and such girls have been chosen to dance"; and proud and pleased they are.

"That Moqui man has been here to teach them a song in the Moquino language."

"Who knows when the dance will come out? They say the boys are very slow learning the songs; they are not practising with girls yet."

"Compa' Faustino has made some new music, very beautiful."

"Last night they had the girls in: maybe they will come out Thursday or Friday."

"They have given out the macaw-tails to the fathers of the dancers, to mount them."

"The captains have announced that the dance will come out on Friday."

O that pleasant last day, the eve of the dance! when the rattles and the fox-skins and the turtle-shells are hanging ready in the houses; when the plaza has been swept, and the cacique is shut up "in the secret chamber of his house," performing his function, and the high officers have been with him there to make up the great headdress of feathers for the girls; when the dancers are washing their long hair, and all the people wash theirs too, to fit them for their part in the ceremony. In the morning the dying groans of goats are heard, and in the evening the ovens glow like stars, and the smell of baking makes the town festive. When the morning of the dance comes, it only remains to put on fine clothes and sit in the sun, while the war captain and his assistants hurry to and fro between their houses and the estufa.

And now at last the drum throbs, and the bells and rattles sound upon the air with a sweet dry clashing, and the dance has come out. In single file they move across the plaza—thirty lads dressed, painted and feathered alike; bodies and limbs painted grey, white kilts and white streaming girdles, eagle feathers and macaw tails on their heads, eagle-down scattered on their flowing hair, red tassels swinging from their garters, fox-skins dangling from their belts behind, green branches on their necks and shoulders, rattles and green branches in their hands. Here comes the first of the women dancers, and here the second; in a stiff square dress of black and colours, and a huge arch of feathers in a corncob handle. Soberly, looking straight before them, they file to the first of their dancing-places in the plaza. Now they re-form, and move in echelon as the cranes fly. Now they are in line for the dance, facing their drummer. Two steps forward, two long shakes of rattles:

o wó ho wo
e yé he yi;

then they break into their full song, and all their scarlet tassels and white painted knees flash rhythmically up and down.

On the heights of the mountains
in every direction
the piñon cloud boys
spread their arms abroad in beauty.

On the shady side of the mountains
in every direction

the piñon cloud boys
have flowers of mist upon them.

In all the mountains
in the depths of a lake
the clouds are issuing:
the mist spreads wide on high:
hither they are coming.

In all the mountains
from the depths of the lake
the clouds are issuing:
the mist spreads from above:
they have come, they are here.

In truth, the dancers are clouds—boy-clouds and maiden-clouds. Now the two girls leave their places in the singing, stamping line, to dance up and down the length of it, passing and re-passing each other in a zig-zag trail, as clouds move before the thunder clap. Now they glide back into their places. No dancer gives a look, a thought to the spectators. They stare straight before them, with narrowed eyes and open mouths. The rattles are shaken in their hands, the green boughs toss, and their white knees flash; and the drum thuds, and the deep song swells and falls.

There far away in the lake of Tamo
the mist is spread on high:
the cloud boys are coming:
They give their breath to us:
by their help we are singing in beauty,
we boys of Khapo.

Two captains walk along the line, on the watch to pick up a fallen feather or tie a garter that comes loose. From time to time, one of them gives a little yelping cry, like a distant view-halloo. The old men, the high officers of the town, stand silent, very near. Their eyes never leave the dance. The people are silent, too; only now and then the words break from someone with a deep happy sigh, "Saawondi ívi jaréndi!"—"beautiful is their dancing!"

Emotion is there: the town throbs with emotion as it throbs to the drum; emotion rises and falls with the singing in great waves that flood the heart; but emotion that flows in ordained channels. It is not left to discharge itself at random by individual vagaries or in formless riot: it is informed with sacred ideas; it is expressed in actions foreseen and foreordained; prescribed, expected, prepared. A sense of beauty and completeness, of absolute rightness, of expectation utterly fulfilled, sinks deep into the heart. All is as it should be: every man is in his function: they are doing as the clouds do, and as the fathers did long ago. All the beauty, all the order of the dances is according to the pattern of things in the heavens. And the people—we who watch the dance from the housetops—the married people, the women and children, all these gay blanketed figures standing out against the sky—are no mere spectators. Our looking-on at the dance is an act of assistance enjoined on us and regulated. We do not look on carelessly, but as worshippers look on at the Mass. By our assistance now, as well as by our expectancy through the days of preparation, we take our part in it and share the blessing.

In the intervals of the dance the performers file away to the estufa, where the cacique and others of his college await them, to pronounce sacred formulas and to give formal counsels "how they ought to live." The people go to their houses to feast on bread and cakes and boiled meat and dried peaches and pumpkins. All the visitors from other pueblos are called into the houses and fed; for we are Khapo and not at all like those people in the story, to whom the Twin Heroes came on the day of a dance and found so little hospitality that they turned town and people and all into stone! No, we should like all the Indians in New Mexico to taste our food; on feast-days our plaza is more crowded with strangers than any other; the hungry Apaches come to us, and go away with their blankets full of bread. But first the women take baskets full of food to the dancers in the estufa, and to the cacique, whose day it is—a ritual act

of giving by which they relieve and express their emotion most pleasantly and naturally.

And now the dance has come out three times, and this is the end: you will see it no more this year. Do not watch to the very last as they climb the ladder to the estufa; and do not be sad, for all is as it should be. You should only be satisfied; it is over, and it is beautiful.... There go the boys, racing down to wash off their paint in the river, and then they will come back to common life and be clouds no longer. The winter dusk is closing in; come into the warm house and give the boys their supper, and we can talk over the dance—how long and beautiful it was, and how many visitors came and from how far away.

Everyone is tired. "Who knows, we shall get some sleep tonight," says the governor; "for ten nights now I have hardly slept."

Good night.

Listen. What is that?

It is the rain.

[For the sake of brevity, I have compressed the description of the Pueblo dance, omitting, for instance, the "vespers" and the early morning appearance of it. It is at these undress performances that the *capitanes* give the view-halloo, so curiously reminiscent of the cat-calling to excite the Mohave-Apache dancers. I do not know that the story of the Twin Heroes is told at this particular Pueblo.... B.F.M.]

Animal Dance

The Animal Dance included impersonators of buffalo, elk, deer, antelope, and mountain sheep. It was distinct from the similarly named old Tewa dance in which only buffalo took part, and also the recently introduced Hopi Buffalo Dance. It corresponded to the Deer, Antelope, Mountain Sheep, and Buffalo rite of San Ildefonso, described by Parsons (1929: 198–99); it was also "quite similar" to Keresan dances of the same type or name [86].

The dance was classified as a "big dance," and before the schism was performed by either moiety. Recently it has been associated with the Summer group. It was danced on Santa Clara Day, San Antonio Day, or in conjunction with the Edge of Spring ceremony. Formerly it was customary to alternate it with the Kwitara, Tablita, or Relay Race on either Santa Clara or San Antonio Day. This rotation lapsed, however, and the Animal Dance was selected by the Summer Moiety and performed on Santa Clara Day from 1937 to 1939, and again in 1948, 1950, 1953, and on March 3, 1957 (Kurath 1958b: 445–46). In 1951, as noted by Lange, it was danced by a group belonging to the Winter Moiety [9, 18, 37, 50, 52]. [It is of interest to note, however, that the 1951 performance was given by four buffalo dancers, four maidens, and a chorus of about a dozen, including four drums. There were no other animals impersonated, and it would seem that the 1951 dance was a Buffalo, rather than an Animal Dance, despite the commentary which appears under the heading of Buffalo Dance, where Hill was told that the last performance was given prior to 1926, at least by the Summer Moiety. CHL].

The dance principals were formerly members of the Hunt Society. Since the obsolescence of that group, dancers have come from the Winter Society when the Winter Moiety performed, or were Bear Society members, selected by the cacique, when the dance was given by the Summer people. The number of performers varied; in recent years it has been reduced. Formerly, when the Hunt Society was still active, it was not uncommon for each animal to be represented by a half dozen or more dancers [8, 13, 18].

A hunter or hunt leader acted as leader or director. (This was formerly the leader of the Hunt Society; now, it is a temporary appointee.) He wore a yellow-dyed buckskin shirt and leggings, moccasins, and a breechclout. A white buckskin was tied over his right shoulder, going under his left arm. The hunter carried a quiver on his back, a bow and arrow in his right hand (Figure 31), and a sprig of evergreen in his left. His eyes, nose, and mouth were outlined in black, and the remainder of the face was white. The hair was worn loose and decorated with either cotton or eagle plumes (Figure 32).

The headdress of the male buffalo impersonators was of buffalo hide, with red-dyed goat hair attached to and extending down the back. Eagle plumes were tied to the tips of the horns and at intervals on the headdress. Eagle feathers were appended at the back (Figure 33). The headdress was secured with a strap under the chin, and in back at the waist. The dancer wore a yellowish-ochre kilt, ornamented with a black plumed serpent, a sash, and plain moccasins surmounted by horsehair anklets. Strips of buffalo hide were suspended from turquoise arm bands at the biceps, and from ligatures below the knees. In the right hand the dancer carried a gourd rattle; in the left, a wooden red and blue "lightning stick" with an eagle feather suspended from either end. The faces and bodies were painted black with white crosses added to the chest, shoulders, and back. The lower arms were colored white, as were the legs a short distance above the knee.

Female buffalo dancers (these were actually men [8]) wore a black manta embroidered in red and green if the dance was given in winter; a white one, if the dance occurred in summer (Figure 34). The manta was secured at the waist by a white sash, on which were designs in red, green, and black. A kilt was worn over the manta on the chest. This passed over the right shoulder and under the left arm, and was secured at the back. Wrapped moccasins with skunkskin guards were worn on the feet. A "mountain sign" surmounted by an eagle plume was carried in each hand (Figure 35). A sun symbol was affixed to the back (Figure 36). A hexagonal ornament terminating in eagle feathers was worn on the head (Figure 37). Only the buffalo were accompanied by "female" impersonators.

Elk dancers wore a plain white shirt, a black kilt with a broad purplish border, a sash, turquoise arm bands, white wide-meshed knitted stockings, red yarn garters, moccasins with white buckskin uppers and black cowhide soles, and skunkhide anklets. A strip of red material was tied around the leg above the anklets, and hung down the front of the moccasin like the tongue of a shoe.

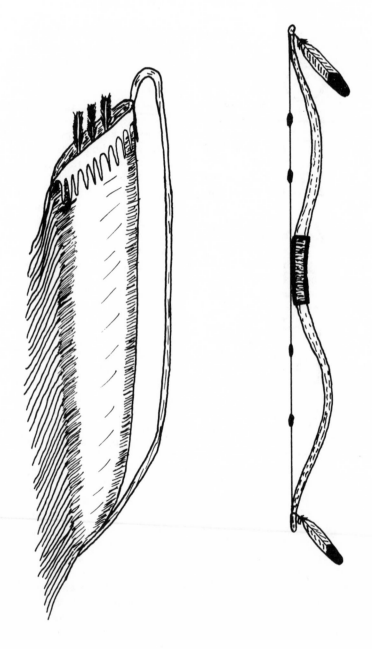

Figure 31. Animal Dance: Hunter's bow and quiver.

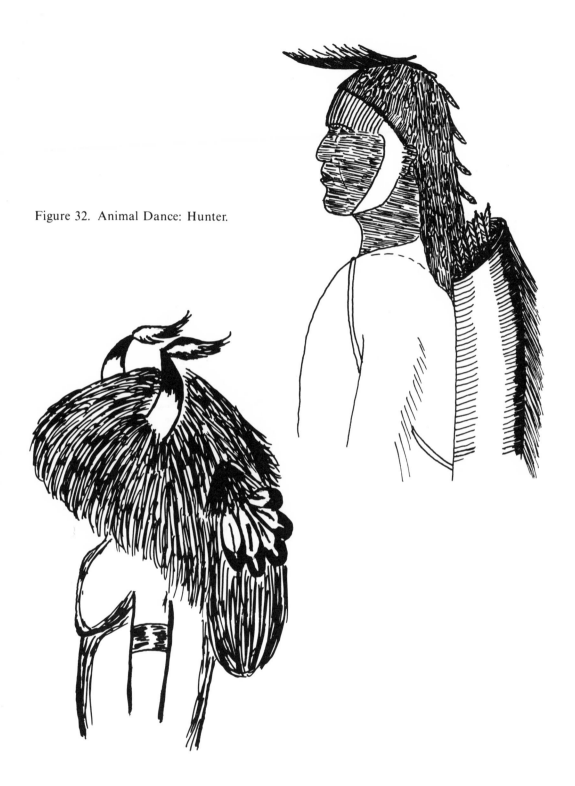

Figure 32. Animal Dance: Hunter.

Figure 33. Animal Dance: Buffalo dancer.

The front of the headdress consisted of a yellow, fan-like shield of yucca strips projecting upward from the forehead. In back of this were attached elk horns, with eagle plumes suspended from their tips. Projecting down the back from the headdress was red-dyed goat hair, to which were attached four feathers. The face of the impersonator was painted black. He carried a stick in either hand to simulate the forelegs of the animal; these had turkey feathers and evergreen sprigs attached near their centers.

Deer dancers wore costumes identical to those of the elk, with the exception that deer horns were used on the headdress (Figure 38).

The costume of the mountain sheep was different from that of the elk in the details of the headdress, and in that a white kilt with a broad red border was substituted for the black one with purple borders. The front of the mountain sheep headdress consisted of a fan-like strip of painted hide, the lower half turquoise, the upper half black (Figure 39). "Genuine horns were used unless there were more than six dancers; then horns were made" [13, 18].

Antelope costumes (Figure 40) were simi-

Figure 34. Animal Dance: "Female" buffalo dancer.

Figure 35. Animal Dance: Mountain signs carried by "female" buffalo dancer.

Figure 36. Animal Dance: Sun symbol worn by "female" buffalo dancer.

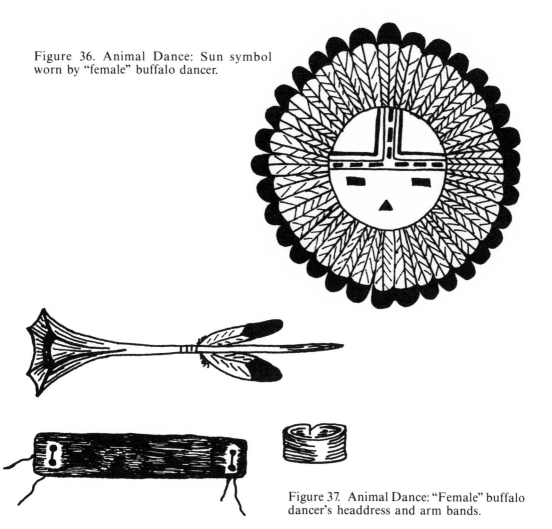

Figure 37. Animal Dance: "Female" buffalo dancer's headdress and arm bands.

lar to those of the elk except for the following items: the tail feathers of the Western red-tailed hawk were substituted for those of the eagle, and antelope horns for elk; the body of the dancer was covered from elbow to knee with heavy underwear, colored yellow and white in imitation of the animal's hide.

The dance began before sunrise, between four and five-thirty in the morning. Male members of the pueblo came from the kiva and houses, and marched toward the foothills, singing of the progress of the animals toward the pueblo. Various geographical locations, progressively nearer the pueblo, were mentioned in the songs. Finally the village was named, and the animals appeared from the foothills. They came in the following order: the hunter, four male and four female buffalo, two elk, two deer, two mountain sheep, and two antelope. The antelope were always impersonated by young boys who were extremely active, and who continually ran in and out and around the group.

The dancers, followed by the chorus, entered the village, and there they were greeted by the women. One group sprinkled cornmeal toward the incoming animals, others came forward to meet them and "feel" them, in order to get power and insure themselves of good luck.

The dance was enacted four times, twice in the morning and twice in the afternoon, in four different parts of the pueblo. The song and tempo changed as they moved from one location to another (see Kurath 1958b: 445–46). After each performance, the dancers retired to the kiva or a designated house to rest. Food was served in the interval between the second and third appearances.

During the latter part of the terminal dance, a shot was fired. This was a signal that all the animals but the buffalo were released, and they immediately ran toward the hills. Any woman who wished was privileged to pursue them, and if she was successful in catching one of the impersonators, she received a gift of meat from the individual she caught. She in turn tendered him a gift, usually an item of clothing. The pursuits were in earnest, some continuing for distances of three to four miles.

Buffalo Dance

The Buffalo Dance (Ko o *share*) proper of the Eastern Pueblos had not been held in recent years at Santa Clara. Informants remembered it vaguely, and stated that it was last given by the Summer Moiety on San Antonio Day sometime prior to 1926. It might also be given at the "Edge of Spring" [45].

Ten to twenty dancers of both sexes participated. Male impersonators painted their faces and bodies black; white crosses were added to the body decoration. The male headdress consisted of a strip of hide with a buffalo horn on one side and a bundle of feathers on the other. Women carried turkey feathers [9, 13, 18, 21, 37].

Mountain Sheep Dance

The Mountain Sheep Dance (Ku wa *share* or Pin ku wa *share*) has not been performed for some time. Recently it has been associated with the Winter group [8, 13, 18, 21]; however, according to one informant [9], it was formerly given by either moiety. It was danced on Santa Clara Day [13, 18] and in January or February [37]. According to another informant [14], it was performed whenever a Tablita, or Corn Dance was held, the moieties alternating in their appearance—the Summer danced the Tablita and the Winter, the Mountain Sheep Dance.

The principals included two male (four males [14]) and two female impersonators and a hunter. These were accompanied by drummers and a chorus [13, 18, 21].

Male impersonators wore a headdress with mountain sheep horns, a white shirt, kilt, belt, and crocheted cotton hose. Their faces were painted black. Women wore a white manta. The hunter's face was painted black. He was dressed in buckskin, and carried a bow, arrows, and quiver [13, 18, 21].

Unlike the Animal Dance, the female impersonators did not enter the pueblo from the hills, but joined the males upon their arrival in the village [13, 18].

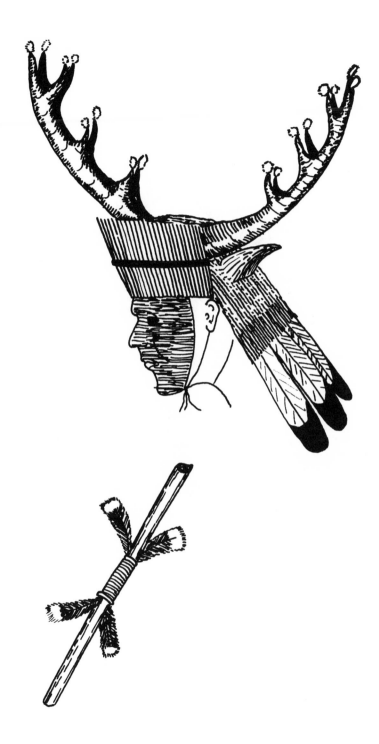

Figure 38. Animal Dance: Deer dancer—headdress and stick for legs.

Figure 39. Animal Dance: Mountain sheep dancer—headdress and stick for legs.

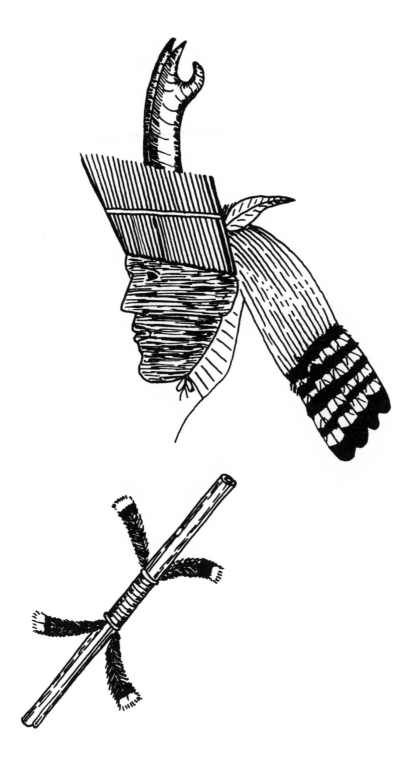

Figure 40. Animal Dance: Antelope dancer—headdress and stick for legs.

Deer Dance

Formerly, according to informants [21, 50], the Santa Clara possessed a Deer Dance (Pai *share*, old Tewa type) which paralleled that performed at San Juan Pueblo. In this version only men participated, and there were no drummers or chorus. It was classed as a "big" dance, and was associated with the Summer Moiety—possibly earlier also with the Winter Moiety. This ritual has lapsed and in part has been replaced by an introduced "little" Deer Dance (see "Little Dances").

Horse Dance

The last occurrence of the Horse Dance (Ka va ju) was sometime prior to 1920. Santa Clara appears to have been the only Tewa pueblo to perform it, although one informant [18] had heard that it was danced at Tesuque. It was one of the alternative selections for presentation on Santa Clara Day. According to Jeançon, it was performed at the time of Ka-ve-Na, the "Edge of Spring" ceremony. He stated that it was phallic in emphasis, and that a large part of it was performed in the kiva. The rite belonged to the Winter Moiety, and only members of the Winter Society participated as principals. According to an informant [50], it was introduced between 1890 and 1900 by a Jemez Indian who married a Santa Clara woman.

The performance began at the termination of the mass in the church. The principal (probably representing Santiago), wearing the framework of the horse, carrying a sword, and with his face below the eyes masked with a black scarf (Figure 41), appeared from one of the houses (probably that of the Winter cacique), and was led, accompanied by a snare drummer, to the church. There was no singing. Here a procession of villagers formed, carrying figures of saints. The horse danced ahead of this group and led it to the bower, where the saints' figures were placed on the altar.

There were four appearances, and in each case the person who played the roles of the horse and rider and the one who led the horse were changed. The horse danced in each of the four plazas on each occasion. Villagers offered it cornmeal during the dance, and embraced it "to get power." On the final round the procession formed again, and was led back to the church by the horse [9, 13, 18, 21].

Relay Race

The relay race (E[n] *share*) was, as Opler has shown, characteristic of the Tanoan peoples and the Jicarilla Apache (see Opler 1944). At Santa Clara, it was classified as a "big dance," and was performed on San Antonio Day or Santa Clara Day, alternating with the Corn Dance, Kwitara, or Animal Dance [13, 18]; or with the Corn Dance or Kwitara [37, 50]; or with the Corn Dance [40]. The last informant indicated that the situation described by him was in force "when we were still together," i.e., before the political break, and that the selection then was determined by the Summer and Winter caciques. A somewhat similar situation appears to have occurred at San Juan Pueblo (see Parsons 1929: 233).

This ritual has lapsed at Santa Clara in recent years. Its last occurrence appears to have been in the 1930s; one was held about 1938 [37]. As indicated elsewhere, some features of the event were related to war and the functions of the War and Scalp societies.

The war captains, formerly the "outside chief" and his assistants, were responsible for organizing the race and selecting the runners. An equal number of married and unmarried males were chosen for each team, and formerly there was equal representation from each moiety [22, 37]. Since the factional development, participants from the Winter Moiety have been in the minority [13, 18] (see Parsons 1929: 234). At the last performance, only members of the Summer Moiety participated [37].

As soon as selections were made, practice began; this was in itself a ritual. According to some informants [13, 18], it consumed two weeks; according to another [50], there was no fixed period, but normally ten or twelve days were involved; according to a fourth [31], the practice lasted four days. Presumably all may have been correct, since one of the oldest informants in the pueblo

Figure 41. Horse Dance: Impersonation of Santiago.

[35] indicated that this preliminary feature, the serg ha? (literally, "man song") was a conditioning rite for warriors held prior to forays into the Navajo country, and that the number of days involved was variable. "Several days before departing for the Navajo country, long ago, men formed in the serg ha? formation each evening and danced in preparation for war. The relay, serg ha? formation, is the same as the one then formed."

Practice was held each evening. At about six or seven o'clock, a drummer and a variable number of people gathered at the northern end of the village, at P'o K'ege ("edge of water place"), and a similar group and drummer at the southern edge of the village, at Nunge K'ege ("bottom place"). The two groups were designated as "north side" and "south side," respectively. Runners associated with the "north side" went to oxurg woge, an arroyo, located three-quarters of a mile to a mile north of the village; those of the "south side," to the edge of P'oci Pa^{n}ge, a mesa a similar distance south of the village. Once they reached their respective positions, the runners ran back and joined their groups.

When all had returned, the northern delegation worked their way to the eastern end of the racetrack in the "principal plaza" (with the cottonwood); the southern, to the western end of the racetrack. Once in position, the groups began to drum and sing. Both runners and elders of each team took part in the songs. After they had sung for some time, they worked slowly toward each other, still singing, passed at the center of the race course, and then reversed positions. When this was achieved, the music ended. The participants then dispersed and went to their homes [9, 22]. Prior to the political schism, members of each delegation repaired to the village kiva, later to their moiety kivas, and were thanked and encouraged to better efforts by the caciques [22].

The actual race was preceded by several preliminary features: purification of the course and runners, and a mass in the Church. The purification of the course and the shrines at either end of the course, by members of the Bear societies, took place during the night prior to the race, an hour or so before the race, or immediately before it started. Informants [13, 29] stated that two men of the Bear societies start in the east, and when they reach the west, two others run back, carrying feathers to clear the course and bless it. Then the race starts. Parsons (1929: 234-35) said that the Bear members go out and purify the course, exorcising with eagle feathers. This was several hours before the race.

Runners were also purified by members of the Bear societies in a rite which involved the laying on of hands, and by bathing in the river. Bathing was accomplished before sunup on the day of the race; this feature was also a preliminary to each practice period [22]. Finally, when the mass was completed, the principal event took place.

The two teams emerged from the kiva, more recently kivas, and went to their respective places at either end of the race course; the "north side" at the eastern end, the "south side" at the western end [9, 22]. A man in each group carried a pole (see also Parsons 1929: 234). According to an informant [9], these poles were identical to the poles used in the scalp dance, and from which the scalps were hung. The top of each pole was surmounted by a gourd in which two eagle feathers were placed. Other feathers and a cloth banner were suspended at the base of the gourd [4, 22]. Below the banner, a fox skin was attached. According to Parsons, the red (or yellow [37]) standard was associated with the western, the white with the eastern group. This was confirmed by the informant [37]. According to another [43], new poles were made for each occasion, the old ones being incorporated in the roofs of the kivas. The fox skins, feathers, and ornaments were reused. According to yet another informant [31], poles were merely stored in the kivas until needed.

Costumes worn by the runners were not standardized. Frequently, however, one side of the body was colored white, the other black. Often the black areas were spotted in white and the white areas in black. Eagle down was worn in the hair, and two eagle feathers were worn at the forehead, held upright by a headband [37].

The initial features of the race duplicated activities performed in the plaza during practice. The teams gathered around their poles, drumming and singing began, and after an interval, each team danced slowly toward the other, passing at the center of the course and taking up reversed positions. When this serg ha?, preliminary portion, had been completed, the race began.

According to one informant [31], a muzzle-loading rifle was discharged, and according to another [37], they counted to four; at any rate, at a signal, two men from the east began running toward the opposite group. One [31] stated that the swiftest contestants ran first; however, another [35] indicated that the oldest members of each team were the initial runners. As each completed the course, he touched the hand of another team member, and a second pair began running; this was repeated until all had participated [31]. The number of laps each person ran was decided before the race; this might be only one, or each person might traverse the course two or three times [4, 35]. A reenactment of the serŋ ha? formation terminated the performance.

Throughout the race, spectators exhorted the runners to better efforts. This was especially true of the older women, who lined the race course, shouting, "try, try," and throwing food to the runners.

The term race is probably a misnomer, since there was no concern with winning. The specific objectives of the event were strengthening and conditioning the men and performing imitative magic. It was believed that by running the sun would be affected and its return northward hastened, i.e., that the winter period would be shortened and spring would arrive earlier.

"LITTLE DANCES" OF THE SUMMER AND WINTER MOIETIES

Preparations for "little dances" followed the general pattern of those for "big dances," though on a reduced scale. Preliminary or terminal religious features were normally absent or attenuated. Decisions to "bring out" a "little dance" originated in small secular groups, and approval from the religious was usually unnecessary, except in the cases of the Foot Light and Kwitara dances. Feeding the dancers was the immediate concern of close relatives, although appreciative villagers might contribute. Only in connection with the "song composer" or a substitute did the preparatory features of "little dances" approach those of the "big dances" in complexity, and then only in certain instances.

The prominent role of "song composer" or substitute associated with "little dances" was consistent and not surprising in view of the Santa Clara predilection for innovation. It is best illustrated in those cases where dances were given honoring visitors. Songs were created indicating the delight of the hosts and often containing specific reference

to individual guests. For example, the songs of the Yan dewa, cited later, were of this type. They were composed in honor of a group of Tewa-Hopi who visited Santa Clara in 1926–27. They not only expressed joy, friendship, and relationship to the guests, but also selected an individual named "Bird" for particular attention [18, 29].

"Foot Light" Dance

The "Foot Light," or "Foot Lifting" dance (An tege *sh*are) was held in the spring prior to Ash Wednesday, or on Easter Sunday following a kachina performance. Permission to give the dance was obtained from either moiety cacique [43, 50].

Men only participated. These formed a single line, danced, and sang to the time of gourd rattles [27, 29, 52]. There were no drums or chorus [43, 50]. Songs and costumes, according to informants [27, 43, 50], were similar to those of the San Juan Turtle Dance. No k'osa were associated with this dance [27, 50]; however, if the leader of the dance happened to belong to a clown organization, he gave the "call" of the Kòsa as he "led out" the file of men [50].

It is probable that this dance once played a more prominent role than at present. (One informant [86] seemed surprised that this was considered a "little dance," pointing out that the same ceremony was "quite sacred" at both San Ildefonso and Tesuque. WWH) Recently, it has been considered the property of the Summer Moiety. At San Juan Pueblo, according to Parsons (1929: 186), it was a Winter dance. Formerly, however, both moieties participated [14, 29, 50, 52]. According to one informant [9], it was danced once at the Gallup Inter-Tribal Ceremonials. However, on that occasion only twelve persons took part, and the dancers were accompanied by the musical rasp.

Yan Dewa

The Yan dewa, popularly designated as the "Sun Basket Dance" (Traŋ tuŋ *sh*are), was danced to satisfy tourist curiosity [29,

37, 52]; on almost any occasion, such as Santa Clara Day, in 1948 (see Parsons 1929: 194); whenever there was a slack period in economic endeavor; when visitors from other pueblos were entertained on Christmas night or during February or March (Parsons 1929: 188) or on Kings' Day [21, 29, 50, 52]. It was danced by the progressive Winter group on Kings' Day (January 6) in 1950. On this occasion the dance team performed at the house of each newly elected officer. The same group gave the dance on February 24, 1957 (Kurath 1958a: 18). The dance principals were two men and two women, the latter carrying baskets, assisted by a chorus and one drummer. Parsons (1929: 194) listed this as a Kόsa dance. However, an informant [27] denied that k'osa were associated with the performance. Presumably this discrepancy resulted from the fact that in recent years the cacique who may and should bless the dancers was affiliated with a rival faction. He therefore did not perform his offices, which were absorbed by the k'osa. This dance was definitely associated with the Winter Moiety, although, as noted by Parsons, it was once performed in Santa Fe by the Summer Moiety.

In 1926 or 1927 the dance was given in honor of some visiting Tewa from Hano. On this occasion, as was customary in dances of this type, sections of the songs were rephrased to compliment the visitors and to honor a particularly distinguished member of the visiting party named "Bird," as mentioned.

The Yan dewa songs, like those of most dances, were rendered in two parts: the first, while the group was in motion; the second, while stationary. The informant [72] was vague about the initial portion of the first part; however, it appears to have conformed to a standardized pattern. Mention was first made of the cardinal points; then reference was made to the flora of the area and its condition. No particular plants were singled out for comment, but the flora in general was mentioned. When this was completed, the same "melody" was sung, but without words.

Following this the composition developed for the specific occasion was rendered:

Friends, Friends, Friends, Friends,
You we have seen, You; we have
    become glad.
We who are uncles,
Also we are brothers.

A short interval of song without words.

Uncle Bird, uncle Bird,
Here we have become glad.

This was followed by other lines which the informant was unable to recall. The second part of the song was without words, but with variations in time and tone. The dancers, accompanied by the chorus and drummer, performed in each of the four plazas. After each round, they returned to the kiva. Two appearances were made in the morning and two in the afternoon [72].

The Yan dewa was danced by the Winter Moiety on Santa Clara Day, August 12, 1948. On this occasion there were several innovations, the principal ones being the inclusion of an extra pair of dancers and a second drummer. The three women wore white shirts, silk scarfs, and white embroidered mantas. Each carried a woven Hopi plaque with red-dyed angora wool attached to the edge. The men were costumed in white shirts, kilts with embroidered edges, and hip-length, openwork, knitted white stockings. In their right hands each carried a gourd rattle; in their left, a staff about three feet long. Two eagle feathers were attached to the top, and there were turkey feathers at the center above the grip. On this occasion the group danced once in each plaza (at each of four appearances) [43, 50].

Prisoner's Dance

The Prisoner's Dance (Parg share) was predominantly a social function, and was danced at any time by members of either moiety. It was often held on the weekend or following a wedding. Parsons (1929: 216) reported its performance on Easter.

The obligation to present or sponsor a Prisoner's Dance was usually incurred on the occasion of an individual's first participation in a "big" dance. During the course of the performance a friend or relative came forward and tied a ribbon on him or her, or presented the candidate with a gift. It was then incumbent upon that person to sponsor a Parg *sh*are at a later date [37, 43, 50].

The dance was held in the sponsor's house, and he was responsible for arranging for the drummer and singers and notifying the pueblo of the event. Usually young boys and girls were the active participants. Ordinary clothing was worn; there was no costuming. The dancers formed in couples and performed two movements. In the first part, the girl remained stationary, and the boy danced backward and forward before her. In the second part, the tempo was accelerated; the boy placed a hand on the girl's shoulder, and they circled. This was repeated, with the boy placing his hand on the other shoulder of the girl [43, 50].

Parsons (1929: 316–17) gave a description of this dance for the Tewa generally, and suggested that it was of Navajo origin. This was not acknowledged by Santa Clara informants [43, 50], although the dance resembled, in part, the Navajo War Dance (Anadji).

Kwitara

The Kwitara, or "Frence War Dance" (Frençe *sh*are; see also Ute, Comanche, and Kiowa Dances) was relegated to the category of "small" dances. In recent years its most common designation has been "Comanche Dance" [86]. It was said to have little religious significance, in spite of the fact that it was performed periodically on one of the more important days of the ritual calendar, i.e., San Antonio Day. Parsons (1929: 208) reported it on this occasion in 1926; it was held on that day by the Summer group in 1941. It was also danced on that date in 1952 and 1958. It could also be performed on Kings' Day [50]. This was possibly the dance witnessed by Keech on Santa Clara Day in 1937, despite the discrepancy in names (see Appendix D; see also Appendix C).

The dance was obviously of foreign origin, probably from the Plains. The tempo was certainly reminiscent of that area, rather than Puebloan. Costuming was variable, and exemplified much of that which has come to be associated with the American Indian stereotype, primarily Plains in character (Figure 42).

The 1941 performance began at 11:30 A.M., about an hour after the pueblo had attended mass. Prior to this, a bower, or shrine, had been erected in one of the plazas. As soon as the mass was celebrated, a number of women hurried to the altar, secured various Christian images, filed out, and deposited these on the altar in the bower. The altar consisted of a table covered by a white cloth and with a low rail in front, upon which lighted candles were placed. The images were flanked by vases of flowers. Throughout the dance, some members of the pueblo sat in the bower and recited the rosary. Subsequently the dancers, on each of their four appearances in this plaza, performed before the shrine. This procedure was standard for those rituals occurring on San Antonio Day and Santa Clara Day.

The chorus, some carrying drums, first appeared in plaza three and formed a single line. The faces of all were colored a light red, and some had a diagonal stripe of deeper red on each cheek. Headgear consisted of brightly colored scarves or Stetson hats. All wore brightly colored silk shirts.

Accompanying the chorus were four men who acted as dance directors. These might include the war captains, pika, the governor, or other officers of the faction responsible for the dance. Their duties included clearing a space for the dancers to perform, retrieving bits of down, feathers, or other parts of costume that fell during the dance, and advising the participants (see also Parsons 1929: 208).

The chorus sang softly to the time of the drums for about five minutes before the appearance of the dancers. These entered in a double file, a woman behind each man, twenty couples in all. The faces and bodies of the men were painted, each in a different design and in a variety of colors. All wore kilts, belts, and clouts, but again there was no attempt at uniformity of costume. Some wore Plains-type headdresses or brightly colored ribbons around the head. Each carried in his left hand a "banner" (Plains type) consisting of a pole with a strip of bright colored cloth attached. In their right

Figure 42. Kwitara Dance: Male dancer.

hands they carried a weapon—a stone-headed club, a bow, or a gun (Figure 43).

The women wore silk or rayon dresses of bright colors and moccasins with white, wrapped leggings attached. Feathers were worn in the hair and carried in each hand (Figure 44).

Dance leaders were chosen on the basis of experience and age. This was followed fairly consistently down the files; those near the center tended to be the younger and poorer dancers. Those at the end of the files were often children making their first public appearance.

Each individual began to dance as soon as he or she passed the center of the chorus. This first dance movement was called "progressing dance" (pun *share*) and had its own song; it was characteristic of the opening stages of most plaza performances. In it the dancers moved first obliquely to the right, then to the left. The tempo was slower than in subsequent movements. When the leaders of the two files reached the end of the plaza, they turned in and were followed by their respective groups, which they led back toward the chorus.

The first movement was completed when the leaders arrived near the chorus.

The second movement, Kwitara *share*, was introduced by a new song. When this began, the leaders again turned in on the file. In the initial stages, the song and drumming were soft and the tempo slow. These were gradually accelerated, the dancing becoming faster and more frenzied, until a climax was reached. After this the lines reversed themselves again, repeated the movement, and at its termination went to the next plaza.

During the day, four separate appearances were made, and on each occasion four plazas were visited. A new set of songs was sung with each appearance, and after each the dancers repaired to the Summer kiva to rest. A longer break was taken after the first two enactments, about 1:30 P.M., during which the dancers ate. Food was furnished and brought to them in the kiva by the women of the conservative faction of the Summer Moiety, which had sponsored the dance.

A special terminal feature was added when the fourth round was completed. A new song was begun, and the dancers who were assembled before the Summer kiva began to dance while ascending the ladder. Each male executed a series of steps on each rung, meanwhile blocking his female partner, who was immediately behind him, attempting to pass him and enter the kiva. Finally all disappeared in the kiva, and the dance was finished [29, 52].

Navajo Dance

The Navajo Dance (Wan save *share*) was purely social in nature. It might be performed at any time for purposes of amusement, and there appears to have been no standardized form of the dance. Any one of several Navajo Dances might be imitated—for example, the Night Chant, or the Feather Dance, or the Mountain Chant [9]. Santa Clara informants [29, 43, 50] did not consider it in any way related to the Pan *share*, or Prisoner's Dance.

Ute Dance

The Ute Dance (Uta *share*) was performed by either moiety, usually on Christmas Eve or Christmas night (Parsons 1929: 215), or at other periods during the Christmas season. It was predominantly social in nature. Informants [29, 43, 50] stated that Ute, Comanche, Kiowa, and Kwitara were all war dances, and similar except for the songs. Costuming was of minimal importance; "you wore what you had on hand." All agreed that these performances were derived from the Plains.

Comanche Dance

See comments regarding the Ute Dance. Parsons described an enactment of this dance held on December 29, 1925 (1929: 215–16). As noted, this was often called the Kwitara Dance.

Kiowa Dance

See Ute Dance.

Figure 43. Kwitara Dance: Male dancer.

Figure 44. Kwitara Dance: Female dancer.

Bow and Arrow Dance

The Bow and Arrow Dance (A' share) was also danced during the Christmas period [50], by the younger boys in January on Holy Innocence Day [29, 52], or at any time during the spring [69]. It had not been performed for a considerable time, although one of the informants [9] had seen his father dance it. The participants held a bow in one hand and a rattle in the other. Another informant [86] believed this may once have been a "big dance."

Shield Dance

The Shield Dance (Ti di share) was a "small dance" which might be selected for performance on Kings' Day. It was no longer current, and some members of the tribe had never seen it performed in the pueblo—"only practiced before a group went to Denver" [43, 50, 69].

It was danced by a group of six or seven men. These were dressed in breechclouts only, or in breechclouts and leggings. Their bodies and faces were variously painted. Headdresses and feathers were worn, the composition of which depended upon personal whim. In the left hand each dancer carried a shield; in the right, a spear or bow and arrows. The dancers performed in a circle and were accompanied by a chorus standing in single file [14, 27].

Deer Dance

A recent, introduced version of the Deer Dance (Pae share) was danced by the Winter Moiety during the Christmas season, according to several informants [29, 43, 69], and by the Summer Moiety on different occasions, according to other informants [27, 37]. The Summer type was said to be of Jemez derivation and to have Jemez songs [27]; the Winter type, to be of Hopi provenience [43, 69].

The Deer Dance was performed by the Winter group in 1939. Participants included two male and two female dancers, a hunter, drummers, and a chorus. Men wore a headdress of antlers tipped with eagle down, with a fan-like shield of yucca strips, painted yellow, projecting upward from the forehead. They were dressed in white shirts, black kilts, white belts, crocheted open-work hose, red yarn garters, and moccasins with skunkskin guards. Each carried two lengths of wood to simulate the forelegs of the animal. Fir boughs were tied to these. Women wore no headdress. They were attired in white mantas and wore moccasins with wrapped leggings attached. Skunkskin guards were worn over the moccasins [43, 69].

The dance group performed four times, twice each in the morning and afternoon. On each occasion they danced in each of the four plazas. At the completion of the round, they returned to the kiva to rest.

The Deer Dance song consisted of two major parts. The first part was sung as the performers progressed from the kiva to the particular plaza. It had five verses; the first four mentioned the arrival of the dancers at sacred locations, each progressively closer to the village. The final verse told of their entering the pueblo, and was timed to coincide with the arrival of the group in the plaza. The first stanza was as follows:

On top of Tsikumo Ping (sacred flint,
  or obsidian-covered mountain)
The group (literally confusion or
  chaos) have come together
The old does and bucks
To Santa Clara they are coming.
With sacred personages (Kachina)
  they are coming.
With lightning they are coming
With thunder they are coming
With floods they are coming
With fog they are coming
Here have they arrived
  o he e e ehe ehe e
  e e e e ehe ehe
  e yeh yeh e ei e ei e
  e e ohe ohe he ho

The four subsequent verses were identical to the first except that new sacred locations—Puje Ping ("meeting place of cottontails?"), Pu Ping, Be He, Ka Po Ge (Santa Clara)—were substituted for "the sacred obsidian-covered mountain."

The second part of the song consisted only of syllables:

ya a ya a ya ala beye e
ya ya ya ala be ye e
ya a ya ya ala beyee
be ye e e be ye e e e [72]

Two aspects of the song are worthy of note. First, while the dance was avowedly introduced, the song followed the standard Santa Clara pattern. Second, while the dance was relegated to the "little" category, the religious emphasis is still apparent in the rain prayer implicit in the songs.

Hopi Buffalo Dance

The Hopi Buffalo Dance was performed by the Summer Moiety on Christmas Day, Kings' Day (it was danced on January 3, 1954), or any time between Easter Sunday and San Antonio Day. It was danced March 3, 1957 (Kurath 1958a: 18). Since it was a recently introduced dance from a foreign source, its religious significance was minimal; on occasion, it was enacted for pay for tourists. "The Fred Harvey people would call up and arrange for the dance to be given" [69].

The Hopi Buffalo Dance was first held at Santa Clara on Kings' Day, 1926. It was introduced by Philip Dasheno, a First Mesa Tewa (from Hano), who had married into the pueblo. He and others from Santa Clara had witnessed it during the period of the Snake Dance the previous year. When the decision was made to hold the dance, John Naranjo brought in some Hopi Indians to coach the Santa Clara participants (see Parsons 1929: 196–97).

The dance principals were five in number: two men, two women, and "a hunter" (see also Kurath 1958b: 440). These were accompanied by three or four drummers. The male impersonators wore a two-horned buffalo headdress, a kilt, and a white belt; their bodies were painted black. According to Parsons (1929: 197), they wore an ordinary shirt and, in addition, crocheted hose. In one hand they carried a lightning stick; in the other, a gourd rattle with turkey feathers affixed to the top. Female impersonators wore a band around the head, from which was suspended, in front, a fringe of horse hair, which hung to the level of the mouth. They were dressed in white embroidered mantas. In their right hands they carried eagle and turkey feathers; in their left, gourds. From the end of the gourds, feathers from various species of birds projected. According to Parsons (1929: 197), women also wore a flower headdress and a sun tablet at their backs. The "hunter" was attired as in the Animal Dance [43, 50].

This dance was performed on Christmas Eve, 1944. On that occasion, three men took part, two representing male and one, a female buffalo. It was said that the dance was organized on such short notice that no women could be recruited to fill the female roles. Costumes were similar to those described above. The dance team performed during the evening and night in front of various houses—not in the plazas.

Pipe Dance

Parsons (1929: 222) gave a short description of a Pipe Dance (Sako *share*). My own informants were unable to verify its occurrence [13, 29, 37, 50]. According to one informant [37], the "pipe" might refer to the tomahawk, since most were combined weapons and pipes.

Hoop Dance

The Hoop Dance (Tembe *share*) was danced occasionally on Christmas Eve and at other times to satisfy tourist demand. Informants [13, 29, 50] agreed that it represented a recent acquisition.

Dog Dance

The Dog Dance (Tse *share*) might be danced by either moiety. It was commonly performed on Kings' Day, and was said to be danced also during Easter. Descriptions of the dance by informants [13, 29, 37, 50] coincided with those of Parsons (1929: 223). As nearly as could be ascertained, the last occurrence of this dance at Santa Clara was the one cited by Parsons in 1926.

Belt Dance (Ba'a *share*)

This was performed by the Summer Moiety on Christmas Eve, Kings' Day, or during Easter. Informants [13, 29, 50] agreed that it was a recent acquisition and of predominantly social import. Parsons did not list this dance; presumably it was introduced after 1927 (1929: 236).

Participants included two men and two women (occasionally four couples), a drummer, and chorus. The chorus circled around the drummer while the dance was in progress. The men danced before the women, carrying a woven belt [13, 29, 52].

Butterfly Dance

The Butterfly Dance (Thi *share*, Pu ga nini) might be performed at any time. Two men and two women danced [13, 14, 29]. The men wore kilts; macaw feathers were attached at the back of their heads and projected above them. Their bodies were painted, the color varying with individual preference. In their hands, they carried a stone axe. The women wore wings consisting of a double row of feathers down the back. Antennae were secured to their heads [27].

According to an informant [27], this dance represented an old form at Santa Clara. However, this may have been an error, since three other informants [13, 29, 50] stated that it had been recently introduced from San Juan. This view is substantiated by Parsons (1929: 191); another informant [86] tended to support the first viewpoint, however, pointing out that Nambé had just revived what they called a Spring Dance, which was really the *old* Kiva Butterfly Dance, done in connection with some masked ceremonies.

Willow Behind or Rainbow Dance

The Willow Behind or Rainbow Dance (Fe an ge *share*, or Qua te be) could be performed anytime—spring, summer, or during the Christmas period [13, 29, 50]. Parsons (1929: 224) witnessed it on Christmas Day, 1927, and it was held on Kings' Day in 1945. It was identified with the Summer Moiety according to one informant [50]; with both moieties, according to another [27].

This dance appears to be one in which considerable improvising was allowed. Parsons (1929: 224-25) gave an adequate account of the 1927 performance; a shorter description was provided by Fergusson (1931: 60-61); see also Keech (1937b: Appendix D). My own descriptions are fragmentary and do not agree in all respects with Parsons. It is possible that the Willow Behind Dance and Rainbow Dance were two separate dances, as was suggested by an informant [8] who had witnessed a performance in 1930.

According to another informant [62], the number of participants was variable. Each wore a fan-shaped headdress and carried a four-colored cardboard, or canvas, rainbow in his hands. Other informants [61, 72] stated that two men and two women participated, and that the men carried colored semicircles representing the rainbow. In 1945 two men and two women took part. Except for the headdresses, costumes were similar to those worn in the Hopi Buffalo Dance. The headdresses consisted of roughly semicircular pieces of cardboard, about two feet in diameter, painted to imitate the rainbow. The dance took place in the plazas [72].

Eagle Dance

The Eagle Dance was avowedly a social affair—any religious connotation being minimal. It could be and was performed at any time, frequently occurring between Easter and San Antonio Day as a "fill in," or on Christmas Day [62, 69]. It was often danced on short notice at the request of the Hunter Clarkson or Fred Harvey tours for the edification of tourists. Moiety ownership was not involved [43, 50].

Parsons witnessed the Eagle Dance on Christmas Day of 1927, and her description agrees with those of current informants, although some additional information on the two forms (see Parsons 1929: 206-7) was collected. According to informants [13, 43, 69] the dance illustrated in Parsons's frontispiece represented an older version. In the more recent one, introduced by a group of visiting Hopi, performers wore a body covering of black-dyed underwear [43, 69].

Corn Dance

As mentioned above, informants [29, 40, 50] distinguished between this and the "Santo Domingo type." One [50] believed that it represented an introduction—probably from the Hopi. It was usually danced during the Christmas season, and was considered to be the property of the Winter Moiety. It was performed by four men on Christmas eve in 1944. Costuming and dance steps were similar to those of the "big" Corn Dance [18, 29].

Cow Dance

According to an informant [69], this "little dance" was given for the first time at Santa Clara in 1949. It was introduced by Kenneth Shupla, a Hopi married to a Santa Clara woman. A substantial account of the performance was recorded by Fay (1952: 186-88). He assigned the dance to the Winter Moiety, although Shupla's wife belonged to the Summer group.

Matachina

This is a dance of European provenance (see Parsons 1939: 852-56; Kurath 1957: 259-64). Its introduction at Santa Clara Pueblo was attributed to Poseyemu, "the Dew God," and it was called Po se ye mu bu *sha*re, "Poseyemu, his dance" [40, 50] (see also Parsons 1929: 217). Details concerning this messiah on the innovation of the dance were contained in the widespread Montezuma legend. The Matachina was an allegorical performance, reflecting the dualistic aspect of Christianity and the eventual triumph of good over evil. The role of Montezuma was played by the *monarcha (monarca)*. Malinche, Cortes' mistress, represented the principles of innocence, purity, and good; the bull, the forces of evil.

The Matachina was performed periodically in the holiday season from Christmas through Kings' Day. It appears to have occurred somewhat sporadically. Jeançon (1904-30) gathered some data on it in 1900,

and examined a photograph taken at Santa Clara in 1902. According to informants [43, 50], it was danced sometime between 1910 and 1915. A group of Santa Clara performed it while on a visit to Colorado in 1928 (Jeançon 1904-30). According to one informant [72], it was danced in 1938 or 1939; it was also held in 1952. On these occasions, visitors from San Juan Pueblo coached the dancers and formed part of the chorus [43, 50]. A performance was given at Puyé in 1963; this was the "Indian" version, with drums rather than stringed instruments [86].

Both moieties formerly took part, but after the schisms only the Summer group participated. Most of the following description was derived from the 1952 dance.

The ensemble consisted of from ten to twelve dancers arranged in two files, the *monarcha* (Montezuma), *malinche,* the bull, the chorus of three or four persons, and the orchestra. The latter was variously constituted, sometimes including a violinist, guitar player, and snare drummer; at other times, and particularly in recent years, the stringed instruments have been replaced by native drums.

The *monarcha* wore a crown ornamented in the front with a cross, beads, and costume jewelry. The cross was supposed to be silver, but in 1952 was tin. Colored ribbons were suspended from the crown, and in the front there was a fringe of black beads, which covered the upper part of the face. The lower part, from the nose down, was covered by a scarf. Clothing consisted of a pleated white or colored silk shirt, a plain or beaded vest, and in recent times, ordinary modern trousers. A scarf was pinned to the back of the vest, forming a kind of cape. His moccasins were beaded, and his armbands consisted of colored ribbons. In his left hand the *monarcha* carried a tripartite wooden symbol of different colors; in his right, a rattle made from a tin can, covered with a scarf.

The dancers were clothed in brightly colored shirts, plain or beaded vests, flannel or woolen leggings with beaded strips down the sides, and beaded moccasins. Around their waists they wore garish fringed shawls and belts, to which sleigh bells were attached. Colored ribbons were worn for arm bands. Each dancer wore a miter-like headgear, or crown, with an eagle feather on each side. A bead fringe was suspended from the front of the miter, and covered the upper part of the dancer's face. Below the nose, the face was covered with a silk handkerchief. Each dancer carried a tin-can rattle and a three-pronged symbol [50, 69].

Jeançon's descriptions from 1902 agree substantially with the details above. He did, however, give additional details, some of which are indicative of changes that have occurred over the years (1904–30):

> The costumes of the dancers consist of a mitre-shaped helmet on the head with a large feather on each side of the head, from which depend long strings of black beads which cover about three-fourths of the upper part of the face. Sometimes the mitres are made of cowhide and again they may be made of pasteboard; they are always covered with blue or red cloth and embroidered. Some have only a border of beads and a cross of gilt beads in the center, others only have a border. Sometimes a piece of black cloth hangs from the edge of the back of the mitre down over the shoulders. A bright colored shirt is worn, and over the shoulders, hanging down the back, is a long cape of light cloth, calico or other such material which may be stamped with gay colors or solid black. A fancy kilt was formerly worn over long cotton pants, but one rarely sees this now. A picture taken of the dance about 1902 shows the dancers wearing bead embroidered woolen leggings such as are often worn in Indian dances, also some made of buckskin. . . .

Malinche wore a communion gown consisting of a white silk or taffeta dress and a white veil. Her crown was made from artificial flowers. Her moccasins were standard Pueblo type with wrapped tops. She carried nothing in her hands. Jeançon, presumably referring to 1902, stated that with the exception of the veil, the *malinche* was dressed in native costume.

The *abuelos,* or grandfathers, wore long-nosed, miter-like masks of cowhide. According to Jeançon, these were equipped with horsehair wigs. Scarves were tied around the neck below the mask. The remainder of the costume consisted of shirt, vest, tight trousers, chaps, and cowboy boots. They carried whips in one hand and lassos at their sides [9, 69]. Jeançon described them as being dressed in ragged costumes.

The bull wore a shirt, blue jeans, and modern shoes. On his head was the headskin of a cow or calf with horns attached. This reached down as far as the eyes. At the rear was suspended an angora goathide; this extended down the back. Apparently, considerable variability occurred in the bull's costume. Jeançon described him as wearing a striped sweater, and indicated that at other times he wore a dried cowhide with head skin attached, or merely strips or fragments of cowhide.

Early in the morning of the day of the dance, the *abuelos* gathered the dancers and took them to a house where they could costume and prepare themselves, and where they waited until the performance was to begin. When all was ready, the *abuelos* entered the plaza and "called out" the dancers, who left their headquarters, formed two files, and danced to the area where they would perform. The *monarcha* and *malinche* were between the two lines of dancers. The *malinche's* position was immediately in back of the *monarcha* [9, 69].

The tempo of the initial portion of the dance was slow. The files swung out in a half circle and then back. Following this, the tempo increased, and a quadrille-like movement was executed. The *monarcha, malinche,* and the first dancer in one of the lines danced diagonally between the two files until they reached the end of the opposite line. The last man in this file then danced forward and occupied the position vacated by the head of the opposite line. This routine was continued, alternating files, until the two lines were completely reversed. When this was accomplished, the *monarcha* and *malinche* seated themselves, and the bull entered [9, 69]. According to Jeançon, during the above interval, and the succeeding portion of the dance, the *abuelos* engaged in various forms of buffoonery. They burlesqued the actions of the directors of the regular dances, drove the spectators back with their whips, and indulged in other pranks. Another side play involved the bull, who pretended to become enraged at (or to attack) the *malinche*. When frustrated in this effort, he took his spite out on the *abuelos*, kicking and throwing dirt and offal on them.

The above dance routine was then re-enacted, the bull in this case acting as the dance leader. When all the dancers had assumed their original positions, the snare drummer beat a roll on his drum. The *abuelos* rushed in, attacked the bull, and threw him to the ground. This appears to have been optional; in some cases the bull was shot by an individual appointed for that purpose. The *abuelos* next castrated the bull and presented the testicles to a woman in the audience.

Next the two dance files knelt on one knee. The *malinche* took the tripartite symbol of the *monarcha*, and with the *abuelos* danced forward and back between the two lines. This movement was repeated, and this time the *malinche* carried the *monarcha's* rattle.

When this was completed, the *abuelos* approached the seated *monarcha*, and in approved shamanistic fashion, each rubbed or massaged one of his legs. The movements were downward, and the "evil" was accordingly driven out through the feet, caught by the *abuelos*, and thrown away.

After this the *monarcha* ordered the chorus to sing, and he and the *malinche*, followed by one file, bisected the other line to form a cross. This movement was then repeated with the other dance file. Both files then reversed themselves, and the *monarcha* and *malinche*, dancing backward, led the two groups toward the chorus. The tempo of the dance was increased, and finally, in single file, the participants danced out of the plaza. This terminated the rite [9, 69].

Ghost Dance

The Santa Clara Indians were aware of the 1890 Ghost Dance, but it was never adopted by them. According to an infor-mant [9], a brother of Edward Dozier's grandfather attempted to introduce it, but failed. This man had visited the Ute and was indoctrinated by them and had received certain "tokens." On his return to Santa Clara, he persuaded a group to take part in the dance. Women were excluded. Shortly thereafter he became ill, and the rite was abandoned. "They said he got sick because of the tokens, so the idea did not go over" [9].

SOCIETIES

Clowns and Clown Societies

Three categories, or levels, of clowns existed at Santa Clara Pueblo. The most important were the representatives of the widespread Pueblo Indian societies, the Kòsa and Kwirana. A second group were the Pini (or Pinini) and the Putsato. These were not organized in formal bodies, but were appointed, on a temporary basis, when the occasion demanded. The pini served as substitutes for the kòsa or kwirana; the putsato performed at the time of a Pú xwe"re" ceremony and perhaps on other occasions. Finally, there were the Savadjo, commissioned to perform at stated intervals; again, no formal organization was involved.

Other current designations for clowns were *chiffonete*, *entremesero*, and *abuelo*. These terms, obviously derived from non-Indian sources, were nevertheless used by the Tewa and by some of the Tiwa, as well as by Spanish-Americans. *Chiffonete* was a generic appellation for clowns at Santa Clara, Taos, and Picuris pueblos. The word *entremesero*, from the Spanish *entremese-ar*, to act in a farce or interlude, was an alternative term for Kòsa. The Spanish *abuelo*, "grandfather," was used to designate the Savadjo proper, and related forms [18, 40, 69].

The clowning complex at Santa Clara, like those of the Pueblo tribes and the Southwest in general, was not a unique phenomenon, but was related both in behavior and function to that current in western North America. All the basic themes designated by Steward (1930: 187–207) occurred at Santa Clara Pueblo, although in some instances phrased to conform to local pattern. These included burlesque and ridicule of the sacred, and disregard for folkways and mores. Practical joking was common. Humor based on sex and obscenity was highly developed, including suggested or pantomimed abnormal social or private behavior. Gluttony and filth eating were frequently practiced by clowns. Comedy based upon illness, sorrow, misfortune, and the important activities of daily life was present. Foreigners, particularly Anglos and Spanish-Americans, were often the butt of humor; individuals were mimicked, and their unfamiliar cultural habits satirized and parodied.

At Santa Clara Pueblo, these universal themes were normally expressed through the medium of esoteric groups whose members appeared in ludicrous and grotesque masks, paintings, or costumes. These individuals frequently employed inverted speech ("talked backward," i.e., said the opposite of what they were told or asked to do). Privileged license and familiarity were common. This not only took the form of joking and criticism of individuals and current affairs, but also might include physical attacks on the persons of individuals. In short, clowns had the right to berate and lampoon the public at large, including respected political and religious officials, and to mock the most serious and sacred religious characters and performances [40, 61, 64, 69, 72, 73].

Clown humor tended to be highly stereotyped, although performers made up their own dialogues to fit the occasion [73]. [There is evidence that the same plots and themes were used over and over again, not only at Santa Clara, but also at neighboring pueblos. See Laski (1958: 40–41). WWH] When such humor focused on specific persons, it was referred to as "song making." The individual who was the butt of the joke was considered fortunate, since his or her selection was believed to insure benefits in the form of good health and abundant crops. "A person might be embarrassed, but would be glad to be joked" [69, 73]. Retaliation by the victim, at any time, was prohibited. Subsequent mention, directly or indirectly, of the episode by fellow villagers to the individual criticized was considered the height of bad form.

Much of the above is confirmed by observances made by Jeançon (1904–30) during his period of residence at Santa Clara. He stated that:

> These two societies [K'osa and Kwirana, WWH] are seen in public as clowns, playing all sorts of pranks and acting the fool, generally. In some of their public appearances they also indulge in scatalogic rites which are extremely foul and repulsive and no attempt will be made to describe them in this paper. Their less offensive capers take the form, mainly, of playing jokes upon the people gathered to witness a dance or ceremony. Under this cover, however, they are performing rites which have a serious intent.

The clowns had special privileges in being exempt from any restraint when appearing in public; no one was immune to their pranks. Even the highest dignitaries of the village had to undergo anything the clowns chose to inflict upon them, although this was rarely done. Generally the victim was especially selected as someone they wished to teach a lesson, or some bystander who did not suspect their intent. Occasionally, non-Indians who had made themselves offensive or obnoxious during a festival were disciplined in some ridiculous manner by the clowns.

Clown functions were manifold and had deeper implications than the immediate and obvious ones connected with sporadic public appearances. Their roles were intimately bound up with the religious, social, and political life of the people.

In the religious sphere their cooperation was necessary in the performance of many kiva and some public ceremonies, both at Santa Clara and other Tewa pueblos. At kachina performances they introduced the preliminary rites, envisaged the coming of supernaturals, in part served as dance directors and assistants to the impersonators, on occasion helped get out the dancers, and acted as an informal police body during the ceremonies. They were believed to be intimately associated with general health, fertility, rain, and perhaps formerly with warfare. According to Jeançon (1904-30), "...they are closely associated with rites of fertility, growing and maturing of crops, rain, snow, and other matters..."

Retreats were held in the homes of the society leaders on or about the middle of each month at the equinoctial and solstitial periods, and prior to any major ceremony in which a clown society participated. At such times private rituals were performed for community welfare and benefits. Pledging and initiation into clown societies was an esoteric function, and often included curing.

The comic relief contributed by clowns was important to the success of any ceremonial. It not only constituted a form of social release, but by contrast added to the effectiveness of the ritual. Whether consciously or not, the Santa Clara Indians were aware that the recurring climaxes in religious dramas could be sustained for only limited periods of time. Paralleling the most sophisticated theatrical techniques, they injected buffoonery to relieve tension. Individual performances by clowns in this and other capacities were marked by a high degree of histrionic ability, and were finished productions.

The sociopolitical role of clowns was most apparent in the area of social control and socialization; they were an important mechanism by which cultural ideals and mores were kept constantly in the foreground, and also a means of enforcing conformity. They acted as a stabilizing and conservative influence upon both old and young. Much of their humor was based on fact; as a result, few adults cared deliberately to flout social or religious convention, when they knew that such acts would ultimately be commented upon and ridiculed in public.

This function is best exemplified in their roles in connection with kachina enactments and at outside dances. The effectiveness of clowns in molding the behavior of the younger members of the community resulted from the fear they engendered. With parental cooperation, the clowns were established as realistic "bogies" who could and did administer corporal punishment.

Parenthetically, they also functioned psychotherapeutically, in that they offered a culturally approved vehicle for the expression of aggression against villagers and foreigners.

[The following two sections, The Kwirana Society and The K'osa Societies, contain material that is of rather special significance and, at the same time, is also somewhat puzzling, or at least surprising.

Elsewhere, Hill has commented on the matter of inter-Puebloan relationships, including "genealogies" of society affiliations, i.e., societal associations between or among the individual Pueblo tribes, even crossing linguistic boundaries. These two sections provide specific details on these matters; in this respect, the data are relatively unique in Puebloan ethnology.

The surprising, or puzzling, aspects of the discussion stem from the particular relationships reported by Hill. The affiliation of the Santa Clara Kwirana Society was to the Cochiti K'osa, or Koshare (Ku-sha'li) Society, not to the Cochiti Kwe'rana, as one might anticipate or, for a cultural "outsider," as it "ought to be."

A common practice in the literature has been to equate the Keresan Koshare with the Tewa K'osa. The black-and-white-striped body painting, the single or dual topknot, or horn, of whitened hair and cornhusks, the black breechclout, and the bandoliers of rabbit fur and/or various seeds are characteristics commonly shared by these clowns. The typical pranks and buffoonery indulged in by these performers add to the general similarities.

In contrast, the Keresan Kwe'rana do not clown, and they appear in their ceremonial "best" clothing, rather than anything resembling the distinctive garb of the K'osa. Finally, the Keresan Kwe'rana have a special relationship with the Pumpkin Kiva (although individual members need not belong to that kiva). In turn, the Pumpkin Kiva is comparable to the Summer people of the Tewa, whereas the Keresan Koshare have ties with the Turquoise Kiva, comparable to the Winter people of the Tewa. Accordingly, the contrast of these Keresan Kwe'rana, as, for example, at

Cochiti (Lange 1959: 307–9; see also pp. 298–307 for a discussion of the Ku-sha'li Society) is most striking when one reads Hill's account of the Santa Clara Kwirana and K'osa societies. CHL]

The Kwirana Society

The Kwirana, Tema, or Cochiti K'osa Society had been extinct for some time. Evidence indicates that it lapsed between the early period of Jeançon's contacts (1900–12) at Santa Clara Pueblo and the beginning of Parsons's fieldwork there in 1923.

The society was composed of both men and women, and included affiliates from both the Summer and Winter moieties. Women played subsidiary roles and did not engage in buffoonery. Members were recruited through trespass or trapping, and vows made either before or at birth or during illness [25, 40, 53]. (See also Jeançon 1904–30.) According to Jeançon, a father, not necessarily a member of the society, after consultation with his wife, would pledge a son at birth. When the child matured, he joined the organization. He also stated that the kwirana sometimes drew a ring of ashes near an area frequented by children at play. A watcher was appointed, and when a boy stepped over the boundary, i.e., trespassed, he was trapped and was seized. Later he became a member.

Headquarters for the Santa Clara Kwirana Society was located at the Keresan pueblo of Cochiti; after a year of training, novices were initiated at that village. However, according to one informant [71], during his father's time (1850s?) the Cochiti kwe'rana visited Santa Clara to hold an initiation. Reciprocal obligations formerly existed between the two societies, one taking part in the rites of the other, and vice versa, as the occasion demanded [25, 40, 53].

Little information was available on the functions of the Kwirana Society at Santa Clara Pueblo. Jeançon stated that their relations with the Winter Moiety were identical to those of the K'osa with the Summer Moiety; both groups acted cooperatively and together, regardless of the ceremony and time of year. In this connection it should be indicated that the Cochiti Kwirana role at Santa Clara probably included features not practiced at the home village. There they functioned predominantly in managerial and directorial capacities; they did not costume themselves or engage in public buffoonery (Lange 1959: 307–8).

The kwirana costume included the following features. They wore a headdress terminating in a point; this was accomplished by wrapping the hair in rags and inserting it through a hole in a skullcap. The body and face were painted a dirty gray, with the eyes and mouth outlined in black. They wore a necklace consisting of seed pods and a blue "shell" pendant, probably indicating their affiliation with the Winter Moiety. On the chest they wore strings of fruit, cookies, and doughnuts. They wore a brown kilt, and a ragged manta covered the shoulders and back. They were barefoot. Characteristically, the hands were folded over the chest. The intent was to create a poverty-stricken image [25, 40, 53] (see also Jeançon [1904–30]).

Just prior to 1940, a Santa Clara man was initiated into the Kwirana Society at Tesuque Pueblo. It was not ascertained whether this individual had ever performed at his own village.

The K'osa Societies

Two chapters of the K'osa, the Nambé and the San Juan, existed at Santa Clara. While diminished in active membership, they were still functional in 1941. The occurrence of the dual organization within the K'osa group appears unique for Santa Clara, and there is evidence for the recent introduction of the San Juan group (Parsons 1929: 129). It is probable that this dichotomy resulted from the lapsing of the Kwirana Society between 1912 and 1923. Such a procedure would be perfectly consistent with the emphasis of the Tewa Indians on the necessity for balanced organization, and their penchant for thinking by analogy.

In 1941 the Nambé society consisted of six members—four males and two females. Five of these belonged to the Summer Moiety. The sixth, a female Winter affiliate, was inactive, having married outside the pueblo. Three males constituted the San Juan group: two Winter and one Summer. The

Summer member was inactive, having moved to Oklahoma. One of the remaining members was only partially active, by reason of physical disability. The lack of female members in the San Juan society may be a further indication of its recency. Female affiliates appear to have had no public functions other than the furnishing and preparation of food, in harmony with the Santa Clara view of women as second-class citizens in the religious area [25, 29, 40, 53].

Each society had a leader or head and, if the membership complement permitted, a right and left arm. Meetings and private rites were held at the home of the head [29, 40, 53]. Before the Kwirana became extinct, and prior to the division of the K'osa into two units, the K'osa Society functioned as a cooperative counterpart of that organization. Although they were associated with the Summer Moiety, they operated during all ceremonies.

Recruitment

Membership cut across moiety lines. Recruits were obtained through vows before or at birth and during illness, and by trapping and trespass. Presumably the pledging pattern for those vowed before or at birth paralleled that of the Summer and Winter societies.

Vows made during illness appear to have followed two courses. The person in poor health might wait until he recovered and then petition the society. More often, however, the society was requested to conduct a curing ceremony, and upon recovery the patient began a novitiate which eventually led to initiation. In a sense these rites constituted a pledging to the organization.

Such a curing ritual was described by two informants [40, 45]. According to them, local members, at times supplemented by individuals from San Juan or Nambé, depending upon the branch involved, gathered at the house of the leader and donned their ceremonial costumes. The women wore the old-type blue manta without underclothing, and were barefoot. The men wore a breechclout, clown headdress, and were painted.

When all were ready, they went to the home of the patient. An altar was erected, and each member in turn gave the ailing person sacred water to drink. This was followed by other ceremonies.

When these were completed, the patient, accompanied by the society, was led through all parts of the village. If he was too ill to walk, he was carried. During this procedure, the members sang; "the K'osa have sets of songs appropriate for curing, initiation, and calling the kachina" [43]. When the trip had been completed, the patient was taken to his home, and the society went to the house of their leader and removed their costumes and paint. Visiting members returned to their home village.

A similar, though somewhat more elaborate rite was described by Parsons (1929: 226–27):

> In 1922 a sick girl in Santa Clara— Tsiowana muhete (lightning moving) or Sofia Naranjo—told her parents she wanted to be cured by the *kossa*. So, after her mother had cried about it [(414) As a grave and exacting enterprise that anybody would cry over. ECP], her father took some corn meal and a cigarette to *kossa sendo* [society head, WWH] who then went to Nambé to notify the Tewa *kossa* there that they were to come to Santa Clara to give water *(poku)* to the sick girl. They gave her water to drink from their medicine bowl. All, including the girl, went to Nambé, and thence all the *kossa*, excepting *kossa sendo* who stayed with the girl, went to *Katepokwinge* [Nambé Lake, WWH]. With them went also an Outside chief. Here, in the lake, each *kossa* was tied by a belt and by others dipped four times into the lake which is very deep. Then they returned towards Nambé bringing with them from the lake the *ohuwa* [kachina, or kachina's power, WWH]. The Outside chief went on ahead, to tell *kossa sendo* they were coming. The sick girl had bathed and wearing one dress (i.e., with no cotton slip under the *manta*), barefoot and with her hair flowing was in the plaza, where the *pufona ohuwa* [this probably

referred to a Bear Society member, WWH] cured her by taking out from her body with his bear paws [(415) The same practice is carried out at Isleta and, no doubt, elsewhere. ECP] what had been sent into it to make her sick. From a corn stalk the *kossa* sprinkled her with water.

The *kossa* made a circle of ashes in which they put what was taken out from her and with pine *(ko'si)* from the mountains they burned it up. In this fire even a stone could be reduced to ashes. The ashes were blown by the *kossa* to *tapayachiamu* to carry off, and he was asked "not to make her sick again." In spite of these words I am not certain that it was the tutelary spirit of the *kossa* who was supposed to have sent the sickness. Possibly Benina meant to say that *tapayachiamu* was asked not to let the patient be made sick again.

Trespass was defined as intrusion during the performance of private rites by the society. An informant [31] stated that if the San Juan K'osa were in retreat and an outsider blundered in, he was obligated to join the organization. Presumably such violations of privacy were not always unintentional, since most societies in retreat were guarded by war captains.

Trapping was accomplished in a variety of ways. According to Jeançon (1904–30), the artifice used by the kwirana in connection with children at play was also employed by the k'osa. Adults were frequently trapped in the course of public performances by the societies. The society often drew a circle of ashes, within which many of their activities were conducted. According to informants [29, 40], this was always done at San Juan during the Turtle Dance on December 25 and 26, which was attended by San Juan k'osa from Santa Clara. If outsiders crossed this line, they were obligated to join. As in the case of trespass, the question of intent was not always clear; some may have "volunteered." "Others really objected to joining" [29, 40].

Regardless of the means by which a candidate became eligible, he or she was required to have a sponsor. Sponsors need not have been society members, and usually were not. A father, grandfather, or uncle was preferred, but if these relatives were lacking, any reputable member of the community was selected. This person made the initial contact with the society, presented the head with cornmeal, tobacco, and feathers, and petitioned on behalf of the candidate. He continued to act in a liaison capacity until the novice was initiated.

Initiations

Initiation was always preceded by a year's novitiate and training, during which the candidate was subjected to a variety of restrictions. Food tabus were enforced, and he was expected to remain continent. Theoretically he was not to leave the village during this period. Actually this meant that he was expected to spend the night in the pueblo and receive instruction in role impersonation and the esoteric rites of the group. Each evening he made and deposited prayer plumes with cornmeal at the shrines located at the four cardinal directions. If at the end of a year the candidate qualified, he was initiated in the village associated with the headquarters of the society—either Nambé or San Juan [30, 40, 45, 50].

No data were obtained on the initiation ceremonies of the San Juan K'osa. However, a relatively full account of those at Nambé was secured from a member [64], and this was supplemented by another informant [73]. Presumably the San Juan rites paralleled those of Nambé. A third informant [55] stated that in both instances initiates were submerged four times in the waters of mountain lakes located in the vicinity of the villages.

The informant [64] joined the Nambé K'osa in 1918. Prior to the influenza epidemic of that year, a number of persons at Santa Clara Pueblo were seriously ill; several of his maternal uncles died. When he contracted a sore throat, which was the principal symptom of the disease, he decided to join the clown society to insure his recovery. Since he lacked relatives who would normally have acted as sponsors, he asked a member who later was Winter cacique to act in that capacity. This man went to Nambé and met with the society. He gave the head tobacco, cornmeal, and feathers, and informed him that he "had a new son who was ill and wished to become a k'osa." The petition was accepted, and the society agreed to visit Santa Clara, in order to determine whether the candidate possessed the proper qualifications for membership.

When they arrived at Santa Clara, they interviewed the informant [64] and presumably assured themselves tentatively of his eligibility. They informed him that he must undergo a year's novitiate, and that during that time he would be subjected to various restrictions and proscriptions. These stressed religious orthodoxy and included strict adherence to native ideals, deference to all religious organizations, and the concomitant, respect for elders of the community. He was told not to leave the pueblo, i.e., to be available each evening to receive instructions. Furthermore, he was expected to remain continent and to refrain from drinking. Finally, he was informed that if he met these probationary requirements, he would be initiated at the end of the year.

At the end of the novitiate, the informant [64], accompanied by his "grandfather and grandmother" (sponsors) and other relatives, went to Nambé. They took with them sacred meal, blue cornmeal, bread, meat, and other food, turkey, yellow warbler, and oriole feathers, and eagle down, which they presented to the head of the Nambé K'osa.

The informant was told to go to the kiva, remove his clothes, and be prepared to remain there for four days. During this interval he was allowed to eat only cornmeal and to drink only sacred water. He was not permitted to lie down, but was required to sleep in a sitting position. He could leave the kiva only at night to relieve himself. Throughout this retreat, he was continually guarded by a member of the society. Those k'osa not assigned to guard duty remained at the group's headquarters and "worked." This involved, among other things, the construction of prayer plumes from the feathers given to the head of the society, and the assembling of material essential for the initiation.

On the fourth day all k'osa went to the kiva. On arrival the leader placed a pouch filled with pollen around the informant's neck. He was told to replenish the pollen whenever it became depleted. Next, members began construction of a K'osa headdress. The material for this was furnished by the society leader. The front was made from undressed deerskin, the back from undressed mountain lion hide. During this rite the informant was requested to smoke, and was given tobacco mixed with deer marrow. When the headdress was completed, the society again went into retreat.

Very early on the morning of the fifth day, the informant, accompanied by two members of the society, departed for "Nambé Lake," east of the pueblo. He was barefoot and wore only a breechclout and blanket. He carried cornmeal, tobacco, and the prayer plumes made by the k'osa.

Upon arrival at the lake the clowns sang. Spinden (1933: 88, 120) recorded one of these songs. It referred to the k'osa going in and under the lake, to the area where thunder, lightning, and rain were located.

> Toward Leaf Lake we are going,
> Under the farthest lightning we are
>   going,
> Under the thunder we are going,
> Even now we are arriving.

When the songs terminated, the informant was told to wade into the lake, reach down, and secure some "mud scum." His first attempt was unsuccessful; he obtained only black mud. He repeated his effort a second and third time and met with failure. "He has to be a man and be brave." On the fourth attempt [the ritually compulsive number, WWH] he was completely submerged by the two k'osa, and succeeded. He placed some of the "mud scum" in his pollen pouch and carried the rest in his hand. The three then began the return trip to the pueblo. En route they stopped at a cattail swamp, and the two k'osa collected more "mud scum."

The trio arrived at Nambé just at daybreak. The informant was taken to the kiva and told to sit in a corner. A line, a half circle of ashes, was drawn around him, and he was not allowed to pass beyond it. Next he was given tobacco to smoke, and the members proceeded to instruct him concerning the society and his role.

Following this, the headdress was painted with alternating stripes of "mud scum" and white clay. While this was in progress, the head took a bowl of sacred water, added "mud scum" and meal, and stirred it with a stone fetish. When the elements were thoroughly mixed, the fetish was given to the informant, who placed it in his pouch.

Next the leader filled a stone pipe with tobacco, lighted it, and gave it to the informant to smoke. When he finished, it was passed to the members, who smoked in turn. Next the head took the pipe and stirred the mixture of water, "mud scum," and meal. Then he dipped it in the liquid and sprinkled, "blessed," the newly made headdress, initiate, and the members. The bowl containing the sacred mixture was then passed to the informant, who drank from it, followed in turn by the K'osa members.

During these rites the clowns sang and prayed. "The songs and prayers told the initiate that he had been successful; that he had won a better life; that his request to join the society had come from the heart, and that they were looking forward to an increase in membership. There was more."

When all had drunk of the mixture, the head announced that the villagers had been informed of the initiation and had gathered; that the informant would be presented to them; and that a feast was to be held in his honor.

The informant was then allowed to stand and stretch, and to pass beyond the semicircular line of ashes. Meanwhile, yucca was brought, and members chewed it to make it pliable; this was later used for the wristlets worn by the society. Concurrently the leader went to a roll of bedding near the wall and removed a pair of new moccasins, a turtle shell rattle with dew claws suspended from the top, a necklace of plant pods called "K'osa berries," and strips of black cotton cloth for wristlets. According to another informant [21], these cotton wristlets constituted the only difference between the Nambé and San Juan K'osa.

Another member presented the informant [64] with a necklace of oranges, apples, sopaipillas, and cookies. He was told not to eat these, but merely to taste them, and to throw them to the villagers as he returned to the kiva. The leader dipped this and all other items of costume and equipment in the sacred mixture.

Next the informant's face and body were painted, and he donned his headdress and the remainder of his costume. Before he was presented with the moccasins, the head tore a piece from the side of the left one and burned it. Some of the resulting ash was placed in the sacred mixture; the rest was dabbed on the black stripes on the body and headdress and the black wristlets, "wherever there was black." He was told that some day that was where he was going, "to the ashes." The informant was instructed to burn the moccasins when they were worn out and to rub the ashes on their replacements.

According to Jeançon (1904–30), the standard costume of the k'osa was intended to create the image of a ragged beggar. The body was painted in alternating horizontal stripes of black and white; the face was white, with the eyes and mouth outlined in black. The headdress, as mentioned earlier, was of deer and mountain lion hide. It had two horns, terminating in corn tassels, and was also striped black and white. The necklace was of seed pods. In addition to this, strings of fruit, cookies, and doughnuts were worn on the chest. The kilt was brown and had a sheepskin secured to the back, which contained the k'osa's "lunch." Above the moccasins were rag anklets and cowhoof rattles. Rags were also tied about the waist. Wristlets and garters were black.

When the initiate was costumed, the rest followed suit or repainted themselves. When all were ready, one member mounted the top of the kiva, announced that they were "coming out," and performed some humorous acts. Meanwhile, several of the group emerged, went to a house, and remained outside singing. When a certain song was begun, the leader and the remainder of the society emerged from the kiva. "They sang and made fun. They were happy and gay. They tossed the new member about. They carried him on their shoulders to show that they were glad."

As soon as they appeared, the first group hid. From time to time, a member of that group checked the progress of the initiate's contingent, and at a certain point they reappeared. The initiate's group then went into hiding, and the first group performed. This alternation was repeated three times. On the fourth occasion, both groups joined in the plaza, where they danced, shouted, and "made fun." During the course of these observances, the female k'osa took food to the kiva.

When the rites in the plaza were terminated, the clowns, accompanied by the secular officials, the priestly hierarchy of the moieties, and members of other societal organizations, returned to the kiva. Here all welcomed and prayed for the initiate. Next he was informed by the K'osa that the food tabus were lifted, and that he might eat anything he wished. "You have missed much food during your retreat." Since k'osa "talk backward," i.e., say the opposite of what is meant, this was a command to eat nothing at all. However, the secular officials, caciques, leaders of the Bear societies, and the head of the Women's Scalp Society told him to ignore this edict and to eat sparingly. Finally, he was informed that a kachina enactment would be held in four days, and that until that time he must remain at the home of the K'osa head.

Following this all ate. Those who were not members feasted at homes of K'osa families. When all had eaten, male and female K'osa members returned to the plaza. The leader brought the bowl containing the sacred mixture; others carried food and gifts. Here the society danced and "made fun." During the rite, members threw food and gifts to the audience, which included visitors from Santa Clara. From time to time, the k'osa drank from the bowl containing the sacred mixture. On each occasion they gestured toward the six cardinal points.

When dancing was completed, the K'osa returned to the kiva, where the initiate was instructed further. He was told, "Now you are a member you must be obedient. You must come to Nambé whenever you are needed. You must participate in all our work. You must not hesitate regardless of personal desire or weather—snow, hail, or rain; you must come and bring your equipment." When night fell, the informant [64], accompanied by two members and carrying his equipment, made another trip to the lake. On arrival he threw the yucca and black cloth wristlets into the water, after which his companions submerged him four times. They said, "Here is a place [the lake, WWH] that you should come if you ever need guidance or help. Here you should come and make your request. Here are members like you. Those who are gone are here."

Following this, the informant said a prayer asking for a "betterment of his life," and gave thanks for the recovery of his health. Next he threw cornmeal into the lake, and purified himself by running his hands from his head down his body. "He unshells or unscales himself like a snake sheds its skin. He makes these motions and is purified and throws the scales [symbolically, WWH] into the lake." After this, the three returned to the kiva, and the remainder of the society membership went to the lake to bathe.

When this was completed, they joined the trio in the kiva; the initiate then left for the house of the K'osa leader. Upon his arrival, he was greeted and congratulated by relatives and friends from Santa Clara. This contingent normally left for their village the next morning, but returned to attend the kachina ceremony three days later. Food tabus were now lifted, and the initiate and the guests feasted.

During the four days the kachina were in retreat, the informant [64] remained at the house of the leader. He was further instructed by members in the various roles played by the k'osa. On the fourth night he visited the headquarters of the kachina, accompanied by the two clowns selected to visualize the coming of the kachina. Here they ascertained the name of the lake from which the kachina would emerge.

Later in the evening they donned their costumes and went to the kiva to play their roles. The initiate "made fun," but took no part in visualizing the emergence of the kachina. "He watches and learns." When the kachina departed for the last time, he turned to the audience and said, "not to live," i.e., the equivalent of "long life to you" [64].

Next the trio went to the headquarters of the kachina. By this time, the masks had been removed. The trio prayed to them and offered meal to the six directions. They then returned to the home of the leader, where the initiate was reminded again of his obligations and duties as a member of the society. Finally, all k'osa, carrying their costumes and equipment, made another pilgrimage to the lake and bathed. "This shows the ceremony is complete."

The next morning the initiate left for Santa Clara. Before he departed, he received a substantial number of gifts, which included such items as cornmeal, food, cloth, and buckskin [64].

Ceremonies of the San Juan and Nambé K'osa

Like other religious groups, the San Juan and Nambé K'osa functioned both as separate units and as integral parts of general moiety ceremonies and dances. According to informants [31, 40], the k'osa were eligible to perform during any dance, and to take part in any ceremony; their activities in connection with pledging, curing, initiation, and "hidden dances" have already been described.

Attention should be called again to the reciprocal obligations which existed between each group and its parent society at Nambé or San Juan. Like the curing societies, their operations extended beyond their own village; however, this was in turn compensated for by assistance from the sponsoring units. When they journeyed to another village, they were always accompanied by a war captain or his representative. This dignitary was dressed in war paraphernalia, which included bow and arrows, or gun, and shield [29, 40, 45, 69].

The appearance of the k'osa at public or outside dances has been limited in recent years. According to one informant [69], during his lifetime they have appeared only twice, both times at Basket Dances. This has resulted from diminished membership and of the physical disability of some of the members. Factionalism has also taken its toll, since only those belonging to the faction

sponsoring the dance have taken part. However, they or their substitutes have still functioned on occasion. Their appearance at outside dances has not necessarily included "fun making." More frequently, they have acted entirely in a directorial or managerial capacity.

Jeançon's generalized remarks on k'osa-kwirana activities during outside dances are pertinent, since they provide examples of social censure, as well as of a variety of humor themes lacking in more esoteric performances. According to Jeançon (1931b: 45–49),

They sometimes enter the house of a woman who is notoriously slovenly about her house duties and person, and tumble everything about in a chaotic mass, exposing dirty corners, and other features of her remissness to her duties; some things, such as dirty pots, remnants of clothing, etc., may be entirely destroyed by breaking or tearing them to pieces. The woman herself may be subjected to considerable mauling and mishandling whereby her festival clothes and ornaments are damaged. The victim does not always take this kindly, and shows her resentment by screaming and fighting her tormentors; this only lends zest to the occasion and she always retires defeated. The rebuke is obvious to those who know about it.

The public burlesques of the White man are amusing spectacles, although on some occasions, particularly when the Catholic Mass is burlesqued it is in rather bad taste from the viewpoint of the Christian. Clowns dressed to represent the priest, acolyt[e]s and other celebrants of the Mass go through a burlesque of the service, often mimic[k]ing the peculiarities and mannerisms of their parish priest. The costumes, made of rags, sacking and such other materials as are at hand are ridiculous. Crude pots and plates are substituted for the objects used in the Christian rites. The words of the service are distorted and singing is always of a boisterous and inharmonious character.

Possibly this burlesque of a rite to which they subscribe with great devotion is a remnant of the time when they first came in contact with the Spaniards, and thought by such means to be able to counteract any serious impression made upon the minds of the Indians. Again, it may be a further carrying out of the idea of concealing, during a public performance, and under the guise of ridicule, a greater respect for their own religion. Although the latter idea is inconsistent with the White man's way of reasoning it is not so to the Indian mind. The idea of concealing, under the guise of ridicule or of depreciation, of things, rites, etc., of value is very common with all primitive peoples.

Less offensive burlesqueing may consist of assuming the White Man's attire, exaggerating costumes, actions, and so on, and particularly mimicking personages who are pompous, dictatorial or who have other mannerisms that mark them as distinct from the average. Often their best friends are held up to ridicule in these pranks but it is all done in the spirit of fun and rarely with any malice.

Sometimes a recent event is re[en]acted with full details, such as a law court, wedding or other occasion. At such times the spectators are impressed into service and must represent the culprit, bride and groom or any one the clowns desire them to represent. The clowns, of course, are always the judge, priest or any other person of prominence, and burlesque these with great precision. A scene of this kind may take several hours to enact. A favorite play that is often used is to seat two old Mexicans or an old Mexican and an old Indian, and make them argue, at length, about nothing. If the argument is not noisy enough the clowns push and annoy the men, urging them to greater effort. This is always a source of great enjoyment to the Indians assembled.

Again, the clowns may steal into a house and scatter meal to the six regions to bring a special blessing upon it and its owner, or they may deposit, in a secret corner of the room, a prayer plume or fetish, again for a special purpose.

A more recent description was provided by an informant [72] who witnessed a Turtle Dance at San Juan Pueblo in 1940. Six k'osa took part on that occasion, including representatives from the Santa Clara chapter.

The k'osa came out in the middle of the afternoon and went to the south, or principal plaza in the pueblo. Here they outlined a white square. The sides of the square were thirty or forty feet in length. In the square and immediately in front, the k'osa made most of their fun to amuse the spectators. The audience consisted of local and visiting Pueblo Indians, neighboring Spanish-Americans, a few Apache, and several Anglo tourists. These formed a semicircle beyond the square.

After considerable comic dialogue, most of which was obscene in nature, and after exaggerated deliberation, the k'osa built a fire in the square and began roasting a hen which had been neither plucked nor dressed. The dialogue was conducted chiefly in Tewa, with occasional orations in Spanish and a few words of English injected from time to time. While the chicken was cooking, one of the clowns secured a pole. At one end was tied an assortment of dirty rags. At intervals he dipped the rags into the fire and then rushed into the audience, scattering soot and dust over the spectators.

Other k'osa went into the crowd and dragged an Apache man and woman into the square and performed a mock marriage over them. Realizing that further struggling would only accentuate their embarrassing situation, the Apache submitted with good grace. One k'osa impersonated a bishop; two others, acolytes. The couple were told to kneel before the "bishop." The "bishop," assuming a serious demeanor, held an old newspaper in one hand and proceeded to read the service. At intervals he stopped and blessed the couple.

The readings were in the main unintelligible, but occasionally a sentence was clear and understandable. One such was as follows: "Recuerdan de esto, si no que se va para el infierno (Remember his; if not, you may go to eternal fire)." This brought peals of laughter from the spectators, but the "bishop" remained serious and continued.

Every so often the "bishop" genuflected. Each time his knee touched the ground, one of the "acolytes" lifted up his kilt and surveyed his posterior—with a grimace at his fellow K'osa. Occasionally the other "acolyte" removed the "bishop's" hat (a square cap made of braided corn husks) and replaced it, as was done when a high pontifical mass was being celebrated. The mock marriage consumed about an hour, the Apache finally being dismissed after being admonished in both Tewa and English. The k'osa then retrieved the half-cooked chicken from the fire, pulled it apart, and began to consume it in a gluttonous manner.

The Turtle Dancers appeared before the K'osa square two or three times during the afternoon and early evening and danced. At each appearance, the k'osa amused themselves with the *abuelos* who accompanied the dancers. After some discussion the clowns decided to request the *abuelos* to dance. There followed much whispering between the k'osa and the *abuelos*. Each time a k'osa whispered in the ear of an *abuelo* that individual drew the lash of the whip he carried taut along the stock and, holding it vertically before his face, shook it while he listened. He nodded his head in agreement or disagreement as he listened. After much whispering and diplomatic endeavor, during which the k'osa waved their arms and grimaced with disgust, the *abuelos* finally agreed to dance.

Immediately one k'osa began orating and reading in Spanish from a newspaper, exaggerating upon the capabilities and dancing genius of the *abuelos*. Some derogatory statements were also made, and at such times the *abuelos*

rushed threateningly toward the k'osa, snapping their whips but never actually striking the clowns.

While the oration was being given, another k'osa took off his cap and went through the audience collecting contributions for the *abuelos*. When this collection had been made and the oration completed, one k'osa took a drum and began singing. The two *abuelos* fell into step and in unison expertly performed a dance. At the conclusion of the dance, the k'osa applauded loudly, and one delivered an oration praising the *abuelos*.

The *abuelos* were then dismissed and another parley was held. After much discussion, which included many oaths and much laughter, it was decided that a bullfight should be staged. Again a k'osa gave an oration elaborating on the strength and viciousness of the two bulls which were about to fight. When the speech was completed, the two chosen to fight got on their hands and knees, about fifty feet apart, and faced each other. With bellows they advanced, stopping to shake their heads in the manner of infuriated bulls, and to throw dirt over their shoulders in apparent anger. Meanwhile, some of the k'osa urged them on, speculated on the winner, and attempted to place bets. One got astride one of the impersonators and pretended to ride.

While this was taking place, one clown chased another about the square, riding the pole with the rags as if it were a horse. Each time he caught up with his partner, he took the pole and pretended pederasty.

Finally the two bulls came together, butted, bellowed, pushed each other, threw dirt, and rolled on the ground. The other k'osa shouted, applauded their efforts, and patted their favorites. Finally they lost interest in the fight and began to amuse themselves in other ways.

One clown arranged the kilt of another to simulate pregnancy. He pretended surprise and enthusiasm at the discovery, shouting to his companions,

"Look, he is pregnant." They came and seriously scrutinized and examined the first man, who rolled on the ground in pretended pain. Acts of the type described continued for the remainder of the evening.

Little information other than that detailed under Initiations was obtained on the subject of private ceremonies of the K'osa. It was known that they "worked" one day during each month, and that they held retreats at solstices and equinoxes, and before participating in general moiety ceremonies. Presumably their activities paralleled those of other organizations.

Formerly k'osa may have made up one of the teams participating in ceremonial shinny before that activity became secularized. More recently, k'osa, at least on one occasion, have substituted for a cacique. This occurred when that particular dignitary refused to function because the group sponsoring a dance belonged to the opposite faction of the moiety. They arrived at the house from which the dancers would emerge, carrying a bag which contained haje, eagle wing feathers, and other items. This was placed in the corner of the room with a circular, terraced bowl of sacred water and a basket of meal. As the dancers donned their costumes, the k'osa dipped the eagle feathers in the sacred water and sprinkled each dancer in turn, as well as members of the chorus and any officials who were present. Then all drank from the bowl while the k'osa prayed and admonished them. As each participant left, he took a pinch of cornmeal from the basket and threw it before him as he went through the doorway [43, 73].

The Pini, or Pinini

The pini, or pinini, acted as temporary substitutes for the k'osa and kwirana. No society organization was involved. Their appearance has been frequent in recent years, with the extinction of the Kwirana Society, the diminution of K'osa membership, and the continuation of factionalism. For exam-

ple, the ceremony on Good Friday night, 1941, was sponsored by the conservative group of the Summer Moiety. The available k'osa were affiliated with the Winter Moiety and the progressive element of the Summer Moiety, and refused to serve. Therefore, pini were appointed to play the roles of the k'osa. Selection was based on the histrionic ability of the individuals [9, 13, 29].

Pini costumes differed radically from those of the k'osa. The face was painted reddish, and the upper part of the chest, back, and arms were the same color, but spotted with rings of black. The remainder of the body was black, except for the arms from the elbows down and the hands, which were colored white. They wore a black skull cap. Attached to the front and chin strap of this cap was a cornhusk mask. This consisted of a husk cylinder extending from the chin over the nose and above the cap, terminating in a corn tassel. Fixed to this were husk circles outlining the mouth and eyes. The kilt and moccasins were brown; the garters and wristlets, black. The necklace consisted of fruit and cookies. A sheepskin containing food was tied to the back [9, 13].

The Putsato

The putsato, "white or dusty buttocks," like the pini, performed the roles of clowns and dance directors on a temporary basis. Their activities were restricted to outside performances; they did not function in the kiva, and therefore their prestige was not as great as that of the pini. A difference of opinion existed as to the scope of their functions. According to two informants [13, 29], they could be assigned to duty in connection with any outside plaza dance. However, others [9, 21] stated that they were associated only with the Women's Scalp Society and P'u xwe^{n}re^n. Possibly their role has been extended in recent years.

The body of a putsato performer was painted white, as were the face and hair, the latter being brought to a point on top of the head. The mask was similar to that of the pini. Moccasins were brown, the kilt black, wristlets and garters yellow. A sheepskin containing food was tied to the back.

The Savadjo

Savadjo was a generic term applied to a variety of impersonators who appeared in the pueblo at various intervals. [See Ortiz (1969: 158–62) for a discussion of the "Tsave Yoh" among the Tewa, but primarily at San Juan Pueblo. CHL] Included in this group were the savadjo proper, Poker-old-man, Pour-water-on-the-head-old-woman, Willow-draggers, Hand-thrower, Thorns-to-apply, Pitch-to-apply, and the *abuelos* of the Matachina Dance. Their principal role was a disciplinary one. In their capacity as realistic "bogeys," they frightened and punished recalcitrant children. However, they might also be critical of adults who were nonconformists. They also served as temporary appointees. According to one informant [31], they were selected by the war captain; another [73] believed they were chosen by the cacique. In any event, they represented an effective means of social control in the hands of vested interests. [The derivation and historical antecedents of this group have remained uncertain. An interesting discussion of this problem, as well as the clown complex in general, was presented by Parsons and Beals (1934: 491–514). See also Ortiz 1969: 158–62. WWH]

Parsons's statement (1924b: 150), outlining the role of this group in the socialization process for the Tewa generally, was confirmed by my Santa Clara data. According to Parsons,

Tsabiyu [savadjo, WWH] is the children's bugaboo. "Tsabiyu will come to whip you or take you," the old people will say to a refractory child, or to a crying child; "Tsabiyu will hear you from k'osena," his home in the eastern mountains. And a child may be told that Tsabiyu has said that he has ears in the chimney. "Knock and I will come," says he. So to a crying child or a lazy one, a mother might say, "I am going to knock on the chimney." "Don't do it, mother," begs the child. The mother may go as far as to pick up a stick to tap with. When it looks like snow in the eastern mountains, people say to the children, "Tsabiyu is coming"; or after snowing,

they say, "Tsabiyu is under the snow, he won't come." At the Christmastide dances Tsabiyu actually does appear. There are two of him, one a man of the Winter People, wearing a white shirt and in white mask; the other, a man of the Summer People, in yellow shirt and black mask. Over [above] their mask, a wig, and under [below] it, a collar of foxskin. They wear trousers and shoes, and carry a horse whip and a sack. They chase the children, and they visit from house to house to collect bread for their sack. As early as November people begin to tell the children that Tsabiyu is getting ready his sack in the mountains.

The Savadjo Proper, or Willow-draggers

According to an informant [40], the savadjo proper, or Willow-draggers (djan whair), appeared in the fields during the fall of the year. "They came when the melons were ripe." Parents appraised children of their presence, and they were threatened with punishment by these supernaturals if they stole produce. Whether they existed as a threat or a reality was not clear.

They also appeared in the village on Christmas Eve. At that time, they visited the various houses and punished children who had been disobedient during the year. Parents frequently intercepted them and asked them to come to their homes. "They frighten the disobedient children with their willow whips and make feints at taking them to their homes to bake them" [40]. "They whipped undisciplined children and made them say that they would always take part in a moiety dance when asked. When the child said 'yes,' it was always obligated to dance in the future" [21].

An account of one of their appearances was obtained from an informant [18]:

The only member of the savadjo group that I have seen were the two "Willow-draggers" who came just at dusk when the Christmas fires (nufu) were dying out. They padded along noiselessly, keeping to the shadows of the houses. I followed at a safe distance behind with a group of older boys. We would not have dared follow even at a distance a few years before; we would have been reported and whipped for our boldness. Both "Willow-draggers" carried whips. They entered a house, and we peeked through the window. We saw a man holding his ten-year-old son in his arms. The boy was obviously frightened. The mother sat at one side with her face in her hands, apparently crying. We heard the father say in an angry voice, "He is very disobedient. He never does anything he is told. He is very bad." The "Willow-draggers" advanced toward the child with their whips, but at this moment we were discovered and ran away. We were told that the child was made to dance; that if he did not obey or if he talked back, he was stripped and whipped.

The Willow-draggers, who always appeared in pairs, were identically costumed. They wore white buckskin suits covered with tunics. The masks were black; the noses, thin and sharp; the ears, thin and pointed. Gray horsehair was fixed to the top of the mask. Earrings were of selenite. Each wore a foxskin around the neck. The butts of a bundle of willows were held in each hand, the tips allowed to drag on the ground behind [29, 52].

According to Santa Clara informants [29, 52, 71], San Juan Pueblo had both Black-faced and White-faced Savadjo, which were equated with the Willow-draggers by Santa Clara Indians. These were apparently regular participants in the clowning performances which accompanied the Turtle Dance at San Juan. What appears to have occurred is that the costumes of the *abuelos* (clowns or cowboys) of the Matachina had been somewhat modified, and their roles extended to include an addition ceremony. However, the typical features of the *abuelos* remained; they carried whips with lashes; they did not speak, but indicated acquiescence or refusal by movements of their heads or whips; and they were continually in motion, i.e., performing a shuffle-like dance [29, 52, 71].

So far as could be ascertained, the Santa Clara *abuelos* took part only in the Matachina Dance.

Poker-old-man

Poker-old-man (Ho do dje sendo) appeared during the shinny game held following the Edge of Spring ceremony, in January or February. One informant [69] stated that he was also called "Old-man-with-cedar-bark" (Kung whi po di sendo), because of the bundle of that material he carried on his back. He was always accompanied by Pour-water-on-the-head-old-woman. Appearance of the Savadjo characters have been sporadic in recent years, and the last time these two were reported was in 1933 and 1934 [40, 45, 50]. According to another [52], they may also appear in the fall.

The impersonator was masked. Horsehair covered the top of the mask, and tied to this was one down feather of an eagle. This indicated that the character was a supernatural and not a witch. "Witches wear two feathers." A foxskin collar adorned the neck. The remainder of the costume consisted of buckskin leggings and a shirt, or a robe of buffalo hide. At the back was a bundle of cedar bark [52].

Poker-old-man and Pour-water-on-the-head-old-woman arrived in the village from the river to the east. As soon as they appeared in the village, children were hidden or guarded by their parents. They danced for a while in the plaza [50]. Poker-old-man attempted to prod the children with his stick. If he caught an unchaperoned child, he placed it in an oven, took cedar bark from his bundle, lit a fire, and pretended to roast the child [43]. He was believed to have cannibalistic propensities. "When he came, my father took me and went to the top of the house. He tried to follow, and my father pushed the ladder out. The old man really frightens children, though some of the older boys make fun of him" [52].

Pour-water-on-the-head-old-woman

Pour-water-on-the-head-old-woman (Ho ho dje kwidjo) appeared with and at the same time as Poker-old-man, normally in the spring, about the time of the vernal equinox [40, 45, 50, 52]. They came from the vicinity of the river, just before sundown [43]. The impersonator was a man. "She" wore a turquoise-blue mask. The hair hung loose. The arms were painted white; the legs, covered with yellow ochre. No footgear was worn. The body was covered with a white woven dress. A kilt served as a shawl. In "her" arms, "she" carried a jar of sacred water.

The arrival of this figure and "her" partner was often signalized by the disturbance which they created among the horses. Unlike Poker-old-man, "she" was looked upon as benevolent and kind to children. "She" climbed the ladders to house rooftops where the people were watching, and gave them water to drink. "If you drink from the jar, you will be healthy." It was imperative that "she" keep constantly in motion, running from place to place and dancing while people drank. When the jar was empty, it was refilled at the spring west of the village [52].

Hand-throwers

The Hand-throwers (Mong whae ri), paired savadjo, came in late summer or early fall, just prior to the harvest. They were masked figures. Each carried a spherical rawhide container filled with sand or earth and closed with a drawstring. Their role was that of preventing theft of farm produce, particularly by children [29, 40, 43, 50]. They also entertained the people [40].

When they arrived in the village from the fields, all immediately went indoors. When the Hand-throwers caught anyone outside the house, they threw the rawhide containers at them [43, 50, 71].

An interesting case of nonconformance to pueblo mores and of punishment in connection with these impersonators took place in the latter part of the nineteenth century:

It is told of Jesús Silva, the father of Tonita Silva, that unlike the rest of the village, he remained on his house roof working when the Hand-throwers appeared. He pretended not to see them and continued to put his corn away.

One, seeing him, asked why he did not follow pueblo custom and go into the house. Jesús replied that the corn needed storing, and he saw no reason why he should run away from one of the members of his own village. When the Hand-thrower moved to strike him, Silva dodged, grabbed the container, threw it into the plaza, unmasked the impersonator, and drove him from his home. For this, Silva and his near relatives were banished from the pueblo and went to live in the "refugee village of Abiquiu" [72].

Thorns-to-apply

Thorns-to-apply (Wha kan yu), a masked figure, accompanied by Pitch-to-apply, appeared in the village just prior to the harvest. The visit was always a surprise one, and anyone caught outdoors had burrs rubbed in their hair. Again, protecting farm theft seems to have been their dominant role [21].

Pitch-to-apply

Pitch-to-apply (Wha kan yu) was paired with Thorns-to-apply, and functioned in the same manner, except that piñon pitch instead of thorns was rubbed in the hair [21].

DISEASE, MEDICINE, AND CURING SOCIETIES

Concern with health and well-being, while not overtly displayed, was always in the foreground of Santa Clara consciousness. It represented one of the major themes of the culture, and was responsible for directing and channeling much of people's behavior. Individuals had constantly to scrutinize their own actions for digressions and omissions which might result in supernatural retribution in the form of misfortune, accident, illness, or death. Besides self-engendered dangers, there were others that had to be guarded against, equally potent, which stemmed from the machinations of antisocial persons .

Added to this, there was some appreciation of the connection between natural causes and ill health. The result was the conception of a hazardous world, fraught with insecurity, which generated considerable anxiety and tension. This expressed itself in continued self-analysis and a distrust and suspicion of those with whom the person came in everyday contact. Amelioration of and protection from these and normal dangers formed a major part of the therapeutic and prophylactic activity of the various esoteric societies and of unaffiliated secular practitioners.

Theories of Disease

Consistent with the above, illness, accident, and misfortune were ideally interpreted in terms of breach of tabu or witchcraft. Breach of tabu was the most frequently encountered explanation of disease; however, object intrusion was also popular. Secondary were illnesses attributed to witchcraft without intrusion, i.e., contagious magic. To this category were often relegated cases where it was difficult to determine specific responsibility. Soul loss, in its classic sense, with resulting disability, appears to have been absent. Illnesses or deaths from natural causes, old age, or accident were recognized, but their role was incidental in the overall theory of disease, though important in its treatment. Herein lay one of the major inconsistencies between theory and practice in Santa Clara culture, a situation probably typical of most, if not all, Pueblo Indian cultures.

All the Pueblos had esoteric societies whose primary, or at least secondary objective was to cure. At Santa Clara, and probably among other Pueblos, witchcraft and breach of tabu were accepted explanations of most disease origins. These were basic assumptions, whose existence was unquestioned and upon which rested most beliefs associated with medicine. Yet in the face of this, the bulk of the medical practice was performed by individuals, both men and women, who were not necessarily society members, or if members, ones who functioned apart from and outside the jurisdiction of the societies. There is no evidence that these midwives, herbalists, masseurs, etc., took much if any cognizance of the teleological factors of breach of tabu or witchcraft.

The above is an excellent example of what Linton (1936: 273–74) termed cultural alternatives. According to the cultural ideal, the most acceptable explanation of disease was either breach of tabu or witchcraft; the most highly considered means of effecting a cure, and the one carrying the greatest social approval, was enlisting the help of one or another of the esoteric societies. However, because of reasons of convenience, expense, time factor, or individual or factional preference, a third alternative, that of natural causes and cure by home remedies, was the one most frequently adopted.

Any interpretation of these alternatives is difficult. Like all American Indians, the people of Santa Clara Pueblo lacked scientific knowledge of disease cause. However, a case can also be made that the esoteric societies were concerned substantially with those ills which were of psychic origin, i.e., those caused by anxieties associated with the supernatural, wheras secular practitioners dealt primarily with those of somatic or accidental nature. There is no evidence that the people of Santa Clara were aware of this dichotomy, and there is some question as well that they would accept it. Nevertheless, those illnesses either attributed to breach of tabu or interpreted as the result of witchcraft, those which from our point of view stressed anxieties on the part of the individual, were treated by societies. Those ailments of prosaic nature, for example, toothache, headache, stomachache, minor cuts, etc., were apt to be treated by household members or secular individuals. It is suggested that a re-examination of the whole field of Pueblo medicine is in order. In turn, this re-examination could well result in a re-evaluation of the concepts of disease, as well as the placement of curing societies in their proper perspective. At the least, the re-examination would undoubtedly uncover culture change in recent years, and the impact of various health programs.

Self-diagnosis was practiced, but frequently, and particularly where serious sickness was involved, this function was performed by the household head or by a member of a regularly constituted society.

Positive therapeutic practice was common; however, preventative measures were equally important. The latter took the form of individual prayers for protection, apologies for past and future transgressions, and rituals both preventative and purificatory, which might be engaged in by a few individuals or the complete membership of the pueblo.

Breach of Tabu

Breach of tabu encompassed any type of nonsanctioned or antisocial behavior, any digression from the ideally conceived way of life, or a nonconformity of any kind. Lapses of this nature were overwhelmingly the concern of the religious area of the culture, or if secular in type, were resolved in religious terms.

Rationalization for this belief, and its association with the religious life of the individual, rested in the instructions given during the kachina initiations. The "wisdom" and "power" conferred upon candidates at that time included instruction in the ideal way of life and a definite responsibility for maintaining it.

> When you join the kachina and are made a man, good and evil are revealed to you. You learn the prayers and the right way of life. Kachina initiates are instructed and cautioned, and therefore prepared to fight evil. They are taught to behave in the right way and to pray in the right way. Somehow or other a man may forget to follow instructions. He may only have failed to listen attentively. He violates something. He becomes ill. Any kind of disease may be caused by evil thoughts in one's own person, even a broken leg. There is only one thing he can do—that is, go to one of the society members. They will right the wrong [69].

Intent was a recognized factor in appraising the seriousness of the offense. "A person who has been made a man (kachina) violates knowingly, but he who has not been made a man does not know the difference between good and evil; he is not as blameworthy as

the former" [69]. In breaches committed by kachina initiates, and this would normally include all adult males, intent was always taken for granted. By accepting the responsibilities of initiation, they placed themselves in greater jeopardy than ordinary persons, i.e., women, children, and the uninitiated. "If a person consciously violated something, the people might will that he become ill" [43]. It is also interesting to note that in all specific instances given of illness or death resulting from breach of tabu, only cases involving adult males were cited.

Women, children, and the uninitiated, on the other hand, were not considered socially responsible. For this reason they were potentially more dangerous, but were not condemned to the same degree for violations. "Women just do not know what to avoid. They are more dangerous than men. They are the ones who cause many violations" [43]. "Both men and women can be helped, however; societies merely right the wrong and caution the patients to pay more attention to their prayers" [69].

Examples of possible breaches of tabu are the following: sacrilegious thoughts; lack of attention to religious instructions, which might result in ritual mistakes; violation of food tabus or continence while engaged in ceremonial activity [69]; failure to perform in ceremonial activity when requested; failure to live up to religious standards as outlined in the kachina initiation; giving information to anthropologists [21]; and practicing witchcraft [39, 51]. While witchcraft was designated as a religious violation, the attitudes toward it were different enough so that it has been discussed in a separate section.

Cases of death attributed to breach of tabu were numerous; this was a favorite rationalization for the sudden demise of persons apparently in the best of health and often in the prime of life. It is interesting that, without exception in the cases cited, death took place while the individual was unattended, and under inexplicable circumstances.

> 'A' was a k'osa. He had been irrigating. When they found him, he had fallen into the mud of the ditch. They could not

explain his death, so they said he must have been guilty of some wrongdoing.

'B' belonged to the Jemez Bear Society. He was employed by a paleontologist. A rock fell on him, and he got blood poison and died. He had done wrong in working for this man.

'C' was a member of the Oyike. He left the society. He was found dead in bed. He had been there a week. They said the reason that he died was because he left the society.

'D' was an old man, a member of the Bear Society and an important religious figure in the village. He was perfectly well. The next day he was found dead in bed. They said he must have violated a tabu [21].

In all of the above examples of breach of tabu, and in all cases of deaths, the violations were religious ones.

Deaths resulting from having practiced witchcraft were also cited. In these cases the "power" essential in the performance of sorcery was *retroactive*, or rationalized. Diagnostic features such as wounds were always present in these instances, and made possible the assigning of death to that cause. While sorcery was considered the epitome of antisocial behavior, and certainly a religious violation, it appears to have been relegated to a category somewhat distinct from that involving ordinary breaches of tabu.

That individuals were constantly aware of the dangers arising from a breach of tabu was evidenced by the number of precautionary prayers asking for the protection of the supernaturals, and for protection against a person's own shortcomings. "Every place you go, you would say prayers. When you pray, you say, 'Let me do as those who are not mortals (i.e., the supernaturals) do.' When you pray, you say, 'That I may not break my leg, fall into a cactus, etc., etc.; guard me also against all things I have forgotten to mention'" [9]. Another example of this precautionary attitude was expressed as follows:

A man is sent by a cacique of Santa Clara with a message to a cacique at Tesuque. He delivers the message, but he thinks he may have forgotten part of it. Harm could befall him if he misrepresented the cacique. To protect himself, he adds a kind of prayer at the end, "This is what I remember I was told to say to you. I am a mere mortal and liable to error. Therefore, what I may have forgotten, I include" [9].

While the contraction of an illness was a matter of grave concern, there is no evidence that those in poor health were feared, avoided, or abandoned. In fact, observations and accounts by informants [9, 21, 50] indicate the contrary. The immediate family devoted considerable time to sympathizing and caring for any member who was sick, and there is no indication from any source that such efforts were resented by either party. Furthermore, if the illness was protracted, groups beyond the immediate kin could be called upon for assistance. This was particularly true in the economic sphere, and must have been an important factor in lessening the anxiety of any person who, because of illness, found himself or herself unable to provide for the family. In these instances, a gift of tobacco was presented to the head of the person's moiety. The cacique immediately appointed individuals to do whatever work was necessary, and all possibility of hardship was virtually eliminated. "In one instance, a man, because of a lengthy illness, was unable to build a house. Moiety members dismantled a house in the mountains, brought it to the village, and reconstructed it for the person" [50].

Witchcraft

When misfortune, accident, illness, or death could not be readily rationalized in terms of some religious breach of tabu, witchcraft was usually invoked to satisfy the sense of causality. The theory of witchcraft stemmed from a belief in the ability of individuals to acquire supernatural power and control it for their own uses, as well as transfer it to others. Some confusion existed in the minds of informants as to the exact nature of the power associated with sorcery.

At times, power was conceived of as a

single, impersonal principle. On other occasions, a dualistic attitude was present, and a clear-cut distinction was made between power used for good and power used for evil. One informant [9] stated, "Wisdom, the good type, is gained through joining societies." Later he cited an instance in which two members of the Bear Society were suspected of witchcraft, and the death of one explained on that basis, i.e., breach of tabu. This suggests that membership in a society was no barrier to antisocial behavior, and possibly that the same power might be used to kill as well as cure and protect. This observation was confirmed in an account of a ceremony (sori wokan, a "large treatment") where, preliminary to the rite, the cacique, war captain (outside chief), and governor all admonished the members of the Bear societies, telling them that they "must use their power for good, never for evil, never for witchcraft" [9]. On still another occasion, the first informant said, "One must always be alert, because you might think that you were getting good wisdom (power) but discover later this friend was giving you the wrong kind" [21]. Here again, while dualism is evident, an inability to distinguish between powers of good and evil was expressed at the outset.

In general, however, the derivation of power and its use for good were associated with esoteric societies, and the antisocial counterparts with individuals or nebulous groups which practiced witchcraft. Perhaps the confusion was the result of four hundred years of contact with Christianity and the inconsistencies inherent in the dualistic concepts of that faith.

Whatever the theories concerning witchcraft, its existence and potency were unquestioned cultural realities. The anxiety witchcraft occasioned was expressed in a variety of ways. First, an inordinate amount of ritual, both of a preventative and purificatory nature, was leveled at the eradication of witches and protection against them. Second, any discussion of witchcraft was accompanied by an obvious uneasiness on the part of even the most sophisticated informants. In some cases, an attempt to introduce the topic was met with an obviously falsified denial of any knowledge of the subject. A similar reluctance to discuss

witches and witchcraft has been reported by Kluckhohn (1944: 9–12) for the Navajo, by Lange (1959: 252) for the Cochiti, and by others for additional cultures. It is a widespread phenomenon—seemingly for virtually identical reasons.

In rare instances, the anxiety was openly voiced, "the belief is strong and they (witches) are greatly feared. Much illness is caused by witchcraft" [12]. "A great deal of individual sickness is caused by witchcraft. Some evil one has made people sick. I do not know how witching is done. I have heard people say that they have seen witches, but I have never seen one" [9]. Some reticence on the subject was attributed to the fear of incurring the displeasure of witches and being made to suffer as a result. Also, a too intimate knowledge of the procedures of sorcery might lead to one's being suspected of the practice; this inevitably involved social retribution in some form.

Anyone suspected of witchcraft was feared and shunned. This was not only because they might use their power to harm, but also because, under the guise of friendship, they might transmit power to an unwitting person. Unwitting acquisition of the power of sorcery was guarded against for several reasons. One was the consequences of antisocial behavior. Another was the belief that the acceptance of the power involved a contractual obligation to participate in human sacrifice and cannibalism, both traits extremely repugnant from the point of view of Santa Clara culture. Finally, there was the conviction that the possession of such power was potentially hazardous to the possessor. First, it represented a breach of tabu of a special kind. Second, it was believed that such power often boomeranged, or backfired.

The above attitudes of suspicion and fear of consequences are well illustrated in a personal experience of one informant [73], which he recounted in connection with a discussion of witchcraft:

I saw a Bear Society member standing alone by the corrals. He beckoned to me, so I asked him what he was doing there. He said he was waiting for a certain woman. (He was a widower; she was a widow). He said, "I have a lot of property in my home, and I want one to inherit it." He asked me to intercede and get the woman to talk to him about becoming his wife. He said, "If you will do this, I will give you power." I did not do it. It frightened me. The mention of power frightened me. You may get power, but it may endanger you, shorten your life.

Contractual aspects are illustrated in statements about the practice of witchcraft in other pueblos. Nambé and San Ildefonso were considered to be headquarters for witches, and this was given as the reason for the loss of population, or at best its static condition, in those villages.

> They had too much wisdom, which they were using against themselves. They had to make human sacrifices in payment for this wisdom. Once some Santa Clara people went to a fiesta at San Ildefonso. They were seated, eating, in a home. Apparently it was the home of the leader of the witches. When the food was passed, they found in the stew the finger of a small child. They knew from that a small child had been sacrificed to the witches [73].

Belief in the backfire consequences of witchcraft is illustrated in the following account, as well as in the tales at the end of this section. In this case a man died of an injury considered too slight to explain death from this cause.

> During a game a man was hit in the leg with a shinny stick. His leg became infected, and he died. They said that he had been doing evil and had been injured; that his disembodied form had returned to his body with this injury. The shinny injury was an excuse. He just stood there and allowed himself to be hit. He was a Zia married to a Santa Clara woman [13, 72].

Identification and discovery of witches were matters of considerable moment. First among the categories of those suspect were foreigners, members of certain other pueblos, close relatives, persons suspected of jealousy, nonconformists, wealthy individuals, and those possessing inordinate skills. Spanish- and Anglo-Americans were particularly associated with the concept of the evil eye. Persons from Nambé and San Ildefonso were viewed with skepticism because of the reputation for sorcery possessed by those tribes. Nambé was alleged to have killed half of its own population by misuse of wisdom [73]. Note also that in the case just cited as an example of the boomerang effects of witchcraft, the man was from Zia Pueblo, and had married into Santa Clara Pueblo.

While no specific cases of witchcraft practiced on close relatives could be obtained, several informants [29, 39, 43, 52] testified to its frequent occurrence. Jealousy was an equally frequent rationalization for ills attributed to sorcery. Thus a woman afflicted with sore eyes was told by a midwife that it was caused by a woman who envied her ability to make excellent pottery, who wished to prevent her from continuing her craft. "She would have to go to the Bear Society" [51].

Nonconformists included any individuals who deviated from the cultural ideal. Members of the progressive group at the time of the political schism of 1894 were accused of witchcraft [43]. Actually, while the wealthy and skilled were specially mentioned as suspects, they also represented nonconformists in terms of Santa Clara culture, and were penalized for excessive individualism.

Cases of witchcraft suspicion surrounding relatives, the jealous, and the nonconformist of whatever type, have had interesting implications. First, they constituted an unconscious recognition of the existence of aggression in another person. Second, the mere fact of leveling accusations was a culturally sanctioned outlet for the accuser's own aggressive tendencies. Furthermore, they illustrate most clearly the role of witchcraft as a latent weapon for indirect social control and the restraint of aggressive action.

While suspicion and accusation were frequent, actual identification of witches was rare, or at best post facto. The difficulties accompanying their recognition were multiplied by the concepts of their nocturnal habits and shapeshifting, and also because they were thought to be invisible except under unusual circumstances. During ceremonies, members of the Bear societies were able to perceive them; in such cases they were dispersed, or at some rituals, captured and brought to the kiva. As they were dragged toward this edifice, however, they were said to diminish progressively in size, until only the figure of a doll remained. The public at large saw only this, which was little help in discovering living culprits.

Positive criteria for identification were present in only a few instances. Owl feathers were associated with witchcraft, probably because they do not seem to have been used in legitimate, or orthodox ceremonies. The possession of such feathers would be taken as a reliable indication that the person was a witch [72].

According to another [61], identification was possible if the individual wore two down feathers on top of the head. "If you meet a witch, you try to grab the left feather. Then the witch will die. If you took the one on the right, you would die."

Information on the methodology of sorcery was meager. This, as mentioned, may well have been through fear of being accused of witchcraft if one knew too much. Witches were believed to congregate from time to time to hold meetings, at which they planned actions against their victims. On these occasions, they presumably practiced the sacrifices and cannibalism noted earlier. Such meetings were always held at night, and it was thought that most, though not all, of their antisocial activities took place after sundown and before dawn [39, 52, 72].

> If they did not finish their evil work before dawn, and the sun caught them, they would be unable to move, and would fall down. People would find them then. People who went early for water would find these witch figures (dolls) in the village or along the roads, where they had fallen dead [52].

This explanation of the occurrence of these dolls was probably found in the rites of the Bear societies. The dolls were definitely responsible for fortifying the belief in the existence of witchcraft.

The ability to shift shapes and the existence of were-animals were accepted parts of the sorcery complex; were-deer and were-rabbits were most mentioned. "He or she might take the form of an animal, or retain his or her own shape" [61, 72]. Much, but not all, of the evil was thought to be accomplished while in these disembodied states.

According to Jeançon (1900–08), the soul left the body while it was asleep and actually lived what were called dreams. During their absences, souls could be caught by a witch and the body impregnated by shooting a disease into it, or by insertion into the mouth, ears, eyes, nose, or vagina. It then went from the place of insertion to some other part of the body, where it lodged until withdrawn by the healer.

While descriptions of actual practices were lacking, it was explicit from accounts of curing and from parenthetical remarks that intrusion, imitative and contagious magic, and a belief in the evil eye were all envisaged. Bear Society members removed a variety of foreign materials by sucking, brushing, and massage.

Hair cuttings and combings were guarded or destroyed. "Whenever you were through cutting hair, you gather it all up and burn it. They said if you left it around, the witches would get hold of it and harm you." "If they want to harm you, they touch you when there is a crowd at a dance." "Witches especially attended these large gatherings, and practiced sorcery on their victims."

It is not clear whether intent was always associated with illness caused by the evil eye. As mentioned earlier, Spanish- and Anglo-Americans were believed most dangerous. Children were the most susceptible to this form of magic. "If someone looks at a child, it might hurt it. They would take the child away if they were looking at it" [73].

It is evident from the number of precautionary measures taken that witches were thought capable of causing harm in other ways than by afflicting individuals.

Corrals and fields were ritually purified, lest livestock and crops suffer. On one occasion, when grasshoppers damaged crops, witch dolls were found, stuffed with these insects. Precisely how this type of harm was effected was not learned.

Organized protection against witchcraft took various forms. The most extensive measures have been described under the activities of the Bear societies. Lesser procedures included warning children to stay in at night, and the use of amulets [18, 61]. A favorite protective device consisted of the root of a plant called oka wafe. This was carried in the pocket, purse, or belt, especially by school children. It also protected a person from robbery or losing money [43, 45]. Rosaries, santos, and holy water were also believed to serve these same purposes [39, 51].

The following five tales of witches and witchcraft represent more or less standard versions, with certain elements suggesting European derivation. Included are three tales collected by Jeançon during the period of 1900–08.

I. This is a story of man and wife. The wife made a lot of bread. They had children. They cooked a lot of food. The children wondered. One day they would have a lot of food; the next day they would have none. They would be practically starving. The children asked the parents what happened to the food; they said yesterday we had plenty. The father said you know there were a lot of people that came yesterday. We had to feed them. This happened several times. The oldest boy was suspicious. He knew there were not enough people to have consumed all this food. That night he pretended to sleep. He saw his parents, his mother dressing in her best clothes and wrapping up all the food. The parents left with the food. The boy followed them to the hills. There were all kinds of people from different places. He knew they were witches.

II. If you ever come in contact with a witch you will know. It is like this: if you

are hunting rabbits or deer you may come across one. It will run a little way and stop. You shoot and miss. It keeps this up, and finally you are all tired out. It is a were-rabbit or deer. Sometimes you will wound it. It will disappear. You go around a corner, and there is a man sitting.

A man is hunting rabbits. He finds tracks. He comes close to the rabbit. It runs from the bushes and leads him on and on. Finally after a long chase he may have wounded the rabbit and been following the blood. He comes around the bushes, and there is a man or woman sitting on a deer or rabbit skin. The witch tells the hunter, "I am your friend—you know me well. Why should you kill me?" The hunter says, "I have to kill you; otherwise I will die." So the witch is killed and left there. The hunter comes home. The hunter must not tell anyone until the witch is actually dead. The hunter will see the dead witch when he comes back to the village. The witch will be walking about. What the witch is doing is looking for a plausible manner of death. What people in [the] village will say is that he died from a fall from a wagon or from a house; or the witch might accidentally shoot himself. He finds a manner of dying. After this the hunter can tell people he was out witching and killed him. He might tell it if the death was of an unexplainable type, uncalled for, or if there was only a small wound, and people wondered why death took place.

III. The woman and the boy. A woman was going with a boy to the house of the witches. She told the boy to go in—not be frightened. She said, "Go to the fireplace and get some ashes and throw them into the pot." They went to the place where the witches were meeting. The boy came to the door but did not do as the woman told him, as he saw his father sitting in the crowd. The boy went out again, and the old woman followed him and asked him why he didn't do as she told him to do. Then she told the boy that they would sacrifice their lives because he did not obey her. That is how they have fever and sickness.

IV. The running boy and his doll. There was a boy that was a swift runner, and he made himself a doll. This doll was a running companion of the boy. He was a swift runner, and no one ever overtook him. He talked to the doll day and night, and on the third night he again talked to him. On the fourth night, he went west, taking the doll with him. They went quite a distance from the village, and he placed the doll on the ground. The doll changed to a man and spoke to the boy and told him to be a man.

They began to run, and the doll was not strong enough to keep up with the boy. The doll told the boy to run fast. When they reached the end of the racecourse, they raced back to the start. The rag doll was just about even with the boy. As they raced the third time, the doll told him to run fast, and then asked the boy, "Why did you make me?" The boy said, "Because I am a swift runner and no one has ever caught me." Then the doll told the boy, "You must run after me, and we will run until I tell you to stop. I could run almost anywhere and go anyplace. I do not care whatever it is or whoever it is, I can outrun it." The fourth time they raced and they were running very fast, and the doll came abreast of the boy and passed him. They kept on running, and the doll turned around and called to the boy to run faster.

They were running, running, running, and arrived on the highest point of the mountain. The doll, as soon as he got there, stepped to one side. The boy came after him. The doll knocked the boy backwards from the mountain top and killed him. That is the kind of a doll the witches make.

Jeançon (1900–08) had the following note concerning this tale:

It would seem from this story that black magic sometimes reacts upon those who make it. The informant was carefully questioned as to who made the doll and always the answer was that the boy had made it. Then the question was asked, "Was the boy a witch?" The answer was that he was not exactly a witch, but that he knew something about black magic but not enough to protect himself against the power he had raised in the doll. Therefore the doll took advantage of him and killed him. To the Indian, the moral of the tale appears to be that the uninstructed should not tamper with magic of any kind. Often white magic may react and evil be brought about when good was intended because the practitioner was inexperienced.

V. The story of the Nambé girl who went to San Juan Pueblo. They were living in a kiva at Nambé. There was a girl, and she thought her father and mother did not care for her because they were so strict with her. They never let her go out without someone with her, and they watched her all the time. They would not let her talk to the boys or young men, and they made her wear old clothes all the time. She was not a bad girl, but they acted like she was a bad girl.

One time she asked if she could go to see her cousin who lived at San Juan, and her parents said yes. The girl liked to go to her cousin's house, and she went there. Her cousin was glad to see her, and the girls talked about many things. The girl noticed that her cousin had a fine manta and belt, and moccasins, and many beads. She asked, "My cousin, where did you get all those pretty things?" Her cousin laughed and said, "Yes, I know what you think; you think I am a bad girl and that the boys give all these things because I let them do what they want to do, but that is not so. I know how to get these things in another way. If you wish, you can have just as many pretty things as I have." The girl was very much interested and asked her cousin how she could get them. Her cousin said, "There are some very nice people that live in a cave in the hills back of the pueblo, and they like to do nice things for poor people. If you will go with me tonight, I will tell them about you and then they will give you the things you want."

The girl asked what she would have to do to pay for the things, and her cousin told her. "You must keep secret where you got the things as they do not want anyone to know where you got them. That is all."

That night after everyone was asleep, the two girls sneaked out of the village and went to the cave in the hill. It was very dark, and the wind was blowing. The girl was frightened, but her cousin laughed and said that there was nothing to be afraid of. When they got to the cave, they found many people gathered around a big black pot that was boiling over the fire. The girl was very shy, and her cousin took her by her hand and took her over where an old grandfather and grandmother were sitting. She said to them, "This is my cousin, and I told her about how kind you people are, and she has come for some pretty clothes and things."

The old people were nice to her and made the girl sit down with them and talked nicely to her. Soon she forgot to be frightened and looked around. Then she saw that the door of the cave was closed, and she did not know how she could get out again. She was frightened again, but the old people just laughed at her and said it was all right.

Then all the people began to sing, and one man got up and stirred the fire. He began to scatter black cornmeal and put owl's feathers on the floor. Then the girl knew where she was; she was in the witches' cave. She was terribly frightened, but she wished to have the pretty clothes and things and thought she could get them and deceive the witches. Soon two witches came over and took her to a corner of the cave. They took her clothes off and put some fine new ones on her and also many beads and pretty things. Then they took her back to the place where she had been sitting. Everyone told her how nice she looked, and she felt happy until one

witch came to her and said, "Now we are going to work, and we need a heart from someone; you must go and get the heart of the person in your family that you love the best." The girl began to cry and said she could not do it as it was far to Nambé and she could not get back in time. She said she could not kill the person she loved the best. The witch said, "You have our clothes and pretty things on, and you must do what we say or we will take your heart. You can see that big owl over there in the corner; he can carry you to Nambé and back in a few minutes. Your people are all asleep, and it will be easy for you to do what we want you to do. Now do not waste more time, or we will kill you and take your heart out." The girl thought, perhaps she could deceive the witches and so she said, "All right, I will go." They took her to the owl, and she got on his back and it flew to Nambé with her. When she arrived, she found everyone asleep. The owl stayed outside when she went in the house. She looked around and saw the old cat asleep and took a knife and cut out its heart. Then she hurried and went out and got on the owl's back, and they flew back to the witches' cave. She gave the heart to the chief of the witches. He looked at it for a minute, and then became angry and said to the girl, "You have tried to deceive us. This is not a man's heart, because it belongs to an animal. You must go back and get us a man's heart."

The girl was terribly frightened, and she ran out and got on the owl's back and told him to hurry and fly back to Nambé. She killed a rooster and took his heart to the witches. This time the witch chief was even angrier and said that they would kill her if she did not bring them a man's heart. She went back to Nambé a third time, and this time she killed her dog and brought his heart. The chief was angrier than before and said that now they were going to take out her heart.

The girl was afraid and cried, but she thought how her father and mother looked when she was home and saw them asleep. Then she said, "Yes, it is all right, you can take my heart because I will not give you the heart of my father or my mother, and so you can take mine." The witch chief said, "Yes, all right, we will take your heart, but we will not kill you just now. We will take your heart out, and you can live for a year, but then you will die. You can keep the pretty clothes and other things for you belong to us now." The girl cried a great deal and was very unhappy, but she did not know what she could do.

When she got back to Nambé and her people saw all the fine things that she had they thought she had been immoral with the young men of San Juan and that these were the presents that the young men had given her. They were mean to her again. She said to her father and mother, "You do not love me, and so I am going away." She went to several other villages, but in a year she came back to Nambé. She used to be a pretty girl, but now she was thin and ugly and very sad. Then she got sick, and one night she died. What the witches had said was true; she had died within a year.

The question of the provenance of many elements of the witchcraft complex among the Indians of the Southwest is still unanswered. Concepts such as that of the evil eye or witch doll are of undoubted European derivation; cases like the belief in were-animals are less clear-cut. The picture is further obscured, since the cult of sorcery still flourishes among the descendants of the Spanish colonists in the area. It can be said, however, that the alleged foreign elements, if they are indeed foreign, have become so deeply imbedded in the matrix of Southwestern culture that the native population considers them part of the aboriginal configuration.

MEDICINE SOCIETIES

In spite of the fact that the bulk of the cures at Santa Clara Pueblo were accomplished by unaffiliated persons and were of the "home remedy" type, both curative practice and preventative medical treatment were ideally considered to be in the hands of the several societies. Relief derived through the employment of one of these agencies carried with it religious and social approval, and had psychic advantages lacking in secular or lay treatment. Most prominent of the curing groups were the Bear societies: the Jemez Bear (Wan ke'), Tesuque Bear (Téchuge ke'), and formerly the Cochiti Bear (Tema ke', or Keres tcaiani). These societies, while having generalized religious scope, were looked upon primarily as curing and purificatory organizations. Their major preoccupation was with the eradication of witches and the prevention and relief of diseases and misfortunes associated with sorcery. They were, however, considered capable of curing any type of illness or injury, regardless of its cause.

In contrast with Keresan and Western Pueblo medicine societies, the functions of those at Santa Clara were unspecialized. While certain members were known for their proficiency in certain areas of treatment, cures for specific types of illnesses were not associated with particular societies.

Thus, while having no monopoly, the Bear groups were credited with alleviating sores, infections, colds, fevers, earaches, toothaches, headaches, sore eyes, stomach disorders, fright, shock, and effects of the evil eye. They also treated sprains and set broken bones, and on occasion, might be called in cases of protracted and difficult labor [25, 50, 61].

Other regularly constituted religious groups, except the kachinas, also engaged in curing and disease prevention. Here emphasis was on those illnesses resulting from breach of tabu. Membership and initiation into the Pay-oj-ke, or Pondjo-oke, the Oyike, the clown, and the scalp fraternities were often dictated by reasons of health, although this curing element was subordinate to the principal functions of the societies. Cures were established as a part of the initiation rites.

Nonsociety practitioners included such gifted and specially trained persons as herbalists, masseurs, midwives, and those who treated snake bite and the effects of the evil eye. These and experienced elders of the kin group accounted for the major portion of given medical treatment [15, 18, 25, 50, 61].

Possessional shamanism appears to have been lacking at Santa Clara Pueblo. Bear Society members, and also members of other societies, acted merely as intermediaries between the secular and spiritual worlds. The former interceded with various animals; no such clear-cut relationship was apparent with the latter groups, although a generalized concept of rapport with supernaturals was explicit. Curers normally achieved the desired result by the execution of learned routines.

Ecstatics, while present, were of limited occurrence. Cultivated trances, so far as is known, occurred only among the principal actors at occasions when Bear societies purified the whole village. In these ceremonies, the society member who captured the final witch succumbed to a trance before leaving for his objective. During the same ritual, the leader of the Bear Society occasionally assumed a trance state. "While dancing, he would fall down as if he were dead. The other members try to bring him back. He goes into the earth to see the members of the Bear Society who have died. The rest of the members slap him with their bear-paw gauntlets to bring him back. The society cannot leave until they bring him back" [61]. The role of the vision at Santa Clara Pueblo has already been discussed, in connection with society membership.

The curing complex, like ceremonial buffoonery, fell within the general North American Indian patterns of behavior and function, and was not unique for the village or area. The only reasonably distinctive feature was the organization of qualified practitioners into esoteric groups, and even this was not unique, but was shared by tribes of California, the Southern Plains, and the Northeastern Woodland. The familiar pattern included the belief that animals, particularly the bear, were intimately associated with, if not frequently responsible for cures. Curing techniques focused on the exorcising or extraction of foreign materials and evil influences of more incorporeal nature. This was accomplished by sucking, massaging, brushing, and the use of emetics. Cures were also implemented by asperging, fumigating, by the application or administration of herbal, mineral, animal, and other medicines, and by the laying on of hands. Preventative medicine, purification, and prophylaxis were common. Cures were normally accompanied by songs, prayers, and dancing. Remuneration for service rendered was expected and invariably forthcoming [45, 50, 61].

BEAR SOCIETIES

There were two medicine societies at Santa Clara Pueblo, the Jemez Bear (Wan ke') and the Tesuque Bear (Téchuge ke'). While four informants (all elderly) stated that these organizations had existed as long as anyone could remember, there is evidence that shifts and realignments had taken place at an earlier period.

Formerly, a chapter of the Cochiti Flint Society (Tema ke') operated at Santa Clara. This was confirmed by informants, Parsons (1929: 122), Jeançon (1900–30), and Lange (1959: 259). According to Lange's informants, the Cochiti Flint Society had functioned as the parent organization, but was later superseded by the Jemez Bear Society. There was no information concerning the time when this transfer was accomplished, or the reasons which led to this new affiliation, although Lange's data (p. 260) suggest the beginnings of obsolescence of the Flint Society at Cochiti. Evidence from Santa Clara informants indicates that the shift had taken place sometime prior to the turn of the century.

Neither Parsons (1929: 122) nor Jeançon (1900–08) were aware of the existence of more than one medicine society during their residence at Santa Clara. In Parsons's case this is understandable, since information given her on this subject was, at best, fragmentary. She stated that there was only one group, the Pa' pafuna, "Fire," Society. Incidentally, the man she cited as the right arm of that organization was head of the Jemez Bear Society in 1940.

Jeançon knew of the Jemez Bear Society, but said it was the only society. Considering his intimate knowledge of the culture, this oversight is difficult to explain. In 1940 informants listed seven members of the

Tesuque Bear Society; five of these were over seventy years of age, and were most probably operative during the period of residence in the village of Parsons and Jeançon. Furthermore, reciprocal relationships were maintained with Tesuque Pueblo. The Jemez roster included twelve members. Three elderly informants stated that formerly there were more Tesuque members than Jemez, but that this was no longer true.

A fact that may have obscured the true situation in recent years, as memberships diminished, was the tendency of the two societies to combine when village-wide ceremonies were involved. Another circumstance which may have influenced Jeançon's thinking was that the members of the two societies were all affiliates of the Summer Moiety. Earlier there had been one exception: an inactive, nonresident Winter man. If Jeançon had been aware of this, he could easily have arrived at the conclusion that he was dealing with a single unit, particularly since he used the terms clan, moiety, and society interchangeably.

The author agrees with Lange (1959: 260) that "These interpueblo ties [between societies, WWH], a subject about which relatively little is known, are worthy of future investigation."

There were only minor differences in behavior, function, and composition of the two societies at Santa Clara Pueblo. Informants had difficulty in envisaging distinguishing features other than the obvious associations with the villages of Jemez and Tesuque. Jemez Bear members underwent a preliminary training period and terminal initiation at Jemez. A similar procedure was followed by Tesuque Bear members at that pueblo. Other differences mentioned by informants were that the songs of the Jemez Society were in Towa rather than Tewa, and that their altars differed in shape from those of the Tesuque group. The Tesuque Bears did not dance during the period when members were exorcising or extracting from a patient; the Jemez Bears did. The Jemez painted their faces red; the Tesuque did not. The Tesuque insisted that for four days after a cure, the patient be accompanied at all times by a relative; no such instructions were given by the Jemez.

Membership in either society was arrived at in a variety of ways. A child might be pledged at or before birth by one of its parents; when it grew up, it was obligated to join. "Before a child was born, a mother might say that if it were a boy and lived, she would give it to a Bear Society." These vows appear to have been binding on the individual. Only two cases were recorded (one of a man and one of a woman), in which the persons failed to live up to the terms of the pledge. Actually, compulsion was strong, since failure to join constituted a breach of tabu, and made the recalcitrant individual subject to supernatural retribution.

Vows were also made during illness, and if cured, the patient was obligated to join the society effecting the cure. There is no evidence that members were acquired by trespass or trapping. According to Jeançon (1904-30), a similar situation prevailed during his residence.

Both males and females belonged to the societies, although the ritual role of women was definitely a subordinate one. Membership cut across both moiety and political lines. During the period of fieldwork, the Jemez Bear Society consisted of twelve members (seven males, five females— one had not completed initiation and one was inactive; eleven were of the Summer Moiety and one, inactive, from the Winter Moiety). The Tesuque Bear Society had nine members (seven males, two females—one male, inactive; all were from the Summer Moiety).

It was denied that affiliation with a Bear Society was a prerequisite for caciqueship.

Initiations were preceded by a year's novitiate and training, during which the candidate remained at the village, i.e., returned each evening and spent the night there. Presumably, he was under instruction during this period. The terminal initiation, as well as some instruction, took place in the village associated with the headquarters of the society. Only one lapse from this practice was cited: according to one informant [72], two brothers were initiated into the Tesuque Bear Society at Santa Clara Pueblo, not at Tesuque. The informant pointed out that this was the result of a dispute, and was definitely an unusual occurrence.

No details of current training or of the initiation rites were obtainable. However, some indication of the scope of those associated with the Jemez Bear Society is provided by Jeançon (1900–08):

> They must take four days to go [to Jemez, WWH], during which time they stop at certain shrines and make offerings of meal, feathers, and kindred objects. The actual period of instruction varies, some times four months are consumed in this work [according to my informant, two to three months, WWH]. Upon their return, which again must take four days with accompanying sacrifices on the way, they hold a retreat of four days in some secret place, usually the house of the Bear Society leader. Here they fast and use herbs as purgatives and emetics. These are chewed and swallowed. An infusion is also made of them and drunk. After the retreat, they must conduct a full healing ceremony before they are entitled to practice.

Members initiated at Jemez were expected to participate from time to time in the ceremonies of that pueblo. Those of Tesuque recognized a similar obligation. In turn, Bears from those villages performed reciprocal services at Santa Clara Pueblo.

BEAR SOCIETY CEREMONIES

The religious obligations of the Bear societies were broad in scope, although their cooperative participation in general moiety ceremonies was less than that of other religious groups. They performed purificatory rites at such communal enterprises as the ditch opening in the spring, and on those occasions when relay races were held. They held retreats at the homes of their leaders at or near the middle of each month, at the solstice and equinoctial periods, and prior to any major ceremony in which they were participants; at such times rites were performed for general village benefit and well-being. They were subject to call by private individuals or village officials to perform rituals of purificatory or curative nature, or both. According to one informant [61], the principal ceremony of the Jemez group took place in the "middle of the year," June or July; that of the Tesuque group, early in the spring.

Informants [31, 69] denied any association of the Bear societies with rain bringing, warfare, etc., insisting that their role was curative or preventative.

Two types of religious performances of the Bear societies are recognizable. The basis for the dichotomy is whether the rituals were primarily curative or preventative, i.e., purificatory. Predominantly curative rites were concerned with removing the malignant consequences of witchcraft, with therapeutic practice, and less frequently, with counteracting the effects of breach of tabu. Such ceremonies focused on a patient.

In those of a preventative-purificatory nature, the "patient," while present, was normally in excellent health, and his role was a passive one. Such ceremonies were directed toward the eradication of witches themselves, the removal of their potentially malign influences, and any other generalized evil which might jeopardize the well-being of persons or things.

All ceremonies actually combined both of these major objectives; however, there was no confusion as to those actions which were curative (pivah) and those which were purificatory (fehreh), and the rite always emphasized one or the other [9].

Ceremonies varied in magnitude from a simple rite held for an individual by a single member of a Bear Society, to a cooperative effort of both societies on behalf of the whole pueblo. When a Bear member, or members, or societies, functioned as individual entities, distinctions were made on the basis of the number of participants and the amount of territory encompassed. Thus the rites were categorized as a "treatment, or cure, with food or meal" (hu coɳ wogi wokaɳ); "treatment, or cure, with house"; "treatment or cure with yard"; and "large treatment" (sori wokaɳ). These differences do not appear to have been applicable to situations in which Bear societies cooperated with other esoteric organizations for general village welfare, i.e., the monthly "work" period, purification of the ditch or race course, etc.

A "cure, or treatment, with food or meal" was the least complicated rite. It might be preponderantly either curative or purificatory, but it was usually curative. It often involved only one member of a Bear Society, the patient, and his or her immediate family. The practitioner or practitioners went to effect the cure in the evening of the same day on which the request was made.

A "cure, or treatment, with house" normally involved the participation of the complete membership of one of the Bear societies. If illness was the immediate reason for the ritual, curative factors were emphasized; if not, purification was stressed. In either case, it was a more inclusive ceremony than the first. It incorporated a wider kin group than the immediate family, and the house was treated, as well as the patient. The cure or treatment took place the evening following the day of the request.

A "treatment, or cure, with yard" was similar to "treatment, or cure, with house," except that the sphere of the purificatory scope was enlarged to include the immediate area outside the house, the corrals and livestock belonging to the family, and in some cases their fields. More often than not this ritual was preponderantly purificatory. An interval of one day elapsed between the request and the ceremony.

A "large cure, or treatment" usually necessitated the cooperative efforts of both Bear societies. It was pueblo-wide in scope, encompassing not only the village, but all the territory and shrines under its jurisdiction and use. Its emphasis was definitely purificatory. A four-day retreat was held prior to the ceremony [9, 13, 21].

Requests for performance of Bear Society rituals were directed to individual members with special skills, or to the leader of the society, as the occasion demanded. In cases of illness, a parent or a near relative made the request. If the illness or accident was not serious and easily recognizable, a single member of the society, noted for proficiency in that particular field of medicine, was contacted. In more complicated sicknesses or when general purification was desired, the leader of the society was approached. A

"large treatment" was always requested by an official of the secular government or one of the heads of the religious hierarchy.

In cases of minor illness, diagnosis might be made by the patient or some near relative. In the former case, cause and selection of the society might be determined by a dream or "vision." When the sickness was complicated or protracted, members of the Bear Society might be called in to make the diagnosis [9, 13].

According to Jeançon (1900–08), when the Bear Society arrived, all persons but the patient were sent from the room. The leader of the society asked the patient about his illness, where the pain was located, and other symptoms; the time of the first attack was also inquired into. Then the patient was asked about quarrels or differences he might have had with neighbors or people outside the village. Usually there was some friction between villagers or with neighboring Mexicans. If this was the case, the illness was diagnosed as resulting from the practice of witchcraft by the person or persons with whom the patient had quarreled. When no specific cause could be established, the illness was attributed to the witch society, without naming a particular person.

If it was established that the person was the victim of witchcraft, the leader attempted by scrying to discover the name of the witch and the circumstances connected with the actual bewitchment. He gazed into a bowl containing water from one of the sacred lakes of the region, or better still, from the Lake of Emergence. In the bowl he was believed to be able to see persons, events, and past and future happenings. Usually the Bear leader designated some unimportant villager or an unpopular Mexican as the guilty person. If no individual could be blamed, responsibility for the sorcery was said to emanate from the witch society. Diagnostic rites could be performed during the day, but healing ceremonies had to be held at night (Jeançon 1900–08).

Requests for assistance were highly formalized, and followed the pattern indicated earlier. They were always accompanied by a gift of cornmeal, tobacco, and feathers; it was understood that subsequent payment in meal, commensurate with the magnitude of the ceremony, would also be made [9, 13]. A difference of opinion existed as to whether a request for a ceremony could be denied. According to one informant [13], the leader of the society consulted with the group, and if the ill person was suspected of being a witch, the request was denied. Another informant [22] stated that societies were obligated to treat even a witch, if he or she was ill. The second informant, an older man, was presumably correct, since his statement is confirmed by Jeançon (1900–08). According to Jeançon, the belief existed that if a member of a Bear Society, for any reason, refused to attempt a cure or exercise his healing powers on behalf of a patient, that member would die during the ensuing year, of the same disease which had afflicted the ailing person. He stated that several cases were known in which coincidences of this type had occurred.

Cure with Food

A "cure with food or meal" was the least complex of the curing and/or purificatory rites. To some extent, the designation "cure with food" is misleading, since all Bear ceremonials requested by individuals and for general purification entailed payment in cornmeal, and in all but a "cure with meal or food," the Bear societies were fed at the termination of the ritual.

These rites were primarily for the cure of individual illnesses. One to three Bear members participated, usually only one being chosen, for his proficiency in treating the particular manifestation or illness. Exorcism, fumigation, and asperging of various types were practiced, but never extraction. "You have extraction only in cases where more than three members were present" [9]. The informant also stated that an altar was built, but that the "mothers" were not used. Other informants [13, 21], and also Jeançon (1900–08), made no reference to altars in their accounts of cures of this type.

Several accounts of individual cures by Bear members were obtained. It was apparent, and was confirmed by informants [9, 21], that witchcraft was not always the causal

factor in these cases. Some were explained on the basis of shock or fright. Commonly a person would become ill because of a fright; this might be produced by someone shouting behind a person, or from falling into a pit. For days afterward, the person would not sleep, or would lose interest in life. In such cases a member of a Bear Society would be called [9]. Other ailments, including stomach disorders and fevers, were also treated by individual members [9, 13, 25].

Usually some home remedies were first attempted; if these failed, help from the societies was solicited. Individual curing rites varied in complexity, according to the need, as determined by the practitioner. A patient suffering from shock might merely be given a stone fetish (kaji) wrapped in a cloth, and be told to secure it about his waist. This was worn for four days, occasionally longer if the cure was slow. During this period the patient was accompanied at all times; this precaution was taken in case the illness stemmed from sorcery. No witch would approach a person so guarded in an attempt to "reinfect him." This type of treatment was administered by a Tesuque Bear, since the Jemez did not guard the patient. At the end of the period, when health was restored, the fetish was returned, with the gift of a basket of cornmeal [9].

In cases of more aggravated or serious illness, treatments were more extensive. A favorite for curing cases of shock involved fumigation and asperging. The Bear member arrived with his bear-paw container. Occasionally he was accompanied by members of his household, who might assist. Normally he did not remove his clothing, as was customary in more complicated rites. He felt the pulse of the patient and diagnosed the case as fright or shock. He then requested that one of the stands, or bowls, in which a pot bottom was rested during the construction of a pot, be filled with live coals from the fireplace. Next he pulled several bear hairs from the outside of his ceremonial container, or took mountain lion hairs and placed them on the coals. The patient was instructed to kneel before the bowl and to inhale; a blanket was placed over him in order that the smoke from the hair would permeate his whole being.

As the fumigation progressed, the Bear member addressed a prayer to the patient in archaic Tewa (again this cure was Tesuque, not Jemez, since the language was Tewa), saying, "think only good thoughts, try as a woman, try as a man, think only one thought. Then our old people, forefathers who were one path [i.e., who were not tainted by European belief and Christianity] will help you."

When the prayer was completed, the blanket was removed, and the coals taken from the container. The ash remaining from the hair was placed in another bowl, and water was added. The Bear member asperged some of this solution on the patient's head and on his hands and feet, which were placed together. The patient then drank the remaining liquid from the bowl. Next he was given a fetish to be worn at the waist, and relatives were admonished to guard him until the cure was complete. This terminated the ceremony [9].

While rituals of the above type were normally conducted by a Bear member, lay persons could perform them if they were cognizant of the routine. One such was described by an informant [43].

In this case the patient was a child who had been frightened. Her uncle, the informant's father, administered the cure. While not a member of the Bear groups, he was an Oyike (Winter Society) member. In general, the performance paralleled that described above. However, these differences occurred: the practitioner got under the blanket with the patient and blew on the coals to keep them burning; other children were told to get under the blanket in order to receive the benefits of the smoke; the patient was not asperged, but the ash and water mixture was rubbed on her forehead, face, and chest. Finally, no prayer was said. The treatment was repeated on four successive nights. According to the informant, the practitioner was enabled to confirm his diagnosis if the coals burned brightly as the patient was led toward the bowl.

Other cures also involved asperging as their principal feature. Illnesses of infants were frequently diagnosed as resulting from the membrane covering the unclosed sutures of the skull, falling in and touching the brain. This problem was remedied in the following manner. Assistance from a Bear member was solicited; in this case, it was a woman, the grandmother of the informant, who was a specialist in this type of cure. She placed a finger in the mouth of the child, pushed upward on the roof and blew on the head four times. Then a mixture of sea shells and water were asperged on the head. Finally the remainder of the solution was given to the child to drink [52].

Jeançon (1900–08) witnessed the individual treatment of a child during his stay in the village, and described it as follows:

A small boy about four years old had been ailing for several days probably due to a slight cold augmented by an oversupply of cheap candy. The mother tried simple home remedies but the child drooped and slept or was in a stupor most of the time. The writer suggested a dose of salts, but this was refused. At last after a consultation between the parents it was decided to appeal to a member of the Bear Society. In such a simple case it was not necessary to ask for the Bear leader or more than one member. The healer came and after some objections to the writer's presence finally agreed to his remaining during the ceremony.

The healer stripped to his breechclout and drew gauntlets of bear skin with the hair on them over his hands. These reached almost to his elbows. A pot of embers was prepared, and after scattering meal to the six directions, a pungent herb was thrown on the hot coals. The healer took the pot of embers in his hands and presented it to the four cardinal points, then told the mother to hold the child over the fumes. Four times the child was passed through the fumes, beginning at the east, then north, then west, and then south. During this time prayers were said to the Prey Animals of the cardinal points to frighten away the disease.

After this the child was laid on the bed. A bowl of hot water was produced.

The bowl was part of the healer's equipment. Herbs were thrown into the hot water, more prayers were said, and meal again scattered to the six directions. As the medicine cooled, the healer stirred it with a stone fetish carved to represent a bear. When cool it was given to the child to drink. (The writer suspects that it was a purgative for the child later had copious passages of the bowels and got well rapidly.)

While the child was drinking, prayers were said, this time directed particularly to the bear. Then the fetish was blessed with meal and put into a buckskin bag containing more cornmeal. (Fetishes are fed white cornmeal in winter and blue cornmeal in the summer, the colors being representative of the seasons.) The bag was then tied in a bandage around the boy's abdomen, to be worn there until he was well; then he was put back to bed again. The fetish was returned to the healer after the boy was well.

The mother presented the healer with a basket of blue cornmeal immediately after the child was fumigated. (The healing took place in the summer.) When the fetish was returned to its owner, another basket of meal accompanied it as a last gift.

According to one informant [13], Bear Society members were immediately cognizant if there were individuals present during a cure who were skeptics or nonbelievers. "If you attend one of these cures and intend to describe it to an outsider, are thinking bad, or do not believe the Bear members know this, they will come over wearing their bear paws and slap you like a bear. I have seen this happen."

A "cure, or treatment, with house" ceremony was a one-night performance held to cure a patient and/or purify a kin group and house. The following is a description of a cure by the Tesuque Bear Society.

When illness occurred or the need for purification arose, some older member of a household, usually the household head, approached the leader of one of the Bear societies and made a request for a treatment.

The petition was submitted near evening. It was accompanied by a gift of feathers (fo), tobacco, and sacred meal (k'an bowa). The request for a "treatment with house" implied that the services of several members, if not the total membership of the society, would be required, and also that a payment for services rendered would be made in food and cornmeal. Because of diminished society membership in recent years, it was not unusual for the leader of one society to ask assistance of the other, and for both groups to participate in the cure.

If the petition was accepted, the household head returned, and the immediate family prepared for the ceremony, which would occur on the following night. The room in which the Bears would work was cleared of furniture and swept. Women prepared food and ground meal. Other members of the kin group were notified of the ceremony and invited to attend; if they accepted, they were obligated to bring meal.

Guest relatives arrived about twilight the following evening. They and the immediate family bathed in the river to purify themselves. All wore a breechclout and blanket. The Bears arrived at dark, similarly attired. "Their breechclouts were broader." Each carried a bear-paw gauntlet, which contained their ceremonial paraphernalia. These they placed along the wall beside the door.

Upon arrival the Bear leader and helpers began to construct the altar (o'wing). He worked in the center, and on either side were three or four assistants. While they engaged in this work, the petitioner rolled cornhusk cigarettes and distributed them to those Bear members who were not occupied. The altar proper was outlined in white cornmeal. It consisted of an enclosed grid with an opening, or "trail," at the front, and with outward curving prongs of lightning projecting forward on either side. When this preliminary work was completed, the leader handed each member his bear-paw gauntlet. They in turn untied these containers, took out the "mothers" (djia), removed their buckskin wrappings, and passed them to the leader, who placed them in a line at the back of the altar. Next they presented their stone fetishes (kadje) to the leader. These he placed on the intersections of the meal lines which formed the grid. Next two "flint" knives were put in the opening of the altar. Finally a basket of sacred meal was placed on the left of the opening and a bowl of sacred water on the right in front; this completed the altar.

The members seated themselves behind it in a line, holding a gourd rattle in one hand and two eagle wing feathers in the other. The leader rose and gave a formal talk, dealing with the reasons for the requested treatment. He said, "The patient has felt sickness and has seen fit to call the Bear Society." The leader mentioned the sick person by name and also by "clan name." He said, "We have come because you have asked us; you have remembered us; you have thought of us; we have come. Some power prompted the patient to call us." The selection of the society was not due to the patient, who was considered a passive participant; the active role was played by the power. The power prompted the patient to ask for the society. The Bear leader mentioned the names of the animals; the members acted as intermediaries between the patient and these (tsi wi). The Bears were their representatives; they did not do the actual curing—the animals cure. "The Bears merely acted as agents of the animals and petitioned them to help the patient" [9]. When the leader completed his talk, the petitioner arose, thanked the leader and society for coming, and repeated much of what had been said by the leader. The talk given by the leader and the response by the man who requested the ceremony consumed twenty or thirty minutes.

As soon as the household head completed his speech, the Bears began a chant, keeping time with gourd rattles. The chant consisted of four songs. During the first three, two men went to the fireplace, obtained ashes, placed them in two piles in front of the altar, and stood before them. In one hand each held an eagle's feather; in the other, an eagle's feather and rattle. They swayed back and forth and shook the rattles. During the songs, reference was made to the disease-causing object. On each such occasion, the men dipped the tips of the feathers in the ashes, snapped the tips together, and made exorcising motions toward the west. Each time they completed this rite, they made a circuit of the room, performing the same act.

During this period anyone in the room who wished came to the altar, took sacred meal from the basket, offered it to (sprinkled it on) the "mothers" and stone fetishes, and recited a prayer requesting the quick recovery of the patient.

When the fourth song began, the petitioner passed cigarettes to all members except the leader. He next procured a splinter of wood from the fire and presented it to the first man in the line, who lighted his cigarette and passed it to the next, etc. All puffed furiously, and soon the room was filled with smoke—individuals were barely visible. Members began to cough and growl like bears and to howl like wolves. This was initiated in soft, low tones, but gradually increased in loudness and tempo.

This continued for some time. Finally all except the leader and women members, which latter acted as helpers but took no part in the individual cure, arose. One by one they came to the front of the altar, raised their hands above their heads, and drew in power, "embraced power to themselves." The leader sat by the altar and chanted. Members next made a circuit of the room, stopping before individuals reaching out from time to time "to pull in evil and blow it away." Their progress was accompanied by growls and howls. Some purified several individuals at once, others, only one person; all went to the patient or to the petitioner, if a patient was lacking. Some used eagle feathers to draw out the evil, others their cupped hands. Those with feathers snapped the tips together and dispelled the evil toward the west, "as if to say, 'Navajo take it all.'" The others performed similar gestures with their hands. When all had returned to the altar, the leader arose and duplicated their actions.

Next all Bears but the leader approached the patient or petitioner, who was seated on a sheepskin before the fireplace. Some had their stone fetishes, which they had procured from the altar, others wore their bear-paw gauntlets, and some were without ceremonial equipment. If the principal was seriously ill, he or she was placed on a mattress and covered with a blanket, and a relative was delegated to assist the patient. This man helped the ill person to a sitting position, and supported him during the actual cure.

Bear members with stone fetishes made gestures of embracing evil and blowing it away. Some took a fetish in one hand, placed a gauntlet on the other, dipped it in the sacred water, went to the patient, placed both the fetish and gauntlet on the person's head, drew out the evil, and dispelled it. Others practiced the laying on of hands, "felt the patient with their hands or bear-paws." Still others massaged and rubbed the patient's arms, legs, and various parts of the body, concentrated the evil in one spot, and then sucked it out through their cupped hands or gauntlets and swallowed it. "One had a special trick; he would place his foot on the patient, draw the object out with his toes, and exhibit it."

"When a member swallowed evil, he arose and came to the altar and walked back and forth in front of it, staggering as if he were drunk, and attempted to vomit the disease cause. The noises he made were very realistic. Finally he vomited it beside the altar. If it was a particularly large object, it might be dragging along the floor behind him and coming out his mouth at the same time. The things extracted included long rags, lengths of yucca tied together, rocks, down feathers, broken glass, sticks, cattail fuzz, etc.—all sorts of filth. The cattail fuzz was blown out in a cloud" [9, 50, 52].

When the patient had been exorcised and purified, treatment might also be given to other members of the household. "If anyone went to sleep during the ceremony, one of the Bear members would go over and slap him" [50].

During these proceedings the leader remained by the altar, chanting. He was joined from time to time by unoccupied members of the society. Finally, when all had completed their work, the leader rose, gathered in evil from the altar, and blew it away. Next he performed this exorcising rite on various members of the household. Finally he extracted an object from the patient, vomited it by the altar, and returned to his place.

The treatment of the patient was followed by a purification of the house. Some members climbed to the roof, others went to the inner rooms. A great tumult was raised; all stomped about, shouting and imitating the cries of animals. Finally they returned one by one, each with an object. Some brought a doll or a bundle of wrapped rags. "This was a witch" (tcu ge ii). Others brought dead hawks or owls; these were occasionally captured alive and killed at the altar. All items collected from the house were placed on the pile of evil objects (tam wa). Then the room and personnel were again exorcised. During this and the purification of the house, the leader remained by the altar.

When the house was cleansed, cigarettes and a lighted splinter were again passed by the petitioner. The leader instructed the man on his right or left to destroy the pile of evil. This person approached the altar, and with a chert or obsidian knife (tsi wi, lower tone than the word for animal) began to reduce it to small pieces. "He cuts or tears up all the objects and scrapes the rocks with his knife. Then he rakes the knife over the bits in a circular motion. This was the cue to begin another set of songs."

If the pile was small, the torn bits were placed in the operator's breechclout; if large, a shawl was borrowed and the pieces were wrapped in that. While the singing continued, he made a counterclockwise circuit of the room and left the house. Once outside, he proceeded toward the west until he found a chamiso bush whose limbs drooped and touched the ground. He lifted these, dug a hole, deposited the evil items, covered them, allowed the limbs to drop into place, and returned to the house.

On entering, he took his place and joined in the singing. Two more songs were sung, and in each one the evil objects were mentioned. This was a signal for two men to repeat the earlier exorcising rite with ashes. At the end of the song, all members drew in evil with their eagle feathers and dispelled it toward the west. When the song terminated, cigarettes were passed. The leader rose, took two eagle feathers and a stone fetish from the altar, dipped the latter in sacred water, and went to the patient. He placed the feathers and fetish first on the patient's head, then on his shoulders, chest, back, knees, feet, and hands. Each time he placed them on the body, he blew on them four times. Next he presented the fetish to the patient, telling him that it would "watch over and care for him" for the next four days. Finally he exorcised the patient with the feathers four times and returned to the altar.

This completed the cure and/or purification proper, which had consumed a time period from nightfall until midnight or later. The terminal features included talks by the Bear leader and petitioner, and payment for the services. The speech by the leader was long and repetitious. He said that what the patient wanted had been granted, that the Bear Society had done all that they could, and that the cure itself was in the hands of the animals" (tsi wi). When he finished, the petitioner formally thanked the society. Then members of the immediate family brought baskets of cornmeal and food, and placed them in two rows before the altar. There was at least one basket of meal for each society member.

After this, the Bear members at either end of the line retrieved the bear-paw gauntlets and gave them to their owners. The leader dismantled the altar. He first gave the "mothers" to the members, who wrapped them in buckskin and replaced them in the containers. After this the stone fetishes were returned and stored. The remainder of the altar paraphernalia was taken by the leader, leaving only the meal lines which outlined the altar proper. Members of the family who wished came forward, took pinches of this meal, and rubbed it over their bodies. The small children rolled in the remainder.

After this the leader, followed by members of the society, arose, went to the baskets, and took a pinch of meal or food from each container. In turn each threw some in the fireplace, and the remainder out the door of the house. "This was called feeding the spirits and the impersonated animals. Spirits (po wa ha) were the souls of all living things, literally water-wind-breath. If a man built a camp he would make this offering. The ants, birds, bears, etc. would eat this."

After the offering was made, the society returned and ate as much as they wished. When all had satisfied their hunger, they asked for clothes or shawls in which to wrap the meal tendered in payment. Those who had relatives present as guests obtained these items for them. Others borrowed them from household members and later returned them. Then, after a warning from the leader, that for the next four days the patient must be accompanied at all times by some relative, the society departed.

When the society left, the household head invited anyone who wished to come forward and eat. Those who were not hungry left for their homes. The remainder ate, and departed after thanking the household head, who in turn thanked them for attending.

No other action was taken until the fourth day after the ceremony. At that time the ceremonial restrictions were lifted from the patient, and the petitioner returned the stone fetish, accompanied by the gift of a basket of cornmeal, to the leader of the Bear Society; this completed the cure. Cures followed the same pattern whether they involved a man, woman, or child [9, 13, 52].

Two informants [9, 52] indicated that cures were formerly held in the kivas as well as in homes. Possibly this was the older and preferred pattern; Jeançon's evidence tends to confirm this. He gave a partial description of a curing rite by the Jemez Bear Society, which contains additional facts lacking in the preceding account.

According to him (Jeançon 1900–08), whenever the Bear Society functioned as a whole, the treatment was held in the kiva, if it was possible to move the patient. When the patient arrived, he was made as comfortable as possible, and the society prepared its paraphernalia. During the preparation, several members went outside and disguised themselves in rags, occasionally adding grotesque headdresses. Then they proceeded a short distance from the kiva, hooting like owls and howling like coyotes and wolves. All villagers except those in the kiva remained indoors, since it was believed that the disease, when driven from the patient, could pass to another individual.

The paraphernalia used in the kiva consisted of the "plume fetish (djia) called the chief Bear medicine"; a carved stone figure of a bear painted yellow; a square or rectangular bowl; a "kiva bell," or kotiti; two pipes (one elbow, one tubular); the dried skin of a bicolored blackbird; and a buckskin bag containing smaller buckskin receptacles, in which were stored medicines, tobacco, roots, and other herbs used in the ceremony.

Male members of the society were attired in a woven, blue apron (breechclout) secured by a woven red belt. They wore a bear-claw necklace, and in their hair, the plume of an eagle. Bear-paw gauntlets with claws attached, reaching almost to the elbow, were worn by all men except the leader (Ke'patowa sendo, "bear impersonator old man"). All participants were barefoot, their bodies and faces painted red.

The Bear leader wore a yellow apron. Most of the time, he sat on a red blanket and supervised the activities of others. Over his heart was a medicine bag, which contained his most potent material. This was suspended by a buckskin thong running over the right shoulder and under the left arm. He wore a bear-claw necklace, and like the others was painted red. In his hand he held two eagle wing feathers for brushing away disease.

Women members were dressed in black mantas passing over the right shoulder and under the left arm. These were secured at the waist with a woven belt. The hair was worn in two braids, one on either side of the head; an eagle plume was secured to the top of the head. In her right hand, each woman carried a long, unchipped obsidian blade; this was used in the witch chase, and later for cutting up witches. In her other hand, she had a large, chipped obsidian spear point (tsi wi).

Jeançon (1904–30) had the following comments on the tsi wi:

> The writer found one of these during the excavations at Po-shu, in 1919. Later while in Santa Fe preparing the material from the excavations for shipment to Washington, a member of the Bear Society came in and saw the blade. He went into raptures over it, handling it with great reverence and breathing in the "strength and spirit" from the point of the spear-head. He begged to be allowed to purchase it, offering a good price, but had to be refused as it was government property.
>
> In 1911 the writer found a spear-head about 16 inches long and 3 inches wide in the Rio Oso excavations at Pesede-ouinge. It was painted green with red

bands at the point, middle, and butt. One of the Indian laborers said it was the same as that used by the Bear Society and that it was probably used by them in the prehistoric days. While there is nothing definite to indicate that the Bear Society goes back that far, yet it is possible that this might be the case. They undoubtedly had healing societies at that time.

The interior of the kiva was lighted only by a fire in the fireplace. The spectators sat around the base of the walls.

When all was ready, messengers were sent to ascertain if any witches were hovering about; they returned and reported that such was the case. Then followed a long ritual, the details of which were not known to Jeançon (1900–08), but which involved the use of prayers, incantations, songs, sacred meal, smoking, and sacred water, for the purpose of gaining control of the witches.

> During this time, members of the Bear Society worked themselves into a highly emotional state. The men growled like bears, clawed the air about the patient, pretended to grasp the witches; the women also imitated the growls of bears, flourished the cutting edges and stabbed with the spear heads, to cut and rend the evil influences. Suddenly the Bear Chief took his bowl of medicine water and gave each member of the society a drink. After this they rushed up the ladder to the roof, screaming and shouting, and pretended to frighten the evils away. They descended into the plaza and sought out those impersonating the witches, struck them, and pretended to cut and destroy them, all the time shrieking, "We are bears, we are real bears, and we are killing the witches." This continued until all the evil ones were killed or driven off. The impersonators of the witches divested themselves of their rags and returned to the kiva with their companion members. Then all of them, headed by the leader, rushed to Santa Clara Creek shouting, "We are bears." When they reached the water, they all plunged in to

wash off the disease and evil influences. The river was thought to carry these underground and bury them.

Upon their return to the kiva, the patient was again prayed over, fumigated, and otherwise treated to ensure the cure. Later he was carried home or, if too feeble, remained in the kiva the balance of the night attended by relatives and friends.

House Blessing Ceremony

A variant of the "cure, or treatment, with house" was the "house blessing ceremony" (Te wha, ove, uru to, toni; "house to, prayer plumes, to place in"). This was performed when a new home was completed. By and large it paralleled the ritual previously described, but was nonetheless considered distinct in character by the villagers [9, 50]. According to another [43], one faction of the Winter Moiety recently has called upon the Catholic priest to bless a new home, instead of the Bear societies.

Early in the morning, the household head or another member of the family went to the leader of one of the Bear societies (in this case the Tesuque), with a gift of tobacco, feathers, and cornmeal, and requested that prayer plumes be placed in the new home, and that it be purified. The society began "work" as soon as possible after the request. According to one informant [50], the work presumably consisted of preparing prayer plumes to be used in the ritual.

In the meantime, household members ground meal and prepared food. Relatives were notified of the coming rite, and were invited to attend; those who accepted brought baskets of meal. All lay participants bathed in Santa Clara Creek, and on arrival at the house divested themselves of their clothing.

When the gathering was complete, the Bear Society arrived. The leader immediately began the construction of the altar, while another member addressed the group. He explained the purpose of their visit, saying that they represented the actual bears, "deities" (tsi wing pa rei). During this talk, the one who had requested the ceremony made cigarettes and passed them to the society members.

When the talk was completed, the petitioner arose and responded; his address paralleled the first one. By this time the altar was erected, and "a cure, or treatment, with house," previously described, was enacted, after which the society departed until mid-morning of the next day.

Upon their return, they requested the family to vacate the premises; they then entered and performed the rite. The informant [50] was uncertain as to the details of their activities, but assumed that they buried prayer plumes and possibly other objects of ceremonial significance in the four corners of the principal room. Following this, the family returned and were instructed to plaster over the areas where the society had dug. "That is all."

According to another informant [21], this ritual was also held if a home became "ruined, spoiled, or haunted" (na ha' po?). (This same term was used to refer to persons who were drunk.) When a member of a household died, it was mandatory that someone remain in the home at all times for four days after the death. If this tabu was disregarded, the dwelling was believed to be "haunted." "You might hear noises in corners or at the windows" [43]. In such cases, the Bear societies were called upon to perform a rite of purification.

Cure with Yard

A "cure with yard" was similar to a "cure with house," except that it included a purification of the corrals, livestock, crops, and landholdings of the household group, as well as of the house and kin group. Presumably, the relationship group might be larger and the payment, accordingly, more substantial.

Large Treatment

A "large treatment" (sori wokang) was an annual ritual with predominantly purificatory and preventative emphases. It was held in the spring, in March or April, prior to the commencement of the agricultural cycle, to cleanse the tribal territory and everything it contained of witches and their malignant influences. It appears to have been associated with the transfer of the religious responsibilities from the Winter to the Summer Moiety. On occasion a ritual called the "meeting of waters" (Poje) was performed in conjunction with a "large treatment." While the latter could be held alone, the former could not; if a "meeting of waters" ceremony took place, the performance of a "large treatment" was mandatory.

There is evidence that a ceremony of this type, or one very similar, was current in many of the pueblos. For examples, White (1932: 53; 1935: 139–41; 1942: 206–7; 1962: 227–28) and Lange (1959: 261–62, 330–31) have provided descriptions of rites for San Felipe, Santo Domingo, Santa Ana, Zia, and Cochiti, which roughly parallel the following. Santa Clara informants [21, 45, 50] stated that an identical ceremony, in which Santa Clara Bears participated, was held each spring at both San Ildefonso and Tesuque. Similar rites were indicated for Jemez (see also Parsons 1925: 75).

According to one informant [9], the war captain decided if a "large treatment" was needed. When the decision was reached, a request for the ceremony was made of either of the Bear societies by the Summer cacique (perhaps, before the split, also by the Winter cacique), the war captain (outside chief), the governor, or the head of the Women's Scalp Society. Whoever made the formal request, accompanied by a gift of cornmeal, feathers, and tobacco, sponsored the performance and acted in the capacity of patient. This person was not necessarily ill, and presumably was not, but served to satisfy the requisite role in the curing portion of the ritual.

In recent times the annual aspect of the ceremony has lapsed. Also, with the reduction in the membership in the Bear societies, it has become customary for both groups to participate. The head of whichever society was petitioned took meal, feathers, and tobacco to the leader of the other, and requested the cooperation of that group. Assistance was also solicited from the Bear societies of Tesuque and San Ildefonso pueblos. A member of the Bear Society, accompanied by a war captain, journeyed to these villages with the petition.

This interpueblo assistance was reciprocal, and the Jemez and Tesuque Bear societies of Santa Clara performed at San Ildefonso and Tesuque, respectively, at their annual "large treatment" [21, 45, 50]. The same relations apparently did not exist with Jemez Pueblo.

A "large treatment" consumed four days. The following account is based upon an enactment in which the Jemez Bears were the directing group [50]. The war captain petitioned the leader of the Jemez Bear Society, who in turn asked aid of the Tesuque group. The head of the Jemez Society then took a gift of tobacco to the war captains, who guarded and assisted during the proceedings.

When these preliminaries had been accomplished, the Bears went into retreat, in this case at the house of the leader of the Jemez Bears, and began their "work." The windows of the house were covered, and the exits were guarded day and night by the war captains. The "work" of the first thirty-six hours consisted of preparing prayer plumes during the day and purifying shrines each night. This was known as nan sipu wo kong, a free translation of which is "to apply medicine to the earth at a shrine."

On the first night the six shrines the greatest distance from the village were visited. These included Ca-wi?, in the south; Fú p'inne, "Fruit of the Yucca Baccata Mountain," in the west; Tun wae joi, "Height Place," and Sun daro tei, for which directions were not obtained. A team composed of two Bear members, a war captain, and an assistant, or "carrier" (o'n honde?i, also called wrapper) went to each. The shrines were purified, prayer plumes deposited, and the captured witches placed in the "bundle" of the carrier. One informant [50] described the procedure as follows: "They picked up a witch at Tca wi [the south shrine] and another at Sun daro tei [another shrine] on the first night. The two Bears ran ahead and left the war captain and the carrier behind. The war captain ran ahead of the carrier, but waited from time to time for him to catch up. The carrier tired quickly because of his burden. Both coming and going, the Bear members emitted growls and calls" [50].

On arrival in the village, the parties went

to the house of the leader of the Bear Society. Members remained at the house. The "carriers" deposited the witches, and with the war captains, went to their respective homes to sleep.

The routine of the second and third days and nights paralleled that of the first. Six shrines, located progressively nearer the village, were purified each night. New members were chosen for the visiting teams on each occasion, and the house guards were changed daily.

Early in the evening of the fourth and final night, members of the Bear societies repaired to the kiva and began the construction of the altar. In recent years the Summer kiva has been used, but the ceremony was formerly held in the kiva of either moiety. The altar was located in the northwest portion of the room, north of the center posts. It was constructed of earth colors, and was U-shaped in outline. The interior portion of the U contained intersecting lines, spaced at intervals to form a grid. On either side, toward the front and extending outward, was a lightning bolt. A cornmeal trail led from the front to the foot of the kiva ladder. The "mothers" (djia) were arranged in a line at the back of the altar. They were flanked on either side by decorated, terraced plaques of wood. The stone fetishes belonging to the various members were placed on the intersections of lines forming the grid.

Within the lines were placed various items of ceremonial paraphernalia. At the center in the rear was a rectangular, terraced pottery container filled with sacred water; just to the right was a pipe. In the adjacent spaces on either side were the two kutiti stones, or "bells." To the right, in the next space, was a stone knife. Forward and on the left side of the altar was a basket of sacred meal for the use of Bear members only. In the front of the altar to the left of the meal trail was another basket of sacred meal for the use of nonsociety participants. Hanging above the altar was a wooden cross with arms of of equal length; feathers were suspended from the ends and at intervals along their length. During the ceremony this cross was kept constantly in motion. When not in use, the bear-paw gauntlets were lined

up on either side of the altar.

While the altar was under construction, the secular officials of the village, members of the Pay-oj-ke, probably Oyike, the Women's Scalp Society, and "the elders" brought cornmeal to a house adjacent to the kiva. This meal was placed in large receptacles and given to the Bear members following the rite.

When the altar was completed, male members of the Bear societies arranged themselves in back of it, along the west wall; female members, along the north wall between the altar and the fireplace. Two male members stood at the foot of the ladder. When all was in readiness, word was sent that the ceremony was to begin, and the audience began to arrive at the kiva.

Men were garbed in breechclouts and blankets; women, in mantas or dresses. All removed their footgear on entering, and went to their places in the south and west sections of the kiva. The Summer cacique sat next to the fireplace. The last to arrive were the secular officers of the village. They entered in order of rank: the governor, lieutenant governor, *alguacil,* war captains, and *fiscales.* These dignitaries were dressed in their best clothing—either buckskin or purchased. However, all wore moccasins. The governor, lieutenant governor, and war captain carried their canes of office; the captains and *fiscales,* bows and arrows.

When they reached the floor of the kiva, one of the two Bear members stationed at the foot of the ladder made a purifying gesture with two eagle feathers before each in turn; the other Bear member took the canes, bows, and arrows. These he placed next to the bear-paw containers located on either side of the altar. The group, in single file, followed the cornmeal trail from the front of the ladder to the altar, formed a line facing it, and each offered it a pinch of cornmeal. This completed, they turned and seated themselves in front of the altar. A Bear member came forward and presented them with cigarettes.

When all were settled and smoking, the governor arose and spoke. His talk dealt with the reason for the request of "the large treatment." He said, "The village and shrines are contaminated with evil, and we want such things to disappear." Whenever he paused, one or another of the Bear members said, "Yes, that is the way." This talk was followed by two others in a similar vein, by the war captain and the Summer cacique. All three spokesmen warned the members of the Bear societies that they should use their power always for good, never for evil; that they should never use it for witchcraft. Finally the leader of the Bear Society (in this case Jemez) arose and concurred with the preceding men, bidding the members of the Bear societies to act as instructed. At the conclusion of these remarks, the secular officials arose, retrieved their canes, bows, and arrows, and left the kiva [50].

While the exit was in progress, members of the Bear societies shook their rattles and began chanting. Both male and female members sang. The chant was in the Jemez (Towa) language, and described incidents in the progress of stone fetishes from a lake in the north to the pueblo of Santa Clara. (This was very similar to the calling of the kachinas.) It consisted of six parts.

During the initial stages of this performance, individuals in the audience who desired to make offerings came forward and sprinkled meal on the altar. In the meantime, the war captain returned, clad only in a breechclout, seated himself in the southeast section of the kiva, and began to roll cigarettes.

When the fourth song was completed, the Bear member who was to play the principal role in the ceremony, i.e., the capturer of the final and most dangerous witch, arose; he went to the altar (owing), picked up a kutiti, dipped it in the bowl of sacred water, walked to the north section of the kiva, and struck the kutiti a blow with the stone beater. He then returned to the altar, still tapping the kutiti, redipped it in the sacred water, and repeated the same action at the five other cardinal points. When this was completed, he wandered from place to place, beating the kutiti in time with the chant, until the end of the song.

When the fifth song was completed, the kutiti was replaced on the altar; this marked the start of the sixth and final part of the chant. The Bear member donned a pair of bear-paw gauntlets and, accompanied by a female member carrying a basket of meal, began to dance about the kiva. By this time the songs indicated that the fetishes had reached a point not too distant from the village, and he went to the north side of the kiva and gazed in that direction. Seeing nothing, he returned to the altar and looked into the bowl of sacred water to ascertain their progress. This was repeated several times (three or five?). On the fourth or sixth occasion, Santa Clara Pueblo (Kapo winge) was finally mentioned in the song. He leapt into the air with arms outstretched, clasped his hands together, captured the fetish, returned to the altar, and dropped it in the bowl of sacred water. "You can hear it hit the bowl" [50]. This performance was repeated at the other five cardinal points.

Following the capture of the fetishes, the war captain arose and went to the society members seated on the south and north sides of the altar, distributing and lighting the cigarettes he had made. All smoked furiously, and in a short while began grunting, growling, howling, and hooting in imitation of bears, wolves, and owls. The male Bear members, with the exception of the leader, arose one by one, some taking eagle feathers from the altar, and began to mingle with the audience. The leader and the female members remained where they were and began chanting.

Those with feathers "drew out" the evil from individual villagers and "blew it away toward the west." Those without feathers gathered the evil in their cupped hands and disposed of it in the same manner. When all had been cleansed, the feathers were placed by the altar. Then each member drew on his bear-paw gauntlets.

Again they went through the audience, and this time rubbed the bodies of individuals with the paws, concentrating the evil in one area. They next placed their mouth at the upper part of the gauntlet, extracted the evil objects by sucking, and swallowed them. As each extraction was completed, the Bear danced groggily to the altar. Here he was met by one of the female members, who placed one arm around his stomach and with the other patted his back upward to assist him, while still dancing in time with the chanting, in vomiting the various evil objects. All vomiting was accompanied by sound effects which lent realism to the rite. The various objects spewed forth were collected and placed by the altar.

The war captain, the "patient" sponsor of the ceremony, was given special attention and thoroughly purified. Pairs of Bear members made house calls on any villagers who were ill and unable to attend the ceremony, in order that they too could receive the benefits of the treatment. Others visited the plazas, corrals, exteriors of homes, livestock, and fields, and purified them. Before leaving, they marked the palms of their hands and the soles of their feet with charcoal [61]. The witches and evil which they gathered were placed in a pile between the altar and fireplace, the "cures" were finally completed, and the society members returned one by one and seated themselves behind the altar.

When all were in their places, one who was to act as assistant to the principal witch-catcher came forward and drew a cornmeal circle in front and slightly to the north of the altar. At this juncture all members bowed their heads and were silent, "as if they were sad and in mourning for something." He then returned, took two eagle feathers, and presented their tips to one of the seated members. This man grasped the tips of the feathers and was led by the first to the meal circle and seated there. Next the member went to the Bear leader and received eagle down feathers, which he placed on the bowed head of the seated man. After this, the assistant took a pipe from the altar and coals from the fire, and presented them to the head of the Bear Society. The head lighted the pipe, puffed on it, and gave it to the man first in line behind him; the pipe was smoked by each member in turn, passing from left to right. The assistant retrieved the pipe at the end of the line, blew smoke on the fetishes and altar, went to the man in the circle, and placed the pipe in his mouth. This principal puffed on the pipe and slowly went into a trance. As he fell backward, he was helped by the assistant.

The assumption of the trance was the signal for chanting to begin. Again the songs were in Jemez. The assistant took the "fetish that sparkles" (kuatsa) from the altar, dipped it in sacred water, carried it to the prostrate man, and began to move it slowly above his body from feet to head. This continued for almost the duration of the first song. Near the end, the man in the trance began to reach feebly for the iridescent stone. The assistant raised the fetish higher; the man struggled into a sitting position. Finally he attempted to get to his feet, and succeeded after several tries. The assistant moved away and the Bear member followed, his eyes on the sparkling fetish. At this point, the second song began.

This song referred to the various cardinal points. North was mentioned first, and the two men went to that section of the kiva. The assistant lifted the other man to the ceiling, and he brought forth a hank of yucca. The two wrestled over the yucca, each attempting to outdo the other in tearing it apart. When it was finally reduced to bits, they struggled with the pieces toward the altar, and threw them with obvious anger on the pile of witches and other objects of evil which had been taken from the shrines. This was repeated at all the other cardinal points. The hank from the zenith was discovered in the main ridgepole of the kiva; the final one, at the nadir, under the seat of the war captain.

Following this purification, another song was begun. The assistant, still holding the fetish, led the principal to the altar, and the latter put on his bear-paw gauntlets. Both made a circuit of the room, during which they motioned toward themselves with their hands and drew in power ("people power") from the audience. After the fourth circuit, they rushed up the ladder and out of the kiva.

The singing continued after their departure. A Bear woman arose, took cornmeal from the altar, went to the foot of the ladder, turned, and began dancing along the trail to the altar, sprinkling meal as she danced. Her progress was slow; she danced in place until the song tempo changed, then edged forward a few inches, then when the tempo changed again, danced in place. When she reached the altar, she sprinkled it with meal and began again at the foot of the ladder. Her final arrival at the altar was timed to coincide with the return of the men who were sent for the principal witch. From time to time, members of the audience also came forward and offered meal at the altar.

In the meantime the head of the Bear Society gazed at intervals into the bowl of sacred water; he reported the fortunes of the witch hunt and encouraged the hunters. This scrying performance was a highly dramatic interlude. Much after the manner of a broadcaster at a football game, he described the search for the principal witch called "the heart" (pín, "the heart of all evil" [50], "the cacique of the witches" [61]), its discovery, and final capture.

This account was graphic and detailed. When "the heart" was encountered, a terrific fight ensued. The principal succeeded in getting his hands on the witch, but the latter broke free. Another attempt was made, and "the heart" invoked its power; the pursuer was described as being dragged through swamps, cactus, or dens of snakes, and tied with yucca rope [50, 61]. "The witches would tie him up that way" [61]. As he and his assistant were confronted with each succeeding difficulty, they were advised and encouraged by the Bear leader. He urged them on saying, "Be men, you are the first bear (of the Emergence Myth), the first mountain lion (of the Emergence Myth)," etc. As the difficulties increased, the assistant returned, drew more power from the people, and rushed out to continue the battle. Somewhat later both returned, gathered still more power, and left again, accompanied by two more Bear members. According to an informant [61], it was occasionally necessary for the Bear leader to leave and assist before the final capture was accomplished; sometimes even he was not capable of the feat, and others were sent to help.

The chanting, which was continuous during the hunt, finally ceased, and the leader or his substitute, who had been looking into the sacred water, announced the capture of "the heart." Almost immediately sounds of the returning party were heard at the hatchway of the kiva. Two members met them as they descended the ladder. "The witch cried as it was brought into the kiva" [61]. One member took "the heart," and the other purified the men who had gone to assist. These left immediately.

The assistant helped the principal witch hunter into the kiva. The latter gave every evidence of being utterly exhausted from his battle. His arms rested on the shoulders of the assistant, and he was half carried by him to the altar and seated in front of it [50]. Evidence substantiating the leader's account of the chase was always in view. Depending upon the description, the hunter might be covered with mud from the swamp, have remains of yucca cordage hanging from him, cactus in his hair, or rattlesnakes or racers tied about his neck [50, 61].

As soon as the principal was seated before the altar, a special song was begun. The assistant took "the heart" by a yucca cord around its neck and danced it down the meal trail in time to the music. By the end of the song, he had reached the altar and placed his burden before it. Witches were thought to be normal size until brought into the kiva; "They shrink as they are brought in. When they reach the floor of the kiva, they were figures about a foot high. They had long hair, were dressed in buckskin, and looked like men. Some were stuffed with bark; others, with feathers or hay. Once when grasshoppers were numerous in the fields and ruining the crops, all the witches collected at the 'large treatment' contained these" [61].

The leader took the witch and examined it. Each Bear then came forward and slapped "the heart," after which it was placed on the pile of "evil" (tom wa). This was the signal for a new song. The assistant went to the witch and began to take it apart piece by piece, examining each piece and cutting it up with a reddish stone knife (ci wi). At the same time, two members of the society were performing in a like manner on the pile of "evil." Some parts they threw in the fire, others they saved. When the assistant had reduced the principal witch to the last piece, he found an "object" and called out, "It is good!" This was addressed to the group at large, but particularly to the society leader. It indicated that the effectiveness of the cure was assured.

The "object" (evil) and remains of the witch were next treated. A female member went to the fire and filled a bowl with hot coals and placed the evil on these. The war captain (patient) came to the altar and, bending over the bowl, allowed the smoke from the disintegrating evil to permeate his body. Next the ash remains of the witch were placed in a bowl and sacred water poured over them. This was presented to the war captain, who drank some of the solution, rubbed some over his body, and then returned to his place by the fire.

By this time the two Bear members who were engaged in cutting up the pile of evil had completed their task. They requested shawls, placed the remains in these, and brought the bundles to the altar. Another song was begun immediately, in which the "evil" was mentioned at six different places. At each instance, two members of the Bear Society, beginning at the altar, progressed along either side of the kiva, snapping eagle feathers to purify the area. They completed the circuit and met in the south. In the first four instances, as the evil was referred to, the two men who had wrapped the bundles performed similar "blowing away motions" over them. At the fifth mention, they rushed from the kiva, carrying the bundles, and returned just as the other two had completed the sixth and final circuit. As the song ended, all society members, both male and female, snapped their feathers four times. Then cigarettes were distributed and lighted, and the above act was repeated while smoking.

This completed the ceremony proper. The women, including those who were members of the Bear Society, left, and then returned with baskets of meal and other food; these were placed on the floor on either side of the cornmeal trail. The secular officers returned and, as on their previous entrance, were relieved of their canes, bows, and arrows, and then seated themselves before the altar. Cigarettes were passed. Next the governor spoke and expressed his appreciation and that of the village for the work done by the societies. His talk was followed by similar addresses from the war captain and the Summer cacique. The leader of the Bear Society then spoke, saying, "All has been accomplished as you wished." After this, various members of the community expressed thanks, and indicated that the food was an offering or gift, in appreciation for the work.

Following the speeches, the Bear member who had acted as assistant arose and took a pinch of cornmeal or other food from each basket. Part of this he sprinkled on the altar and fire and the remainder outside the kiva. At the conclusion of this procedure, the canes, bows, and arrows were returned to the secular officers, who departed immediately.

Their departure was a signal for the society members to gather their ceremonial equipment and place it in bear-paw containers, and to dismantle the altar, leaving only the cornmeal which outlined the various sections. When this was accomplished, members of the audience who wished to came forward and rubbed themselves with the meal which remained. Children often rolled in these altar remains, as well. This concluded the ceremony, and the public departed for home; by this time it was almost daylight [50, 61]. "Only the Bears know what happens to the food that is left" [50].

Meeting of Waters

The Meeting of Waters (Poje) ceremony, as mentioned earlier, was occasionally held as a preliminary to a large treatment. When the two rites were integrated, there were minor alterations and some additions to the introductory stages of the large treatment.

Conditions surrounding the request for a purification were similar, except that a Meeting of Waters was included in the petition. Another alteration occurred during the retreat; the number of shrines purified was reduced from six to three. On the first night, the purifying teams went to Ca' wi?, Fú p'inne ("Fruit of the Yucca Baccata Mountain"), and Tun wae joi ("Height Place"), which were at the greatest distance from the pueblo. On the second night, shrines somewhat closer to the village, K'u nu k'wazhe ("Rock Ash Top"), Pu quise buge, Famu tun waei ("Enclosure Place"? or "High Yucca Glauca"?) were visited. Finally, on the third night, those nearest the village, Tepu janae ("Foundation Just Beyond"—all three were called by the same name) were purified.

On the fourth night, the villagers waited in their homes until the altar was constructed and the Bear societies were in readiness. The signal was finally given, and all rushed to the kiva ladder and climbed to the roof. When they came to the hatchway, they removed their clothing, bundled it up, and descended.

As they entered the kiva, the Meeting of Waters began. At the foot of the ladder, each individual stepped into a hoop; two Bear members raised and lowered this several times, to the accompaniment of a ritual which the informant was unable to recall. When this was completed, another Bear presented the tips of two eagle feathers to the person. He or she grasped these in either hand, and was led by the member, who held the shafts, to the west side of the kiva. There he walked through a section covered with wet, red clay.

Subsequent to this, another society member took black earth obtained from the bottom of a swamp and drew crosses on the backs and palms of the villagers' hands, the tops and soles of their feet, and on their shoulders. Finally, still another Bear member secured a roadrunner (o'go'wi) feather in the person's hair.

This completed the Meeting of Waters ceremony. Participants retrieved their clothing, which they had placed at the foot of the ladder, dressed, took their places either on the north or south side of the kiva, and the ceremony of a "large treatment" was enacted [9, 50].

MISCELLANEOUS RITES OF THE BEAR SOCIETIES

There were several specialized, minor co-operative rites of a purificatory nature in which the Bear societies participated. The most important were those connected with the opening of the irrigation ditch and the purification of the race course.

Purification of the Irrigation Ditch

Clearing the principal ditch of weeds and other encumbrances was begun in March.

Before water was turned into the main artery, various rites were performed by delegates from the moieties and Bear societies; those of the Bear societies were held the night before the opening. The societies went into retreat "work," and each chose a representative whose duty it was to traverse the ditch and purify it [25, 45, 73]. Information on the rites of purification was not obtained, but presumably they paralleled those performed in other instances of prophylaxis.

Purification of the Race Course

On those occasions (intermittently, but on San Antonio Day—June 13, or Santa Clara Day—August 12) when relay races were held, both the race course and the runners were purified by members of the Bear societies. As in the case of the ditch opening, the rite was performed the night prior to the event [31, 45, 50]. After the retreat, a member selected from each society, equipped with eagle feathers, started at either end of the course and traversed it, passing at the center. As they ran, they snapped the feathers to purify the area [31, 43, 50]. One informant [69] believed that prayer plumes or bear fur were buried on the course, but indicated that this was only hearsay.

The author witnessed the public portion of this rite at San Juan Pueblo. The only difference at this village was that the ritual immediately preceded the race.

At Santa Clara, individual runners were purified by Bear members. This was accomplished by a laying on of hands [25, 45].

SECULAR MEDICAL PRACTICE

Whether this title is applicable in a literal sense is questionable. A large number of persons who practiced curing, herbalism, massage, midwifery, etc., within kin groups were also religious society affiliates. Conversely, society members were equally conversant with the above practices. The real distinction lay in whether therapeutic measures were accomplished at home or by near relatives in an informal situation, or were part of an organized group procedure.

Herbalists and Masseurs

Some people of the village, because of their knowledge of "remedial" plants, other medicines, and massage, acquired considerable reputations as curers, herbalists, and masseurs. These callings were open to both men and women. Membership in one of the Bear societies or other esoteric organizations was not a prerequisite to practice; however, if one were a member of such a group, it was taken as self-evident that he or she possesed some knowledge of materia medica.

The efforts of herbalists and masseurs proper were mostly confined to the application and practice of home remedies on immediate kin, although occasionally they were called upon by outsiders. The illnesses treated were usually straightforward ones: digestive disorders, headaches, fevers, sores, cuts, etc. They were presumably considered to result from natural causes, rather than from witchcraft or breach of tabu.

Types of treatment and the administration of medicines are indicated in the discussion of ailments and therapeutics. It should be borne in mind that this same knowledge was shared and applied in the course of society rituals [13, 18, 23, 44].

Midwives

There were at least three midwives at Santa Clara Pueblo during the period of investigation. All three were members of the Winter Moiety; however, the assumption of this profession did not depend upon moiety affiliation [18, 29]. Nor were they necessarily members of the Bear societies. Aside from ministrations during parturition, these midwives might advise women on recommended food and activity during the prenatal period [40]. They were said to be able to cure barrenness [13] and also to prevent conception [45]. The latter was achieved, according to accounts, by drinking an infusion prepared from Osage orange, and was believed to cause permanent sterility [45]. Because of their general knowledge, midwives were often called in to cure a variety of ailments,

particularly children's diseases. All three at Santa Clara functioned as both herbalists and masseuses.

Snake Bite

Information on snake bite cures was essentially lacking or in the realm of hearsay. Informants [23, 27, 52] agreed that there were formerly individuals at Santa Clara Pueblo who had the necessary knowledge of medicines and methods to cure snake bites, but that there were none at present.

According to one [23], the curer secured yucca baccata, mountain amole (or Spanish bayonet, P'a), and "dug out" the wound with the points of the leaves. Next, with the help of assistants, two snakes were secured. "They dug them out." In each case the curer seized the snake by the throat, forced open its jaws, spit into its mouth, and threw it to the ground. "Both snakes swelled up and died. These people have a special power to kill snakes." In the incident described, the cure was applied to a burro, but it was said to be effective also for humans.

An account of a cure at San Juan Pueblo by a member of the Cochiti Bear Society was given by another informant. The victim had reached into a burrow to secure a rabbit, and had been bitten by a rattlesnake. By the time he reached the pueblo, his arm was badly swollen. The Bear Society member cut hair from a girl and tied it around the arm above the bite. Next he made a series of punctures along the arm with points of yucca baccata leaves. "The water dripped down from his arm into a bowl. In a day or two the arm began to shrivel, but in about three days he was well" [69].

The Evil Eye

Illnesses resulting from the "evil eye" might be cured by the Bear societies or by secular members of the community. In the latter case, the modus operandi was of undoubted European provenance. Cures could be effected only by women named Juanita. The practitioner broke two chicken eggs into a bowl; only chicken eggs might be used. The bowl was placed by the bedside of the patient, almost invariably a child, and allowed to remain there overnight. In the morning it was examined; if the eggs had "foam on their eyes [yolks]," it was an indication that the illness was caused by the "evil eye." In these instances, the practitioner took the bowl and eggs and buried them in the center of the road leading from the village. This established the cure "to do eye done" (otsing) [69].

Ailments and Therapeutics

The following comprises a partial list of ailments, disorders, and injuries collected from informants and source materials; stomach disorders, including diarrhea, colic, vomiting, and gas; colds and sore throats; infections, cuts, and open sores; eye infections; venereal disease and urinary disabilities; bodily aches, rheumatism, sore parts of the body but not open sores, bruises, sore muscles; swellings; internal injuries; pain; headache; toothache; earache; fever; coma; measles; sprains, dislocations, and fractures; gunshot wounds; baldness.

Therapeutic measures other than the rituals previously described were known and applied in cures for the above. Many of these included the use of herbs, as well as animal and mineral substances. However, such remedies cannot be assigned the role of specifics, since the teleological factors contributing to the disability were not always recognized. Furthermore, in the cures established by societies, medicines as such were relegated to a minor position in comparison with religious ritual.

While there was no necessary correlation between the number and variety of remedies for a particular disorder and the frequency of occurrence of the ailment, some relationship may be assumed. Cures for digestive and related ailments were four or five times as numerous as those for most complaints, and approximately three times greater than any other category of illnesses. These data may indicate that the diet at Santa Clara Pueblo was far from optimum; this has been substantiated, at least in part, by a number of investigations (for example, see Eggan and Pijoan 1943; Hawley, Pijoan, and Elkin 1943).

Extending this reasoning, toxic conditions of various kinds were the next most numerous reasons for physical incapacity. These included open sores, surface infections, colds, and sore throats. This is not an unreasonable assumption, since sanitary conditions were and continue to be adverse; similarly, common knowledge of contagion, or the communicability of disease, was generally lacking.

In relation to the number of separate cures, the incidence of headaches was inferred to be the next most frequent complaint. The list of medicines applied to ailments other than those above was relatively meager.

The following includes a list of disabilities, materials believed to have therapeutic value in each instance, and the manner in which these were administered. The list of curative materials represents a relative minimum, since most informants either refused or were reluctant to divulge knowledge of this type. This aversion resulted first from its religious association; second, since the ability to cure carried considerable prestige, individuals hesitated to make public secret information which had contributed to their high position in the community.

Medicinal plants, and presumably other materials of this type, were invariably gathered under ritualistic conditions. When supplies became low or were exhausted, a society set a date on which those members who wished went on a collecting trip. It was customary to visit the more distant shrines in the course of such a journey [69].

Stomach Disorders

A large number of plants were used to alleviate generalized stomach ailments. They included: *Monarda menthaefolia,* horsemint (tsu tsigi' irɐ), which was eaten green [45], or the dried leaves were ground, mixed with water, and drunk [23, 45]; *Lappula floribunda,* stickseed (oki), the ground leaves of which were mixed with warm water and drunk [23, 45]; *Peritoma serrulatum,* Rocky Mountain bee plant (guaco, or qwa), the leaves of which were boiled and the liquid drunk [23, 65]; *Kallstroemia brachystylis,* "star stalk," (ago yo fe), the leaves of which were steeped in hot water and the liquid drunk [23, 65]. According to Robbins, Harrington, and Freire-Marreco (1916: 56–57), the roots were used as a remedy for diarrhea. [This publication was purportedly a general study of Tewa ethnobotany. Citations have been limited to those designated as from Santa Clara Pueblo. Readers should consult the original for broader applications. WWH]

A drink was prepared from the plant osa pu [23, 45]. It was taken only by men, since it was very bitter [45]; however, according to another [48], it was one of the plants employed to cure diarrhea in children. This ailment was said to coincide with teething. The plant was boiled, after which a cloth was dipped in the liquid and given to the child to suck. The roots of "wolf stalk" (hungo fe) were ground, mixed with warm water, and the liquid drunk. According to two informants [48, 49], it was employed in the same manner as osa pu to cure diarrhea in teething children. The fruit of yucca baccata was boiled, and the liquid drunk [23, 44]. The root of "blue root" (pu tsa wae i, imuto pu) was dried, ground, boiled, and drunk. The roots of *Achillea lanulosa,* yarrow sneezeweed (pa urro fe), were boiled or steeped in hot water and drunk. The leaves of mint (povi wang) and "mountain flower" (ping povi wang) were boiled and drunk by women [23, 44]. The leaves of Tsi ma ha, Spanish *chimaha,* were boiled, and the liquid drunk. The needles of *Juniperus monosperma,* one-seeded juniper (hung), were ground and boiled, and the infusion drunk [23, 44]. The leaves of *Chrysothamnus bigelovii,* rabbitbrush ("green rabbit bush," fung shung), were boiled and the water drunk. According to Robbins, Harrington, and Freire-Marreco (1916: 62), the galls of this plant (pu be e, "rabbit bush, ball, small") were ground and drunk in water. This was considered a good, though strong, medicine. A plant designated as "rabbitbrush" (fu tse to) was given in small quantities to cure horses, but was too strong for men [25]. *Artemisia filifolia,* a silver sage ("mist or fog stalk," so vox uafe), was boiled in water and drunk [25]. Robbins, Harrington, and Freire-Marreco (1916: 45) stated that all New Mexican sages were used at Santa Clara Pueblo for the treatment of indigestion, but that *Artemisia tridentata,* Rocky Mountain sage, was considered the most effective, though disagreeably strong; the leaves were chewed and swallowed. It was useful in dispelling gas. The leaves of *Xanthium commune,* cocklebur (n wae djo ka), were ground and mixed with warm water; the liquid was strained through a cloth and drunk to cure vomiting. Robbins, Harrington, and Freire-Marreco (1916: 49) confirmed this use and stated that it was also a remedy for diarrhea. A small part of a root of *Quamoclidion multiflora,* four-o'clock, was ground, mixed with warm water, and given to babies suffering from colic [25]. Small amounts of Chamisa (fung) leaves were boiled and given to horses to cure them of colic [25, 45].

Colds and Sore Throats

Plants and their application for the cure of colds and sore throats included the following: *Gutierrezia longifolia* (ko ya ya), the shoots of which were ground and boiled; the patient bathed in the solution and was then wrapped in blankets and put to bed. The plant was believed to induce sweating and cure the cold [23]. *Artemisia tridentata,* Rocky Mountain sage, was used in the same manner. The leaves of this plant, according to Robbins, Harrington, and Freire-Marreco (1916: 45), were also chewed and swallowed to relieve persons with "a constant feeble cough with ineffectual expectoration." The roots of the "blue root" plant were ground, water was added, and the paste was rubbed on the chest to cure coughs [23]. According to Robbins, Harrington, and Freire-Marreco (1916: 106), coughs were cured by placing a mixture of tobacco, oil, and soot in the hollows of the patient's neck, and a cross of tobacco on the chest. The same authors stated that tobacco snuff was used to cure discharges from the nose (p. 106) and that the liquid from a mixture of charcoal and hot water was a remedy for cough and sore throat. The mixture was stirred, allowed to settle, and the liquid drunk (p. 28). Sore throats were also treated by eating a mixture of wild rose (ka'a) petals and fat, or by drinking a mixture of water and the dried leaves of *Monarda menthae-*

folia, horsemint (pp. 57–58). Dried horsemint leaves were worn about the neck in buckskin or calico containers for the same purpose (pp. 57–58).

Infections, Cuts, and Sores

Plants used in curing infections, cuts, and open sores included the following: *Monarda menthaefolia,* horsemint, and wild rose (ka'a)—the leaves of these two plants were dried, ground, and placed in open sores. Osa pu—the plant was ground, mixed with water, and applied to open sores and cuts; it was used to prevent infections [25]. Cattail *(Typha latifolia)* root (awa pu) and piñon *(Pinus edulis)* sap (t'o kwae) were placed on sores to draw out pus [23, 44].

Kwae ka—portions of this plant were rubbed on open sores. According to one informant [44], this possessed greater curative power than any other herb. *Pentstemon torreyi,* beard-tongue, according to Robbins, Harrington, and Freire-Marreco (1916: 58), was used for dressing sores, and lichens and wild rose petals mixed with grease were used for treating sores about and in the mouth (pp. 48, 68). Ground corn smut mixed with fat was rubbed in sores to dry them up and create scabs [25, 45].

Eye Infections

Eye infections were treated with the following: *Monarda menthaefolia,* horsemint—the leaves were dried, ground, and placed in water to which salt had been added; the eyes were washed with this solution [23, 65]. This was confirmed by data presented by Robbins, Harrington, and Freire-Marreco (1916: 58). *Kallstroemia brachystylis,* "star stalk" (ago yo fe)—the roots were collected and ground after the bark had been removed; the powder was mixed with water and dropped into the eye. Occasionally, *Quamoclidion multiflora,* four-o'clock, was added [45]. Ground watermelon leaves in solution were also used as an eye rinse [27, 44].

Venereal Disease and Urinary Disorders

Urinary disorders resulting from venereal disease or other causes were treated in the following manner: Mormon tea (k'ung te bi), or *Castilleja linariaefolia,* Indian paint-brush, "stalk flower" (pu t'ang fe povi), was boiled and the liquid drunk by those with venereal disease who had difficulty in urinating [23, 25, 44]. According to Robbins, Harrington, and Freire-Marreco (1916: 49), children with urinary disorders were cured by fumigating them with *Xanthium commune,* cocklebur.

Bodily Aches and Rheumatism

Xung dja fe—plants were ground and rubbed on the body; this was believed to be especially efficacious for backache [25].

Sore Parts of the Body But Not Open Sores

Sore areas of the body were treated by rubbing them with a mixture of ground root of *Quamoclidion multiflora,* four o'clock, and water [44].

Bruises

Bruises were treated as follows: wild rose leaves were dried and rubbed on the bruise [44], or according to Robbins, Harrington, and Freire-Marreco (1916: 70), the leaves of "wolf plant" (ku djo pe) or *Taraxacum taraxacum,* common dandelion, "medicine for broken legs" (pot'awo) were ground and mixed with dough, then applied, sometimes tied over the fracture or bruise (p. 61).

Sore Muscles

Sore muscles were alleviated in the following manner: they were rubbed with a paste made from ground leaves of *Kallstroemia brachystylis,* "star stalk," and water; with the *Sphaeralcea lobata,* globe mallow (oda) plant; with a mixture of water and ground roots of osa pu; or with the fruit of the Yucca baccata, "mountain amole."

Swellings

Swellings of the body and limbs were reduced with the following remedies: the ground roots of "wolf stalk" (hung djo fe) mixed with water or the liquid from the boiled flower stems of the "snakeweed" were rubbed on the afflicted areas [44]. According to Robbins, Harrington, and Freire-Marreco (1916: 97), swollen glands in the neck of a child would subside in two or three days if an ear of corn was laid on a warm hearth near the fire, and the patient placed his foot on it and rubbed it to and fro.

Internal Injuries

Two methods were employed to combat internal injuries caused by falls. According to one informant [25], the patient was given corn smut mixed with cornmeal and water. "This acts as an emetic and will bring up any blood caused by the injury." Another [9] stated that blue cornmeal in water was given. "It acts as a physic and will carry out any injury."

Pain

It was believed that drinking a solution of corn pollen and water would eliminate pain [27, 62]. According to Robbins, Harrington, and Freire-Marreco (1916: 97), blue cornmeal and water would relieve palpitation and pains near the heart or diaphragm. The same authors stated that pain in the shins caused by cold weather was relieved by rubbing that portion of the body with warm ashes (p. 29).

Headache

Parts of a variety of plants were applied to cure headaches. These included the green leaves of *Monarda menthaefolia,* horsemint [44]; the ground leaves of *Kallstroemia brachystylis,* "star stalk" [44, 45]; watermelon leaves [23, 27]; and the ground, dried roots of the "blue root," mixed with water [23]. All were rubbed on the forehead and sides of the head; the last plant was considered most effective [23, 44].

The ground, dried leaves of horsemint were drunk as well as rubbed on the patient [44]. According to Robbins, Harrington, and Freire-Marreco (1916: 71), mallow ground to a paste with water and sugar added was applied over the temporal artery and on the forehead between the eyebrows. For headaches resulting from toothache, the head was rubbed with a lather made from *Gilia longiflora,* white gilia, and water. According to Robbins, Harrington, and Freire-Marreco (1916: 61, 71), neuralgic headaches were relieved either by smearing the head with a greasy paste made from the seed of a plant from the Rio Verde Mountains in Arizona, "vegetable head" (pʹekwaʹa), or cooked and mashed beans spread over the face.

Toothache

The root of *Achillea lanulosa,* yarrow, or "sneezeweed," was ground and held next to the tooth to draw out the soreness [23], or the liquid from a crushed white grub, "wood worm" (sung po be) was used [45]. Cavities were filled with juniper pitch [45] (Robbins, Harrington, and Freire-Marreco 1916: 40) or lichen. The latter was said to stop pain generally (p. 68).

Earache

The plant osa was used to cure earache. A small portion of the stalk or a shoot was cut and ground to powder. A cornhusk cigarette was made with the powder, and smoke was blown into the ear. Before the smoke escaped, the opening of the ear was plugged with a corn kernel, formerly wrapped in cotton, more recently, in wool. If the ear was still sore on the following day, the treatment was repeated; if not, the plug was removed. When there was a discharge, osa and another plant were ground to powder and poured into the ear [25]. A similar treatment for discharges of the ear was described by Robbins, Harrington, and Freire-Marreco (1916: 67). In this treatment, the spores of the fungus *Geaster* sp., earthstar, "earth swelling" (nam pu), were blown into the ear through a tube of corn husk or paper.

Fever

Fevers were broken by an internal and external application of *Monarda menthaefolia,* horsemint. Dried ground leaves were drunk in water, and green leaves were rubbed on various parts of the body. A similar treatment was described by Robbins, Harrington, and Freire-Marreco (1916: 58). *Achillea lanulosa,* yarrow, or "sneezeweed," was used in somewhat the same way. Dried roots were ground, mixed with a small amount of water, and rubbed on the chest; this powder was also boiled and given to the patient to drink.

Coma

"If a person was in a dazed condition from illness," he was given ground root bark of the *Kallstroemia brachystylis,* "star stalk" to drink.

Measles

Ashes were dusted over the eruptions with a cloth, to soothe the irritation of those who had measles (Robbins, Harrington, and Freire-Marreco 1916: 29).

Sprains

The principal method of treating sprains was by massage; masseurs were called and treated the patient [21, 25, 29]. A more complicated cure was also described [25]: a man was selected to treat the patient. This person went to the mountains early in the morning and gathered leaves from the "oak leaf" (kwa ka, a small plant about a foot high); these were ground to powder. The curer visited the patient at the same time each day for twelve days, and rubbed this preparation on the afflicted area. The same remedy was applied to gunshot wounds. The "oak leaf" was said to draw out the shot [25].

Dislocations and Fractures

In recent years, dislocations have been attended by outside doctors [9, 50]; formerly they were cared for by villagers. Some men had sufficient knowledge of anatomy to replace dislocations and set fractures. Casts were applied to dislocations after massage, or to fractures as soon as the break was set. Casts were made from a mixture of *Nuttallia multiflora, Taraxacum taraxacum* (common dandelion), and yeast (see also Robbins,

Harrington, and Freire-Marreco 1916: 57, 61). Casts were removed when the practitioner considered the injury healed [25, 45].

Gunshot Wounds

See Sprains.

Baldness

Baldness was prevented by washing the hair in a boiled solution of *Phoradendron juniperinum,* mistletoe (hun se pere) [25]. According to Robbins, Harrington, and Freire-Marreco (1916: 103), cottonseed was crushed, chewed, and applied to a child's head to prevent baldness.

OTHER SOCIETIES

Hunt Society

While some aboriginal functions of the Hunt Society were still performed by temporary appointees and members of other ceremonial groups at Santa Clara Pueblo, the society itself had lapsed. When it became inactive was not determined, but presumably this occurred about the turn of the last century. The uncle of one of the informants [69], who was fifty-six in 1940, was said to have been the last member. The reasons for its obsolescence are obscure; one contributing factor, however, was the gradually diminishing importance of wild game as a factor in subsistence, and the attendant increase in communal hunting and fishing.

The organization of the society was similar to that of other societies. The leader was the P'ing xarg zho, "mountain lion man." His two assistants were known as the right arm and left arm [21, 36, 45, 50]. The group was known as the "fathers of all game" [45].

Members were acquired through dedication at birth or by vows during illness. The neophyte underwent a probationary period of a year, during which period he learned the esoteric duties of the society. His training was surrounded with restrictions: the candidate could not leave the pueblo, i.e., he had to be home every night; also he was not allowed to cut his hair; and he had to wear buckskin clothing [25, 45].

Preliminary stages of Hunt Society initiations were held either at Santa Clara Pueblo or at some other village, depending upon the local strength of the society at the time. If membership was small, the group journeyed to another village and solicited its cooperation. Details of the rites were lacking. Part of the initiation included visits to sacred springs and a considerable number of shrines. "You need a large group to visit the number of shrines involved."

The terminal portion of the initiation took place at Santa Clara Pueblo, in conjunction with an induction into the Women's Scalp Society. The principal female impersonator and dancer in the P'u xwe^{n}re^n was the Hunt Society initiate (see Women's Scalp Society). Inferentially, curing was part of the initiation procedure.

Under aboriginal conditions, the society functioned in a variety of cooperative capacities. They went into retreat each month, and also at the equinoctial and solstice periods; at these times they "worked" for the general health and well-being of the pueblo, but were particularly charged with the responsibility for repairing shrines and keeping them in good order, especially those associated with the increase of wild game. Much of their retreat period appears to have been spent in the mountains of these sacred locations.

Jeançon (1904–30) stated:

Hunting shrines are often found in remote places in the mountains. Such a shrine was visited by the writer in 1904 in a canyon between Frijoles and Colorado canyons. It consisted of a sort of bower of small poles, the sides and top thatched with boughs of cottonwood with the eastern face open to the canyon. All around the three walls were miniature bows and arrows, brass cartridges, miniature lances and one or two small animal fetishes carved from stone. All of the objects were decorated with gaily colored feathers from birds and some of them had one or more finely chipped arrowheads tied to them with cotton string. There were traces of sacred meal on the dirt of the floor but seemingly no one had visited the shrine recently. Our guide, Juan Gonzales of San Ildefonso, told us it was a Cochiti hunting shrine as this part of mountains was in their traditional grounds. Since the decline of the communal hunts at Santa Clara there are almost no hunting shrines there anymore, and what there are consist of simple circles of stones that are only dressed when an individual or several persons go hunting in the mountains.

The Hunt Society organized, directed, and was in overall charge of all ritual hunts, such as the rabbit hunt which preceded a kachina dance in the hills. "The head instructed and admonished the village before the hunt" [29]. According to other informants [23, 50, 52], the society was also in charge of all communal hunts and fishing ventures. However, this applied only in a spiritual sense to buffalo and antelope hunting, which were supervised by the outside chief (war captain) or a person delegated by him. This was consistent with the pattern of authority, since this dignitary held jurisdiction over activities at a distance from the village; furthermore, the continuing religious responsibilities of the Hunt Society head precluded his extended absence from the pueblo, which these two hunting ventures entailed.

Individuals and small groups always made contact with the society before departure on a hunting trip. A gift of cornmeal and feathers was presented to the head of the society, requesting assistance. The leader or other society members "worked" and deposited prayer plumes and meal at various shrines to insure the success of the venture [31, 45].

It was the obligation and privilege of the society to conduct and perform all animal dances, ko share [43, 45, 50]. When the moiety hierarchy selected one of these ceremonies, a gift of cornmeal was taken to the leader of the Hunt Society, and a request for "a dance of wild game" was made. The leader granted permission for the dance and informed the moiety membership that they were obligated to perform.

According to one informant [18], the P'íng xang *zho* was delegated the duty of whipping the kachinas prior to a performance. "When the evergreens and yucca were brought by the kachinas, the P'íng xang *zho* whipped each performer once with the yucca. Then the yucca and evergreens were distributed to the performers." Hunt society members did not play the parts of djen sendo during a kachina ceremonial [31].

As indicated earlier, the Hunt Society has become extinct. With its lapse, many of its ritual and other functions likewise disappeared; others, however, were retained and carried out by other religious or even secular individuals, usually on a temporary, appointive basis.

Discontinued functions include rites performed at the monthly, solstice, and equinoctial "work" periods, some of the duties connected with the success of individual and small hunting parties, and much, if not all, of the preliminary ceremonialism associated with the Hunt Society's appearance in ritual and communal hunts, the P'u xwe͏ⁿre͏ⁿ, and animal dances. Retained were their essentially practical services: the direction of communal and ritual hunts, and performance in the animal and P'u xwe͏ⁿre͏ⁿ dances. The latter represented, as in the case of the Clown and Bear societies, a reintegration; a shift was made, and the essential cooperative duties of the society were distributed. A balance was thus maintained, and the functions of the Women's Scalp Society and moiety ceremonialism continued unimpaired.

To the war captain and his assistants was delegated responsibility for the direction of communal hunting and fishing. A group of men would request the war captain's assistance, or ask him to appoint a leader for a specific hunt [40]. Ritual hunts were directed by a person appointed by the hierarchy of the moiety responsible for the ceremony. There is no indication that in recent times this role was other than temporary.

Performance in animal dances was complicated by village and moiety factionalism. When the animal dance was given by the Winter Moiety, performers were chosen from the membership of the Oyike, or Winter Society. This represented the conservative element within the moiety, led by the former right arm, (as of 1948) the nominal but unofficial Winter cacique. This person "owned' (stored) the masks (headdresses) and designated those who were to dance [15, 21, 31, 50]. Summer Moiety animal dancers were selected by the cacique from the membership of the Bear societies. One informant [73] commented that in recent years the same people have played the same roles. There is some evidence that the animal dances by the Summer Moiety were a fairly recent innovation, and that they were formerly considered property of the Winter Moiety [15, 21, 50].

The dancer and female impersonator in the P'u xwe͏ⁿre͏ⁿ, as indicated in the description of that dance, was no longer a Hunt Society initiate, but a person selected by members of the Women's Scalp Society.

At least some of the ritual duties connected with success in hunting have been absorbed by the caciques. Orthodox hunters went to them prior to a hunt, and they prepared "bundles" of feathers and deer fat, which insured good luck [9, 69].

War Society

The men's War Society (C'e o?ke) lapsed many years ago. According to one informant [50], the last member was the grandfather of the former Summer cacique who died in 1952. There is considerable evidence, however, that rites associated with this organization once formed an important adjunct to the total ceremonial complex at Santa Clara Pueblo. In spite of the obsolescence of warfare, the attendant extinction of the War Society, and the current waning of the Women's Scalp Society, many scraps of esoteric behavior associated with the war complex were still retained, and some public ritual was still extant, in attenuated or altered form.

Several informants [4, 15, 27, 35, 40] agreed that the society had been composed of those who had taken scalps. Variants on this idea were contributed by others [50, 65]. According to the former, membership was acquired through being the first to reach and jump on a fallen enemy; "If a Navajo was shot, the first man to jump on him became 'C'e oʔke.' This would not necessarily be the man who had killed or wounded the enemy." The other [65] stated that touching a Navajo's bow and arrow was forbidden, and that if a person violated this tabu he was obligated to join the society. Presumably all three methods of affiliation were in vogue.

Little was known of the internal organization of the society; presumably it followed the standard Santa Clara societal pattern. There was a head and probably a right and left arm. The duties of the head were primarily religious in nature, and he did not lead war parties. This was an obligation of the "outside chief," who, depending upon circumstances, might or might not be a member of the society [29, 44, 50].

Only fragmentary accounts of the ritual activities of the society were available. However, it was known that they conducted ceremonies prior to the departure of warriors on raids, engaged in rites upon the return of a war party, which involved a victory celebration and purification, and took part in the initiations of their own members as well as in those of the Hunt Society and the Women's Scalp Society.

Some of the rites held prior to the departure of a war party still existed in vestigial form as a part of the Relay Race, and have been described in that discussion. This was the "man song" (serg ha?), which opened and closed the race. From four days to two weeks before leaving, warriors formerly gathered each night, and under the direction of the War Society, raced and performed the "man song" each evening. On these occasions, the scalps were carried on a short pole, or the pole might be placed in the middle of the plaza and the "man song" performed around it.

Song themes which accompanied the rite normally dealt with victory. Spinden (1933: 99, 123) has recorded one of these:

> Next after comes Coyote, Stretched-
> Out-in-Dew,
> Next after braves of yesterday or the
> day before!

To Blue Earth town of the Navahos
we go
And arriving we shall kill. So that
is why
Coyote, Stretched-Out-in-Dew, sits
straight and ready.
Wi-ya-he, a-ude-a-a. The next scalp!

Navaho youths! your fault alone it is
That now you die fallen along your
house.
Your fault alone it is that now you die
Fallen along your house with earth-
streaked thighs,
That now your mouths are stopped
and streaked with earth.
Ho-o-wi-na, a-ye-a-a. The next
scalp!

Sometimes, however, an element of self-commiseration was present, as exhibited in the following, attributed by Spinden (1933: 78, 116) to the Tewa in general:

> So we have bad luck
> For we are men,
> You have good luck now
> For you are women!
> To Navaho towns we go
> Ready for war, Goodbye!

According to informants [4, 15, 22, 44], the "man song" held both prior and subsequent to a raid obviated the necessity of practice or physical training. It was believed that by participating the men received the power to kill, and victory was assured; it was considered a ceremony of spiritual conditioning.

Another series of rituals was held upon the return of a war party. These involved several distinct actions. The initial performance was a victory celebration honoring the warriors. The returning party, escorted by the welcoming group, was met in the pueblo by the head of the Women's Scalp Society, who expressed the pueblo's enmity for the defeated by publicly chewing and stamping upon the scalps. Inferentially, this person took charge of the trophies, which were then suspended from a pole in the order in which they had been acquired. According to one informant [40], all scalps previously taken were added to the new ones; according to others [35, 62], only the fresh ones were used. Recognition by the War Society (C'e o?ke), in the form of a special name, was accorded the man who had taken the first scalp.

Inconsistencies in informants' accounts render the next actions problematical. According to one [15], the pole was erected in the center of the pueblo and a dance consuming the remainder of the day was held around this symbol of victory. Both men and women participated. The men discharged their bows and guns at the scalps, and both sexes shouted insults and boasts expressing such thoughts as, "We can do as well as any people in obtaining scalps," or "We have power to kill the enemy." According to other accounts [4, 14], once the scalps were hung, the formal "man song" dance was begun. In this the pole was carried, and the participants were limited to members of the War Society and the Women's Scalp Society. It is probable that both activities occurred: a shorter period of informal exultation, followed by the formalized serg ha?, "man song."

When these events were terminated, all members of the war party began a period of four days of ritual purification. What these rites entailed was unknown; presumably, the novices were instructed in the duties of the society. During this time they remained continent, and their food was limited to various preparations made from corn.

When this period was concluded, the final ceremony, that of initiation, took place. This was a public performance, the P'u xwe^n re^n, which included initiations into the Women's Scalp Society and the Hunt Society, as well as into the War Society. It is described under the Women's Scalp Society, which is discussed next.

Nothing could be learned of the ritual functions of the society, aside from those associated with warfare. It can only be inferred that they followed the same pattern as those for other societies. Undoubtedly they "worked" for the success and protection of warriors while they were in the field. However, this responsibility was and continues to be shared by other groups. During World War II, the Bear societies were particularly active in this capacity. They "treated" the men before their departure to the services and gave them amulets (k'a je) to ward off danger [22, 31, 55].

Women's Scalp Society

The Women's Scalp Society (Punuha), while not possessing its earlier vitality, still functioned at Santa Clara Pueblo. It was closely associated in former times with the Hunt Society and the War Society, and it was looked upon as a female adjunct of the War Society. After those organizations lapsed, its overall functions have been curtailed. Its recent activities paralleled those of other secret organizations. According to Parsons (1929: 136), there were four members in 1923. In the 1940s, membership consisted of three persons [9, 25, 45].

The paraphernalia of the group was stored in her portion of the house of the head. When she died, her sister inherited the house, but since she was not a member of the society, she did nothing about the materials. At her death her daughter, who was also a nonmember, went to the council and asked that the paraphernalia be removed. "She offered them three dollars to take it away." It was stored in the home of the husband of the present head [21, 43].

Membership was achieved in a variety of ways, and cut across both moiety and political lines. Children were pledged or dedicated to the society before or at birth. When they matured, they were initiated. Adults vowed themselves to the society during illness. Some joined the group upon recovery; others associated themselves with it immediately, and their illness was treated by the society [9, 25]. "A woman would join the society through sickness. She would say to herself, 'If I get well, I will join the society.' When she recovered, she joined. Some persons entered the society while they were still ill. In this case they were treated by the society and cured" [4]. "It was known that the scalps had curative power" [23].

The pledging ceremony incorporated many of the elements of a curing or purificatory rite. Pledges were visited at their homes by members of the society, and were bathed with medicinal herbs and given an infusion of herbs to drink [45]. At this time the novices were informed when they would be initiated. Initiations were held during the full moon of January, according to one informant [45]; about every fifteen years, in November, according to Parsons (1929: 212). Probably both statements are correct. The apparent inconsistency is resolved if the evidence presented for the P'u xwe^{n}re^n is accepted, i.e., that Women's Scalp Society members were initiated with and at the same time as War or Hunt Society members. This would allow for considerable latitude in the time when the ceremony might be held.

Ordinarily a novice underwent a probationary training period of a year. During this time the candidate might not leave the pueblo, i.e., had to return every night. She was to eat only aboriginal foods. She was especially warned against quarreling with relatives. Terminal initiation rites formed a part of the P'u xwe^{n}re^n.

The direction of society activities was in the hands of the leader, the Punuha qui djo, "old woman," or "old woman uncared for" [9].

The duties of the Women's Scalp Society corresponded closely to those of parallel groups. They went into retreat each month, and under the direction of their leader, the Punuha qui djo, "worked" for the general welfare of the pueblo [31, 45]. They also "worked" for a day and a night at the solstice periods, and probably also at the equinoxes [69].

Little on activities during retreats was available. Members "worked" alone at the home of their leader [55]. They made prayer plumes, which they deposited at shrines, and they worked with the scalps and masks [25, 50, 55]. Retreats were guarded by the war captains. "When they are working, they yell like crows or coyotes. At times they burst out laughing. They sing and chant in the dark" [50].

Their principal responsibility was the custodianship of the scalps, which were stored in jars on rooftops. Part of their ritual duties consisted of "feeding" them crusts of blue cornmeal mush, sprinkling them with cornmeal, singing to them, and depositing prayer plumes in the jars [25, 27, 35, 44, 50, 55].

One of their songs was recorded by Spinden (1933: 108):

> Down yonder at their village
> The Navaho youths lie scalped
> The young men of Santa Clara
> Those blue-bird skins stripped off.

Their proper treatment was considered essential, since they were believed to be intimately associated with the general welfare of the village. Scalps had "power," the supernatural power of the enemy which had been transferred to the pueblo, and subsequently expressed itself in terms of prosperity, health, and good fortune. "Scalps are not dangerous. Everyone wants to see them. They give power to the pueblo. If you obtain scalps, villagers from other pueblos will visit you. You do the same if they get scalps. I should not say this, but it would be a good thing if the soldiers brought scalps back today [World War II, WWH]" [23].

The curing aspects of the Women's Scalp Society were mentioned in the discussion of pledging; detailed information on the rites was not obtained.

Cooperation with other ritual groups has been limited, at least in recent years. Formerly, this group was closely associated with the War Society and Hunt Society. As indicated earlier, they greeted returning war parties and conducted victory rites and ceremonies. Their initiations formed part of those of the War Society and/or Hunt Society. Their only contemporary cooperative effort, however, was the assistance they provided during the "water immersion" (po ku) of the Summer Moiety. It was not learned whether they also cooperated at Winter Moiety initiations.

The climax of the initiation rites of the Women's Scalp Society was the enactment of a P'u xwe^{n}re^n. Formerly, this dance also served as the terminal ceremony for the induction of members into the War and Hunt societies, as noted.

One such ceremony took place in November 1923. Parsons's account (1929: 212), derived from her informants, is as follows:

> *P'u xwere.* This is a two-day initiation war dance which is performed

nowadays only at Santa Clara, where it is in charge of the women *tse'oke.* The four men who dance are appointed by the *tse'oke kwiyo,* war society old woman. Women dress as men, and men as women, some of them making up as pregnant women, and these sing, "Some of those boys made me pregnant." The men in masquerade do women's work, fetching water, baking bread outdoors in the ovens on street or roof, and carrying dinner to the dancers. [The war dances of the Cheyenne were in charge of the "half women–half men." ECP] The women masqueraders with cloths in their hands to clean the ovens go from door to door and sing, "I am scared, let's run away." People give them bread. "You are lazy. You don't bring us wood, you don't hunt deer, you bring nothing to us," the men say to the women. In the dance, women sing for the men. They sing *kapohenu* and refer to earrings of cotton, full of vermin from the hair. Other women carry baskets of bread on their head, and throw it, saying, "My *pare* (elder brother or sister) is dancing and I throw this bread." As a matter of fact they throw things, too, "corn, dishes, everything." According to the Santa Clara tale of how puwere is danced as a Scalp dance four days after the return of the warrior women bringing scalps. The women send word to their parents to prepare food in abundance to throw. [The implicit idea is or was to offer food to the scalp. ECP]

Subsequently, the rite was held in 1925 or 1926, and in 1928. According to informants [4, 25, 40, 50], recent performances have represented degenerated versions, "less serious than they formerly were."

Before the disappearance of the War and Hunt societies, one or both of these groups cooperated and assured the full participation of the whole pueblo. Recently, participants have been more or less dragooned into service, and the total number has decreased. The role of principal female impersonator, and the person who danced opposite the Scalp Society initiate, was played by either a War or Hunt society

initiate. Recently, this part has been played by relatives of Scalp Society members [25, 35]. Finally, the pole carrying the suspended scalps was no longer used in the ceremony [35, 50, 69].

Preparations for the modern versions of the P'u xwe^{n}re^n were begun about a month prior to the actual performance. Under the leadership of the Scalp Society head, members and other women of the pueblo began practicing songs; practice was held at the home of the head. About two weeks before the ceremony, the female impersonators ("female partners," nung) were chosen. Men were loath to play these female roles, and avoided being asked, if possible. In order to circumvent this reluctance, society members made their requests ahead of any public announcement, before the men suspected that such a rite was to be held. If invited, a man could not refuse to perform, and requests were made under circumstances which prevented the party from escaping, if he suspected the intent, or in a public gathering, where he would be too embarrassed to refuse [50].

Four days before the dance, the society went into retreat [50, 69]. Formerly, the War and Hunt societies also went into retreat. During this period all three groups made prayer plumes, and each night deposited them at shrines. Scalp Society members sang to the scalps and fed them crusts of blue cornmeal mush. Society members who would be principals practiced their parts, particularly those who played the roles of male and female impersonators [25, 69].

While the intent of the ritual was serious, the exchange of male and female roles by members of the Scalp, War, and Hunt societies, and more recently by selected male relatives of Scalp Society members, was the occasion for considerable hilarity and amusement for the whole village. Each sex, in enacting the part of the other, exaggerated and accentuated particular aspects of role and behavior for purposes of comedy. Much of the humor was broadly sexual in nature. This is also apparent in Parsons's account (1929: 212), and implicit in Kellogg's description of a similar performance given at San Ildefonso Pueblo in May, 1932 (1932: 1–4). Any doubt of the effectiveness of this performance was dispelled by watching the obvious enjoyment of informants and interpreters as the situations were described.

Each morning of the first three days, Women's Scalp Society members, dressed as and impersonating men, harnessed horses and went to the mountains for wood. The wood had previously been cut and conveniently placed by men. When the wagons were loaded, the women returned to the village. Their arrival was a noisy one; they whistled, sang, and shouted. "Many wore straw hats and were smoking. They yelled at the horses, whipped them, and called them by name" [9, 18]. Each turned the wood over to a female impersonator.

On one day turkeys were reported to be in the hills. The head of the Hunt Society formally made this announcement, ordering all men, i.e., women, to go to the mountains and bring game to serve the initiates [25]. The male impersonators immediately left on foot and horseback, carrying bows and arrows and guns. They killed the birds, which had been staked out for them. "Sometimes domestic turkeys were set free" [25, 29]. When they returned carrying the game, the women of the pueblo rushed up to them after the manner of greeting returning hunters [9].

In the meantime, their male counterparts in women's costumes pursued female occupations. The head of the Hunt Society ordered them to grind corn and bake bread for the initiates [25]. While they worked, women of the village sang corn grinding songs. The tempo of the songs was increased, in order that the men would work harder and faster. Older men dressed as women directed the work. "One of these had a beard! One of the corn grinders wore a huge sun bonnet and high-topped, white shoes" [9].

Others of the female impersonators baked bread in the outside ovens. "One wore a shawl, and as he took the bread from the oven, he held the ends of the shawl in his teeth, just as women do when they are in a hurry. Some wore short skirts, and when they leaned over they exposed their buttocks" [9, 50].

On the evening of the third day an "Apache dance" (save share) was held. This was formerly performed by members of the Women's Scalp Society and the War Society. It took place on the race course, and was similar to one of the initial stages of the present-day relay race. Two groups faced each other, with male impersonators in front, females in back. The dance began in the east, and the group moved westward. It terminated when the west end of the course was reached.

On the fourth day, the P'u xwe^{n}re^n proper was held. Four principal female impersonators were dressed in mantas; three of the four wore belts. Each had a bundle of grass tied to the back of his hair, feathers in his hair, and a gray-fox skin on his left arm.

The dancer without the belt, formerly the Hunt Society or War Society initiate, went to the headquarters of the Women's Scalp Society. On arrival he was given a belt, after which he conducted the four principal male impersonators of the society to the plaza where the dance was held. These four women were dressed in male, Plains-type costumes, made of buckskin, and carried bows and arrows. One of the four was the initiate. The remainder of the male impersonators followed to the dance plaza. They were also dressed in Plains-type costumes of either buckskin or flannel.

The first stage of the dance was known as oho share. The Women's Scalp Society initiate, formerly the initiate of the Hunt Society or War Society, and the male impersonators took part in this. The male impersonators formed a group, and the initiate danced in and out through this body. Music was furnished by the chorus of female impersonators.

The second part of the dance was the P'u xwe^{n}re^n. The participants arranged themselves in the following manner:

X Drummer	XXXX Relatives XXXX of the XXXX dancers
XXXXXX	Male impersonators kneeling
X	Female impersonator—initiate of the War or Hunt Society

```
          X Masked Scalp Society
            initiate
X X X X X X Male impersonators
            kneeling
X X X X X X Female
            impersonators
X X X X X X Relatives of the
            dancers
```

Groups composed of relatives of the dancers were located beside the drummer, behind the line of female impersonators. They and the female impersonators carried clothing, baskets of food, and other gifts, which were tossed to the dancers as the ritual began. "Everyone rushes for them, food, clothing, and toys. My grandmother had a whole shawl full. I had to have my uncle carry them" [72]. The male impersonators knelt as before a metate, and during the course of the dance moved their arms backward and forward as if grinding corn. The Women's Scalp Society initiate was masked. Several informants [9, 35, 50] agreed that the mask consisted of the head skin of a pig with an ear of corn inserted in the mouth. However, one [50] added that there were two other masks used by subsequent dancers; one of these was the headskin of a goat, and the other, that of a calf. In the mouth of the calf was inserted a bundle of grass.

When the dance began, men stationed on rooftops fired guns as rapidly as possible. Those individuals who carried food, clothing, or other gifts tossed them to the dancers. The principal female impersonator, the War Society or Hunt Society initiate, danced forward toward the Women's Scalp Society initiate and then back to his original position; this was repeated four times in all. On the second repetition, he was handed a knife-shaped wooden paddle by the Scalp Society initiate. This was symbolic of the knife used in scalping. He carried it on this round of the dance, returning it on the third. When the fourth number was completed, an intermission was taken. Participants returned to their respective headquarters [9, 50].

There is some evidence that, in recent years, the wooden scalping knife has been substituted for the scalp pole; there is also a possibility that it was used only by Hunt Society initiates. According to two informants [35, 43], the man who danced alone, carrying the scalps, was the one who had taken a Navajo scalp, or, if several scalps had been taken, the one who had taken the most.

The dancers made three subsequent appearances. Performances in each case were similar to the first, except that the Scalp, War, or Hunt Society initiates were replaced on each occasion by one of the three remaining female impersonators, and by one of the male impersonators carrying bow and arrows [9, 35, 55]. According to one [9], the latter might wear any one of the masks. After the fourth appearance, a feast was held in which the whole village participated. This concluded the ceremony [4, 9, 25].

Appendix A

[This Appendix contains five Santa Clara genealogies (I, II, III, IV, and V) which were compiled by Hill in the course of his field-work. Only minimal reference was made to them in his discussion; he undoubtedly planned to do more with the data contained in them. For example, there are various letters and numbers (tf, tmZ, fJA, mw, mN, tfw, mL, m!, !, fSp, fA, etc.) in the genealogical charts for which no explanation has been found. They have been retained rather than deleted.

In spite of their incomplete nature and lack of context, the genealogies have been included in this volume for the additional details they provide concerning mid-twentieth century Santa Clara Pueblo. CHL]

GENEALOGY I

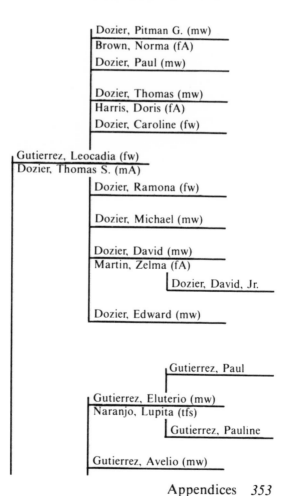

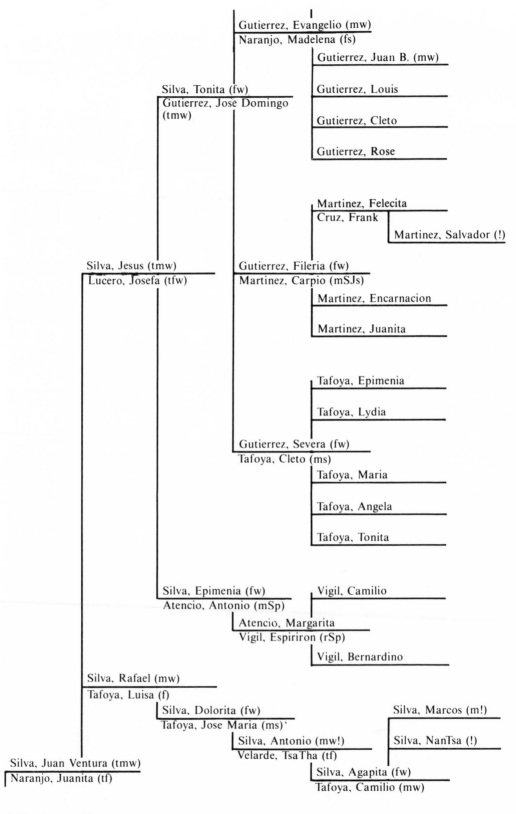

Gutierrez, Evangelio (mw)
Naranjo, Madelena (fs)

Gutierrez, Juan B. (mw)

Gutierrez, Louis

Silva, Tonita (fw)
Gutierrez, José Domingo
(tmw)

Gutierrez, Cleto

Gutierrez, Rose

Martinez, Felecita
Cruz, Frank

Martinez, Salvador (!)

Silva, Jesus (tmw)
Lucero, Josefa (tfw)

Gutierrez, Fileria (fw)
Martinez, Carpio (mSJs)

Martinez, Encarnacion

Martinez, Juanita

Tafoya, Epimenia

Tafoya, Lydia

Gutierrez, Severa (fw)
Tafoya, Cleto (ms)

Tafoya, Maria

Tafoya, Angela

Tafoya, Tonita

Silva, Epimenia (fw)
Atencio, Antonio (mSp)

Vigil, Camilio

Atencio, Margarita
Vigil, Espiriron (rSp)

Vigil, Bernardino

Silva, Rafael (mw)
Tafoya, Luisa (f)

Silva, Dolorita (fw)
Tafoya, Jose Maria (ms)`

Silva, Marcos (m!)

Silva, Antonio (mw!)
Velarde, TsaTha (tf)

Silva, NanTsa (!)

Silva, Juan Ventura (tmw)
Naranjo, Juanita (tf)

Silva, Agapita (fw)
Tafoya, Camilio (mw)

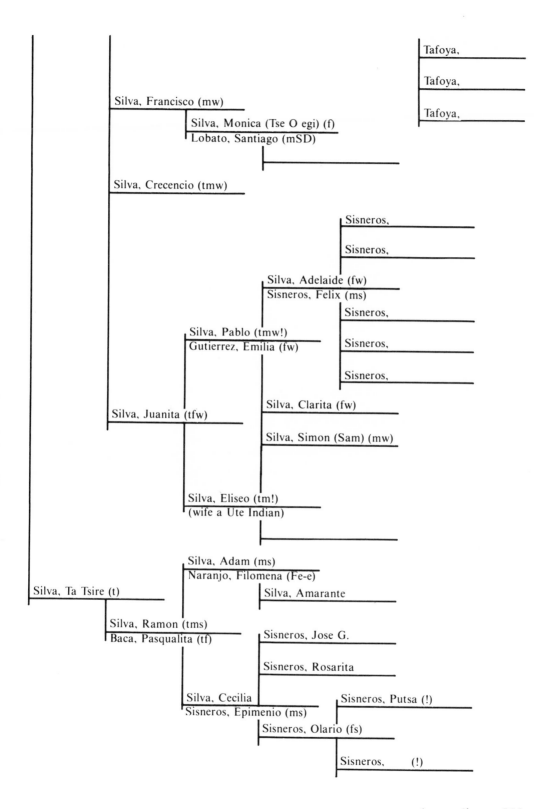

Silva, Francisco (mw)
Silva, Monica (Tse O egi) (f)
Lobato, Santiago (mSD)

Tafoya,
Tafoya,
Tafoya,

Silva, Crecencio (tmw)

Silva, Adelaide (fw)
Sisneros, Felix (ms)

Sisneros,
Sisneros,

Sisneros,

Sisneros,

Sisneros,

Silva, Pablo (tmw!)
Gutierrez, Emilia (fw)

Silva, Clarita (fw)

Silva, Simon (Sam) (mw)

Silva, Juanita (tfw)

Silva, Eliseo (tm!)
(wife a Ute Indian)

Silva, Adam (ms)
Naranjo, Filomena (Fe-e)

Silva, Amarante

Silva, Ta Tsire (t)

Silva, Ramon (tms)
Baca, Pasqualita (tf)

Sisneros, Jose G.

Sisneros, Rosarita

Silva, Cecilia
Sisneros, Epimenio (ms)

Sisneros, Putsa (!)

Sisneros, Olario (fs)

Sisneros,   (!)

GENEALOGY II

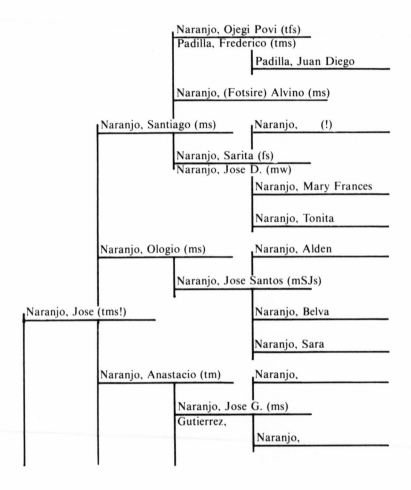

Naranjo, Ojegi Povi (tfs)
Padilla, Frederico (tms)
Padilla, Juan Diego

Naranjo, (Fotsire) Alvino (ms)

Naranjo, Santiago (ms)
Naranjo,   (!)

Naranjo, Sarita (fs)
Naranjo, Jose D. (mw)

Naranjo, Mary Frances

Naranjo, Tonita

Naranjo, Ologio (ms)
Naranjo, Alden

Naranjo, Jose Santos (mSJs)

Naranjo, Jose (tms!)
Naranjo, Belva

Naranjo, Sara

Naranjo, Anastacio (tm)
Naranjo,

Naranjo, Jose G. (ms)
Gutierrez,

Naranjo,

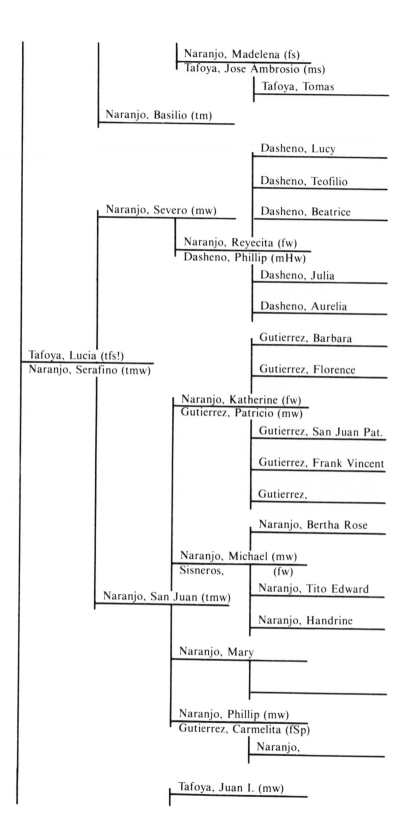

Naranjo, Madelena (fs)
Tafoya, Jose Ambrosio (ms)
Tafoya, Tomas

Naranjo, Basilio (tm)

Dasheno, Lucy

Dasheno, Teofilio

Naranjo, Severo (mw)   Dasheno, Beatrice

Naranjo, Reyecita (fw)
Dasheno, Phillip (mHw)
Dasheno, Julia

Dasheno, Aurelia

Gutierrez, Barbara

Gutierrez, Florence

Tafoya, Lucia (tfs!)   Naranjo, Katherine (fw)
Naranjo, Serafino (tmw)   Gutierrez, Patricio (mw)
Gutierrez, San Juan Pat.

Gutierrez, Frank Vincent

Gutierrez,

Naranjo, Bertha Rose

Naranjo, Michael (mw)
Sisneros,   (fw)
Naranjo, Tito Edward
Naranjo, San Juan (tmw)

Naranjo, Handrine

Naranjo, Mary

Naranjo, Phillip (mw)
Gutierrez, Carmelita (fSp)
Naranjo,

Tafoya, Juan I. (mw)

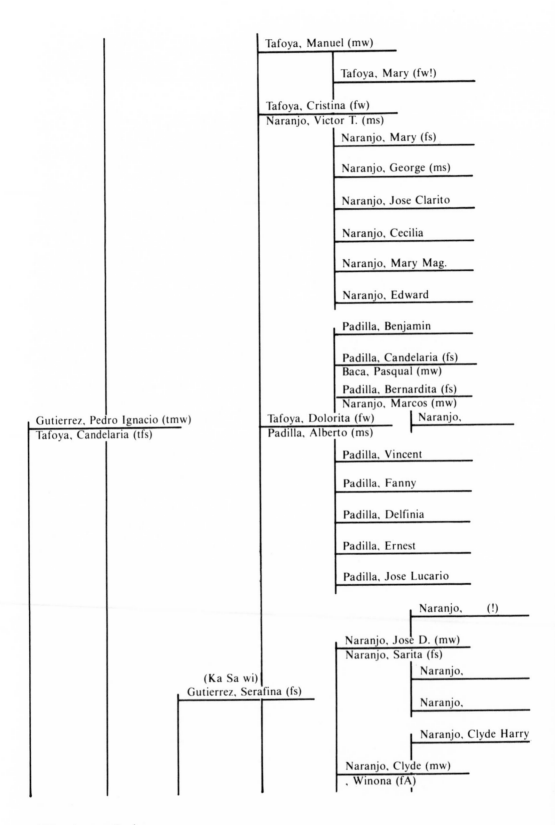

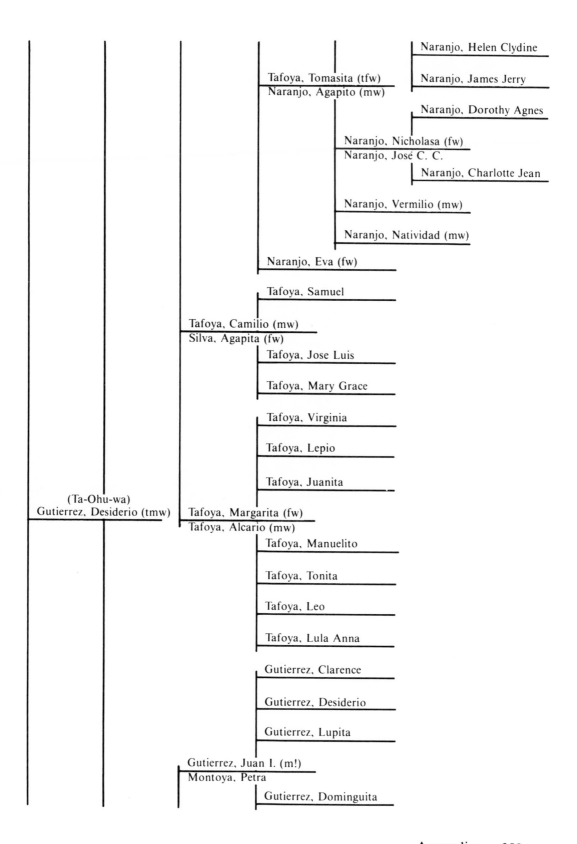

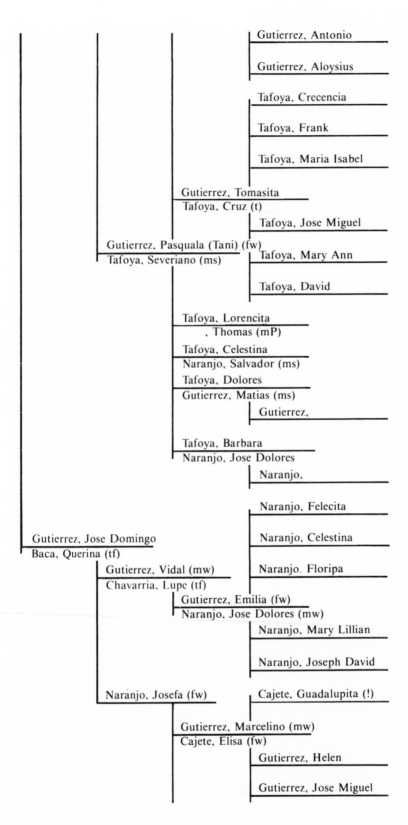

Gutierrez, Antonio

Gutierrez, Aloysius

Tafoya, Crecencia

Tafoya, Frank

Tafoya, Maria Isabel

Gutierrez, Tomasita
Tafoya, Cruz (t)

Tafoya, Jose Miguel

Gutierrez, Pasquala (Tani) (fw)
Tafoya, Severiano (ms)

Tafoya, Mary Ann

Tafoya, David

Tafoya, Lorencita
, Thomas (mP)
Tafoya, Celestina
Naranjo, Salvador (ms)
Tafoya, Dolores
Gutierrez, Matias (ms)

Gutierrez,

Tafoya, Barbara
Naranjo, Jose Dolores

Naranjo,

Naranjo, Felecita

Naranjo, Celestina

Gutierrez, Jose Domingo
Baca, Querina (tf)

Gutierrez, Vidal (mw)
Chavarria, Lupe (tf)

Naranjo. Floripa

Gutierrez, Emilia (fw)
Naranjo, Jose Dolores (mw)

Naranjo, Mary Lillian

Naranjo, Joseph David

Naranjo, Josefa (fw)

Cajete, Guadalupita (!)

Gutierrez, Marcelino (mw)
Cajete, Elisa (fw)

Gutierrez, Helen

Gutierrez, Jose Miguel

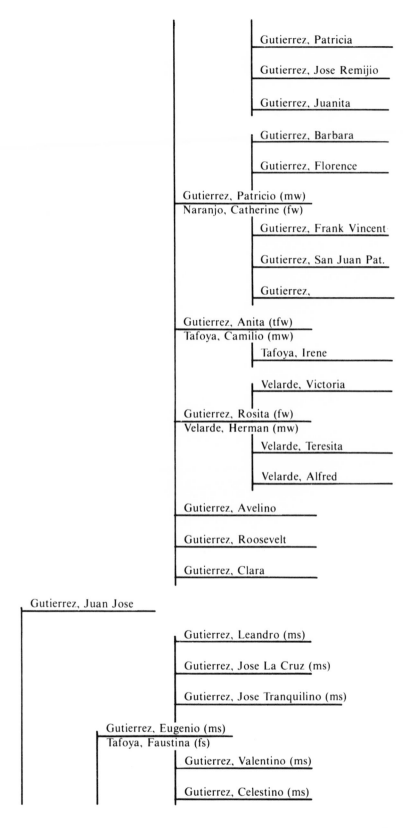

Gutierrez, Patricia

Gutierrez, Jose Remijio

Gutierrez, Juanita

Gutierrez, Barbara

Gutierrez, Florence

Gutierrez, Patricio (mw)
Naranjo, Catherine (fw)

Gutierrez, Frank Vincent

Gutierrez, San Juan Pat.

Gutierrez,

Gutierrez, Anita (tfw)
Tafoya, Camilio (mw)

Tafoya, Irene

Velarde, Victoria

Gutierrez, Rosita (fw)
Velarde, Herman (mw)

Velarde, Teresita

Velarde, Alfred

Gutierrez, Avelino

Gutierrez, Roosevelt

Gutierrez, Clara

Gutierrez, Juan Jose

Gutierrez, Leandro (ms)

Gutierrez, Jose La Cruz (ms)

Gutierrez, Jose Tranquilino (ms)

Gutierrez, Eugenio (ms)
Tafoya, Faustina (fs)

Gutierrez, Valentino (ms)

Gutierrez, Celestino (ms)

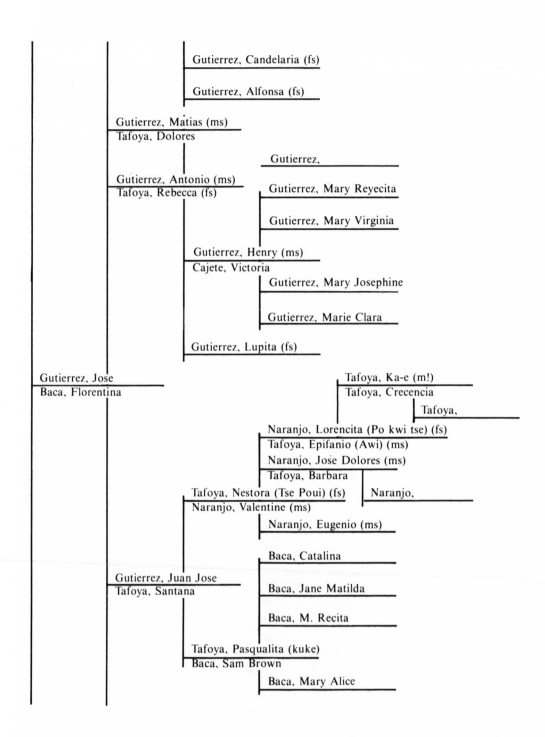

Gutierrez, Candelaria (fs)

Gutierrez, Alfonsa (fs)

Gutierrez, Matias (ms)
Tafoya, Dolores

Gutierrez,

Gutierrez, Antonio (ms)
Tafoya, Rebecca (fs)

Gutierrez, Mary Reyecita

Gutierrez, Mary Virginia

Gutierrez, Henry (ms)
Cajete, Victoria

Gutierrez, Mary Josephine

Gutierrez, Marie Clara

Gutierrez, Lupita (fs)

Gutierrez, Jose
Baca, Florentina

Tafoya, Ka-e (m!)
Tafoya, Crecencia

Tafoya,

Naranjo, Lorencita (Po kwi tse) (fs)
Tafoya, Epifanio (Awi) (ms)
Naranjo, Jose Dolores (ms)
Tafoya, Barbara

Tafoya, Nestora (Tse Poui) (fs)
Naranjo, Valentine (ms)

Naranjo,

Naranjo, Eugenio (ms)

Baca, Catalina

Gutierrez, Juan Jose
Tafoya, Santana

Baca, Jane Matilda

Baca, M. Recita

Tafoya, Pasqualita (kuke)
Baca, Sam Brown

Baca, Mary Alice

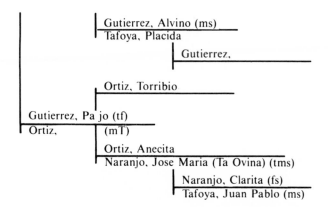

Gutierrez, Alvino (ms)
Tafoya, Placida
Gutierrez,

Ortiz, Torribio

Gutierrez, Pa jo (tf)
Ortiz,   (mT)
Ortiz, Anecita
Naranjo, Jose Maria (Ta Ovina) (tms)
Naranjo, Clarita (fs)
Tafoya, Juan Pablo (ms)

GENEALOGY III

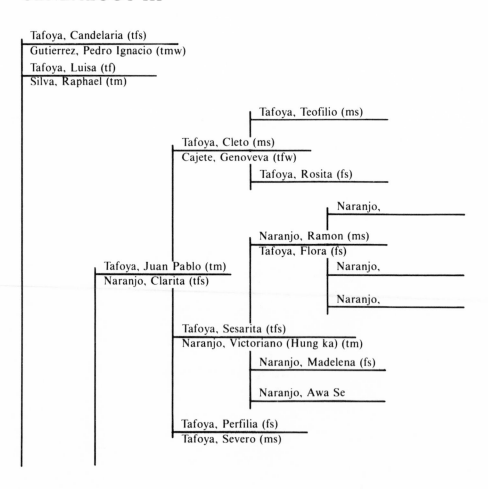

Tafoya, Candelaria (tfs)
Gutierrez, Pedro Ignacio (tmw)
Tafoya, Luisa (tf)
Silva, Raphael (tm)

Tafoya, Teofilio (ms)

Tafoya, Cleto (ms)
Cajete, Genoveva (tfw)

Tafoya, Rosita (fs)

Naranjo,

Naranjo, Ramon (ms)
Tafoya, Flora (fs)

Naranjo,

Naranjo,

Tafoya, Juan Pablo (tm)
Naranjo, Clarita (tfs)

Tafoya, Sesarita (tfs)
Naranjo, Victoriano (Hung ka) (tm)

Naranjo, Madelena (fs)

Naranjo, Awa Se

Tafoya, Perfilia (fs)
Tafoya, Severo (ms)

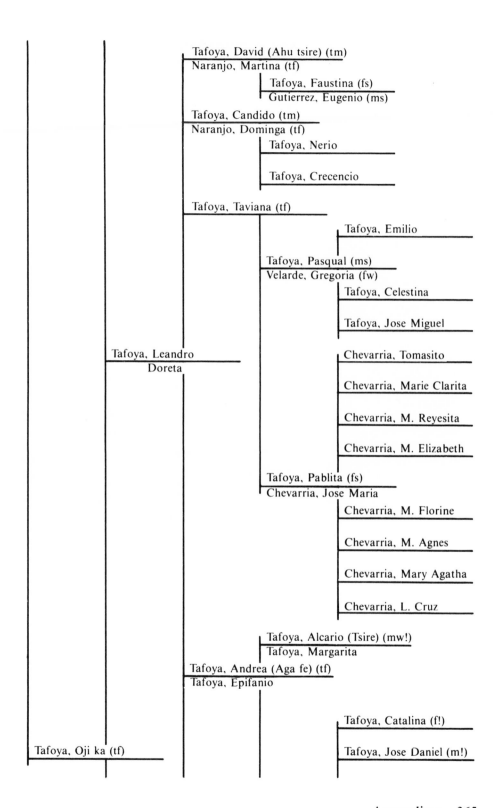

Tafoya, David (Ahu tsire) (tm)
Naranjo, Martina (tf)
Tafoya, Faustina (fs)
Gutierrez, Eugenio (ms)
Tafoya, Candido (tm)
Naranjo, Dominga (tf)
Tafoya, Nerio

Tafoya, Crecencio

Tafoya, Taviana (tf)

Tafoya, Emilio

Tafoya, Pasqual (ms)
Velarde, Gregoria (fw)
Tafoya, Celestina

Tafoya, Jose Miguel

Tafoya, Leandro
Doreta

Chevarria, Tomasito

Chevarria, Marie Clarita

Chevarria, M. Reyesita

Chevarria, M. Elizabeth

Tafoya, Pablita (fs)
Chevarria, Jose Maria
Chevarria, M. Florine

Chevarria, M. Agnes

Chevarria, Mary Agatha

Chevarria, L. Cruz

Tafoya, Alcario (Tsire) (mw!)
Tafoya, Margarita
Tafoya, Andrea (Aga fe) (tf)
Tafoya, Epifanio

Tafoya, Catalina (f!)

Tafoya, Jose Daniel (m!)

Tafoya, Oji ka (tf)

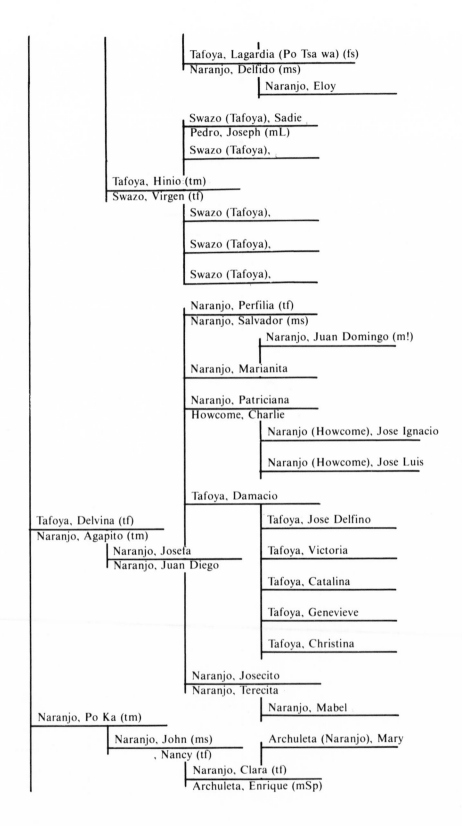

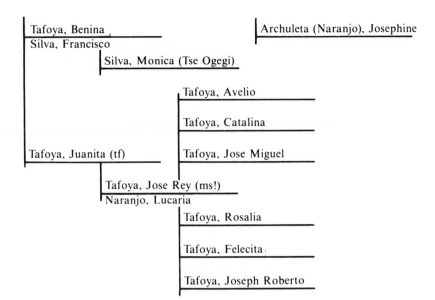

Tafoya, Benina
Silva, Francisco

Archuleta (Naranjo), Josephine

Silva, Monica (Tse Ogegi)

Tafoya, Avelio

Tafoya, Catalina

Tafoya, Juanita (tf)

Tafoya, Jose Miguel

Tafoya, Jose Rey (ms!)
Naranjo, Lucaria

Tafoya, Rosalia

Tafoya, Felecita

Tafoya, Joseph Roberto

GENEALOGY IV

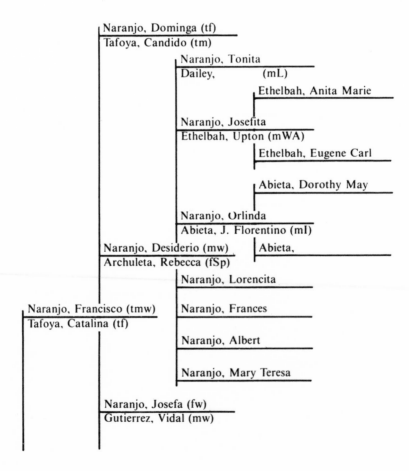

Naranjo, Dominga (tf)
Tafoya, Candido (tm)

Naranjo, Tonita
Dailey,   (mL)

Ethelbah, Anita Marie

Naranjo, Josefita
Ethelbah, Upton (mWA)

Ethelbah, Eugene Carl

Abieta, Dorothy May

Naranjo, Orlinda
Abieta, J. Florentino (mI)

Naranjo, Desiderio (mw)   Abieta,
Archuleta, Rebecca (fSp)

Naranjo, Lorencita

Naranjo, Francisco (tmw)   Naranjo, Frances
Tafoya, Catalina (tf)

Naranjo, Albert

Naranjo, Mary Teresa

Naranjo, Josefa (fw)
Gutierrez, Vidal (mw)

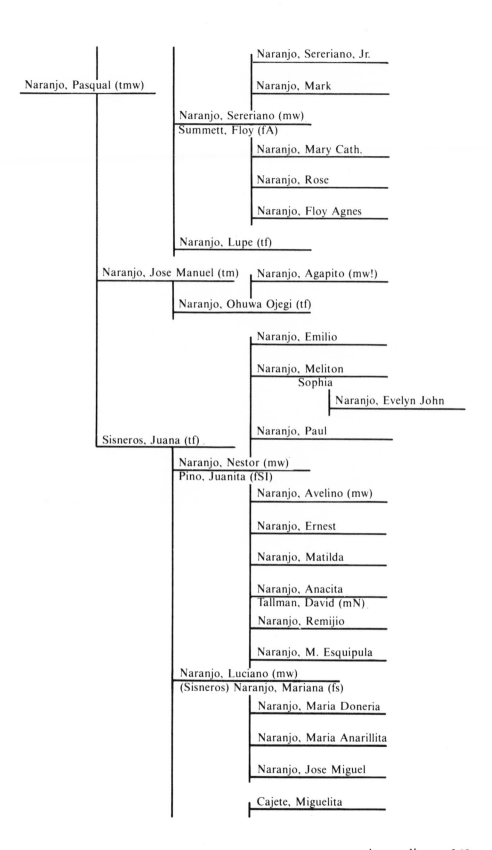

Naranjo, Pasqual (tmw)

Naranjo, Sereriano (mw)
Summett, Floy (fA)

Naranjo, Sereriano, Jr.

Naranjo, Mark

Naranjo, Mary Cath.

Naranjo, Rose

Naranjo, Floy Agnes

Naranjo, Lupe (tf)

Naranjo, Jose Manuel (tm)

Naranjo, Agapito (mw!)

Naranjo, Ohuwa Ojegi (tf)

Naranjo, Emilio

Naranjo, Meliton
Sophia

Naranjo, Evelyn John

Naranjo, Paul

Sisneros, Juana (tf)

Naranjo, Nestor (mw)
Pino, Juanita (fSI)

Naranjo, Avelino (mw)

Naranjo, Ernest

Naranjo, Matilda

Naranjo, Anacita
Tallman, David (mN)
Naranjo, Remijio

Naranjo, M. Esquipula

Naranjo, Luciano (mw)
(Sisneros) Naranjo, Mariana (fs)

Naranjo, Maria Doneria

Naranjo, Maria Anarillita

Naranjo, Jose Miguel

Cajete, Miguelita

Cajete, Clara

Cajete, Alexander

Naranjo, Maria (fw)
Cajete, Olejandro (tmw)

Cajete, Francisco (m!)

Cajete, Pauline (f!)

Naranjo, Serafino
Tafoya, Lucia

Naranjo, Alfonso

Singer, Lawrence Pat

Naranjo, Florencia
Singer, Laurence

Singer, James

Naranjo, Geronimo (mw)
Herrera, Dominga

Singer, Ruby

Naranjo, Clemente

Naranjo, Dolores (tm)
Cajete, Romana (tf)

Naranjo, Della May

Naranjo, Juan B.
Mirabal, Mary

Naranjo, Bernard

Naranjo, Jose D. D. (mw)
Baca, Senada (f½SI)

Naranjo, Marcus
Tafoya, Bernardita

Naranjo,

Naranjo, Donaciano (Ohuwa T'se) (ms)
Baca, Ago yo Sa wi

Naranjo, Dorothy Agnes

Naranjo, José C. C. (m!)
Naranjo, Nicolasa

Naranjo, Diego (tm)
Chevarria, Povi Tani (tf)

Naranjo, Charlotte Jean

Naranjo, Margarita I.

Naranjo, Averisto (Hang fe)
(Tsi T'ung) (tf)

Naranjo, Isabel

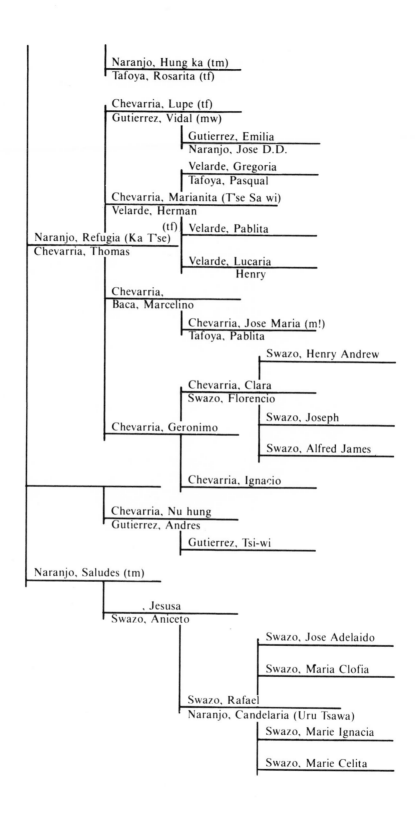

Naranjo, Hung ka (tm)
Tafoya, Rosarita (tf)

Chevarria, Lupe (tf)
Gutierrez, Vidal (mw)

Gutierrez, Emilia
Naranjo, Jose D.D.

Velarde, Gregoria
Tafoya, Pasqual

Chevarria, Marianita (T'se Sa wi)
Velarde, Herman
          (tf)   Velarde, Pablita

Naranjo, Refugia (Ka T'se)
Chevarria, Thomas   Velarde, Lucaria
                               Henry

Chevarria,
Baca, Marcelino

Chevarria, Jose Maria (m!)
Tafoya, Pablita

Swazo, Henry Andrew

Chevarria, Clara
Swazo, Florencio

Swazo, Joseph

Chevarria, Geronimo
                    Swazo, Alfred James

Chevarria, Ignacio

Chevarria, Nu hung
Gutierrez, Andres

Gutierrez, Tsi-wi

Naranjo, Saludes (tm)

, Jesusa
Swazo, Aniceto

Swazo, Jose Adelaido

Swazo, Maria Clofia

Swazo, Rafael
Naranjo, Candelaria (Uru Tsawa)

Swazo, Marie Ignacia

Swazo, Marie Celita

GENEALOGY V

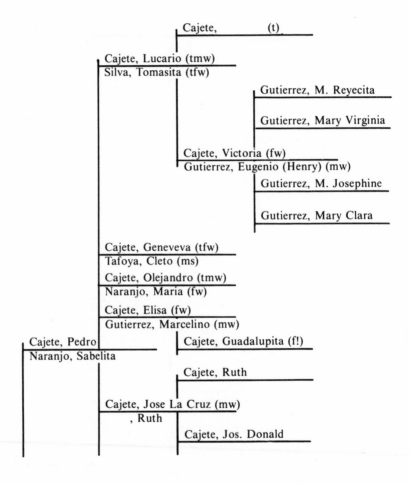

Cajete,   (t)

Cajete, Lucario (tmw)
Silva, Tomasita (tfw)

Gutierrez, M. Reyecita

Gutierrez, Mary Virginia

Cajete, Victoria (fw)
Gutierrez, Eugenio (Henry) (mw)

Gutierrez, M. Josephine

Gutierrez, Mary Clara

Cajete, Geneveva (tfw)
Tafoya, Cleto (ms)
Cajete, Olejandro (tmw)
Naranjo, Maria (fw)
Cajete, Elisa (fw)
Gutierrez, Marcelino (mw)

Cajete, Pedro
Naranjo, Sabelita

Cajete, Guadalupita (f!)

Cajete, Ruth

Cajete, Jose La Cruz (mw)
, Ruth

Cajete, Jos. Donald

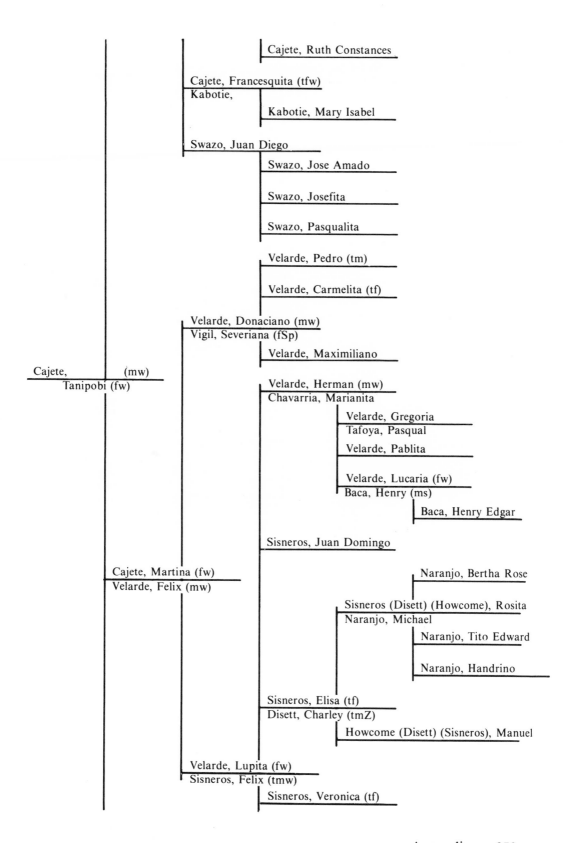

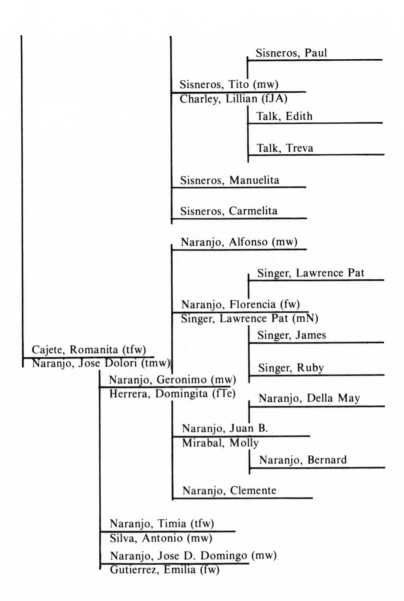

Appendix B

[A typewritten copy of the constitution for Santa Clara Pueblo, approved December 14, 1935, was found among Hill's papers associated with his fieldwork there. Since this document figured prominently in the events related in Chapter 9, the five-page statement is included here. CHL].

CONSTITUTION AND BYLAWS OF THE PUEBLO OF SANTA CLARA

We, the people of Santa Clara Pueblo, in order to establish justice, promote the common welfare and preserve the advantages of self-government, do ordain and establish this Constitution.

ARTICLE I. JURISDICTION

This Constitution shall apply within the exterior boundaries of Santa Clara Pueblo Grant and to such other lands as are now or may in the future be under the jurisdiction of the Pueblo of Santa Clara. This Constitution shall apply to and be for the benefit of all persons who are members of the Pueblo of Santa Clara.

ARTICLE II. MEMBERSHIP

Section 1. Conditions of Membership

The membership of the Santa Clara Pueblo shall consist as follows:

(a) All persons of Indian blood whose names appear on the census roll of the Santa Clara Pueblo as of November 1, 1935, provided that within one year from the adoption and approval of this Constitution corrections may be made in the said roll by the Pueblo Council with the approval of the Secretary of the Interior.

(b) All persons born of parents both of whom are members of the Santa Clara Pueblo.

(c) All children of mixed marriages between members of the Santa Clara Pueblo and non-members, provided such children have been recognized and adopted by the Council.

(4) All persons naturalized as members of the Pueblo.

Section 2. Naturalization

Indians from other Pueblos or reservations may become members of the Pueblo, with the assent of the Council, by naturalization. To do this they must (1) go before the Pueblo Council and renounce allegiance to their tribe and declare intention of becoming members of the Santa Clara Pueblo. They shall swear that from that date on they will not receive any benefits from their people, except through inheritance. (2) A year later they shall go before the Pueblo Council again, swear allegiance to the Pueblo of Santa Clara and receive membership papers; Provided, they have kept their promise from the time of their first appearance before the Pueblo Council.

ARTICLE III. ORGANIZATION OF THE PUEBLO COUNCIL

Section 1. Officers

The governing power of the Pueblo of Santa Clara shall be vested in the Pueblo Council which shall consist of the following officers:

Officers	Number
Governor	1
Lt. Governor	1
Representatives	8
Secretary	1
Treasurer	1
Interpreter	1
Sheriff	1

and such other officers as the Council may recognize or appoint.

Section 2. Election of Governor, Lt. Governor, Secretary, Treasurer, Interpreter, and Sheriff

On the first Saturday of each year an election shall be held within the Pueblo of Santa Clara, at which a Governor, Lt. Governor, Secretary, Treasurer, Interpreter, and Sheriff shall be elected by secret ballot to serve for the ensuing year.

Section 3. Who may vote.

Every member of the Pueblo of Santa Clara who is of sane mind and over 18 years of age, may vote at any election. Any member who is absent from the Pueblo on the date of any election shall have the right to vote by mail under such rules as may be prescribed by the Pueblo Council.

Section 4. Candidates

Candidates for Governor, Lt. Governor, Secretary, Interpreter, and Sheriff shall be nominated at least fifteen (15) days before the date upon which each election is held. Nominations for the first election shall be made by the recognized parties now existing within the Pueblo. Thereafter, nominations shall be made in a manner prescribed by the Council of the Pueblo.

Section 5. Representatives

Two representatives shall be appointed to the Pueblo Council upon the date of the first election, for a term of one year by each of the four recognized parties now existing within the Pueblo, and in all future elections eight representatives shall be chosen in a manner to be prescribed by the Council.

Section 6. Manner of Elections

All nominations for office and elections shall be made and held in a manner prescribed by the Council of the Pueblo.

ARTICLE IV. THE PUEBLO COUNCIL AND ITS POWERS

Section 1. Legislative Power

The legislative power shall be vested in the Pueblo Council, and the said power shall be exercised in accordance with, and not to conflict with, the Constitution or any laws of the United States of America.

The Pueblo Council shall have the following rights and powers:

1. To employ legal counsel, the choice of counsel and fixing of fees to be subject to the approval of the Secretary of the Interior.

2. To prevent the sale, disposition, lease or encumbrance of Pueblo lands, interests in lands, or other tribal assets.

3. To negotiate with the Federal, State and local govenments, and with the councils and governing authorities of other pueblos or Indian tribes.

4. To advise the Secretary of Interior with regard to all appropriation estimates or Federal projects for the benefit of the Pueblo prior to the submission of such estimates to the Bureau of the Budget and to Congress.

5. To enact ordinances, not inconsistent with the Constitution and Bylaws of the Pueblo, for the maintenance of law and order within the Pueblo and for the punishment of members and the exclusion of non-

members violating any such ordinances, for the raising of revenue and the appropriation of available funds for Pueblo purposes, for the regulation of trade, inheritance, land-holding, and private dealings in land within the Pueblo, for the guidance of the officers of the Pueblo in all their duties, and generally for the protection of the welfare of the Pueblo and for the execution of all other powers vested in the Pueblo by existing law: Provided that, any ordinance which affects persons who are not members of the Pueblo shall not take effect until it has been approved by the Secretary of the Interior or some officer designated by him.

6. To delegate any of the foregoing powers to appropriate officers of the Pueblo, reserving the right to review any action taken by virtue of such delegated power.

Section 2. Judicial Power

The Pueblo Council shall also adjudicate all matters coming before it over which it has jurisdiction. In all controversies coming before the Pueblo Council, the Council shall have the right to examine all witnesses and ascertain full details of the controversy, and after the matter shall have been sufficiently commented upon by the interested parties, the Council shall retire to a private place to make a decision. All of the members of the Council except the Governor and the Lt. Governor shall have the right to vote upon a decision, and a majority shall rule. In the event of a tie, the Governor shall have the right to cast a vote, thereby breaking the tie. It shall be the duty of the Governor and Lt. Governor to express to the other members of the Pueblo Council their views regarding the case before a vote is taken.

Section 3. Common Law of Pueblo

With respect to all matters not covered by the written Constitution, Bylaws and ordinances of the Pueblo of Santa Clara, nor by those laws of the United States of America which are applicable to the Pueblo of Santa Clara, the customs and usages of the Pueblo, civil and criminal, as interpreted by the Council, shall have the force of law.

ARTICLE V. THE GOVERNOR, HIS POWERS AND DUTIES

The Governor shall be the executive head of the Pueblo Government. It shall be his duty to enforce the laws of the Pueblo, civil and criminal, written and unwritten. If any person considers that any ruling of the Governor is unjust, he shall have the right to demand through any representative of the Pueblo Council or directly to the Pueblo Council that the matter be brought before the Pueblo Council for adjudication at the next meeting of said officers.

ARTICLE VI. VACANCIES AND IMPEACHMENTS

Section 1. Vacancies

Should any vacancy occur in any of the offices or any Member of the Council, the Council shall, by a majority vote, have the right to name a successor for the said office, except that in the event the office of the Governor becomes vacant for any reason, then and in that event the Lt. Governor shall thereupon become the Governor with all duties and powers of the said office, and further, that the successor to any Pueblo representative appointed by a particular group shall be chosen by the same group.

Section 2. Impeachment

Any officer charged with grave offenses may be tried before the other members of the Council. The manner of conducting impeachments shall be prescribed by the Council. The Council shall act as the trial court and if they decide, by a two-thirds vote, to remove the accused member from office he will be removed.

ARTICLE VII. LAND

Section 1. Pueblo title

Title to all lands of the Pueblo, whether assigned to the use of individuals or withheld for the common use of the members of the Pueblo, shall forever remain in the Pueblo itself and not in the individual members thereof. All the members of the Pueblo are declared to have an equal right to make beneficial use, in accordance with ordinances of the Council, of any land of the Pueblo not heretofore or hereafter assigned to individual members.

For the purpose of this Article the word "member" shall be defined by the Council.

Section 2. Individual Rights of Possession

The right of full possession shall be guaranteed to every member of the Pueblo, holding lands assigned to him by the Pueblo Council, for cultivation or other purposes; Provided, that no member holding said lands shall sell or will same to an alien. All lands assigned to individuals of the Pueblo must be completely fenced within three years. Any violation of the above provision shall be sufficient cause for the Council to dispossess him of said land. He shall have the right, however, to rent to a Pueblo member or, with the approval of the Council, to an alien, all lands under his possession, for a term not to exceed two years. He shall have the right to sell his interest in said lands to any other member of the Pueblo after his assignment has been finally approved, subject to such regulations as the Council may prescribe.

Section 3. Council to have Power of Granting Assignments

When any member of the Pueblo desires a piece of unimproved Pueblo land, he shall select his land, and then make his application for same to the Council of the Pueblo. If the Council decides to grant him the land, or any part thereof, they shall mark out the boundaries of same. The Grantee shall, thereafter have full possession of said land, unless the Council shall, in accordance with the Constitution, Bylaws and ordinances of the Pueblo, dispossess him of the same.

Section 4. Prior Assignments Recognized

All assignments of land heretofore made by the Pueblo authorities are hereby recognized and confirmed.

ARTICLE VIII. AMENDMENTS

No amendments or changes shall be made in the Constitution or Bylaws of the Pueblo except by a decision of the general Pueblo. At the request of the Council the Secretary of the Interior shall submit any proposed amendment to the said Constitution or Bylaws to a vote of the people. If such amendment is approved by a majority of the qualified voters of the Pueblo, 21 years or over, voting at an election in which at least 30 percent of those entitled to vote shall vote, it shall be submitted to the Secretary of the Interior, and if he shall approve the same it shall become effective.

Appendix C

[This brief dance description by Roy A. Keech (1937a), "The Rainbow Dance (At Santa Clara, N.M., Aug. 12, 1937)" appeared in a relatively obscure periodical, *National Archaeological News*. A photocopy of the original was fortunately made available through the courtesy of the Peabody Museum, Tozzer Library, Harvard University. Because of that and because of the details provided on this ceremony performed some four decades ago, the reproduction of the full account here seems justified. CHL]

How this ceremony gets its name is very difficult to guess. Possibly it is a special ceremony in honor of the Rainbow Woman, a very sacred priestess of each pueblo, and probably the most powerful of all the Pueblo officials.

Formations, postures, and rhythms seemed the same as for the Green Corn Dance (a harvest ceremony of thanksgiving). The costume, too, was much the same.

The men wore their hair loose, with blue or green little birds' feathers on top of the head. One baldric of conus shells crossed the bodies from the right shoulder to the left hip. Strings of various kinds of beads were draped at the neck. Wide, light green leather bands were on each upper arm. Naked to the waist, nine of their bodies were painted bluish-black, with thighs and upper arms to match; calves and forearms painted a grayish-white. (These men and their partners, I believe, were Winter People.) The other men were painted a reddish-orange and grayish-white. (These were certainly Summer People.) All these men wore the regulation Pueblo dance kilts, white, rain sash with knotted cords dangling at right knees, fox pelt, beaded moccasins, and skunk-skin masks at ankles. Some of them wore leather straps with sleigh bells below the knees. Each man carried a goard [*sic*] rattle, painted to match his body, in his right hand and several short sprigs of evergreen in his left.

The women wore *tablitas* (as in the Green Corn Dance). These were all exactly alike (an unusual feature); square except where they come down over the sides of the heads, with the usual three points at the top of the boards tipped with eagle down; painted light green, with the Greek letter *tau* cut out with jigsaw. In most other details the women's costumes were similar to those worn for the Blue Corn Dance, except that the *petones* were worn in the regulation manner—pinned to the shoulders in back, and falling loosely down the back of the dress. This manner of wearing the *petones* showed to better advantage the beautiful embroidery on the bottom of the dresses and the red dance belts. They wore their white wrap leggings, instead of dancing barefoot as they should in all summer ceremonies.

One drummer in bright orange silk shirt and green headband led the rhythm, followed by nine men in the chorus. There was no rain wand, no Koshares or Karinas [Kwiranas] (members of the Pueblo medicine societies), no leader who could be observed. The Governor of the Pueblo followed this group from plaza to plaza; he wore store clothes and carried his cane of office.

On the whole, there was not the same seriousness shown by the people of Santa Clara in regard to their ceremonies as is shown in most of the Pueblo villages. No cameras were smashed, or even taken into custody. Camera fiends were allowed to ride their hobby for the payment of five dollars into the tribal treasury. Also, several young white girls were allowed to stand on top of a kiva and look down in while the dance group was inside. In most any other pueblo this means being escorted by Indian officials to one's car and ordered out of the village, or a white man runs the risk of very rough treatment for the same offense.

Just a short note about *kivas:* This is a Hopi word, meaning sacred ceremonial chamber. Most of them are round, drum-shaped, though always some have been square, and having no windows or doors. Originally the kivas were subterranean. Today most of them are built on top of the ground, or partly so. To enter the kiva, the Indians go up a rough pole ladder to the roof, and then down another ladder through a large square hole. Inside is a low stone or adobe bench that goes all the way around the wall. There is also a stone altar and fire box in which a fire is kept perpetually burning from the beginning of the year until new fire is made at the beginning of the next year.

Formerly each clan had its own kiva. But today most tribes have only two, one for each people (Summer and Winter). The women enter only for ceremonial purposes, or to carry food to their men. The men, however, use them for council chambers, to assemble for the making of ceremonial materials, as a place to weave (in the few pueblos where this craft is still continued), and sometimes even for social gatherings. As the Christian's religion center is his church, so the Pueblo's religion center is his kiva. Few white people have ever entered a kiva in a living pueblo. The writer has entered just one—in a Hopi village.

Appendix D

[A short article by Roy A. Keech (1937b), "The Blue Corn Dance (At Santa Clara, N.M., August 12, 1937)" was published in the *National Archaeological News*. A typescript of the article was found among Hill's Santa Clara papers; at the top of the page, he had written, *"Kwitara, Probably,"* and in another part of the upper margin, "Pogo Sare [37]." A photocopy of the article was obtained through the kind cooperation of the Peabody Museum, Tozzer Library, Harvard University. Since the account appeared in a relatively scarce journal, and since it contains numerous details concerning this ceremony of some four decades ago, the reproduction of it here in its entirety seems well justified. CHL]

The dancers emerged from the Summer *kiva* about eleven o'clock, and filed to the main dance *plaza*. There were eight men and eight women, counting boys and girls. There was no visible leader. The drummer led the procession with his large war drum. Behind him came the nine men of the chorus, all wearing "store pants" and gay silk shirts, with bright headbands.

Upon arriving at the main plaza, the dancers formed in two lines, with the drummer and the chorus off to one side. The drum took up the rhythm of the dance; the chorus formed a circle around it, and chanted in unison.

The men dancers were naked from the waist up, except for a deerskin, slit and worn poncho fashion, the necks of the skins dangling between the men's knees, and the tails between the men's shoulderblades. The hair of the pelts was worn outside. On the tops of their heads the men wore four long feathers; some were eagle, some turkey, and some pheasant. These were worn fanwise, extending backward and slightly upward. Just in front of the big feathers were little bunches of small feathers: parrot, bluebird, woodpecker, and downy eagle. From the waists hung the regulation dance kilt, open at the right side; the rain-sash, dangling at the right side to the knees; the fox pelt hanging from the rear of the belt, tail downward. On their feet were beautifully beaded low moccasins, with the regulation skunk-skin masks over these, the white stripe in the middle so that a black stripe nearly touched the ground to keep all evil out of the ceremony. The bodies, arms, and legs below the knees were painted a blackish-blue to represent the blue corn meal. The faces were painted with vivid red spots on either cheek, or in some cases with wide red bands across the upper cheeks and nose. Bluish-black goard [*sic*] rattles in their right hands, evergreen in left.

The women were wearing three white-tipped eagle feathers fanwise, erect from the back of the heads, and bound there with beaded head-bands. Bright red spots on either cheek. Many necklaces of silver, coral, and shell beads. They all wore the old style heavy, black, wool Pueblo-weave dress, but with beautiful embroidery in red and green around the bottoms; arms and left shoulders showed the silk dresses underneath. Fastened between the shoulder blades were cardboard discs of two-foot diameter. In the center of these large discs were painted six-inch sun symbols with fringe of orange or red horse hair, and extending outward from these suns, like spokes of a wheel, were eagle or turkey tail feathers, with more fringe from the edge of the disc. The *petones* (large, bright colored silk scarfs with lace edges) were tied over the right shoulders, so that they hung under the left arms, covering the left side, front and back, but leaving a narrow strip of the black dress showing down the right side. The *petones* reached to just above the knees, leaving a few inches of the red and green embroidery of the black dress showing below. The woman [*sic*] and girls all wore the white moccasins (turned slightly up at the toes) and white wrap-leggings. They also wore the skunk-skin masks at their ankles. The women carried short spruce boughs in each hand, with which they kept the rhythm of the big drum.

Two of the male and two of the female dancers were children, probably not over ten or twelve years of age, though perfectly costumed to match their elders. All of the dancers were young people.

The men and boys began by dancing rather wildly for a ceremony of this sort. They pranced high, turning from side to side, each occasionally circling his female partner. By the middle of the afternoon they had tamed their steps somewhat, not from fatigue, but to match the slower rhythm of the drum.

The women's steps were, except at the very beginning, mincing, only the heels seeming to lift from the ground. The posture was good, denoting a background of hundreds, perhaps thousands, of years without heels, and the balancing of *ollas* full of precious water from the springs and brooks. The general attitude of these women, however, was not the usual demureness of the Pueblo woman and girl. Perhaps this was due to the fact that every one taking part in this ceremony had bobbed hair. (It is not all good that they have learned from their white sisters!) Perhaps it was due to the fact that Santa Clara has the most beautiful girls and women (as a tribe) of all the Pueblos.

This group danced in the main plaza for probably half an hour; then they moved on to another plaza to make room for a group of Rainbow dancers which filed in from the Winter kiva. One group of dancers followed the other group from plaza to plaza all the rest of the day until sunset, when both groups danced together in the main plaza; then both groups filed to their respective kivas to remove their dance costumes, and the men and boys went to the river to wash off their paint.

The Blue Corn Dance is one of the least known and least frequent of all the Pueblo ceremonies, being done as I was told by a friend in the Pueblo, only once in seven years.

Editor's Note: Roy A. Keech, author of the Blue Corn Dance, contributes articles frequently to the News. His most recent and noted series was that of Zuni Vocabulary written and complied solely by himself.

Glossary

abuelo grandfather

alguacil constable or other minor official; sheriff

arroyo stream bed with deep-cut sides, common in semidesert or desert areas

Bear societies general, or specific, reference to the curing or medicine societies, bears being credited with particularly effective curing powers

cacique a word of Arawakan (Caribbean) origin, applied by Spanish officials to Indian religious leaders. The Pueblo cacique was the primary authority in all matters—both sacred and profane. Among Tewa tribes, there were two, one for the Summer Moiety and one for the Winter

campo santo cemetery

canal gutter, eavestrough

canoa canoe or boat; in New Mexico, also a trough

capitán de (la) guerra war captain

carreta cart

Cibobe in the tribal origin tale, the Place of Emergence, in the north

descanso ritual sometimes held when a person died away from the pueblo; it did not matter if the body was returned or not

encomendero holder of a land grant or other favor from the crown

entrada authorized expedition for exploration, settlement, or other purpose

entremesero clown, player of farces or interludes

fiscal minister, officer; in New Mexico, commonly associated with management of the church building and other property

genízaro Indians, generally non-Puebloan, who adopted a Hispanicized way of life in New Mexico, the descendants often of Indians who were purchased or captured from nomadic tribes

gobernador, governador governor

interino interim, provisional, or temporary official

junta general general council or assembly

K'osa the Koshare, or Kossa Society and individual members; counterpart of the Kwirana; affiliated with the Summer Moiety at Santa Clara Pueblo

kutiti (kotiti) stones, or "bells" sometimes referred to as "kiva bells," long, slender stones (1.5" by 10") that rang when struck together in the course of rituals

Kwirana counterpart of the K'osa Society; refers to the society or to individual members; associated with the Winter Moiety at Santa Clara Pueblo

madrina, madrinha godmother

malinche maiden who dances in Matachina and other ceremonies

mano handstone used in grinding corn and other material; one- and two-hand forms

manta one-piece cotton, or woolen, dress, blanket, or cover; most commonly black, with red and/or green trim. Also, a white form, with black and red top and bottom borders

Matachín(a) dance performed in various pueblos and Spanish villages, portraying the conflict between good and evil; accompaniment more typically is violin rather than drum *matalote* male dancer in Matachina and war dances

metate grinding stone on which corn and other materials are reduced to meal or powder

monarcha (Montezuma) important figure portrayed in Matachina dances

Oyike Winter Moiety, the Winter Society, or the headman of the Winter people; the Winter cacique (also known as Oyike sendo)

padrino, padrinho godfather

Pay-oj-ke Summer Moiety, the Summer Society, or the headman of the Summer people; the Summer cacique (also known as Po̜ an tur̜g *zho̜rg*)

penitente member of a brotherhood, a lay religious organization related to the Roman Catholic Church in the American Southwest, especially in northern New Mexico and southern Colorado

Pini, Pinini temporary substitutes for either

Putsato temporary dance directors, or clowns; similar in function to the *pini*

P'u xwe^{n}re^n ceremony closely associated with the Hunt Society, the War Society, and the Women's Scalp Society

ramada a covering of leafy branches for shade; may be attached to house as a porch or portal, or may be a separate structure

Savadjo generic term applied to a variety of impersonators; primarily, these figures were "bogeys," disciplinarians, although they were considered clowns as well

sori wokan "large cure or treatment," by the medicine societies

teniente deputy or assistant official

veloria the wake, generally held at the home of the deceased; a *veloria* may also be held as part of the dedication of a new house, or at other times "for the general good"

viga one of the several beams used for roof support

Bibliography

Aberle, Sophie D.
  1948   The Pueblo Indians of New Mexico: Their Land, Economy and Civil Organization. Memoirs of the American Anthropological Association, No. 70. 93 pp.

Adair, John
  1945   The Navajo and Pueblo Silversmiths. Norman: University of Oklahoma Press. 220 pp.

Adams, Eleanor B., and Fray Angelico Chavez
  1956   The Missions of New Mexico, 1776: A Description by Fray Francisco Atanasio Domínguez. Albuquerque: University of New Mexico Press. 387 pp.

Aitken, Barbara [Freire-Marreco]
  1930   Temperament in Native American Religion. Journal of the Royal Anthropological Institute, 60:363–87.
  1949   A Note on Pueblo Belt-Weaving. Man 49:37.

American Guide Series
  1940   New Mexico: A Guide to the Colorful State. New York: Coronado Cuarto Centennial Commission and the University of New Mexico, Hastings House. 458 pp.

Bailey, Florence M.
  1928   Birds of New Mexico. Washington: Judd and Detweiler. 807 pp.

Bailey, Vernon
  1913   Life Zones and Crop Zones of New Mexico. Washington: Bureau of Biological Survey, North American Fauna 35. 100 pp.

Bandelier, Adolph F.
  1890   The Delight Makers. New York: Dodd, Mead & Co. 490 pp. (Reprinted 1916, Dodd, Mead & Co.; 1918, Fanny R. Bandelier; 1946, Dodd, Mead & Co.; 1971, Harcourt Brace Jovanovich.
  1890-92 Final Report of Investigations among the Indians of the Southwestern United States, Carried on Mainly in the Years from 1880 to 1885. 2 vols. Archaeological Institute of America, American Series, III and IV. 319 pp. and 591 pp..
  1892   An Outline of the Documentary History of the Zuñi Tribe. Journal of American Ethnology and Archaeology III (iv). 115 pp.
  1893   The Gilded Man (El Dorado) and Other Pictures of the Spanish Occupancy of America. New York: D. Appleton and Company. 302 pp. (Reprinted 1962, Rio Grande Press, Chicago.
  1910   Documentary History of the Rio Grande Pueblos of New Mexico: I. Bibliographic Introduction. Archaeological Institute of America, Papers of the School of American Archaeology 13: 1–28

Barton, Robert S.
  1953   The Lincoln Canes of the Pueblo Governors. Lincoln Herald 55(4):24–29

Bienenstok, Theodore
1950   Social Life and Authority in the
        East European Jewish Shtetel
        Community. Southwestern
        Journal of Anthropology 6(3):
        238–54.
Bloom, Lansing B., ed.
1936   Bourke on the Southwest X.
        New Mexico Historical Review
        11 (3):217–82.
Brophy, William A., and Sophie D. Aberle,
        et al.
1966   The Indian: America's Unfin-
        ished Business. Norman: Uni-
        versity of Oklahoma Press. xix +
        236 pp.
Brown, Donald Nelson
1960   Taos Dance Classification. El
        Palacio 67(6):203–9.
Bryan, Kirk
1925   Date of Channel Trenching (Ar-
        royo Cutting) in The Arid
        Southwest. Science 62:338–44.
1929   Flood-water Farming. Geogra-
        phical Review 19: 444–56.
1941   Pre-Columbian Agriculture in
        the Southwest, As Conditioned
        by Periods of Alluviation. Asso-
        ciation of American Geogra-
        phers, Annals 31:219–42.
Chavez, Fray Angelico, O.F.M.
1957   Archives of the Archdiocese of
        Santa Fe. Academy of American
        Franciscan History, Biblio-
        graphic Series III. 283 pp.
Culin, Stewart
1907   Games of the North American
        Indians. 24th Annual Report of
        the Bureau of American Ethnol-
        ogy. 843 pp.
Dale, Edward Everett
1949   The Indians of the Southwest: A
        Century of Development under
        the United States. Norman: Uni-
        versity of Oklahoma Press. xvi +
        283 pp.
Dennis, Wayne, and Marsena G. Dennis
1940   Cradles and Cradling Practices
        of the Pueblo Indians. American
        Anthropologist 42(1):107–15.
Dorroh, J.H. Jr.
1946   Certain Hydrologic and Climat-
        ic Characteristics of the South-

west. Albuquerque: University
of New Mexico Publications in
Engineering 1. 64 pp.
Douglas, Frederic H.
1939   Weaving in the Tewa Pueblos.
        Denver: Denver Art Museum,
        Leaflet 90: 157–60.
1940   Main Types of Pueblo Cotton
        Textiles. Denver: Denver Art
        Museum, Leaflets 92–93: 165–
        72.
Douglass, W.B.
1917   Notes on the Shrines of the Tewa
        and Other Pueblo Indians of
        New Mexico. Washington:
        Proceedings, 19th International
        Congress of Americanists:
        344–78.
Dozier, Edward P.
1954a   The Hopi-Tewa of Arizona.
        Berkeley: University of Califor-
        nia Publications in American
        Archaeology and Ethnology
        44(3):259–376.
1954b   Spanish-Indian Acculturation in
        the Southwest: Comments.
        American Anthropologist
        56:680–83.
1961   The Rio Grande Pueblos. Pp.
        96–186 in Perspectives in
        American Indian Culture
        Change (ed. by Edward H.
        Spicer). Chicago: University of
        Chicago Press.
1966   Hano: A Tewa Indian Com-
        munity in Arizona. New York:
        Holt, Rinehart and Winston.
        104 pp.
1970a   The Pueblo Indians of North
        America. Holt, Rinehart and
        Winston. xv + 224 pp.
1970b   Making Inferences from the
        Present to the Past. Pp. 202–13
        in Reconstructing Prehistoric
        Pueblo Societies (ed. by William
        A. Longacre). Albuquerque:
        University of New Mexico Press.
Dozier, Thomas S.
n.d.   Statement to the Trade for 1907.
        Pamphlet, privately printed, 6
        pp.
n.d.   About Indian Pottery. Denver:
        Eames Bros. 14 pp.

Dutton, Bertha P.
1975　Indians of the American Southwest. Englewood Cliffs: Prentice-Hall. 298 pp.

Eggan, Fred, and Michel Pijoan
1943　Some Problems in the Study of Food and Nutrition. America Indigena 3(1):9–22.

Ellis, Florence Hawley
1954　Spanish-Indian Acculturation in the Southwest: Comments. American Anthropologist 56:678–80.

Faris, Chester E.
1952　Pueblo Governors' Canes. Mimeo. 8 pp.

Fay, George E.
1952　Some Notes on the Cow Dance, Santa Clara Pueblo. El Palacio 59:186–88.

Fenneman, Nevin M.
n.d.　Map: Physical Divisions of the United States. Washington: U.S. Department of the Interior, Geological Survey.

Fergusson, Erna
1931　Dancing Gods: Indian Ceremonials of New Mexico and Arizona. New York: Alfred A. Knopf. xxvi + 276 pp. (Reprinted 1957, Albuquerque: University of New Mexico Press).

Fewkes, J. Walter
1920　Fire Worship of the Hopi Indians. Annual Report, Smithsonian Institution, 1920:589–610.
1922　The Use of Idols in Hopi Worship. Annual Report, Smithsonian Institution, 1922:377–97.

Ford, Richard I.
1972　An Ecological Perspective on the Eastern Pueblos. Pp. 1–17 in New Perspectives on the Pueblos (ed. by Alfonso Ortiz). Albuquerque: University of New Mexico Press.

Ford, Richard I., Albert H. Schroeder, and Stewart L. Peckham
1972　Three Perspectives on Puebloan Prehistory. Pp. 19–39 in New Perspectives on the Pueblos (ed. by Alfonso Ortiz). Albuquerque: University of New Mexico Press.

Foster, George M.
1953　Relationships between Spanish and Spanish-American Folk Medicine. Journal of American Folklore 66:201–17.
1960　Culture and Conquest: America's Spanish Heritage. New York: Viking Fund Publications in Anthropology 27. 272 pp.

Franciscan Fathers
1910　An Ethnologic Dictionary of the Navaho Language. St. Michaels, Arizona. 536 pp.

Freire-Marreco, Barbara (See also Aitken, Barbara)
1911　Two American Indian Dances. The Sociological Review IV(4): 324–37.

Gjevre, John A.
1969　Chili Line: the Narrow Rail Trail to Santa Fe. Espanola, N.M.: Rio Grande Sun Press. 82 pp.

Hack, John T.
1942　The Changing Environment of the Hopi Indians of Arizona. Peabody Museum of American Archaeology and Ethnology Papers 35(1). 85 pp.

Hammond, George P., and Agapito Rey
1940　Narratives of the Coronado Expedition, 1540–1542. Albuquerque: University of New Mexico Press. 413 pp.
1953　Don Juan de Oñate: Colonizer of New Mexico, 1595–1628. 2 vols. Albuquerque: University of New Mexico Press. Pp. 1–584 and 585–1187.
1966　The Rediscovery of New Mexico, 1580–1594. Albuquerque: University of New Mexico Press. 341 pp.

Harper, Allan G., Andrew R. Cordova, and Kalervo Oberg
1943　Man and Resources in the Middle Rio Grande Valley. Albuquerque: University of New Mexico Press. 156 pp.

Harrington, John Peabody
1916　The Ethnogeography of the Tewa Indians. 29th Annual

Report of the Bureau of American Ethnology: 29–636.

Hawley, Florence
1950   Big Kivas, Little Kivas, and Moiety Houses in Historical Reconstruction. Southwestern Journal of Anthropology 6(3): 286–302.

Hawley, Florence, Michel Pijoan, and C.A. Elkin
1943   An Inquiry into Food Economy and Body Economy in Zia Pueblo. American Anthropologist 45(3):547–56.

Henderson, Junius, and John Peabody Harrington
1914   Ethnozoology of the Tewa Indians. Bureau of American Ethnology Bulletin 56. 76 pp.

Hewett, Edgar L.
1906   Antiquities of the Jemez Plateau, New Mexico. Bureau of American Ethnology Bulletin 32. 55 pp.
1908   Archaeology of the Rio Grande Valley. Out West 31:3–29.
1930   Ancient Life in the American Southwest. Indianapolis: The Bobbs-Merrill Company. 392 pp.

Hewett, Edgar Lee, Junius Henderson, and Wilfred W. Robbins
1913   The Physiography of the Rio Grande Valley, New Mexico, in Relation to Pueblo Culture. Bureau of American Ethnology Bulletin 54. 76 pp.

Hill, W. W.
1938   The Agricultural and Hunting Methods of the Navaho Indians. Yale University Publications in Anthropology 18. 194 pp.
1940   Navaho Salt Gathering. University of New Mexico Bulletin, Anthropological Series 3:3–25.
1948   Navaho Trading and Trading Ritual: A Study of Cultural Dynamics. Southwestern Journal of Anthropology 4(4):371–96.
n.d.   Correspondence, 1940–1972. Papers of W.W. Hill. Albuquerque.

Hodge, Frederick Webb
1907–10 Handbook of American Indians North of Mexico. 2 vols. Bureau of American Ethnology Bulletin 30. 972 and 1,221 pp..

Hodge, Frederick Webb, George P. Hammond, and Agapito Rey
1945   Fray Alonso de Benavides' Revised Memorial of 1634. Albuquerque: University of New Mexico Press. 368 pp.

Hoebel, E. Adamson
1960   The Authority Systems of the Pueblos of the Southwestern United States. Akten des 34. Internationalen Amerikanisten-kongresses, Wien:555–63.

Horgan, Paul
1975   Lamy of Santa Fe: His Life and Times. New York: Farrar, Straus and Giroux. 523 pp.

Jeançon, Jean Allard
1904–30 Field notes on Santa Clara Pueblo. Ms. in papers of W.W. Hill, Albuquerque. Some notes, mostly for 1906, at Denver Art Museum.
1926   A Rectangular Ceremonial Room. The Colorado Magazine (The State Museum, Denver) 3(4):133–37.
1931a   Santa Clara and San Juan Pottery. Denver Art Museum Department of Indian Art Leaflet 35. 4 pp. (Reprinted 1945)
1931b   Santa Clara: A New Mexico Tewa Pueblo. Ms. in papers of W.W. Hill, Albuquerque. 100 pp.

Keech, Roy A.
1937a   The Rainbow Dance (At Santa Clara, N.M., Aug. 12, 1937). National Archaeological News. 1(8):19–21.
1937b   The Blue Corn Dance (At Santa Clara, N.M., August 12, 1937). National Archaeological News 1(9):26–28.

Kellogg, Harold
1932   It's an Old Indian Custom. El Palacio 33(1):1–4.

Kluckhohn, Clyde
1944   Navaho Witchcraft. Peabody

Museum of American Archaeology and Ethnology Papers 22 (2). 149 pp. (Reprinted by Beacon Press, Boston, 1967; 3rd printing, 1970, xxii + 254 pp.)

Kluckhohn, Clyde, W.W. Hill, and L.W. Kluckhohn
1971 Navaho Material Culture. Cambridge, Mass.: Harvard University Press, xiv + 488 pp.

Kurath, Gertrude P.
1957 The Origin of the Pueblo Indian Matachinas. El Palacio 64(9–10):259–64.
195a Plaza Circuits of Tewa Indian Dancers. El Palacio 65(1):16–26.
1958b Game Animal Dances of the Rio Grande Pueblos. Southwestern Journal of Anthropology 14(4):438–48.

Kurath, Gertrude Prokosch, with Antonio Garcia
1970 Music and Dance of the Tewa Pueblos. Museum of New Mexico Research Records 8. viii + 309 pp.

Lambert, Marjorie F.
1954 Paa-ko, Archaeological Chronicle of An Indian Village in North Central New Mexico. School of American Research Monograph 19, Parts I–V. 183 pp.

Lange, Charles H.
1952 The Feast Day Dance at Zia Pueblo, New Mexico, August 15, 1951. Texas Journal of Science 4(1):19–26.
1957 Tablita, or Corn, Dances of the Rio Grande Pueblo Indians. Texas Journal of Science 9(1):59–74.
1959 Cochiti: A New Mexico Pueblo, Past and Present. Austin: University of Texas Press. 618 pp. (Reprinted by Arcturus Books, Southern Illinois University Press, Carbondale, 1968)

Lange, Charles H., and Carroll L. Riley, eds.
1966 The Southwestern Journals of Adolph F. Bandelier, 1880–1882. Albuquerque: University of New Mexico Press. 462 pp.
1970 The Southwestern Journals of Adolph F. Bandelier, 1883–1884. (With the assistance of Elizabeth M. Lange) Albuquerque: University of New Mexico Press. 528 pp.

Lange, Charles H., Carroll L. Riley, and Elizabeth M. Lange, eds.
1975 The Southwestern Journals of Adolph F. Bandelier, 1885–1888. Albuquerque: University of New Mexico Press. 702 pp.
n.d. The Southwestern Journals of Adolph F. Bandelier, 1889–1892. Ms. in press.

Laski, Vera
1958 Seeking Life. American Folklore Society Memoirs 50. 91 pp.

Le Free, Betty
1975 Santa Clara Pottery Today. Albuquerque: University of New Mexico Press. 114 pp.

Linton, Ralph
1936 The Study of Man: An Introduction. New York: D. Appleton-Century. 503 pp.

Longacre, William A., ed.
1970 Reconstructing Prehistoric Pueblo Societies. Albuquerque: University of New Mexico Press. 247 pp.

Lowie, Robert H.
1937 The History of Ethnological Theory. New York: Farrar and Rinehart. 296 pp.

Mahood, Ruth I.
1961 Photographer of the Southwest: Adam Clark Vroman, 1856–1916. Los Angeles: The Ward Ritchie Press. 127 pp.

Opler, Morris E.
1944 The Jicarilla Apache Ceremonial Relay Race. American Anthropologist 46(1):75–97.

Ortiz, Alfonso
1969 The Tewa World. Chicago: University of Chicago Press. 197 pp.
1972 New Perspectives on the Pueblos. Albuquerque: University of New Mexico Press. 340 pp.

Parsons, Elsie Clews
  1924a   Tewa Kin, Clan, and Moiety. American Anthropologist 26(3):333–39.
  1924b   Tewa Mothers and Children. Man 24:148–51.
  1929   The Social Organization of the Tewa of New Mexico. Memoirs of the American Anthropological Association 36. 309 pp.
  1939   Pueblo Indian Religion. 2 vols. Chicago: University of Chicago Press. Pp. 1–549, 551–1275.
Parsons, Elsie Clews, and Ralph L. Beals
  1934   The Sacred Clowns of the Pueblo and Mayo-Yaqui Indians. American Anthropologist 36(4): 491–514.
Poore, Henry R.
  1894   Condition of 16 New Mexico Pueblos, 1890. Report on Indians Taxed and Indians Not Taxed in the United States (except Alaska) at the Eleventh Census: 1890. Department of the Interior, Census Office, 52nd Congress, 1st Session, H. Misc. Doc. No. 340, Part 15:424–60.
Reed, Erik K.
  1949   Sources of Upper Rio Grande Pueblo Culture and Population. El Palacio 56(6):163–84.
  1950   Eastern-Central Arizona Archaeology in Relation to the Western Pueblos. Southwestern Journal of Anthropology 6(2):120–38.
Riley, Carroll L.
  1963   Color-Direction Symbolism. An Example of Mexican-Southwestern Contacts. América Indígena 23(1):49–60.
Robbins, Wilfred Williams, John Peabody Harrington, and Barbara Freire-Marreco
  1916   Ethnobotany of the Tewa Indians. Bureau of American Ethnology Bulletin 55. 124 pp.
Sando, Joe S.
  1976   The Pueblo Indians. San Francisco: The Indian Historian Press. 248 pp.

Scholes, France V.
  1937   Church and State In New Mexico, 1610–1650. Historical Society of New Mexico, Publications in History 7. 206 pp.
  1942   Troublous Times in New Mexico, 1659–1670. Historical Society of New Mexico, Publications in History 11. 276 pp.
Schroeder, Albert H.
  1968   Shifting for Survival in the Spanish Southwest. New Mexico Historical Review 43(4):291–310.
  1972   Rio Grande Ethnohistory. Pp. 41–70 in New Perspectives on the Pueblos (ed. by Alfonso Ortiz). Albuquerque: University of New Mexico Press.
Schroeder, Albert H., and Dan S. Matson
  1965   A Colony on the Move: Gaspar Castaño de Sosa's Journal, 1590–1591. Santa Fe: The School of American Research. 196 pp.
Scully, Vincent
  1975   Pueblo: Mountain, Village, Dance. New York: Viking. 398 pp.
Smith, Anne M.
  1966   New Mexico Indians: Economic, Educational and Social Problems. Santa Fe: Museum of New Mexico Research Records No. 1. 165 pp.
Spicer, Edward H.
  1954   Spanish-Indian Acculturation in the Southwest. American Anthropologist 56(4):663–84.
Spier, Leslie
  1924   Zuñi Weaving Technique. American Anthropologist 26(1):64–85.
Spinden, Herbert J.
  1911   The Making of Pottery at San Ildefonso. American Museum Journal 11:192–96.
  1915a   Home Songs of the Tewa Indians. American Museum Journal 15:73–78.
  1915b   Characteristics of Tewa Mythology. American Anthropologist 17:372.

1933   Songs of the Tewa. New York: The Explorers' Club. 125 pp. (Reprinted, 1975, by Sunstone Press, Santa Fe, with Introduction by Margaret D. Ortiz and Sandra Prewitt Edelman, Foreword by Alice Marriott; 144 pp.)

n.d.   Notes on the Rio Grande Pueblos, 1909–1913. Ms. in papers of W. W. Hill, Albuquerque. 379 pp.

Stevenson, James
1883a   Illustrated Catalogue of the Collections Obtained from the Indians of New Mexico and Arizona in 1879. Bureau of Ethnology, Second Annual Report: 307–422.

1883b   Illustrated Catalogue of the Collections Obtained from the Indians of New Mexico in 1880. Bureau of Ethnology, Second Annual Report: 423–65.

Stevenson, Matilda Coxe
1904   The Zuñi Indians: Their Mythology, Esoteric Fraternities, and Ceremonies. Bureau of American Ethnology, Twenty-Third Annual Report: 3–634.

1912   Field Notes. Ms. Washington, D.C.: Smithsonian Institution.

1913   Studies of the Tewa Indians of the Rio Grande Valley. Smithsonian Miscellaneous Collections 40(30):35–41.

1914   Strange Rites of the Tewa Indians. Smithsonian Miscellaneous Collections 63(8): 73–83.

1916   The Sun and the Ice People among the Tewa of New Mexico. Smithsonian Miscellaneous Collections 65(6):73–78.

Steward, Julian H.
1930   The Ceremonial Buffoon of the American Indian. Papers of the Michigan Academy of Science, Arts and Letters 14:187–207.

Stubbs, Stanley A.
1950   Bird's-Eye View of the Pueblos. Norman: University of Oklahoma Press. 122 pp.

Wendorf, Fred
1954   A Reconstruction of Northern Rio Grande Prehistory. American Anthropologist 56(2):200–27.

Wendorf, Fred, and Erik K. Reed
1955   An Alternative Reconstruction of Northern Rio Grande Prehistory. El Palacio 62(5–6):131–73.

White, Leslie A.
1932   The Pueblo of San Felipe. Memoirs of the American Anthropological Association 38. 69 pp.

1935   The Pueblo of Santo Domingo, New Mexico. Memoirs of the American Anthropological Association 43. 210 pp.

1942   The Pueblo of Santa Ana, New Mexico. Memoirs of the American Anthropological Association 60. 360 pp.

1943   Punche: Tobacco in New Mexico History. New Mexico Historical Review 18(4):386–93.

1962   The Pueblo of Sia, New Mexico. Bureau of American Ethnology Bulletin 184. xii + 358 pp.

Williamson, Ten Broeck
1937a   The Jemez Yucca Ring-basket. El Palacio 42(7–9):37–39.

1937b   The Jemez Yucca Ring-basket. Indians at Work 5(2):33–35. (Reprint of 1937a)

Index

than in Winter, 218
—: kivas, 204
—: membership, normal male and female affiliation aboriginally, 208; patrilineal bias in, 208
Mountain lion man (Pirg xarg *zho*): Hunt Society head, 343
Mountain Sheep Dance ("Big Dance"), 274

Nambé K'osa Society, differentiated from San Juan K'osa in having black cotton wristlets, 300; reciprocal obligations with parent society at Nambé Pueblo, 302. *See also* K'osa.
Nambé Pueblo, known as center for witchcraft, 313
Names, relatively lacking in significance, 131
Naming, customs and changes in, 131–34; ceremonies in, 132–34
Navajo Dance ("Little Dance"), 285
Navajo Indians: enemies of the Santa Clara, not liked by them, 233

Old age: emphasis on seniority and respect for elders, 170–71
Oñate, Don Juan de: 1598 expedition of, and settlement among Tewas by, 6–7
Ortiz, Alfonso, xxix
Outside chief, or war captain: role of, 182, 184, 186; physical punishment by, 184–85
Ovens, baking, 77–78
Owl feathers: closely associated with witchcraft, 314, 317
Ownership, 19–21
Oxen: used in agricultural work, 109–10
Oxu wa. *See* Summer Moiety Subgroupings and Winter Moiety Subgroupings.
Oyike. *See* Winter Moiety Subgroupings.
Oyike sendo. *See* Winter chief.
Oyike Society. *See* Winter Society.

Pain, treatment of body (secular medicine), 342
Pajarito Plateau, xxvi
Parfleches: various forms and uses of, 92
Parsons, Elsie Clews, xxviii–xxix, xxxi
Patrilineal bias in moiety membership, 208
Pay-oj-ke. *See* Summer Moiety Subgroupings.
Pay-oj-ke Society. *See* Summer Society.
Peace: formal negotiations for, 70

Pens: eagle, 56–57; chicken, 79
Peralta, Don Pedro de: governor, 7
Personal adornment: male and female, 103
Personal property, 20–21
Phonetic table: explanation and discussion by Winter Laite, xxii–xxiii
Pika. See Church warders.
Pini, or Pinini, 232, 243; temporary replacements for K'osa, 305
Pini costumes: distinct from K'osa, 305
Pirg xarg *zho. See* Mountain Lion Man.
Pipe Dance ("Little Dance"), 289
Pitch-to-apply (Savadjo), 308
Po e turg *zhon. See* Summer Chief.
Pogo Share ("Big Dance"), 264–68
Poje. *See* Meeting of Waters Ceremony.
Poker-old-man (Savadjo), 307
Po'ku, initiation ceremonies. *See* "Water immersion."
Political organization: characteristics of, 181–82; changes in, 181; ramifications of, 181
Political schisms: events of 1894, 1935, 1940, and 1941, 193; depositions regarding, taken by David Dozier, 1935, 193–94; by Edward Dozier, 1935, 194–96
Porcupine quill decoration, 106
Postnatal practices, 128–29
Pottery: categories of, 89; used in rituals, 90
Pottery making, 83–90; changes in, 83; ritual in, 84
Pour-water-on-the-head-old-woman (Savadjo), 307–8
Premarital relationships, 152–53
Prenatal beliefs and practices, 125–26
Preparation of food for dances, 259
Prestige: form of status defined and discussed, 164–67
Principales, 190
Prisoner's Dance ("Little Dance"), 282–83
Progressive-Conservative factions: defined, 191; discussion of, 197–201
"Private, or personal, law": forms of, 147–48
Property: real, 19–20; personal, 20–21
"Public law": forms of, 146–47
Puebloan concept of balance: examples of, at Santa Clara, 186
Pueblo Indian Revolt of 1680, 7, 24
Punishment by war captains, 187; for nonconformity, 195–96; for disregarding masked impersonators, 308
Punuha. *See* Women's Scalp Society.
Purification by Bear Societies: of irrigation

ditch, 337; of race course, 337. *See also* Cure with food, Cure with yard.

Putsato, 305

P'u xwere Dance: sexes dress in clothes of opposite sex, 349, 350, 351. *See also* Women's Scalp Society.

Puyé, xxvi, xxx

Quirana Society. *See* Kwirana Society.

Rainbow Dance. *See* Willow-Behind Dance.

Rainbow Dance of August 12, 1937, 379–80

Ramadas, 78

Real property, 19–20

Reconquest, 1691–96, by Governor Don Diego de Vargas, 7–8

Relay Race ("Big Dance"), 278–81, 337; vestige of war rites, 346

Religious rites: individual activities in, 255–56

Residence patterns: post-marriage, 161; recent changes, 161

Religious awe: acquisition of, by child, 144–45

Reverse behavior in K'osa initiations, 301. *See also* Contrary behavior.

Riley, Carroll L., xxx

Rites of passage: primarily associated with kachinas, 123, 151

Rito de los Frijoles, xxvi

Robbins, Wilfred W., xxvi

Robes, 98

Rodríguez, Fray Agustín: expedition of 1581, 6

Salt gathering, 61; in Estancia Valley, 254–55

Sando, Joe S., xxx

San Ildefonso Pueblo: known as center for witchcraft, 313

San Juan K'osa Society: distinguished from Nambé K'osa by lack of black cotton wristlets, 300; reciprocal obligations with parent society at San Juan Pueblo, 312. *See also* K'osa.

San Juan Pueblo, xxxi

Santa Clara Indians: relations—with Navajo Indians, 8; with Plains Indian tribes, 8; with Spaniards, 1700s to 1821, 8

Santa Clara Pueblo: geographic location of, 1

—: grant and reservation, history of, 2, 9

—: history of, sixteenth century Spanish contacts, 6–7; culture change of nineteenth century, 8–9; under American government, 1846, 9–17; twentieth century developments, 14–17

—: mission (church) archives at, 13–14

—: names for, 1; population figures for, 1

—: prehistory of, 5–6

Santa Clara Reservation: history of, 2, 9; soils of, 2; weather records for, 2–3; fauna of, 3; flora of, 3; life zones of, 3

Santiago, impersonation of. *See* Horse Dance.

Savadjo: disciplinary "bogeys," 306; comprised of various impersonations, general remarks, 306–8

Savadjo Proper, or Willow-draggers, 306–7

Scalps: handling of, 346–47; "feeding" of, 347, 348. *See also* War Society, Women's Scalp Society.

Schisms at Santa Clara Pueblo: of 1894, 199; of 1934–35, 199–201; within Winter Moiety, 212; in ceremonial structure, 257

Scrying: in ceremonial diagnoses of witchcraft, 322, 333, 335

Scully, Vincent, xxx

Seasonal shifts between Summer and Winter Societies, 211–12

Secular medical practice, 337–43; personnel and procedures commonly with religious associations, 337

Sewing: sex division in, 107

Sheriff (*alguacil,* or left arm): named by governor, 188, 189

Shield Dance ("Little Dance"), 288

Shinny. *See* Ceremonial Shinny.

"Shooter": role of, during consecration of the mass, 190

Silversmithing, 103

Skin dressing, 103–5

Snake bite, treatment of (secular medicine), 338

Social controls, xviii; forms and exercise of, 146–51; role of tribal council in, 148; role of the Savadjo in, 306–8

Socialization mechanisms, 123–24. *See also* Values, acquisition of.

Social norms: enforcement mechanisms, 148–51

Solstice Ceremonies: general remarks concerning, 252

Song composers for ceremonials, 257–58
Sore body parts but not open sores, treatment of (secular medicine), 341
Sore muscles, treatment of (secular medicine), 341
Spaniards: sixteenth century contacts with Santa Clara Pueblo, 6–7
Spanish-American influences: in ownership and inheritance, 21; in agricultural practices, 24–25, 37; designation of hot and cold foods and other objects, 39; foodstuffs, 40; in basket weaving, 91; in names and naming, 131; in burial rites, 175–76; in *Matachina* Dance, 291–93; in ceremonial clowning, 293; in witchcraft, 318
Spanish-Americans, as scapegoats in the appraisal and fending off of witchcraft, 322
Spanish language at Santa Clara Pueblo, xvii–xviii
Spinden, Herbert J., xxvii, xxx
Sprains, treatment of (secular medicine), 343
Status: general remarks regarding, 164–65
Status of women, 169–70; bases of differentiation, 169–70
Stevenson, Colonel James, xxvi
Stevenson, Matilda Coxe, xxvii
Stirling, Matthew W., xvii, xxix
Stomach disorders, treatment of (secular medicine), 339–40
Stone containers: rarity of, 91
Storage structures/areas, 78, 82
Stubbs, Stanley A., xxix
Summer Chief (Po e tuŋ *zh*on, Summer cacique, or Summer priest), 183; responsibilities of, 211; induction ceremony for, 225–26
Summer Kachina Society: initiation ceremony of, 218–19; Good Friday "Hidden Dance" (ivaxi) of, 227–40; "Hidden Dance" of, in hills, 240–41; Winter "Hidden Dance" of, 241–42
Summer Moiety: ceremonial dominance of, over Winter Moiety, 182; subgroupings (initiated members [Xa *zh*e]; kachina members [Oxu wa]; managing society [Pay-oj-ke]), 208; initiation ceremony of, 213–16
Summer Society (Pay-oj-ke), 182–82; elite group within Summer Moiety, 210; pledging and initiation ceremonies of,

220–22; "Edge of Spring" Ceremony of, 27, 28, 211, 227, 247–50; Solstice ceremonies of, 252–53; monthly retreats of, 253–54; ditch opening ceremony of, 254; salt gathering rites of, 254–55
Swellings, treatment of (secular medicine), 341–42

Tablita, or Corn, Dance ("Big Dance"), 263–64
Tafoya, Joseph Filario, xxx
Tales of witchcraft, 315–18
Taos-Isleta pueblos, xxxi
Taos Pueblo, xxxi
Tesuque Bear Society, 319–21
Tewa language at Santa Clara Pueblo, xviii
Theories of disease, 309–10
Thorns-to-apply (Savadjo), 308
Threshing floors, 78–79
Toothache, treatment of (secular medicine), 342
Toys: limited in variety and number, 137–38
Trading: recent increase in importance, 62; religious aspects of, 62; with Spaniards and Spanish-Americans, 63; with other Pueblo tribes, 63, 64–65; with Plains Indian tribes, 63–64, 65, 66, 67–68; practices, 64–68
"Trapping": as secret society recruiting method, 219, 251, 296, 297, 298, 320
Trespass: ceremonial, 253. *See also* "Trapping."
Twins: unfavorable attitudes toward, 125
Tyuonyi (Frijoles Canyon), xxvi

Unaffiliated persons (punuŋ ge?i), 208
Uninitiated persons (punuŋ ge?i), 208
Ute Dance ("Little Dance"), 285

Values, acquisition of, 140–44
Vargas. *See* de Vargas, Don Diego.
Venereal disease and urinary disorders, treatment of (secular medicine), 341
Vows as a means of gaining K'osa Society membership, 297
Vroman, A.C., xxvi

War captain(s): selection of, 186–87; functions of, 187; origin of, 188
War Equipment. *See* Hunting and War Equipment; *see also* Fighting Equipment.
Warfare: economic considerations in, 68;

DATE DUE

FEB 1 8 2009			